1993 THE COMPLETE HANDBOOK OF BASEBALL

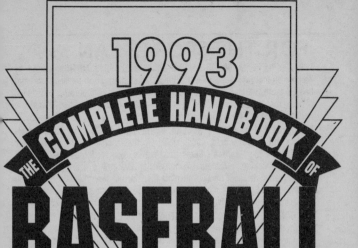

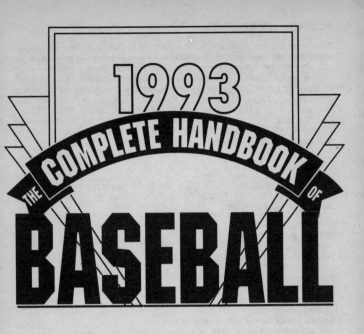

1993 THE COMPLETE HANDBOOK OF BASEBALL

EDITED BY

ZANDER HOLLANDER

AN ASSOCIATED FEATURES BOOK

A SIGNET BOOK

ACKNOWLEDGMENTS

You can't tell the players without a scorecard! Thanks to free agency and expansion, the most bizarre offseason in history promises to produce an intriguing year for fan and player alike. Our own preseason awards—for operating under chaotic conditions—go to associate editor Howard Blatt, contributing editor Eric Compton, stats maven Lee Stowbridge and the writers listed on the contents page. We also thank Dot Gordineer of Libra Graphics, Seymour Siwoff and Bob Rosen of the Elias Sports Bureau, Kevin Mulroy, Sue Powderly, Jerry Todd, Lisa Vaughn, Linda Spain, Phyllis Hollander, Katy Feeney, Phyllis Merhige, Susan Aglietti, MLB-IBM Information System and Westchester Book Composition.

Zander Hollander

PHOTO CREDITS: Cover—Wide World. Inside photos—George Gojkovich, Ira Golden, Vic Milton, Mitch Reibel, Wide World and the major-league team photographers.

SIGNET
Published by the Penguin Group
Penguin Books USA Inc., 375 Hudson Street,
New York, New York 10014, U.S.A.
Penguin Books Ltd, 27 Wrights Lane,
London W8 5TZ, England
Penguin Books Australia Ltd, Ringwood,
Victoria, Australia
Penguin Books Canada Ltd, 10 Alcorn Ave.,
Toronto, Ontario, Canada M4V 3B2
Penguin Books (N.Z.) Ltd, 182-190 Wairau Road,
Auckland 10, New Zealand

Penguin Books Ltd, Registered Offices:
Hamondsworth, Middlesex, England

First Signet Printing, March, 1993
10 9 8 7 6 5 4 3 2 1

Printed in the United States of America

CONTENTS

THE TWO BARRY BONDS ▪ by Bob Hertzel 6

O CANADA! O ALOMAR! ▪ By Kevin Kernan 14

THE ECK: FROM FEAR
TO A'S SAVING GRACE ▪ By Ron Kroichick 22

GOOD LUCK!
ROCKIES, MARLINS ▪ By Eric Compton 30

INSIDE THE NL ▪ By John Belis and Kevin Kernan . . . 40

Chicago Cubs	42	Atlanta Braves	126
Florida Marlins	54	Cincinnati Reds	138
Montreal Expos	66	Colorado Rockies . . .	150
New York Mets	78	Houston Astros	161
Philadelphia Phillies . .	91	Los Angeles Dodgers . .	173
Pittsburgh Pirates . . .	103	San Diego Padres . . .	186
St. Louis Cardinals . . .	114	San Francisco Giants . . .	197

INSIDE THE AL ▪ By Tom Pedulla and Tony DeMarco . 210

Baltimore Orioles	212	California Angels	290
Boston Red Sox	223	Chicago White Sox . . .	300
Cleveland Indians	235	Kansas City Royals . . .	311
Detroit Tigers	245	Minnesota Twins	322
Milwaukee Brewers . . .	256	Oakland Athletics	332
New York Yankees . . .	266	Seattle Mariners	343
Toronto Blue Jays	278	Texas Rangers	354

YEAR-BY-YEAR LEADERS 366

ALL-TIME RECORDS 384

WORLD SERIES WINNERS 385

1992 WORLD SERIES SUMMARY 388

OFFICIAL 1992 NATIONAL LEAGUE STATISTICS 390

OFFICIAL 1992 AMERICAN LEAGUE STATISTICS 416

AMERICAN LEAGUE SCHEDULE 440

NATIONAL LEAGUE SCHEDULE 444

Editor's Note: The material herein includes trades and rosters up to the final printing deadline.

"I Gotta Be Mad To Be Bad"

MEET THE TWO BARRY BONDS

By BOB HERTZEL

It is March 1991, in the Bradenton, Fla., spring training camp of the Pirates and Barry Bonds is burning.

An MVP award-winning 1990 season followed by a loss in salary arbitration has lit a fire within Bonds that will fuel him for the entire season. He has already said he wouldn't re-sign with Pittsburgh for $100 million as a free agent after the 1992 season. At the moment, he is a ticking time bomb, an incident waiting to happen.

Out on the field, aimlessly going through his drills, angry at the world, Bonds observes a club public relations executive asking a photographer friend of Bonds to leave a restricted area and launches into a profanity-laced tirade. When Bill Virdon attempts to intervene, Bonds simply changes his target, getting into it with the Pirate coach. As this happens, manager Jim Leyland comes to the support of his coach and verbally lashes into Bonds.

"I've kissed your bleep for three bleeping years here and I'm sick of this." shouts Leyland. "If you guys don't want to be here, then get the hell out."

The ugly scene—a far cry from a Father Knows Best lecture—is captured by national television crews and delivered into America's living rooms via videotape many times during the season.

Meet Barry Bonds, angry, young man against the world.

It is March 1992, again in spring training camp, and Barry Bonds is bonding.

Veteran sportswriter Bob Hertzel wrote his first story about Barry Bonds when he was in his first pro season at Prince William, Va., and has covered him throughout his career with the Pirates.

He slugged, fielded and ran his way to MVP.

Walking out on the same practice field, he is followed by his two-year-old son Nikolai. Bonds is dressed in blue-jean coveralls with his baseball cap on backwards—just like the one atop his son's head. An autograph seeker calls to Bonds.

Clearly enjoying the cultivation of a closer relationship with his son than he had managed as a boy with his famous, busy, ballplaying father Bobby, Barry says to the autograph seeker, "After I'm through having fun with my son."

Meet Barry Bonds, caring, soft-hearted, family man.

Which is "the real Barry Bonds?" The answer, of course, is both.

If you ask the NL's Most Valuable Player in two of the last three seasons, this versatile 28-year-old left fielder whom the Giants bestowed with a six-year, $43.75-million deal as a free agent last winter will tell you the mellow, easygoing family man must disappear when it's time to take the field.

When it comes to playing baseball, Bonds has lived by one credo: "I gotta be mad to be bad."

Bonds became another in a long line of Pirate tough guys like Dock Ellis, Dave Parker and John Candelaria. He has always recharged his competitive juices by being a man against the world and has made no pretenses about it—not even in his younger days as a college star at Arizona State.

"Oh, yeah, he had a rep on him coming out of high school, alright," said his college coach Jim Brock. "The word was: 'Don't touch. Bad kid.' Seemed like everyone, the recruiters included, was out to get him for one thing or another. But when I met him at the airport and saw that twinkle in his eye, I said, 'This can't be the kid whom everyone is down on.' I came to really care about Barry—and believe me, I'm not the kind of coach who gets close to his players.

"Right away, though I could see that Barry wasn't a master at making people like him. He was drafted higher than the other kids on the team [in the second round in June 1982 by the Giants, of all people, who weren't ready to pay the price for him back then]. He had turned down more money than they had and frankly he wasn't interested in living that down. Whether it was because of that or because that team liked to go out and party and Barry didn't, a kind of silent conspiracy started . . . The jealousy parlayed into a sort of 'the hell with Barry' thing and he got frozen out."

The isolation was not new to him, because Barry Bonds was accustomed to not needing anyone. As the young son of Bobby, much-travelled superstar and five-time 30-30 man, Barry Bonds kidded with Willie McCovey and cavorted with Willie Mays, his

Bobby Bonds as a young Giant in the late '60s.

idol. However, for eight months of the year, while Bobby was off somewhere hitting 332 homers and stealing 461 bases, Barry was growing up without his dad.

"I never understood why he didn't spend more time with me," said Barry, acknowledging they didn't become close until he was in college. "We're best of friends now. We play golf and talk all the time. But back then, I missed not having him at my games and so on."

Barry will wear his dad's old number, 25. Mays gave Barry

permission to don his treasured 24, but fan reaction caused Barry to switch.

Bobby will be at Barry's games this season, because the elder Bonds is the newly hired hitting instructor for his first former team, the Giants. Now he will be right beside his son to offer the guidance, advice and support he had previously given him on the telephone.

"Barry knows I've been there," said Bobby. "I've stood 60 feet, 6 inches from Bob Gibson and Don Drysdale. There is no situation that comes up for Barry that I haven't gone through myself at one time—the hitting aspect, the mental aspect, any aspect."

There are few aspects of hitting, catching and throwing a baseball that Barry hasn't already mastered. In 1992, playing under the pressure of prospective free agency, without his friend Bobby Bonilla to share the run-producing load, Bonds led the Pirates to a third straight NL East title by hitting .311 with 34 homers and 103 RBI. He scored 109 runs, walked 127 times (32 of them intentional) and won a Gold Glove on the way to becoming the 10th NL player to win more than one MVP award.

Now, he'll be the centerpiece for the Giants' new ownership, who wanted him so badly that, after paying $100 million to buy the club from Bob Lurie, they anted up nearly half of that again to outbid the Yankees and several other clubs for Bonds' services. With an average salary of more than $7.29 million, Bonds surpassed the Cubs' Ryne Sandberg at the top of baseball's earnings list in December. Of course, no one has to tell Barry that money and talent don't guarantee happiness or friends, two things he has sometimes found hard to come by.

There was the flap over calling teammate Andy Van Slyke "Pittsburgh's Great White Hope" and the stir he caused when he accused teammate Jeff King of not playing through the pain of a back injury in the 1990 NLCS—six months before King required major disk surgery. And, of course, there was that famous square-off with Leyland.

"My dad only told me a couple of things in the way of advice about baseball," Barry said. "He told me to play the game as long as I could, because it all goes so fast. And he told me to keep my mouth shut. I guess that second one got by me."

Still, Bonds believes that, because he has said some intemperate things while wearing his angry game face, he is widely misunderstood.

"A lot of times I can come across as a bad person, because I'm doing things that get Barry Bonds prepared for a game," he said. "I go to the ballpark, work myself up, in anger, thinking I want that pitcher. Then when I say to guys, 'Leave me alone,' they say 'What's your problem? Every single day, you come in mad.' Then, on the days, I come in laughing, it's 'You're not applying yourself' or 'How come you're not focused?'

"I can't smile things off like Bobby Bonilla did. I have to be mad and hungry. That's the way I play best."

Though Bonds has been portrayed as the quintessential modern, self-obsessed player, he is more acutely aware of his debts to pioneers like Jackie Robinson than are a lot of his black contemporaries. When the Pirates had a "Turn Back the Clock" promotion last year in which the Reds and Pirates wore their 1939 uniforms, Bonds wore one red sock and one black sock as a tribute to Robinson and the Negro League players who were excluded in those days.

However, the face he chooses to show the media is almost always that of the angry young man.

"I like people," he said. "My friends give me my space and my privacy. The media, they sometimes want to step over the line . . . They think they can defeat me, but they're not going to. I've always been able to separate the controversy from my ballplaying."

And no one can find fault with his ballplaying, especially last year—until October, when he got off to another awful start in the NLCS, strengthening the perception of him as one of the game's most glaring postseason non-performers, especially in the clutch. He felt at least part of the problem was that the media-circus atmosphere of the playoffs made his normal pre-game preparations impossible to maintain.

"[Usually] I lay down before a game and close my eyes," he said. "A lot of times people think I'm sleeping before a game, but I'm not. I take myself away from baseball and try to block everything around me . . . the fans, the announcers, the players, the umpires, the media. I block it all out and just see what is in front of me.

"I try to visualize the pitcher, his motion, the release point. It's not a trick. I watch the pitcher in the bullpen from the dugout before the game. I visualize that motion coming to me. I start timing everything from that point. There is so much happening [during the postseason], I'm a different person. I have to be left alone. I have to be by myself. I'm not making excuses, but you don't get that time alone in the postseason."

After Game 4 last October, Bonds—desperately wanting to give the city of Pittsburgh and Leyland the going-away gift of a

World Championship—was so upset with his failures at the plate that he even dropped the tough-guy routine long enough to seek the fatherly advice of his manager, friend and sympathizer.

He knew he could be looking at his final game as a Pirate in Pittsburgh the next day and couldn't accept what was happening. He walked into Leyland's office, sat quietly in a corner while Leyland talked to the media and waited for a moment alone with him. Bonds' face was long, his mood pensive.

"I felt bad for my team, for the city, for Jim Leyland. I couldn't understand how I could be so outstanding for 162 games and then disappear," he said. "I just didn't want it to end that way."

"He feels bad, like he let me down, like he let the whole club down. I tried to tell him that isn't the case," said Leyland after their talk. "I think there's some uncertainty there about where he's going to be playing, about whether or not we're going to be together again."

Maybe Leyland was right about Bonds being upset at the prospect of leaving a city and a manager he had grown to love for literally greener pastures. As a result, perhaps he wasn't enjoying what Leyland said should've been "the best time of his life."

"I told him, 'You have to remember the rainbow is not green,' " said Leyland. "You know, you hear players say 'I have to take care of my family.' That really gets me. With $27 million, you can take care of Guam."

After leaving Leyland, Bonds called his buddy Bonilla, back home in Bradenton, and talked with him until the wee hours. It was 6 A.M. before he got to bed prior to one of the most important games of his career. While the media spent the day analyzing his postseason failures, Bonds slept all day.

And that night, in front of a large Game 5 crowd in Pittsburgh that included Bonilla—flown to Pittsburgh for the occasion by Barry's wife Sun—Bonds' life changed. He was greeted not by booing, but rather by one of the warmest ovations Three Rivers Stadium has ever granted anyone. Pirate fans, chanting "Stay, Barry, stay," were also thanking him for the memories.

And the angry young man against the world, who has always acted like he needed no one, suddenly realized that he had been adopted by everyone.

Bonds finally had a Barry Bonds game in October with two hits and a great catch. He now understands that it need not be him against the world. Maybe he has come to the conclusion he no longer needs to be mad to be bad.

Or maybe Barry Bonds the Giant will be as mad and bad as ever.

He has averaged 36 stolen bases over seven seasons.

O Canada! O Alomar! The Making of A National Hero

By KEVIN KERNAN

This was the scene before Game 5 of the World Series in the SkyDome. Toronto outfielder Dave Winfield was alongside the batting cage, warning reporters not to get too close or else they might get lumped by his lumber as he took some serious practice swings.

All around Winfield other grim-faced Blue Jays were getting ready for that night's encounter against the Braves by tuning up the finer points of their game.

Behind the team's dugout, however, in a tunnel leading to the Toronto clubhouse, there sat one relaxed Blue Jay, wearing a blue sweat top, uniform pants, a headband and a Gold Glove smile. For Roberto Alomar, this was a moment to sit back and enjoy. So there he was, propped on a box joking with a handful of fans.

It was difficult to tell who was having more fun, Alomar or the blessed backstage fans.

Why shouldn't Alomar look as comfortable as a cat sitting in front of a cozy fire? After all, he was at his home while the rest of the ballplayers were just visiting the SkyDome. For Alomar, it's a leisurely five-minute walk and a freight-elevator ride from home plate to his suite at the SkyDome Hotel.

Isn't it only fitting that Alomar, whose life has been surrounded by the game since the day he was born, lives in a ballpark? Isn't

---

Kevin Kernan escaped the harsh New York winters six years ago to follow the Sun, and the Padres, for the San Diego Union and Tribune. *He was a witness to the rise of Alomar in the budding star's years as a Padre.*

Roberto Alomar celebrates flight of the Blue Jays.

that what baseball is all about—going home?

"It's a great place to live," Alomar said of the SkyDome Hotel, "I show up and play."

Show up and play second base the way no one else in the game can. Watching Alomar roam around second is like watching a stone skip over a pond. He covers everything from the right-field line to behind second base all in an instant, always pushing the envelope, making plays other second baseman can only dream about.

Offensively, Alomar energizes the Blue Jays' attack. The switch-hitter led the team in hitting with a .310 average during the regular season and then guided the Blue Jays to their first World Championship, winning MVP honors in the ALCS and slamming The Home Run in Game 4 against Dennis Eckersley. During the World Series, he was outstanding in the field and came up with a three-hit performance in the Game 6 clincher.

"Robbie is a century player," said his former agent Scott Boras. "At the end of the century, when you put together the best teams of each decade over the past 100 years, he'll be there."

All that, and he's only 25. In this age of negativity, Alomar is that rare athlete who not only plays the game with style and substance, but enjoys himself on the field. The faithful fans in Toronto recognize that and have responded to him warmly. The former Padre has found the perfect home. The Blue Jays are baseball's nouveau riche and Alomar is their brightest star.

He sparkles like the Toronto skyline, expensive and sleek, brimming with confidence and unlimited potential. Since being traded by San Diego to Toronto along with Joe Carter for Fred McGriff and Tony Fernandez in the 1990 winter meetings, Alomar has taken over the city and much of the country.

"He's the next Prime Minister," reliever Tom Henke said. "If he would run, he would win. I'm not kidding. He's that popular. I've never seen a player as well-liked as Robbie and I've never seen anybody play second base like Robbie."

"Alomar is a manager's player," noted Oriole skipper Johnny Oates. "He's a situation-type player who is an offensive threat. He can drive the ball, but he also will give himself up to manufacture a run and give them a chance to get out front in a hurry. He's a .300 hitter who can hit a few home runs and steal bases, but he's not concerned about those numbers. You can see that in the way he will do whatever it takes to get the man on base in scoring position. You don't find a lot of impact players with that mentality. It's impressive."

Toronto, the city, has been a lot more than Alomar expected. "This is a great place to play," he said. "I didn't know that when I was traded. I thought it would be just like Montreal. I miss San Diego, but I'm a Blue Jay now."

He will always have his Padres memories, though. In his locker in the spacious Blue Jays clubhouse, there's a special picture of Robbie, brother Sandy and dad, Sandy Sr.

All three are wearing those broad Alomar smiles.

And all three are wearing Padre uniforms. Brown uniforms.

Alomars at 1990 All-Star Game: Dad, Roberto, Sandy Jr.

It's a picture from another era.

"Considering everything that's happened with the Padres," Alomar said matter-of-factly, "the trade was the best thing that could have happened to me. I'm just glad I'm in Toronto."

So are his Blue Jay teammates and the rest of Canada.

Before the ninth inning of the Blue Jays' pennant-clinching victory over the A's, Carter walked up to Alomar behind second base and gave him a hug. "I just told Robbie that I was glad that he was traded here with me," Carter said of that special moment, adding the Padres will always regret dealing Alomar. "He could be in the Hall of Fame someday."

"Robbie has been everything we expected and more," said Toronto GM Pat Gillick, who pulled the trigger on the deal.

Remarked manager Cito Gaston, "I just don't know what else to say about Robbie. He's one of the finest second basemen I've ever seen and one of the most unselfish players I've seen, especially in the way he gives himself up to win a ballgame. It's so unusual to see that in a young player. Without him, we'd never be where we are today."

Legendary Cubs scout Hugh Alexander, who has been in baseball more than 50 years, knows quality when he sees it. "Alomar gets my MVP vote," Alexander said, picking Alomar over Eckersley, who came away with MVP honors. "He's always there when something happens: gets a double, steals, dives to get a ground ball. He's everywhere."

Alomar is everywhere off the field, too. He's on CHSC—the Canadian Home Shopping Channel—at 1 A.M. You can buy an official autographed Robbie Alomar baseball or a Robbie Alomar plaque with an autographed picture. "Wouldn't that look great in your den?" offered the well-groomed talking head doing the sales pitch. Then there's the limited edition World Series autographed ball, which is "sure to be a collector's item."

Wake up in the morning and Alomar is on the radio. Throughout the playoffs and World Series a local station was beating to death a catchy tune called "Rockin' Robbie," tweet-tweeting sweet praise to Alomar.

And, oh yes, his biography, *Second to None*, was due to hit the bookstores in time for spring training.

In 1991, Alomar's first season in Toronto, he was named the Labatt's "Blue" Player of the Year and was honored by the Toronto baseball writers as the Jays' MVP when he batted .295 and won his first of what should be many Gold Gloves. The Jays rewarded Alomar with a four-year deal worth $18.5 million.

"I don't think I would have gotten that in San Diego," he said, knowing the Padres' financial problems. This past season, Alomar responded with better numbers, batting .310 with a team-high 87 walks, 76 RBI, 105 runs scored, 27 doubles, eight triples and 49 stolen bases.

The key to understanding Alomar's contributions is that he makes the play when it is most needed. Nothing is done for numbers. Everything is done for one purpose—winning. Thirteen times during the season he stole third base. He hit .354 with runners in scoring position and an incredible .444 with the bases loaded. During the ALCS, he batted .423. On the field, he is always thinking. His father, Sandy, who spent 15 years in the majors as an infielder, taught him well. "Robby knows how to play the game," Sandy said. "He is a very smart player."

Detroit manager Sparky Anderson called him "the most complete player in the game today."

The charismatic Alomar also knows how to play the game off the field. His marketing representative, John Boggs of San Diego, said Alomar would have a windfall off-season, making somewhere in "the high six figures." Alomar not only owns a Gold Glove, but he possesses the golden touch. His endorsements include McDonalds, Zubaz, a casual clothing company; Cooper sporting goods and a board game called Baseball Mania, which was recently named one of the "Top 15 International Games."

How he came about endorsing such a game is typical Alomar. On a winter day he ran into the game's inventors in the SkyDome lobby, cleared off a narrow table, played the game, loved it and decided to endorse it.

Living downtown at the SkyDome has been a plus for Alomar in many ways. He absorbs the flavor of the city like no other athlete in Toronto and few in America.

"Robbie has got a Michael Jordan-type mystique most definitely in Canada," Boggs added. "Now the challenge is to bring that across the border. The beauty of Canada and Toronto is the intensity of the fans there. They love their Blue Jays. So, for the more visible players, it's an incredible marketing place. It's a gold mine because of the intensity of the fans, because of the fact it's a winning franchise and it's a first-class franchise. Everywhere you go, it's the Blue Jays. They wear the Blue Jay colors. What I find, too, is that there is a tremendous corporate involvement in Canada. The Canadian entities of U.S.-based corporations are very tied in, tuned in to the Blue Jays. In every aspect, the Blue Jays are like a national team."

And Alomar has become their national hero.

"He has captured the hearts of the Canadians," Boggs said. "He has charisma. He's young, he's good-looking and he's single. And he's personable. I've been with him in Toronto and there is one thing that Roberto Alomar does that is really indicative—he takes care of his fans. He is not aloof in any way. He will sign autographs. He will take time to stop for people to do whatever it takes."

Alomar said the reason for his kindness to fans is simple. "I was a fan once," he said. "You have to realize that. I know what it's like. Without the fans I am nothing in this game. I treat the fans the way they treat me. If you are good to them, they'll be good to you. They are the ones who pay to see you play. I never thought I would get this popular. So now that I have the chance to meet so many fans and do so many endorsements, why not do it? I never thought I'd be in the World Series, either; that's why it was so much fun."

Alomar's enthusiasm for the game may be his greatest attribute. From the day he walked on the field as a rookie with the Padres in 1988, it was obvious that he loved playing baseball. All it took was one look at his uniform pants, covered with grass stains before the games even started, to see that he was different than most players. Alomar may still be the only player in the majors who gets dirty during batting practice diving for balls.

"I still love to do that when we play on grass," he said with child-like wonder. "The name of this game is fun. The only way to have fun is by enjoying the game and letting that feeling take over."

Alomar said he is a fan of the game and all he has to do to

Free-swinging Roberto found a happy home in the dome.

prove that is to look at a 1977 Blue Jays yearbook. That was the first year of the Blue Jays' existence. One picture in the yearbook shows outfielder Otto Velez talking with two young fans. The fans aren't identified, but they are Roberto and his brother Sandy.

"I think that picture was taken in Texas," Alomar said. "We were always around the ballpark."

Alomar remembers another ballplayer's son always playing with their group—Barry Bonds. "We had a lot of fun," he said.

While his father was off playing for the Braves, White Sox, Angels, Yankees and Rangers, Roberto spent most of his time back home in Puerto Rico with his mother Maria. He gives her credit for a lot of his success.

"She taught us discipline, that's for sure," Alomar said with a laugh. "She was the one who made sure we went to school. She was the one who took us to Little League. She took care of us. She taught us how to be responsible at an early age. A lot of my friends growing up, they went the wrong way and didn't get anywhere. I always went the right way and look where I am now. If those guys had gone the right way, they'd be here, too."

Like a good son, Roberto still listens when given advice by his parents. Whether it's Little League or the majors, baseball has always been a game of fathers and sons. Before Game 4 when Alomar drilled that game-tying, ninth-inning homer off Eckersley, the father told the son that he was not concentrating enough during infield practice. "He told me to take infield like it was the game," Roberto recalled. "I listen to my dad. He is the best advisor I ever had. He and my mother have seen me play since I was a kid. They are the ones who know when I'm going good and when I'm going bad. They know what to say."

"I've always talked to him," Sandy Sr. said. "Sometimes because of his age he takes things for granted. Sometimes he has to be reminded about the little things."

The conversation hit home. Alomar went 4-for-5 in Game 4, hoisting the home run and starting a key rally in the eighth with a double that knocked out starter Bob Welch as the Blue Jays recorded the largest comeback in postseason play.

"Everybody remembers the homer, but that double might have been just as important," Roberto says.

The home run will be a magic moment forever in post-season history. As Alomar made contact he raised his hands to the heavens in triumph and, in that second, an indelible image was created.

"I wasn't trying to show anybody up," Alomar said of his salute. "I was just reaching to the moment. It was just such a great feeling. Without that home run we don't win the game. If we lose that game, we might lose the series because they won the next game and would have been ahead, 3-2."

Gordon Lakey, the Blue Jays' special assignment scout and Gillick's right-hand man, may have said it best when he said that blast was heard around the baseball world. "That is the second-biggest home run in our lifetime by a second baseman," Lakey noted.

The first, of course, was hit by Pittsburgh's Bill Mazeroski, the famed ninth-inning homer off the Yankees' Ralph Terry in Game 7 of the 1960 World Series.

After all his success, Alomar was asked how could Toronto, how could Canada, honor him even more.

"I don't know," he answered with a slight grin. "Maybe they can name the hotel after me."

The Alomar. Has a nice championship ring to it.

The Eck: From Fear to A's Saving Grace

By RON KROICHICK

The irony bounced around the SkyDome. As the Blue Jays were about to secure their first American League pennant, a derisive chant began in right field, near the Athletics' bullpen, and spread slowly throughout the stadium:

"We Want Eck! We Want Eck!"

Dennis Eckersley's arrival almost invariably has meant impending defeat for opposing teams, but this time the taunting Toronto faithful were savoring their team's rare and recent achievement: puncturing Eck's cloak of armor in a shocking Game 4 finish from which Oakland couldn't recover.

"Somebody's got to be the hero and somebody's got to be the goat," Eckersley said. "It's not like I had a horrible season."

Actually, Eckersley had another phenomenal season in 1992. The veteran reliever's outrageous numbers—51 saves in 54 chances, 7-1 record, 1.91 ERA—carried him to both the American League Cy Young Award and MVP designation. Only three other relief pitchers have been MVPs: Jim Konstanty, Phillies, 1950; Rollie Fingers, Brewers, 1981, and Willie Hernandez, Tigers, 1984.

Although his playoff disappointment left a nasty stain on his season, it was not nasty enough to overshadow the remarkable revival story of an alcoholic once headed toward the junkyard for starting pitchers who instead became the premier reliever in the

---

Ron Kroichick covers the A's for the Sacramento Bee. *Because he never had Eck-like control, his pitching career ended with his days as Little Leaguer.*

Dennis Eckersley owns the world in the ninth inning.

game. "I have such a passion for what I do because I look at it as my second chance," he said.

Now, six years after joining Oakland, Eckersley finishes victories as reliably as the Star-Spangled Banner precedes them. He leads the major leagues with 220 saves over the last five seasons, far ahead of second-place Bobby Thigpen (177) of the White Sox.

Along the way, Eckersley has helped the A's win four AL West titles. It started in 1988, when manager Tony La Russa and pitching coach Dave Duncan anointed Eckersley as Oakland's full-time closer.

He blossomed that season, earning 45 saves and instant recognition as a top closer. Now, he doesn't expect a single late-inning lead to get away.

"I think I throw harder at times than I did in '88," Eckersley said last season. "I'm in better shape, physically. And I walk out there expecting to be good. In '88, I was surprising myself."

Last season, Eckersley converted his first 36 save opportunities. The A's did not lose a game in which he participated until August 25. He and victory were joined at the hip. The closer's job has evolved through the years from multi-inning work to the ninth-inning specialty duty to which Eckersley seems to be uniquely suited.

One of the keys to his domination has been his ability to ruthlessly paint the corners of home plate with his pitches. Eck's career strikeout-to-walk ratio of 3.12 is the third-highest in baseball history, behind only Juan Marichal and Ferguson Jenkins. Last season, Eckersley walked 11 and struck out 93.

The natural question seems to be how long can Eckersley continue to dominate hitters? He's 38 years old, with retirement nowhere on the horizon. He signed a two-year, $7.5-million contract extension last July. The A's have a $4-million option for 1995—and Eckersley hopes they'll want to exercise it.

"My desire to be the best I can be is as great as ever," he said last season. "If I can hold up physically, I hope I can perform at this level for the next three years. I feel indebted to the A's because of what they did for my career."

Eckersley compares his job to that of a field-goal kicker in football. You wait around, watch your team move into position to win . . . and then assume full responsibility.

"People are always relying on you to close it out," Eckersley said. "If you don't, it's devastation."

Devastation does not visit often, but it showed up during Game 4 of last October's ALCS. The Blue Jays battered Eckersley in the eighth and ninth, turning likely defeat into improbable triumph.

Dennis and Nancy on the day he won the Cy Young Award.

Roberto Alomar struck the telling blow, a two-run, game-tying home run in the ninth. Losing can be even harder to swallow for someone whom defeat finds so rarely.

"It took me a long time to get over it," Eckersley says. "I almost had to leave the Bay Area and go on with my life. I know I disappointed a lot of people, including myself."

For a man who had to save himself before he could save any games, bouncing back from adversity is nothing new. As a recovering alcoholic, he has learned to conquer "the fear of being responsible." But, first, Eckersley had to hit rock bottom. It happened in December 1986, when he saw a videotape of himself—drunk—in front of his young daughter, Mandee. Vividly awakened to his problem, he checked into a treatment center in Newport, R.I. He departed six weeks later. *Sober. Wiser. More patient. In control.*

"The treatment made me accept a lot of things about myself,"

Eckersley says. "That goes in every part of my life—at home and especially in my profession. It gives you a much greater appreciation. That's what it did for me. It gave me a second chance in life. I'm glad I got a chance before it was too late."

Alcoholism led his older brother, Wallace, into a life of trouble. Wallace now is in prison, convicted of the kidnapping and attempted murder of a Colorado woman in 1987.

Dennis, meanwhile, has found domestic tranquility with his second wife Nancy, three-year-old son Jake, and Mandee, his teenage daughter from his first marriage. He owns homes in the Bay Area and in Boston, Nancy's hometown.

When Eckersley retires from baseball, he wants people to remember more than his sliders on the corner and more than his phenomenal run as the best relief pitcher in the universe. Eckersley wants people to remember his troubled path. "For the most part, I'm proud of how I turned my career around," he said. "More than anything, that's what my life represents. There is hope. You can change your life. That's why I talk about it. It gives people hope."

And it gives Eckersley some humility in the face of his notable achievements.

Since becoming Oakland's full-time closer in 1988, Eck has converted 220 saves in 248 chances (88.7 percent). His ERA is 1.90. His strikeout-to-walk ratio of 378-to–38 falls somewhere between unfathomable and unfair.

Eckersley throws hard and his control borders on unreal. But he refuses to let his ego stand in his way.

"He listens," Terry Steinbach, his catcher, said. "He never puts himself above that. Sometimes, you're leery of giving your opinion to a guy with his credentials. But he always listens."

While waiting for the call, Eckersley finds comfort in his routine: Run like a maniac before the game. Watch five innings on television in the clubhouse. Sit in the dugout for an inning or two. Jog to the bullpen in the eighth. By the time Eckersley reaches the mound, his cool, casual manner has faded away. He is intense, purposeful, even brash. He works quickly, like a machine.

He becomes "The Eck."

"I hate to say I don't know the guy, but I am different out there," he said. "It's amazing what this game does to you."

Eckersley's mind clicks away as he analyzes hitters the way Tony Gwynn studies pitchers. Though he essentially throws only two pitches—the fastball and the slider—he mixes speeds and locations masterfully.

"He's very smart," former Seattle second baseman Harold

Reynolds said. "I saw him twice in a week and he pitched me different each time—with the same result. I struck out. I faced him the second time and I said to myself, "OK, I know what he did to me the other day in Oakland. I figured I'd jump on it. Then he changed his speeds. Awww."

Eckersley's fastball flirts with the 90-mile-per-hour mark, which is fast, but not Roger Clemens fast. He does not really overpower hitters. They are instead carved into neat pieces because of Eckersley's gift for spotting pitches precisely where he wants to throw them.

This reputation for throwing strikes accompanies him to the pitcher's mound. Umpires know they might as well keep their right arms raised to save some energy.

Sometimes, the reputation helps. He struck out Chili Davis last season on a pitch several miles inside. It was a called strike, leaving Davis flabbergasted and renewing hushed talk of how Eckersley's control intimidates umpires.

One opposing hitter, asked the size of Eckersley's strike zone, smiled and spread his arms far apart. Really far apart. "It's huge," the hitter said.

White Sox outfielder Tim Raines figures Eckersley has earned the favor of the umps. Hang around the plate long enough and you get the calls.

"It's sort of like it was with Pete Rose," Raines said. "Two strikes and there's a pitch down the middle—if Pete doesn't swing, it has to be a ball. Eck is the most effective pitcher in baseball on the corners . . . Somehow it seems like he never gives you a good pitch to hit. And, once you get two strikes, you're at his mercy."

Eckersley has always gestured at hitters following strikeouts. He insists it's his way of releasing emotion. A's broadcaster Ray Fosse—who caught Eckersley's no-hitter with Cleveland in 1977, even recalls him shouting at dawdling hitters to "get in there."

Eckersley swaggered through 12 eventful seasons as a starting pitcher. The tour took him from Cleveland to Boston to the Chicago Cubs. There was the no-hitter, one 20-win season, several ordinary seasons . . . and plenty of wild nights.

Those days, as a starter, he picked his spots. These days, Eckersley never knows when the A's will need him. So he now channels once-wayward energy into exercise.

"He doesn't smoke, drink or carouse," Fosse said. "He's smart enough to know he can't do that. He finally woke up and realized it. It takes quite a man to realize it and get on with the rest of his life."

Dennis, with Storm Davis, looks for the right stuff in 1988.

Manager Tony La Russa and pitching coach Dave Duncan protect Eckersley's right arm as if it were a precious jewel. They know he has thrown nearly 3,000 innings in his 18-year career. Because he rarely enters games before the ninth inning and almost never works more than one inning, hitters see his funky, side-winding delivery only once per game. La Russa never overuses Eckersley. Never!

Eckersley appreciates the way La Russa and Duncan pamper him. As he said, smiling mischievously, when he signed his contract extension, "If I go somewhere else, they might expect me to pitch two innings."

So he remains in Oakland, nicking corners with his fastball in the city where he was born. His parents, Bernice and Wally, attend most A's home games and find joy in watching him pitch amid trying times for the family.

It all traces to his biggest save. Himself.

COLORADO ROCKIES™

Good Luck! Colorado Rockies, Florida Marlins

By ERIC COMPTON

Welcome to the Year of Expansion as the National League's first-year Colorado Rockies and Florida Marlins attempt to answer that age-old expansionist question: "Can anyone here play this game?"

Judging by the history of newly assembled teams—this year's duo is the first in major league baseball since the Seattle Mariners and Toronto Blue Jays in 1977—the Rockies and Marlins shouldn't expect miracles.

With an initial investment of $95 million per franchise, Colorado principal owners Jerry (trucking magnate) McMorris and John (beverage entrepreneur) Antonucci and their Florida counterpart Wayne (Blockbuster Video) Huizenga bravely go to bat in

---

Eric Compton of Newsday *is a contributing editor of the Handbook.*

a new world governed by balls and strikes and all the unknowns that have challenged the Finleys, Veecks, Rupperts, Busches and Steinbrenners before them.

There is no living in the past for either team. Oh, Denver can point with nostalgia to its minor league Bears of yore (Zephyrs, more recently) and a procession of players who passed through Denver on the way to the bigs (ex-Bears Tony Kubek, Bobby Richardson, Ryne Duren, Don Larsen, Art Fowler, irresistible Marv Throneberry, Woodie Held, Norm Siebern, Tim Raines, Tim Wallach, Darrell Johnson, Graig Nettles and ex-Zephyrs Barry Larkin, Chris Sabo, Rob Dibble, Eric Davis, Paul O'Neill, for instance).

How welcome these Denver alumni (the retireds in their prime, naturally) would be in the Rockies lineup for their first major league game on April 5 against the New York Mets at Shea Stadium and their first home opener on April 9 against the Montreal Expos at homer-prone Mile High Stadium.

Miami and its South Florida neighbors have had minor league teams going back to the 1912 Miami Magicians. Since then there have been Tourists, Wahoos, Flamingos, Tarpons, Indians, Sun Sox and, since 1956, with occasional relocation, the Marlins.

Along the way, the minor league Marlins have rostered an assortment of future major leaguers and one ageless legend, Satchel Paige, who posted a 31-22 record when he was still pitching in his mid-fifties or so, from 1956 through 1958.

Among the grads who graced Marlin lineups were Fergie Jenkins, Alex Johnson, Johnny Oates (now the Orioles' manager), Dennis Martinez, Eddie Murray and Jose Canseco (1-for-9 in his six-game Marlin career in 1982).

A fan's fantasy would have these former Marlins jump-starting

FLORIDA MARLINS EXPANSION DRAFT

No.	Pos.	Player, Team, '92 Stats	'92 Salary
ROUND 1			
1.	OF	Nigel Wilson, Toronto: AAA, .274, 26 HR, 69 RBI	$109,000
2.	RHP	Jose Martinez, N.Y. Mets: (AA) 5-2, 1.71 ERA	N/A
3.	2B	Bret Barberie, Montreal: .232, 1 HR, 24 RBI	$129,000
4.	RHP	Trevor Hoffman, Cincinnati: (AAA) 4-6, 4.27 ERA, 65⅓ IP	$109,000
5.	RHP	Patrick Rapp, San Francisco: 0-2, 7.20 ERA	$109,000
6.	LHP	[a]Greg Hibbard, Chi. White Sox: 10-7, 4.40 ERA, 176 IP	$210,000
7.	CF	Chuck Carr, St. Louis: .219, 3 RBI, 10 SB	$109,000
8.	RF	Darrell Whitmore, Cleveland: (A) .280, 10 HR, 52 RBI	N/A
9.	C	[b]Eric Helfand, Oakland: (A) .289, 10 HR, 44 RBI	N/A
10.	RHP	Bryan Harvey, California: 0-4, 2.83 ERA, 13 SV	$3,125,000
11.	IF-OF	Jeff Conine, Kansas City: .253, 0 HR, 9 RBI	$109,000
12.	RHP	Kip Yaughn, Baltimore: (AA) 7-8, 3.48 ERA	N/A
13.	CF	Jesus Tavarez, Seattle: (AA), .258, 3 HR, 25 RBI	N/A
ROUND 2			
1.	OF	Carl Everett, N.Y. Yanks: (A), .230, 2 HR, 19 RBI	N/A
2.	RHP	Dave Weathers, Toronto: 0-0, 8.10 ERA	$121,000
3.	RHP	John Johnstone, N.Y. Mets: (AA) 7-7, 3.74 ERA, 149⅓ IP	$109,000
4.	SS	Ramon Martinez, Pittsburgh: (A) .289, 3 HR, 30 RBI	N/A
5.	C	Steve Decker, San Francisco: .163, 0 HR, 1 RBI	$130,000
6.	RHP	Cris Carpenter, St. Louis: 5-4, 2.97 ERA, 88 IP	$150,000
7.	RHP	Jack Armstrong, Cleveland: 6-15, 4.64 ERA, 166⅔ IP	$400,000
8.	RHP	Scott Chiamparino, Texas: 0-4, 3.55 ERA, 25⅓ IP	$112,000
9.	RHP	[c]Tom Edens, Minnesota: 6-3, 2.83 ERA, 76⅓ IP	$137,000
10.	RHP	Andres Berumen, Kansas City: (A) 5-2, 2.65 ERA, 57⅔ IP	N/A
11.	RHP	[d]Robert Person, Chi. White Sox: (A) 5-7, 3.59 ERA, 105⅓ IP	N/A
12.	RHP	Jim Corsi, Oakland: 4-2, 1.43 ERA, 44 IP	$125,000
13.	RHP	Richie Lewis, Baltimore: 1-1, 10.20 ERA, 6⅔ IP	$109,000
ROUND 3			
1.	LHP	[e]Danny Jackson, Cubs-Pitt: 8-13, 3.84 ERA, 201⅓ IP	$2,425,000
2.	C	Bob Natal, Montreal: (AAA) .302, 12 HR, 50 RBI	$109,000
3.	RHP	Jamie McAndrew, L.A.: (AA) 3-4, 3.50 ERA, 50½ IP	$109,000
4.	OF	Junior Felix, California: .246, 9 HR, 72 RBI	$590,000
5.	OF	Kerwin Moore, Kansas City: (AA) .235, 4 HR, 17 RBI	$109,000
6.	RHP	Ryan Bowen, Houston: 0-7, 10.96 ERA, 33⅔ IP	$125,000
7.	LHP	Scott Baker, St. Louis: (A) 10-9, 1.96 ERA, 151⅔ IP	N/A
8.	IF	[f]Chris Donnels, N.Y. Mets: .174, 0 HR, 6 RBI	$120,000
9.	IF	Monty Fariss, Texas: .217, 3 HR, 21 RBI	$109,000
10.	LHP	Jeff Tabaka, Milwaukee: 9-5, 2.52 ERA, 92 IP	N/A

a-Traded to Chicago Cubs for Gary Scott and Alex Arias; b-Traded to Oakland for Walt Weiss and Scott Baker; c-Traded to Houston for Brian Griffiths and Hector Carrasco; d-Not offered contract; e-Traded to Philadelphia for Joel Adamson and Matt Whisenant; f-waived and claimed by Astros

COLORADO ROCKIES EXPANSION DRAFT

No. Pos.	Player, Team, '92 Stats	'92 Salary
ROUND 1		
1. RHP	David Nied, Atlanta: 3-0, 1.17 ERA, 23 IP	$109,000
2. 3B	Charlie Hayes, N.Y. Yanks: .257, 18 HR, 66 RBI	$280,000
3. RHP	Darren Holmes, Milwaukee: 4-4, 2.55 ERA, 42⅓ IP	$130,000
4. OF	Jerald Clark, San Diego: .242, 12 HR, 58 RBI	$200,000
5. OF	[a]Kevin Reimer, Texas: .267, 16 HR, 58 RBI	$210,000
6. 2B	Eric Young, L.A.: .258, 1 HR, 11 RBI	$109,000
7. 2B	[b]Jody Reed, Boston: .247, 3 HR, 40 RBI	$1,600,000
8. LHP	Scott Aldred, Detroit: 3-8, 6.78 ERA, 65 IP	$130,000
9. OF	Alex Cole, Pittsburgh: .278, 10 RBI, 7 SB	$162,500
10. C	Joe Girardi, Chi. Cubs: .270, 1 HR, 12 RBI	$300,000
11. RHP	Willie Blair, Houston: 4-7, 4.00 ERA, 78⅔ IP	$134,000
12. C	Jay Owens, Minnesota: (AA) .267, 4 HR, 30 RBI	N/A
13. RHP	Andy Ashby, Philadelphia: 1-3, 7.54 ERA, 37 IP	$109,000
ROUND 2		
1. SS	Freddie Benavides, Cincinnati: .231, 1 HR, 17 RBI	$120,000
2. 2B	Roberto Meija, L.A.: (A) .248, 12 HR, 40 RBI	N/A
3. RHP	Doug Bochtler, Mon.: (AA) 6-5, 2.32 ERA, 77⅔ IP	N/A
4. LHP	Lance Painter, S.D.: (AA) 10-5, 3.53 ERA, 163⅓ IP	N/A
5. LHP	Butch Henry, Houston: 6-9, 4.02 ERA, 165⅔ IP	$109,000
6. RHP	Ryan Hawblitzel, Chi. Cubs: (AA) 12-8, 3.76 ERA	N/A
7. IF	Vinny Castilla, Atlanta: .250, 0 HR, 1 RBI	$109,000
8. RHP	Brett Merriman, Calif.: (AAA) 1-3, 1.42 ERA, 31⅔ IP	N/A
9. 3B	Jim Tatum, Milwaukee: .125, 0 HR, 0 RBI	$109,000
10. RHP	Kevin Ritz, Detroit: 2-5, 5.60 ERA, 80⅓ IP	$125,000
11. C	Eric Wedge, Boston: .250, 5 HR, 11 RBI	$109,000
12. RHP	Keith Shepherd, Philadelphia: 1-1, 3.27 ERA, 22 IP	$109,000
13. RHP	Calvin Jones, Seattle: 3-5, 5.69 ERA, 61⅔ IP	$132,500
ROUND 3		
1. C	Brad Ausmus, N.Y. Yanks: (AAA) .242, 35 RBI	$109,000
2. RHP	Marcus Moore, Tor.: (AA) 5-10, 5.59 ERA, 106⅓ IP	N/A
3. RHP	Armando Reynoso, Atlanta: 1-0, 4.70 ERA, 7⅔ IP	$111,500
4. RHP	Steve Reed, San Francisco: 1-0, 2.30 ERA, 15⅔ IP	$109,000
5. RHP	Mo Sanford, Cincinnati: (AAA) 8-8, 5.68 ERA, 122 IP	$112,000
6. IF	Pedro Castellano, Chi. Cubs: (AAA) .248, 2 HR	$109,000
7. RHP	Curt Leskanic, Minn.: (AAA) 1-2, 9.98 ERA, 15⅓ IP	N/A
8. RHP	Scott Fredrickson, S.D.: (AA) 4-7, 3.19 ERA, 73⅓ IP	N/A
9. OF	Braulio Castillo, Philadelphia: .197, 2 HR, 7 RBI	$109,000
10. LHP	Denis Boucher, Cleveland: 2-2, 6.37 ERA, 41 IP	$116,000

a-Traded to Milwaukee for Dante Bichette; b-Traded to Los Angeles for Rudy Seanez the Florida entry when it hosts the Los Angeles Dodgers in its major league debut on April 5 at Joe Robbie Stadium.

The real world, of course, began with the expansion draft on November 17 when the new teams revealed their strategy: Denver—focus on the present; Florida—accent on the future.

A day after signing veteran Cardinal first baseman Andres Galarraga, Rockies GM Bob Gebhard and manager Don Baylor made 23-year-old Brave pitcher David Nied the No. 1 pick in the draft. But their 12 other picks in the first round, beginning with Yankee third baseman Charlie Hayes, all have had major league experience, if not overwhelming credentials.

On the other hand, Florida GM Dave Dombrowski and manager Rene Lachemann zoomed in on minor league prospects, led by Blue Jay outfielder Nigel Wilson. A prominent exception was veteran Angel reliever Bryan Harvey. And they landed six-year A's shortstop Walt Weiss in a trade.

Dombrowski conceded that the Rockies might be able to field a better team in the beginning, but that "we have the talent ready to break in at the major league level."

Summed up Colorado executive VP John McHale, Jr.: "We wanted to be competitive just as fast as we can and we wanted guys who will stay with us for a number of years—and we think we did that."

For detailed scouting reports and profiles of the new franchises, see Rockies (starting on page 150) and Marlins (starting on page 54.)

EXPANSION TEAM HIGHS, LOWS

Los Angeles Angels (1960)

One of two expansion teams to join the American League in 1960, the Angels were 70-91 in their first season . . . Became the talk of the baseball world in 1961, winning 86 games and staying in the AL race until September . . . Became known as the California Angels in 1965 as they prepared for a move from Dodgers Stadium to Anaheim Stadium in 1966 . . . Finished under .500 in nine of 10 seasons before winning their first divisional title in 1982, when they finished 93-69. Took a 2-0 lead over Milwaukee before losing three straight in best-of-five series . . . Won another divisional title in 1986 with a 92-70 record, but blew three-games-to-one lead and lost to Red Sox . . . Have never been in a World Series.

Washington Senators (1960)

Joined American League as expansion replacement for the old Senators franchise, which relocated in Minnesota as the Twins . . . Finished first year with 61-100 record for ninth place in 10-team league . . . Did not finish within eight games of .500 until 1969, when Ted Williams managed them to 86-76 mark and fourth place in six-team division . . . Moved to Texas and became the Rangers in 1972, but switch of scenery did not mean switch of fortunes . . . Best seasons came in 1977 and 1978, when they had back-to-back second-place finishes and won 94 and 87 games, respectively . . . Only franchise (other than Mariners) never to have played a post-season game.

Houston Colt .45s (1962)

Joined the National League when it went from eight to 10 teams . . . Finished first season with 64-98 record, ahead of established Cubs and expansionist Mets . . . Changed nickname to Astros in 1965, when team moved from Colt Stadium to the Astrodome, the first indoor baseball facility in the world . . . Did not finish higher than eighth or with more than 72 wins until 1969, when league expanded again. That season, Harry Walker managed them to 81-81 record and fifth place in six-team National League West . . . Did not win their first division title until 1980, when they beat Dodgers in one-game playoff after finishing 92-70. They went on to lose five-game playoff series to Phillies . . . Won another NL West title in 1986, when they won team-record 96 games. There was another disappointment in the playoffs, though, as the Mets defeated them in six games.

New York Mets (1962)

The Mets fielded the worst team in history when they lost a record 120 of 160 games in their first season . . . But after seven dreadful years in which they never finished higher than ninth, they amazed the baseball world by winning the World Series in 1969. The Miracle Mets, as they were called, won 100 regular-season games, three more in a playoff series against the Braves, and then capped off the year with a five-game victory over the Orioles in the Series . . . Won another pennant in 1973 though they finished only three games over .500. Again they won a playoff series, over Cincinnati, before losing a seven-game World Series to Oakland . . . After hitting bottom with three last-place finishes in the late 1970s, the Mets rebuilt in the 1980s and became champions again in 1986, when they won a club-record 108 games, defeated the Astros in the playoffs and the Red Sox in the World Series . . . A 100-win season brought them another division title in 1988, but they lost a seven-game playoff series to the Dodgers.

Montreal Expos (1969)

Entered the National League along with San Diego and had a dismal first season, finishing 52-110, 48 games behind the champion Mets . . . They improved to 73 wins the following season and had back-to-back 79-win seasons in 1973 and 1974 . . . Became a contender when the team moved from Jarry Park into Olympic Stadium in 1979. They won a club-record 95 games that season and won 90 more in 1980 . . . The Expos appeared in their first playoff in the strike-shortened 1981 season. They defeated the Phillies in a five-game divisional series before losing to the Dodgers in a five-game NLCS. They have not been back to the playoffs since.

San Diego Padres (1969)

The Padres entered the league with the Expos and coincidentally had the same 52-110 mark in their first season . . . Finished last in their first six seasons and didn't record more than 63 victories until 1975, when they finally escaped the NL West cellar with a 71-91 record that ranked them fourth . . . Did not finish higher than fourth until 1984, when they finished a surprising 92-70 that produced their first division crown . . . The Padres spotted the Cubs a two-game lead in the best-of-five playoffs before winning three games in a row to advance to their first World Series. The magic ended there, though, as the Tigers won in five games.

Kansas City Royals (1969)

Entered the American League West in 1969 and became one of the most successful expansion teams ever . . . After 69 and 65 victories their first two years, the Royals were 85-76, good for a second-place finish, in 1971 . . . It wasn't until five years later, though, that the Royals made the playoffs. They won three straight division titles from 1976 through 1978, but were beaten by the Yankees in the playoffs each time . . . After a second-place finish in 1979, the Royals won the West in 1980 and finally disposed of the Yankees in a three-game sweep in the playoffs before losing to the Phillies in a six-game World Series . . . They also won divisional titles in 1984 and 1985. In 1984 they were beaten by Detroit in the playoffs, but the following year they came back from a three-games-to-one deficit in both the playoffs and World Series to defeat Toronto and St. Louis, respectively, and win their first championship.

Seattle Pilots (1969)

Spent only one season in Seattle before being shifted to Milwaukee and renamed the Brewers in 1970 . . . Pilots finished 64-98 for last place in their inaugural campaign . . . Did not win more than 76 games in any of their first nine seasons before breaking through with 93 wins and a third-place finish in 1978 . . . Their first postseason action came in the strike-shortened 1981 season, when they were beaten by the Yankees in a five-game divisional series . . . There was no stopping them the next season, though, as they won the East with a 95-67 record and then came back from a 2-0 deficit to upend California in the playoffs. The Brewers took a three-games-to-two lead in the World Series before losing to the Cardinals.

Toronto Blue Jays (1977)

The American League expanded to Canada in 1977 and the Blue Jays received a rude welcome as they went 54-107 their first season and followed that with four more last-place finishes . . . Their rush to the top started in 1983, when they posted the first of consecutive 89-73 seasons . . . They won their first East Division title in 1985 with a 99-62 record, but lost a seven-game playoff series to the Royals . . . First-place finishes in 1989 and 1991 also ended in playoff defeats before the Blue Jays reached the pinnacle in 1992. They won the East Division for the fourth time, ousted Oakland in a six-game playoff and then brought Canada its first World Championship with a six-game triumph over the Braves.

Seattle Mariners (1977)

Baseball returned to the Pacific Northwest when the expansion Mariners joined the American League West . . . The team was 64-98 in its first season but did not finish in last place, thanks to the Oakland A's, who were a half-game behind them . . . After five more dismal seasons, the Mariners had an upward turn in 1982, when a 76-86 record brought them a fourth-place finish . . . But they fell back into the cellar in 1983 and did not finish above .500 until 1991, their 15th season, when an 83-79 mark meant fifth place.

How Expansion Teams Fared in First Year

1961	W	L	Pct.	GB	Pos.
Los Angeles Angels[1] (AL)	70	91	.435	38½	8th
Washington Senators[2] (AL)	61	100	.379	47½	9th
1962					
Houston Colt .45s[3] (NL)	64	96	.400	36½	8th
New York Mets (NL)	40	120	.250	60½	10th
1969					
Montreal Expos (NL)	52	110	.321	48	6th
San Diego Padres (NL)	52	110	.321	41	6th
Kansas City Royals (AL)	69	93	.426	26	4th
Seattle Pilots[4] (AL)	64	98	.395	33	6th
1977					
Seattle Mariners (AL)	64	98	.395	38	6th
Toronto Blue Jays (AL)	54	107	.335	45½	7th

1-Now California Angels; 2-Texas Rangers in 1972; 3-Now Astros; 4-Milwaukee Brewers in 1970.

Expansion Team Managers and Marks

Manager	Team	Tenure	W-L	PCT.
Bill Rigney	Los Angeles Angels	1961-69	625-707	.469
Mickey Vernon	Washington Senators	1961-63	135-227	.373
Harry Craft	Houston Colt .45s	1962-64	191-280	.406
Casey Stengel	New York Mets	1962-65	175-404	.302
Gene Mauch	Montreal Expos	1969-75	499-627	.443
Preston Gomez	San Diego Padres	1969-72	180-316	.363
Joe Gordon	Kansas City Royals	1969	69-93	.426
Joe Schultz	Seattle Pilots	1969	64-98	.395
Roy Hartsfield	Toronto Blue Jays	1977-79	166-318	.343
Darrell Johnson	Seattle Mariners	1977-80	226-362	.384

No. 1 Picks of Past Expansion Drafts

Year	Team	Player	Pos.	Previous Team
1960	L.A. Angels	Eli Grba	P	N.Y. Yankees
1960	Washington	Bobby Shantz	P	N.Y. Yankees
1961	Houston	Ed Bressoud	SS	San Francisco
1961	New York	Hobie Landrith	C	San Francisco
1968	Kansas City	Roger Nelson	P	Baltimore
1968	Seattle	Don Mincher	1B	California
1968	Montreal	Manny Mota	OF	Pittsburgh
1968	San Diego	Ollie Brown	OF	San Francisco
1976	Seattle	Ruppert Jones	OF	Kansas City
1976	Toronto	Bob Bailor	SS	Baltimore

Note: Teams began play the following year.

INSIDE THE
NATIONAL LEAGUE

By JOHN BELIS and KEVIN KERNAN
Bridgewater (N.J.) Courier-Post — *San Diego Union*

PREDICTED ORDER OF FINISH

East	West
Montreal Expos	Atlanta Braves
St. Louis Cardinals	Cincinnati Reds
New York Mets	Houston Astros
Chicago Cubs	San Francisco Giants
Pittsburgh Pirates	Los Angeles Dodgers
Philadelphia Phillies	San Diego Padres
Florida Marlins	Colorado Rockies

Playoff Winner: Atlanta

EAST DIVISION

	Team	Owner	1992	Morning Line Manager
1	**EXPOS** Scarlet, white & royal blue Best in weak field	Claude Brochu	W 87 L 75	3-1 Felipe Alou
2	**CARDINALS** Red & white Close all the way	August A. Busch III	W 83 L 79	4-1 Joe Torre
3	**METS** Orange, white & blue Last chance to win	N. Doubleday/F. Wilpon	W 72 L 90	8-1 Jeff Torborg
4	**CUBS** Royal blue & white Will fade in stretch	Stanton Cook	W 78 L 84	10-1 Jim Lefebvre
5	**PIRATES** Old gold, white & black Not enough horses	Mark Sauer	W 96 L 66	15-1 Jim Leyland
6	**PHILLIES** Crimson & white Find a way to lose	William Y. Giles	W 70 L 92	20-1 Jim Fregosi
7	**MARLINS** Blue, silver, orange & black Totally outclassed	H. Wayne Huizenga		200-1 Rene Lache-mann

EXPOS prevail at the wire, but **CARDS** are in contention from start to finish as **METS** and **CUBS** fall short. **PIRATES** can't compete. **PHILLIES** disappoint again and **MARLINS** are left at the gate.

Peachtree Classic

117th Running. National League Race. Distance: 162 games plus playoff. Payoff (based on '92): $114,962.16 per winning player, World Series; $84,259.13 per losing player, World Series. A field of 14 entered in two divisions.

Track Record: 116 wins—Chicago, 1906

WEST DIVISION

	Team	Owner	1992	Morning Line / Manager
1	**BRAVES** Royal blue & white Armed and dangerous, again	W. Bartholomay/S. Kasten	1992 W 98 L 64	2-1 Bobby Cox
2	**REDS** Red & white A Big Red hitting machine	Marge Schott	1992 W 90 L 72	4-1 Tony Perez
3	**ASTROS** Orange & white Rapidly making strides	Drayton McLane, Jr.	1992 W 81 L 81	15-1 Art Howe
4	**GIANTS** White, orange & black Still a little short	Peter Magowan	1992 W 72 L 90	40-1 Dusty Baker
5	**DODGERS** Royal blue & white Time for another tuneup	Peter O'Malley	1992 W 63 L 99	50-1 Tommy Lasorda
6	**PADRES** Brown, gold & white Should enter a claimer	Tom Werner	1992 W 82 L 80	100-1 Jim Riggle-man
7	**ROCKIES** Purple, silver & black Too young to race	J. McMorris/J. Antonucci		500-1 Don Baylor

In a stirring finish, **BRAVES** hold on to beat talented field as **REDS** pound on the door and **ASTROS** move up in class. **GIANTS** fade down the stretch and **DODGERS** stumble out of the gate. **PADRES** can't stay with the pack while **ROCKIES** are just along for the ride.

CHICAGO CUBS

TEAM DIRECTORY: Chairman: Stanton Cook; Exec. VP-Baseball Operations: Larry Himes; VP-Scouting and Player Development: Al Goldis; Dir. Media Rel.: Sharon Pannozzo; Trav. Sec.: Jimmy Bank; Mgr.: Jim Lefebvre. Home: Wrigley Field (38,712). Field distances: 355, l.f. line; 400, c.f.; 353, r.f. line. Spring training: Mesa, Ariz.

SCOUTING REPORT

HITTING: The Cubs finished 10th in the NL in runs (593) last season and now they're without free-agent defector Andre Dawson, who has been their big run producer for the last six years. That will put an even greater burden on Ryne Sandberg (.304, 26, 87), who remains one of the most consistent players in baseball. Mark Grace (.307, 9, 79) improved all of his offensive statistics in 1992 and is becoming a better hitter as he matures.

Shawon Dunston has a big bat for a shortstop, but he's questionable because of a bad back which required surgery and limited him to just 18 games. Sammy Sosa (.260, 8, 25 in only 67 games) is coming back from a broken left ankle. Derrick May (.274, 8, 45) showed promise, especially during the second half, as he established himself in left field. Steve Buechele (.261, 9, 64) might put an end to the Cubs' 20-year search for a third baseman.

Perennial free agent Candy "Have Bat, Will Travel" Maldonado (.272, 20, 66 with the Blue Jays) will add pop to the lineup, but he can't replace Dawson as an all-around player or clubhouse presence. Neither can aging former Athletic Willie Wilson (2.70, 0, 37, 28 steals). Rick Wilkins (.270, 8, 22) is a pretty fair hitter for a catcher.

PITCHING: The Cubs made a concerted effort to improve their pitching last winter, adding four solid veterans. But they also lost Cy Young winner Greg Maddux to free agency and he was their first 20-game winner in 15 years. Free-agent addition Jose Guzman (16-11, 3.66 with the Rangers) inherits Maddux' role as the staff ace. Greg Hibbard (10-7, 4.40 with the White Sox) is another key newcomer as the Cubs virtually stole him in a trade with the Marlins on expansion draft day.

Mike Morgan (16-8, 2.55) is coming off a very good first season as a Cub and is almost unbeatable at Wrigley Field. Frank

Cub first baseman enjoyed return to Grace in '92.

Castillo (10-11, 3.46) reached double figures in victories despite pitching in bad luck. Mike Harkey (4-0, 1.89) might be a terrific pitcher if he could only stay healthy. He is coming back from shoulder surgery and a ruptured knee tendon which limited him to 11 starts over the last two seasons.

Chicago's bullpen converted just 36 of 55 save opportunities in 1992, but that should change with the addition of Randy Myers (3-6, 4.29, 38 saves with the Padres) and Dan Plesac (5-4, 2.96 with the Brewers) via free agency. Bob Scanlan (3-6, 2.89, 14 saves) and Paul Assenmacher (4-4, 4.10, 8 saves) are relief holdovers.

FIELDING: Substituting Maldonado for Dawson in right hurts the outfield defense, but the infield looks very good. Grace won a Gold Glove while leading all NL first basemen in putouts and assists. Sandberg saw his string of Gold Gloves snapped at nine, but he still led all second basemen in total chances and he has gone 2½ years without a throwing error. Dunston has a gun at shortstop and Buechele didn't make an error at third base over the last two months.

CHICAGO CUBS 1993 ROSTER

MANAGER Jim Lefebvre

Coaches—Billy Connors, Chuck Cottier, Jose Martinez, Tony Muser, Tom Trebelhorn, Billy Williams

PITCHERS

No.	Name	1992 Club	W-L	IP	SO	ERA	B-T	Ht.	Wt.	Born
45	Assenmacher, Paul	Chicago (NL)	4-4	68	67	4.10	L-L	6-3	210	12/10/60 Allen Park, MI
47	Boskie, Shawn	Iowa	0-0	7	3	3.68	R-R	6-3	200	3/28/67 Hawthorne, NV
		Chicago (NL)	5-11	92	39	5.01				
52	Bullinger, Jim	Iowa	1-2	22	15	2.45	R-R	6-2	185	8/21/65 New Orleans, LA
		Chicago (NL)	2-8	85	36	4.66				
49	Castillo, Frank	Chicago (NL)	10-11	205	135	3.46	R-R	6-1	195	4/1/69 El Paso, TX
33	Dickson, Lance	Iowa	0-1	2	2	19.29	R-L	6-1	185	10/19/69 Fullerton, CA
—	Guzman, Jose	Texas	16-11	224	179	3.66	R-R	6-3	195	4/9/63 Puerto Rico
22	Harkey, Mike	Peoria	1-0	12	17	3.00	R-R	6-5	235	10/25/66 San Diego, CA
		Iowa	0-1	23	18	5.56				
		Charlotte	0-1	8	5	5.63				
		Chicago (NL)	4-0	38	21	1.89				
37	Hibbard, Greg	Chicago (AL)	10-7	176	69	4.40	L-L	6-0	190	9/13/64 New Orleans, LA
32	Hollins, Jessie	Charlotte	3-4	70	73	3.20	R-R	6-3	215	1/27/70 Conroe, TX
		Chicago (NL)	0-0	5	0	13.50				
35	McElroy, Chuck	Chicago (NL)	4-7	84	83	3.55	L-L	6-0	195	10/1/67 Port Arthur, TX
36	Morgan, Mike	Chicago (NL)	16-8	240	123	2.55	R-R	6-2	210	10/8/59 Tulare, CA
—	Myers, Randy	San Diego	3-6	80	66	4.29	L-L	6-1	208	9/19/62 Vancouver, WA
—	Plesac, Dan	Milwaukee	5-4	79	54	2.96	L-L	6-5	215	2/4/62 Gary, IN
—	*Robinson, Jeff	Chicago (NL)	4-3	78	46	3.00	R-R	6-4	200	12/13/60 Santa Ana, CA
30	Scanlan, Bob	Chicago (NL)	3-6	87	42	2.89	R-R	6-8	215	8/9/66 Los Angeles, CA
51	Slocumb, Heathcliff	Chicago (NL)	0-3	36	27	6.50	R-R	6-3	220	6/7/66 Jamaica, NY
		Iowa	1-3	42	47	2.59				
42	*Smith, Dave	Chicago (NL)	0-0	14	3	2.51	R-R	6-1	195	1/21/55 San Francisco, CA
50	Stevens, Dave	Charlotte	9-13	150	89	3.91	R-R	6-4	205	3/4/70 Fullerton, CA
46	Swartzbaugh, Dave	Charlotte	7-10	165	111	3.65	R-R	6-2	195	2/11/68 Middletown, OH
43	Wendell, Turk	Iowa	2-0	25	12	1.44	S-R	6-2	175	5/19/67 Pittsfield, MA

CATCHERS

No.	Name	1992 Club	H	HR	RBI	Pct.	B-T	Ht.	Wt.	Born
—	Lake, Steve	Philadelphia	13	1	2	.245	R-R	6-1	199	3/14/57 Inglewood, CA
7	Pedre, George	Iowa	75	6	34	.253	R-R	6-0	205	10/12/66 Culver City, CA
		Chicago (NL)	0	0	0	.000				
9	Walbeck, Matt	Charlotte	116	7	42	.301	S-R	5-11	185	10/2/69 Sacramento, CA
2	Wilkins, Rick	Iowa	43	5	28	.277	L-R	6-2	215	6/4/67 Jacksonville, FL
		Chicago (NL)	66	8	22	.270				

INFIELDERS

No.	Name	1992 Club	H	HR	RBI	Pct.	B-T	Ht.	Wt.	Born
24	Buechele, Steve	Pitt.-Chi. (NL)	137	9	64	.261	R-R	6-2	200	9/26/61 Lancaster, CA
12	Dunston, Shawon	Chicago (NL)	23	0	2	.315	R-R	6-1	175	3/21/63 Brooklyn, NY
17	Grace, Mark	Chicago (NL)	185	9	79	.307	L-L	6-2	190	6/28/64 Winston-Salem, NC
6	Sanchez, Rey	Iowa	26	0	3	.342	R-R	5-9	170	10/5/67 Puerto Rico
		Chicago (NL)	64	1	19	.251				
23	Sandberg, Ryne	Chicago (NL)	186	26	87	.304	R-R	6-2	185	9/18/59 Spokane, WA
—	Shields, Tommy	Rochester	130	10	59	.302	L-R	6-0	180	8/14/64 Fairfax, VA
25	Viera, Jose	Winston-Salem	111	18	58	.274	R-R	6-1	180	3/26/68 Dominican Republic
16	Vizcaino, Jose	Chicago (NL)	64	1	17	.225	R-S	6-1	180	3/26/68 Dominican Republic

OUTFIELDERS

No.	Name	1992 Club	H	HR	RBI	Pct.	B-T	Ht.	Wt.	Born
28	Dauphin, Phil	Charlotte	113	10	43	.254	L-L	6-1	180	5/11/69 St. Mary's, OH
—	Maldonado, Candy	Toronto	133	20	66	.272	R-R	6-0	195	9/5/60 Puerto Rico
27	May, Derrick	Chicago (NL)	96	8	45	.274	L-R	6-4	225	7/14/68 Rochester, NY
		Iowa	11	2	8	.367				
39	Ramsey, Fernando	Iowa	129	1	38	.269	R-R	6-1	175	12/20/65 Panama
		Chicago (NL)	3	0	2	.120				
19	Roberson, Kevin	Iowa	60	6	34	.305	S-R	6-4	210	1/29/68 Decatur, IL
18	Smith, Dwight	Chicago (NL)	60	3	24	.276	L-R	5-11	195	11/8/63 Tallahassee, FL
		Iowa	2	0	1	.250				
21	Sosa, Sammy	Chicago (NL)	68	8	25	.260	R-R	6-0	185	11/12/68 Dominican Republic
		Iowa	6	0	1	.316				
—	Wilson, Willie	Oakland	107	0	37	.270	S-R	6-3	200	7/9/55 Montgomery, AL

*Free agent offered arbitration

OUTLOOK: If all the new pitchers produce, Jim Lefebvre's Cubs should improve on last year's 78-84 fourth-place finish and they might even contend in this weak division. But it's hard to feel good about a team that just lost Maddux and Dawson.

CUB PROFILES

MARK GRACE 28 6-2 190 Bats L Throws L

Gold Glove first baseman re-dedicated himself and dramatically improved offensive numbers ... Finished ninth in batting, 10th in on-base percentage (.380), fourth in hits and tied for seventh in doubles ... Reached career high in extra-base hits (51) ... Reached base via hit or walk at least 200 times during each of first five seasons ... Committed error Sept. 16 to snap career-high 102-game errorless streak ... Made just four errors in 1992: two bad throws, one bobbled grounder and one dropped popup ... Errorless streak began following two-error game at Los Angeles May 18 ... Had three hitting streaks of at least 10 games, including season-high 13-gamer from June 5-21 ... Born June 28, 1964, in Winston-Salem, N.C. ... Cubs' 24th pick in 1985 draft ... Named Eastern League MVP after driving in 101 runs for Pittsfield (AA) in 1987 ... Finished among NL's top 10 batters four of last five years ... Earned $2.2 million in 1992.

Year	Club	Pos.	G	AB	R	H	2B	3B	HR	RBI	SB	Avg.
1988	Chicago (NL) ..	1B	134	486	65	144	23	4	7	57	3	.296
1989	Chicago (NL) ..	1B	142	510	74	160	28	3	13	79	14	.314
1990	Chicago (NL) ..	1B	157	589	72	182	32	1	9	82	15	.309
1991	Chicago (NL) ..	1B	160	619	87	169	28	5	8	58	3	.273
1992	Chicago (NL) ..	1B	158	603	72	185	37	5	9	79	6	.307
	Totals		751	2807	370	840	148	18	46	355	41	.299

RYNE SANDBERG 33 6-2 185 Bats R Throws R

"Ryno" seems assured of finishing career in Cubs uniform after signing four-year, $28.4-million contract extension prior to last season ... Future Hall of Famer is revered for work habits and professional demeanor as well as for his production ... Perennial All-Star had Gold Glove streak snapped at nine straight in 1992 by Pirates' Jose Lind ... Perhaps the most consistent second baseman in history ... Went 2½ years without committing throwing error ... Joined Charlie Gehringer as only second basemen with 500 or more assists in six seasons . . . Joined Juan Samuel as only second basemen with at least 60 extra-base hits in four straight seasons . . . Scored 100 or more runs last four years . . . Ranks fourth in career homers among second basemen . . . Had 20th two-homer game Sept. 1 against Dodgers . . . Tied club record with eight consecutive hits from July 29-Aug. 1 . . . Born Sept. 18, 1959, in Spokane, Wash. . . . Phillies' 20th draft pick in 1978 . . . Traded to Cubs before 1982 season . . . Earned $2.1 million in 1992.

Year	Club	Pos.	G	AB	R	H	2B	3B	HR	RBI	SB	Avg.
1981	Philadelphia . . .	SS-2B	13	6	2	1	0	0	0	0	0	.167
1982	Chicago (NL) . .	3B-2B	156	635	103	172	33	5	7	54	32	.271
1983	Chicago (NL) . .	2B-SS	158	633	94	165	25	4	8	48	37	.261
1984	Chicago (NL) . .	2B	156	636	114	200	36	19	19	84	32	.314
1985	Chicago (NL) . .	2B-SS	153	609	113	186	31	6	26	83	54	.305
1986	Chicago (NL) . .	2B	154	627	68	178	28	5	14	76	34	.284
1987	Chicago (NL) . .	2B	132	523	81	154	25	2	16	59	21	.294
1988	Chicago (NL) . .	2B	155	618	77	163	23	8	19	69	25	.264
1989	Chicago (NL) . .	2B	157	606	104	176	25	5	30	76	15	.290
1990	Chicago (NL) . .	2B	155	615	116	188	30	3	40	100	25	.306
1991	Chicago (NL) . .	2B	158	585	104	170	32	2	26	100	22	.291
1992	Chicago (NL) . .	2B	158	612	100	186	32	8	26	87	17	.304
	Totals		1705	6705	1076	1939	320	67	231	836	314	.289

DERRICK MAY 24 6-4 225 Bats L Throws R

Previous Cubs' management nearly gave up on this former first-round draft choice, but new GM Larry Himes and manager Jim Lefebvre gave him a chance and he began paying dividends in 1992 . . . Was almost traded to Padres late in 1991 by former GM Jim Frey, but Himes called off deal shortly after taking over . . . Outfielder credits Lefebvre with teaching him to pull ball . . . Half of his eight homers were three-run shots . . . Had first two-homer game June 19 at Philadelphia, recording five RBI . . . Hit second career pinch-homer July 16 off Pirates' Doug Drabek . . . Had four-hit game Sept. 14 against Mets . . . Sizzled during 2½-week stretch in June, batting .348 with three homers and 11 RBI . . . Began season at Iowa (AAA), but was recalled in April when Cubs were scratching for runs . . . Born July 14, 1968, in Rochester, N.Y. . . . Son of former major league outfielder Dave May . . . Ninth player chosen overall in 1986 draft . . . Earned $109,000 in 1992.

Year	Club	Pos.	G	AB	R	H	2B	3B	HR	RBI	SB	Avg.
1990	Chicago (NL) . .	OF	17	61	8	15	3	0	1	11	1	.246
1991	Chicago (NL) . .	OF	15	22	4	5	2	0	1	3	0	.227
1992	Chicago (NL) . .	OF	124	351	33	96	11	0	8	45	5	.274
	Totals		156	434	45	116	16	0	10	59	6	.267

SHAWON DUNSTON 30 6-1 175 Bats R Throws R

Talented shortstop was off to fast start until his season abruptly ended because of bad back . . . Underwent surgery in mid-May to repair herniated disc . . . Injury allowed Cubs to discover shortstops Rey Sanchez and Jose Vizcaino . . . Has volunteered to become outfielder this season if it would help club . . . His rifle arm and extraordinary athletic ability make anything possible . . . Participated in extensive swimming therapy as part of rehabilitation . . . Had .342 on-base percentage before being sidelined . . . Enjoyed best April of career, hitting .327 in 14 games, despite being hampered by sore hamstring . . . Began season as leadoff hitter . . . Born March 21, 1963, in Brooklyn, N.Y. . . . First player chosen in 1982 draft, after batting .790 with 37 stolen bases for Thomas Jefferson High . . . In first full big league season in 1986, he led NL shortstops with 17 homers . . . Earned $2.1 million in 1992.

Year	Club	Pos.	G	AB	R	H	2B	3B	HR	RBI	SB	Avg.
1985	Chicago (NL) . .	SS	74	250	40	65	12	4	4	18	11	.260
1986	Chicago (NL) . .	SS	150	581	66	145	36	3	17	68	13	.250
1987	Chicago (NL) . .	SS	95	346	40	85	18	3	5	22	12	.246
1988	Chicago (NL) . .	SS	155	575	69	143	23	6	9	56	30	.249
1989	Chicago (NL) . .	SS	138	471	52	131	20	6	9	60	19	.278
1990	Chicago (NL) . .	SS	146	545	73	143	22	8	17	66	25	.262
1991	Chicago (NL) . .	SS	142	492	59	128	22	7	12	50	21	.260
1992	Chicago (NL) . .	SS	18	73	8	23	3	1	0	2	2	.315
	Totals		918	3333	407	863	156	38	73	342	133	.259

STEVE BUECHELE 31 6-2 200 Bats R Throws R

Acquired from Pirates last July 11 for Danny Jackson . . . Became 60th different Cub to play third base since end of Ron Santo era in 1973 . . . Hit .249 with eight homers and 43 RBI with Pirates . . . In first 16 games with Cubs, he batted .339 with three three-hit games and four two-hit games . . . Exploded against former teammates July 28, hitting double, triple and first homer as Cub . . . Committed just six errors as Cub and none after July 29 . . . Has been traded in midseason two straight years . . . Helped Pirates win 1991 division title after Aug. 30 acquisition from Rangers . . . Signed four-year, $11-million deal, then was traded again during first year of contract because Pirates were desperate for pitching . . . Born Sept. 26, 1961, in Lancaster, Cal.

. . . Played three years at Stanford University, leading Cardinals to 1982 College World Series . . . Rangers' fifth choice in 1982 draft . . . Earned $2.6 million in 1992.

Year	Club	Pos.	G	AB	R	H	2B	3B	HR	RBI	SB	Avg.
1985	Texas	3B-2B	69	219	22	48	6	3	6	21	3	.219
1986	Texas	3B-2B-OF	153	461	54	112	19	2	18	54	5	.243
1987	Texas	3B-2B-OF	136	363	45	86	20	0	13	50	2	.237
1988	Texas	3B-2B	155	503	68	126	21	4	16	58	2	.250
1989	Texas	3B-2B	155	486	60	114	22	2	16	59	1	.235
1990	Texas	3B-2B	91	251	30	54	10	0	7	30	1	.215
1991	Texas	3B-2B-SS	121	416	58	111	17	2	18	66	0	.267
1991	Pittsburgh	3B	31	114	16	28	5	1	4	19	0	.246
1992	Pitt-Chi (NL) . . .	3B	145	524	52	137	23	4	9	64	1	.261
	Totals		1056	3337	405	816	143	18	107	421	15	.245

SAMMY SOSA 24 6-0 175 Bats R Throws R

First season as Cub was interrupted twice by injuries . . . Sustained broken bone in right hand when hit by Dennis Martinez pitch and was disabled from June 13-July 27 . . . In first at-bat after being activated, he homered off Pirates' Doug Drabek on first pitch . . . Had second career two-homer game June 10 in St. Louis . . . Went 15-for-39 after coming off DL, including one game-winning hit and two game-tying hits . . . Only nine games after returning from hand injury, he broke left ankle when he fouled pitch off foot Aug. 6 . . . Promising young outfield talent with speed and strong arm . . . Looking to strengthen defense before last season, Cubs traded George Bell to White Sox for him and pitcher Ken Patterson . . . Still needs to cut down on strikeouts . . . Manager Jim Lefebvre compared his center-field play to that of Ken Griffey Jr. . . . Born Nov. 12, 1968, in San Pedro de Macoris, D.R. . . . Signed by Rangers in 1985 . . . Earned $180,000 in 1992.

Year	Club	Pos.	G	AB	R	H	2B	3B	HR	RBI	SB	Avg.
1989	Tex.-Chi. (AL)	OF	58	183	27	47	8	0	4	13	7	.257
1990	Chicago (AL) . .	OF	153	532	72	124	26	10	15	70	32	.233
1991	Chicago (AL) . .	OF	116	316	39	64	10	1	10	33	13	.203
1992	Chicago (NL) . .	OF	67	262	41	68	7	2	8	25	15	.260
	Totals		394	1293	179	303	51	13	37	141	67	.234

MIKE MORGAN 33 6-2 210 **Bats R Throws R**

An excellent free-agent pickup, he enjoyed his finest season during first year as Cub . . . Finished sixth in ERA race, fourth in winning percentage and innings pitched . . . Especially effective at Wrigley, where he was 9-2 with five complete games . . . In 21 career starts at Wrigley, he is 13-2 with 1.35 ERA . . . Won career-high seven straight decisions from May 2-June 26, longest streak by a Cub pitcher in four years . . . Named NL Pitcher of the Month in May, going 5-0 with 2.32 ERA . . . Pitched two-hit shutout Sept. 17 against Phillies and was also involved in three combined shutouts . . . Had rough start, going 0-2 with 5.63 ERA in four April outings . . . Won six of last seven decisions . . . Born Oct. 8, 1959, in Tulare, Cal. . . . Selected by Athletics in first round of 1978 draft . . . Made big league debut one week after graduating from high school, losing 3-0 complete game to Orioles . . . Made only All-Star appearance in 1991 . . . Earned $2,875,000 in 1992.

Year	Club	G	IP	W	L	Pct.	SO	BB	H	ERA
1978	Oakland	3	12	0	3	.000	0	8	19	7.50
1979	Oakland	13	77	2	10	.167	17	50	102	5.96
1982	New York (AL)	30	150⅓	7	11	.389	71	67	167	4.37
1983	Toronto	16	45⅓	0	3	.000	22	21	48	5.16
1985	Seattle	2	6	1	1	.500	2	5	11	12.00
1986	Seattle	37	216⅓	11	17	.393	116	86	243	4.53
1987	Seattle	34	207	12	17	.414	85	53	245	4.65
1988	Baltimore	22	71⅓	1	6	.143	29	23	70	5.43
1989	Los Angeles	40	152⅔	8	11	.421	72	33	130	2.53
1990	Los Angeles	33	211	11	15	.423	106	60	216	3.75
1991	Los Angeles	34	236⅓	14	10	.583	140	61	197	2.78
1992	Chicago (NL)	34	240	16	8	.667	123	79	203	2.55
	Totals	298	1625⅓	83	112	.426	783	546	1651	3.87

JOSE GUZMAN 29 6-3 195 **Bats R Throws R**

Put together his best major league season just two years removed from scrap heap . . . Established career highs in victories, innings and strikeouts . . . Led Rangers in whiffs and was second behind Kevin Brown in wins and innings as well as starts and complete games (5) . . . Returned in 1991 after missing previous two seasons because of career-threatening shoulder injuries . . . Was cut in spring training that year . . .

Signed minor league contract and was recalled May 23 . . . Went on to win 13 games, including nine after the All-Star break . . . Earned $1.365 million in 1992 . . . Signed originally by Rangers as free agent in February 1981 . . . Born April 9, 1963, in Santa Isabel, P.R. . . . Became free agent last winter and signed four-year, $14.35-million contract with Cubs.

Year	Club	G	IP	W	L	Pct.	SO	BB	H	ERA
1985	Texas	5	32⅔	3	2	.600	24	14	27	2.76
1986	Texas	29	172⅓	9	15	.375	87	60	199	4.54
1987	Texas	37	208⅓	14	14	.500	143	82	196	4.67
1988	Texas	30	206⅔	11	13	.458	157	82	180	3.70
1989	Texas					Injured				
1991	Texas	25	169⅔	13	7	.650	125	84	152	3.08
1992	Texas	33	224	16	11	.593	179	73	229	3.66
	Totals	159	1013⅔	66	62	.516	715	395	983	3.90

FRANK CASTILLO 24 6-1 195 Bats R Throws R

Established himself as Cubs' No. 3 starter, pitching more innings and making more starts than anyone except Greg Maddux and Mike Morgan . . . Frequently pitched in bad luck . . . Went nearly two months without victory before winning twice in one week in late August . . . Cubs scored total of just 13 runs in his first 10 losses . . . Struggled with release point on change-up, contributing to slump . . . Finished strong after record dipped to 6-10 . . . Reached double figures in victories by beating Expos on final day of season . . . Born April 1, 1969, in El Paso, Tex. . . . Cubs' sixth-round pick in 1987 draft . . . Named Appalachian League Player of the Year after going 10-1 with 2.29 ERA for Wytheville in 1987 . . . His four complete games in 1991 were most by a Cub rookie since Dennis Lamp pitched six in 1978 . . . Won first three big league decisions . . . Earned $150,000 in 1992.

Year	Club	G	IP	W	L	Pct.	SO	BB	H	ERA
1991	Chicago (NL)	18	111⅔	6	7	.462	73	33	107	4.35
1992	Chicago (NL)	33	205⅓	10	11	.476	135	63	179	3.46
	Totals	51	317	16	18	.471	208	96	286	3.78

DAN PLESAC 31 6-5 215 Bats L Throws L

Immediately strengthened Cubs' bullpen when he signed two-year, $3.2-million contract as free agent during winter meetings . . . Figures to be used as setup man for fellow free-agent import Randy Myers . . . Holds Brewers' all-time record with 365 games pitched . . . Also has team-record 133 career saves, but just one of them came in 1992 . . . Made 40 relief appearances and four starts last year, holding opponents to .229 batting average as he made successful transition to setup role . . . Born Feb. 4, 1962, in Gary, Ind. . . . Selected by Brewers in first round of 193 draft . . . Named to three straight All-Star teams from 1987-89 . . . Set Brewers' single-season save record in 1989 with 33 . . . After 311 straight relief appearances, he made first major league start Aug. 10, 1991, and finished that season in Brewers' rotation, getting 10 starts . . . Earned $2.76 million in 1992.

Year	Club	G	IP	W	L	Pct.	SO	BB	H	ERA
1986	Milwaukee.	51	91	10	7	.588	75	29	81	2.97
1987	Milwaukee.	57	79⅓	5	6	.455	89	23	63	2.61
1988	Milwaukee.	50	52⅓	1	2	.333	52	12	46	2.41
1989	Milwaukee.	52	61⅓	3	4	.429	52	17	47	2.35
1990	Milwaukee.	66	69	3	7	.300	65	31	67	4.43
1991	Milwaukee.	45	92⅓	2	7	.222	61	39	92	4.29
1992	Milwaukee.	44	79	5	4	.556	54	35	64	2.96
	Totals.	365	524⅓	29	37	.439	448	186	460	3.21

RANDY MYERS 30 6-1 208 Bats L Throws L

Padre free agent joined Cubs in December with three-year, $11-million contract . . . Came to Padres, along with his grenades and knives, from Reds in deal for Bip Roberts prior to last season . . . Saved a career-high 38 games, ranking second in NL and that was second-highest total in club history to Mark Davis' 44 in 1989 . . . After giving up game-tying homer to Andre Dawson June 2, he lost his closer's duties for a month . . . That decision was one of the reasons manager Greg Riddoch lost his job . . . After regaining closer's role, he saved 16 straight over next seven weeks, posting a 1.45 ERA during that stretch . . . Despite his soldier-of-fortune reputation, critics say there isn't enough attack in his pitching and that he nibbles too much . . . Mr. October is 2-0 with four saves lifetime in postseason . . . Born Sept. 19, 1962, in Vancouver, Wash . . . Mets' No. 1 pick in secondary phase of 1982 draft . . . Made $2.35 million last year . . . Owns 131 career saves . . . Saved total of 50 games for Mets in 1988 and 1989.

Year	Club	G	IP	W	L	Pct.	SO	BB	H	ERA
1985	New York (NL).	1	2	0	0	.000	2	1	0	0.00
1986	New York (NL).	10	10⅔	0	0	.000	13	9	11	4.22
1987	New York (NL).	54	75	3	6	.333	92	30	61	3.96
1988	New York (NL).	55	68	7	3	.700	69	17	45	1.72
1989	New York (NL).	65	84⅓	7	4	.636	88	40	62	2.35
1990	Cincinnati	66	86⅔	4	6	.400	98	38	59	2.08
1991	Cincinnati	58	132	6	13	.316	108	80	116	3.55
1992	San Diego.	66	79⅔	3	6	.333	66	34	84	4.29
	Totals.	375	538⅓	30	38	.441	536	249	438	3.06

GREG HIBBARD 28 6-0 190 Bats L Throws L

Nothing spectacular here, but a solid No. 3 or No. 4 starter . . . These days you can do a lot worse . . . Moved across Chicago over the winter, with brief stopover in Florida . . . Was selected in expansion draft by Marlins, who dealt him to Cubs for Gary Scott and Alex Arias . . . Won 10-plus games in each of last three seasons with White Sox, but ERA was above 4.00 in last two . . . Part of White Sox steal from KC in December 1987, when he was obtained along with Melido Perez and two other minor league pitchers for Floyd Bannister and Dave Cochrane . . . Deal was engineered by current Cubs GM Larry Himes, which makes two times Himes has traded for him . . . A 16th-round pick of Royals in 1986 . . . Born Sept. 13, 1964, in New Orleans . . . Earned $210,000 in 1992.

Year	Club	G	IP	W	L	Pct.	SO	BB	H	ERA
1989	Chicago (AL)	23	137⅓	6	7	.462	55	41	142	3.21
1990	Chicago (AL)	33	211	14	9	.609	92	55	202	3.16
1991	Chicago (AL)	32	194	11	11	.500	71	57	196	4.31
1992	Chicago (AL)	31	176	10	7	.588	69	57	187	4.40
	Totals	119	718⅓	41	34	.547	287	210	727	3.78

TOP PROSPECTS

JESSIE HOLLINS 23 6-3 215 Bats R Throws R

During first full season in bullpen, he emerged as major prospect at Charlotte (AA) . . . Rated 10th-best prospect in Southern League by *Baseball America* after finishing third in saves with 25 . . . Held opponents to .230 batting average . . . Imposing size and above-average fastball fostered comparisons to Lee Smith . . . Made major league debut Sept. 19 . . . Selected by Cubs in 40th round in 1988 . . . Tied for New York-Penn League lead in victories while going 10-3 with 115 strikeouts in 97 innings for Geneva (A) in 1990 . . . Born Jan. 27, 1970, in Conroe, Tex.

FERNANDO RAMSEY 27 6-1 175 Bats R Throws R

A sprinter who never played organized baseball until six years ago, he had breakthrough season in 1992, representing Iowa in Triple-A All-Star Game . . . Led Iowa in stolen bases (39) and batted .269 before September callup to Chicago . . . Represented

Panama as sprinter in 1984 Olympics . . . Drafted by Cubs in 33rd round of 1987 draft, out of New Mexico State . . . Cubs' roving instructor Jimmy Piersall claims, "He can play center field as well as anyone in baseball." . . . Led Southern League in hits and led all outfielders in putouts and assists with Charlotte (AA) in 1991 . . . Born Dec. 20, 1965, in Rainbow, Panama.

MANAGER JIM LEFEBVRE: Became 43rd manager in Cubs' history and presided over transitional season under first-year GM Larry Himes . . . Cubs traded George Bell, cutting payroll and improving clubhouse relations but hurting offense . . . Plans for a running game were short-circuited by injuries to Shawon Dunston and Sammy Sosa . . . Had to deal with massive team slump during first two months as Cubs were shut out four straight times in one stretch, scoring just 21 runs in 11 games . . . Maintained his cool and team responded, battling back from eight games under .500 (42-50) to high-water mark of four over (68-64) before settling in to finish fourth at 78-84 . . . Was winningest manager in Seattle history (233-253 in three years) . . . Fired after 1991 season despite leading Mariners to their first winning record (83-79) . . . Began managerial career in 1978 in Pioneer League . . . Coached for Dodgers, Giants and Athletics . . . Was Giants' director of player development in 1983-84 . . . Named Pacific Coast League Manager of the Year in 1985 and 1986 at Phoenix . . . Named 1965 NL Rookie of the Year as Dodger infielder . . . Played eight seasons and batted .251 as switch-hitter in 922 major league games . . . Born Jan. 7, 1942, in Inglewood, Cal. . . . Overall managerial record is 311-337.

ALL-TIME CUB SEASON RECORDS

BATTING: Rogers Hornsby, .380, 1929
HRs: Hack Wilson, 56, 1930
RBI: Hack Wilson, 190, 1930
STEALS: Frank Chance, 67, 1903
WINS: Mordecai Brown, 29, 1908
STRIKEOUTS: Ferguson Jenkins, 274, 1970

FLORIDA MARLINS

TEAM DIRECTORY: Owner: H. Wayne Huizenga; Exec. VP/GM: David Dombrowski; VP-Business Oper.: Richard Anderson; VP Communications: Dean Jordan; Dir. Scouting: Gary Hughes; Dir. Player Dev.: John Boles; Dir. Media Rel.: Chuck Pool; Trav. Sec.: John Panagakis; Mgr.: Rene Lachemann. Home: Joe Robbie Stadium (48,000). Field distances: 335, l.f. line; 380, l.c.; 410, c.f.; 380, r.c.; 345, r.f. line. Spring training: Melbourne, Fla.

SCOUTING REPORT

HITTING: Florida looked to the future during the expansion draft and most of the Marlins' top choices are probably at least a year away from the majors. No. 1 pick Nigel Wilson (.274, 26, 69 for Double-A Knoxville) is a future star, but he probably won't be seen in Miami before September. For 1993, the Marlins will try to get by with retreads.

Miami native Orestes Destrade, who has won three straight home-run titles in Japan, figures to be the first baseman and cleanup hitter. The Marlins are hoping he can be another Cecil Fielder. Junior Felix (.246, 9, 72 with the Angels) will also be in the middle of the lineup. Free-agent signee Dave Magadan (.283, 3, 28 with the Mets) is another name player, but he is coming off two straight injury-marred seasons. Free-agent recruit Benito Santiago (.251, 10, 42 with the Padres) isn't as prized as he once was, but he remains one of the better hitting catchers in baseball.

Veteran shortstop Walt Weiss (.212, 0, 21 with the Athletics) has been injury plagued for four straight seasons. Second baseman Bret Barberie (.232, 1, 24 with the Expos) had a disappointing rookie season, but has potential. Center fielder Chuck Carr (.308, 3, 28, 53 steals for Triple-A Louisville) provides speed at the top of the lineup. Jeff Conine (.302, 20, 72 for Triple-A Omaha) can play the outfield or first base and Monty Fariss (.217, 3, 21 with the Rangers) is a typical expansion team player.

PITCHING: The Marlins selected pitchers with 21 of their 36 picks in the expansion draft but, again, they were aiming toward the future and most of those picks probably won't help much this year.

Jack Armstrong (6-15, 4.64 with the Indians) could be the Opening Day starter, but he hasn't had a good season since 1990. Free-agent import and knuckleballer Charlie Hough (7-12, 3.93

Benito Santiago brings temperament and talent to Marlins.

with the White Sox) is 45, but he'll give the rotation some stability if he can stay healthy for another season. Other starters might include Pat Rapp (7-8, 3.05 for Triple-A Phoenix), Ryan Bowen (0-7, 10.96 with the Astros), David Weathers (1-4, 4.66 for Triple-A Syracuse) or Scott Chiamparino, who pitched at five levels for the Rangers in 1992.

Florida's bullpen looks more promising than its starting staff. Bryan Harvey (0-4, 2.83, 13 saves with the Angels) was one of the top closers in baseball, but he's coming off arthroscopic elbow surgery. Jim Corsi (4-2, 1.43 with the Athletics) could be a setup

FLORIDA MARLINS 1993 ROSTER

MANAGER Rene Lachemann
Coaches—Marcel Lachemann, Vada Pinson, Doug Rader, Frank Reberger, Cookie Rojas

PITCHERS

No.	Name	1992 Club	W-L	IP	SO	ERA	B-T	Ht.	Wt.	Born
77	Armstrong, Jack	Cleveland	6-15	167	114	4.64	R-R	6-5	215	3/7/65 Englewood, NJ
29	Berumen, Andres	Appleton	5-2	58	52	2.65	R-R	6-1	205	4/5/71 Mexico
46	Bowen, Ryan	Houston	0-7	34	22	10.96	R-R	6-0	185	2/10/68 Hanford, CA
		Tucson	7-6	122	94	4.12				
44	Carpenter, Cris	St. Louis	5-4	88	46	2.97	R-R	6-1	185	4/5/65 St. Augustine, FL
49	Carrasco, Hector	Asheville	5-5	78	67	2.99	R-R	6-2	175	10/22/69 Dominican Republic
43	Chaimparino, Scott	Gulf Coast	0-1	7	5	0.00	L-R	6-2	205	8/22/66 San Mateo, CA
		Port Charlotte	1-1	12	8	2.31				
		Tulsa	0-0	19	18	1.93				
		Oklahoma City	2-1	31	9	2.87				
		Texas	0-4	25	13	3.55				
41	Corsi, Jim	Tacoma	0-0	29	21	1.23	R-R	6-1	220	9/9/61 Newton, MA
		Oakland	4-2	44	19	1.43				
40	Griffiths, Brian	Jackson	3-9	97	91	3.80	R-R	6-2	190	5/29/68 Portland, OR
34	Harvey, Bryan	California	0-4	29	34	2.83	R-R	6-2	215	6/2/63 Chattanooga, TN
51	Hoffman, Trevor	Chattanooga	3-0	30	31	1.52	R-R	6-1	200	10/13/67 Bellflower, CA
		Nashville	4-6	65	63	4.27				
—	Hough, Charlie	Chicago (AL)	7-12	176	76	3.93	R-R	6-2	190	1/5/48 Honolulu, HI
42	Johnstone, John	Binghamton	7-7	149	121	3.74	R-R	6-3	195	11/25/68 Liverpool, NY
18	Lewis, Richie	Rochester	10-9	159	154	3.28	R-R	5-10	175	1/25/66 Muncie, IL
		Baltimore	1-1	7	4	10.80				
37	Martinez, Jose	St. Lucie	6-5	123	114	2.05	R-R	6-2	155	4/1/71 Dominican Republic
		Binghamton	5-2	58	39	1.71				
31	McAndrew, Jamie	San Antonio	3-4	50	35	3.58	R-R	6-2	190	9/2/67 Williamsport, PA
		Albuquerque	1-3	29	9	5.83				
—	McClure, Bob	St. Louis	2-2	54	24	3.17	R-L	5-11	188	4/29/53 Oakland, CA
48	Rapp, Pat	Phoenix	7-8	121	79	3.05	R-R	6-3	195	7/13/67 Jennings, LA
		San Francisco	0-2	10	3	7.20				
38	Tabaka, Jeffery	El Paso	9-5	82	75	2.52	R-L	6-2	195	1/17/64 Barberton, OH
35	Weathers, Dave	Syracuse	1-4	48	30	4.66	R-R	6-3	205	9/25/69 Lawrenceburg, TN
		Toronto	0-0	3	3	8.10				
45	Yaughn, Kip	Hagerstown	7-8	116	106	3.48	R-R	6-0	180	7/20/69 Walnut Creek, CA

CATCHERS

No.	Name	1992 Club	H	HR	RBI	Pct.	B-T	Ht.	Wt.	Born
55	Decker, Steve	Phoenix	127	8	74	.282	R-R	6-3	210	10/25/65 Rock Island, IL
		San Francisco	7	0	1	.163				
13	Natal, Bob	Indianapolis	104	12	50	.302	R-R	5-11	190	11/13/65 Long Beach, CA
		Montreal	0	0	0	.000				
09	Santiago, Benito	San Diego	97	10	42	.251	R-R	6-1	185	3/9/65 Puerto Rico

INFIELDERS

No.	Name	1992 Club	H	HR	RBI	Pct.	B-T	Ht.	Wt.	Born
24	Arias, Alex	Iowa	114	5	40	.279	R-R	6-3	185	11/20/67 New York, NY
		Chicago (NL)	29	0	7	.293				
—	Berroa, Geronimo	Cincinnati	4	0	0	.267	R-R	6-0	195	3/18/65 Dominican Republic
		Nashville	151	2	22	.328				
6	Barberie, Bret	Montreal	66	1	24	.232	S-R	5-11	180	8/16/87 Long Beach, CA
		Indianapolis	17	3	8	.395				
19	Conine, Jeff	Omaha	120	20	72	.302	R-R	6-1	220	6/27/66 Tacoma, WA
		Kansas City	23	0	9	.253				
—	Destrade, Orestes	Seibu	119	41	87	.266	S-R	6-4	210	5/8/62 Cuba
—	Magadan, Dave	New York (NL)	91	3	28	.283	L-R	6-3	205	9/30/62 Tampa, FL
27	Martinez, Ramon	Salem	154	3	30	.289	S-R	6-2	165	9/8/69 Dominican Republic
20	Scott, Gary	Iowa	93	10	48	.263	R-R	6-0	175	8/22/68 New Rochelle, NY
		Chicago (NL)	15	2	11	.156				
22	Weiss, Walt	Tacoma	3	0	3	.231	S-R	6-0	175	11/28/63 Tuxedo, NY
		Oakland	67	0	21	.212				

OUTFIELDERS

No.	Name	1992 Club	H	HR	RBI	Pct.	B-T	Ht.	Wt.	Born
21	Carr, Chuck	Arkansas	29	1	6	.261	S-R	5-10	165	8/10/68 San Bernardino, CA
		Louisville	116	3	28	.308				
		St. Louis	14	0	3	.219				
3	Everett, Carl	Ft. Lauderdale	42	2	9	.230	S-R	6-0	181	6/3/70 Tampa, FL
		Prince William	7	4	9	.318				
4	Fariss, Monty	Texas	36	3	21	.217	R-R	6-4	205	10/13/67 Cordell, TX
		Oklahoma City	56	9	38	.299				
47	Felix, Junior	California	125	9	72	.246	S-R	5-11	165	10/3/67 Dominican Republic
7	Moore, Kerwin	Baseball City	59	1	10	.236	S-R	6-1	190	10/29/70 Detroit, MI
		Memphis	42	4	17	.235				
2	Pose, Scott	Chattanooga	180	2	45	.342	L-R	5-11	165	2/11/67 Davenport, IA
17	Tavarez, Jesus	Jacksonville	101	3	25	.258	R-R	6-0	170	3/26/71 Dominican Republic
11	Whitmore, Darrell	Kinston	124	10	52	.280	L-R	6-1	210	11/18/68 Front Royal, VA
30	Wilson, Nigel	Knoxville	143	26	69	.274	L-L	6-1	185	1/12/70 Canada

man or a closer. Cris Carpenter (5-4, 2.97 with the Cardinals) can pitch middle or short relief.

FIELDING: Weiss is an excellent shortstop and Carr covers a lot of ground in center field. Santiago has an outstanding arm, but he led all NL catchers with 12 errors. Barberie, who spent most of his time at third base last year and played poorly, committed just one error in 26 games at second. Felix has a strong arm in right field. Magadan is below average at third.

OUTLOOK: This is a typical first-year expansion team, trying to survive with borderline major leaguers and a handful of recognizable names. It'll be a long season and Rene Lachemann's Marlins are likely to lose 100 games and finish last.

MARLIN PROFILES

BENITO SANTIAGO 27 6-1 185 Bats R Throws R

Free at last after being embroiled in contract problems throughout his career in San Diego, he signed two-year, $7.2-million pact with Marlins in December . . . Fractured the little finger on his right hand sliding into second in St. Louis May 31 . . . Second time in three years a broken bone put him on the disabled list . . . Rejoined the team July 11 . . . A fan favorite everywhere but San Diego as he was voted onto NL All-Star team for fourth time . . . Did not have a passed ball all season . . . His throwing suffered, though . . . Only caught 26 percent of attempted base-stealers after nailing 35 percent in 1991 . . . Has not improved much since rookie season because of lack of coaching and desire to work on his shortcomings . . . One of the more misunderstood players in the majors . . . Made $3.3 million in 1992 . . . Born March 9, 1965, in Ponce, P.R. . . . Padres signed him as a free agent in September 1982.

Year	Club	Pos.	G	AB	R	H	2B	3B	HR	RBI	SB	Avg.
1986	San Diego	C	17	62	10	18	2	0	3	6	0	.290
1987	San Diego	C	146	546	64	164	33	2	18	79	21	.300
1988	San Diego	C	139	492	49	122	22	2	10	46	15	.248
1989	San Diego	C	129	462	50	109	16	3	16	62	11	.236
1990	San Diego	C	100	344	42	93	8	5	11	53	5	.270
1991	San Diego	C-OF	152	580	60	155	22	3	17	87	8	.267
1992	San Diego	C	106	386	37	97	21	0	10	42	4	.251
	Totals		789	2872	312	758	124	15	85	375	62	.264

WALT WEISS 29 6-0 175 Bats S Throws R

Outstanding defensive shortstop plagued by injuries past four years with Athletics . . . Missed six weeks of 1992 season with strained rib-cage muscle . . . Slumped after returning to lineup and had career-worst batting average . . . Benched for four of six ALCS games against Blue Jays . . . Committed career-high 19 errors . . . Protected by A's in expansion draft but traded to Marlins immediately following draft in exchange for catcher Eric Helfand . . . Instantly became Marlins' highest-paid position player . . . Born Nov. 28, 1963, in Tuxedo, N.Y. . . . Selected by A's in first round of 1985 draft . . . Named 1988 AL Rookie of the Year after committing just one error in second half of season . . . Injury problems began in 1989 when he tore cartilage in right knee . . . Suffered cartilage damage to left knee during 1990 ALCS . . . Missed final 109 games of 1991 with torn ligaments in left ankle . . . Earned $760,000 in 1992.

Year	Club	Pos.	G	AB	R	H	2B	3B	HR	RBI	SB	Avg.
1987	Oakland	SS	16	26	3	12	4	0	0	1	1	.462
1988	Oakland	SS	147	452	44	113	17	3	3	39	4	.250
1989	Oakland	SS	84	236	30	55	11	0	3	21	6	.233
1990	Oakland	SS	138	445	50	118	17	1	2	35	9	.265
1991	Oakland	SS	40	133	15	30	6	1	0	13	6	.226
1992	Oakland	SS	103	316	36	67	5	2	0	21	6	.212
	Totals		528	1608	178	395	60	7	8	130	32	.246

DAVE MAGADAN 30 6-3 205 Bats L Throws R

Free agent signed minor league contract with Marlins in December . . . Ranks second on Mets' career batting list yet has never established himself as everyday player . . . Criticized for lack of power, speed and range . . . Forced to leave first base after Mets signed Eddie Murray, he beat out Bill Pecota to win third-base job and did adequate work defensively, making some spectacular plays . . . Tied career best with 12-game hitting streak from April 19-May 2 . . . Season ended Aug. 8 in Chicago as he suffered fractured right wrist when hit by relay throw from Cubs shortstop Rey Sanchez . . . Injuries have cut short two straight seasons . . . Underwent arthroscopic surgery on both shoulders Sept. 13, 1991 . . . Born Sept. 30, 1962, in Tampa . . . Mets' second-round pick in 1983 draft . . . Led NCAA with .525 batting average for University of Alabama in 1983 . . . Finished third in

NL batting race in 1990, posting second-best average in Mets' history . . . Earned $1.4 million in 1992.

Year	Club	Pos.	G	AB	R	H	2B	3B	HR	RBI	SB	Avg.
1986	New York (NL)	1B	10	18	3	8	0	0	0	3	0	.444
1987	New York (NL)	3B-1B	85	192	21	61	13	1	3	24	0	.318
1988	New York (NL)	1B-3B	112	314	39	87	15	0	1	35	0	.277
1989	New York (NL)	1B-3B	127	374	47	107	22	3	4	41	1	.286
1990	New York (NL)	1B-3B	144	451	74	148	28	6	6	72	2	.328
1991	New York (NL)	1B	124	418	58	108	23	0	4	51	1	.258
1992	New York (NL)	3B-1B	99	321	33	91	9	1	3	28	1	.283
	Totals		701	2088	275	610	110	11	21	254	5	.292

BRET BARBERI 25 5-11 180 Bats S Throws R

Third player selected by Marlins in expansion draft and first with major league experience . . . Spent most of 1992 season with Expos but had disappointing offensive numbers . . . Replaced Tim Wallach at third base in controversial spring training move by former manager Tom Runnells . . . Became only sixth different Opening-Day third baseman in Montreal history . . . Started 57 games at third base and 17 at second . . . Optioned to Indianapolis (AAA) in June and batted .395 in 10 games . . . Returned to Expos and batted .250 following All-Star break . . . Had three-hit games July 24 against Dodgers and Aug. 5 against Cubs . . . Born Aug. 16, 1967, in Long Beach, Cal. . . . Selected by Expos in seventh round of 1988 draft . . . Batted .312 at Indianapolis in 1991, earning promotion to Montreal, where he excelled . . . Homered from both sides of plate in same game against Phillies and had four-hit game against Pirates . . . Earned $129,000 in 1992.

Year	Club	Pos.	G	AB	R	H	2B	3B	HR	RBI	SB	Avg.
1991	Montreal	INF	57	136	16	48	12	2	2	18	0	.353
1992	Montreal	3B–2B-SS	111	285	26	66	11	0	1	24	9	.232
	Totals		168	421	42	114	23	2	3	42	9	.271

JUNIOR FELIX 25 5-11 165 Bats S Throws R

Great start fizzled into another subpar season, with Angels and he landed with Marlins as a third-round pick in expansion draft . . . Posted career-low batting average . . . Struck out 128 times and drew only 33 walks . . . Stole only eight bases in 16 attempts, far below his potential . . . Did drive in a career-high 72 runs, but was among league leaders in May, only to drop out of sight . . . Earned $590,000 in 1992 . . . Originally signed as free agent in 1986 . . . Discovered at age 18 at a track meet. Hadn't played baseball since childhood when signed . . . Still playing catch-up fundamentally . . . Outfielder was acquired by Angels from Blue Jays with Luis Sojo for Devon White and Willie Fraser prior to 1991 season . . . Born Oct. 3, 1967, in Laguna Sabada, D.R.

Year	Club	Pos.	G	AB	R	H	2B	3B	HR	RBI	SB	Avg.
1989	Toronto	OF	110	415	62	107	14	8	9	46	18	.258
1990	Toronto	OF	127	463	73	122	23	7	15	65	13	.263
1991	California	OF	66	230	32	65	10	2	2	26	7	.283
1992	California	OF	139	509	63	125	22	5	9	72	8	.246
	Totals		442	1617	230	419	69	22	35	209	46	.259

CRIS CARPENTER 27 6-1 185 Bats R Throws R

Rubber-armed reliever figures to be setup man in Marlins' bullpen . . . Selected off Cardinals' roster with Marlins' sixth pick in second round of expansion draft . . . Came up to St. Louis as starting pitcher in 1988 but hasn't started big-league game since 1989 . . . Finished second among Cardinal relievers in 1992 in innings pitched and appearances . . . Set personal bests in ERA, games and innings pitched . . . Earned only major league save May 23 while tossing three scoreless innings against Astros . . . Held opponents to .220 average . . . Gave up no runs in final 13 appearances covering 12⅓ innings . . . Born April 5, 1965, in St. Augustine, Fla. . . . Cardinals' first round draft choice in 1987 . . . Saved 11 games for Louisville (AAA) in 1989 . . . Fanned 100 batters in 143 innings at Louisville in 1990 . . . His 10 victories in 1991 were most by a Cardinal reliever since Al Hrabosky won 13 in 1975 . . . Earned $150,000 in 1992.

Year	Club	G	IP	W	L	Pct.	SO	BB	H	ERA
1988	St. Louis.	8	47⅔	2	3	.400	24	9	56	4.72
1989	St. Louis.	36	68	4	4	.500	35	26	70	3.18
1990	St. Louis.	4	8	0	0	.000	6	2	5	4.50
1991	St. Louis.	59	66	10	5	.714	47	20	53	4.23
1992	St. Louis.	73	88	5	4	.556	46	27	69	2.97
	Totals.	180	277⅔	21	15	.583	158	84	253	3.66

CHUCK CARR 24 5-10 165 Bats S Throws R

Speedy outfielder has not yet proven he can hit major league pitching . . . Chosen by Marlins with sixth pick in expansion draft off Cardinals' roster . . . Played at three levels in 1992, progressing from Arkansas (AA) to Louisville (AAA) to St. Louis . . . Batted .308 in 96 games at Louisville before September callup . . . Was 10-for-12 in stolen base attempts for Cardinals . . . Made 14 starts in St. Louis, playing all three outfield positions . . . Had career-high three hits and two stolen bases against Expos Sept. 28 . . . Born Aug. 10, 1968, in San Bernardino, Cal. . . . Picked by Reds in ninth round of 1986 draft . . . Signed with Mariners as free agent in 1987 and traded to Mets before 1989 season . . . Stole 47 bases in 1989 and 48 in 1990 at Jackson (AA) . . . Voted best outfielder and most exciting player by Texas League managers in 1990 . . . Hamstring injury ruined his 1991 season . . . Traded to Cardinals before 1992 season.

Year Club	Pos.	G	AB	R	H	2B	3B	HR	RBI	SB	Avg.
1990 New York (NL)	OF	4	2	0	0	0	0	0	0	1	.000
1991 New York (NL)	OF	12	11	1	2	0	0	0	1	1	.182
1992 St. Louis.....	OF	14	64	8	14	3	0	0	3	10	.219
Totals.......		30	77	9	16	3	0	0	4	12	.208

JIM CORSI 31 6-1 210 Bats R Throws R

Could be setup man or closer in Marlins' well-stocked bullpen . . . Grabbed off Athletics' roster with Marlins' 25th pick in expansion draft . . . Signed free-agent minor league contract with A's in March 1992 after spending previous year with Astros . . . Opened season in Tacoma (AAA), where he saved 12 games in 26 appearances and compiled 1.23 ERA . . . Recalled to Oakland and picked up second major league victory June 12 at Texas . . . Did best pitching following All-Star break, going 3-1 in 27 games and allowing just two earned runs for 0.76 ERA in second half . . . Allowed no earned runs over final 14 appearances . . . Permitted 9 of 24 inherited runners to score . . . Opponents batted .275 . . . Has never pitched full season in big leagues . . . Only major league start came in 1988 . . . Born Sept. 9, 1961, in Newton, Mass. . . . Pitched at St. Leo College near Tampa . . .

Picked by Yankees in 24th round of 1982 draft... Earned $125,000 in 1992.

Year	Club	G	IP	W	L	Pct.	SO	BB	H	ERA
1988	Oakland	11	21⅓	0	1	.000	10	6	20	3.80
1989	Oakland	22	38⅓	1	2	.333	21	10	26	1.88
1991	Houston	47	77⅔	0	5	.000	53	23	76	3.71
1992	Oakland	32	44	4	2	.667	19	18	44	1.43
	Totals	112	181⅓	5	10	.333	103	57	166	2.78

JACK ARMSTRONG 28 6-5 215 Bats R Throws R

A second-round choice from Cleveland in expansion draft... Still looking to fulfill promise... Was largely disappointing after he was acquired with Scott Scudder and Joe Turek from Cincinnati for Greg Swindell prior to last season... Opened year in rotation, going 2-13 with 5.43 ERA before he was sent to bullpen... Dropped six straight starts from June 21-July 18 to trigger demotion... Did best work in relief, compiling 3-0 record with 1.16 ERA compared to 3-15, 5.44 as a starter... Career fortunes plunged after he was NL's starting pitcher in 1990 All-Star Game... Was 11-3 with a 2.28 ERA to earn that honor, but went 1-6 with a 5.96 ERA in second half... Born March 7, 1965, in Englewood, N.J.... Holds economics degree from Oklahoma... Earned $237,000 in 1992.

Year	Club	G	IP	W	L	Pct.	SO	BB	H	ERA
1988	Cincinnati	14	65⅓	4	7	.364	45	38	63	5.79
1989	Cincinnati	9	42⅔	2	3	.400	23	21	40	4.64
1990	Cincinnati	29	166	12	9	.571	110	59	151	3.42
1991	Cincinnati	27	139⅔	7	13	.350	93	54	158	5.48
1992	Cleveland	35	166⅔	6	15	.286	114	67	176	4.64
	Totals	114	580⅓	31	47	.397	385	239	588	4.62

BRYAN HARVEY 29 6-2 215 Bats R Throws R

Elbow trouble and all, Marlins made this dominating Angel closer their 10th pick in expansion draft... Earned his 13th and final save May 30, when he appeared on his way to another 40-save season... Went on disabled list a week later... Came back June 22, but was back on DL two weeks later... Rolaids Reliever of the Year in 1991, when he saved 46 games and posted 1.60 ERA. That save total is fourth-highest in history . . . Also allowed only 51 hits and 17 walks in 78⅔ innings in 1991 . . . Fastball-forkball combination is all he needs, other than his health . . . Earned $3,125,000 in 1992 . . . Signed as free agent by Angels, in August, 1984, out of a tryout camp . . . Was playing softball with father on nationally ranked Howard's Furniture team at the time . . . Born June 2, 1963, in Chattanooga, Tenn.

Year	Club	G	IP	W	L	Pct.	SO	BB	H	ERA
1987	California	3	5	0	0	.000	3	2	6	0.00
1988	California	50	76	7	5	.583	67	20	59	2.13
1989	California	51	55	3	3	.500	78	41	36	3.44
1990	California	54	64⅓	4	4	.500	82	35	45	3.22
1991	California	67	78⅔	2	4	.333	101	17	51	1.60
1992	California	25	28⅔	0	4	.000	34	11	22	2.83
	Totals.	250	307⅔	16	20	.444	365	126	219	2.49

SCOTT CHIAMPARINO 26 6-2 205 Bats L Throws R

Solid pitching prospect had career sidetracked by reconstructive elbow surgery while with Rangers in 1991 . . . Began 1992 season on disabled list before going to extended spring program in June . . . Put on medical rehab assignment in Gulf Coast League July 12 and continued rehab with stops at Port Charlotte (A), Tulsa (AA) and Oklahoma City (AAA) . . . Recalled to Texas Aug. 31 and lost all four big league starts despite pitching well . . . Selected by CBS-TV as Player of the Game while pitching seven-inning four-hitter at Toronto Sept. 19 . . . Also worked seven innings against Yankees Sept. 6 in first major league appearance since May 25, 1991 . . . Selected by Marlins with eighth pick in second round of expansion draft . . . Born Aug. 22, 1966, in San Mateo, Cal. . . . Athletics' fourth choice in 1987 free-agent draft . . . Traded to Rangers Sept. 4, 1990, completing deal for Harold Baines . . . Earned $112,000 in 1992.

Year	Club	G	IP	W	L	Pct.	SO	BB	H	ERA
1990	Texas	6	37⅔	1	2	.333	19	12	36	2.63
1991	Texas	5	22⅓	1	0	1.000	8	12	26	4.03
1992	Texas	4	25⅓	0	4	.000	13	5	25	3.55
	Totals.	15	85⅓	2	6	.250	40	29	87	3.27

TOP PROSPECTS

NIGEL WILSON 23 6-1 185 Bats L Throws L

Blue Jays were high on this native of Canada, but Marlins made him their first pick in the expansion draft . . . Batted .274 with 26 home runs and 69 RBI for Knoxville (AA) . . . Placed second in organization in home runs . . . Outfielder showed speed with 13 stolen bases . . . Sixty-seven of his 143 hits went for extra bases . . . Needs to make more contact . . . Struck out 137 times in as many games . . . Born Jan. 12, 1970, in Oshawa, Ont. . . . Signed as a free agent in July 1987.

PAT RAPP 25 6-3 195 Bats R Throws R

Marlins' fifth pick in expansion draft . . . Worked out of bullpen and was a starter for Giants' farm at Phoenix (AAA), where he posted 7-8 mark with 3.05 ERA . . . PCL is hitter's heaven, so ERA was impressive, ranking third overall in league and best among Phoenix pitchers with more than 100 innings . . . Was 2-1 with an 0.98 ERA over his first 11 appearances . . . Pitched in three games for Giants and was 0-2 during an 18-day stint in majors last season . . . Selected in 15th round of 1989 draft . . . Born July 13, 1967, in Jennings, La. . . . His one-year-old son, Ryan Patrick, is named after Nolan Ryan . . . Chosen in first round of expansion draft as Marlins' fifth pick overall.

ALEX ARIAS 25 6-3 185 Bats R Throws R

Joined Marlins from Cubs with Gary Scott in November trade for Greg Hibbard . . . Injuries to shortstops Shawon Dunston, Rey Sanchez and Jose Vizcaino gave him his big chance with Cubs . . . Called up Aug. 26, he batted .293 in 32 major league games, including 5-for-5 performance against Pirates Sept. 7 . . . Batted .279 with 23 doubles for Iowa in first Triple-A season . . . Selected by Cubs in third round of 1987 draft . . . Led Midwest League in triples (11), putouts, assists and double plays with Peoria (A) in 1989 . . . Led Southern League shortstops in fielding percentage with Charlotte (AA) in 1991 . . . Born Nov. 20, 1967, in New York.

MATT WHISENANT 21 6-3 200 Bats S Throws L

Rated by *Baseball America* as fifth-best prospect in the South Atlantic League (A) while pitching for Spartanburg Phillies in 1992 . . . Had league's best fastball, striking out 151 batters in 151 innings, and going 11-7 with 3.23 ERA . . . Considered by some to have best arm in Phillies' organization . . . Acquired by Marlins with pitcher Joel Adamson following expansion draft in trade for Danny Jackson . . . Selected by Phillies in 18th round of 1989 draft . . . Born June 8, 1971, in Los Angeles.

JEFF CONINE 26 6-1 220 **Bats R Throws R**

First baseman rebounded from injury-plagued 1991 and was plucked from Royals' system in first round of expansion draft by Marlins . . . Hit .253 in 91 at-bats with Royals, but didn't hit a home run . . . Made strong showing with Omaha (AAA), hitting .302 with 20 homers and 72 RBI . . . Hit .320 with 15 homers and 95 RBI for Memphis (AA) in 1990 . . . Picked in 58th round of 1987 draft . . . Born June 27, 1966, in Tacoma, Wash.

MANAGER RENE LACHEMANN: After waiting eight years for another major league managing job, Lachemann faces challenge of building expansion Marlins from ground up . . . Solid baseball man who relates well to people . . . Florida management feels he has enough practice and hunger to succeed with brand new team . . . Ability to speak Spanish earned him bonus points because of Miami's large Hispanic community . . . Named Marlins' manager Oct. 23, 1992 after spending six seasons as A's coach . . . Also served two years as Red Sox third-base coach and has coached in five ALCS and four World Series . . . Until now, has spent entire career in AL . . . Managed Mariners (1981-83) and Brewers (1984) . . . Has .430 winning percentage and his clubs never finished higher than fourth place . . . Signed three-year contract with Marlins worth about $1 million . . . Beat out seven other candidates who were interviewed . . . Born May 4, 1945, in Los Angeles . . . Spent three seasons as A's catcher in both Kansas City (1965-66) and Oakland (1968) . . . In just 281 major league at-bats, he hit .210 with nine doubles, nine homers and 33 RBI . . . Managed in minors (1973-81) and in Winter Leagues (1976-81) . . . Overall major league managerial record is 207-274.

MONTREAL EXPOS

TEAM DIRECTORY: Pres.-General Partner: Claude Brochu; VP/GM: Dan Duquette; VP-Baseball Oper.: Bill Stoneman; Dir. Media Rel.: Richard Griffin; Dir. Media Services: Monique Giroux; Trav. Sec.: Erik Ostling; Mgr.: Filipe Alou. Home: Olympic Stadium (43,739). Field distances: 325, l.f. line; 375, l.c.; 404, c.f.; 375, r.c.; 325, r.f. line. Spring training: West Palm Beach, Fla.

SCOUTING REPORT

HITTING: This is probably the best group of young hitters in baseball and nearly everybody came up through the Montreal farm system. Still, the Expos need to improve on last year's total of 648 runs, which was only fifth-best in the NL.

The outfield, with Larry Walker, Marquis Grissom and Moises Alou, has three potential superstars. Walker (.301, 23, 93) is already an All-Star, one of the most feared left-handed hitters in the league, the winner of a Silver Slugger Award and the Expos' Player of the Year. Grissom (.276, 14, 66, 78 steals) has led the majors in stolen bases the last two years, yet he's ticketed to be the No. 3 hitter because of his extra-base power. Alou (.282, 9,

All-Star Larry Walker has clout and a Gold Glove.

56) was outstanding in a part-time role, so the Expos traded Ivan Calderon to make room for him in left field.

Delino DeShields (.292, 7, 56, 46 steals) can be far more effective as a leadoff hitter now that he has cut down on his strikeouts and learned to hit lefties. Wil Cordero takes over for the departed Spike Owen at shortstop after hitting .302 in a late-season trial. Tim Wallach (.223, 9, 59) put up the worst numbers of his career and was traded in December to the Dodgers. Greg Colbrunn (.268, 2, 18 in just 52 games) could be a big producer at first base.

PITCHING: Dennis Martinez is the only big name on this staff, yet the Expos ranked second in the NL with a 3.25 ERA and led the majors by holding opponents to a .238 batting average. At 37, Martinez (16-11, 2.47) is still a horse, as he pitched 226 innings last year and opposing hitters batted just .211 against him. There's no reason to believe he can't do it again. Ken Hill (16-9, 2.68) had an outstanding first season in Montreal, establishing himself among baseball's elite. Chris Nabholz (11-12, 3.32) is also back along with Brian Barnes (6-6, 2.97). Mike Gardiner (4-10, 4.75 with the Red Sox) hopes to step in for the traded Mark Gardner.

Montreal's bullpen was a big reason for the Expos' surprising showing in 1992. John Wetteland (4-4, 2.92, 37 saves) is the club's first bona fide closer since Jeff Reardon left town six years ago. Wetteland posted the second-best save total in Expos' history. Mel Rojas (7-1, 1.43, 10 saves) was equally important as a setup man, making 68 relief appearances during his first full season in the majors. Jeff Fassero (8-7, 2.84) is another big cog in the bullpen, pitching in 70 games last year and finishing 22 of them.

FIELDING: Walker is a Gold Glove winner in right field, throwing out 16 runners last season and committing just two errors. Grissom covers a lot of ground in center field and Wallach, a former Gold Glover at third base, is gone. DeShields has greatly improved his play at second base, making just 15 errors last year after committing a league-high 27 in 1991. Cordero looks like a natural at shortstop.

OUTLOOK: Felipe Alou's Expos need more production from their corner infielders and need big seasons again from pitchers Martinez, Hill, Wetteland and Rojas. If everything falls into place, the Expos will be as good as anybody in this wide-open division and they could surpass last season's 87-75, second-place performance.

MONTREAL EXPOS 1993 ROSTER

MANAGER Felipe Alou

Coaches—Pierre Arsenault, Tommy Harper, Tim Johnson, Joe Kerrigan, Jerry Manuel, Luis Pujols

PITCHERS

No.	Name	1992 Club	W-L	IP	SO	ERA	B-T	Ht.	Wt.	Born
54	Arteaga, Ivan			Did not play			L-R	6-2	230	7/20/72 Venezuela
53	Ausanio, Joe	Buffalo	6-4	84	66	2.90	R-R	6-1	205	12/9/65 Kingston, NY
47	Barnes, Brian	Indianapolis	4-4	83	77	3.69	L-L	5-9	170	3/25/67 Roanoke Rapids, NC
		Montreal	6-6	100	65	2.97				
56	Batista, Miguel	W. Palm Beach	7-7	135	92	3.79	R-R	6-0	197	2/19/71 Dominican Republic
		Pittsburgh	0-0	2	1	9.00				
46	Bottenfield, Kent	Indianapolis	12-8	152	111	3.43	S-R	6-3	225	11/14/68 Portland, OR
		Montreal	1-2	32	14	2.23				
51	Cornelius, Reid	Harrisburg	1-0	23	17	3.13	R-R	6-0	185	6/2/70 Thomasville, AL
61	Eischen, Joe	W. Palm Beach	9-8	170	167	3.08	L-L	6-1	190	5/25/70 West Covina, CA
13	Fassero, Jeff	Montreal	8-7	86	63	2.84	L-L	6-1	195	1/5/63 Springfield, IL
—	Gardiner, Mike	Boston	4-10	131	79	4.75	S-R	6-0	200	10/19/65 Canada
34	Heredia, Gil	Phoenix	5-5	81	37	2.01	R-R	6-1	190	10/26/65 Nogales, AZ
		SF-Mont.	2-3	45	22	4.23				
		Indianapolis	2-0	18	10	1.02				
44	Hill, Ken	Montreal	16-9	218	150	2.68	R-R	6-2	175	12/14/65 Lynn, MA
37	Hurst, Jonathan	Indianapolis	4-8	119	70	3.77	R-R	6-3	175	10/20/66 New York, NY
		Montreal	1-1	16	4	5.51				
32	Martinez, Dennis	Montreal	16-11	226	147	2.47	R-R	6-1	180	5/14/55 Nicaragua
52	Mathile, Mike	Harrisburg	12-5	186	89	2.86	R-R	6-4	220	11/24/68 Toledo, OH
43	Nabholz, Chris	Montreal	11-12	195	130	3.32	L-L	6-5	212	1/5/67 Harrisburg, PA
62	Picota, Len	Harrisburg	4-3	72	38	1.88	R-R	6-1	200	7/23/66 Panama
50	Risley, Bill	Indianapolis	5-8	96	64	6.40	R-R	6-2	210	5/29/67 Chicago, IL
		Montreal	1-0	5	2	1.80				
27	Rojas, Mel	Indianapolis	2-1	8	7	5.40	R-R	5-11	185	12/10/66 Dominican Republic
		Montreal	7-1	101	70	1.43				
60	Thomas, Mike	Rockford	5-9	113	108	3.58	L-L	6-2	200	9/2/69 Sacramento, CA
26	Valdez, Sergio	Indianapolis	4-2	62	41	3.75	R-R	6-1	190	9/7/65 Dominican Republic
		Montreal	0-2	37	32	2.41				
57	Wetteland, John	Montreal	4-4	83	99	2.92	R-R	6-2	195	8/21/66 San Mateo, CA
20	Young, Pete	Indianapolis	6-2	43	34	3.51	R-R	6-0	225	3/19/68 Meadville, MS
		Montreal	0-0	20	11	3.98				

CATCHERS

No.	Name	1992 Club	H	HR	RBI	Pct.	B-T	Ht.	Wt.	Born
63	Fitzpatrick, Rob	W. Palm Beach	86	8	37	.256	R-R	5-11	190	9/14/68 Ridgewood, NJ
24	Fletcher, Darrin	Montreal	54	2	26	.243	L-R	6-1	199	10/3/66 Elmhurst, IL
		Indianapolis	13	1	9	.255				
19	Laker, Tim	Harrisburg	99	15	68	.242	R-R	6-3	195	11/27/69 Encino, CA
		Montreal	10	0	4	.217				
65	Santana, Raul	Rockford	84	10	51	.208	R-R	5-10	207	2/9/72 Dominican Republic
—	Spehr, Tim	Omaha	85	15	42	.253	R-R	6-2	205	7/2/66 Excelsior Springs, MO

INFIELDERS

5	Berry, Sean	Omaha	126	21	77	.287	R-R	5-11	210	3/22/66 Santa Monica, CA
		Montreal	19	1	4	.333				
58	Bolick, Frank	Jacksonville	0	13	42	.268	S-R	5-10	175	6/28/66 Ashland, PA
		Calgary	79	14	54	.288				
14	Cianfrocco, Archi	Montreal	56	6	30	.241	R-R	6-5	200	10/6/66 Rome, NY
		Indianapolis	18	4	16	.305				
15	Colbrunn, Greg	Indianapolis	66	11	48	.306	R-R	6-0	190	7/26/69 Fontana, CA
		Montreal	45	2	18	.268				
12	Cordero, Wilfredo	Indianapolis	64	6	27	.314	R-R	6-2	185	10/3/71 Puerto Rico
		Montreal	38	2	8	.302				
4	DeShields, Delino	Montreal	155	7	56	.292	L-R	6-1	170	1/15/69 Seaford, DE
59	Lansing, Mike	Harrisburg	135	6	54	.280	R-R	6-0	175	4/3/68 Rawlins, WY

OUTFIELDERS

18	Alou, Moises	Montreal	96	9	56	.282	R-R	6-3	190	7/3/66 Atlanta, GA
9	Grissom, Marquis	Montreal	180	14	66	.276	R-R	5-11	190	4/17/67 Atlanta, GA
25	Stairs, Matt	Indianapolis	107	11	56	.267	L-R	5-9	175	2/27/69 Canada
		Montreal	5	0	5	.167				
23	Vander Wal, John	Montreal	51	4	20	.239	L-L	6-2	190	4/29/66 Grand Rapids, MI
33	Walker, Larry	Montreal	159	23	93	.301	L-R	6-3	215	12/1/66 Canada

EXPO PROFILES

LARRY WALKER 26 6-3 215 Bats L Throws R

Canadian-born right fielder has developed into rising superstar . . . Hits for average, power and production with compact stroke . . . Gold Glove outfielder with devastating arm . . . Finished seventh in homers, tied for seventh in RBI, ranked sixth in slugging percentage (.506) and 10th in total bases (267) . . . Made first All-Star appearance . . . Established career highs in batting average, doubles, triples, homers and RBI . . . Had pair of two-assist games against Mets June 9 and Sept. 18 . . . Threw out Padres' Tony Fernandez at first base on apparent single July 4 . . . Batted .413 during 23-game stretch in September with 11 doubles, four homers and 25 RBI . . . Had four-hit, five-RBI game at Cincinnati Aug. 31 . . . Hit 10 homers against lefties . . . Homered in three straight games spanning April and May . . . Born Dec. 1, 1966, in Maple Ridge, B.C. . . . Signed by Expos as non-drafted free agent in 1984 . . . Earned $975,000 in 1992.

Year	Club	Pos.	G	AB	R	H	2B	3B	HR	RBI	SB	Avg.
1989	Montreal	OF	20	47	4	8	0	0	0	4	1	.170
1990	Montreal	OF	133	419	59	101	18	3	19	51	21	.241
1991	Montreal	OF-1B	137	487	59	141	30	2	16	64	14	.290
1992	Montreal	OF	143	528	85	159	31	4	23	93	18	.301
	Totals		433	1481	207	409	79	9	58	212	54	.276

MARQUIS GRISSOM 25 5-11 190 Bats R Throws R

Baseball's top base-stealer for two straight seasons . . . Won NL stolen-base race by a mile over teammate Delino DeShields . . . Career-high 78 steals came in just 91 attempts . . . Also finished fifth in runs, sixth in hits, fifth in doubles and ninth in total bases (273) . . . Ranks third on Expos' all-time stolen-base list . . . Had straight steal of home Aug. 23 against Reds, first by an Expo in four years . . . Center fielder moved into leadoff spot April 23 and stayed there for next 51 starts . . . For remainder of season, he led off whenever DeShields was out of lineup . . . Had spectacular game in pennant race showdown against Pirates Sept. 16, notching three hits, including triple and homer, two steals and three runs and throwing out runner at plate . . . Homered in consecutive games April 18-19 . . . Born April 17, 1967, in

Atlanta . . . Batted .448 for Florida A&M in 1988 . . . Expos' third pick in 1988 draft . . . Earned $300,000 in 1992.

Year	Club	Pos.	G	AB	R	H	2B	3B	HR	RBI	SB	Avg.
1989	Montreal	OF	26	74	16	19	2	0	1	2	1	.257
1990	Montreal	OF	98	288	42	74	14	2	3	29	22	.257
1991	Montreal	OF	148	558	73	149	23	9	6	39	76	.267
1992	Montreal	OF	159	653	99	180	39	6	14	66	78	.276
	Totals		431	1573	230	422	78	17	24	136	177	.268

DELINO DeSHIELDS 24 6-1 170 Bats L Throws R

After disappointing sophomore season, second baseman came to camp last year with renewed determination and turned in solid performance . . . Homers and stolen bases were down slightly, but everything else improved . . . Most dramatic change was his ability to make contact more often . . . Fanned 108 times after leading NL in strikeouts with 151 in 1991 . . . Also hit 100 points higher against lefties than in '91 . . . Finished second behind teammate Marquis Grissom in NL stolen-base rankings and tied for sixth in triples . . . Had best RBI production ever by an Expo second baseman . . . Fourth on Expos' all-time steals list . . . Led off game with homer for fourth time in career April 13 against Cardinals' Rheal Cormier . . . Missed 11-game stretch in September with strained muscle in side . . . Hit inside-the-park homer April 9 against Pirates . . . Expos' Player of the Month for July, hitting .376 . . . Born Jan. 15, 1969, in Seaford, Del. . . . Expos' first pick in 1987 draft . . . Earned $302,500 in 1992.

Year	Club	Pos.	G	AB	R	H	2B	3B	HR	RBI	SB	Avg.
1990	Montreal	2B	129	499	69	144	28	6	4	45	42	.289
1991	Montreal	2B	151	563	83	134	15	4	10	51	56	.238
1992	Montreal	2B	135	530	82	155	19	8	7	56	46	.292
	Totals		415	1592	234	433	62	18	21	152	144	.272

MOISES ALOU 26 6-3 190 Bats R Throws R

Bounced back from shoulder surgery which wiped out his 1991 season . . . Enjoyed solid rookie year while playing for his father Felipe . . . Started games at all three outfield positions and was Expos' best pinch-hitter . . . Most memorable at-bat was 14th-inning grand slam that beat Pirates Sept. 23 and kept Expos' flickering pennant hopes alive . . . Got plenty of playing time because of Ivan Calderon's injury . . . Hit three-run homer to beat Reds' Rob Dibble Aug. 21 . . . Disabled with strained left hamstring July 7 and missed 18 games . . . Had five hits during June 5 doubleheader against Cubs . . . Hit first major league homer May 27 against Astros' Mark Portugal . . . Went 4-for-4 during first start in center field May 18 against Reds . . . Born July 3, 1966, in Atlanta . . . Pirates' first pick in 1986 draft . . . Traded to Expos for Zane Smith in 1990 . . . Earned $110,500 in 1992.

Year	Club	Pos.	G	AB	R	H	2B	3B	HR	RBI	SB	Avg.
1990	Pitt.-Mont.	OF	16	20	4	4	0	1	0	0	0	.200
1991	Montreal				Injured							
1992	Montreal	OF	115	341	53	96	28	2	9	56	16	.282
	Totals		131	361	57	100	28	3	9	56	16	.277

Marquis Grissom terrorized foes with 78 steals.

KEN HILL 27 6-2 175 Bats R Throws R

Joined Expos prior to last season in trade with Cardinals that solidified Montreal's starting rotation . . . Established himself among top pitchers in NL . . . Finished eighth in ERA, seventh in winning percentage and opponents' batting average (.230) and tied for eighth in shutouts (3) . . . Won career-best seven straight decisions . . . Had streak of 24 consecutive innings snapped Sept. 4 . . . Pitched four-hit shutout against Astros Aug. 30 . . . Lost 1-0 game to Reds Aug. 23 without surrendering earned run . . . Fanned career-high 10 batters July 10 against Giants . . . Pitched one-hit shutout against Mets June 8, allowing only infield single by pitcher Anthony Young . . . Also threw four-hit blank against Mets in debut with Montreal April 10 . . . Born Dec. 14, 1965, in Lynn, Mass. . . . Signed by Tigers as non-drafted free agent in 1986 and came to Expos from St. Louis for Andres Galarraga . . . A bargain at $620,000 in 1992.

Year	Club	G	IP	W	L	Pct.	SO	BB	H	ERA
1988	St. Louis	4	14	0	1	.000	6	6	16	5.14
1989	St. Louis	33	196⅔	7	15	.318	112	99	186	3.80
1990	St. Louis	17	78⅔	5	6	.455	58	33	79	5.49
1991	St. Louis	30	181⅓	11	10	.524	121	67	147	3.57
1992	Montreal	33	218	16	9	.640	150	75	187	2.68
	Totals	117	688⅔	39	41	.488	447	280	615	3.62

DENNIS MARTINEZ 37 6-1 180 Bats R Throws R

Can be overbearing because of outspoken manner and controversial opinions, but is still a fierce competitor and among the most respected pitchers in baseball . . . Last season, he posted NL's fifth-best ERA, tied for third in victories and ranked fourth in opponents' batting average (.211) . . . Very popular in his native Nicaragua, he pledged $100,000 and organized relief effort to aid countrymen in recovering from destructive tidal waves . . . Picked for third straight All-Star Game . . . Pitched 3,000th inning May 27 and is only the sixth active pitcher to reach that total . . . Pitched two-hitter against Braves May 22 . . . Born May 14, 1955, in Granada, Nicaragua . . . Signed with Orioles in 1973 and became first Nicaraguan-born player in majors . . . Traded to Expos for Rene Gonzales in 1986 . . . Named Expos' Player of the

Year in 1991, a season highlighted by his perfect game against Dodgers . . . Earned $3.33 million in 1992.

Year	Club	G	IP	W	L	Pct.	SO	BB	H	ERA
1976	Baltimore	4	28	1	2	.333	18	8	23	2.57
1977	Baltimore	42	167	14	7	.667	107	64	157	4.10
1978	Baltimore	40	276	16	11	.593	142	93	257	3.25
1979	Baltimore	40	292	15	16	.484	132	78	279	3.67
1980	Baltimore	25	100	6	4	.600	42	44	103	3.96
1981	Baltimore	25	179	14	5	.737	88	62	173	3.32
1982	Baltimore	40	252	16	12	.571	111	87	262	4.21
1983	Baltimore	32	153	7	16	.304	71	45	209	5.53
1984	Baltimore	34	141⅔	6	9	.400	77	37	145	5.02
1985	Baltimore	33	180	13	11	.542	68	63	203	5.15
1986	Baltimore	4	6⅔	0	0	.000	2	2	11	6.75
1986	Montreal	19	98	3	6	.333	63	28	103	4.59
1987	Montreal	22	144⅔	11	4	.733	84	40	133	3.30
1988	Montreal	34	235⅓	15	13	.536	120	55	215	2.72
1989	Montreal	34	232	16	7	.696	142	49	227	3.18
1990	Montreal	32	226	10	11	.476	156	49	191	2.95
1991	Montreal	31	222	14	11	.560	123	62	187	2.39
1992	Montreal	32	226⅓	16	11	.593	147	60	172	2.47
	Totals	523	3159⅔	193	156	.553	1693	926	3050	3.62

JOHN WETTELAND 26 6-2 195 Bats R Throws R

Given first opportunity to be major league closer, he responded by saving 37 games in 46 opportunities . . . Came to Montreal in winter trade with Reds and was final piece in Expos' 1992 puzzle . . . Saved six of Expos' first 10 victories in September . . . Stranded 78 percent of inherited runners . . . Had second-best single-season save total in Expos' history . . . Saved both ends of July 7 doubleheader against former teammates in Los Angeles . . . Pitched three shutout innings to beat Giants in 12 innings July 9 . . . Lone major league save prior to last year came in 1989 . . . Fanned seven of 11 batters he faced Sept. 24 against Pirates . . . Born Aug. 21, 1966, in San Mateo, Cal. . . . Selected by Dodgers in secondary phase of January 1985 draft . . . Went 20-for-20 in save opportunities for Albuquerque (AAA) in 1991 . . . Earned $156,000 in 1992 . . . Dodgers traded him to Reds, who shipped him to Montreal for Dave Martinez and Scott Ruskin.

Year	Club	G	IP	W	L	Pct.	SO	BB	H	ERA
1989	Los Angeles	31	102⅔	5	8	.385	96	34	81	3.77
1990	Los Angeles	22	43	2	4	.333	36	17	44	4.81
1991	Los Angeles	6	9	1	0	1.000	9	3	5	0.00
1992	Montreal	67	83⅓	4	4	.500	99	36	64	2.92
	Totals	126	238	12	16	.429	240	90	194	3.52

MEL ROJAS 26 5-11 185 Bats R Throws R

Unsung hero in Expos' bullpen during first full season in big leagues . . . Led Expos in ERA and was second in appearances . . . Finished with 10 saves and all seven victories came in relief . . . Allowed just one run in 19 innings from Aug. 21-Sept. 19 . . . During that month, he held batters to 2-for-31 with runners in scoring position . . . Led all NL relievers in ERA and inherited runners stranded (83 percent) . . . Had 21-inning shutout streak snapped July 16 . . . Retired 16 straight batters in May . . . Born Dec. 10, 1966, in Santo Domingo, D.R. . . . Nephew of manager Felipe Alou . . . Signed by Expos as free agent in 1985 . . . Became relief pitcher for Jacksonville (AA) in 1989, but returned to starting role with Indianapolis (AAA) in 1990 . . . Has never started a major league game . . . Had one save for Expos in 1990 and six in 1991 . . . Came on strong during final month of 1991, going 2-0 with four saves and 1.03 ERA in 13 appearances.

Year	Club	G	IP	W	L	Pct.	SO	BB	H	ERA
1990	Montreal	23	40	3	1	.750	26	24	34	3.60
1991	Montreal	37	48	3	3	.500	37	13	42	3.75
1992	Montreal	68	100⅔	7	1	.875	70	34	71	1.43
	Totals	128	188⅔	13	5	.722	133	71	147	2.48

TOP PROSPECTS

WIL CORDERO 21 6-2 185 Bats R Throws R

Expos' shortstop of the future . . . Sure hands, quick first step, accurate arm and good instincts . . . Youngest player ever to be named MVP of Puerto Rican Winter League in 1992 . . . Batted .314 with 11 doubles, six homers and 27 RBI in just 52 games for Indianapolis (AAA) . . . Called up to Montreal July 24 and batted .302 in 45 games . . . Hit first major league homer Sept. 18 in New York . . . Signed by Expos as free agent in 1988 and became youngest player ever invited to Expos' major league camp in 1989 . . . Born Oct. 3, 1971, in Mayaguez, P.R.

TIM LAKER 23 6-3 195 Bats R Throws R

Big catcher was rated fifth-best prospect in Eastern League by *Baseball America* . . . Spent most of season at Harrisburg (AA), where he improved defensively and showed dramatic gains offensively . . . Reached personal highs in homers (15) and RBI (68) while batting .242 with 19 doubles . . . Promoted to Montreal and singled against Atlanta's Tom Glavine on first major league pitch Aug. 19 . . . Expos' sixth pick in 1988 draft . . . Led Midwest League catchers in assists in 1990 . . . Born Nov. 27, 1969, in Encino, Cal.

GREG COLBRUNN 23 6-0 190 Bats R Throws R
Once considered a future Gary Carter, he had to forsake catching when elbow surgery sidelined him for entire 1991 season . . . Underwent tendon transfer and ligament reconstruction . . . Made impressive comeback as first baseman in 1992, batting .306 with 19 doubles and 11 homers in 57 games for Indianapolis (AAA) . . . Promoted to Montreal and singled in first at-bat against Giants' Rod Beck . . . First homer also came off Beck . . . Disabled for two weeks in August with strained muscle in back . . . Settled in as Expos' No. 5 hitter during pennant race and finished with 18 RBI . . . Expos' sixth pick in 1987 draft . . . Born July 26, 1969, in Fontana, Cal.

MIKE LANSING 24 6-0 175 Bats R Throws R
Rated second-best prospect in Eastern League by *Baseball America* after batting .280 with 19 doubles and 54 RBI for Harrisburg (AA) . . . Finished second in league with 45 stolen bases . . . Steady defensive shortstop . . . Back injury during junior year at Wichita State scared off major league scouts . . . Selected in sixth round of 1990 draft by independent Miami Miracle of Florida State League . . . Batted .286 for Miami in 1991 with 20 doubles and 29 stolen bases . . . Expos bought his contract in September 1991 . . . Born April 3, 1968, in Rawlins, Wy.

MANAGER FELIPE ALOU: Became first Dominican-born

manager in major league history when he replaced Tom Runnells May 22 . . . Expos were off to 17-20 start, but he led young team in stunning turnaround, keeping them in pennant race into late September before finishing second to Pirates at 87-75 . . . Provided welcome change from overbearing Runnells . . . Stressed intensity and aggressiveness, but never put pressure on his players . . . Assumed first big league managing job

Workhorse Dennis Martinez is ready for 18th season.

just 10 days after 57th birthday . . . Managed in Winter Leagues for 12 seasons, winning Caribbean World Series in 1990 with Escogido of Dominican League . . . Member of Expos organization for 17 years . . . Managed at West Palm Beach (A), Memphis (AA), Denver (AAA), Wichita (AAA) and Indianapolis (AAA), compiling 844-751 record in 12 minor league seasons . . . His teams finished first three times and won two championships . . . Born May 12, 1935, in Haina, D.R. . . . Had 17-year major league playing career, batting .286 with 206 homers for Giants, Braves, Athletics, Yankees and Brewers . . . Made major league history in September 1963 by appearing in same outfield with younger brothers Matty and Jesus . . . Led NL in hits, runs and total bases in 1966 . . . Played in three All-Star Games . . . Became 31st player in history to reach 2,000 hits and 200 home runs . . . Major league managerial record is 70-55.

ALL-TIME EXPO SEASON RECORDS

BATTING: Tim Raines, .334, 1986
HRs: Andre Dawson, 32, 1983
RBI: Tim Wallach, 123, 1987
STEALS: Ron LeFlore, 97, 1980
WINS: Ross Grimsley, 20, 1978
STRIKEOUTS: Bill Stoneman, 251, 1971

NEW YORK METS

TEAM DIRECTORY: Chairman: Nelson Doubleday; Pres.: Fred Wilpon; Sr. VP-Consultant: Frank Cashen; Exec. VP/GM/COO: Al Harazin; Asst. VP-Baseball Oper.: Gerry Hunsicker; Dir. Minor Leagues: Steve Phillips; Dir. Pub. Rel.: Jay Horwitz; Trav. Sec.: Bob O'Hara; Mgr.: Jeff Torborg. Home: Shea Stadium (55,601). Field distances: 338, l.f. line; 371, l.c.; 410, c.f.; 371, r.c.; 388, r.f. line. Spring training: Port St. Lucie, Fla.

SCOUTING REPORT

HITTING: Surely, the Mets will generate more offense than they did in 1992, when they were arguably the least productive and most boring team in baseball. Their .235 team batting average was easily the worst in the majors and they ranked ninth in the NL with 599 runs.

Bobby Bonilla (.249, 19, 70) should benefit from the lessons he learned during his first difficult season in New York. Howard Johnson (.223, 7, 43) is coming off the worst season of his career and certainly will do better if he's injury-free. Eddie Murray (.261, 16, 93) was the Mets' most productive hitter in 1992, but the question is whether he can come close to duplicating those numbers at age 37. Vince Coleman suffered through his second straight injury-riddled year, stealing just 24 bases, and free-agent signee Joe Orsulak (.289, 4, 39 with the Orioles) could wind up stealing his job.

Tony Fernandez (.275, 4, 37 with the Padres) was the Mets' major off-season acquisition and he represents a significant offensive improvement at shortstop. Second baseman Jeff Kent (11 homers in 305 at-bats), acquired late in the season from Toronto in the David Cone deal, also should provide good pop for a middle infielder. Ryan Thompson (.282, 14, 46 for Triple-A Syracuse) looked impressive during a September trial and will be given the opportunity to win the center field job.

FIELDING: On paper, the Mets have a good rotation, but there are still major question marks. Dwight Gooden (10-13, 3.67) made a remarkable recovery from rotator cuff surgery, but he's no longer a dominant pitcher. Bret Saberhagen (3-5, 3.50) saw his first NL season ruined by a finger injury that limited him to 15 starts. He has always been a much better pitcher in odd-numbered years and the Mets hope that trend continues.

Bobby Bonilla aims to silence those Bronx cheers.

Sid Fernandez (14-11, 2.73) was the Mets' most pleasant surprise in 1992, finally living up to his potential while showing maturity and confidence. Pete Schourek (6-8, 3.64) is a capable fourth starter and free-agent signee Frank Tanana (13-11, 4.39 with the Tigers) will provide innings.

John Franco (6-2, 1.64, 15 saves) remains a top bullpen closer, but he's coming off elbow surgery. Anthony Young (2-14, 4.17, 15 saves) showed flashes of brilliance as Franco's replacement, but he faded badly in September. Mike Maddux (2-2, 2.37, 5 saves with the Padres) was acquired to strengthen the bullpen, which could also be bolstered by Rule V draft pick Mike Draper (37 saves for Triple-A Columbus).

FIELDING: The Mets tied for eighth in the NL with a .981 fielding percentage in 1992 and there are still some soft spots. Murray's range is extremely limited at first base and Johnson figures to make numerous throwing errors in his return to third base. Coleman is not a good left fielder and Bonilla is just adequate in right. The team looks solid up the middle with Todd Hundley catching, Kent and Fernandez as the DP combination and Thompson in center.

OUTLOOK: The Mets protected their veterans in the expansion draft, indicating that they still consider themselves contenders. If the injured players bounce back, Jeff Torborg's team should do better than last year's 72-90, fifth-place finish.

NEW YORK METS 1993 ROSTER

MANAGER Jeff Torborg

Coaches—Mike Cubbage, Barry Foote, Dave LaRoche, Tom McCraw, Mel Stottlemyre

PITCHERS

No.	Name	1992 Club	W-L	IP	SO	ERA	B-T	Ht.	Wt.	Born
63	Castillo, Juan	St. Lucie	11-8	154	80	2.58	R-R	6-5	205	6/23/70 Venezuela
43	Dewey, Mark	Tidewater	5-7	54	55	4.31	R-R	6-0	207	1/3/65 Grand Rapids, MI
		New York (NL)	1-0	33	24	4.32				
50	Fernandez, Sid	New York (NL)	14-11	215	193	2.73	L-L	6-1	215	10/12/62 Honolulu, HI
31	Franco, John	New York (NL)	6-2	33	20	1.64	L-L	5-10	185	9/17/60 Brooklyn, NY
16	Gooden, Dwight	New York (NL)	10-13	206	145	3.67	R-R	6-3	210	11/16/64 Tampa, FL
53	Hillman, Eric	Tidewater	9-2	91	49	3.65	L-L	6-10	225	4/27/66 Gary, IN
		New York (NL)	2-2	52	16	5.33				
40	Innis, Jeff	New York (NL)	6-9	88	39	2.86	R-R	6-1	168	7/5/62 Decatur, IL
51	Maddux, Mike	San Diego	2-2	80	60	2.37	L-R	6-2	190	8/27/61 Dayton, OH
18	Saberhagen, Bret	New York (NL)	3-5	98	81	3.50	R-R	6-1	200	4/11/64 Chicago Heights, IL
48	Schourek, Pete	Tidewater	2-5	53	42	2.73	L-L	6-5	205	5/10/69 Austin, TX
		New York (NL)	6-8	136	60	3.64				
—	Tanana, Frank	Detroit	13-11	187	91	4.39	L-L	6-3	195	7/3/53 Detroit, MI
38	Telgheder, David	Tidewater	6-14	169	118	4.21	R-R	6-3	212	11/11/66 Middleton, NY
49	Vitko, Joe	Binghamton	12-8	165	89	3.49	R-R	6-8	210	2/1/70 Somerville, NJ
		New York (NL)	0-1	5	6	13.50				
19	Young, Anthony	New York (NL)	2-14	121	64	4.17	R-R	6-2	200	1/19/66 Houston, TX

CATCHERS

No.	Name	1992 Club	H	HR	RBI	Pct.	B-T	Ht.	Wt.	Born
64	Fordyce, Brook	Binghamton	118	11	61	.278	R-R	6-1	185	5/7/70 New London, CT
9	Hundley, Todd	New York (NL)	75	7	32	.209	S-R	5-11	185	5/27/69 Martinsville, VA
22	O'Brien, Charlie	New York (NL)	33	2	13	.212	R-R	6-2	200	5/1/61 Tulsa, OK

INFIELDERS

No.	Name	1992 Club	H	HR	RBI	Pct.	B-T	Ht.	Wt.	Born
36	Baez, Kevin	Tidewater	83	2	33	.236	R-R	6-0	170	1/10/67 Brooklyn, NY
		New York (NL)	2	0	0	.154				
23	Bogar, Timothy	Tidewater	134	5	38	.279	R-R	6-2	198	10/28/66 Indianapolis, IN
1	Fernandez, Tony	San Diego	171	4	37	.275	S-R	6-2	175	6/30/62 Dominican Republic
65	Huskey, Butch	St. Lucie	125	18	75	.254	R-R	6-3	244	11/10/71 Anadarko, OK
12	Kent, Jeff	Toronto	46	8	35	.240	R-R	6-1	185	3/7/68 Bellflower, CA
		New York (NL)	27	3	15	.239				
61	Ledesma, Aaron	St. Lucie	120	2	50	.263	R-R	6-2	200	6/3/71 Union City, CA
7	McKnight, Jeff	Tidewater	108	4	43	.307	S-R	6-0	180	2/18/63 Conway, AR
		New York (NL)	23	2	13	.271				
33	Murray, Eddie	New York (NL)	144	16	93	.261	S-R	6-2	222	2/24/56 Los Angeles, CA
62	Navarro, Tito	Tidewater	Injured				S-R	5-10	165	9/12/70 Puerto Rico

OUTFIELDERS

No.	Name	1992 Club	H	HR	RBI	Pct.	B-T	Ht.	Wt.	Born
25	Bonilla, Bobby	New York (NL)	109	19	70	.249	S-R	6-3	240	2/23/63 New York, NY
5	Burnitz, Jeromy	Tidewater	108	8	40	.243	L-R	6-0	190	4/14/69 Westminster, CA
11	Coleman, Vince	New York (NL)	63	2	21	.275	S-R	6-1	185	9/22/61 Jacksonville, FL
		St. Lucie	8	0	2	.364				
8	Gallagher, Dave	New York (NL)	42	1	21	.240	R-R	6-0	184	9/20/60 Trenton, NJ
		Tidewater	3	0	0	.250				
20	Johnson, Howard	New York (NL)	78	7	43	.223	S-R	5-10	195	11/29/60 Clearwater, FL
6	Orsulak, Joe	Baltimore	113	4	39	.289	L-L	6-1	203	5/31/62 Glen Ridge, NJ
13	Reed, Darren	Indianapolis	1	0	0	.333	R-R	6-1	205	10/16/65 Ventura, CA
		W. Palm Beach	10	2	12	.250				
		Montreal	14	5	10	.173				
		Minnesota	6	0	4	.182				
44	Thompson, Ryan	Syracuse	121	14	46	.282	R-R	6-3	200	11/4/67 Chesterton, MD
		New York (NL)	24	3	10	.222				
34	Walker, Chico	Chi.(NL)-NY(NL)	73	4	38	.289	S-R	5-9	185	11/26/58 Jackson, MS

MET PROFILES

TONY FERNANDEZ 30 6-2 175 Bats S Throws R

Mets are grateful Padres' ownership demanded budget cuts, so he and his $2.3-million salary were sent to New York for Wally Whitehurst, D.J. Dozier and minor leaguer . . . One of game's top shortstops, he landed in San Diego in deal that brought Fred McGriff from Toronto for Roberto Alomar and Joe Carter prior to 1991 . . . After making career-high 20 errors in 1991, he committed just 11 last season and only one over last 58 games to rank third in NL with .983 fielding percentage . . . Named to NL All-Star team for first time after three AL All-Star gigs . . . Did not like playing at Jack Murphy Stadium . . . Posted career-best 19-game hitting streak at end of season . . . Born June 30, 1962, in San Pedro de Macoris, D.R. . . . Because of his poor background, he learned to play the game by using cardboard cut-out gloves made by his brother. That's probably the reason he has such soft hands . . . Extremely sensitive individual . . . Originally signed as free agent by Blue Jays, April 24, 1979 . . . Made $2.1 million in 1992.

Year	Club	Pos.	G	AB	R	H	2B	3B	HR	RBI	SB	Avg.
1983	Toronto	SS	15	34	5	9	1	1	0	2	0	.265
1984	Toronto	SS-3B	88	233	29	63	5	3	3	19	5	.270
1985	Toronto	SS	161	564	71	163	31	10	2	51	13	.289
1986	Toronto	SS	163	687	91	213	33	9	10	65	25	.310
1987	Toronto	SS	146	578	90	186	29	8	5	67	32	.322
1988	Toronto	SS	154	648	76	186	41	4	5	70	15	.287
1989	Toronto	SS	140	573	64	147	25	9	11	64	22	.257
1990	Toronto	SS	161	635	84	175	27	17	4	66	26	.276
1991	San Diego	SS	145	558	81	152	27	5	4	38	23	.272
1992	San Diego	SS	155	622	84	171	32	4	4	37	20	.275
	Totals		1328	5132	675	1465	251	70	48	479	181	.285

BOBBY BONILLA 30 6-3 240 Bats S Throws R

Right fielder endured difficult first season in New York after signing five-year, $29-million contract as free agent . . . Became whipping boy for Shea Stadium fans as Mets struggled offensively all year . . . Played with aching right shoulder and underwent arthroscopic surgery Sept. 17 to repair labral tear and torn bicep tendon . . . Also was disabled from Aug. 3-19 with fractured rib . . . Ex-Pirate openly feuded with New York media and his season became public relations disaster . . . Took the most heat for phone call to press box, complaining about error, while Mets were being routed by Cubs June 25 . . . Highlight of season came Opening Night, when he hit two homers in St. Louis . . . Tied club record with homers in four consecutive games, from Aug. 19-23 . . . Hit grand slam June 1 against Giants . . . Hit dramatic three-run, ninth-inning homer to beat Reds' Rob Dibble Aug. 30 . . . Led Mets in homers and was second in RBI . . . Born Feb. 23, 1963, in New York . . . Signed with Pirates as non-drafted free agent in 1981 . . . Earned $6.1 million in 1992.

Year	Club	Pos.	G	AB	R	H	2B	3B	HR	RBI	SB	Avg.
1986	Chicago (AL) . .	OF-1B	75	234	27	63	10	2	2	26	4	.269
1986	Pittsburgh	OF-1B-3B	63	192	28	46	6	2	1	17	4	.240
1987	Pittsburgh	3B-OF-1B	141	466	58	140	33	3	15	77	3	.300
1988	Pittsburgh	3B	159	584	87	160	32	7	24	100	3	.274
1989	Pittsburgh	38-1B-OF	163	616	96	173	37	10	24	86	8	.281
1990	Pittsburgh	OF-3B-1B	160	625	112	175	39	7	32	120	4	.280
1991	Pittsburgh	OF-3B-1B	157	577	102	174	44	6	18	100	2	.302
1992	New York (NL)	OF-1B	128	438	62	109	23	0	19	70	4	.249
	Totals		1046	3732	572	1040	224	37	135	596	32	.279

JEFF KENT 25 6-1 185 Bats R Throws R

Faced difficult situation as rookie when traded from Blue Jays to Mets with Ryan Thompson for David Cone Aug. 27 . . . Had to change leagues, leaving first-place Jays for also-ran Mets . . . Encountered hostility from fans, coolness from teammates and skepticism from media because he was replacing popular Cone . . . Arrived in New York Aug. 28 and immediately became Mets' everyday second baseman, playing both games of doubleheader . . . After slow start with Mets, he turned in solid final weeks, hitting safely in 13 of last 17 starts with nine runs and 10 RBI . . . Had four-hit game Oct. 2 against Pirates . . . Had three-hit games June 22 against Rangers, July 6 against Angels and Sept. 8 against Phillies . . . Has size and pop to be productive middle infielder . . . Born March 7, 1968, in Bellflower, Cal. . . . Selected by Blue Jays in 21st round of 1989 draft . . . Led Southern League in doubles (34) and was team MVP for Knoxville (AA) in 1991 . . . Earned $109,000 in 1992.

Year	Club	Pos.	G	AB	R	H	2B	3B	HR	RBI	SB	Avg.
1992	Toronto	3B–2B–1B	65	192	36	46	13	1	8	35	2	.240
1992	New York (NL)	2B–3B-SS	37	113	16	27	8	1	3	15	0	.239
	Totals		102	305	52	73	21	2	11	50	2	.239

HOWARD JOHNSON 32 5-10 195 Bats S Throws R

Suffered through the most disappointing season of career . . . Had huge dip in all offensive categories one year after putting together best power production numbers in Mets' history . . . Offensive problems were compounded by struggles in center field . . . Finally moved to left at midseason, his fifth position as a Met . . . Could wind up back at third base . . . Hit no homers after June 27 . . . Suffered hairline fracture of right wrist July 28 and was disabled Aug. 2, ending his season . . . Subsequently underwent surgery on both knees and left shoulder . . . Tied career high with five RBI against Expos April 19 . . . Born Nov. 29, 1960, in Clearwater, Fla. . . . Selected by Tigers in secondary phase of 1979 draft . . . Traded to Mets for Walt Terrell before 1985 season . . . Set club record for doubles in 1989 while also reaching career highs in batting average, hits and stolen bases . . . Led NL in homers and RBI while driving in club-record 117 runs in 1991 . . . Earned $2.27 million in 1992.

Year	Club	Pos.	G	AB	R	H	2B	3B	HR	RBI	SB	Avg.
1982	Detroit	3B-OF	54	155	23	49	5	0	4	14	7	.316
1983	Detroit	3B	27	66	11	14	0	0	3	5	0	.212
1984	Detroit	3B-SS-1B-OF	116	355	43	88	14	1	12	50	10	.248
1985	New York (NL)	3B-SS	126	389	38	94	18	4	11	46	6	.242
1986	New York (NL)	3B-SS-OF	88	220	30	54	14	0	10	39	8	.245
1987	New York (NL)	3B-SS-OF	157	554	93	147	22	1	36	99	32	.265
1988	New York (NL)	3B-SS	148	495	85	114	21	1	24	68	23	.230
1989	New York (NL)	3B-SS	153	571	104	164	41	3	36	101	41	.287
1990	New York (NL)	3B-SS	154	590	89	144	37	3	23	90	34	.244
1991	New York (NL)	3B-OF-SS	156	564	108	146	34	4	38	117	30	.259
1992	New York (NL)	OF	100	350	48	78	19	0	7	43	22	.223
	Totals		1279	4309	672	1092	225	17	204	672	213	.253

EDDIE MURRAY 37 6-2 222 Bats S Throws R

Enhanced Hall of Fame credentials with solid offensive season after leaving Dodgers to sign with Mets as free agent . . . Only Met big gun who remained healthy and productive all season . . . Led club in batting average, runs, doubles and RBI . . . Has played at least 150 games six straight years and 14 times in career . . . Has missed just 81 games in 16 seasons . . . Tied with Darrell Evans for 22nd place on all-time homer list . . . Tied with Tris Speaker for 26th place in RBI . . . Hit grand slams June

2 against Giants' Trevor Wilson and Sept. 4 against Reds' Tim Belcher . . . Tied for third all-time in slams (17) with Jimmie Foxx and Ted Williams . . . Ranks second among active players in home runs . . . Has hit .429 with 247 RBI in bases-loaded situations . . . Age is evident in first baseman's diminished range . . . Born Feb. 24, 1956, in Los Angeles . . . Selected by Orioles in third round of 1973 draft . . . Earned $4.1 million in 1992 . . . Was not on protected list for expansion draft, but Mets' gamble worked.

Year	Club	Pos.	G	AB	R	H	2B	3B	HR	RBI	SB	Avg.
1977	Baltimore	OF-1B	160	611	81	173	29	2	27	88	0	.283
1978	Baltimore	1B-3B	161	610	85	174	32	3	27	95	6	.285
1979	Baltimore	1B	159	606	90	179	30	2	25	99	10	.295
1980	Baltimore	1B	158	621	100	186	36	2	32	116	7	.300
1981	Baltimore	1B	99	378	57	111	21	2	22	78	2	.294
1982	Baltimore	1B	151	550	87	174	30	1	32	110	7	.316
1983	Baltimore	1B	156	582	115	178	30	3	33	111	5	.306
1984	Baltimore	1B	162	588	97	180	26	3	29	110	10	.306
1985	Baltimore	1B	156	583	111	173	37	1	31	124	5	.297
1986	Baltimore	1B	137	495	61	151	25	1	17	84	3	.305
1987	Baltimore	1B	160	618	89	171	28	3	30	91	1	.277
1988	Baltimore	1B	161	603	75	171	27	2	28	84	5	.284
1989	Los Angeles . . .	1B-3B	160	594	66	147	29	1	20	88	7	.247
1990	Los Angeles . . .	1B	155	558	96	184	22	3	26	95	8	.330
1991	Los Angeles . . .	1B-3B	153	576	69	150	23	1	19	96	10	.260
1992	New York (NL)	1B	156	551	64	144	37	2	16	93	4	.261
	Totals		2444	9124	1343	2646	462	32	414	1562	90	.290

VINCE COLEMAN 31 6-1 185 Bats S Throws R

A major disappointment since signing four-year deal with Mets as free agent following 1990 season . . . Once the most feared base-stealer in baseball, but injuries have ruined his game . . . Outfielder spent huge portions of last two seasons on disabled list . . . Strained left hamstring four games into 1992 season and was disabled from April 10-May 1 . . . Immediately went back on DL with torn left rib cage muscle from May 2-28 . . . Lost another month, from June 27-July 27, after re-injuring hamstring . . . Ejected by umpires for protesting strike calls twice within three days, he compounded second ejection by arguing with manager Jeff Torborg, resulting in two-game suspension Sept. 2-3 . . . Set club record with five walks against Pirates Aug. 10 . . . Broke club single-game mark with four stolen bases against Cardinals June 26 . . . Born Sept. 22, 1961, in Jacksonville, Fla.

. . . Cardinals' 10th pick in 1982 draft . . . Set rookie record with 110 stolen bases in 1985 . . . Earned $3.2 million in 1992.

Year	Club	Pos.	G	AB	R	H	2B	3B	HR	RBI	SB	Avg.
1985	St. Louis	OF	151	636	107	170	20	10	1	40	110	.267
1986	St. Louis	OF	154	600	94	139	13	8	0	29	107	.232
1987	St. Louis	OF	151	623	121	180	14	10	3	43	109	.289
1988	St. Louis	OF	153	616	77	160	20	10	3	38	81	.260
1989	St. Louis	OF	145	563	94	143	21	9	2	28	65	.254
1990	St. Louis	OF	124	497	73	145	18	9	6	39	77	.292
1991	New York (NL)	OF	72	278	45	71	7	5	1	17	37	.255
1992	New York (NL)	OF	71	229	37	63	11	1	2	21	24	.275
	Totals		1021	4042	648	1071	124	62	18	255	610	.265

DWIGHT GOODEN 28 6-3 210 Bats R Throws R

"Doc" suffered first losing record of career yet made remarkable recovery from rotator cuff surgery . . . Seemed to get stronger and better in September, pitching complete games to win two of last three starts . . . Threw career-low 88 pitches in complete game 2-1 win over Pirates Oct. 3 . . . Only setback came at midseason, when he went on DL for three weeks with inflammation of right shoulder . . . Mets scored just 11 runs in his 13 losses . . . Pitched at least six innings in 25 of 31 starts . . . Also had outstanding year at plate, batting .264 with three doubles, a triple, a homer and nine RBI . . . Became second Met pitcher to record pinch-hit single Aug. 10 against Pirates . . . Hit fifth career homer Aug. 24 against Giants while also snapping career-high four-game losing streak . . . Born Nov. 16, 1964, in Tampa . . . Mets' first pick in 1982 draft and fifth player taken overall . . . NL Rookie of the Year in 1984 . . . Became youngest pitcher ever to win Cy Young in 1985 . . . Earned $4.9 million in 1992.

Year	Club	G	IP	W	L	Pct.	SO	BB	H	ERA
1984	New York (NL)	31	218	17	9	.654	276	73	161	2.60
1985	New York (NL)	35	276⅔	24	4	.857	268	69	198	1.53
1986	New York (NL)	33	250	17	6	.739	200	80	197	2.84
1987	New York (NL)	25	179⅔	15	7	.682	148	53	162	3.21
1988	New York (NL)	34	248⅓	18	9	.667	175	57	242	3.19
1989	New York (NL)	19	118⅓	9	4	.692	101	47	93	2.89
1990	New York (NL)	34	232⅔	19	7	.731	223	70	229	3.83
1991	New York (NL)	27	190	13	7	.650	150	56	185	3.60
1992	New York (NL)	31	206	10	13	.435	145	70	197	3.67
	Totals	269	1919⅔	142	66	.683	1686	575	1664	2.99

SID FERNANDEZ 30 6-1 215 Bats L Throws L

Always an enigma, "El Sid" finally lived up to potential in 1992, becoming Mets' most effective, most consistent starter . . . Lost weight during offseason and kept it off . . . Stayed in shape by riding stationary bicycle and it resulted in better stamina for late innings . . . Also showed surge in confidence and better control . . . Stayed ahead of hitters, threw better change-ups and didn't wilt in sixth inning . . . Began season as No. 4 starter, but he was No. 1 by September . . . Tied career highs with six complete games and 32 starts . . . Was durable, missing just one start with tender elbow . . . Fourth in NL in strikeouts . . . Tied for second in opponents' batting average (.210) . . . Mets averaged just 2.1 runs in his 11 losses . . . Born Oct. 12, 1962, in Honolulu . . . Dodgers' third-round pick in 1981 . . . Traded to Mets for Carlos Diaz and Bob Bailor after 1983 season . . . Opponents batted .191 against him in 1988 and .200 in 1990 . . . Earned $2.2 million in 1992.

Year	Club	G	IP	W	L	Pct.	SO	BB	H	ERA
1983	Los Angeles.	2	6	0	1	.000	9	7	7	6.00
1984	New York (NL).	15	90	6	6	.500	62	34	74	3.50
1985	New York (NL).	26	170⅓	9	9	.500	180	80	108	2.80
1986	New York (NL).	32	204⅓	16	6	.727	200	91	161	3.52
1987	New York (NL).	28	156	12	8	.600	134	67	130	3.81
1988	New York (NL).	31	187	12	10	.545	189	70	127	3.03
1989	New York (NL).	35	219⅓	14	5	.737	198	75	157	2.83
1990	New York (NL).	30	179⅓	9	14	.391	181	67	130	3.46
1991	New York (NL).	8	44	1	3	.250	31	9	36	2.86
1992	New York (NL).	32	214⅔	14	11	.560	193	67	162	2.73
	Totals.	239	1471	93	73	.560	1377	567	1092	3.17

FRANK TANANA 39 6-3 195 Bats L Throws L

Went from Tiger free agency to Mets for $1.5 million . . . Smart veteran continues to win . . . Reached double figures in victories for eighth time in nine seasons . . . Ranks fourth among active pitchers with 233 lifetime victories . . . Had 96-81 record with Tigers . . . Rebounded after going 1-3 with 7.07 ERA in first six starts . . . Moved to bullpen for two weeks . . . Returned to post 11-8 mark with 4.02 ERA from May 19 through end of season . . . Was overpowering early in career . . . Ranks 14th all-time with 2,657 career strikeouts . . . Has made outstanding adjustment to lost velocity . . . Understands importance of taking over inside part of plate . . . Detroit native was born July 3,

1953 . . . Angels' first-round pick in 1971 draft . . . Earned $1.7 million in 1992.

Year	Club	G	IP	W	L	Pct.	SO	BB	H	ERA
1973	California	4	26	2	2	.500	22	8	20	3.12
1974	California	39	269	14	19	.424	180	77	262	3.11
1975	California	34	257	16	9	.640	269	73	211	2.63
1976	California	34	288	19	10	.655	261	73	212	2.44
1977	California	31	241	15	9	.625	205	61	201	2.54
1978	California	33	239	18	12	.600	137	60	239	3.65
1979	California	18	90	7	5	.583	46	25	93	3.90
1980	California	32	204	11	12	.478	113	45	223	4.15
1981	Boston	24	141	4	10	.286	78	43	142	4.02
1982	Texas	30	194⅓	7	18	.280	87	55	199	4.21
1983	Texas	29	159⅓	7	9	.438	108	49	144	3.16
1984	Texas	35	246⅓	15	15	.500	141	81	234	3.25
1985	Texas-Detroit	33	215	12	14	.462	159	57	220	4.27
1986	Detroit	32	188⅓	12	9	.571	119	65	196	4.16
1987	Detroit	34	218⅔	15	10	.600	146	56	216	3.91
1988	Detroit	32	203	14	11	.560	127	64	213	4.21
1989	Detroit	33	223⅔	10	14	.417	147	74	227	3.58
1990	Detroit	34	176⅓	9	8	.529	114	66	190	5.31
1991	Detroit	33	217⅓	13	12	.520	107	78	217	3.77
1992	Detroit	32	186⅔	13	11	.542	91	90	188	4.39
	Totals	606	3984	233	219	.515	2657	1200	3847	3.63

JOHN FRANCO 32 5-10 185 Bats L Throws L

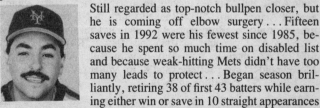

Still regarded as top-notch bullpen closer, but he is coming off elbow surgery . . . Fifteen saves in 1992 were his fewest since 1985, because he spent so much time on disabled list and because weak-hitting Mets didn't have too many leads to protect . . . Began season brilliantly, retiring 38 of first 43 batters while earning either win or save in 10 straight appearances . . . Held opponents to .049 average in April and May . . . Had six straight wins before suffering first loss June 28 in St. Louis . . . Allowed just two runs in first 21 appearances . . . Disabled from June 28-Aug. 1 with inflammation of left elbow . . . Pitched season-high four consecutive days from Aug. 8-12 before elbow problems returned . . . Disabled again Aug. 26 and underwent open surgery Sept. 29 to repair flexor tendon . . . Born Sept. 17, 1960, in Brooklyn, N.Y. . . . Dodgers' fifth choice in 1981 draft . . .

Traded to Reds in 1983 and to Mets for Randy Myers before 1990 season . . . Has 226 career saves . . . Earned $3.3 million in 1992.

Year	Club	G	IP	W	L	Pct.	SO	BB	H	ERA
1984	Cincinnati	54	79⅓	6	2	.750	55	36	74	2.61
1985	Cincinnati	67	99	12	3	.800	61	40	83	2.18
1986	Cincinnati	74	101	6	6	.500	84	44	90	2.94
1987	Cincinnati	68	82	8	5	.615	61	27	76	2.52
1988	Cincinnati	70	86	6	6	.500	46	27	60	1.57
1989	Cincinnati	60	80⅔	4	8	.333	60	36	77	3.12
1990	New York (NL)	55	67⅔	5	3	.625	56	21	66	2.53
1991	New York (NL)	52	55⅓	5	9	.357	45	18	61	2.93
1992	New York (NL)	31	33	6	2	.750	20	11	24	1.64
	Totals	531	684	58	44	.569	488	260	611	2.49

BRET SABERHAGEN 28 6-1 200 Bats R Throws R

First season as Met turned into injury nightmare as he suffered tendinitis in index finger of pitching hand . . . Never won another game after leaving May 15 start in Los Angeles following fifth inning . . . Disabled May 16 and didn't pitch again until July 21 . . . Three starts later, on Aug. 1, injury resurfaced and he returned to DL until Sept. 7 . . . After two relief appearances, he made four more starts, pitching very effectively and pain-free . . . Went eight innings in each of last three starts, never giving up more than two runs . . . Allowed just 15 earned runs in final 13 starts . . . Pitched 26 consecutive scoreless innings spanning April and May . . . Picked up first NL victory and shutout against Astros April 29 . . . Ranked fourth in NL in strikeouts at time of injury . . . Born April 11, 1964, in Chicago Heights, Ill. . . . Won AL Cy Young in 1985 and 1989 . . . Royals' 19th pick in 1982 . . . Obtained from Royals with Bill Pecota for Kevin McReynolds, Gregg Jefferies and Keith Miller prior to last season . . . Earned $2.95 million in 1992.

Year	Club	G	IP	W	L	Pct.	SO	BB	H	ERA
1984	Kansas City	38	157⅔	10	11	.476	73	36	138	3.48
1985	Kansas City	32	235⅓	20	6	.769	158	38	211	2.87
1986	Kansas City	30	156	7	12	.368	112	29	165	4.15
1987	Kansas City	33	257	18	10	.643	163	53	246	3.36
1988	Kansas City	35	260⅔	14	16	.467	171	59	271	3.80
1989	Kansas City	36	262⅓	23	6	.793	193	43	209	2.16
1990	Kansas City	20	135	5	9	.357	87	28	146	3.27
1991	Kansas City	28	196⅓	13	8	.619	136	45	165	3.07
1992	New York (NL)	17	97⅔	3	5	.375	81	27	84	3.50
	Totals	269	1758	113	83	.577	1174	358	1635	3.23

TOP PROSPECTS

BOBBY JONES 23 6-4 210 Bats R Throws R

Named Eastern League's top prospect by *Baseball America* . . . In first full season of pro ball, he went 12-4 with 1.88 ERA for Binghamton (AA) . . . Fanned 144 in 158 innings while yielding just 118 hits and 43 walks . . . Turned in impressive performance against White Sox in Hall of Fame game exhibition, retiring first 19 batters . . . Sports outstanding change-up and excellent control . . . Didn't get September callup, because it would have made him eligible for expansion draft . . . Mets' second pick in 1991 draft after leading Fresno State to College World Series, going 16-2 with 1.88 ERA . . . Born Feb. 10, 1970, in Fresno, Cal.

RYAN THOMPSON 25 6-3 200 Bats R Throws R

Acquired from Toronto along with Jeff Kent in David Cone deal Aug. 27, he might finally solve Mets' problem in center field . . . Led Syracuse (AAA) with 74 runs while hitting .282 with 20 doubles, seven triples, 14 homers, 46 RBI and 10 stolen bases . . . Joined Mets Sept. 1 and was immediately inserted into first big league game . . . Hit first homer Sept. 22 against Cubs and had two-homer game six days later against Phillies . . . Hit safely in eight of last 10 starts . . . Strong-armed outfielder with speed and pop, but needs to cut down on strikeouts . . . Selected by Blue Jays in 13th round of 1987 draft . . . Born Nov. 4, 1967, in Chestertown, Md.

ERIC HILLMAN 26 6-10 225 Bats L Throws L

Tallest player in Mets history, but not an overpowering pitcher . . . Must keep ball down to be effective . . . Won seven of last eight starts for Tidewater (AAA) before being called up to New York . . . Made first major league start Aug. 11, shutting out Pirates for eight innings . . . Also won second start, holding Giants to five hits in 8⅓ innings . . . Was hit hard in September, finishing with 2-2 record and 5.33 ERA . . . Mets' 17th pick in 1987 draft . . . Born April 27, 1966, in Gary, Ind.

BROOK FORDYCE 22 6-1 185 Bats R Throws R

Unless Todd Hundley improves his hitting, this youngster could eventually become Mets' No. 1 catcher . . . Named 10th-best prospect in Eastern League by *Baseball America* . . . Once considered strictly an offensive player, he has made rapid improvement behind plate, throwing out 39 percent of would-be base-stealers for Binghamton (AA) while batting .278 with 28 doubles, 11 homers and 61 RBI . . . Mets' third pick in 1989 draft . . . Led South Atlantic League in slugging percentage in 1990 . . . Named to Florida State League all-star team in 1991 . . . Born May 7, 1970, in New London, Conn.

MANAGER JEFF TORBORG: Hailed as homecoming hero when he left White Sox to become Mets' manager, he endured toughest season of career as team collapsed and finished fifth . . . Combination of injuries, season-long slump, lack of speed, shaky defense and poor fundamentals doomed Mets to 72-90 finish in his first season . . . Somehow, he managed to keep club in contention until early August, when Bret Saberhagen, Bobby Bonilla and Howard Johnson all went down with injuries the same weekend . . . An 0-6 trip through Pittsburgh and Chicago sealed Mets' fate . . . Scored points Sept. 1, standing up to Vince Coleman in on-the-field confrontation and suspending outfielder for two games . . . Criticized by veterans for his excessive pregame meetings, rigid team rules and devotion to percentage baseball . . . Also took heat for doing daily pregame and postgame radio shows . . . Born Nov. 26, 1941, in Westfield, N.J. . . . Set NCAA record with .537 batting average during senior year at Rutgers . . . During 10 seasons with Dodgers and Angels, he caught three no-hitters . . . Managed Indians from 1977-79 and White Sox from 1989-91 . . . Named AL Manager of the Year after winning 94 games in 1990 with youngest team in big leagues . . . Overall managerial record is 479-526.

ALL-TIME MET SEASON RECORDS

BATTING: Cleon Jones, .340, 1969
HRs: Darryl Strawberry, 39, 1987, 1988, 1990
RBI: Howard Johnson, 117, 1991
STEALS: Mookie Wilson, 58, 1982
WINS: Tom Seaver, 25, 1969
STRIKEOUTS: Tom Seaver, 289, 1971

PHILADELPHIA PHILLIES

TEAM DIRECTORY: Pres.: William Y. Giles; Exec. VP: David Montgomery; VP/GM: Lee Thomas; Player Pers. Adm.: Ed Wade; VP-Pub. Rel.: Larry Shenk; Mgr. Media Rel.: Gene Dias; Trav. Sec.: Eddie Ferenz; Mgr.: Jim Fregosi. Home: Veterans Stadium (64,538). Field distances: 330, l.f. line; 408, c.f.; 330, r.f. line. Spring training: Clearwater, Fla.

SCOUTING REPORT

HITTING: Scoring should be no problem for the Phillies, especially if they can stay healthy. Their 686 runs in 1992 were the second-highest figure in the NL and that was accomplished despite placing a club-record 17 players on the disabled list.

Catcher Darren Daulton (.270, 27, 109) won the league RBI title while having a career year. If he comes close to duplicating those numbers in 1993, the Phillies should be in great shape. The Phils also need healthy seasons from John Kruk and Lenny Dykstra. Kruk (.323, 10, 70) underwent shoulder surgery in October and spent the winter rehabilitating and working out in an effort to

Darren Daulton became fourth catcher to lead NL in RBI.

get his weight down. Dykstra (.301, 6, 39, 30 steals) is the catalyst at the top of the lineup, but he's coming off two straight injury-plagued years. A broken thumb and a broken hand limited him to 85 games last season. Wes Chamberlain (.258, 9, 41) also missed six weeks with a sprained ankle.

Third baseman Dave Hollins (.270, 27, 93) is a proven run producer and utility infielder Mariano Duncan (.267, 8, 50) can provide a big boost whenever he is in the lineup. Free-agent imports Pete Incaviglia (.266, 11, 44 with the Astros) and Milt Thompson (.293, 4, 17 with the Cardinals) could be a productive tandem platooning in left field.

PITCHING: Despite leading the NL with 27 complete games in 1992, the Phillies' pitching staff was a disaster area, giving up a league-high 717 runs. Yet, the Phils are going into 1993 with essentially the same cast of characters, except for Danny Jackson (8-13, 3.84 with the Cubs and Pirates)—and he hasn't had a winning season since 1988.

Terry Mulholland (13-11, 3.81) is still the ace, but he must bounce back from arthroscopic knee surgery. Curt Schilling (14-11, 2.35) was the biggest surprise of 1992, but he must prove that he can do it again. Ben Rivera (7-4, 3.07) also showed great promise while making 14 starts. Tommy Greene (3-3, 5.32) needs to rebound from shoulder tendinitis. Jose DeJesus (10-9, 3.42 in 1991) lost an entire season after rotator-cuff surgery.

Mitch Williams (5-8, 3.78, 29 saves) remains a force in the bullpen. The Phillies also traded for David West (1-3, 6.99 with the Twins), a one-time phenom who has been a bust. Tyler Green, the Phillies' No. 1 draft choice from 1991, is trying to come back from arthroscopic shoulder surgery. If he's healthy, he might pitch long relief and then ease into the rotation.

FIELDING: No Gold Gloves here. Only the Dodgers committed more errors than the Phillies (131) last year. Hollins made 18 errors at third base, Daulton had 11 errors and 12 passed balls and Chamberlain had just three assists in 73 games. Mickey Morandini is solid at second base and a healthy Dykstra improves the outfield defense. Juan Bell still must prove himself at shortstop.

OUTLOOK: The Phillies have had just one winning record in the last nine seasons. Staying healthy is essential if Jim Fregosi's team expects to improve on last year's 70-92, sixth-place finish. At least the birth of the Marlins guarantees that the Phils will get out of the basement.

PHILADELPHIA PHILLIES 1993 ROSTER

MANAGER Jim Fregosi

Coaches—Larry Bowa, Denis Menke, Johnny Podres, Mel Roberts, Mike Ryan, John Vukovich

PITCHERS

No.	Name	1992 Club	W-L	IP	SO	ERA	B-T	Ht.	Wt.	Born
47	Abbott, Kyle	Philadelphia	1-14	133	88	5.13	L-L	6-4	195	2/18/68 Newburyport, MA
		Scranton	4-1	35	34	1.54				
—	Andersen, Larry	San Diego	1-1	35	35	3.34	R-R	6-3	205	5/6/53 Portland, OR
55	Ayrault, Bob	Scranton	5-1	25	30	4.97	R-R	6-4	235	4/27/66 S. Lake Tahoe, CA
		Philadelphia	2-2	43	27	3.12				
—	Borland, Toby	Scranton	0-1	28	25	7.24	R-R	6-6	182	5/29/69 Quitman, LA
		Reading	2-4	42	45	3.43				
51	Brantley, Cliff	Scranton	3-1	31	26	1.76	R-R	6-1	215	4/12/68 Staten Island, NY
		Philadelphia	2-6	76	58	4.60				
31	Brink, Brad	Reading	1-1	14	12	3.29	R-R	6-2	203	1/20/65 Roseville, CA
		Scranton	8-2	111	92	3.48				
		Philadelphia	0-4	41	16	4.14				
21	Combs, Pat	Philadelphia	1-1	19	11	7.71	L-L	6-4	213	10/29/66 Newport, RI
		Scranton	5-7	125	77	3.61				
54	DeJesus, Jose	Philadelphia		Injured			R-R	6-5	213	1/6/65 Brooklyn, NY
50	DeLeon, Jose	St. L.-Phil.	2-8	117	79	4.37	R-R	6-3	226	12/20/60 Dominican Republic
—	Farmer, Mike	Clearwater	3-3	53	41	1.87	S-L	6-1	175	7/3/68 Gary, IN
—	Fletcher, Paul	Reading	9-4	127	103	2.83	R-R	6-1	185	1/14/67 Galliapolis, OH
		Scranton	3-0	23	26	2.78				
49	Greene, Tommy	Philadelphia	3-3	64	39	5.32	R-R	6-5	225	4/6/67 Lumberton, NC
		Reading	0-0	2	2	9.00				
		Scranton	2-1	22	21	2.49				
43	Howell, Ken	Philadelphia		Injured			R-R	6-3	237	11/28/60 Detroit, MI
27	Jackson, Danny	Chi.(NL)-Pitt.	8-13	202	97	3.84	R-L	6-0	205	1/5/62 San Antonio, TX
45	Mulholland, Terry	Philadelphia	13-11	229	125	3.81	R-L	6-3	207	3/9/63 Uniontown, PA
—	Parris, Steve	Reading	5-7	85	60	4.64	R-R	6-0	180	12/17/67 Joliet, IL
		Scranton	3-3	51	29	4.03				
—	Ritchie, Wally	Scranton	1-0	17	12	2.70	L-L	6-2	183	7/12/65 Glendale, CA
		Philadelphia	2-1	39	19	3.00				
34	Rivera, Ben	Atl.-Phil.	7-4	117	77	3.07	R-R	6-6	210	1/11/69 Dominican Republic
		Scranton	2-0	12	10	0.00				
38	Schilling, Curt	Philadelphia	14-11	226	147	2.35	R-R	6-4	215	11/14/66 Anchorage, AK
—	West, David	Portland	7-6	102	87	4.43	L-L	6-6	240	9/1/64 Memphis, TN
		Minnesota	1-3	28	19	6.99				
41	Williams, Mike	Reading	1-2	16	12	5.17	R-R	6-2	196	7/29/69 Redford, VA
		Scranton	9-1	93	59	2.43				
		Philadelphia	1-1	29	5	5.34				
28	Williams, Mitch	Philadelphia	5-8	81	74	3.78	L-L	6-4	205	11/17/64 Santa Ana, CA

CATCHERS

No.	Name	1992 Club	H	HR	RBI	Pct.	B-T	Ht.	Wt.	Born
10	Daulton, Darren	Philadelphia	131	27	109	.270	L-R	6-2	195	1/3/62 Arkansas City, KS
35	Lindsey, Doug	Scranton	57	4	27	.208	R-R	6-2	200	9/22/67 Austin, TX
23	Pratt, Todd	Reading	44	6	26	.333	R-R	6-3	195	2/9/67 Bellevue, NE
		Scranton	40	7	28	.320				
		Philadelphia	13	2	10	.283				

INFIELDERS

No.	Name	1992 Club	H	HR	RBI	Pct.	B-T	Ht.	Wt.	Born
—	Batiste, Kim	Philadelphia	28	1	10	.206	R-R	6-0	193	3/15/68 New Orleans, LA
		Scranton	70	2	29	.260				
—	Bell, Juan	Rochester	48	3	23	.218	S-R	5-11	170	3/29/68 Dominican Republic
		Philadelphia	30	1	8	.204				
7	Duncan, Mariano	Philadelphia	153	8	50	.267	R-R	6-0	185	3/13/63 Dominican Republic
15	Hollins, Dave	Philadelphia	158	27	93	.270	S-R	6-1	205	5/25/66 Buffalo, NY
17	Jordan, Ricky	Philadelphia	84	4	34	.304	R-R	6-3	205	5/26/65 Richmond, CA
		Scranton	5	0	2	.263				
29	Kruk, John	Philadelphia	164	10	70	.323	L-L	5-10	200	2/9/61 Charleston, WV
—	Lockett, Ron	Reading	91	5	36	.228	L-L	6-1	189	9/5/72 Chicago, IL
12	Morandini, Mickey	Philadelphia	112	3	30	.265	L-R	5-11	175	4/22/66 Kittanning, PA

OUTFIELDERS

No.	Name	1992 Club	H	HR	RBI	Pct.	B-T	Ht.	Wt.	Born
33	Amaro, Ruben	Philadelphia	82	7	34	.219	S-R	5-10	175	2/12/65 Philadelphia, PA
		Scranton	20	1	10	.294				
44	Chamberlain, Wes	Philadelphia	71	9	41	.258	R-R	6-2	219	4/13/66 Chicago, IL
		Scranton	42	4	26	.331				
4	Dykstra, Len	Philadelphia	104	6	39	.301	L-L	5-10	180	2/10/63 Santa Ana, CA
—	Incaviglia, Pete	Houston	93	11	44	.266	R-R	6-1	230	4/2/64 Pebble Beach, CA
—	Jackson, Jeff	Clearwater	72	6	36	.242	R-R	6-2	185	1/2/72 Chicago, IL
		Reading	20	0	6	.185				
—	Longmire, Tony			Injured			L-R	6-1	197	8/12/68 Vallejo, CA
3	Murphy, Dale	Philadelphia	10	2	7	.161	R-R	6-4	200	3/12/56 Portland, OR
—	Nuneviller, Tom	Reading	51	4	23	.309	R-R	6-3	210	5/15/69 Sellersville, PA
—	Thompson, Milt	St. Louis	61	4	17	.293	L-R	5-11	200	1/5/59 Washington, DC
52	Williams, Cary	Scranton	83	7	40	.223	R-R	6-3	190	11/17/64 Florence, AL

PHILLIE PROFILES

DARREN DAULTON 31 6-2 195 Bats L Throws R

Easily the best-hitting catcher in baseball . . . Became only fourth catcher in history to lead NL in RBI . . . Reached career highs in homers, RBI, hits and walks . . . Broke Stan Lopata's 36-year-old club record for homers by a catcher . . . Broke Bo Diaz's team record for RBI by a catcher . . . Batted .319 at Veterans Stadium with 17 homers and 63 RBI, the most homers and RBI ever at Vet by a lefty . . . First Phils catcher to steal 10 or more bases since Jimmie Wilson in 1927 . . . Has stolen 21 bases in 23 attempts since 1990 . . . Notched most RBI by Phils lefty since Chuck Klein had 120 in 1933 . . . Tied for fourth in home-run race, ranked fourth in slugging percentage (.524), tied for sixth in on-base percentage (.385) and ranked sixth in walks (88) . . . Born Jan. 3, 1962, in Arkansas City, Kan. . . . Selected by Phillies in 25th round of 1980 draft . . . His 1991 season was ruined by injuries suffered in Lenny Dykstra's car crash . . . Earned $2.4 million in 1992.

Year	Club	Pos.	G	AB	R	H	2B	3B	HR	RBI	SB	Avg.
1983	Philadelphia . . .	C	2	3	1	1	0	0	0	0	0	.333
1985	Philadelphia . . .	C	36	103	14	21	3	1	4	11	3	.204
1986	Philadelphia . . .	C	49	138	18	31	4	0	8	21	2	.225
1987	Philadelphia . . .	C–1B	53	129	10	25	6	0	3	13	0	.194
1988	Philadelphia . . .	C–1B	58	144	13	30	6	0	1	12	2	.208
1989	Philadelphia . . .	C	131	368	29	74	12	2	8	44	2	.201
1990	Philadelphia . . .	C	143	459	62	123	30	1	12	57	7	.268
1991	Philadelphia . . .	C	89	285	36	56	12	0	12	42	5	.196
1992	Philadelphia . . .	C	145	485	80	131	32	5	27	109	11	.270
	Totals		706	2114	263	492	105	9	75	309	32	.233

JOHN KRUK 32 5-10 200 Bats L Throws L

Rotund figure and hillbilly act suggest he's comic caricature, but he has developed into feared hitter . . . Likes to joke about lack of conditioning, yet he tied for third in batting race, finished second in on-base percentage (.423) and fifth in walks (92) . . . Reached career highs in average, hits, doubles, runs and walks . . . Sidelined late in season with sore right shoulder . . . Batted .355 in his last 18 games . . . Hit .314 against lefties . . . Became first Phillie first baseman to hit over .300 since Von

Hayes in 1986 . . . Steadily improving hitter who has batted .308 since becoming a Phillie, June 3, 1989 . . . Has .309 career average at Veterans Stadium . . . His most famous line: "I'm not an athlete. I'm a baseball player." . . . Born Feb. 9, 1961, in Charleston, W. Va. . . . Padres' third pick in secondary phase of 1981 draft . . . Traded to Phillies with Randy Ready for Chris James . . . Earned $2.3 million in 1992.

Year	Club	Pos.	G	AB	R	H	2B	3B	HR	RBI	SB	Avg.
1986	San Diego	OF-1B	122	278	33	86	16	2	4	38	2	.309
1987	San Diego	OF-1B	138	447	72	140	14	2	20	91	18	.313
1988	San Diego	1B-OF	120	378	54	91	17	1	9	44	5	.241
1989	S.D.-Phil.	OF-1B	112	357	53	107	13	6	8	44	3	.300
1990	Philadelphia . . .	OF-1B	142	443	52	129	25	8	7	67	10	.291
1991	Philadelphia . . .	1B-OF	152	538	84	158	27	6	21	92	7	.294
1992	Philadelphia . . .	1B-OF	144	507	86	164	30	4	10	70	3	.323
	Totals		930	2948	434	875	142	29	79	446	48	.297

LENNY DYKSTRA 30 5-10 180 Bats L Throws L

Plays baseball and sometimes approaches life with reckless abandon . . . Phillies can't win without him, but they can't keep "Nails" healthy . . . Spent five stints on disabled list over past two seasons, missing 176 games . . . Phillies were 40-45 with him in lineup and 30-47 without him in 1992 . . . Hit by a pitch, center fielder suffered fractured thumb on Opening Day . . . Also disabled in July with strained right hamstring . . . Season ended Aug. 15 when he fractured left hand diving into first base to beat out single . . . Batted .333 in his last nine games and matched career high with four-hit game at Montreal Aug. 6 . . . Had 14-game hitting streak in June . . . Has 81-percent career success rate stealing bases . . . Born Feb. 10, 1963, in Santa Ana, Cal. . . . Mets' 12th pick in 1981 draft . . . Traded to Phillies with Roger McDowell for Juan Samuel, June 18, 1989 . . . Car crash interrupted 1991 season . . . Earned $2.3 million in 1992.

Year	Club	Pos.	G	AB	R	H	2B	3B	HR	RBI	SB	Avg.
1985	New York (NL)	OF	83	236	40	60	9	3	1	19	15	.254
1986	New York (NL)	OF	147	431	77	127	27	7	8	45	31	.295
1987	New York (NL)	OF	132	431	86	123	37	3	10	43	27	.285
1988	New York (NL)	OF	126	429	57	116	19	3	8	33	30	.270
1989	N.Y.(NL)-Phil.	OF	146	511	66	121	32	4	7	32	30	.237
1990	Philadelphia . . .	OF	149	590	106	192	35	3	9	60	33	.325
1991	Philadelphia . . .	OF	63	246	48	73	13	5	3	12	24	.297
1992	Philadelphia . . .	OF	85	345	53	104	18	0	6	39	30	.301
	Totals		391	3219	533	916	190	28	52	283	220	.285

MARIANO DUNCAN 30 6-0 185 Bats R Throws R

Valuable contributor during first year in Philadelphia . . . A regular without a regular position, he split time at shortstop, second base and left field . . . Finished with more at-bats than any Phillie except Dave Hollins . . . Tied for second-most doubles in NL . . . Stole 16 straight bases and 23 in 24 attempts overall . . . Had 13-game hitting streak in June . . . Had nine three-hit games and one four-hit game and went 5-for-5, including homer, May 3 against Giants . . . Career-best 14-game hitting streak was snapped April 28 in San Diego . . . Batted .404 with nine doubles during streak . . . Born March 13, 1963, in San Pedro de Macoris, D.R. . . . Signed as free agent with Dodgers in 1982 . . . Traded to Reds with Tim Leary for Kal Daniels and Lenny Harris in 1989 . . . Has made seven trips to disabled list . . . Signed with Phillies as free agent following 1991 season . . . Earned $2 million in 1992.

Year	Club	Pos.	G	AB	R	H	2B	3B	HR	RBI	SB	Avg.
1985	Los Angeles . . .	SS–2B	142	562	74	137	24	6	6	39	38	.244
1986	Los Angeles . . .	SS	109	407	47	93	7	0	8	30	48	.229
1987	Los Angeles . . .	SS–2B-OF	76	261	31	56	8	1	6	18	11	.215
1989	LA-Cin.	SS–2B-OF	94	258	32	64	15	2	3	21	9	.248
1990	Cincinnati.	2B-SS-OF	125	435	67	133	22	11	10	55	13	.306
1991	Cincinnati.	2B-SS-OF	100	333	46	86	7	4	12	40	5	.258
1992	Philadelphia . . .	OF-2B-SS-3B	142	574	71	153	40	3	8	50	23	.267
	Totals		788	2830	368	722	123	27	53	253	147	.255

DAVE HOLLINS 26 6-1 205 Bats S Throws R

During first full season as everyday player, he became one of top hitting third basemen in majors . . . Tied teammate Darren Daulton for third in homer race . . . Tied for seventh in RBI, second in runs and eighth in total bases (275) . . . Played 31 straight errorless games . . . Set club records in homers and RBI by switch-hitter, breaking Buzzy Arlett's mark from 1931 . . . Also set major league record for switch-hitters by being hit by pitch 19 times . . . Suspended by league four days for charging mound Sept. 24 after being hit by Bob Scanlan pitch, starting six-minute, bench-clearing brawl . . . Returned from suspension on final day of season to hit two-run homer against Cardinals . . . Extremely intense competitor who has been compared to Pete Rose . . . Born May 25, 1966, in Buffalo . . . Padres' sixth pick in 1987 draft . . . Drafted by Phillies from San Diego, Dec. 4, 1989 . . . Earned $180,000 in 1992.

Year	Club	Pos.	G	AB	R	H	2B	3B	HR	RBI	SB	Avg.
1990	Philadelphia . . .	3B–1B	72	114	14	21	0	0	5	15	0	.184
1991	Philadelphia . . .	3B–1B	56	151	18	45	10	2	6	21	1	.298
1992	Philadelphia . . .	3B–1B	156	586	104	158	28	4	27	93	9	.270
	Totals		284	851	136	224	38	6	38	129	10	.263

MICKEY MORANDINI 26 5-11 175 Bats L Throws R

Stepped into record book last Sept. 20, becoming first second baseman to turn unassisted triple play in regular season . . . Grabbed line drive by Pirates' Jeff King, stepped on second base to double up Andy Van Slyke and tagged out Barry Bonds . . . It was first unassisted triple play in big leagues since Ron Hansen's in 1968 and first in NL since Jim Cooney's in 1927 . . . Only ninth unassisted triple play in history . . . Turned in solid overall performance during first full season in majors with 59-game errorless streak . . . Had career-high 10-game hitting streak in September and nine-game streak in July . . . Hit safely in seven straight at-bats from Sept. 6-8 . . . Had four-hit games April 14 at New York and Sept. 6 at Atlanta . . . Tied for sixth in NL in triples . . . Phillies felt he needed to build up strength to help him endure 162-game season . . . Born April 22, 1966, in Kittanning, Pa. . . . Phillies' fifth choice in 1988 draft . . . Earned $180,000 in 1992.

Year	Club	Pos.	G	AB	R	H	2B	3B	HR	RBI	SB	Avg.
1990	Philadelphia . . .	2B	25	79	9	19	4	0	1	3	3	.241
1991	Philadelphia . . .	2B	98	325	38	81	11	4	1	20	13	.249
1992	Philadelphia . . .	2B-SS	127	422	47	112	8	8	3	30	8	.265
	Totals		250	826	94	212	23	12	5	53	24	.257

TERRY MULHOLLAND 30 6-3 207 Bats R Throws L

Phillies' ace led NL with 12 complete games and ranked eighth in innings pitched despite being sidelined down the stretch with knee injury . . . Averaged just 1½ walks per start . . . Made four straight starts without surrendering walk from July 21-Aug. 5 . . . Went 9-1 from May 5-July 4 . . . Has devastating pickoff move, making it nearly impossible to steal a base . . . Picked off 14 runners . . . First Phillie to have double-digit wins in consecutive seasons since Shane Rawley (1986-87) . . . Bothered by gimpy knees, he won just twice during six-week stretch late in season . . . Problems began Aug. 5, when he had to leave game in St. Louis after just three innings with flu . . . Also sustained broken knuckle trying to field grounder June 20 . . . Selected by Giants in first round of 1984 draft . . . Traded to Phillies for Steve Bedrosian in 1989 . . . Born March 9, 1963, in Uniontown, Pa. . . . Earned $1.25 million in 1992.

Year	Club	G	IP	W	L	Pct.	SO	BB	H	ERA
1986	San Francisco	15	54⅔	1	7	.125	27	35	51	4.94
1988	San Francisco	9	46	2	1	.667	18	7	50	3.72
1989	S.F.-Phil.	25	115⅓	4	7	.364	66	36	137	4.92
1990	Philadelphia	33	180⅔	9	10	.474	75	42	172	3.34
1991	Philadelphia	34	232	16	13	.552	142	49	231	3.61
1992	Philadelphia	32	229	13	11	.542	125	46	227	3.81
	Totals	148	857⅔	45	49	.479	453	215	868	3.87

BEN RIVERA 24 6-6 210 — Bats R Throws R

Big rookie right-hander went from top to bottom when Braves traded him to Phillies last May, but it turned into golden opportunity . . . Strictly a reliever in Atlanta, he was 0-1 with 4.70 ERA in eight appearances before trade . . . Quickly stepped into Phils' rotation, becoming one of their most effective starters and finishing with third-best ERA on club . . . Earned first big league victory Aug. 7, holding Expos to one run on four hits through eight innings . . . Pitched seven shutout innings and fanned eight Mets in next start, en route to first complete game . . . Started 14 games, completed four and had one shutout . . . Has overpowering fastball and throws curve and straight change for strikes . . . Disabled from July 8-29 with strained right groin . . . Born Jan. 11, 1969, in San Pedro de Macoris, D.R. . . . Signed with Braves as free agent in 1985 . . . Traded to Phillies for pitcher Donnie Elliott . . . Earned $109,000 in 1992.

Year	Club	G	IP	W	L	Pct.	SO	BB	H	ERA
1992	Atl.-Phil.	28	117⅓	7	4	.636	77	45	99	3.07

CURT SCHILLING 26 6-4 215 — Bats R Throws R

Acquired from Houston for Jason Grimsley in April, he came out of nowhere to lead Phillies in ERA and victories . . . Began season in middle relief . . . Hadn't started a major league game since 1989, but filled void when other starters were injured . . . Moved into rotation in May, replacing Tommy Greene . . . Had fourth-best ERA in NL, tied for second in complete games (10), tied for third in shutouts (4) and boasted lowest opponents' batting average (.201) . . . Pitched 29 consecutive scoreless innings from July 22-Aug. 1 . . . Went 3-1 with 2.03 ERA in July . . . Born Nov. 14, 1966, in Anchorage, Alaska . . . Selected by Red Sox in second round of January 1986 draft . . . Traded to Orioles with Brady Anderson for Mike Boddicker in 1988 . . . Traded to Astros for Glenn Davis in 1991 . . . Started just five of first 100 games before joining Phils . . . Earned $205,000 in 1992.

Year	Club	G	IP	W	L	Pct.	SO	BB	H	ERA
1988	Baltimore	4	14⅔	0	3	.000	4	10	22	9.82
1989	Baltimore	5	8⅔	0	1	.000	6	3	10	6.23
1990	Baltimore	35	46	1	2	.333	32	19	38	2.54
1991	Houston	56	75⅔	3	5	.375	71	39	79	3.81
1992	Philadelphia	42	226⅓	14	11	.560	147	59	165	2.35
	Totals	142	371⅓	18	22	.450	260	130	314	3.05

MITCH WILLIAMS 28 6-4 205 Bats L Throws L

"Wild Thing" never seems to do things the easy way, but he's still a quality bullpen closer . . . Saved 29 games in 37 opportunities in 1992 . . . Had a hand in 49 percent of Phillies' 70 wins . . . His 11-inning scoreless streak in June was longest by a Phillie reliever . . . Named Rolaids Relief Pitcher for June, saving nine games in 10 chances . . . Ranked fifth in NL in saves . . . Has knack for pitching himself into and out of trouble, driving managers to distraction . . . "I guess it's worse for the manager," he says. "My stomach hurts when we lose, but his hurts even if we win." . . . Surrendered game-winning homer to Terry Pendleton June 1, first home run he'd given up in 52 appearances . . . Born Nov. 17, 1964, in Santa Ana, Cal. . . . Padres' eighth pick in 1982 draft . . . Traded from Cubs to Phillies on eve of 1991 season for Chuck McElroy and Bob Scanlan . . . Owns 143 major league saves . . . Earned $3.2 million in 1992.

Year	Club	G	IP	W	L	Pct.	SO	BB	H	ERA
1986	Texas	80	98	8	6	.571	90	79	69	3.58
1987	Texas	85	108⅔	8	6	.571	129	94	63	3.23
1988	Texas	67	68	2	7	.222	61	47	48	4.63
1989	Chicago (NL)	76	81⅔	4	4	.500	67	52	71	2.64
1990	Chicago (NL)	59	66⅓	1	8	.111	55	50	60	3.93
1991	Philadelphia	69	88⅓	12	5	.706	84	62	56	2.34
1992	Philadelphia	66	81	5	8	.385	74	64	69	3.78
	Totals	502	592	40	44	.476	560	448	436	3.39

DANNY JACKSON 31 6-0 205 Bats R Throws L

Wound up being traded to Phillies after Marlins, in prearranged deal, made him their 27th pick in expansion draft . . . Still struggling to regain his 23-win stuff of 1988, he split 1992 season between Cubs and Pirates and finished with fourth straight non-winning record . . . Traded for Steve Buechele July 11 as Pirates needed veteran left-hander to bolster pitching staff for pennant drive . . . Was 4-9 with Cubs and went 4-4 for Pirates . . . Flopped badly in NLCS, getting chased after giving up four runs in second inning of Game 2 . . . Pitched division-clinching victory against Mets Sept. 27 . . . Gave up just five earned runs in first four starts for Pirates . . . Had 5-14 record with Cubs . . . Went 20 consecutive starts without a victory as a Cub until he beat Expos June 5 . . . Born Jan. 5, 1962, in San Antonio . . . First player chosen overall, by Royals, in secondary phase of January 1982 draft . . . Signed with Cubs as free agent following 1990 season . . . Finished second in 1988 Cy Young voting . . . Earned $2,625,000 in 1992.

Year	Club	G	IP	W	L	Pct.	SO	BB	H	ERA
1983	Kansas City	4	19	1	1	.500	9	6	26	5.21
1984	Kansas City	15	76	2	6	.250	40	35	84	4.26
1985	Kansas City	32	208	14	12	.538	114	76	209	3.42
1986	Kansas City	32	185⅔	11	12	.478	115	79	177	3.20
1987	Kansas City	36	224	9	18	.333	152	109	219	4.02
1988	Cincinnati	35	260⅔	23	8	.742	161	71	206	2.73
1989	Cincinnati	20	115⅔	6	11	.353	70	57	122	5.60
1990	Cincinnati	22	117⅓	6	6	.500	76	40	119	3.61
1991	Chicago (NL)	17	70⅔	1	5	.167	31	48	89	6.75
1992	Chi (NL)-Pitt.	34	201⅓	8	13	.381	97	77	211	3.84
	Totals.	247	1478⅓	81	92	.468	865	598	1462	3.83

TOMMY GREENE 25 6-5 225 Bats R Throws R

Up-and-coming career was temporarily sidetracked in 1992, when he was shelved from May 13-Aug. 31 with tendinitis in right shoulder after making just six starts . . . Returned to rotation Sept. 8 and pitched five shutout innings against Mets . . . Pitched seven innings against Cubs April 8, his longest outing until Sept. 24, when he again went seven innings against Chicago . . . Made six starts down the stretch, going 1-2 . . . Had first-inning problems in April when his combined first-inning ERA was

13.50 . . . Born April 6, 1967, in Lumberton, N.C. . . . Selected by Braves in first round of 1985 draft . . . Traded to Phillies with Dale Murphy for Jeff Parrett, Jim Vatcher and Victor Rosario, Aug. 3, 1990 . . . Braves' Minor League Pitcher of the Year in 1986 . . . Spent first full season in majors in 1991, finishing among NL leaders in strikeouts, shutouts (2), winning percentage and opponents' batting average (.230) . . . Earned $255,000 in 1992.

Year	Club	G	IP	W	L	Pct.	SO	BB	H	ERA
1989	Atlanta	4	26⅓	1	2	.333	17	6	22	4.10
1990	Atl.-Phil.	15	51⅓	3	3	.500	21	26	50	5.08
1991	Philadelphia	36	207⅔	13	7	.650	154	66	177	3.38
1992	Philadelphia	13	64⅓	3	3	.500	39	34	75	5.32
	Totals	68	349⅔	20	15	.571	231	132	324	4.04

TOP PROSPECTS

MIKE LIEBERTHAL 21 6-0 170 Bats R Throws R

Phillies' first-round draft pick in 1990 has made rapid strides as catcher and hitter . . . Batted .286 with 16 doubles and 37 RBI in just 308 at-bats for Reading (AA) before being promoted to Scranton (AAA) . . . Named ninth-best prospect in Eastern League by *Baseball America* . . . Displays good catching instincts and relates well to pitchers . . . Batted .305 with 17 doubles and 31 RBI in 72 games for Spartanburg (A) in 1991 . . . Born Jan. 18, 1972, in Glendale, Cal.

TODD PRATT 26 6-3 195 Bats R Throws R

Good hitter who is still learning to catch . . . Selected by Phillies from Baltimore organization in December 1991 Rule 5 draft . . . Began 1992 season at Reading (AA), where he underwent extensive tutoring behind the plate . . . Batted .333 with six homers in 41 games before being promoted to Scranton (AAA), where he hit .320 with nine doubles and seven homers . . . Called up to Philadelphia July 28 and batted .283 with two homers in 16 major league games . . . Had four-RBI game against Braves Aug. 30 . . . Selected by Red Sox in sixth round of 1985 draft . . . Born Feb. 9, 1967, in Bellevue, Neb.

MANAGER JIM FREGOSI: Management did not blame him

for Phillies' last-place finish and, at midseason, his contract was extended through 1993 . . . The 70-92 finish marked Phillies' sixth straight losing season, the longest current non-winning streak in NL . . . With club-record 17 players on disabled list and 17 rookies on roster before late-season callups, his hands were tied . . . Was praised for ability to communicate with players, but he couldn't halt Phillies' steady slide as they went 10-12 in April, 12-13 in May, 12-15 in June and 11-18 in July before dropping out of sight while losing nine of first 11 games in August . . . Replaced Nick Leyva as Phils' manager April 23, 1991 and presided over turnaround as Phils played 10 games over .500 after All-Star break to finish third . . . Also managed Angels from 1978-81 and White Sox from 1986-88 . . . Won 1979 AL West title . . . Batted .265 during 18-year major league career . . . Was six-time All-Star shortstop . . . Played with Angels, Mets, Rangers and Pirates . . . Hit 151 homers and drove in 706 runs . . . Held eight Angels' career records . . . Born April 4, 1942, in San Francisco . . . Overall managerial record is 574-642.

ALL-TIME PHILLIE SEASON RECORDS

BATTING: Frank O'Doul, .398, 1929
HRs: Mike Schmidt, 48, 1980
RBI: Chuck Klein, 170, 1930
STEALS: Juan Samuel, 72, 1984
WINS: Grover Alexander, 33, 1916
STRIKEOUTS: Steve Carlton, 310, 1972

PITTSBURGH PIRATES

TEAM DIRECTORY: Pres./CEO: Mark Sauer; GM: Ted Simmons; VP-Pub. Rel.: Rick Cerrone; Dir. Media Rel.: Jim Trdinich; Trav. Sec.: Greg Johnson; Mgr.: Jim Leyland. Home: Three Rivers Stadium (58,729). Field distances: 335, l.f. line; 375, l.c.; 400, c.f.; 375, r.c.; 335, r.f. line. Spring training: Bradenton, Fla.

SCOUTING REPORT

HITTING: The Pirates are facing life without NL MVP Barry Bonds and it doesn't figure to be easy. The Bucs led the league with 693 runs in 1992, but Bonds scored 109 of them and drove in 103. Pittsburgh, which was bent on payroll slashing last winter, also must replace Jose Lind, Alex Cole, Gary Varsho and Cecil Espy.

Andy Van Slyke (.324, 14, 89) is the one remaining big gun, but he no longer has Bonds protecting him. Shortstop Jay Bell (.264, 9, 55) is very productive for a middle infielder and had a league-high, 22-game hitting streak last year. Jeff King (.231, 14, 65) will have to play a much bigger role in 1993. Newly signed Lonnie Smith from the Braves (.247, 6, 33) and rookie Al Martin (.305, 20, 59 for Triple-A Buffalo) will vie for Bond's spot in left field.

The new, improved Andy Van Slyke hits lefties, too.

Carlos Garcia (.303, 13, 70 for Buffalo) might be an offensive improvement over Lind at second base. Lloyd McClendon (.253, 3, 20) figures to get more playing time and the Pirates need more production from Orlando Merced (.247, 6, 60). Platoon catcher Don Slaught (.345, 4, 37) might get an opportunity to play more, despite Mike LaValliere's superior defensive skills.

PITCHING: Pittsburgh ranked third in the NL with a 3.35 team ERA and 20 complete games in 1992, but this was another area that took a heavy hit when Doug Drabek left as a free agent and Danny Jackson was lost in the expansion draft.

The Bucs are counting on a full recovery by Zane Smith (8-8, 3.06), who was limited to 22 starts last year and underwent arthroscopic shoulder surgery. Rookie knuckleballer Tim Wakefield (8-1, 2.15) saved the Pirates last season after being promoted in late July and Pittsburgh has to hope that he's the real thing. Randy Tomlin (14-9, 3.41) usually puts up good numbers, although opponents batted a healthy .282 against him in 1992. Veteran Bob Walk (10-6, 3.20) has shuttled between starting and relieving, but he figures to play a more important role now and the question is whether he's up to it.

Pittsburgh's bullpen has been a trouble area, as was evident in the NLCS when all three Pirate victories over the Braves came on complete games. Stan Belinda (6-4, 3.15, 18 saves) is back, but he's not considered a premier closer and Pirates fans won't forget that he blew the save in Game 7 of the NLCS. Free-agent signees Alejandro Pena (1-6, 4.07, 15 saves with the Braves) and John Candelaria (2-5, 2.84, 5 saves with the Dodgers) are being counted on to help.

FIELDING: For years, the Pirates have been winning games with their gloves, but now they've lost two Gold Glove winners in left fielder Bonds and second baseman Lind. Van Slyke is still golden in center field and Bell is solid at shortstop, but Slaught is below average behind the plate. Garcia, a fine shortstop prospect, must play second base, young Kevin Young is a question mark at third and King probably has to move across the diamond to first.

OUTLOOK: Pirates manager Jim Leyland is a magician and he has fooled everybody by winning three straight division titles. But this time, he has simply lost too many horses. It's difficult to see any way that Pittsburgh could approach last year's 96-66 record.

PITTSBURGH PIRATES 1993 ROSTER

MANAGER Jim Leyland

Coaches–Terry Collins, Rich Donnelly, Milt May, Ray Miller, Tommy Sandt, Bill Virdon

PITCHERS

No.	Name	1992 Club	W-L	IP	SO	ERA	B-T	Ht.	Wt.	Born
50	Belinda, Stan	Pittsburgh	6-4	71	57	3.15	R-R	6-3	187	8/6/66 Huntingdon, PA
—	Candelaria, John	Los Angeles	2-5	25	23	2.84	R-L	6-6	225	11/6/53 Brooklyn, NY
61	Cole, Victor	Buffalo	11-6	116	69	3.11	R-R	5-10	160	1/23/68 Russia
		Pittsburgh	0-2	23	12	5.48				
26	Cooke, Steve	Carolina	2-2	36	38	3.00	R-L	6-6	220	1/14/70 Kanai, HI
		Buffalo	6-3	74	52	3.75				
		Pittsburgh	2-0	23	10	3.52				
—	DeLos Santos, M.	Augusta	7-8	96	103	2.25	R-R	5-10	200	7/13/70 Dominican Republic
—	Hope, John	Salem	11-8	176	106	3.47	R-R	6-3	195	12/21/70 Ft. Lauderdale, FL
—	Johnston, Joel	Kansas City	0-0	3	0	13.50	R-R	6-4	220	3/8/67 West Chester, PA
		Omaha	5-2	75	48	6.39				
66	Minor, Blas	Buffalo	5-4	96	60	2.43	R-R	6-3	195	3/20/66 Merced, CA
		Pittsburgh	0-0	2	0	4.50				
—	Moeller, Dennis	Omaha	8-5	121	56	2.46	R-L	6-2	195	9/15/67 Tarzana, CA
		Kansas City	0-3	18	6	7.00				
32	Neagle, Denny	Pittsburgh	4-6	86	77	4.48	L-L	6-2	215	9/13/68 Gambrills, MD
—	Pena, Alejandro	Atlanta	1-6	42	34	4.07	R-R	6-1	203	6/25/59 Dominican Republic
—	Robertson, Rich	Salem	3-0	37	27	3.41	L-L	6-4	175	9/15/68 Nacogdioches, TX
		Carolina	6-7	125	107	3.03				
30	Rodriguez, Rosario	Buffalo	0-1	2	1	15.43	R-L	6-0	205	7/8/69 Mexico
—	Shouse, Brian	Carolina	5-6	77	80	2.44	L-L	5-11	180	9/26/68 Effingham, IL
41	Smith, Zane	Pittsburgh	8-8	141	56	3.06	L-L	6-1	205	12/28/60 Madison, WI
29	Tomlin, Randy	Pittsburgh	14-9	209	90	3.41	L-L	5-10	170	6/14/66 Bainbridge, MD
43	Wagner, Paul	Carolina	6-6	122	101	3.03	R-R	6-1	185	11/14/67 Milwaukee, WI
		Buffalo	3-3	39	19	5.49				
		Pittsburgh	2-0	13	5	0.69				
49	Wakefield, Tim	Buffalo	10-3	135	71	3.06	R-R	6-2	195	8/2/66 Melbourne, FL
		Pittsburgh	8-1	92	51	2.15				
17	Walk, Bob	Pittsburgh	10-6	135	60	3.20	R-R	6-3	217	11/26/56 Van Nuys, CA
—	Zimmerman, Mike	Carolina	4-15	153	106	3.82	R-R	6-0	180	2/6/69 Brooklyn, NY

CATCHERS

No.	Name	1992 Club	H	HR	RBI	Pct.	B-T	Ht.	Wt.	Born
12	LaValliere, Mike	Pittsburgh	75	2	29	.256	L-R	5-9	210	8/18/60 Charlotte, NC
14	Prince, Tom	Buffalo	64	9	35	.262	R-R	5-11	185	8/13/64 Kankakee, IL
		Pittsburgh	4	0	5	.091				
11	Slaught, Don	Pittsburgh	88	4	37	.345	R-R	6-1	190	9/11/58 Long Beach, CA

INFIELDERS

3	Bell, Jay	Pittsburgh	167	9	55	.264	R-R	6-0	185	12/11/65 Pensacola, FL
—	Foley, Tom	Montreal	20	0	5	.174	L-R	6-1	175	9/9/59 Columbus, GA
51	Garcia, Carlos	Buffalo	129	13	70	.303	R-R	6-1	185	10/15/67 Venezuela
		Pittsburgh	8	0	4	.205				
7	King, Jeff	Pittsburgh	111	14	65	.231	R-R	6-1	180	12/26/64 Marion, IN
		Buffalo	10	2	5	.345				
6	Merced, Orlando	Pittsburgh	100	6	60	.247	S-R	5-11	170	11/2/66 Puerto Rico
27	Richardson, Jeff	Buffalo	95	3	29	.290	R-R	6-2	180	8/26/65 Grand Island, NE
—	Sandoval, Jose	Mexico City	142	26	89	.283	R-R	5-11	170	8/25/69 Mexico
46	Shelton, Ben	Carolina	86	10	51	.234	R-L	6-3	210	9/21/69 Chicago, IL
22	Wehner, John	Buffalo	60	7	27	.269	R-R	6-3	205	6/29/67 Pittsburgh, PA
		Pittsburgh	22	0	4	.179				
36	Young, Kevin	Buffalo	154	8	65	.314	R-R	6-3	210	6/16/69 Alpena, MI
		Pittsburgh	4	0	4	.571				

OUTFIELDERS

47	Bullett, Scott	Carolina	140	8	45	.270	L-L	6-2	190	12/25/68 Martinsburg, WV
		Buffalo	4	0	0	.400				
35	Clark, Dave	Buffalo	77	11	55	.304	L-R	6-2	210	9/3/62 Tupelo, MS
		Pittsburgh	7	2	7	.212				
28	Martin, Albert	Buffalo	128	20	59	.305	L-L	6-2	220	11/24/67 West Covina, CA
		Pittsburgh	2	0	2	.167				
23	McClendon, Lloyd	Pittsburgh	48	3	20	.253	R-R	6-0	212	1/11/59 Gary, IN
25	Pennyfeather, William	Carolina	67	6	25	.337	R-R	6-2	215	5/25/68 Perth Amboy, NJ
		Buffalo	38	1	12	.238				
		Pittsburgh	2	0	0	.222				
—	Smith, Lonnie	Atlanta	39	6	33	.247	R-R	5-9	170	12/22/55 Chicago, IL
—	Thomas, Keith	Salem	103	16	51	.277	R-R	6-1	180	9/12/68 Chicago, IL
		Carolina	23	4	15	.295				
18	Van Slyke, Andy	Pittsburgh	199	14	89	.324	L-R	6-2	195	12/21/60 Utica, NY

PIRATE PROFILES

ANDY VAN SLYKE 32 6-2 195 Bats L Throws L

Five-time Gold Glove center fielder enjoyed outstanding year, because he finally learned to hit lefties . . . His .299 batting average against left-handers was 81 points higher than previous career mark . . . Also reached career highs in doubles and hits . . . Led majors in multi-hit games (65) . . . Led NL in doubles, finished second in batting, seventh in slugging percentage (.505), ninth in on-base percentage (.381), third in runs, triples and total bases (310) and tied for first in hits . . . Had 11 assists . . . Tripled and doubled in Game 4 of NLCS and hit seventh-inning sacrifice fly to drive home winning run in Game 3 . . . Went 8-for-29 in playoffs with three doubles and four RBI . . . Reached double figures in doubles, triples and homers for third time . . . Born Dec. 21, 1960, in Utica, N.Y. . . . Cardinals' first pick in 1979 draft . . . Traded to Pirates in package for Tony Pena, prior to 1987 season . . . *Sporting News'* 1988 Player of the Year . . . Earned $4.25 million in 1992.

Year	Club	Pos.	G	AB	R	H	2B	3B	HR	RBI	SB	Avg.
1983	St. Louis	OF-1B-3B	101	309	51	81	15	5	8	38	21	.262
1984	St. Louis	OF-1B-3B	137	361	45	88	16	4	7	50	28	.244
1985	St. Louis	OF-1B	146	424	61	110	25	6	13	55	34	.259
1986	St. Louis	OF-1B	137	418	48	113	23	7	13	61	21	.270
1987	Pittsburgh	OF-1B	157	564	93	165	36	11	21	82	34	.293
1988	Pittsburgh	OF	154	587	101	169	23	15	25	100	30	.288
1989	Pittsburgh	OF-1B	130	476	64	113	18	9	9	53	16	.237
1990	Pittsburgh	OF	136	493	67	140	26	6	17	77	14	.284
1991	Pittsburgh	OF	138	491	87	130	24	7	17	83	10	.265
1992	Pittsburgh	OF	154	614	103	199	45	12	14	89	12	.324
	Totals		1390	4737	720	1308	251	82	144	688	220	.276

JAY BELL 27 6-0 185 Bats R Throws R

Steady shortstop and dependable No. 2 hitter reached career highs in hits and doubles in 1992 . . . Had league-high 22-game hitting streak from Aug. 24-Sept. 17 . . . Batted .322 over his last 39 games with 10 doubles, four triples, four homers and 21 RBI . . . Committed just four errors over final 70 games . . . Tied teammate Barry Bonds for ninth place in doubles . . . Delivered game-winning single in 13th inning to beat Expos Sept. 17 in pivotal NL East showdown . . . Hit clutch seventh-inning double in Game 3 of NLCS . . . Belted three-run homer in Game 6 . . . Went 5-for-29 in playoffs with four RBI . . . Has 22 career NLCS hits, breaking Willie Stargell's club record . . . Born Dec. 11, 1965, at Eglin AFB, Fla. . . . Twins' first pick in 1984 draft . . . Traded to Indians in 1985 and sent to Pirates for Felix Fermin prior to 1989 season . . . Only third Pirate shortstop to hit more than 15 homers in a season . . . Earned $875,000 in 1992.

Year	Club	Pos.	G	AB	R	H	2B	3B	HR	RBI	SB	Avg.
1986	Cleveland	2B	5	14	3	5	2	0	1	4	0	.357
1987	Cleveland	SS	38	125	14	27	9	1	2	13	2	.216
1988	Cleveland	SS	73	211	23	46	5	1	2	21	4	.218
1989	Pittsburgh	SS	78	271	33	70	13	3	2	27	5	.258
1990	Pittsburgh	SS	159	583	93	148	28	7	7	52	10	.254
1991	Pittsburgh	SS	157	608	96	164	32	8	16	67	10	.270
1992	Pittsburgh	SS	159	632	87	167	36	6	9	55	7	.264
	Totals		669	2444	349	627	125	26	39	239	38	.257

JEFF KING 28 6-1 180 Bats R Throws R

Batting behind Barry Bonds, he played crucial role during Pirates' pennant drive . . . His career was resurrected after Steve Buechele was traded to Cubs at midseason . . . Began season with Pirates, but was optioned to Buffalo (AAA) July 4 when he was hitting .187 . . . Recalled July 14 and batted .268 in second half with eight homers and 45 RBI . . . Had career-best 11-game hitting streak in September and reached career high in RBI . . . Made 65 starts at third base, 30 at first base, 22 at second, three at shortstop and one in right field . . . Hit record-tying four doubles in NLCS . . . Went 3-for-4, including RBI double, in Game 5 . . . Overall, he was 7-for-29 in playoffs . . . Born Dec. 26, 1964, in Marion, Ind. . . . First player selected overall in 1986 draft, following junior year at University of Arkansas . . . *The Sporting News'* College Player of the Year in 1986 . . . Earned $225,000 in 1992.

Year	Club	Pos.	G	AB	R	H	2B	3B	HR	RBI	SB	Avg.
1989	Pittsburgh	1B-3B-2B-SS	75	215	31	42	13	1	5	19	4	.195
1990	Pittsburgh	3B-1B	127	371	46	91	17	1	14	53	3	.245
1991	Pittsburgh	3B	33	109	16	26	1	1	4	18	3	.239
1992	Pittsburgh . .	3B-2B-1B-SS-OF	130	480	56	111	21	2	14	65	4	.231
	Totals		365	1175	149	270	52	5	37	155	14	.230

DON SLAUGHT 34 6-1 190 Bats R Throws R

Platoon catcher made strong bid for No. 1 job with career-high batting average in 1992... Batted .415 during 21-game stretch in September... Threw out 19 of 64 runners attempting to steal (30 percent)... Began season on disabled list with strained muscle in rib cage... Hit bases-empty homer off Tom Glavine in Game 3 of NLCS and had two-run double off Glavine to break open Game 6... Went 4-for-12 in playoffs and tied for club lead with five RBI, although he started only against lefties... Had sizzling 21-for-53 stretch spanning May and June ... Born Sept. 11, 1958, in Long Beach, Cal.... Selected by Royals in seventh round of 1980 draft... Traded from Yankees to Pirates for Jeff Robinson and Willie Smith following 1989 season... Spent time on disabled list during each of four seasons as a Pirate... Played four years at UCLA, where his teammates included Matt Young, Tim Leary and Mike Gallego... Earned $1.67 million in 1992.

Year	Club	Pos.	G	AB	R	H	2B	3B	HR	RBI	SB	Avg.
1982	Kansas City ...	C	43	115	14	32	6	0	3	8	0	.278
1983	Kansas City ...	C	83	276	21	86	13	4	0	28	3	.312
1984	Kansas City ...	C	124	409	48	108	27	4	4	42	0	.264
1985	Texas	C	102	343	34	96	17	4	8	35	5	.280
1986	Texas	C	95	314	39	83	17	1	13	46	3	.264
1987	Texas	C	95	237	25	53	15	2	8	16	0	.224
1988	New York (AL)	C	97	322	33	91	25	1	9	43	1	.283
1989	New York (AL)	C	117	350	34	88	21	3	5	38	1	.251
1990	Pittsburgh	C	84	230	27	69	18	3	4	29	0	.300
1991	Pittsburgh	C-3B	77	220	19	65	17	1	1	29	1	.295
1992	Pittsburgh	C	87	255	26	88	17	3	4	37	2	.345
	Totals		1004	3071	320	859	193	26	59	351	16	.280

MIKE LaVALLIERE 32 5-9 210 Bats L Throws R

Coming off least productive season of six-year Pirate career... Platooned at catcher with Don Slaught, who overshadowed him offensively ... Still considered a top defensive backstop, he committed just three errors in 92 games... Threw out 33 of 103 runners attempting to steal ... Received career-high 14 intentional walks ... Put together 15-for-33 hot streak late in season... Had three RBI game Aug. 9 against Cardinals... Played three games in NLCS, going 2-for-10 with no RBI and no extra-base hits... Born Aug. 18, 1960, in Charlotte, N.C.... Signed by Phillies as non-drafted free agent in 1981 . . . Signed by Cardinals as free agent in 1985 . . . Traded to Pirates along with Andy Van Slyke and Mike Dunne for Tony Pena April 1, 1987 . . . Won 1987 Gold Glove while leading majors by throwing out 43 percent of base-stealers . . . Led NL catchers in 1991 with .998 fielding percentage, committing just one error . . . Earned $1.85 million in 1992.

Year	Club	Pos.	G	AB	R	H	2B	3B	HR	RBI	SB	Avg.
1984	Philadelphia . . .	C	6	7	0	0	0	0	0	0	0	.000
1985	St. Louis	C	12	34	2	5	1	0	0	6	0	.147
1986	St. Louis	C	110	303	18	71	10	2	3	30	0	.234
1987	Pittsburgh	C	121	340	33	102	19	0	1	36	0	.300
1988	Pittsburgh	C	120	352	24	92	18	0	2	47	3	.261
1989	Pittsburgh	C	68	190	15	60	10	0	2	23	0	.316
1990	Pittsburgh	C	96	279	27	72	15	0	3	31	0	.258
1991	Pittsburgh	C	108	336	25	97	11	2	3	41	2	.289
1992	Pittsburgh	C-3B	95	293	22	75	13	1	2	29	0	.256
	Totals		736	2134	166	574	97	5	16	243	5	.269

RANDY TOMLIN 26 5-10 170 Bats L Throw L

In second full major league season, he was Pirates' second-leading winner while reaching career highs in victories, starts and innings pitched . . . Was not given playoff start and was ineffective in two relief appearances, compiling 6.75 ERA . . . NL Pitcher of the Month in June, going 5-1 with 2.22 ERA . . . Won first four starts of 1992 while registering 1.67 ERA . . . Went 0-3 with 10.13 ERA in next four starts before putting together career-best six-game winning streak . . . Born June 14, 1966, in Bainbridge, Md. . . . Selected by Pirates in 18th round of 1988 draft . . . Made jump from Double-A to majors in August 1990 and pitched complete-game victory over Phillies in debut . . . Allowed two earned runs or fewer in 10 of his first 12 big league starts . . . Led Pirates in ERA and was eighth in NL in 1991 . . . Earned $180,000 in 1992.

Year	Club	G	IP	W	L	Pct.	SO	BB	H	ERA
1990	Pittsburgh	12	77⅔	4	4	.500	42	12	62	2.55
1991	Pittsburgh	31	175	8	7	.533	104	54	170	2.98
1992	Pittsburgh	35	208⅔	14	9	.609	90	42	226	3.41
	Totals	78	461⅓	26	20	.565	236	108	458	3.10

BOB WALK 36 6-3 217 Bats R Throws R

Veteran's finest moment came in Game 5 of NLCS when he was surprise starter and pitched three-hit complete game . . . Also relieved in Game 2 and surrendered fifth-inning grand slam to Ron Gant . . . Compiled sparkling 0.71 ERA at Three Rivers Stadium during 12-start stretch between mid-May and mid-September . . . Was Pirates' third-leading winner while making 19 starts and 17 relief appearances . . . Completed just one start during regular season, but finished seven games out of bullpen and had two saves . . . Among current NL pitchers with at least 10 decisions each year, he is only one with six straight winning seasons (1987-92) . . . Spent two stints on disabled list with groin injury . . . Born Nov. 26, 1956, in Van Nuys, Cal. . . . Phillies' third pick in secondary phase of 1976 draft . . . Won Game 1 of 1980 World Series as rookie . . . Released by Braves and signed by Pirates in 1984 . . . Earned $1,225,000 in 1992.

Year	Club	G	IP	W	L	Pct.	SO	BB	H	ERA
1980	Philadelphia	27	152	11	7	.611	94	71	163	4.56
1981	Atlanta	12	43	1	4	.200	16	23	41	4.60
1982	Atlanta	32	164⅓	11	9	.550	84	59	179	4.87
1983	Atlanta	1	3⅔	0	0	.000	4	2	7	7.36
1984	Pittsburgh	2	10⅓	1	1	.500	10	4	8	2.61
1985	Pittsburgh	9	58⅔	2	3	.400	40	18	60	3.68
1986	Pittsburgh	44	141⅔	7	8	.467	78	64	129	3.75
1987	Pittsburgh	39	117	8	2	.800	78	51	107	3.31
1988	Pittsburgh	32	212⅔	12	10	.545	81	65	183	2.71
1989	Pittsburgh	33	196	13	10	.565	83	65	208	4.41
1990	Pittsburgh	26	129⅔	7	5	.583	73	36	136	3.75
1991	Pittsburgh	25	115	9	2	.818	67	35	104	3.60
1992	Pittsburgh	36	135	10	6	.625	60	43	132	3.20
	Totals	318	1479	92	67	.579	768	536	1457	3.82

TIM WAKEFIELD 26 6-2 195 Bats R Throws R

Best Cinderella story of 1992 . . . Became rookie sensation and playoff hero after being called up to big leagues in late July . . . A weak-hitting first baseman in minors, he developed knuckleball and was converted into pitcher mid-way through 1989 season . . . Pitched brilliantly for Pirates down the stretch, giving up three runs or fewer in 12 of 13 major league starts . . . Pitched complete-game six-hitter, striking out 10 and allowing no earned runs against Cardinals in major league debut July 31

. . . Had four complete games in regular season and pitched complete-game victories in Games 3 and 6 of NLCS . . . Became only second pitcher to throw two complete games in same NLCS . . . Pitched five-hitter in Game 3, becoming first rookie starter to win NLCS game since Charlie Hudson (1983) . . . Born Aug. 2, 1966, in Melbourne, Fla. . . . Pirates' eighth draft choice in 1988.

Year	Club	G	IP	W	L	Pct.	SO	BB	H	ERA
1992	Pittsburgh	13	92	8	1	.889	51	35	76	2.15

ZANE SMITH 32 6-1 205 Bats L Throws L

Must bounce back from offseason arthroscopic shoulder surgery . . . Sidelined for most of stretch drive, he was not included on Pirates' postseason roster . . . Received injections late in season in last-ditch effort to relieve aching shoulder . . . Spent two stints on disabled list following All-Star break . . . Just before being sidelined in July, he allowed one earned run in 23-inning stretch . . . Had eight straight winless starts spanning May and June, going 0-5 . . . Born Dec. 28, 1960, in Madison, Wis. . . . Selected by Braves in third round of 1982 draft . . . Traded to Expos in 1989 and came to Pirates in Aug. 8, 1990 deal for Scott Ruskin, Willie Greene and Moises Alou . . . Helped Pirates win divisional title that year, going 6-2 with 1.30 ERA in 11 games . . . Finished second in 1990 NL ERA race . . . Led 1991 Pirates in complete games and had lowest walk-to-strikeout ratio in majors . . . Earned $2,525,000 in 1992.

Year	Club	G	IP	W	L	Pct.	SO	BB	H	ERA
1984	Atlanta	3	20	1	0	1.000	16	13	16	2.25
1985	Atlanta	42	147	9	10	.474	85	80	135	3.80
1986	Atlanta	38	204⅔	8	16	.333	139	105	209	4.05
1987	Atlanta	36	242	15	10	.600	130	91	245	4.09
1988	Atlanta	23	140⅓	5	10	.333	59	44	159	4.30
1989	Atl.-Mont.	48	147	1	13	.071	93	52	141	3.49
1990	Mont.-Pitt.	33	215⅓	12	9	.571	130	50	196	2.55
1991	Pittsburgh	35	228	16	10	.615	120	29	234	3.20
1992	Pittsburgh	23	141	8	8	.500	56	19	138	3.06
	Totals.	281	1485⅓	75	86	.466	828	483	1473	3.53

TOP PROSPECTS

CARLOS GARCIA 25 6-1 185 Bats R Throws R

Picked by *Baseball America* as best Triple-A shortstop in baseball . . . Batted .303 with 28 doubles, nine triples, 13 homers, 70 RBI and 21 stolen bases for Buffalo . . . Called up to Pittsburgh Aug. 31, so that he'd be eligible for playoffs . . . Has instincts, hands and arm to play shortstop in big leagues, but Jay Bell is blocking his path in Pittsburgh . . . Signed with Pirates as non-drafted free agent in 1987 . . . Underwent arthroscopic surgery on left shoulder following 1991 season and it improved his ability to turn on pitches . . . Born Oct. 15, 1967, in Tachira, Venezuela.

DENNIS MOELLER 25 6-2 195 Bats R Throws L

Acquired from Royals with Joel Johnston in November trade for Jose Lind . . . Left-hander made four starts with Royals, going 0-3 with 7.00 ERA as he battled wildness . . . Went five shutout innings against Oakland Aug. 2, but was hit hard in other three outings . . . Went 8-5 with 2.46 ERA for Omaha (AAA) last season . . . Royals' 17th-round pick in 1988 draft . . . Signed by current Royals pitching coach Guy Hansen, he's from same high school that produced Bret Saberhagen . . . Born Sept. 15, 1967, in Tarzana, Cal.

KEVIN YOUNG 23 6-3 210 Bats R Throws R

Made tremendous strides during first Triple-A season and was rated No. 1 prospect by American Association managers . . . Batted .314 with 29 doubles, six triples, eight homers, 65 RBI and 18 stolen bases for Buffalo . . . Line-drive, gap hitter . . . Also showed improvement as third baseman . . . Has above-average speed and arm . . . Went 4-for-7 as late-season callup to Pittsburgh . . . Pirates' seventh pick in 1990 draft . . . Hit combined .328 at three levels in 1991 . . . Born June 16, 1969, in Alpena, Mich.

AL MARTIN 25 6-2 220 Bats L Throws L

Left Braves' organization following 1991 season to sign with Pirates as minor league free agent and it immediately paid dividends . . . Named by *Baseball America* as eighth-best prospect in American Association and also selected to Triple-A all-star team . . . Led league in triples (15) and slugging percentage (.557) while batting .305 with 16 doubles, 20 homers and 20 stolen bases for Buffalo . . . Good outfielder with both leg speed and bat speed . . . Braves' seventh pick in 1985 draft . . . Born Nov. 24, 1967, in West Covina, Cal.

STEVE COOKE 23 6-6 220 Bats R Throws L

Made rapid rise through Pirates' system in 1992 . . . Struck out 38 batters in 36 innings for Carolina (AA) . . . Went 6-3 with 3.75

ERA in just 13 starts for Buffalo (AAA) before promotion to Pittsburgh . . . Pitched seven shutout innings of three-hit ball against Cardinals Sept. 21 after relieving injured Bob Walk . . . Went 2-0 with one save in 11 big league appearances . . . Has above-average fastball and throws curves for strikes, but best pitch is straight change . . . Pirates' 35th-round pick in 1989 draft . . . Born Jan. 14, 1970, in Kanai, Hawaii.

MANAGER JIM LEYLAND: Added to growing reputation by leading overachieving Pirates to 96-66 finish and third straight divisional title . . . Won despite depleted roster as Bobby Bonilla left as free agent, John Smiley was traded and Bill Landrum was released . . . His team became only second NL club in history to win three consecutive divisional races . . . Pirates were in first place from June 2 and had sole possession after July 31 . . . Pirates dominated their two major preseason challengers, going 15-3 vs. Cardinals and 14-4 vs. Mets . . . Club beat back challenge from pesky Expos, wrapping up title Sept. 27 . . . Called it his most satisfying season . . . Came within one out of upsetting more talented Braves in NLCS . . . A players' manager who runs loose clubhouse and rarely takes credit for team's success . . . Career minor leaguer, he managed 11 seasons in Tigers' system, winning three league championships . . . Named Manager of the Year in Florida State League in 1977 and 1978 and American Association in 1979 . . . After four seasons as White Sox third-base coach under Tony La Russa, he became Pirates manager in 1986 and finished last . . . Began rebuilding process, winning 88 games in 1988 . . . Named NL Manager of the Year in 1990 . . . Born Dec. 15, 1944, in Toledo, Ohio . . . Major league managerial record is 593-541.

ALL-TIME PIRATE SEASON RECORDS

BATTING: Arky Vaughan, .385, 1935
HRs: Ralph Kiner, 54, 1949
RBI: Paul Waner, 131, 1927
STEALS: Omar Moreno, 96, 1980
WINS: Jack Chesbro, 28, 1902
STRIKEOUTS: Bob Veale, 276, 1965

ST. LOUIS CARDINALS

TEAM DIRECTORY: Chairman: August A. Busch III; Vice Chairman: Fred L. Kuhlmann; Pres./CEO: Stuart Meyer; VP/GM: Dal Maxvill; Dir. Player Pers.: Mike Jorgensen; Dir. Pub. Rel.: Jeff Wehling; Mgr. Pub. Rel.: Brian Bartow; Trav. Sec.: C.J. Cherre; Mgr.: Joe Torre. Home: Busch Stadium (56,627). Field distances: 330, l.f. line; 402, c.f.; 330, r.f. line. Spring training: St. Petersburg, Fla.

SCOUTING REPORT

HITTING: The Cardinals led the NL with a .262 batting average, but ranked sixth with just 631 runs in 1992.

Center fielder Ray Lankford (.293, 20, 86, 42 steals) has emerged as one of the top all-around players in baseball, but he needs to cut down on his league-high 147 strike-outs. Felix Jose (.295, 14, 75) took over as the cleanup hitter and demonstrated serious power. Bernard Gilkey (.302, 7, 43) came on strong during the second half. Re-signing shortstop Ozzie Smith (.295, 0, 31, 43 steals) turned out to be the Cardinals' most important winter move. He's a key offensive component with over 2,000 career hits and 500 stolen bases.

The rest of the infield remains a question mark. Todd Zeile (.257, 7, 48) was briefly demoted to Louisville (AAA). He'll be challenged for the third-base job by Tracy Woodson (.296, 12, 59 for Louisville) and Stan Royer (.282, 11, 77 for Louisville). Second baseman Jose Oquendo was limited by injuries to 14 games and both Luis Alicea (.245, 2, 32) and Geronimo Pena (.305, 7, 31) are waiting in the wings. Rod Brewer (.288, 18, 86 for Louisville) could be the starting first baseman, although he showed no power during a September trial. Ozzie Canseco (.266, 22, 57 for Louisville) is another possibility. Catcher Tom Pagnozzi (.249, 7, 44) holds his own offensively.

PITCHING: This is a solid staff which compiled the fourth-best ERA (3.38) in the NL, but the Cardinals lack a dominant ace. They would get a tremendous boost if Joe Magrane (1-2, 4.02) could return to his superstar form of 1989 after being sidelined nearly two full years following elbow surgery.

Bob Tewksbury (16-5) has become the Cardinals' ace as he parlayed uncanny control and pitching smarts into the NL's second-best ERA at 2.16. Rheal Cormier (10-10, 3.68) won seven straight decisions to close 1992, his first full season in the majors.

The sign on Bob Tewksbury's corner says 'Don't walk.'

Donovan Osborne (11-9, 3.77) was the Cards' biggest surprise, in only his third year of professional baseball. Omar Olivares (9-9, 3.84) is another young pitcher with promise. Mark Clark (3-10, 4.45) is coming off a tough rookie year.

Lee Smith (4-9, 3.12, 43 saves) remains one of the top closers in the business, though he will miss having free-agent defector Todd Worrell and expansion draft loss Cris Carpenter as his setup men. Mike Perez (9-3, 1.84) did an outstanding job in middle relief as a rookie. Rene Arocha (12-7, 2.70 for Louisville) should be ready. Mike Milchin, coming off an injury-plagued season at Louisville, will get a chance to be the prime lefty in the bullpen.

FIELDING: The Cardinals' tradition of great defense continues. Smith is a 13-time Gold Glove winner at shortstop while Pagnozzi has won two straight Gold Gloves behind the plate. Lankford led all NL outfielders in putouts and Oquendo is solid at second base, making this team exceptionally strong up the middle.

OUTLOOK: A lack of power might be the Cardinals' only serious weakness but, playing in spacious Busch Stadium, they can overcome that by using speed and defense to better last year's 83-79, third-place finish. With improved clutch hitting, Joe Torre's team could win the division.

ST. LOUIS CARDINALS 1993 ROSTER

MANAGER Joe Torre
Coaches—Chris Chambliss, Joe Coleman, Dave Collins, Bucky Dent, Gaylen Pitts, Red Schoendienst

PITCHERS

No.	Name	1992 Club	W-L	IP	SO	ERA	B-T	Ht.	Wt.	Born
55	Clark, Mark	Louisville	4-4	61	38	2.80	R-R	6-5	225	5/12/68 Bath, IL
		St. Louis	3-10	113	44	4.45				
65	Compres, Fidel	Arkansas	4-3	58	39	3.28	R-R	6-0	165	5/10/65 Dominican Republic
52	Cormier, Rheal	St. Louis	10-10	186	117	3.68	L-L	5-10	185	4/23/67 Canada
—	Dixon, Steve	Arkansas	2-1	49	65	1.84	L-L	6-0	190	8/3/69 Cincinnati, OH
		Louisville	1-2	20	21	5.03				
—	Eversgerd, Bryan	St. Petersburg	3-2	74	57	2.68	R-L	6-1	190	2/11/69 Centralia, IL
		Arkansas	0-1	5	4	6.75				
32	Magrane, Joe	St. Petersburg	0-1	18	15	1.50	R-L	6-6	230	7/2/64 Des Moines, IA
		Louisville	3-4	53	35	5.40				
		St. Louis	1-2	31	20	4.02				
53	Milchin, Mike	Louisville	2-6	65	37	5.79	L-L	6-3	190	2/28/68 Knoxville, TN
00	Olivares, Omar	St. Louis	9-9	197	124	3.84	R-R	6-1	193	7/6/67 Puerto Rico
31	Osborne, Donovan	St. Louis	11-9	179	104	3.77	L-L	6-2	195	6/21/69 Roseville, CA
42	Perez, Mike	St. Louis	9-3	93	46	1.84	R-R	6-0	187	10/19/64 Puerto Rico
47	Smith, Lee	St. Louis	4-9	75	60	3.12	R-R	6-6	269	12/4/57 Jamestown, LA
39	Tewksbury, Bob	St. Louis	16-5	233	91	2.16	R-R	6-4	208	11/30/60 Concord, NH
—	Urbani, Tom	Arkansas	4-6	65	41	1.93	L-L	6-1	190	1/21/68 Santa Cruz, CA
		Louisville	4-5	89	46	4.67				

CATCHERS

No.	Name	1992 Club	H	HR	RBI	Pct.	B-T	Ht.	Wt.	Born
—	Ellis, Paul	St. Petersburg	67	2	29	.218	L-R	6-2	205	11/12/68 Oxnard, CA
		Arkansas	18	2	8	.228				
—	Fulton, Ed	Louisville	47	12	29	.201	L-R	6-0	195	1/7/66 Danville, VA
		Arkansas	6	0	5	.261				
19	Pagnozzi, Tom	St. Louis	121	7	44	.249	R-R	6-1	190	7/30/62 Tucson, AZ
—	Ronan, Marc	Springfield	81	6	48	.215	L-R	6-2	190	9/19/69 Ozark, AL
—	Villanueva, Hector	Chicago (NL)	17	2	13	.152	R-R	6-1	220	10/2/64 Puerto Rico

INFIELDERS

No.	Name	1992 Club	H	HR	RBI	Pct.	B-T	Ht.	Wt.	Born
18	Alicea, Luis	Louisville	20	0	6	.282	S-R	5-9	177	7/29/65 Puerto Rico
		St. Louis	65	2	32	.245				
—	Andujar, Juan	St. Petersburg	97	2	29	.270	S-R	6-0	150	8/14/71 Dominican Republic
33	Brewer, Rod	Louisville	122	18	86	.288	L-L	6-3	218	2/24/66 Eustis, FL
		St. Louis	31	0	10	.301				
—	Cromer, Tripp	Arkansas	81	7	29	.240	R-R	6-2	165	11/21/67 Lake City, SC
		Louisville	5	1	7	.200				
50	Figueroa, Bien	Louisville	91	1	23	.285	R-R	5-10	170	2/7/64 Dominican Republic
		St. Louis	2	0	4	.182				
8	Jones, Tim	St. Louis	29	0	3	.200	L-R	5-10	175	12/1/62 Sumter, SC
11	Oquendo, Jose	St. Louis	9	0	3	.257	S-R	5-10	171	7/4/63 Puerto Rico
		Louisville	17	0	6	.266				
		Arkansas	3	0	1	.429				
21	Pena, Geronimo	St. Louis	62	7	31	.305	S-R	6-1	195	3/29/67 Dominican Republic
		Louisville	25	3	12	.248				
28	Perry, Gerald	St. Louis	34	1	18	.238	L-R	6-0	201	10/30/60 Savannah, GA
5	Royer, Stan	Louisville	125	11	77	.282	R-R	6-3	221	8/31/67 Olney, IL
		St. Louis	10	2	9	.323				
1	Smith, Ozzie	St. Louis	153	0	31	.295	S-R	5-10	168	12/26/54 Mobile, AL
12	Wilson, Craig	St. Louis	33	0	13	.311	R-R	5-11	208	11/28/64 Anne Arundel, MD
		Louisville	24	0	5	.296				
54	Woodson, Tracy	Louisville	122	12	59	.296	R-R	6-3	216	10/5/62 Richmond, VA
		St. Louis	35	1	22	.307				
27	Zeile, Todd	St. Louis	113	7	48	.257	R-R	6-1	190	9/9/65 Van Nuys, CA
		Louisville	23	5	13	.311				

OUTFIELDERS

No.	Name	1992 Club	H	HR	RBI	Pct.	B-T	Ht.	Wt.	Born
46	Canseco, Ozzie	Louisville	82	22	57	.266	R-R	6-3	220	7/2/64 Cuba
		St. Louis	8	0	3	.276				
—	Coleman, Paul	St. Petersburg	19	1	7	.271	R-R	5-11	200	12/9/70 Jacksonville, TX
23	Gilkey, Bernard	St. Louis	116	7	43	.302	R-R	6-0	190	9/24/66 St. Louis, MO
10	Hudler, Rex	St. Louis	24	3	5	.245	R-R	6-0	195	9/2/60 Tempe, AZ
3	Jordan, Brian	St. Louis	40	5	22	.207	R-R	6-1	205	3/29/67 Baltimore, MD
		Louisville	45	4	16	.290				
34	Jose, Felix	St. Louis	150	14	75	.295	S-R	6-1	221	5/8/65 Dominican Republic
		Louisville	1	0	0	.143				
		St. Petersburg	8	0	2	.444				
16	Lankford, Ray	St. Louis	175	20	86	.293	L-L	5-11	198	6/5/67 Modesto, CA
51	Maclin, Lonnie	Louisville	94	1	38	.324	L-L	5-11	185	2/17/67 Clayton, MO

CARDINAL PROFILES

RAY LANKFORD 25 5-11 198 Bats L Throws L

One of the best all-around players in NL, this center fielder dramatically improved most offensive numbers during second full season . . . Became first Cardinal to hit 20 homers and steal 20 bases since Lou Brock did it 25 years ago . . . Tied for second-most doubles in NL, was eighth in hits and slugging percentage (.480), sixth in stolen bases and seventh in total bases (287) . . . Also led NL with 147 strikeouts . . . Broke Jack Clark's club strikeout record (139 in 1987) . . . Hit first career grand slam Sept. 13 against Cubs . . . Cards' first 40 steals-80 RBI man since Willie McGee had 56 and 82, respectively, in 1985 . . . Had 12-game hitting streak in July . . . Improved on-base percentage from .301 in 1991 to .371 last year . . . Born June 5, 1967, in Modesto, Cal. . . . Cardinals' third pick in 1987 draft . . . Made outstanding debut in 1991, becoming first Cardinal rookie in 92 years with 60 RBI and 40 steals . . . Hit 16 triples for Springfield (A) in 1988 . . . Earned $160,000 in 1992.

Year	Club	Pos.	G	AB	R	H	2B	3B	HR	RBI	SB	Avg.
1990	St. Louis	OF	39	126	12	36	10	1	3	12	8	.286
1991	St. Louis	OF	151	566	83	142	23	15	9	69	44	.251
1992	St. Louis	OF	153	598	87	175	40	6	20	86	42	.293
	Totals		343	1290	182	353	73	22	32	167	94	.274

OZZIE SMITH 38 5-10 168 Bats S Throws R

Probably best defensive shortstop in history, "The Wizard of Oz" has also made major impact as hitter . . . Achieved 2,000th hit, 7,000th assist and 500th stolen base in 1992 . . . Set team record for games played at shortstop . . . Has 15 straight 20-steal seasons and holds NL record for double plays by shortstop . . . At age 37, he led Cardinals in hitting and stolen bases . . . Has five 40-steal seasons . . . Finished fifth among NL stolen-base leaders . . . Extremely popular in St. Louis . . . Made 12th All-Star appearance . . . Had 13-game hitting streak in May . . . Won 13th consecutive Gold Glove . . . Born Dec. 26, 1954, in Mobile, Ala. . . . Padres' fourth pick in 1977 draft . . . Traded to Cardinals for Garry Templeton before 1982 season . . . Committed just eight errors to establish NL record for shortstops in 1991 . . . Earned $2 million in 1992 before testing free-agent waters and then signing one-year contract for $3 million with options for additional years at the same figure.

Year	Club	Pos.	G	AB	R	H	2B	3B	HR	RBI	SB	Avg.
1978	San Diego	SS	159	590	69	152	17	6	1	46	40	.258
1979	San Diego	SS	156	587	77	124	18	6	0	27	28	.211
1980	San Diego	SS	158	609	67	140	18	5	0	35	57	.230
1981	San Diego	SS	110	450	53	100	11	2	0	21	22	.222
1982	St. Louis	SS	140	488	58	121	24	1	2	43	25	.248
1983	St. Louis	SS	159	552	69	134	30	6	3	50	34	.243
1984	St. Louis	SS	124	412	53	106	20	5	1	44	35	.257
1985	St. Louis	SS	158	537	70	148	22	3	6	54	31	.276
1986	St. Louis	SS	153	514	67	144	19	4	0	54	31	.280
1987	St. Louis	SS	158	600	104	182	40	4	0	75	43	.303
1988	St. Louis	SS	153	575	80	155	27	1	3	51	57	.270
1989	St. Louis	SS	155	593	82	162	30	8	2	50	29	.273
1990	St. Louis	SS	143	512	61	130	21	1	1	50	32	.254
1991	St. Louis	SS	150	550	96	157	30	3	3	50	35	.285
1992	St. Louis	SS	132	518	73	153	20	2	0	31	43	.295
	Totals		2208	8087	1079	2108	347	57	22	681	542	.261

FELIX JOSE 27 6-1 221 **Bats S Throws R**

An emerging talent, he gave indication of power potential last Sept. 6, when he became only second player to homer off right-field scoreboard at Busch Stadium . . . Homer traveled estimated 460 feet . . . Right fielder finished second on team to Ray Lankford in homers, RBI, total bases (220) and strikeouts (100) . . . NL Player of the Month for May, batting .346 with four homers and 26 RBI . . . Hit safely in 16 of first 17 games after returning from hamstring injury, including 425-foot homer into Busch Stadium center-field bleachers against Giants May 6 . . . Injury cost him five weeks . . . Born May 8, 1965, in Santo Domingo, D.R. . . . Signed with Athletics as free agent in 1984 . . . Traded to Cardinals for Willie McGee, Aug. 30, 1990 . . . Finished fifth in batting race and second in doubles while leading Cards in slugging percentage (.438) in 1991 . . . Earned $300,000 in 1992.

Year	Club	Pos.	G	AB	R	H	2B	3B	HR	RBI	SB	Avg.
1988	Oakland	OF	8	6	2	2	1	0	0	1	1	.333
1989	Oakland	OF	20	57	3	11	2	0	0	5	0	.193
1990	Oakland	OF	101	341	42	90	12	0	8	39	8	.264
1990	St. Louis	OF	25	85	12	23	4	1	3	13	4	.271
1991	St. Louis	OF	154	568	69	173	40	6	8	77	20	.305
1992	St. Louis	OF	131	509	62	150	22	3	14	75	28	.295
	Totals		439	1566	190	449	81	10	33	210	61	.287

BERNARD GILKEY 26 6-0 190 Bats R Throws R

Put together big second half during first full season in majors . . . All seven of his homers came after July 28 . . . Had four-hit game and four RBI Aug. 11 at Philadelphia . . . Hit two game-winning homers against Expos, including 10th-inning shot Sept. 7 . . . Also hit game-winning blast against Astros Aug. 20 . . . Cards' most frequent left fielder had to share position with Milt Thompson, Brian Jordan and Pedro Guerrero . . . Had back-to-back four-hit games in June . . . Batted .308 in first 17 starts . . . Had three hits in each of his first two starts . . . Born Sept. 24, 1966, in St. Louis . . . Signed with Cardinals as non-drafted free agent in 1984 . . . Led Texas League in stolen bases (53) and runs (104) for Arkansas (AA) in 1989 . . . In 1991, he became Cardinals' first rookie Opening Day left fielder since Stan Musial . . . Rookie season interrupted by broken thumb . . . Earned $135,000 in 1992.

Year	Club	Pos.	G	AB	R	H	2B	3B	HR	RBI	SB	Avg.
1990	St. Louis	OF	18	64	11	19	5	2	1	3	6	.297
1991	St. Louis	OF	81	268	28	58	7	2	5	20	14	.216
1992	St. Louis	OF	131	384	56	116	19	4	7	43	18	.302
	Totals		230	716	95	193	31	8	13	66	38	.270

TODD ZEILE 27 6-1 190 Bats R Throws R

Promising career took slight detour in 1992, when he was sent to Louisville (AAA) for remedial work . . . Took demotion well, batting .311 with five homers and 13 RBI in 21 games . . . Recalled to St. Louis Aug. 31 and hit safely in eight of next 11 games, batting .326 with 10 RBI and two homers . . . Led team in sacrifice flies and was second in walks (68) . . . Drove in just 25 runs from late April until early August and went more than a month without an extra-base hit, prompting his demotion . . . Was hitting .190 with runners in scoring position . . . Had nine-game hitting streak in July . . . Smashed three homers during first five games of season, then didn't hit another until June 21 . . . Born Sept. 9, 1965, in Van Nuys, Cal. . . . Cardinals' third pick in 1986 draft . . . Came up as catcher, but was converted into third baseman during 1990 season . . . Led Cards in homers and RBI in 1991 . . . Earned $300,000 in 1992.

Year	Club	Pos.	G	AB	R	H	2B	3B	HR	RBI	SB	Avg.
1989	St. Louis	C	28	82	7	21	3	1	1	8	0	.256
1990	St. Louis	C–3B–1B-OF	144	495	62	121	25	3	15	57	2	.244
1991	St. Louis	3B	155	565	76	158	36	3	11	81	17	.280
1992	St. Louis	3B	126	439	51	113	18	4	7	48	7	.257
	Totals		453	1581	196	413	82	11	34	194	26	.261

TOM PAGNOZZI 30 6-1 190 Bats R Throws R

Catcher continues to prove he's a better hitter than anybody realized . . . In second season as No. 1 catcher, he more than doubled his career home-run output and was club runnerup in doubles . . . Committed just one error to lead all catchers with phenomenal .999 fielding percentage . . . Lone error came on bizarre throw into left-center when he changed his mind about throwing . . . Started more games than any Cardinal except Ray Lankford . . . Endured midseason slump, going from July 29-Aug. 30 without scoring a run . . . After never hitting a road homer in previous seasons, he blasted four in 1992 . . . First-time All-Star . . . Had eight-game hitting streak in June . . . Born July 30, 1962, in Tucson, Ariz. . . . Cards' eighth pick in 1983 draft . . . His 57 RBI in 1991 were most by a Cardinal catcher since Darrell Porter had 68 in 1984 . . . Also won first Gold Glove in 1991 . . . Earned $967,500 in 1992.

Year	Club	Pos.	G	AB	R	H	2B	3B	HR	RBI	SB	Avg.
1987	St. Louis	C-1B	27	48	8	9	1	0	2	9	1	.188
1988	St. Louis	1B-C-3B	81	195	17	55	9	0	0	15	0	.282
1989	St. Louis	C-1B-3B	52	80	3	12	2	0	0	3	0	.150
1990	St. Louis	C-1B	69	220	20	61	15	0	2	23	1	.277
1991	St. Louis	C-1B	140	459	38	121	24	5	2	57	9	.264
1992	St. Louis	C	139	485	33	121	26	3	7	44	2	.249
	Totals		508	1487	119	379	77	8	13	151	13	.255

BOB TEWKSBURY 32 6-4 208 Bats R Throws R

One of baseball's great success stories, "Tewks" just keeps getting better and better . . . Tossed aside by two organizations because he didn't have overpowering stuff, he has turned into fine pitcher because of uncanny control . . . Reached career high in victories while averaging less than one walk per 11 innings . . . Finished second in ERA, tied for third in victories and was first with .762 winning percentage . . . Led Cardinals in games started, complete games (5) and innings pitched . . . Had 19 walkless starts . . . Made first All-Star appearance . . . Ended first half at 9-3 with 1.87 ERA . . . Assembled streak of 42 walkless innings in July . . . Had game-winning single in 17th inning to beat Expos April 25 after entering game as emergency reliever . . . Born Nov. 30, 1960, in Concord, N.H. . . . Yankees' 19th pick in 1981 draft . . . Signed with Cardinals as minor league free agent following 1988 season . . . Earned $800,000 in 1992.

Year	Club	G	IP	W	L	Pct.	SO	BB	H	ERA
1986	New York (AL)	23	130⅓	9	5	.643	49	31	144	3.31
1987	New York (AL)	8	33⅓	1	4	.200	12	7	47	6.75
1987	Chicago (NL)	7	18	0	4	.000	10	13	32	6.50
1988	Chicago (NL)	1	3⅓	0	0	.000	1	2	6	8.10
1989	St. Louis.	7	30	1	0	1.000	17	10	25	3.30
1990	St. Louis.	28	145⅓	10	9	.526	50	15	151	3.47
1991	St. Louis.	30	191	11	12	.478	75	38	206	3.25
1992	St. Louis.	33	233	16	5	.762	91	20	217	2.16
	Totals.	137	784⅓	48	39	.552	305	136	828	3.22

RHEAL CORMIER 25 5-10 185 Bats L Throws L

Important cog in Cardinals' starting rotation during first full season in majors . . . Survived rough 0-5 start and then was unbeatable in second half, closing season with seven consecutive victories . . . Didn't lose after Aug. 14 . . . Picked up 10th victory and finally evened record on last day of season, scattering nine hits over six innings to beat Phillies . . . Enjoyed exceptional success against Phils, going 3-0 with 1.64 ERA . . . Club runnerup in games started, complete games (3) and strikeouts . . . Had 11-strikeout game at Los Angeles July 10 . . . Pitched four-hitter against Astros Aug. 19 . . . Pitched 20 consecutive scoreless innings from Aug. 25-Sept. 12 . . . Canadian-born pitcher lost four of five decisions to Expos . . . Born April 23, 1967, in Moncton, Canada . . . Cards' sixth choice in 1988 draft . . . Won major league debut against Mets Aug. 15, 1991 . . . Earned $120,000 in 1992.

Year	Club	G	IP	W	L	Pct.	SO	BB	H	ERA
1991	St. Louis.	11	67⅔	4	5	.444	38	8	74	4.12
1992	St. Louis.	31	186	10	10	.500	117	33	194	3.68
	Totals.	42	253⅔	14	15	.483	155	41	268	3.80

LEE SMITH 35 6-6 269 **Bats R Throws R**

Size, mound presence and fastball make him one of the most intimidating relief pitchers of all time . . . Led NL in saves (43) for second straight season . . . Has 355 career saves, second only to Jeff Reardon . . . Sidelined briefly in September with rib cage injury . . . Saved 12 games in August, most by an NL reliever since John Franco saved 13 during one month in 1988 . . . He and Reardon are only pitchers to save at least 20 games for 10 straight seasons . . . Selected to fourth All-Star Game . . . Slowed by shoulder problems in June, giving up eight earned runs in 13 innings while walking seven . . . Surrendered just one walk in April . . . Recorded 1,000th career strikeout May 6 . . . Born Dec. 4, 1957, in Jamestown, La. . . . Cubs' second pick in 1975 draft . . . In 1987, he became first NL reliever with 30 or more saves in four consecutive seasons . . . Traded from Red Sox to Cardinals for Tom Brunansky, May 4, 1990 . . . Earned $2.66 million in 1992.

Year	Club	G	IP	W	L	Pct.	SO	BB	H	ERA
1980	Chicago (NL)	18	22	2	0	1.000	17	14	21	2.86
1981	Chicago (NL)	40	67	3	6	.333	50	31	57	3.49
1982	Chicago (NL)	72	117	2	5	.286	99	37	105	2.69
1983	Chicago (NL)	66	103⅓	4	10	.286	91	41	70	1.65
1984	Chicago (NL)	69	101	9	7	.563	86	35	98	3.65
1985	Chicago (NL)	65	97⅔	7	4	.636	112	32	87	3.04
1986	Chicago (NL)	66	90⅓	9	9	.500	93	42	69	3.09
1987	Chicago (NL)	62	83⅔	4	10	.286	96	32	84	3.12
1988	Boston	64	83⅔	4	5	.444	96	37	72	2.80
1989	Boston	64	70⅔	6	1	.857	96	33	53	3.57
1990	Boston	11	14⅓	2	1	.667	17	9	13	1.88
1990	St. Louis	53	68⅔	3	4	.429	70	20	58	2.10
1991	St. Louis	67	73	6	3	.667	67	13	70	2.34
1992	St. Louis	70	75	4	9	.308	60	26	62	3.12
	Totals	787	1067⅓	65	74	.468	1050	402	919	2.86

DONOVAN OSBORNE 23 6-2 195 **Bats S Throws L**

As non-roster pitcher invited to spring training in 1992, he surprised everybody by making club and becoming Cardinals' second-leading winner . . . In only his third year of pro ball, he made jump from Double-A to majors . . . Posted more impressive numbers in big leagues than in minors, where he had two-year record of 10-16 . . . Registered Cards' third-most strikeouts . . . Made 29 starts and also pitched out of bullpen . . .

Enjoyed most success against Padres, going 3-0 . . . Fanned 10 Giants while suffering first major league loss, 2-0, after winning first three decisions . . . Gave up just one earned run in first 16 innings . . . Cards' first-round pick in 1990 draft . . . Finished seventh in ERA in Texas League and fourth in strikeouts for Arkansas (AA) in 1991, but was just 8-12 in 26 starts . . . Earned $109,000 in 1992 . . . Born June 21, 1969, in Roseville, Cal.

Year	Club	G	IP	W	L	Pct.	SO	BB	H	ERA
1992	St. Louis.	34	179	11	9	.550	104	38	193	3.77

TOP PROSPECTS

RENE AROCHA 26 6-0 180 Bats R Throws R

Rated third-best prospect in American Association by *Baseball America* after going 12-7 with 2.70 ERA for Louisville (AAA) . . . Had league's third-best ERA and third-most strikeouts (128 in 167 innings) . . . Would have been called up to Cardinals, but they didn't want to expose him to expansion draft . . . Defected from Cuban national team in 1991 and signed with Cardinals after they won his rights in a lottery . . . Played on three World Amateur Championship teams . . . Had 100 wins and 1,000 strikeouts in Cuba . . . Born Oct. 24, 1966, in Havana.

OZZIE CANSECO 28 6-3 220 Bats R Throws R

Twin brother of Jose Canseco, he signed minor league contract with Cards after playing in Japan in 1991 . . . Made big splash at Louisville (AAA), hitting 19 doubles and 22 homers in just 98 games . . . Called up to St. Louis Sept. 1 and batted .276 with five doubles in only 29 at-bats before re-aggravating injury to right shoulder . . . Selected by Yankees as pitcher in second round of January 1983 draft . . . Became full-time outfielder in 1986 before being released . . . Signed with Athletics in 1986 and hit 20 homers for Huntsville (AA) in 1990 . . . Born July 2, 1964, in Havana.

STAN ROYER 25 6-3 221 Bats R Throws R

Sure-handed third baseman had another solid year for Louisville (AAA), batting .282 with 31 doubles, 11 homers and 77 RBI . . . Recalled to St. Louis in September for second straight year and had four-hit, four-RBI game against Cubs . . . Batted .323 in 13 games . . . Selected by Athletics in first round of 1988 draft and named by *Baseball America* as top prospect in Northwest League

. . . Traded to Cardinals with Felix Jose and Daryl Green for Willie McGee, Aug. 30, 1990 . . . Born Aug. 31, 1967, in Olney, Ill.

ROD BREWER 27 6-3 218 Bats L Throws L
After injury-plagued 1991 season, he bounced back at Louisville (AAA), leading Cardinals' organization with 86 RBI while batting .288 with 20 doubles and 18 homers . . . First baseman-outfielder had been dropped from Cards' 40-man roster following 1991 season, but he was restored to major league roster Sept. 1 and promoted to St. Louis where he hit .301 in 29 games . . . Had five-hit game against Cubs . . . Cardinals' fifth pick in 1987 draft . . . Born Feb. 24, 1966, in Eustis, Fla.

Ray Lankford has quietly become a versatile trump Card.

MANAGER JOE TORRE: Enormously popular during his

playing days in St. Louis from 1969-74, he has also scored points as manager . . . Kept Cardinals in contention through first half of last season despite series of devastating injuries which began on Opening Night, when Jose Oquendo went down . . . Cards were in first place as late as June 2 . . . Succession of close losses to Pirates doomed pennant chances and led to 83-79 finish . . . Left Angels' broadcast booth to become Cards' manager, Aug. 1, 1990, succeeding Whitey Herzog . . . Made changes during final two months of 1990 season and then surprised experts by leading club to second-place finish in 1991 . . . Compiled .297 lifetime batting average during 18-year playing career with 2,342 hits, 1,185 RBI and 252 homers . . . Invited to nine All-Star Games and named NL MVP in 1971 after hitting .363 with 137 RBI . . . Hit 36 homers for Atlanta in 1966, setting Braves' record for a catcher . . . Traded to Cardinals in 1969 for Orlando Cepeda . . . Named Mets' player-manager May 31, 1977 and accumulated 286-420 record in five seasons . . . Named Braves' manager in 1982 and guided team to division title . . . Three-year record in Atlanta was 257-229 . . . Born July 18, 1940, in Brooklyn, N.Y. . . . Overall managerial record in 734-830.

ALL-TIME CARDINAL SEASON RECORDS

BATTING: Rogers Hornsby, .424, 1924
HRs: Johnny Mize, 43, 1940
RBI: Joe Medwick, 154, 1937
STEALS: Lou Brock, 118, 1974
WINS: Dizzy Dean, 30, 1934
STRIKEOUTS: Bob Gibson, 274, 1970

ATLANTA BRAVES

TEAM DIRECTORY: Chairman: Bill Bartholomay; Pres.: Stan Kasten; Sr. VP/Asst. to Pres.: Hank Aaron; Exec. VP/GM: John Schuerholz; Dir. Scouting and Player Development: Chuck LaMar; Dir. Pub. Rel.: Jim Schultz; Trav. Sec.: Bill Acree; Mgr.: Bobby Cox. Home: Atlanta-Fulton County Stadium (52,007). Field distances: 330, l.f. line; 402, c.f.; 330, r.f. line. Spring training: West Palm Beach, Fla.

SCOUTING REPORT

HITTING: After batting .254 in the regular season, the sixth-best mark in the NL, and .244 in the NLCS, the Braves dropped all the way to .220 against the Blue Jays and that was the difference in the World Series. If not for Deion Sanders, they would have hit .195 in that Series.

Sanders should concentrate only on baseball because the results would be staggering. Tim McCarver's favorite player batted .533 in the World Series and The Neon One also led the majors in triples with 14, even though he had just 303 at-bats. Terry Pendleton (.311, 21, 105) continues to be the Braves' leading man, pacing the team in average, homers and RBI.

Right fielder David Justice hit 21 homers and figures to get better with maturity. Sid Bream (.261, 10, 61) is solid at first, center fielder Otis Nixon (.294, 41 steals) is the spark to the offense while Jeff Blauser (.262, 14, 46) led all NL shortstops in homers. Second baseman Mark Lemke (.227, 6, 26) fell back to earth after his 1991 World Series heroics.

The Braves dominated left-handers, going 34-17 against them last year.

PITCHING: The best staff in the world got much better when Cy Young winner Greg Maddux (20-11, 2.18 ERA with the Cubs) was signed to a five-year, $28-million contract as a free agent in December. The Braves led all of baseball with a 3.14 ERA in 1992 and they also led in complete games (26) and shutouts (24). Maddux will sharpen all of those numbers for Atlanta in 1993.

Maddux will join Cy Young runnerup Tom Glavine (20-8, 2.76), John Smoltz (15-12, 2.85) and Steve Avery (11-11, 3.20) in the rotation. The only way the Fab Four could get better is if GM John Schuerholz resurrects Cy Young himself.

In the bullpen, left-hander Mike Stanton (5-4, 4.10, 8 saves)

Greg Maddux took the tour and chose the city of Atlanta.

and right-hander Mark Wohlers (1-2, 2.55, 4 saves) will get a lot more save opportunities this season. In 12⅓ World Series innings, Stanton has not surrendered a run.

FIELDING: The game always will come down to pitching and defense. The Braves had the best pitching in the majors and only three NL teams had a better fielding percentage than their .982 mark in 1992. Center fielder Nixon can run down everything and made the catch of the year when he robbed Pittsburgh's Andy Van Slyke of a home run July 25. Pendleton is one of the best at third. And the Braves have added ex-Met Bill Pecota as infield backup. Much depends on catcher Greg Olson's comeback from a serious ankle injury, because Olson is an expert at handling a pitching staff.

OUTLOOK: Bobby Cox's club followed its worst-to-first 1991 season by amassing the best record in baseball at 98-64 and winning another pennant, only to fall short again in the World Series. If the Braves keep trying, sooner or later they are going to win one. Having Maddux in the rotation instead of Charlie Leibrandt is the kind of tradeoff that can make it possible.

ATLANTA BRAVES 1993 ROSTER

MANAGER Bobby Cox
Coaches—Jim Beauchamp, Pat Corrales, Clarence Jones, Leo Mazzone, Jimy Williams, Ned Yost

PITCHERS

No.	Name	1992 Club	W-L	IP	SO	ERA	B-T	Ht.	Wt.	Born
33	Avery, Steve	Atlanta	11-11	234	129	3.20	L-L	6-4	190	4/14/70 Trenton, MI
—	Bark, Brian	Greenville	5-0	55	49	1.15	L-L	5-9	160	8/26/68 Baltimore, MD
		Richmond	1-2	42	50	6.00				
—	Borbon, Pedro	Greenville	8-2	94	79	3.06	R-R	6-1	205	11/15/67 Dominican Republic
		Atlanta	0-1	1	1	6.75				
67	Burlingame, Dennis	Greenville	9-9	152	84	3.09	R-R	6-4	200	6/17/69 Woodbury, NJ
48	Davis, Mark	Kansas City	1-3	36	19	7.18	L-L	6-4	210	10/19/60 Livermore, CA
		Atlanta	1-0	17	15	7.02				
—	Elliott, Donnie	Greenville	7-2	104	100	2.08	R-R	6-4	190	9/20/68 Pasadena, TX
40	Freeman, Marvin	Atlanta	7-5	64	41	3.22	R-R	6-7	222	4/10/63 Chicago, IL
47	Glavine, Tom	Atlanta	20-8	225	129	2.76	L-L	6-0	175	3/25/66 Concord, MA
—	Holman, Shawn	Nuevo Larado	12-7	107	39	2.53	R-R	6-1	200	11/10/64 Sewickley, PA
—	Maddux, Greg	Chicago (NL)	20-11	268	199	2.18	R-R	6-0	175	4/14/66 San Angelo, TX
50	Mercker, Kent	Atlanta	3-2	68	49	3.42	L-L	6-2	195	2/1/68 Dublin, OH
63	Murray, Matt	Greenville		Injured			L-R	6-6	200	9/26/70 Boston, MA
—	Potts, Michael	Durham	6-8	128	123	4.02	L-L	5-9	170	9/5/70 Langdale, AL
25	Smith, Pete	Richmond	7-4	109	93	2.14	R-R	6-2	200	2/27/66 Weymouth, MA
		Atlanta	7-0	79	43	2.05				
29	Smoltz, John	Atlanta	15-12	247	215	2.85	R-R	6-3	185	5/15/67 Warren, MI
30	Stanton, Mike	Atlanta	5-4	64	44	4.10	L-L	6-1	190	6/2/67 Houston, TX
43	Wohlers, Mark	Richmond	0-2	34	33	3.93	R-R	6-4	207	1/23/70 Holyoke, MA
		Atlanta	1-2	35	17	2.55				

CATCHERS

No.	Name	1992 Club	H	HR	RBI	Pct.	B-T	Ht.	Wt.	Born
11	Berryhill, Damon	Atlanta	70	10	43	.228	S-R	6-0	205	12/3/63 South Laguna, CA
19	Cabrera, Francisco	Richmond	82	9	35	.272	R-R	6-4	193	10/10/66 Dominican Republic
		Atlanta	3	2	3	.300				
65	Houston, Tyler	Durham	91	7	38	.226	L-R	6-2	210	1/17/71 Las Vegas, NV
8	Lopez, Javier	Greenville	142	16	60	.321	R-R	6-3	185	11/5/70 Puerto Rico
		Atlanta	6	0	2	.375				
10	Olson, Greg	Atlanta	72	3	27	.238	R-R	6-0	200	9/16/60 Marshall, MN

INFIELDERS

2	Belliard, Rafael	Atlanta	60	0	14	.211	R-R	5-6	160	10/24/61 Dominican Republic
4	Blauser, Jeff	Atlanta	90	14	46	.262	R-R	6-0	170	11/8/65 Los Gatos, CA
12	Bream, Sid	Atlanta	97	10	61	.261	L-L	6-4	220	8/3/60 Carlisle, PA
65	Caraballo, Ramon	Greenville	29	1	8	.312	S-R	5-7	150	5/23/69 Dominican Republic
		Richmond	114	2	40	.281				
14	Hunter, Brian	Atlanta	57	14	41	.239	R-L	6-0	195	3/4/68 Torrance, CA
18	Klesko, Ryan	Richmond	105	17	59	.251	R-R	6-3	220	6/12/71 Westminster, CA
		Atlanta	0	0	1	.000				
20	Lemke, Mark	Atlanta	97	6	26	.227	S-R	5-9	167	8/13/65 Utica, NY
—	Oliva, Jose	Tulsa	120	16	75	270	R-R	6-1	200	3/3/71 Dominican Republic
—	Pecota, Bill	New York (NL)	61	2	26	.227	R-R	6-2	190	2/16/60 Redwood City, Ca
9	Pendleton, Terry	Atlanta	199	21	105	.311	S-R	5-9	195	7/16/60 Los Angeles, CA
—	Roa, Hector	Durham	105	8	46	.279	S-R	5-11	170	6/11/69 Dominican Republic
		Greenville	3	0	2	.333				

OUTFIELDERS

5	Gant, Ron	Atlanta	141	17	80	.259	R-R	6-0	172	3/2/65 Victoria, TX
—	Hughes, Troy	Durham	110	16	53	.244	R-R	6-2	173	1/3/71 Mt. Vernon, IL
23	Justice, David	Atlanta	124	21	72	.256	L-L	6-3	195	4/14/66 Cincinnati, OH
17	Mitchell, Keith	Richmond	91	4	50	.226	R-R	5-10	180	8/6/69 San Diego, CA
7	Nieves, Melvin	Greenville	99	18	76	.283	S-R	6-2	186	12/28/71 Puerto Rico
		Atlanta	4	0	1	.211				
1	Nixon, Otis	Atlanta	134	2	22	.294	S-R	6-2	180	1/9/59 Evergreen, NC
24	Sanders, Deion	Atlanta	92	8	28	.304	L-L	6-1	195	8/9/67 Ft. Myers, FL
—	Tarasco, Tony	Greenville	140	15	54	.286	L-R	6-0	185	12/9/70 New York, NY

BRAVE PROFILES

TERRY PENDLETON 32 5-9 195 Bats S Throws R

Third baseman is big reason the Braves have won two straight pennants . . . Called "cornerstone of the club," by GM John Schuerholz, who signed him to four-year, $10.2-million contract as free agent prior to 1991 season . . . Turned in a repeat performance of 1991 MVP season, though he finished second to Barry Bonds in balloting this time . . . Became first Brave third baseman to post back-to-back .300 seasons since 1900 . . . Established career high in RBI and hits, tying Pirates' Andy Van Slyke for most hits in NL . . . His 191 RBI over two seasons are most by a Brave third baseman since Eddie Mathews drove in 215 runs in 1960-61 . . . Set career high with six RBI against Padres April 20 . . . Struggled in NLCS with .233 average and in World Series with .240 mark . . . Leg injuries might have caught up with him . . . Won NL batting title with .319 average his first year as a Brave . . . Hit just .167 in 1991 NLCS . . . Rebounded in that World Series with .367 mark and two homers . . . Born July 16, 1960, in Los Angeles . . . Selected by St. Louis in first round of 1982 draft . . . Earned $3 million last season . . . Won Gold Glove in 1992.

Year	Club	Pos.	G	AB	R	H	2B	3B	HR	RBI	SB	Avg.
1984	St. Louis	3B	67	262	37	85	16	3	1	33	20	.324
1985	St. Louis	3B	149	559	56	134	16	3	5	69	17	.240
1986	St. Louis	3B-OF	159	578	56	138	26	5	1	59	24	.239
1987	St. Louis	3B	159	583	82	167	29	4	12	96	19	.286
1988	St. Louis	3B	110	391	44	99	20	2	6	53	3	.253
1989	St. Louis	3B	162	613	83	162	28	5	13	74	9	.264
1990	St. Louis	3B	121	447	46	103	20	2	6	58	7	.230
1991	Atlanta.	3B	153	586	94	187	34	8	22	86	10	.319
1992	Atlanta.	3B	160	640	98	199	39	1	21	105	5	.311
	Totals		1240	4659	596	1274	228	33	87	633	114	.273

DAVID JUSTICE 26 6-3 195 Bats L Throws L

Right fielder has super talent, but irritates teammates because he sometimes talks a better game than he produces . . . Disappeared in World Series, batting only .158 with a homer and three RBI after solid showing in NLCS with .280 average, three homers and six RBI . . . Became first Brave to hit 20-plus homers in first three full seasons since Bob Horner and Dale Murphy

(1978-80) . . . Drilled 11 homers and drove in 30 runs over final 43 games . . . Struggled until that point . . . Has a tendency to take himself too seriously and takes too many good pitches, because he's looking for the perfect pitch to drive . . . Led NL by grounding into only one DP in 484 at-bats . . . Hit .326 with runners on third . . . Earned $555,000 last season . . . Born April 14, 1966, in Cincinnati . . . Braves' fourth-round pick in 1985 draft.

Year	Club	Pos.	G	AB	R	H	2B	3B	HR	RBI	SB	Avg.
1989	Atlanta.	OF	16	51	7	12	3	0	1	3	2	.235
1990	Atlanta.	1B-OF	127	439	76	124	23	2	28	78	11	.282
1991	Atlanta.	OF	109	396	67	109	25	1	21	87	8	.275
1992	Atlanta.	OF	144	484	78	124	19	5	21	72	2	.256
	Totals		396	1370	228	369	70	8	71	240	23	.269

OTIS NIXON 34 6-2 180 Bats S Throws R

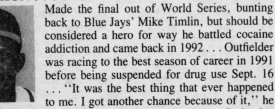

Made the final out of World Series, bunting back to Blue Jays' Mike Timlin, but should be considered a hero for way he battled cocaine addiction and came back in 1992 . . . Outfielder was racing to the best season of career in 1991 before being suspended for drug use Sept. 16 . . . "It was the best thing that ever happened to me. I got another chance because of it," he said . . . Was catalyst of Braves' offense last season . . . Stole nine bases in postseason . . . Batted .296 in World Series and delivered two-out hit in ninth to tie Game 6 . . . Born Jan. 9, 1959, in Evergreen, N.C. . . . Brother Donell played with Mariners, Giants and Orioles . . . Signed by Expos as a free agent in 1988 . . . Selected by Reds in 21st round in 1978 draft . . . Signed three-year deal with Braves worth $8.1 million before last season . . . Acquired from Expos for Jimmy Kremers and Boi Rodriguez, just prior to 1991 season.

Year	Club	Pos.	G	AB	R	H	2B	3B	HR	RBI	SB	Avg.
1983	New York (AL)	OF	13	14	2	2	0	0	0	0	2	.143
1984	Cleveland	OF	49	91	16	14	0	0	0	1	12	.154
1985	Cleveland	OF	104	162	34	38	4	0	3	9	20	.235
1986	Cleveland	OF	105	95	33	25	4	1	0	8	23	.263
1987	Cleveland	OF	19	17	2	1	0	0	0	1	2	.059
1988	Montreal	OF	90	271	47	66	8	2	0	15	46	.244
1989	Montreal	OF	126	258	41	56	7	2	0	21	37	.217
1990	Montreal	OF-SS	119	231	46	58	6	2	1	20	50	.251
1991	Atlanta.	OF	124	401	81	119	10	1	0	26	72	.297
1992	Atlanta.	OF	120	456	79	134	14	2	2	22	41	.294
	Totals		869	1996	381	513	53	10	6	123	303	.257

DEION SANDERS 25 6-1 195 — Bats L Throws L

"Neon" could light up the game if he put his mind to it . . . Outfielder showed world what he is capable of doing by hitting .533 in World Series . . . If Braves had beaten Blue Jays, it would have been fun to watch Tim McCarver present him with MVP trophy . . . Presented McCarver with a Carv-wash during NLCS victory celebration . . . If he decides to give up Falcons and football, All-Pro will be an All-Star . . . Became the first player in major league history to lead his league in triples, despite playing under 100 games . . . Born Aug. 9, 1967, in Ft. Myers, Fla. . . . Signed as a minor league free agent in January 1991 . . . Yanks chose him in the 30th round of 1988 draft . . . Made a base salary of $600,000 in 1992.

Year	Club	Pos.	G	AB	R	H	2B	3B	HR	RBI	SB	Avg.
1989	New York (AL)	OF	14	47	7	11	2	0	2	7	1	.234
1990	New York (AL)	OF	57	133	24	21	2	2	3	9	8	.158
1991	Atlanta.	OF	54	110	16	21	1	2	4	13	11	.191
1992	Atlanta.	OF	97	303	54	92	6	14	8	28	26	.304
	Totals		222	593	101	145	11	18	17	57	46	.245

RON GANT 28 6-0 172 — Bats R Throws R

Bad year ended on a crushing note when he was benched during World Series for Deion Sanders . . . Only got eight at-bats vs. Blue Jays . . . Hit just .182 in NLCS . . . Despite his poor season, outfielder became first Brave in franchise history to record three consecutive years with 30-plus stolen bases and 80-plus RBI . . . Selected to All-Star team for first time . . . Went 30 games without a homer from July 22-Aug. 30 and batted .199 from June 8-Sept. 9 . . . In 1991, he became only the third player in major league history to produce back-to-back 30-homer, 30-steal seasons . . . Set NLCS record with seven stolen bases in 1991 . . . Born March 2, 1965, in Victoria, Tex. . . . Braves' fourth-round selection in 1983 draft . . . Earned $2,650,000 last season.

Year	Club	Pos.	G	AB	R	H	2B	3B	HR	RBI	SB	Avg.
1987	Atlanta.	2B	21	83	9	22	4	0	2	9	4	.265
1988	Atlanta.	2B-3B	146	563	85	146	28	8	19	60	19	.259
1989	Atlanta.	3B-OF	75	260	26	46	8	3	9	25	9	.177
1990	Atlanta.	OF	152	575	107	174	34	3	32	84	33	.303
1991	Atlanta.	OF	154	561	101	141	35	3	32	105	34	.251
1992	Atlanta.	OF	153	544	74	141	22	6	17	80	32	.259
	Totals		701	2586	402	670	131	23	111	363	131	.259

SID BREAM 32 6-4 220 **Bats L Throws L**

One of nicest guys in game turns meek during the World Series . . . Has never driven in a run in 13 World Series games and is batting .154 over that span . . . Stranding 16 runners in scoring position in 1991, but left only one man in scoring position against Blue Jays . . . Every Braves fan will forever remember how he drove his scarred knees from second to home to score winning run on Francisco Cabrera's single in NLCS Game 7 . . . Has undergone six knee operations . . . Smooth first baseman left Pirates as free agent after 1990 season to sign three-year, $5.5-million contract with Braves . . . Born Aug. 3, 1960, in Carlisle, Pa. . . . Earned $2.4 million last season . . . Selected by Dodgers in second round of 1981 draft . . . Traded to Pirates with Cecil Espy and R.J. Reynolds for Bill Madlock, Sept. 9, 1985.

Year	Club	Pos.	G	AB	R	H	2B	3B	HR	RBI	SB	Avg.
1983	Los Angeles . . .	1B	15	11	0	2	0	0	0	2	0	.182
1984	Los Angeles . . .	1B	27	49	2	9	3	0	0	6	1	.184
1985	L.A.-Pitt.	1B	50	148	18	34	7	0	6	21	0	.230
1986	Pittsburgh	1B-OF	154	522	73	140	37	5	16	77	13	.268
1987	Pittsburgh	1B	149	516	64	142	25	3	13	65	9	.275
1988	Pittsburgh	1B	148	462	50	122	37	0	10	65	9	.264
1989	Pittsburgh	1B	19	36	3	8	3	0	0	4	0	.222
1990	Pittsburgh	1B	147	389	39	105	23	2	15	67	8	.270
1991	Atlanta.	1B	91	265	32	67	12	0	11	45	0	.253
1992	Atlanta.	1B	125	372	30	97	25	1	10	61	6	.261
	Totals		925	2770	311	726	172	11	81	413	46	.262

MARK LEMKE 27 5-9 167 **Bats S Throws R**

Earth to Lemke, come back . . . Second baseman hit .211 in World Series after posting .417 mark in 1991 . . . That was the week of his life. After three career triples, he hit three in four at-bats during seven-game battle with Twins . . . Committed only nine errors in 1992 . . . Connected for three homers in nine games from Aug. 6-15, after hitting six homers in his first 369 games . . . Wears Buddy Holly glasses and false teeth . . . Born Aug. 13, 1965, in Utica, N.Y. . . . Made only 49 starts at second during season, but found a home there again during postseason

. . . Earned $250,000 last season . . . A regular Walter Mitty story as Braves' 27th-round selection in 1983 draft.

Year	Club	Pos.	G	AB	R	H	2B	3B	HR	RBI	SB	Avg.
1988	Atlanta.	2B	16	58	8	13	4	0	0	2	0	.224
1989	Atlanta.	2B	14	55	4	10	2	1	2	10	0	.182
1990	Atlanta.	3B-2B-SS	102	239	22	54	13	0	0	21	0	.226
1991	Atlanta.	2B-3B	136	269	36	63	11	2	2	23	1	.234
1992	Atlanta.	2B-3B	155	427	38	97	7	4	6	26	0	.227
	Totals		423	1048	108	237	37	7	10	82	1	.226

JOHN SMOLTZ 25 6-3 185 Bats R Throws R

Led NL in strikeouts . . . Turned out to be Braves' strongest pitcher in postseason, going 2-0 in the playoffs and 1-0 in World Series . . . Has never lost a postseason game . . . Idol is Jack Morris . . . His 15 wins and three shutouts represented career highs . . . Set a franchise record May 24 by striking out 15 Expos. That tied Warren Spahn for most strikeouts by a Brave . . . Turned his 1991 season around after All-Star break . . . Staggered to the break with 2-11 record and 5.16 ERA, but ripped off 12-2 record with 2.62 ERA rest of the way and was spectacular in postseason . . . Earned $1,525,000 last season . . . Born May 15, 1967, in Detroit . . . Signed by Tigers as free agent in September 1985 . . . Traded to Braves by Tigers for Doyle Alexander, Aug. 12, 1987.

Year	Club	G	IP	W	L	Pct.	SO	BB	H	ERA
1988	Atlanta	12	64	2	7	.222	37	33	74	5.48
1989	Atlanta	29	208	12	11	.522	168	72	160	2.94
1990	Atlanta	34	231⅓	14	11	.560	170	90	206	3.85
1991	Atlanta	36	229⅔	14	13	.519	148	77	206	3.80
1992	Atlanta	35	246⅔	15	12	.556	215	80	206	2.85
	Totals.	146	979⅔	57	54	.514	738	352	852	3.50

TOM GLAVINE 27 6-0 175 Bats L Throws L

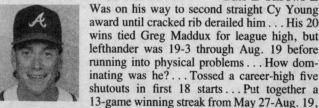

Was on his way to second straight Cy Young award until cracked rib derailed him . . . His 20 wins tied Greg Maddux for league high, but lefthander was 19-3 through Aug. 19 before running into physical problems . . . How dominating was he? . . . Tossed a career-high five shutouts in first 18 starts . . . Put together a 13-game winning streak from May 27-Aug. 19, setting modern-day Braves record and equaling mark set by Charlie Buffinton in 1884 . . . Struggled in NLCS with 0-2 mark and 12.27

ERA, but rebounded in World Series with 1-1 record and 1.59 ERA . . . Is now 0-4 lifetime in NLCS . . . Although he was hammered in All-Star Game, he became the first NL pitcher to start consecutive All-Star Games since Robin Roberts in 1955-56 . . . Captured Cy Young in 1991 . . . Born March 25, 1966, in Concord, Mass. . . . Braves' second-round pick in 1984 draft, he also was fourth-round pick of NHL's Los Angeles Kings . . . Earned $2,925,000 last season.

Year	Club	G	IP	W	L	Pct.	SO	BB	H	ERA
1987	Atlanta	9	50⅓	2	4	.333	20	33	55	5.54
1988	Atlanta	34	195⅓	7	17	.292	84	63	201	4.56
1989	Atlanta	29	186	14	8	.636	90	40	172	3.68
1990	Atlanta	33	214⅓	10	12	.455	129	78	232	4.28
1991	Atlanta	34	246⅔	20	11	.645	192	69	201	2.55
1992	Atlanta	33	225	20	8	.714	129	70	197	2.76
	Totals	172	1117⅔	73	60	.549	644	353	1058	3.60

GREG MADDUX 26 6-0 175 **Bats R Throws R**

Displayed excellent timing in 1992, putting together Cy Young season during walk year . . . Turned down five-year, $28.5-million contract extension at midseason to test free-agent waters and went on to become Cubs' first 20-game winner since Rick Reuschel in 1977 . . . Then, in December, signed five-year, $28-million contract with Braves that was $6 million less than the Yankees' final proposal . . . Tied Braves' Tom Glavine for NL lead in victories, led in innings pitched, tied for second in opponents' batting average (.210), finished third in strikeouts, tied for third in shutouts (4) and tied for fourth in complete games (9) . . . Matched career high with 10 strikeouts July 27 against Pirates and June 30 against Mets . . . Had spectacular July, going 4-1 with 1.13 ERA . . . Made first All-Star appearance . . . Born April 14, 1966, in San Angelo, Tex. . . . Cubs' second-round choice in 1984 draft . . . Finished third in 1989 NL Cy Young voting . . . Won another Gold Glove in 1992 . . . Earned $4.2 million in 1992.

Year	Club	G	IP	W	L	Pct.	SO	BB	H	ERA
1986	Chicago (NL)	6	31	2	4	.333	20	11	44	5.52
1987	Chicago (NL)	30	155⅔	6	14	.300	101	74	181	5.61
1988	Chicago (NL)	34	249	18	8	.692	140	81	230	3.18
1989	Chicago (NL)	35	238⅓	19	12	.613	135	82	222	2.95
1990	Chicago (NL)	35	237	15	15	.500	144	71	242	3.46
1991	Chicago (NL)	37	263	15	11	.577	198	66	232	3.35
1992	Chicago (NL)	35	268	20	11	.645	199	70	201	2.18
	Totals	212	1442	95	75	.559	937	455	1352	3.35

STEVE AVERY 22 6-4 190 **Bats L Throws L**

On the surface it looked like he slipped badly last season, but, in his 11 losses, Braves scored only 25 runs . . . Began season at 2-5 before going on a 7-2 streak from May 30-Aug. 5 . . . Had only one postseason win and ERA was 5.85 . . . Those 223⅔ innings in regular season may have been too much for his young arm to handle . . . His 18 wins in 1991 were most by a 21-year-old in franchise history . . . Destroyed Pirates in 1991 NLCS, winning two games and pitching 16⅓ shutout innings to capture MVP honors . . . Was Braves' first selection as the third player taken overall in 1988 draft . . . Made $355,000 last season.

Year	Club	G	IP	W	L	Pct.	SO	BB	H	ERA
1990	Atlanta	21	99	3	11	.214	75	45	121	5.64
1991	Atlanta	35	210⅓	18	8	.692	137	65	189	3.38
1992	Atlanta	35	233⅔	11	11	.500	129	71	216	3.20
	Totals	91	543	32	30	.516	341	181	526	3.71

TOP PROSPECTS

JAVIER LOPEZ 22 6-3 185 **Bats R Throws R**

The new Benito Santiago . . . Best catching prospect in minors . . . Played nine games for Atlanta, hitting .375, and was put on post-season roster after Greg Olson broke his leg and dislocated his ankle . . . Had outstanding year for Greenville (AA), where he batted .321 with 28 doubles, 16 homers and 60 RBI . . . Born Nov. 5, 1970, in Ponce, P.R. . . . Signed as free agent in November 1987.

CHIPPER JONES 20 6-3 185 **Bats S Throws R**

Shortstop started at Durham (A), where he hit .277 with four homers and 31 RBI in 264 at-bats . . . Earned promotion to Green-ville (AA), where he tore it up, batting .346 with nine homers and 42 RBI in 266 at-bats . . . Definitely the Braves' shortstop of the future . . . Was the No. 1 pick in nation in 1990 draft and is living up to expectations . . . Batted .323 with 15 homers, 24 dou-bles, 11 triples and 98 RBI and scored 104 runs for Macon (A) in 1991 . . . Born April 24, 1972, in Deland, Fla.

RYAN KLESKO 21 6-3 220 Bats L Throws L

First baseman is considered the best power-hitting prospect in organization . . . Spent entire 1992 season with Richmond (AAA) . . . Put up solid numbers, hitting .251 with 17 homers and 59 RBI . . . Hit 14 homers and 22 doubles for Greenville (AA) in 1991, even though he was walked 75 times . . . Born June 12, 1971, in Westminster, Cal. . . . Braves' sixth-round selection in 1989 draft.

MELVIN NIEVES 21 6-2 186 Bats S Throws R

Outfielder has outstanding offensive potential and is considered a Bobby Bonilla-type player . . . Started 1992 season at Durham (AAA), where he hit .302 with eight homers and 32 RBI in 106 at-bats . . . Promoted to Greenville (AA), where he hit .283 in 350 at-bats, slugging 18 homers and driving in 76 runs . . . Born Dec. 28, 1971, in San Juan, P.R. . . . Signed as a free agent in May 1988.

MANAGER BOBBY COX: Even though he has been unable to clear final hurdle and win a world championship, he is one of the best managers around . . . Critics charge he has blown the last two World Series, but without his leadership those teams never would have gotten that far . . . Last year Braves won NL West by eight games and their 98-64 record was best in majors . . . In 1991, he became first to win Manager of the Year awards in both leagues after leading Atlanta to its first pennant . . . When Russ Nixon was fired in 1990, he was put on the hot seat . . . Knows how to get the most out of his players . . . Is patient, understanding and honest . . . Joined Braves in October 1985 as GM, temporarily ending 25-year, on-the-field career as player, coach and manager . . . Spent five years as GM and acquired many of the players that turned the doormat Braves into winners . . . Managed Blue Jays from 1982-85, so World Series was a homecoming . . . Took Toronto team that finished seventh in 1984 to within one game of World Series in 1985 . . . Was named AL Manager of the Year that season . . . Born May 21, 1941, in Tulsa, Okla. . . . Third baseman spent 12 years as a player, 10 of them in the minors, before bad knees ended his career . . . Started managing in Yankee farm system in 1971 . . . In first time around as Braves manager, from 1978-81, he posted 266-323 record . . . Overall major league record is 853-804.

Terry Pendleton made stab at back-to-back MVPs.

ALL-TIME BRAVE SEASON RECORDS

BATTING: Rogers Hornsby, .387, 1928
HRs: Eddie Mathews, 47, 1953
Hank Aaron, 47, 1971
RBI: Eddie Mathews, 135, 1953
STEALS: Otis Nixon, 72, 1991
WINS: Vic Willis, 27, 1902
Charles Pittinger, 27, 1902
Dick Rudolph, 27, 1914
STRIKEOUTS: Phil Niekro, 262, 1977

CINCINNATI REDS

TEAM DIRECTORY: Principal Owner/Pres.: Marge Schott; GM: James Bowden IV; Dir. Scouting: Julian Mock; Dir. Player Development: Sheldon (Chief) Bender; Publicity Dir.: Jon Braude; Trav. Sec.: Joel Pieper; Mgr.: Tony Perez. Home: Riverfront Stadium (52,952). Field distances: 330, l.f. line; 404, c.f.; 330, r.f. line. Spring training: Plant City, Fla.

SCOUTING REPORT

HITTING: New GM Jim Bowden put his stamp on this team by acquiring slugger Kevin Mitchell (.286, 9, 67) from the Mariners. Mitchell, blimp-like in Seattle, promises he will inflate his statistics, not his waistline this season. Mitchell figures to love his return to the NL and the way the ball travels at Riverfront Stadium. However, it should be noted this talented but troubled slugger's production has dropped dramatically in each of the last four years.

The Reds also have added speed and defense in center with Roberto Kelly (.272, 10, 66, 26 steals with the Yankees). Barry Larkin (.304, 12, 78) is the best shortstop in the majors. Add to that Bip Roberts' sparkling play and the Reds have the makings of an exciting team. Roberts (.323, 4, 45, 44 steals) was the Reds' best player last year.

If Chris Sabo (.244, 12, 43) and Hal Morris (.271, 6, 53) can bounce back from their fractured seasons, catcher Joe Oliver (.270, 10, 57) can build upon the best year of his career and youngster Reggie Sanders (.270, 12, 36) continues to improve, the Reds will be the most potent team in baseball. Considering they had the second-highest batting average in the NL last season at .260, they could be scary.

PITCHING: The Reds overhauled their pitching staff last season, but only went from eighth to seventh in ERA, finishing with a 3.46 mark. This season they will have to make up for the losses of Greg Swindell, Norm Charlton and Scott Bankhead.

Charlton was sent to Seattle for Mitchell, but there still is the flame-throwing Rob Dibble in the bullpen. Dibble (3-5, 3.07, 25 saves) is one happy Nasty Boy, because he has the closer's job to himself for the first time. Free-agent addition Greg Cadaret (4-8, 4.25 with the Yankees) might be used as a setup man.

Count on Tim Belcher (15-14, 3.91) to win 20, considering that his teammates scored two runs or fewer in 10 of his losses

Bip Roberts was Mr. Everywhere as renaissance Red.

last season. Jose Rijo (15-10, 2.56) overcame elbow problems to put together another excellent season and is one of the best starters in the majors. Free-agent acquisition John Smiley (16-9, 3.21 with the Twins) makes up for the loss of Swindell. For the first time in five years, Tom Browning (6-5, 5.07) did not pitch 200 innings, because he tore up his left knee in a home-plate collision, but he figures to come back strong in 1993.

FIELDING: Roberts will be at second, the position that is his weakest. Other than that, the infield is strong defensively, because it is anchored by Larkin, whose fielding percentage of .983 was second-best among NL shortstops. When the Reds won it all in '90, they led the league in fielding percentage. They slipped to eighth the following year, but bounced back to tie for second last season with a .984 mark.

OUTLOOK: The architects of the 1990 world champions, Lou Piniella and Bob Quinn, are gone—even though the Reds made a run at the Braves last season, compiling a 90-72 record and earning 16 more wins than the previous year. However, if Mitchell is a dominant player, the Reds will contend for Bowden and rookie manager Tony Perez.

CINCINNATI REDS 1993 ROSTER

MANAGER Tony Perez
Coaches—Dave Bristol, Don Gullett, Dave Miley, Ron Oester, Larry Rothschild

PITCHERS

No.	Name	1992 Club	W-L	IP	SO	ERA	B-T	Ht.	Wt.	Born
59	Ayala, Bobby	Chattanooga	12-6	163	154	3.54	R-R	6-2	190	7/8/69 Ventura, CA
		Cincinnati	2-1	29	23	4.34				
31	Belcher, Tim	Cincinnati	15-14	228	149	3.91	R-R	6-3	210	10/19/61 Sparta, OH
32	Browning, Tom	Cincinnati	6-5	87	33	5.07	L-L	6-1	195	4/28/60 Casper, WY
—	Burke, Tim	New York (AL)	2-2	28	8	3.25	R-R	6-3	205	2/19/59 Omaha, NE
		New York (NL)	1-2	16	7	5.74				
25	Cadaret, Greg	New York (AL)	4-8	104	73	4.25	L-L	6-3	215	2/27/62 Detroit, MI
49	Dibble, Rob	Cincinnati	3-5	70	110	3.07	L-R	6-4	235	1/24/64 Bridgeport, CT
64	Ferry, Mike	Cedar Rapids	13-4	163	143	2.71	R-R	6-3	185	7/26/69 Appleton, WI
54	Foster, Steve	Nashville	5-3	50	28	2.68	R-R	6-0	180	8/16/66 Dallas, TX
		Cincinnati	1-1	50	34	2.88				
45	Hammond, Chris	Cincinnati	7-10	147	79	4.21	L-L	6-1	195	1/21/66 Atlanta, GA
48	Henry, Dwayne	Cincinnati	3-3	84	72	3.33	R-R	6-3	230	2/16/62 Elkton, MD
39	Hill, Milton	Nashville	0-5	74	70	2.66	R-R	6-0	180	8/22/65 Atlanta, GA
		Cincinnati	0-0	20	10	3.15				
—	Landrum, Bill	Montreal	1-1	20	7	7.20	R-R	6-2	205	8/17/58 Columbia, SC
		Indianapolis	1-1	27	23	3.95				
62	Luebbers, Larry	Cedar Rapids	7-0	82	56	2.62	R-R	6-6	190	10/11/69 Cincinnati, OH
		Chattanooga	6-5	87	56	2.27				
55	Powell, Ross	Chattanooga	4-1	57	56	1.26	L-L	6-0	180	1/24/68 Grand Rapids, MI
		Nashville	4-8	93	84	3.38				
40	Pugh, Tim	Nashville	12-9	170	117	3.55	R-R	6-6	225	1/26/67 Lake Tahoe, CA
		Cincinnati	4-2	45	18	2.58				
27	Rijo, Jose	Cincinnati	15-10	211	171	2.56	R-R	6-2	200	5/13/65 Dominican Republic
66	Robinson, Scott	Charleston	8-2	99	80	1.72	R-R	6-2	195	11/15/68 Jasper, AL
		Chattanooga	7-2	83	51	3.80				
28	Ruskin, Scott	Cincinnati	4-3	54	43	5.03	R-L	6-2	195	6/8/63 Jacksonville, FL
41	Service, Scott	Ind.-Nash.	8-2	95	112	1.89	R-R	6-6	235	2/26/67 Cincinnati, OH
		Montreal	0-0	7	11	14.14				
57	Smiley, John	Minnesota	16-9	241	163	3.21	L-L	6-4	200	3/17/65 Phoenixville, PA
65	Spradlin, Jerry	Cedar Rapids	1-0	2	4	7.71	S-R	6-7	220	6/14/67 Fullerton, CA
		Chattanooga	3-3	65	35	1.38				

CATCHERS

No.	Name	1992 Club	H	HR	RBI	Pct.	B-T	Ht.	Wt.	Born
63	Cox, Darron	Chattanooga	84	1	38	.254	R-R	6-1	195	11/21/67 Oklahoma City, OK
9	Oliver, Joe	Cincinnati	131	10	57	.270	R-R	6-3	210	7/24/65 Memphis, TN
6	Wilson, Dan	Nashville	92	4	34	.251	R-R	6-3	190	3/25/69 Arlington Hts., IL
		Cincinnati	9	0	3	.360				

INFIELDERS

No.	Name	1992 Club	H	HR	RBI	Pct.	B-T	Ht.	Wt.	Born
20	Branson, Jeff	Nashville	40	4	12	.325	L-R	6-0	180	1/26/67 Waynesboro, MS
		Cincinnati	34	0	15	.296				
50	Costo, Tim	Chattanooga	102	28	71	.241	R-R	6-5	230	2/16/69 Melrose Park, IL
		Cincinnati	8	0	2	.222				
19	Doran, Bill	Cincinnati	91	8	47	.235	S-R	6-0	180	5/28/58 Cincinnati, OH
15	Greene, Willie	Cedar Rapids	34	12	40	.283	L-R	5-11	180	9/23/71 Milledgeville, GA
		Chattanooga	97	15	66	.278				
		Cincinnati	25	2	13	.269				
—	Gregg, Tommy	Atlanta	5	1	1	.263	L-L	6-1	190	7/29/63 Boone, NC
11	Larkin, Barry	Cincinnati	162	12	78	.304	R-R	6-0	185	4/28/64 Cincinnati, OH
23	Morris, Hal	Cincinnati	107	6	53	.271	L-L	6-4	215	4/9/65 Fort Rucker, AL
		Nashville	1	0	0	.167				
10	Roberts, Rip	Cincinnati	172	4	45	.323	S-R	5-7	168	10/27/63 Berkeley, CA
17	Sabo, Chris	Cincinnati	84	12	43	.244	R-R	6-0	185	1/19/62 Detroit, MI
		Nashville	4	1	1	.364				
—	Samuel, Juan	Los Angeles	32	0	15	.262	R-R	5-11	170	12/9/60 Dominican Republic

OUTFIELDERS

No.	Name	1992 Club	H	HR	RBI	Pct.	B-T	Ht.	Wt.	Born
56	Brantley, Mickey	Tucson	35	1	23	.224	R-R	5-10	185	6/17/61 Catskill, NY
		Nashville	73	7	31	.317				
46	Brumfield, Jacob	Nashville	59	5	19	.284	R-R	6-0	180	5/27/65 Bogalusa, LA
		Cincinnati	4	0	2	.133				
22	Espy, Cecil	Pittsburgh	50	1	20	.258	S-R	6-3	195	1/20/63 San Diego, CA
67	Gordon, Keith	Cedar Rapids	94	12	63	.251	R-R	6-1	200	1/22/69 Bethesda, MD
58	Hernandez, Cesar	Chattanooga	91	3	27	.277	R-R	6-0	160	9/28/66 Dominican Republic
		Nashville	2	0	0	1.000				
		Cincinnati	14	0	4	.275				
36	Kelly, Roberto	New York (AL)	158	10	66	.272	R-R	6-2	192	10/1/64 Panama
7	Mitchell, Kevin	Seattle	103	9	67	.286	R-R	5-11	225	1/13/62 San Diego, CA
16	Sanders, Reggie	Cincinnati	104	12	36	.270	R-R	6-1	180	12/1/67 Florence, SC
42	Varsho, Gary	Pittsburgh	36	4	22	.222	L-R	5-11	190	6/20/61 Marshfield, WI

RED PROFILES

BIP ROBERTS 29 5-7 168 Bats S Throws R

Another player Padres let get away . . . Came to Reds in Randy Myers deal prior to last season and became club's MVP . . . Mr. Versatility led Reds in average, runs, hits, doubles, steals and on-base percentage (.432) and tied for lead in triples . . . Finished fourth in NL in batting . . . Padres said he wasn't durable enough, yet he tied for second among Reds in games played . . . One of top leadoff hitters in game . . . Tied NL record as he became first player since 1943 to notch 10 consecutive hits (over four games, Sept. 19-23) . . . Went hitless in two straight starts only twice all season . . . Started games at four different positions and played more than one position in a game 26 times . . . Made All-Star team for first time and went 2-for-2 with two RBI in San Diego homecoming . . . Born Oct. 27, 1963, in Berkeley, Cal. . . . Signed by Pirates in first round of secondary phase of 1982 draft, but was left unprotected and was taken by the Padres . . . Earned $1.5 million last season.

Year	Club	Pos.	G	AB	R	H	2B	3B	HR	RBI	SB	Avg.
1986	San Diego	2B	101	241	34	61	5	2	1	12	14	.253
1988	San Diego	2B-3B	5	9	1	3	0	0	0	0	0	.333
1989	San Diego	OF-3B-SS-2B	117	329	81	99	15	8	3	25	21	.301
1990	San Diego	OF-3B-SS-2B	149	556	104	172	36	3	9	44	46	.309
1991	San Diego	2B-OF	117	424	66	119	13	3	3	32	26	.281
1992	Cincinnati.....	OF-2B-3B	147	532	92	172	34	6	4	45	44	.323
	Totals		636	2091	378	626	103	22	20	158	151	.299

BARRY LARKIN 28 6-0 185 Bats R Throws R

Rock of the franchise . . . Hit more than .300 for fourth year in a row and no one has done that since Harvey Kuenn in 1953-56 . . . Led all shortstops in batting average, more proof he's the best at his position . . . Became first shortstop to lead Reds in RBI since Leo Cardenas shared the team lead with Deron Johnson in 1966 . . . Finished 10th in NL in hitting with highest full-season mark of his career . . . Knee problems landed him on DL in April . . . Was activated May 8 . . . Hit his stride the next month, batting .340 from June 24 through the end of the season . . . Spanked lefties with .355 mark . . . Batted .338 with runners in scoring position . . . Sparkled in 1990 World Series, hitting .353 . . . Was named Big 10 MVP twice at Michigan . . . Fourth player chosen overall in 1985 draft . . . Born April 28, 1964, in Cincinnati . . . Earned $4.3 million last season.

Year	Club	Pos.	G	AB	R	H	2B	3B	HR	RBI	SB	Avg.
1986	Cincinnati	SS-2B	41	159	27	45	4	3	3	19	8	.283
1987	Cincinnati	SS	125	439	64	107	16	2	12	43	21	.244
1988	Cincinnati	SS	151	588	91	174	32	5	12	56	40	.296
1989	Cincinnati	SS	97	325	47	111	14	4	4	36	10	.342
1990	Cincinnati	SS	158	614	85	185	25	6	7	67	30	.301
1991	Cincinnati	SS	123	464	88	140	27	4	20	69	24	.302
1992	Cincinnati	SS	140	533	76	162	32	6	12	78	15	.304
	Totals		835	3122	478	924	150	30	70	368	148	.296

CHRIS SABO 31 6-0 185 Bats R Throws R

Played all year on a bad ankle and it showed . . . After putting up best numbers of his career in 1991, third baseman saw all of his production figures dip in 1992 . . . They say you shouldn't slide feet first into first and he's living proof. He tried that in second game of the season and was put on DL the next day . . . Required post-season surgery to correct damage . . . Looks like he's from another world, but teammate Rob Dibble says he's "like a Ty Cobb" . . . Batted .331 with 22 doubles, 14 homers and 50 RBI in final 78 games of 1991 season . . . Born Jan. 19, 1962, in Detroit . . . Reds' second-round selection in 1983 draft, out of Michigan . . . Plays third like a goalie and, as a youth, he was goalie on two national championship hockey teams . . . Earned $2,750,000 in 1992.

Year	Club	Pos.	G	AB	R	H	2B	3B	HR	RBI	SB	Avg.
1988	Cincinnati	3B-SS	137	538	74	146	40	2	11	44	46	.271
1989	Cincinnati	3B	82	304	40	79	21	1	6	29	14	.260
1990	Cincinnati	3B	148	567	95	153	38	2	25	71	25	.270
1991	Cincinnati	3B	153	582	91	175	35	3	26	88	19	.301
1992	Cincinnati	3B	96	344	42	84	19	3	12	43	4	.244
	Totals		616	2335	342	637	153	11	80	275	108	.273

HAL MORRIS 27 6-4 215 Bats L Throws L

After he came within one hit of winning NL batting title in 1991, injuries ruined first baseman's season last year . . . Spent two extended stints on disabled list . . . Suffered a fractured right hand when hit by a Charlie Leibrandt pitch April 15, then pulled left hamstring muscle while stretching in on-deck circle in Atlanta Aug. 4 . . . As a result, he played in just 115 games . . . If that wasn't enough, knee injury slowed him all year . . . Had to have surgery Oct. 5 to remove a bone chip . . . Led NL first baseman with .999 fielding percentage . . . Made only one error in 926 total chances . . . One of former GM Bob Quinn's sharpest deals . . . Stole him from Yankees along with Rodney Imes for Tim Leary and Van Snider prior to 1990 season . . . Hit .417 in 1990 NLCS vs. Pirates, but posted .071 mark in World Series . . . Born April 9, 1965, in Fort Rucker, Ala. . . . Eighth-round selection of Yankees in 1986 draft . . . Earned $430,000 last season.

Year	Club	Pos.	G	AB	R	H	2B	3B	HR	RBI	SB	Avg.
1988	New York (AL)	OF	15	20	1	2	0	0	0	0	0	.100
1989	New York (AL)	OF–1B	15	18	2	5	0	0	0	4	0	.278
1990	Cincinnati.	1B-OF	107	309	50	105	22	3	7	36	9	.340
1991	Cincinnati.	1B-OF	136	478	72	152	33	1	14	59	10	.318
1992	Cincinnati.	1B	115	395	41	107	21	3	6	53	6	.271
	Totals		388	1220	166	371	76	7	27	152	25	.304

KEVIN MITCHELL 31 5-11 225 Bats R Throws R

Happy to be back in NL after offseason trade that brought him from Mariners for Norm Charlton . . . Last spring, he came to camp 25 pounds overweight and slumped to worst season . . . Outfielder hit only nine homers and drove in 67 runs in 99 games . . . Missed time due to hand and rib cage injuries . . . Mariners expected so much more when they sent pitchers Billy Swift, Mike Jackson and Dave Burba to Giants for him and Mike Remlinger prior to last season . . . Had averaged 30 homers and 87 RBI over previous five seasons . . . Set career highs with 47 homers and 125 RBI in NL MVP season in 1989 . . . Has missed 112 games in last two seasons . . . Work habits and off-field behavior far from exemplary . . . Made $3,750,000 in 1992 . . . Originally signed by Mets as free agent in November 1980 . . . Born Jan. 13, 1962, in San Diego.

Year	Club	Pos.	G	AB	R	H	2B	3B	HR	RBI	SB	Avg.
1984	New York (NL)	3B	7	14	0	3	0	0	0	1	0	.214
1986	New York (NL)	OF-SS-3B-1B	108	328	51	91	22	2	12	43	3	.277
1987	S.D.-S.F.	3B-SS-OF	131	464	68	130	20	2	22	70	9	.280
1988	San Francisco	3B-OF	148	505	60	127	25	7	19	80	5	.251
1989	San Francisco	3B-OF	154	543	100	158	34	6	47	125	3	.291
1990	San Francisco	OF	140	524	90	152	24	2	35	93	4	.290
1991	San Francisco	OF-1B	113	371	52	95	13	1	27	69	2	.256
1992	Seattle.	OF	99	360	48	103	24	0	9	67	0	.286
	Totals		900	3109	469	859	162	20	171	548	26	.276

JOE OLIVER 27 6-3 210 **Bats R Throws R**

A good example of hard work paying off . . . Catcher has made himself into an solid hitter and is no longer just a platoon player . . . Set career highs in hits, RBI, doubles, runs, games and at-bats . . . It was such a good year he even managed his first triple . . . Had shoulder surgery after the 1991 season . . . His batting average in 1992 was his best for a full season . . . Caught 141 games, the most by a Reds catcher since Johnny Bench caught 141 in 1971 . . . Phils' Darren Daulton was only catcher to drive in more runs . . . Born July 24, 1965, in Memphis, Tenn. . . . Reds' second-round selection in 1983 draft . . . Earned $260,000 last year.

Year	Club	Pos.	G	AB	R	H	2B	3B	HR	RBI	SB	Avg.
1989	Cincinnati	C	49	151	13	41	8	0	3	23	0	.272
1990	Cincinnati	C	121	364	34	84	23	0	8	52	1	.231
1991	Cincinnati	C	94	269	21	58	11	0	11	41	0	.216
1992	Cincinnati	C-1B	143	485	42	131	25	1	10	57	2	.270
	Totals		407	1269	110	314	67	1	32	173	3	.247

ROBERTO KELLY 28 6-2 192 **Bats R Throws R**

Still looking to fulfill star potential in new league, with Reds . . . Acquired from Yanks for Paul O'Neill last winter . . . In 1992, this first-time All-Star couldn't sustain brisk pace he set early . . . Produced half as many homers as he did the year before and connected only three times after June 22 . . . Owned career-high 44 RBI at All-Star break and was named to All-Star team for first time . . . Run production and average both tailed off sharply in second half, however . . . Reached on catcher's interference a major league-record eight times . . . Shifted from center to left for final 43 starts . . . Led Yankees in stolen bases . . . Smart base-runner owns 151 career steals in 199 tries, a 76-percent success rate . . . Born Oct. 1, 1964, in Panama City, Panama . . . Signed as free agent by Yanks in February 1982 . . . Salary was $2.15 million in 1992.

Year	Club	Pos.	G	AB	R	H	2B	3B	HR	RBI	SB	Avg.
1987	New York (AL)	OF	23	52	12	14	3	0	1	7	9	.269
1988	New York (AL)	OF	38	77	9	19	4	1	1	7	5	.247
1989	New York (AL)	OF	137	441	65	133	18	3	9	48	35	.302
1990	New York (AL)	OF	162	641	85	183	32	4	15	61	42	.285
1991	New York (AL)	OF	126	486	68	130	22	2	20	69	32	.267
1992	New York (AL)	OF	152	580	81	158	31	2	10	66	28	.272
	Totals		638	2277	320	637	110	12	56	258	151	.280

REGGIE SANDERS 25 6-1 180 Bats R Throws R

Created a lot of offensive opportunities his first full year in the majors . . . Tied for team lead in triples, ranked second in steals and tied for second in homers . . . His 12 home runs matched the most by a Reds rookie since Gary Redus hit 17 in 1983 . . . Hit four homers in five games, from Aug. 15-19 . . . Like most Reds, he spent time on DL . . . Suffered left hamstring injury in May and severely bruised rib cage in July . . . Reds' seventh-round choice in 1987 draft . . . Born Dec. 1, 1967, in Florence, S.C. . . . Earned $115,000 in 1992 . . . Ex-shortstop has come a long way defensively in outfield . . . Had 11 assists, one less than team leader Paul O'Neill . . . Still needs to get better jump on the ball.

Year	Club	Pos.	G	AB	R	H	2B	3B	HR	RBI	SB	Avg.
1991	Cincinnati	OF	9	40	6	8	0	0	1	3	1	.200
1992	Cincinnati	OF	116	385	62	104	26	6	12	36	16	.270
	Totals		125	425	68	112	26	6	13	39	17	.264

ROB DIBBLE 29 6-4 235 Bats L Throws R

Made a mess in first half of season, going 0-4 with 4.46 ERA and four blown saves in 16 opportunities because of shoulder problems . . . Bounced back in the second half to go 3-1 with a 1.59 ERA and 13 saves in 14 opportunities . . . His 14.1 strikeouts per nine innings topped his 13.6 ratio of 1991 as the highest rate in modern major league history . . . Fanned 60 of the last 111 batters he faced . . . Had 25 saves, boosting career figure to 69 . . . He and Norm Charlton became the first teammates in major league history to record 25 or more saves in same season . . . Opponents hit .193 against him . . . In 1990 NLCS, he struck out 10 of 16 Pirates he faced . . . He did not give up a run in that postseason and surrendered just three hits . . . Born Jan. 24, 1964, in Bridgeport, Conn. . . . First selection in January 1983 draft . . . Earned $1.4 million last season.

Year	Club	G	IP	W	L	Pct.	SO	BB	H	ERA
1988	Cincinnati	37	59⅓	1	1	.500	59	21	43	1.82
1989	Cincinnati	74	99	10	5	.667	141	39	62	2.09
1990	Cincinnati	68	98	8	3	.727	136	34	62	1.74
1991	Cincinnati	67	82⅓	3	5	.375	124	25	67	3.17
1992	Cincinnati	63	70⅓	3	5	.375	110	31	48	3.07
	Totals.	309	409	25	19	.568	570	150	282	2.35

JOSE RIJO 27 6-2 200 **Bats R Throws R**

Reds didn't win the division, but don't blame it on Rijo . . . Led staff in ERA and strikeouts and tied Tim Belcher for wins . . . Set career highs in starts and innings pitched and matched his career high in wins . . . All this, despite spending time on DL with elbow problems . . . Worked under a pitch limit most of the season . . . His record the last two years could have been much better with more support . . . Reds scored just 26 runs in his 21 losses over that span . . . Did not allow a home run in his final seven starts . . . Another player the Yankees let get away . . . Originally signed as free agent by Yanks in 1981, but was sent to A's in Rickey Henderson deal in 1984 . . . A's made huge mistake by dealing him to Reds with Tim Birtsas for Dave Parker following 1987 season . . . Born May 13, 1965, in San Cristobal, D.R. . . . Earned $3,083,333 last season.

Year	Club	G	IP	W	L	Pct.	SO	BB	H	ERA
1984	New York (AL)	24	62⅓	2	8	.200	47	33	74	4.76
1985	Oakland	12	63⅔	6	4	.600	65	28	57	3.53
1986	Oakland	39	193⅔	9	11	.450	176	108	172	4.65
1987	Oakland	21	82⅓	2	7	.222	67	41	106	5.90
1988	Cincinnati	49	162	13	8	.619	160	63	120	2.39
1989	Cincinnati	19	111	7	6	.538	86	48	101	2.84
1990	Cincinnati	29	197	14	8	.636	152	78	151	2.70
1991	Cincinnati	30	204⅓	15	6	.714	172	55	165	2.51
1992	Cincinnati	33	211	15	10	.600	171	44	185	2.56
	Totals.	256	1287⅓	83	68	.550	1096	498	1131	3.26

TIM BELCHER 31 6-3 210 **Bats R Throws R**

First year in Cincinnati could have been much better . . . Led staff in innings pitched and starts and tied Jose Rijo for lead in wins . . . Like Rijo, he did not get enough support . . . Reds scored two runs or fewer in 10 of his losses and were shut out three times . . . Enslaves right-handers, who hit just .178 against him in 1992 . . . Despite career-high number of starts, he got stronger toward the end of the year, winning his last four starts with 1.69 ERA . . . Struck out a career-high 13 Sept. 20 vs. Padres . . . Reds acquired him prior to last season with John Wetteland in deal that sent Eric Davis and Kip Gross to Dodgers . . . Came to Dodgers from A's in September 1987 deal for Rick Honeycutt . . . Was first pick in nation in 1983 by the Twins, but did not sign . . . Became the Yankees' first-round pick in January 1984, but was drafted by Oakland in compensation pool a week later... Born Oct. 19, 1961, in Sparta, Ohio... Made $2.1 million last season.

Year	Club	G	IP	W	L	Pct.	SO	BB	H	ERA
1987	Los Angeles........	6	34	4	2	.667	23	7	30	2.38
1988	Los Angeles........	36	179⅔	12	6	.667	152	51	143	2.91
1989	Los Angeles........	39	230	15	12	.556	200	80	182	2.82
1990	Los Angeles........	24	153	9	9	.500	102	48	136	4.00
1991	Los Angeles........	33	209⅓	10	9	.526	156	75	189	2.62
1992	Cincinnati	35	227⅔	15	14	.517	149	80	201	3.91
	Totals............	173	1033⅔	65	52	.556	782	341	881	3.20

JOHN SMILEY 28 6-4 200 — Bats L Throws L

Twins' free agent signed four-year, $18.4-million contract in December... Tied for Twins' lead in wins... Dealt by Pirates to Minnesota for left-hander Denny Neagle and promising minor-league outfielder Midre Cummings prior to last season... Pirates wanted to get something for him rather than lose him to free agency after 1992 season... Helped replace Jack Morris by throwing staff-leading 241 innings... Pitched two shutouts and five complete games... Earned $3.4 million in 1992 ... Won 20 games in 1991, tying Braves' Tom Glavine for NL lead... Collapsed in 1991 postseason, lasting less than three innings combined in two starts... Selected by Pirates in 12th round of 1983 draft... Born March 17, 1965, in Phoenixville, Pa.

Year	Club	G	IP	W	L	Pct.	SO	BB	H	ERA
1986	Pittsburgh..........	12	11⅔	1	0	1.000	9	4	4	3.86
1987	Pittsburgh..........	63	75	5	5	.500	58	50	69	5.76
1988	Pittsburgh..........	34	205	13	11	.542	129	46	185	3.25
1989	Pittsburgh..........	28	205⅓	12	8	.600	123	49	174	2.81
1990	Pittsburgh..........	26	149⅓	9	10	.474	86	36	161	4.64
1991	Pittsburgh..........	33	207⅔	20	8	.714	129	44	194	3.08
1992	Minnesota..........	34	241	16	9	.640	163	65	205	3.21
	Totals............	230	1095	76	51	.598	697	294	992	3.49

TOP PROSPECTS

TIM PUGH 26 6-6 225 — Bats R Throws R

Remember the name... Posted 4-2 record with 2.58 ERA for Reds as September callup... Power pitcher was 12-9 with 3.55

ERA for Nashville (AAA) . . . In 45 innings for the Reds, he allowed only two homers and 13 walks . . . Could win a spot in rotation this spring . . . Born Jan. 26, 1967, in Lake Tahoe, Cal. . . . Reds chose him in sixth round of 1989 draft, out of Oklahoma State, where he compiled a 33-6 record.

WILLIE GREENE 21 5-11 180 Bats L Throws R

Third baseman was acquired from Expos with Dave Martinez and Scott Ruskin for John Wetteland and Bill Risley prior to last season . . . Lots of power in small package . . . With return of a healthy Chris Sabo, he could be shifted to second or outfield . . . Started the season in Class A and finished it starting at third in Cincinnati . . . Hit 27 homers and drove in 106 runs in minors last season and was named Reds' Minor League MVP . . . Batted .333 over last 10 games with Reds . . . Produced .269 average, two homers and 13 RBI in short major league stint . . . Born Sept. 23, 1971, in Milledgeville, Ga. . . . Originally chosen by Pittsburgh in first round of 1989 draft.

DAN WILSON 24 6-3 190 Bats R Throws R

Catcher is set to back up Joe Oliver this year . . . Was called up from Nashville (AAA) Aug. 31 . . . Hit .251 with four homers and 34 RBI in 106 games for Nashville . . . First major-league hit was pinch-hit RBI single off Tom Glavine Sept. 9 in Atlanta . . . Born March 25, 1969, in Arlington Heights, Ill. . . . Taken in the first round of 1990 draft as the seventh pick overall . . . Selected first team All-America at University of Minnesota.

BOBBY AYALA 23 6-2 190 Bats R Throws R

Could use one year of Triple-A seasoning . . . Was called up from Chattanooga (AA) Sept. 5 and made five starts for Reds, winning his final two decisions and fanning 23 in 29 innings . . . For Chattanooga, he posted 12-6 mark with 3.54 ERA and 154 strikeouts in 163 innings . . . Broke in as a relief pitcher in 1988 and was shifted to starter next season . . . Moved back to the bullpen in 1991 . . . Reds signed him as a free agent in June 1988 . . . Born July 8, 1969, in Ventura, Cal.

MANAGER TONY PEREZ: Was RBI machine of Big Red

Machine, knocking in 90 or more runs nine consecutive years . . . Named successor to Lou Piniella, who had had enough of owner Marge Schott's brand of baseball and quit . . . Has never managed . . . Has worked quietly as Cincinnati coach the last six seasons . . . Hit 379 career homers during his 23-year career, tying him with Orlando Cepeda for record among players from Latin America . . . Born May 14, 1942, in Camaguey, Cuba . . . Was Reds' first-base coach in '87, hitting coach in '88 and '89 and both first-base coach and hitting coach the following year . . . Finished his playing career in Reds' all-time top five in games, at-bats, hits, doubles, homers, extra-base hits, total bases and RBI . . . Also played for Montreal, Boston and Philadelphia . . . Nicknamed "Doggie," he will have to stay out of Schott's doghouse . . . Off to a good start . . . Believes there is room on the field for Schottzie 02, which won over Reds' canine-obsessed owner.

ALL-TIME RED SEASON RECORDS

BATTING: Cy Seymour, .377, 1905
HRs: George Foster, 52, 1977
RBI: George Foster, 149, 1977
STEALS: Bob Bescher, 81, 1911
WINS: Adolfo Luque, 27, 1923
Bucky Walters, 27, 1939
STRIKEOUTS: Mario Soto, 274, 1972

COLORADO ROCKIES

TEAM DIRECTORY: Chairman/CEO: Jerry McMorris; Chairman/CEO/Pres.: John Antonucci; Exec. VP-Baseball Oper.: John McHale Jr.; Sr. VP/GM: Bob Gebhard; Sr. VP/Chief Financial Off.: Kevin Jordan; Sr. VP-Business Oper.: Bernie Mullin; Sr. VP-Pub. Affairs: Dean Peeler; Dir. Player Dev.: Dick Balderson: Dir. Scouting: Pat Daugherty; Dir. Pub. Rel.: Mike Swanson; Trav. Sec.: Peter Durso. Mgr.: Don Baylor. Home: Mile High Stadium (76,100). Field Distances: 335, l.f. line; 375, l.c.; 423, c.f.; 390, r.c.; 370, r.f. line. Spring training: Tucson, Ariz.

SCOUTING REPORT

HITTING: Life is never easy when you're the new kid on the block, but the Rockies made the best of it and drafted a team capable of hitting home runs in the Mile High air of Denver.

While the Marlins drafted extremely young players at the power positions, the Rockies went for experience. The average age of Colorado's outfielders is 27.3 while the Marlins' outfielders average 23.5. Third baseman Charlie Hayes (.257, 18, 66 with the Yankees) hit more homers last season than teammate Don Mattingly. Outfielder Jerald Clark (.242, 12, 58 with the Padres) had a terrific second half and may be another one of those talented players whom San Diego has let slip away.

First baseman Andres Galarraga also has pop and the Rockies are hoping this free-agent signee rebounds from an injury-riddled season that saw him hit 10 homers, drive in 39 runs and bat .243 for the Cards. Outfielder Dante Bichette (.287, 5, 41 with the Brewers) produced a career-high batting average last season and will give the Rockies another solid bat.

The Rockies also own two speedsters in outfielder Alex Cole, who stole 16 bases for the Indians and Pirates last season, and second baseman Eric Young, who stole a total of 146 bases in 1990 and 1991 in the Dodgers' farm system.

PITCHING: This department is always the biggest problem for expansion clubs. In 1977, the last time the majors expanded, the first-year Blue Jays posted a 4.57 ERA while the debuting Mariners put up an embarrassing 4.83 mark.

At least the Rockies have a talented youngster to build around in former Brave David Nied (3-0, 1.17), the top pick in the expansion draft. They also have a potential closer in right-hander

Braves' loss, David Nied, was Rockies' gain as No. 1.

Darren Holmes (4-4, 2.55 with the Brewers), who saved six games last season. Big Mo Sanford (4-0 for Double-A Chattanooga) could surprise as could another ex-Braves pitching prospect, Armando Reynoso (12-9, 2.66) for Triple-A Richmond). Former Astros Willie Blair (5-7, 4.00) and Butch Henry (6-9, 4.02) figure to round out the rotation. Bryn Smith (4-2, 4.64 with the Cards) can definitely help if he's healthy. All in all, pitching coach Larry Bearnarth will have his work cut out for him.

FIELDING: The Rockies are set at the corners with Galarraga, who posted a .991 fielding percentage last season, and Hayes, who made just eight errors in the final 79 games. Young has to improve at second, but veterans Vinny Castilla and Freddie Benavides are solid up the middle. For a fast runner, Cole is a poor fielder. However, Clark may have been the most improved outfielder in the NL last season, committing just three errors and posting 10 assists.

OUTLOOK: This will not be an easy ride for first-time manager Don Baylor, but the Rockies may have enough talent to be respectable. A few general managers could learn some lessons from the way Rockies' boss Bob Gebhard assembled this team. Remember though, since 1961, the average first-year win total for the last 10 expansion teams has been 59.

COLORADO ROCKIES 1993 ROSTER

MANAGER Don Baylor

Coaches—Larry Bearnarth, Ron Hassey, Amos Otis, Jerry Royster, Don Zimmer

PITCHERS

No.	Name	1992 Club	W-L	IP	SO	ERA	B-T	Ht.	Wt.	Born
32	Aldred, Scott	Detroit	3-8	65	34	6.78	L-L	6-4	215	6/12/68 Flint, MI
		Toledo	4-6	86	81	5.13				
43	Ashby, Andy	Philadelphia	1-3	37	24	7.54	R-R	6-5	180	7/1/67 Kansas City, MO
		Scranton	0-3	33	18	3.00				
19	Blair, Willie	Houston	5-7	79	48	4.00	R-R	6-1	185	12/18/65 Paintsville, KY
		Tucson	4-4	53	35	2.39				
50	Bochtler, Doug	Harrisburg	6-5	78	89	2.32	R-R	6-3	185	7/5/70 W. Palm Beach, FL
37	Boucher, Denis	Colorado Springs	11-4	124	40	3.48	R-L	6-1	195	3/7/68 Canada
		Cleveland	2-2	41	17	6.37				
47	Buckley, Travis	Harrisburg	7-7	160	123	2.87	R-R	6-4	210	6/15/70 Overland Park, KS
49	Fredrickson, Scott	Wichita	4-7	73	66	3.19	R-R	6-3	215	8/19/67 Manchester, NH
48	Hawblitzel, Ryan	Charlotte	12-8	175	119	3.76	R-R	6-2	170	4/30/71 West Palm Beach, FL
27	Henry, Butch	Houston	6-9	166	96	4.02	L-L	6-1	195	10/7/68 El Paso, TX
40	Holmes, Darren	Denver	0-0	13	12	1.38	R-R	6-0	199	4/25/66 Asheville, NC
		Milwaukee	4-4	42	31	2.55				
51	Jones, Calvin	Seattle	3-5	62	49	5.69	R-R	6-3	185	9/26/63 Compton, CA
		Calgary	2-0	33	32	3.86				
35	Leskanic, Curt	Orlando	9-11	153	126	4.30	R-R	6-0	180	4/2/68 Homestead, PA
		Portland	1-2	15	14	9.98				
53	Merriman, Brett	Midland	3-4	53	32	2.70	R-R	6-2	180	7/15/66 Jacksonville, FL
		Edmonton	1-3	32	15	1.42				
54	Moore, Marcus	Knoxville	5-10	106	85	5.59	S-R	6-5	195	11/2/70 Oakland, CA
17	Nied, David	Richmond	14-9	168	159	2.84	R-R	6-2	175	12/22/68 Dallas, TX
		Atlanta	3-0	23	19	1.17				
28	Painter, Lance	Wichita	10-5	163	137	3.53	L-L	6-1	195	7/21/67 England
39	Reed, Steve	Shreveport	1-0	29	33	0.62	R-R	6-2	202	3/1/66 Los Angeles, CA
		Phoenix	0-1	31	30	3.48				
		San Francisco	1-0	16	11	2.30				
42	Reynoso, Armando	Richmond	12-9	169	108	2.66	R-R	6-0	186	5/1/66 Mexico
		Atlanta	1-0	8	2	4.70				
31	Ritz, Kevin	Detroit	2-5	80	57	5.60	R-R	6-4	220	6/8/65 Eatontown, NJ
—	Ruffin, Bruce	Milwaukee	1-6	58	45	6.67	R-L	6-2	209	10/4/63 Lubbock, TX
		Denver	3-0	29	17	0.94				
34	Sanford, Mo	Nashville	8-8	122	129	5.68	R-R	6-6	225	12/24/66 Americus, GA
		Chattanooga	4-0	27	28	1.35				
44	Seanez, Rudy	Los Angeles		Injured			R-R	5-10	185	10/20/68 Brawley, CA
52	Shepherd, Keith	Birmingham	3-3	71	64	2.14	R-R	6-2	197	1/21/68 Wabash, IN
		Reading	0-1	23	9	2.78				
		Philadelphia	1-1	22	10	3.27				
—	Smith, Bryn	St. Louis	4-2	21	9	4.64	R-R	6-2	205	8/11/55 Marietta, GA

CATCHERS

No.	Name	1992 Club	H	HR	RBI	Pct.	B-T	Ht.	Wt.	Born
11	Ausmus, Brad	Albany	3	0	1	.167	R-R	5-11	185	4/14/69 New Haven, CT
		Columbus	88	2	35	.242				
7	Girardi, Joe	Chicago (NL)	73	1	12	.270	R-R	5-11	195	10/14/64 Peoria, IL
33	Owens, Jay	Orlando	88	4	30	.267	R-R	6-1	200	2/10/69 Cincinnati, OH
22	Wedge, Eric	Pawtucket	63	11	40	.299	R-R	6-3	215	1/27/68 Fort Wayne, IN
		Boston	17	5	11	.250				

INFIELDERS

12	Benavides, Freddie	Cincinnati	40	1	17	.231	R-R	6-2	185	4/7/66 Laredo, TX
15	Castellano, Pedro	Iowa	59	2	20	.248	R-R	6-1	175	3/11/70 Venezuela
		Charlotte	33	1	15	.224				
9	Castilla, Vinny	Richmond	113	7	44	.252	R-R	6-1	195	7/4/67 Mexico
		Atlanta	4	0	1	.250				
14	Galarraga, Andres	St. Louis	79	10	39	.243	R-R	6-3	235	6/18/61 Venezuela
13	Hayes, Charlie	New York (AL)	131	18	66	.257	R-R	6-0	205	5/29/65 Hattiesburg, MS
8	Mejia, Roberto	Vero Beach	82	12	40	.248	R-R	5-11	160	4/14/72 Dominican Republic
20	Tatum, Jim	Denver	162	19	101	.329	R-R	6-2	200	10/9/67 Grossmont, CA
		Milwaukee	1	0	0	.125				
21	Young, Eric	Albuquerque	118	3	49	.337	R-R	5-9	180	11/26/66 Jacksonville, FL

OUTFIELDERS

10	Bichette, Dante	Milwaukee	111	5	41	.287	R-R	6-3	225	11/18/63 West Palm Beach, FL
—	Boston, Daryl	New York (NL)	72	11	35	.249	L-L	6-3	195	1/4/63 Cincinnati, OH
16	Castillo, Braulio	Scranton	95	13	47	.246	R-R	6-0	160	5/13/68 Dominican Republic
		Philadelphia	15	2	7	.197				
24	Clark, Jerald	San Diego	120	12	58	.242	R-R	6-4	205	8/10/63 Crockett, TX
5	Cole, Alex	Cleveland	20	0	5	.206	L-L	6-2	170	8/17/65 Fayetteville, NC
		Pittsburgh	57	0	10	.278				

ROCKIE PROFILES

CHARLIE HAYES 27 6-0 205 Bats R Throws R

After solving Yankees' long-standing problem at third base, he went unprotected in expansion draft and was grabbed by Rockies as their second pick . . . Acquired by Yankees as player to be named in deal that sent minor league reliever Darrin Chapin to Philadelphia before last season . . . Set career bests in homers and RBI . . . His 139 games at third were most by a Yankee since Mike Pagliarulo played 147 there in 1987 . . . A gifted fielder who has made only 13 errors in last 156 games at position . . . Streaky hitter with tendency to concentrate too much on pulling the ball . . . Given difficult role of succeeding Mike Schmidt in Philadelphia and never fit in . . . Giants' fourth-round pick in 1983 draft . . . Born May 29, 1965, in Hattiesburg, Miss. . . . A bargain at $280,000 in 1992.

Year	Club	Pos.	G	AB	R	H	2B	3B	HR	RBI	SB	Avg.
1988	San Francisco	OF–3B	7	11	0	1	0	0	0	0	0	.091
1989	SF-Phil.	3B	87	304	26	78	15	1	8	43	3	.257
1990	Philadelphia . . .	3B–1B–2B	152	561	56	145	20	0	10	57	4	.258
1991	Philadelphia . . .	3B-SS	142	460	34	106	23	1	12	53	3	.230
1992	New York (AL)	3B–1B	142	509	52	131	19	2	18	66	3	.257
	Totals		530	1845	168	461	77	4	48	219	13	.250

ANDRES GALARRAGA 31 6-3 235 Bats R Throws R

Became first 1992 free agent to switch teams when he signed with Rockies on eve of expansion draft . . . Coming off second straight injury-plagued, subpar season with two different teams . . . Traded to Cardinals from Expos for pitcher Ken Hill following 1991 season . . . Spent 44 days on disabled list with cracked bone in right wrist after being hit by Wally Whitehurst pitch in third game of season . . . Began hitting ball to right-center again during second half and impressed Cardinal hitting coach Don Baylor, who later urged Rockies to sign him . . . Batted over .300 against lefties . . . Hit third career grand slam Aug. 15 at Montreal . . . Born June 18, 1961, in Caracas, Venezuela . . . Signed as free agent with Expos in 1979 . . . Led NL in strikeouts three straight seasons (1988-90) . . . Won Gold Gloves at first base in 1989 and '90 . . . Named to 1988 All-Star team while leading NL in doubles . . . Earned $2.36 million in 1992.

Year	Club	Pos.	G	AB	R	H	2B	3B	HR	RBI	SB	Avg.
1985	Montreal	1B	24	75	9	14	1	0	2	4	1	.187
1986	Montreal	1B	105	321	39	87	13	0	10	42	6	.271
1987	Montreal	1B	147	551	72	168	40	3	13	90	7	.305
1988	Montreal	1B	157	609	99	184	42	8	29	92	13	.302
1989	Montreal	1B	152	572	76	147	30	1	23	85	12	.257
1990	Montreal	1B	155	579	65	148	29	0	20	87	10	.256
1991	Montreal	1B	107	375	34	82	13	2	9	33	5	.219
1992	St. Louis	1B	95	325	38	79	14	2	10	39	5	.243
	Totals		942	3407	432	909	182	16	116	472		.267

DANTE BICHETTE 29 6-3 225 — Bats R Throws R

An inferno the first half of the season when he batted .316 for the Brewers . . . Hit .247 after the break . . . Best month was June when he batted .338 with three homers and 19 RBI . . . Despite second-half slide, still managed to set career highs in average (.287), doubles (27) and stolen bases (18) . . . Hit .346 with runners on third base and two out, second on the Brewers to Scott Fletcher (.360) . . . Came over to Rockies in expansion-day deal for outfielder Kevin Reimer . . . Tied a club record by scoring four runs on June 28 in Baltimore . . . Born Nov. 18, 1963, in West Palm Beach, Fla. . . . Angels selected him in the 17th round of 1984 draft . . . Traded to Milwaukee for Dave Parker prior to the 1991 season . . . Earned $230,000 in 1992.

Year	Club	Pos.	G	AB	R	H	2B	3B	HR	RBI	SB	Avg.
1988	California	OF	21	46	1	12	2	0	0	8	0	.261
1989	California	OF	48	138	13	29	7	0	3	15	3	.210
1990	California	OF	109	349	40	89	15	1	15	53	5	.255
1991	Milwaukee	OF-3B	134	445	53	106	18	3	15	59	14	.238
1992	Milwaukee	OF	101	387	37	111	27	2	5	41	18	.287
	Totals		413	1365	144	347	69	6	38	176	40	.254

JERALD CLARK 29 6-4 205 — Bats R Throws R

After waiting two years for left fielder to hit his stride, Padres didn't protect him in the draft and he was Rockies' fourth choice . . . Batted .283 with eight of his 12 home runs and 43 of his 58 RBI after June . . . Once he and his wife adopted baby daughter, his year turned around . . . Batted just .192 through June . . . With a runner on third and less than two out, he hit .391 . . . Fly-ball hitter should benefit greatly in Mile High Stadium

. . . A poor defensive outfielder entering the season, he became one of the better left fielders in the NL through hard work . . . Spent each day talking with Tony Gwynn about the nuances of the game and that paid off . . . Born Aug. 10, 1963, in Crockett, Tex. . . . Padres selected him in the 12th round of 1983 draft . . . Earned $200,000 in 1992 . . . Brothers Phil and Isaiah were first-round draft choices of Tigers and Brewers . . . Never hit lower than .301 in four years in the minors.

Year	Club	Pos.	G	AB	R	H	2B	3B	HR	RBI	SB	Avg.
1988	San Diego	OF	6	15	0	3	1	0	0	3	0	.200
1989	San Diego	OF	17	41	5	8	2	0	1	7	0	.195
1990	San Diego	1B-OF	53	101	12	27	4	1	5	11	0	.267
1991	San Diego	OF–1B	118	369	26	84	16	0	10	47	2	.228
1992	San Diego	OF–1B	146	496	45	120	22	6	12	58	3	.242
	Totals		340	1022	88	242	45	7	28	126	5	.237

JOE GIRARDI 28 5-11 195 Bats R Throws R

Intelligent player and excellent handler of pitchers . . . That's why the Rockies took him from the Cubs with their 10th pick . . . Owns an industrial engineering degree from Northwestern University, where he earned academic All-America honors three times . . . Threw out 28 of 73 runners . . . Makes contact, batting .270 over 91 games with only one homer and 12 RBI . . . Born Oct. 14, 1964, in Peoria, Ill. . . . His 1991 season was a washout because of a lower back strain . . . Appeared in only 21 games that year . . . His first day back he broke his nose in a home-plate collision with John Kruk . . . Selected by the Cubs in the fifth round of 1986 draft . . . Earned $300,000 in 1992.

Year	Club	Pos.	G	AB	R	H	2B	3B	HR	RBI	SB	Avg.
1989	Chicago (NL) . .	C	59	157	15	39	10	0	1	14	2	.248
1990	Chicago (NL) . .	C	133	419	36	113	24	2	1	38	8	.270
1991	Chicago (NL) . .	C	21	47	3	9	2	0	0	6	0	.191
1992	Chicago (NL) . .	C	91	270	19	73	3	1	1	12	0	.270
	Totals		304	893	73	234	39	37	3	70	10	.262

ALEX COLE 27 6-2 170 Bats L Throws L

Speedster is running out of teams . . . This is outfielder's fifth stop in three years . . . Rockies are looking for him to play center field, but he has yet to show defensive instincts . . . Played in 41 games for Cleveland and batted just .206 with nine stolen bases before he was sent to Pirates on July 3 in exchange for Tony Mitchell and John Carter . . . Batted .278 for Pirates in

64 games with seven stolen bases . . . Born Aug. 17, 1965, in Fayetteville, N.C. . . . Selected by Cardinals in second round of 1985 draft . . . Earned $162,500 last season . . . Rockies made him their ninth choice.

Year	Club	Pos.	G	AB	R	H	2B	3B	HR	RBI	SB	Avg.
1990	Cleveland	OF	63	227	43	68	5	4	0	13	51	.300
1991	Cleveland	OF	122	387	58	114	17	3	0	21	27	.295
1992	Cleveland	OF	41	97	11	20	1	0	0	5	9	.206
1992	Pittsburgh	OF	64	205	33	57	3	7	0	10	7	.278
	Totals		290	916	145	259	26	14	0	49	83	.283

FRED BENAVIDES 26 6-2 185 — Bats R Throws R

Slick-fielding shortstop can also play second base . . . Started 44 games for the Reds, 23 at second, 21 at short . . . Did not make an error at second in 108 chances . . . At times, showed he can handle a bat, too . . . Hit his first major league home run April 14 at Riverfront Stadium off Atlanta's Steve Avery . . . Hit .234 in 21 games from May 8 to July 24 . . . Finished strong, batting .370 over his last 10 games of the year . . . Born April 7, 1966, in Laredo, Tex. . . . Selected by Reds in second round of 1987 draft . . . Attended Texas Christian University, where he played baseball for three years . . . Earned $120,000 last season . . . Was Rockies' first pick in second round.

Year	Club	Pos.	G	AB	R	H	2B	3B	HR	RBI	SB	Avg.
1991	Cincinnati	SS-2B	24	63	11	18	1	0	0	3	1	.286
1992	Cincinnati	2B-SS-3B	74	173	14	40	10	1	1	17	0	.231
	Totals		98	326	25	58	11	1	1	20	1	.246

ERIC YOUNG 26 5-9 180 — Bats R Throws R

Dodgers gave him a look in the second half and didn't like what they saw, so they left him exposed in the draft . . . May have acted too quickly . . . At Albuquerque (AAA), speedy second baseman batted .337 in 94 games with 28 stolen bases but did make 20 errors . . . Is not smooth around the bag . . . In 49-game tryout with Dodgers, he batted .258 with six stolen bases . . . Born Nov. 26, 1966, in Jacksonville, Fla. . . . Selected by the Dodgers in 43rd round of the 1989 draft . . . Dodgers took notice in 1990, when he set a Vero Beach record with 75 stolen bases while helping the team to the Florida State League championship . . . Followed that up with a club-record 71 stolen bases at San Antonio (AA) in 1991 . . . Earned $109,000 in 1992 . . . Was Rockies' sixth pick.

Year Club	Pos.	G	AB	R	H	2B	3B	HR	RBI	SB	Avg.
1992 Los Angeles . . .	2B	49	132	9	34	1	0	1	11	6	.258

VINNY CASTILLA 25 6-1 195 Bats R Throws R

Has utilityman written all over him . . . Played in just 16 games with the Braves, hitting .250 . . . Spent most of the season at Richmond (AAA) . . . Batted .252 with 29 doubles, seven homers and 44 RBI while grounding into 19 double plays there . . . Could surprise and challenge Fred Benavides for starting job at shortstop . . . Born July 4, 1967, in Oacaxa, Mexico . . . Contract was purchased by Braves prior to 1990 season from Saltillo of the Mexican League after he batted .307 and tied for league lead with 13 triples . . . Earned $109,000 in 1992 . . . Was second-round expansion pick.

Year	Club	Pos.	G	AB	R	H	2B	3B	HR	RBI	SB	Avg.
1991	Atlanta.	SS	12	5	1	1	0	0	0	0	0	.200
1992	Atlanta.	3B-SS	9	16	1	4	1	0	0	1	0	.250
	Totals		21	21	2	5	1	0	0	1	0	.238

DAVID NIED 24 6-2 175 Bats R Throws R

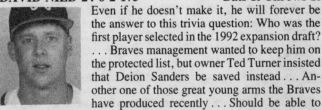

Even if he doesn't make it, he will forever be the answer to this trivia question: Who was the first player selected in the 1992 expansion draft? . . . Braves management wanted to keep him on the protected list, but owner Ted Turner insisted that Deion Sanders be saved instead . . . Another one of those great young arms the Braves have produced recently . . . Should be able to make the jump into the majors, despite his youthful appearance . . . Gave a glimpse of his abilities after September callup by going 3-0 with 1.17 ERA for the Braves, striking out 19 batters in 23 innings . . . Put together a 14-9 record at Richmond (AAA) with a fine 2.84 ERA . . . Struck out 159 batters and walked only 44 in 168 innings . . . Posted a 15-6 record in 1991, splitting his time between Durham (A) and Greenville (AA), striking out 101 batters in 89⅔ innings at Greenville . . . Born Dec. 22, 1968, in Dallas

. . . Selected in the 14th round of 1987 draft . . . Earned $109,000 last season.

Year	Club	G	IP	W	L	Pct.	SO	BB	H	ERA
1992	Atlanta	6	23	3	0	1.000	19	5	10	1.17

DARREN HOLMES 26 6-0 199 Bats R Throws R

Will be given the closer's job after performing setup duties with Milwaukee . . . Did get six saves for Brewers . . . Established personal bests in appearances, victories, ERA and saves . . . Ranked first on the Brewers with a 17-percent inherited-runners ratio and second in games finished (25) and saves . . . Held opponents to a .224 batting average . . . Finished strong, allowing one earned run over his last 20⅔ innings, while compiling a 1.93 ERA in 21 games after the All-Star break . . . No stranger to Denver, he appeared in 12 games there for Milwaukee's Triple-A club . . . Born April 25, 1966, in Asheville, N.C. . . . Acquired by Brewers from the Dodgers prior to the 1991 season for Bret Heffernan . . . Another bad deal for the Dodgers, considering LA's massive bullpen woes . . . Earned $130,000 in 1992 . . . Rockies' third pick.

Year	Club	G	IP	W	L	Pct.	SO	BB	H	ERA
1990	Los Angeles.	14	17⅓	0	1	.000	19	11	15	5.19
1991	Milwaukee.	40	76⅓	1	4	.200	59	27	90	4.72
1992	Milwaukee.	41	42⅓	4	4	.500	31	11	35	2.55
	Totals.	95	136	5	9	.357	109	49	140	4.10

BUTCH HENRY 24 6-1 195 Bats L Throws L

Everything that could go wrong his rookie year did, as he finished 6-9 . . . Astros scored just 13 runs in his nine losses and only one in each of his last five losses . . . Only three other pitchers in league had less support that his 3.37 runs per game . . . If that wasn't enough, he spent the last month of the season sidelined with tendinitis . . . His first major league hit was three-RBI inside-the-park homer vs. Pirates on May 8 . . . Born Oct. 7, 1968, in El Paso, Tex. . . . Earned $109,000 last season . . . Astros acquired him from Cincinnati along with Keith Kaiser and Terry McGriff for Bill Doran on Aug. 31, 1990 . . . Selected by Reds in 15th round of 1987 draft . . . Second-round expansion pick.

Year	Club	G	IP	W	L	Pct.	SO	BB	H	ERA
1992	Houston	28	165⅔	6	9	.400	96	41	185	4.02

Rockies landed gem of draft in ex-Yank Charlie Hayes.

TOP PROSPECTS

KEITH SHEPHERD 25 6-2 197 Bats R Throws R
Rockies selected him 25th in expansion draft . . . Pitching for fifth organization in seven years, he finally hit jackpot when White Sox traded him to Phillies Aug. 10 . . . By September, he was in Philadelphia's bullpen . . . Made 12 appearances, going 1-1 with two saves and 3.27 ERA . . . Picked up first win Sept. 8 against Mets and first save six days later against Expos . . . Made Southern League all-star team while going 3-3 with 2.14 ERA and seven saves for Birmingham (AA) last year . . . Pirates' 11th pick in 1986 draft . . . Had 0.51 ERA and 10 saves for South Bend (A) in 1991 . . . Born Jan. 21, 1968, in Wabash, Ind.

PEDRO CASTELLANO 23 6-1 175 Bats R Throws R
Rockies' 32nd pick in expansion draft . . . Cubs' Minor League Player of the Year and Carolina League MVP with Charlotte (AA)

in 1991 had trouble making jump to Triple-A last year . . . Batted .248 at Iowa before being demoted to Charlotte in July . . . Slowed by thumb injury and also lost two weeks to chicken pox . . . Average third baseman with strong arm . . . Signed with Cubs as nondrafted free agent in 1988 . . . Batted .303 with 25 doubles, 10 homers and 87 RBI for Winston-Salem (A) in 1991 . . . Born March 11, 1970, in Lara, Venezuela.

BRAULIO CASTILLO 24 6-0 160 Bats R Throws R
Was Rockies' 35th pick in expansion draft . . . Showed surprising power in 1992, hitting 13 homers at Scranton (AAA) to tie for tops in Phillies' minor league system . . . Outfielder was recalled to Philadelphia Aug. 17 to replace injured Lenny Dykstra . . . Hit first major league homer Sept. 14 off Expos' Brian Barnes . . . Had three-hit game Sept. 27 against Cardinals . . . Signed with Dodgers as free agent in 1985 . . . Traded to Phillies with Mike Hartley for Roger McDowell, July 31, 1991 . . . Selected to 1989 California League all-star team after hitting 28 doubles and 18 homers . . . Born May 13, 1968, in Ellas Pina, D.R.

MANAGER DON BAYLOR: After years of being leader on the field as a player, he is expected to mold winning attitude in formative years of this franchise . . . Owns plenty of experience at winning . . . Participated in three World Series and seven AL playoffs . . . Former outfielder, first baseman and designated hitter was given a three-year contract, becoming only fourth minority manager in majors . . . His major league playing career spanned 19 years with Orioles, Athletics, Angels, Yankees and Red Sox . . . Hit 338 home runs . . . Was named AL MVP as an Angel in 1979 . . . Had .260 career average and 1,276 RBI and was hit by pitches a record 255 times . . . His idols are Earl Weaver and Gene Mauch . . . Spent last season as the Cardinals' hitting coach after two years in same role with Brewers . . . Born June 28, 1949, in Austin, Tex.

HOUSTON ASTROS

TEAM DIRECTORY: Owner: Drayton McLane Jr.; GM: Bill Wood; Asst. GM: Bob Watson; Coordinator Minor League Instruction: Jimmy Johnson; Dir. Pub. Rel.: Rob Matwick; Trav. Sec.: Barry Waters; Mgr.: Art Howe. Home: Astrodome (54,816). Field distances: 330, l.f. line; 380, l.c.; 400, c.f.; 380, r.c.; 330, r.f. line. Spring training: Kissimmee, Fla.

SCOUTING REPORT

HITTING: Something is happening here. The Astros are on the brink of success with a lineup of young stars like second baseman

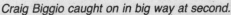

Craig Biggio caught on in big way at second.

Craig Biggio (.277, 6, 39, 38 steals), first baseman Jeff Bagwell (.273, 18, 96), third baseman Ken Caminiti (.294, 13, 62) and center fielder Steve Finley (.292, 5, 55, 44 steals).

Bagwell didn't let the sophomore jinx get to him after winning NL Rookie of the Year honors in 1991 as he ranked among the NL's top ten in four key categories. Bagwell, Biggio and Finley all showed their durability by playing in all 162 games. Only one other player in the majors, Baltimore's Cal Ripken Jr., accomplished the feat.

The Astros hit just .246 and only the Giants and Mets were less potent than that in 1992. Things are getting better, though, considering it was the fourth straight year the Astros' batting average has improved. Outfielder Luis Gonzalez (.243, 10, 55) got off to a dreadful start last year while outfielder Eric Anthony finally showed some power by hitting a team-high 19 homers and driving in 80 runs.

PITCHING: After finishing with a 4.00 ERA in 1991, the Astros dropped to 3.72 last year—but that was the second-worst mark in the league. Only the "beat-me, whip me" Phillies owned an uglier ERA, at 4.11.

The Astros went a long way toward strengthening their weakest link last winter by signing free agents Doug Drabek and Greg Swindell, at a cost of $37 million over four years. Drabek, 15-11 with a 2.77 ERA last season, has been the backbone of the Pirates' staff, winning 52 games the last three years. Swindell compiled an impressive 12-8 record and a 2.70 ERA with the Reds.

The Astros have a solid third starter in Pete Harnisch, who slumped to 9-10 last season with a 3.70 ERA, but still ranked among the NL leaders by holding opponents to a .234 batting average. Returning veteran Mark Portugal (6-3, 2.66) was hampered last season by elbow surgery. Closer Doug Jones (11-8, 1.85) was the biggest bargain in baseball, setting a club record with 36 saves. Jones has plenty of help in the pen with Al Osuna (6-3, 4.23), Joe Boever (3-6, 2.51) and Xavier Hernandez (9-1, 2.11).

FIELDING: In 1991, the Astros were the worst defensive team in the majors, compiling 161 errors. They trimmed that total to 114 errors last season, the third-lowest total in team history, as the Astros finished with a .981 fielding percentage. The most successful defensive move of the season was switching Biggio from catcher to second, but Houston still could use a shortstop.

HOUSTON ASTROS 1993 ROSTER

MANAGER Art Howe

Coaches—Bob Cluck, Matt Galante, Rudy Jaramillo, Ed Ott, Tom Spencer

PITCHERS

No.	Name	1992 Club	W-L	IP	SO	ERA	B-T	Ht.	Wt.	Born
54	Boever, Joe	Houston	3-6	111	67	2.51	R-R	6-1	200	10/4/60 St. Louis, MO
—	Drabek, Doug	Pittsburgh	15-11	257	177	2.77	R-R	6-1	185	7/25/62 Victoria, TX
46	Edens, Tom	Minnesota	6-3	76	57	2.83	L-R	6-2	188	6/9/61 Ontario, OR
43	Grimsley, Jason	Tucson	8-7	125	90	5.05	R-R	6-3	180	8/7/67 Cleveland, TX
27	Harnisch, Pete	Houston	9-10	207	164	3.70	R-R	6-0	195	9/23/66 Commack, NY
31	Hernandez, Xavier	Houston	9-1	111	96	2.11	L-R	6-2	185	8/16/65 Port Arthur, TX
50	Hurta, Bob	Jackson	3-1	46	52	2.33	L-L	6-0	190	11/17/65 Freeport, TX
		Tucson	3-1	21	22	2.61				
23	Jones, Doug	Houston	11-8	112	93	1.85	R-R	6-2	195	6/24/57 Covina, CA
59	Jones, Todd	Tucson	0-1	4	4	4.50	L-R	6-3	200	4/24/68 Marietta, GA
		Jackson	3-7	66	60	3.14				
44	Juden, Jeff	Tucson	9-10	147	120	4.04	R-R	6-7	245	1/19/71 Salem, MA
57	Kile, Darryl	Tucson	4-1	56	43	3.99	R-R	6-5	185	12/2/68 Garden Grove, CA
		Houston	5-10	125	90	3.95				
56	Mallicoat, Rob	Tucson	1-3	50	53	2.32	L-L	6-3	180	11/16/64 St. Helen's, OR
		Houston	0-0	24	20	7.23				
—	*Murphy, Rob	Houston	3-1	56	42	4.04	L-L	6-2	215	5/26/60 Miami, FL
29	Osuna, Al	Houston	6-3	62	37	4.23	R-L	6-2	200	8/10/65 Inglewood, CA
51	Portugal, Mark	Houston	6-3	101	62	2.66	R-R	6-0	190	10/30/62 Los Angeles, CA
38	Reynolds, Shane	Houston	1-3	25	10	7.11	R-R	6-3	210	3/26/68 Bastrop, CA
		Tucson	9-8	142	106	3.68				
49	Scheid, Rich	Van.-Tuc.	4-7	128	82	2.68	L-L	6-3	185	2/3/65 Staten Island, NY
		Houston	0-1	12	8	6.00				
—	Swindell, Greg	Cincinnati	12-8	214	138	2.70	S-L	6-3	225	1/2/65 Fort Worth, TX
53	Williams, Brian	Tucson	6-1	70	58	4.50	R-R	6-2	195	2/15/69 Lancaster, SC
		Houston	7-6	96	54	3.92				

CATCHERS

No.	Name	1992 Club	H	HR	RBI	Pct.	B-T	Ht.	Wt.	Born
10	Eusebio, Tony	Jackson	104	5	44	.307	R-R	6-2	180	4/27/67 Dominican Republic
9	Servais, Scott	Houston	49	0	15	.239	R-R	6-2	195	6/4/67 LaCrosse, WI
6	Taubensee, Eddie	Houston	66	5	28	.222	L-R	6-4	205	10/31/68 Beeville, TX
		Tucson	25	1	10	.338				
36	Tucker, Eddie	Houston	6	0	3	.120	R-R	6-2	205	11/18/66 Greenville, MS
		Tucson	87	1	29	.302				

INFIELDERS

No.	Name	1992 Club	H	HR	RBI	Pct.	B-T	Ht.	Wt.	Born
5	Bagwell, Jeff	Houston	160	18	96	.273	R-R	6-0	198	5/27/68 Boston, MA
7	Biggio, Craig	Houston	170	6	39	.277	R-R	5-11	180	12/14/65 Smithtown, NY
11	Caminiti, Ken	Houston	149	13	62	.294	S-R	6-0	200	4/21/63 Hanford, CA
1	Candaele, Casey	Houston	68	1	18	.213	S-R	5-9	165	1/12/61 Lompoc, CA
17	Cedeno, Andujar	Houston	38	2	13	.173	R-R	6-1	168	8/21/69 Dominican Republic
		Tucson	82	6	56	.293				
—	Donnels, Chris	Tidewater	84	5	32	.301	L-R	6-0	185	4/21/66 Los Angeles, CA
		New York (NL)	21	0	6	.174				
19	Guerrero, Juan	Houston	25	1	14	.200	R-R	5-11	160	2/1/67 Dominican Republic
2	Miller, Orlando	Tucson	9	2	8	.243	R-R	6-1	180	1/13/69 Panama
		Jackson	100	5	53	.265				

OUTFIELDERS

No.	Name	1992 Club	H	HR	RBI	Pct.	B-T	Ht.	Wt.	Born
64	Ansley, Willie	Gulf Coast	13	0	6	.371	R-R	6-2	200	12/15/69 Dallas, TX
		Jackson	29	0	3	.242				
21	Anthony, Eric	Houston	105	19	80	.239	L-L	6-2	205	11/8/67 San Diego, CA
12	Finley, Steve	Houston	177	5	55	.292	L-L	6-2	180	3/12/65 Union City, TN
26	Gonzalez, Luis	Tucson	19	1	9	.432	L-R	6-2	180	9/3/67 Tampa, FL
		Houston	94	10	55	.243				
60	Hatcher, Chris	Osceola	103	17	68	.281	R-R	6-3	220	1/7/69 Anaheim, CA
62	Hunter, Brian	Osceola	146	1	62	.299	R-R	6-2	170	3/5/71 Portland, OR
63	Mota, Gary	Asheville	141	24	90	.291	R-R	6-0	195	10/6/70 Dominican Republic
4	Rhodes, Karl	Tucson	96	2	54	.289	L-L	5-11	170	8/21/68 Cincinnati, OH
		Houston	0	0	0	.000				
22	Simms, Mike	Tucson	114	11	75	.282	R-R	6-4	185	1/12/67 Orange, CA
		Houston	6	1	3	.250				

*Free agent offered arbitration

OUTLOOK: After playing at a .660 pace over the final 50 games last season, the Astros are the team to watch in 1993. They have new ownership, new money and new pitching. Last season, Art Howe's team was thrilled to finish at 81-81. This year, the Astros will be expected to be in the race. It will be interesting to see how they react to such pressure.

ASTRO PROFILES

JEFF BAGWELL 24 6-0 198 — Bats R Throws R

No sophomore jinx for power-hitting first baseman . . . After becoming first Astro to win NL Rookie of the Year honors in 1991, he had another strong season . . . His home run and RBI totals in 1992 were better than those of rookie year . . . Played in all 162 games . . . Boasted the third-best fielding percentage among NL first basemen . . . Launched only the seventh ball ever hit into the Club Level of Atlanta-Fulton County Stadium, July 29 against Tom Glavine . . . Batted .381 with five homers and 22 RBI in last 31 games of season . . . Hit .317 with 10 homers and 38 RBI after sixth inning . . . Stolen from the Red Sox for Larry Andersen, Aug. 31, 1990 . . . Born May 27, 1968, in Boston, and now lives in Houston . . . Chosen by Red Sox in fourth round of 1989 draft . . . Earned $350,000 last year.

Year	Club	Pos.	G	AB	R	H	2B	3B	HR	RBI	SB	Avg.
1991	Houston......	1B	156	554	79	163	26	4	15	82	7	.294
1992	Houston......	1B	162	586	87	160	34	6	18	96	10	.273
	Totals.......		318	1140	166	323	60	10	33	178	17	.283

STEVE FINLEY 28 6-2 180 — Bats L Throws L

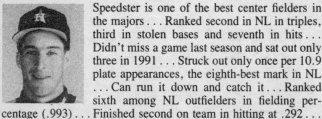

Speedster is one of the best center fielders in the majors . . . Ranked second in NL in triples, third in stolen bases and seventh in hits . . . Didn't miss a game last season and sat out only three in 1991 . . . Struck out only once per 10.9 plate appearances, the eighth-best mark in NL . . . Can run it down and catch it . . . Ranked sixth among NL outfielders in fielding percentage (.993) . . . Finished second on team in hitting at .292 . . . Never went more than three games without a hit . . . Came over from Orioles with Pete Harnisch and Curt Schilling for Glenn Davis prior to 1991 season . . . Earned $1,120,000 last year . . . Selected by Orioles in 14th round of 1987 draft . . . Born March

12, 1965, in Union City, Tenn. . . . Earned degree in physiology from Southern Illinois-Carbondale.

Year	Club	Pos.	G	AB	R	H	2B	3B	HR	RBI	SB	Avg.
1989	Baltimore	OF	81	217	35	54	5	2	2	25	17	.249
1990	Baltimore	OF	142	464	46	119	16	4	3	37	22	.256
1991	Houston	OF	159	596	84	170	28	10	8	54	34	.285
1992	Houston	OF	162	607	84	177	29	13	5	55	44	.292
	Totals		544	1884	249	520	78	29	18	171	117	.276

CRAIG BIGGIO 27 5-11 180 Bats R Throws R

Astros had sense to move him from catcher to second base and it paid off . . . When he made All-Star team last year, he became first player in major league history to make the squad at catcher (in 1991) and second base . . . Too good a runner and too bad a thrower to have stayed behind the plate . . . Chalked up .378 on-base percentage as a leadoff hitter, second-highest figure in NL . . . Ranked seventh in league in runs, fourth in walks and 10th in stolen bases . . . Here's something else that wouldn't have happened if he had stayed at catcher: he played in all 162 games . . . Set a career high in hits . . . Batted .326 during Astros' 28-day Republican Convention trip . . . Intelligent base-runner . . . Stole third 12 times, ranking second to Expos' Marquis Grissom, who did it 24 times . . . Earned $1,375,000 last year . . . Born Dec. 14, 1965, in Smithtown, N.Y. . . . Attended Seton Hall . . . Chosen by Astros in first round of 1987 draft.

Year	Club	Pos.	G	AB	R	H	2B	3B	HR	RBI	SB	Avg.
1988	Houston	C	50	123	14	26	6	1	3	5	6	.211
1989	Houston	C-OF	134	443	64	114	21	2	13	60	21	.257
1990	Houston	C-OF	150	555	53	153	24	2	4	42	25	.276
1991	Houston	C-3B-OF	149	546	79	161	23	4	4	46	19	.295
1992	Houston	2B	162	613	96	170	32	3	6	39	38	.277
	Totals		645	2280	306	624	106	12	30	192	109	.274

KEN CAMINITI 29 6-0 200 Bats S Throws R

Luck finally ran out . . . After missing just 20 games the three previous seasons, he separated his right shoulder 11 games into 1992 season in a collision at third . . . Hitting .308 when he was injured . . . Missed 20 games . . . Had monster seven-game streak in June during which he batted .500 with four doubles, three homers and 10 RBI . . . May be best-fielding third baseman in majors . . . No one else since Brooks Robinson dives, gets up quicker and puts more juice on his throw . . . Fielding percentage of .966 was second-best in NL . . . Likes Dome cooking . . . Batted .329 at home . . . Hit .357 with bases loaded . . . Earned $1.5 million . . . Born April 21, 1963, in Hanford, Cal . . . Astros' third-round pick in 1984 draft, out of San Jose State.

Year	Club	Pos.	G	AB	R	H	2B	3B	HR	RBI	SB	Avg.
1987	Houston	3B	63	203	10	50	7	1	3	23	0	.246
1988	Houston	3B	30	83	5	15	2	0	1	7	0	.181
1989	Houston	3B	161	585	71	149	31	3	10	72	4	.255
1990	Houston	3B	153	541	52	131	20	2	4	51	9	.242
1991	Houston	3B	152	574	65	145	30	3	13	80	4	.253
1992	Houston	3B	135	506	68	149	31	2	13	62	10	.294
	Totals		694	2492	271	639	121	11	44	295	27	.256

LUIS GONZALEZ 25 6-2 180 Bats L Throws R

Got off to a terrible start and was batting .158 May 20, when he was sent down to Tucson (AAA) . . . Corrected his mechanical flaws and was back in Houston June 3 . . . From that point until the All-Star break, he hit .309 with five homers and 20 RBI . . . Managed .271 average overall after his recall . . . Made switch from infield to outfield in 1991 . . . With all the young talent the Astros have put together, he cannot afford to get off to such a slow start again this season . . . Earned $285,000 last season . . . Selected by Astros in fourth round of 1988 draft . . . Born Sept. 3, 1967, in Tampa . . . Attended South Alabama University . . . In 1990, he tied for Southern League in home runs with 24 for Columbus (AA).

Year	Club	Pos.	G	AB	R	H	2B	3B	HR	RBI	SB	Avg.
1990	Houston	3B-1B	12	21	1	4	2	0	0	0	0	.190
1991	Houston	OF	137	473	51	120	28	9	13	69	10	.254
1992	Houston	OF	122	387	40	94	19	3	10	55	7	.243
	Totals		271	881	92	218	49	12	23	124	17	.247

ERIC ANTHONY 25 6-2 205 Bats L Throws L

Finally started to do big things with his big swing . . . Led club and set career high in home runs and established a career high in RBI, too . . . One of only five players with two grand slams last season . . . Struggled through April with a .167 mark before putting it together . . . Still doesn't make enough contact . . . A left-handed version of Pete Incaviglia . . . Struck out 98 times, one fewer that Pete . . . Astros rushed him in 1990 and are still paying the price . . . Became third Houston player to reach Astrodome's upper deck, May 17, 1990 . . . Born Nov. 8, 1967, in San Diego . . . Selected in 34th round of 1986 draft . . . Earned $115,000 last year.

Year	Club	Pos.	G	AB	R	H	2B	3B	HR	RBI	SB	Avg.
1989	Houston......	OF	25	61	7	11	2	0	4	7	0	.180
1990	Houston......	OF	84	239	26	46	8	0	10	29	5	.192
1991	Houston......	OF	39	118	11	18	6	0	1	7	1	.153
1991	Houston......	OF	39	118	11	18	6	0	1	7	1	.153
1992	Houston......	OF	137	440	45	105	15	1	19	80	5	.239
	Totals		285	858	89	180	31	1	34	123	11	.210

AL OSUNA 27 6-2 200 — Bats R Throws L

Arrival of Doug Jones made him a more effective pitcher, because he's not ready to be a closer . . . Workhorse has appeared in 137 games last two seasons . . . In 1991, he was only left-hander in Houston bullpen and it showed . . . Made 71 appearances that season, shattering Astro rookie record set by Charley Kerfeld in 1986 . . . Went 5-1 with a 1.97 ERA at home last season . . . Did not allow a run in his first 11 appearances, but all that extra work must have caught up with him after May . . . Born Aug. 10, 1965, in Inglewood, Cal. . . . Selected by Astros in 16th round of 1987 draft . . . Pitched for Stanford and was winner in championship game of 1987 College World Series . . . Earned $235,000 last year.

Year	Club	G	IP	W	L	Pct.	SO	BB	H	ERA
1990	Houston	12	11⅓	2	0	1.000	6	6	10	4.76
1991	Houston	71	81⅔	7	6	.538	68	46	59	3.42
1992	Houston	66	61⅔	6	3	.667	37	38	52	4.23
	Totals............	149	154⅔	15	9	.625	111	90	121	3.84

MARK PORTUGAL 30 6-0 190 — Bats R Throws R

Elbow injury put a damper on his season . . . Was 5-2 after first 11 starts, but then began to have problems . . . Underwent elbow surgery July 24 to remove bone chips and a bone spur . . . Two months later, he was back on mound . . . Another Dome lover, he posted a 4-0 record with 1.86 ERA at home last season and is 20-8 with a 2.38 ERA at the Astrodome since '89 . . . Held opponents to .213 average and left-handers to .171 mark . . . Was on the mound for one of the funnier baseball incidents . . . On Sept. 14, 1991 in Cincinnati, he surrendered three consecutive home runs, which resulted in back-to-back-to-back fireworks displays. Pitching coach Bob Cluck rushed to the mound and said, "I just came out here to give the guy time to reload his cannon" . . . Born Oct. 30, 1962, in Los Angeles . . . Signed with Twins as amateur free agent in 1980 . . . Traded to Astros for Todd McClure before 1989 season . . . Earned $1,250,000 in 1992.

Year	Club	G	IP	W	L	Pct.	SO	BB	H	ERA
1985	Minnesota	6	24⅓	1	3	.250	12	14	24	5.55
1986	Minnesota	27	112⅔	6	10	.375	67	50	112	4.31
1987	Minnesota	13	44	1	3	.250	28	24	58	7.77
1988	Minnesota	26	57⅔	3	3	.500	31	17	60	4.53
1989	Houston	20	108	7	1	.875	86	37	91	2.75
1990	Houston	32	196⅔	11	10	.524	136	67	187	3.62
1991	Houston	32	168⅓	10	12	.455	120	59	163	4.49
1992	Houston	18	101⅓	6	3	.667	62	41	76	2.66
	Totals	174	813	45	45	.500	542	309	771	4.01

DOUG JONES 35 6-2 195 Bats R Throws R

Yes, there still are bargains in baseball . . . Reliever was signed to make-good minor league contract prior to 1992 season . . . Responded by finishing second to Cards' Lee Smith by just one point for NL Rolaids Relief Man Award . . . Set a club single-season record with 36 saves, giving him career total of 164 . . . His 11 wins were the most by NL reliever and most by an Astros' pitcher, marking first time a reliever has ever led club in wins . . . Finished second in NL in appearances and fifth in relief ERA . . . Also finished 70 games, 12 more than closest NL reliever . . . Converted 24 of his last 27 save opportunities and 36 of 42 overall . . . Made his fourth All-Star appearance . . . Former Indian has three speeds—slow, slower and slowest—but keeps hitters off balance . . . Earned $750,000 for his efforts . . . Born June 24, 1957, in Covina, Cal. . . . Brewers chose him in third round in 1978 draft.

Year	Club	G	IP	W	L	Pct.	SO	BB	H	ERA
1982	Milwaukee	4	2⅔	0	0	.000	1	1	5	10.13
1986	Cleveland	11	18	1	0	1.000	12	6	18	2.50
1987	Cleveland	49	91⅓	6	5	.545	87	24	101	3.15
1988	Cleveland	51	83⅓	3	4	.429	72	16	69	2.27
1989	Cleveland	59	80⅔	7	10	.412	65	13	76	2.34
1990	Cleveland	66	84⅓	5	5	.500	55	22	66	2.56
1991	Cleveland	36	63⅓	4	8	.333	48	17	87	5.54
1992	Houston	80	111⅔	11	8	.579	93	17	96	1.85
	Totals	356	535⅓	37	40	.481	433	116	518	2.82

DOUG DRABEK 30 6-1 185 Bats R Throws R

Pirates' free agent signed four-year, $19.5-million contract with Astros in December . . . Led Pirates in complete games (10) and shutouts (4), but lost three times in NLCS . . . Shut out Braves for eight innings in Game 7 before being victimized by three-run rally in ninth . . . Tied for second-most complete games in NL, tied for third in shutouts, was second in innings pitched, fifth in strikeouts and eighth in opponents' batting average (.231) . . . Often received minimal support, making seven straight starts without a victory from April 22-June 4 . . . Fanned season-high 10 batters against Giants Aug. 30 . . . Always a slow starter, he has 38-40 career record before All-Star break and 61-30 mark in second halves . . . First Pirates starter with five straight winning seasons since Jim Rooker (1973-77) . . . Reached career high in innings pitched . . . Born July 25, 1962, in Victoria, Tex. . . . White Sox' 11th pick in 1983 . . . Traded from Yankees to Pirates in package for Rick Rhoden after 1986 season . . . Named Cy Young winner in 1990 . . . Earned $4.5 million in 1992.

Year	Club	G	IP	W	L	Pct.	SO	BB	H	ERA
1986	New York (AL)	27	131⅔	7	8	.467	76	50	126	4.10
1987	Pittsburgh	29	176⅓	11	12	.478	120	46	165	3.88
1988	Pittsburgh	33	219⅓	15	7	.682	127	50	194	3.08
1989	Pittsburgh	35	244⅓	14	12	.538	123	69	215	2.80
1990	Pittsburgh	33	231⅓	22	6	.786	131	56	190	2.76
1991	Pittsburgh	35	234⅔	15	14	.517	142	62	245	3.07
1992	Pittsburgh	34	256⅔	15	11	.577	177	54	218	2.77
	Totals	226	1494⅓	99	70	.586	896	387	1353	3.11

PETE HARNISCH 26 6-0 195 Bats R Throws R

Something is wrong here . . . Should have had more than nine wins . . . Made a career-high 34 starts and finished eighth in NL in strikeouts and 10th in opponents' batting average with .234 mark . . . Worked six or more innings in 21 starts . . . Allowed three earned runs or fewer 22 times, so he keeps his team in game . . . Had 15 no-decisions, but Astros were 11-4 in those games . . . Things started to turn around in his last eight starts (5-1 with a 2.83 ERA) . . . Struck out 12 Dodgers in last game of season to match a career high . . . Does well in wide-open spaces of the Dome . . . Was 7-4 with 2.75 ERA at home and 2-6 with 5.61 ERA on the road . . . In 1991, opponents hit only .212 against him, best mark in NL . . . Acquired from Orioles with Steve Finley and Curt Schilling for Glenn Davis prior to 1991 season . . . Born Sept. 23, 1966, in Commack, N.Y. . . . Selected by Orioles with compensation pick between first and second rounds of 1987 draft . . . Earned $455,000 last year.

Year	Club	G	IP	W	L	Pct.	SO	BB	H	ERA
1988	Baltimore	2	13	0	2	.000	10	9	13	5.54
1989	Baltimore	18	103⅓	5	9	.357	70	64	97	4.62
1990	Baltimore	31	188⅔	11	11	.500	122	86	189	4.34
1991	Houston	33	216⅔	12	9	.571	172	83	169	2.70
1992	Houston	34	206⅔	9	10	.474	164	64	182	3.70
	Totals	118	728⅓	37	41	.474	538	306	650	3.73

XAVIER HERNANDEZ 27 6-2 185 Bats L Throws R

If you don't have a lot of starters, everyone in your bullpen gets plenty of work . . . Only six other pitchers in NL made more appearances than him . . . One of the biggest surprises of season for Astros . . . His ERA was sixth-best in league among relievers . . . In his last 52 appearances, covering 75⅓ innings, he allowed just 13 earned runs (1.55 ERA) . . . Especially tough with men on base, when opponents only hit .206 against him, the sixth-best mark in NL . . . Born Aug. 16, 1965, in Port Arthur, Tex. . . . Earned $175,000 last season . . . At $2,273 per appearance, he had to be one of best bargains in baseball.

Year	Club	G	IP	W	L	Pct.	SO	BB	H	ERA
1989	Toronto	7	22⅔	1	0	1.000	7	8	25	4.76
1990	Houston	34	62⅓	2	1	.667	24	24	60	4.62
1991	Houston	32	63	2	7	.222	55	32	66	4.71
1992	Houston	77	111	9	1	.900	96	42	81	2.11
	Totals	150	259	14	9	.609	182	106	232	3.58

GREG SWINDELL 28 6-3 225 Bats S Throws L

Thought he had left his troubles behind when he left Cleveland, but five times he came out of a game with the Reds leading only to watch the opposition win . . . Did the same things in NL he had done in AL . . . Control artist's five complete games and three shutouts led Reds . . . His ratio of 1.7 walks per nine innings was third-best in NL . . . Picked off nine baserunners . . . Acquired from Cleveland for Scott Scudder, Jack Armstrong and Joe Turek after 1991 season . . . Two years ago, he led

Indians in innings pitched, strikeouts and complete games . . . Chosen by Cleveland in 1986 draft as second player picked overall . . . Posted 43-8 career mark at University of Texas . . . Born Jan. 2, 1965, in Fort Worth, Tex. . . . Made $2.5 million last year and, as free agent last winter, he signed four-year Houston pact worth $17 million.

Year	Club	G	IP	W	L	Pct.	SO	BB	H	ERA
1986	Cleveland	9	61⅔	5	2	.714	46	15	57	4.23
1987	Cleveland	16	102⅓	3	8	.273	97	37	112	5.10
1988	Cleveland	33	242	18	14	.563	180	45	234	3.20
1989	Cleveland	28	184⅓	13	6	.684	129	51	170	3.37
1990	Cleveland	34	214⅔	12	9	.571	135	47	245	4.40
1991	Cleveland	33	238	9	16	.360	169	31	241	3.48
1992	Cincinnati	31	213⅔	12	8	.600	138	41	210	2.70
	Totals	184	1256⅔	72	63	.533	894	267	1269	3.60

TOP PROSPECTS

ALVIN MORMAN 24 6-3 210 Bats L Throws L

Closer's mechanical flaws were corrected last season and he came out of nowhere to go 8-0 with 15 saves and 1.55 ERA for Asheville (A) . . . Struck out 70 in 75⅓ innings . . . Another good season and he could make the jump to the majors . . . Fastball has been clocked in low 90s . . . Born Jan. 6, 1969, in Rockingham, N.C. . . . Selected in 39th round of 1991 draft.

TODD JONES 24 6-3 200 Bats L Throws R

Converted from starter to reliever last season at Jackson (AA) and posted 25 saves in 30 opportunities . . . Record was 3-7 with a 3.14 ERA . . . Throws smoke . . . Struck out 60 batters in 66 innings . . . Split the year between Osceola (A) and Jackson in 1991, when he was 8-7 overall . . . Selected by Astros as a compensation pick following the first round of 1989 draft . . . Born April 24, 1968, in Marietta, Ga. . . . Rated as one of the top five power pitchers in 1989 draft.

ORLANDO MILLER 24 6-1 180 Bats R Throws R

Slick-fielding shortstop batted .265 with five homers and 53 RBI for Jackson (AA) . . . Fielding is not his problem . . . Has to improve at the plate . . . Named to the South Atlantic All-Star team in 1990 and was selected as league's 10th-best prospect . . . Born Jan. 13, 1969, in Changuinola, Panama . . . Acquired from Yankees for Dave Silvestri prior to 1990 season . . . Signed as a nondrafted free agent by Yankees in 1987.

GARY MOTA 22 6-0 195 **Bats R Throws R**

Famous family has another good player . . . Outfielder batted .296 with 24 homers and 90 RBI for Asheville (A) . . . Youngest of four brothers playing pro ball and he has two younger brothers playing in high school . . . Father Manny played with Dodgers from 1969-80 and 1982 . . . Born Oct. 6, 1970, in Santo Domingo, D.R. . . . Selected by Astros in second round of 1990 draft.

MANAGER ART HOWE: May be nicest manager in baseball

. . . His patience finally paid off last year as Astros finished at 81-81 and only one game back of third-place Padres . . . Club improved by 16 games over 1991 finish . . . His overall record as Astros manager is 307-341. Only Houston managers to post more wins are Bill Virdon (544) and Harry Walker (355) . . . Through all the tough times, he has kept his sense of humor . . . Born Dec. 15, 1946, in Pittsburgh . . . Played on Astros' 1980 NL West champions . . . Came up with Pirates, but was traded for Tommy Helms in 1976 . . . Tenth manager in Houston history . . . This is his 23rd season in pro ball . . . Played baseball and football at University of Wyoming, but his football career ended with a back injury . . . Graduated with degree in business administration . . . Was a computer programmer when he attended Pirates' tryout camp . . . Served as coach for Rangers and gained managerial experience in Puerto Rican League during winters.

ALL-TIME ASTRO SEASON RECORDS

BATTING: Rusty Staub, .333, 1967
HRs: Jimmy Wynn, 37, 1967
RBI: Bob Watson, 110, 1977
STEALS: Gerald Young, 65, 1988
WINS: Joe Niekro, 21, 1979
STRIKEOUTS: J. R. Richards, 313, 1979

LOS ANGELES DODGERS

TEAM DIRECTORY: Pres.: Peter O'Malley; Exec. VP-Player Pers.: Fred Claire; VP-Marketing: Barry Stockhamer; VP-Communications: Tommy Hawkins; Dir. Minor League Oper.: Charlie Blaney; Dir. Scouting: Terry Reynolds; Publicity Dir.: Jay Lucas; Trav. Sec.: Billy DeLury; Mgr.: Tom Lasorda. Home: Dodger Stadium (56,000). Field distances: 330, l.f. line; 370, l.c.; 395, c.f.; 370, r.c.; 330, r.f. line. Spring training: Vero Beach, Fla.

SCOUTING REPORT

HITTING: The Dodgers will tell you that, if not for injuries to Darryl Strawberry (.237, 5, 25) and Eric Davis (.228, 5, 32), there is no way they would have have hit a major league-low 72 homers or produced a .248 average, the fifth-worst mark in baseball, in 1992. Obviously, the key to this season will be keeping those two healthy.

The major offensive bright spot last season was NL Rookie of

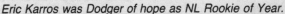

Eric Karros was Dodger of hope as NL Rookie of Year.

the Year Eric Karros (.257, 20, 88), who became the first Dodger rookie to lead the team in homers and RBI and who led the NL in second-half RBI with 55. Reliable Brett Butler (.309, 3, 39) established a career high with 40 bunt singles. Mike Sharperson (.300, 3, 36) didn't quite make fans forget he was acquired at the cost of Juan Guzman, but he had a productive year. Lenny Harris (.271, 0, 30) also contributed offensively. Newcomer Cory Snyder (.269, 14, 57 with the Giants), a free-agent signee, will give the Dodgers more pop and ex-Red Sox second baseman Jody Reed (.247, 3, 40) will supply a little more stability.

PITCHING: The Dodgers, who finished sixth in the NL with a 3.41 ERA, signed free-agent closer Todd Worrell (5-3, 2.11 ERA, 3 saves with the Cards) to a three-year, $9.5-million deal last winter. Here's why: the Dodgers had a major league-low 29 saves last season. Worrell worked as Lee Smith's setup man in St. Louis after coming back from serious elbow and shoulder surgeries. From 1986 through 1989, Worrell compiled 121 saves.

As for getting to Worrell, that won't always be easy. Ramon Martinez (8-11, 4.00) does not look like a healthy pitcher. Orel Hershiser (10-15, 3.67) has made a tremendous comeback and is still smarter than your average pitcher and hitter. The most talented arm on the staff may belong to youngster Pedro Astacio (5-5, 1.98), who recorded four shutouts in 11 starts, the most by a Dodger rookie since Hershiser had four in 1984. No-hit man Kevin Gross (8-13, 3.17) has the talent, but the right-hander has to become more consistent. Knuckleballer Tom Candiotti (11-15, 3.00) did not enjoy having that knuckle defense behind him.

FIELDING: Embarrassing. Humiliating. Horrible. Any of the three will describe the Dodgers' feeble attempts at fielding the baseball last season, when the club committed a major league-high 174 errors. It all begins and ends here. If you can't catch the ball, you can't get them out. Shortstop Jose Offerman led everyone on the planet with 42 errors and Harris made 27, the second most in baseball. Defense is crucial in the close games and the Dodgers were 17-40 in one-run games last year. Former Expo third baseman Tim Wallach should help.

OUTLOOK: After finishing a game out of first in 1991, GM Fred Claire restructured the team and it exploded in his face. The Dodgers finished in last place with a 63-99 record in 1992, the most losses by a Dodger team since 1908. Strawberry and Davis must get healthy. Even so, the chemistry just doesn't seem right for Tommy Lasorda's club to contend in this difficult division.

LOS ANGELES DODGERS 1993 ROSTER

MANAGER Tom Lasorda

Coaches—Joe Amalfitano, Mark Cresse, Joe Ferguson, Ben Hines, Manny Mota, Ron Perranoski, Ron Roenicke

PITCHERS

No.	Name	1992 Club	W-L	IP	SO	ERA	B-T	Ht.	Wt.	Born
56	Astacio, Pedro	Albuquerque	6-6	99	66	5.47	R-R	6-2	174	11/28/69 Dominican Republic
		Los Angeles	5-5	82	43	1.98				
—	Bustillos, Albert	San Antonio	1-0	13	9	0.69	R-R	6-1	233	4/8/68 San Jose, CA
		Albuquerque	1-2	38	23	4.78				
49	Candiotti, Tom	Los Angeles	11-15	204	152	3.00	R-R	6-2	210	8/31/57 Walnut Creek, CA
—	Daspit, James	Vero Beach	6-12	149	109	3.44	R-R	6-7	210	8/10/69 Tacoma, WA
—	Delahoya, Javier	Vero Beach	4-5	80	92	2.81	R-R	6-0	162	2/21/70 Mexico
		San Antonio	2-1	25	24	2.84				
35	Gott, Jim	Los Angeles	3-3	88	75	2.45	R-R	6-4	229	8/3/59 Hollywood, CA
46	Gross, Kevin	Los Angeles	8-13	205	158	3.17	R-R	6-5	215	6/8/61 Downey, CA
57	Gross, Kip	Albuquerque	6-5	108	58	3.51	R-R	6-2	194	8/24/64 Scottsbluff, NE
		Los Angeles	1-1	24	14	4.18				
—	Hansell, Greg	San Antonio	6-4	92	66	2.83	R-R	6-5	213	3/12/71 Bellflower, CA
		Albuquerque	1-5	69	38	5.24				
55	Hershiser, Orel	Los Angeles	10-15	211	130	3.67	R-R	6-3	192	9/16/58 Buffalo, NY
59	James, Mike	Albuquerque	2-1	47	33	5.59	R-R	6-3	182	8/15/67 Ft. Walton, FL
		San Antonio	2-1	54	52	2.67				
45	Martinez, Pedro	Albuquerque	7-6	125	124	3.81	R-R	5-11	152	7/25/71 Dominican Republic
		Los Angeles	0-1	8	8	2.25				
48	Martinez, Ramon	Los Angeles	8-11	151	101	4.00	L-R	6-5	171	3/22/68 Dominican Republic
31	McDowell, Roger	Los Angeles	6-10	84	50	4.09	R-R	6-1	182	12/21/60 Cincinnati, OH
—	Nichting, Chris	San Antonio	4-5	79	81	2.52	R-R	6-1	205	5/13/66 Cincinnati, OH
		Albuquerque	1-3	42	25	7.93				
38	Wilson, Steve	Los Angeles	2-5	67	54	4.19	L-L	6-4	224	12/13/64 Canada
—	Worrell, Todd	St. Louis	5-3	64	64	2.11	R-R	6-5	222	9/28/59 Arcadia, CA

CATCHERS

No.	Name	1992 Club	H	HR	RBI	Pct.	B-T	Ht.	Wt.	Born
61	Baar, Bryan	Albuquerque	19	1	11	.257	R-R	6-3	218	4/10/68 Zeeland, MI
		San Antonio	18	3	11	.137				
41	Hernandez, Carlos	Los Angeles	45	3	17	.260	R-R	5-11	218	5/24/67 Venezuela
25	Piazza, Mike	San Antonio	43	7	20	.377	R-R	6-3	200	9/4/68 Norristown, PA
		Albuquerque	122	16	69	.341				
		Los Angeles	16	1	7	.232				
65	Wakamatsu, Don	Albuquerque	54	2	15	.323	R-R	6-2	200	2/22/63 Hood River, OR

INFIELDERS

No.	Name	1992 Club	H	HR	RBI	Pct.	B-T	Ht.	Wt.	Born
28	Bournigal, Rafael	Albuquerque	128	0	34	.324	R-R	5-11	165	5/12/66 Dominican Republic
		Los Angeles	3	0	0	.150				
—	Busch, Mike	San Antonio	99	18	51	.238	R-R	6-5	241	7/7/68 Davenport, IA
15	Hansen, Dave	Los Angeles	73	6	22	.214	L-R	6-0	195	11/24/68 Long Beach, CA
29	Harris, Lenny	Los Angeles	94	0	30	.271	L-R	5-10	220	10/28/64 Miami, FL
23	Karros, Eric	Los Angeles	140	20	88	.257	R-R	6-4	205	11/4/67 Hackensack, NJ
30	Offerman, Jose	Los Angeles	139	1	30	.260	S-R	6-0	160	11/8/68 Dominican Republic
—	Pye, Eddie	Albuquerque	67	1	25	.302	R-R	5-10	175	2/13/67 Columbia, TN
3	Reed, Jody	Boston	136	3	40	.247	R-R	5-9	165	7/26/62 Tampa, FL
27	Sharperson, Mike	Los Angeles	95	3	36	.300	R-R	6-3	190	10/4/61 Orangeburg, SC
—	Wallach, Tim	Montreal	120	9	59	.223	R-R	6-3	202	9/14/57 Huntington Park, CA

OUTFIELDERS

No.	Name	1992 Club	H	HR	RBI	Pct.	B-T	Ht.	Wt.	Born
7	Ashley, Billy	San Antonio	106	24	66	.279	R-R	6-7	220	7/11/70 Taylor, MI
		Albuquerque	20	2	10	.211				
		Los Angeles	21	2	6	.221				
22	Butler, Brett	Los Angeles	171	3	39	.309	L-L	5-10	160	6/15/57 Los Angeles, CA
33	Davis, Eric	Los Angeles	61	5	32	.228	R-R	6-3	185	5/29/62 Los Angeles, CA
47	Goodwin, Tom	Albuquerque	96	2	28	.301	L-R	6-1	170	7/27/68 Fresno, CA
		Los Angeles	17	0	3	.233				
43	Mondesi, Raul	Albuquerque	43	4	15	.312	R-R	5-11	175	3/12/71 Dominican Republic
		San Antonio	18	2	14	.265				
26	Rodriguez, Henry	Albuquerque	111	14	72	.304	L-L	6-1	200	11/8/67 Dominican Republic
		Los Angeles	32	3	14	.219				
—	Snyder, Cory	San Francisco	105	14	57	.269	R-R	6-3	206	11/11/62 Inglewood, CA
44	Strawberry, Darryl	Los Angeles	37	5	25	.237	L-L	6-6	200	3/12/62 Los Angeles, CA
20	Webster, Mitch	Los Angeles	70	6	35	.267	S-R	6-1	185	5/16/59 Lerned, KS

DODGER PROFILES

DARRYL STRAWBERRY 31 6-6 200 Bats L Throws L

So far, it's been all talk and little action for right fielder . . . Played in just 43 games and had only 156 at-bats because of back problems in 1992 . . . His average, homer total and RBI total were lowest numbers of his career . . . Finally underwent back surgery Sept. 15 . . . Signed five-year, $20.25-million contract as free agent prior to 1991 season . . . Dodgers brought him in to be a leader on and off the field and he hasn't lived up to those expectations . . . Much too talented a player for such little production . . . In 1991, he finished seventh in NL in homers and ninth in RBI . . . That year, shoulder injury limited his first-half production . . . Vulnerable to high, inside heat—and that's why he struck out 34 times last year and 125 times two seasons ago . . . Left Mets as their all-time leader in home runs (252), RBI (733), extra-base hits (469) and runs (662) . . . Born March 12, 1962, in Los Angeles . . . Mets made him first player chosen in 1980 draft . . . Earned $4,050,000 last season.

Year	Club	Pos.	G	AB	R	H	2B	3B	HR	RBI	SB	Avg.
1983	New York (NL)	OF	122	420	63	108	15	7	26	74	19	.257
1984	New York (NL)	OF	147	522	75	131	27	4	26	97	27	.251
1985	New York (NL)	OF	111	393	78	109	15	4	29	79	26	.277
1986	New York (NL)	OF	136	475	76	123	27	5	27	93	28	.259
1987	New York (NL)	OF	154	532	108	151	32	5	39	104	36	.284
1988	New York (NL)	OF	153	543	101	146	27	3	39	101	29	.269
1989	New York (NL)	OF	134	476	69	107	26	1	29	77	11	.225
1990	New York (NL)	OF	152	542	92	150	18	1	37	108	15	.277
1991	Los Angeles . . .	OF	139	505	86	134	22	4	28	99	10	.265
1992	Los Angeles . . .	OF	43	156	20	37	8	0	5	25	3	.237
	Totals		1291	4564	768	1196	217	34	285	857	204	.262

ERIC KARROS 25 6-4 205 Bats R Throws R

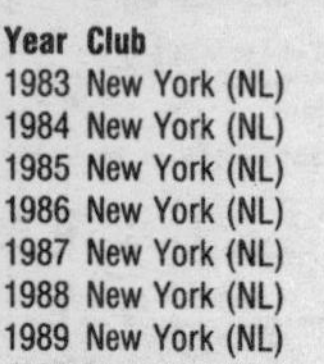

Dodgers finally gave him a chance to play and he ran away with NL Rookie of the Year honors . . . Should have been in starting lineup two years ago . . . First baseman is developing into one of best young power hitters in game . . . No Dodger rookie has hit more homers since Frank Howard blasted 25 in 1960 . . . Born Nov. 4, 1967, in Hackensack, N.J. . . . Played at UCLA, where he earned All-American honors after joining the club as walk-on . . . Earned $124,000 last season . . . Has personality and power to make it big in City of Angels.

Year	Club	Pos.	G	AB	R	H	2B	3B	HR	RBI	SB	Avg.
1991	Los Angeles . . .	1B	14	14	0	1	1	0	0	1	0	.071
1992	Los Angeles . . .	1B	149	545	63	140	30	1	20	88	2	.257
	Totals		163	559	63	141	31	1	20	89	2	.252

CORY SNYDER 30 6-3 206 **Bats R Throws R**

Came back from the baseball dead to have solid season and capped it when, as Giant free agent, he signed with Dodgers in December. . . . Made the team in spring training as non-roster invitee and received bargain-basement salary of $135,000 . . . Giants were his fourth organization in two years . . . His 434-foot homer off Craig Lefferts June 26 enabled Giants from tying a dubious NL record by being shutout three straight times . . . Became only ninth player to reach the left-field loge seats at Jack Murphy Stadium with that blast . . . Named NL Player of the Month for June after hitting .372 with five homers and 24 RBI . . . Right fielder has played every position but pitcher and catcher . . . Indians traded him to the White Sox prior to the 1991 season and then he was dealt to Blue Jays, who released him after the season . . . Born Nov. 11, 1962, in Inglewood, Cal. . . . Indians made him fourth selection overall in 1984 draft.

Year	Club	Pos.	G	AB	R	H	2B	3B	HR	RBI	SB	Avg.
1986	Cleveland	OF-SS-3B	103	416	58	113	21	1	24	69	2	.272
1987	Cleveland	OF-SS	157	577	74	136	24	2	33	82	5	.236
1988	Cleveland	OF	142	511	71	139	24	3	26	75	5	.272
1989	Cleveland	OF-SS	132	489	49	105	17	0	18	59	6	.215
1990	Cleveland	OF-SS	123	438	46	102	27	3	14	55	1	.233
1991	Chi (AL)-Tor. . .	OF-1B-3B	71	166	14	29	4	1	3	17	0	.175
1992	San Francisco	OF-INF	124	390	48	105	22	2	14	57	4	.269
	Totals		852	2987	360	729	139	12	132	414	23	.244

BRETT BUTLER 35 5-10 160 **Bats L Throws L**

Center fielder finished strong and wound up leading club in batting average and finishing eighth in NL . . . Moved to second in the order and did much better in that slot . . . Finished fourth in NL in triples, third in walks (95), third in on-base percentage (.413), seventh in stolen bases . . . Was caught stealing 21 times, second-most times in NL . . . Led NL in sacrifice bunts with 24 . . . Third-hardest hitter in league to double up, he grounded into DP once per 138.3 at-bats . . . Also among NL leaders in triples and multi-hit games (53) . . . For first time in five years, he did not score 100 runs . . . Dodger dropsies even got to him . . . After not committing an error since Sept. 6, 1990, he made two last season . . . Ex-Giant signed three-year, $10-million contract as new-look free agent prior to 1991 season . . . Earned $3,333,333 last season . . . Born June 15, 1957, in Los Angeles . . . Traded by Braves to Indians with Brook Jacoby and Rick Behenna for Len Barker after 1983 season . . . Atlanta's 23rd-round pick in 1979 draft.

Year	Club	Pos.	G	AB	R	H	2B	3B	HR	RBI	SB	Avg.
1981	Atlanta.	OF	40	126	17	32	2	3	0	4	9	.254
1982	Atlanta.	OF	89	240	35	52	2	0	0	7	21	.217
1983	Atlanta.	OF	151	549	84	154	21	13	5	37	39	.281
1984	Cleveland	OF	159	602	108	162	25	9	3	49	52	.269
1985	Cleveland	OF	152	591	106	184	28	14	5	50	47	.311
1986	Cleveland	OF	161	587	92	163	17	14	4	51	32	.278
1987	Cleveland	OF	137	522	91	154	25	8	9	41	33	.295
1988	San Francisco	OF	157	568	109	163	27	9	6	43	43	.287
1989	San Francisco	OF	154	594	100	168	22	4	4	36	31	.283
1990	San Francisco	OF	160	622	108	192	20	9	3	44	51	.309
1991	Los Angeles . . .	OF	161	615	112	182	13	5	2	38	38	.296
1992	Los Angeles . . .	OF	157	553	86	171	14	11	3	39	41	.309
	Totals		1678	6169	1048	1777	216	99	44	439	437	.288

MIKE SHARPERSON 31 6-3 190 Bats R Throws R

Only other Dodger besides Brett Butler to finish at .300 . . . Highlight of his career was being named to All-Star team . . . Dodgers' season got so far out of hand, their only All-Star made just 24 starts over second half . . . After the team collapsed, rookie second baseman Eric Young got most of starts . . . Born Oct. 4, 1961, in Orangeburg, S.C. . . . Acquired from Blue Jays for Juan Guzman, Sept. 21, 1987 . . . No matter what he does, this figures to rank as one of Dodgers' worst all-time trades . . . Blue Jays chose him in secondary phase of 1981 draft . . . Earned $587,500 last season.

Year	Club	Pos.	G	AB	R	H	2B	3B	HR	RBI	SB	Avg.
1987	Toronto	2B	32	96	4	20	4	1	0	9	2	.208
1987	Los Angeles . . .	3B–2B	10	33	7	9	2	0	0	1	0	.273
1988	Los Angeles . . .	2B-3B-SS	46	59	8	16	1	0	0	4	0	.271
1989	Los Angeles . . .	INF	27	28	2	7	3	0	0	5	0	.250
1990	Los Angeles . . .	INF	129	357	42	106	14	2	3	36	15	.297
1991	Los Angeles . . .	INF	105	216	24	60	11	2	2	20	1	.278
1992	Los Angeles . . .	2B-3B-SS	128	317	48	95	21	0	3	36	2	.300
	Totals		477	1106	135	313	56	5	8	111	20	.283

ERIC DAVIS 30 6-3 185 Bats R Throws R

Baseball's version of expensive china . . . Beautiful to look at, but shatters easily . . . Reds became exasperated with outfielder's injury woes and Dodgers went through same problems last season . . . Because of a variety of injuries, he played in just 76 games last season (even Kal Daniels played in more) and in only 89 games in 1991 . . . Was on disabled list twice and did not play after Sept. 5 . . . Underwent right wrist and left shoulder surgery two weeks later . . . When healthy, he plays hard . . . Dodgers thought they were going to win NL West after acquiring him from Reds with Kip Gross for Tim Belcher and John Wetteland prior to last season . . . Like his buddy Darryl Strawberry, he posted lowest numbers of his career in 1992 . . . Led Reds in RBI with 86 in 1990, but has totaled just 65 the last two years . . . Home runs have dropped from 24 to 11 to 5 over last three years . . . Reds' eighth-round pick in 1980 draft . . . Born May 29, 1962, in Los Angeles . . . Earned $3,600,000 in 1992, declared free agency and re-signed for one year at $1 million.

Year	Club	Pos.	G	AB	R	H	2B	3B	HR	RBI	SB	Avg.
1984	Cincinnati	OF	57	174	33	39	10	1	10	30	10	.224
1985	Cincinnati	OF	56	122	26	30	3	3	8	18	16	.246
1986	Cincinnati	OF	132	415	97	115	15	3	27	71	80	.277
1987	Cincinnati	OF	129	474	120	139	23	4	37	100	50	.293
1988	Cincinnati	OF	135	472	81	129	18	3	26	93	35	.273
1989	Cincinnati	OF	131	462	74	130	14	2	34	101	21	.281
1990	Cincinnati	OF	127	453	84	118	26	2	24	86	21	.260
1991	Cincinnati	OF	89	285	39	67	10	0	11	33	14	.235
1992	Los Angeles . . .	OF	76	267	21	61	8	1	5	32	19	.228
	Totals		932	3124	575	828	127	19	182	564	266	.265

JOSE OFFERMAN 24 6-0 160 Bats S Throws R

Perhaps the Dodgers misjudged this shortstop and he will never be as good in the field as they expected . . . Committed a major league-high 42 errors. As a team, Cardinals only committed 94 and they had 6,311 total chances . . . Has never learned how to read the catcher's signs and position himself . . . If he continues to self-destruct at short, he may be moved to outfield

. . . Hitting was better than expected after he batted .195 in 1991 . . . Born Nov. 8, 1968, in San Pedro de Macoris, D.R. . . . Signed as a free agent by Dodgers in July 1986 . . . Earned $135,000 last season . . . Named the *Sporting News'* Minor League Player of the Year in 1990 and had been tabbed best shortstop prospect by *Baseball America* from 1989-91 . . . Hard to believe.

Year	Club	Pos.	G	AB	R	H	2B	3B	HR	RBI	SB	Avg.
1990	Los Angeles . . .	SS	29	58	7	9	0	0	1	7	1	.155
1991	Los Angeles . . .	SS	52	113	10	22	2	0	0	3	3	.195
1992	Los Angeles . . .	SS	149	534	67	139	20	8	1	30	23	.260
	Totals		230	705	84	170	22	8	2	40	27	.241

JODY REED 30 5-9 165 Bats R Throws R

Red Sox' veteran was picked fifth by Rockies in expansion draft, then traded to Dodgers for Rudy Seanez . . . Must search for answers after disappointing season . . . Batted 41 points below lifetime mark at beginning of 1992 . . . Was tried at four different positions in order and didn't respond well to any of them . . . Still a good contact man . . . Was ninth-toughest in AL to strike out, fanning once per 14.2 at-bats . . . Solid second baseman who ranks among leaders at the position in fielding percentage, assists, putouts and total chances . . . Born July 26, 1962, in Tampa . . . Red Sox' eighth-round pick in 1984 draft . . . Holds criminology degree from Florida State . . . Earned $1.6 million in 1992.

Year	Club	Pos.	G	AB	R	H	2B	3B	HR	RBI	SB	Avg.
1987	Boston	SS-2B-3B	9	30	4	9	1	1	0	8	1	.300
1988	Boston	SS-2B-3B	109	338	60	99	23	1	1	28	1	.293
1989	Boston	SS-2B-3B-OF	146	524	76	151	42	2	3	40	4	.288
1990	Boston	2B-SS	155	598	70	173	45	0	5	51	4	.289
1991	Boston	2B	153	618	87	175	42	2	5	60	6	.283
1992	Boston	2B	143	550	64	136	27	1	3	40	7	.247
	Totals		715	2658	361	743	180	7	17	227	23	.280

RAMON MARTINEZ 25 6-5 171 Bats R Throws R

Elbow problems caused him to shut it down the last month of last season . . . Enters 1993 as a major question mark . . . Started 1991 by going 15-6, but is just 10-18 from that point . . . Part of the reason for his struggles is biceps injury, suffered Aug. 20, 1991 after being hit by a line drive off bat of Padres' Jack Howell . . . Bad mechanics may have caught up with him . . .

His fastball didn't have enough zip and he has never mastered the curve . . . On June 4, 1990, he tied Sandy Koufax' all-time Dodger single-game strikeout record with 18 . . . In 1990, he also became youngest Dodger to win 20 since Ralph Branca won 21 at 21 in 1947 . . . Dodgers have to hope that his star hasn't burned out . . . Born March 22, 1968, in Santo Domingo, D.R. . . . Signed as a free agent at 16 . . . Earned $725,000 last season.

Year	Club	G	IP	W	L	Pct.	SO	BB	H	ERA
1988	Los Angeles.	9	35⅔	1	3	.250	23	22	27	3.79
1989	Los Angeles.	15	98⅔	6	4	.600	89	41	79	3.19
1990	Los Angeles.	33	234⅓	20	6	.769	223	67	191	2.92
1991	Los Angeles.	33	220⅓	17	13	.567	150	69	190	3.27
1992	Los Angeles.	25	150⅔	8	11	.421	101	69	141	4.00
	Totals.	115	739⅔	52	37	.584	586	268	628	3.32

TODD WORRELL 33 6-5 222 Bats R Throws R

Cardinal free agent landed three-year, $9.5-million contract with Dodgers in December . . . Comeback Pitcher of the Year in 1992, rebounding from two years of inactivity and two arm operations . . . Returned to bullpen and gave up runs in just eight of 67 relief appearances . . . Played second fiddle to Lee Smith, but still finished 14 games and saved three . . . Became Cards' all-time saves leader with 129, passing Bruce Sutter (127) . . . Picked up record 128th save Sept. 5 against Giants . . . Yielded just one run during 22-inning stretch in July and August . . . Whiffed 50 batters in first 49 innings . . . Eighteen of first 19 outings were scoreless . . . Beat Dodgers April 28 for first big league victory since 1989 . . . Born Sept. 28, 1959, in Arcadia, Cal. . . . Cardinals' first draft choice in 1982 . . . Named 1986 NL Rookie of the Year while leading league with 36 saves . . . Sat out all of 1990 following elbow surgery . . . Underwent rotator cuff surgery in July 1991 . . . Earned $600,000 in 1992.

Year	Club	G	IP	W	L	Pct.	SO	BB	H	ERA
1985	St. Louis.	17	21⅔	3	0	1.000	17	7	17	2.91
1986	St. Louis.	74	103⅔	9	10	.474	73	41	86	2.08
1987	St. Louis.	75	94⅔	8	6	.571	92	34	86	2.66
1988	St. Louis.	68	90	5	9	.357	78	34	69	3.00
1989	St. Louis.	47	51⅔	3	5	.375	41	26	42	2.96
1990	St. Louis.		Injured							
1991	St. Louis.		Injured							
1992	St. Louis.	67	64	5	3	.625	64	25	45	2.11
	Totals.	348	425⅔	33	33	.500	365	167	345	2.56

KEVIN GROSS 31 6-5 215 Bats R Throws R

Authored the one shining moment of the Dodgers' dreadful 1992 season, pitching no-hitter against the Giants Aug. 17 . . . Irony of that performance is that club feels he is best suited to be a closer . . . Wants to remain in rotation . . . Another Dodger pitcher who deserved a better fate . . . Tossed 21 quality starts, the same number as Braves' Tom Glavine. Finished ninth in NL in strikeouts . . . Born June 8, 1961, in Downey, Cal. . . . Signed as a free agent prior to 1991 season . . . Earned $2,216,667 last season . . . Phils chose him in secondary phase of 1981 draft . . . Traded to Montreal for Floyd Youmans and Jeff Parrett prior to 1989 season.

Year	Club	G	IP	W	L	Pct.	SO	BB	H	ERA
1983	Philadelphia	17	96	4	6	.400	66	35	100	3.56
1984	Philadelphia	44	129	8	5	.615	84	44	140	4.12
1985	Philadelphia	38	205⅔	15	13	.536	151	81	194	3.41
1986	Philadelphia	37	241⅔	12	12	.500	154	94	240	4.02
1987	Philadelphia	34	200⅔	9	16	.360	110	87	205	4.35
1988	Philadelphia	33	231⅔	12	14	.462	162	89	209	3.69
1989	Montreal	31	201⅓	11	12	.478	158	88	188	4.38
1990	Montreal	31	163⅓	9	12	.429	111	65	171	4.57
1991	Los Angeles	46	115⅔	10	11	.476	95	50	123	3.58
1992	Los Angeles	34	204⅔	8	13	.381	158	77	182	3.17
	Totals	345	1789⅔	98	114	.462	1249	710	1752	3.89

TOM CANDIOTTI 35 6-2 210 Bats R Throws R

No pitcher appeared more frustrated by Dodgers' horrible defense than this knuckleballer . . . After finishing second in AL with 2.65 ERA in 1991, his mark jumped to 3.00 last year . . . No one in NL lost more games than his 15 . . . Finished 10th in NL in strikeouts . . . Will give you innings . . . Has pitched 200 or more innings the past seven seasons . . . Not an ace, but he is a solid starter . . . Free agent was signed to four-year contract worth $15.5 million before last season . . . Acquired by Blue Jays from Indians with Turner Ward for Mark Whiten, Glenallen Hill and Denis Boucher, June 27, 1991 . . . Was not drafted out of St. Mary's College in 1979 . . . Took him four-plus minor league seasons to get shot with Brewers . . . Career took off after working with Phil Niekro on knuckler with Indians in 1986 . . . Born Aug. 31, 1957, in Walnut Creek, Cal.

Year	Club	G	IP	W	L	Pct.	SO	BB	H	ERA
1983	Milwaukee..........	10	55⅔	4	4	.500	21	16	62	3.23
1984	Milwaukee..........	8	32⅓	2	2	.500	23	10	38	5.29
1986	Cleveland	36	252⅓	16	12	.571	167	106	234	3.57
1987	Cleveland	32	201⅔	7	18	.280	111	93	193	4.78
1988	Cleveland	31	216⅔	14	8	.636	137	53	225	3.28
1989	Cleveland	31	206	13	10	.565	124	55	188	3.10
1990	Cleveland	31	202	15	11	.577	128	55	207	3.65
1991	Clev.-Tor.	34	238	13	13	.500	167	73	202	2.65
1992	Los Angeles.........	32	203⅔	11	15	.423	152	63	177	3.00
	Totals............	245	1608⅓	95	93	.505	1030	524	1526	3.45

OREL HERSHISER 34 6-3 192 Bats R Throws R

His greatest triumph wasn't winning Cy Young in 1988, it was coming back from revolutionary 1990 shoulder surgery . . . Still learning a different style of pitching . . . After fighting back to 7-2 mark in 1991, he went 10-15 last season, tying teammate Tom Candiotti for most losses in NL . . . Only ex-Dodger Tim Belcher allowed more runs than his 101 . . . Only 86 of those runs were earned . . . His 209 hits allowed were 10th-most in NL . . . Was named NLCS and World Series MVP in 1988 . . . Born Sept. 16, 1958, in Buffalo, N.Y. . . . Dodgers' 17th-round selection in 1979 draft . . . Earned $3,333,333 last season.

Year	Club	G	IP	W	L	Pct.	SO	BB	H	ERA
1983	Los Angeles........	8	8	0	0	.000	5	6	7	3.38
1984	Los Angeles........	45	189⅔	11	8	.579	150	50	160	2.66
1985	Los Angeles........	36	239⅔	19	3	.864	157	68	179	2.03
1986	Los Angeles........	35	231⅓	14	14	.500	153	86	213	3.85
1987	Los Angeles........	37	264⅔	16	16	.500	190	74	247	3.06
1988	Los Angeles........	35	267	23	8	.742	178	73	208	2.26
1989	Los Angeles........	35	256⅔	15	15	.500	178	77	226	2.31
1990	Los Angeles........	4	25⅓	1	1	.500	16	4	26	4.26
1991	Los Angeles........	21	112	7	2	.778	73	32	112	3.46
1992	Los Angeles........	33	210⅔	10	15	.400	130	69	209	3.67
	Totals............	289	1805	116	82	.586	1230	539	1587	2.87

TOP PROSPECTS

PEDRO ASTACIO 23 6-2 174 Bats R Throws R

Went 5-5 with 1.98 ERA in 11 starts for Dodgers in second half of 1992 and will move right into rotation . . . Of his wins, four were shutouts . . . Allowed only 18 earned runs in 82 innings . . . His numbers look terrific, but he needs to go around the league a couple times before we get an accurate reading . . . For Albuquerque (AAA), he was only 6-6 with a 5.47 ERA . . . Born Nov. 28, 1969, in Hato Mayor, D.R. . . . Signed as a free agent in November 1987.

PEDRO MARTINEZ 21 5-11 152 Bats R Throws R

Ramon's little brother appeared in just two games with the Dodgers and had 0-1 mark with 2.25 ERA . . . Struck out eight batters in eight innings . . . Underwent postseason reconstructive surgery on non-pitching shoulder . . . Had some right shoulder problems during regular season, which caused him to miss six weeks . . . Put together 7-6 mark with 3.81 ERA for Albuquerque (AAA), where he struck out 124 in 125 innings . . . Signed as a free agent in June 1988 . . . Born July 25, 1971, in Manoguayabo, D.R.

BILLY ASHLEY 22 6-7 220 Bats R Throws R

Outfielder was late-season callup and hit two homers, drove in six runs and batted .221 over 95 at-bats with Dodgers . . . Has to make better contact as he struck out 34 times . . . No Dodger has hit the ball as far in BP since days of Frank Howard . . . In 101 games for San Antonio (AA), he hit .279 and led organization with 24 homers . . . Had 110 strikeouts in 380 at-bats . . . For Albuquerque (AAA), he hit just .211 with 42 strikeouts in 95 at-bats . . . Was on disabled list three times in 1991, slowing his progress . . . Born July 11, 1970, in Taylor, Mich. . . . Dodgers' third-round selection in 1988 draft.

MIKE PIAZZA 24 6-3 200 Bats R Throws R

Catcher is moving up the ladder and not just because Tommy Lasorda is his godfather . . . Late-season call-up batted .232 with one homer and seven RBI in 69 at-bats for Dodgers . . . Started season at San Antonio (AA), where he batted .377 with seven homers and 20 RBI in 31 games . . . Batted .341 with 16 homers and 69 RBI over 91 games at Albuquerque (AAA) . . . Born Sept. 4, 1968, in Norristown, Pa. . . . Dodgers' 62nd-round selection in 1988 draft.

RAUL MONDESI 22 5-11 175 Bats R Throws R

Center fielder of the future . . . Owns excellent arm . . . Suffered wrist and knee injuries last season and had to undergo surgery . . . Has to learn to control his temper . . . In 35 games for Albuquerque (AAA), he hit .312 with four homers and 15 RBI . . . Was demoted to San Antonio because of disciplinary problems and played just 18 games there, hitting .265 . . . Born March 12, 1971, in San Cristobal, D.R. . . . Signed as a free agent in June 1988.

MANAGER TOM LASORDA: Even the greatest baseball salesman in the world had a tough time keeping a positive attitude through embarrassing mess of 1992 season . . . Suffered through a miserable 63-99 last-place finish, worst in his career and worst mark in majors last season . . . Has won six division titles, three pennants and two World Series since replacing Walter Alston 16 years ago . . . Coming to the end of the line as manager, because Bill Russell is being groomed to replace him. This will probably be his last year . . . Managerial record is 1,339-1,199 . . . Not only bleeds Dodger Blue, bleeds Dodger Green, too. This is his 44th year on Dodger payroll . . . Had short-lived major league career as left-handed pitcher (1954-55 with Dodgers and 1955 with Kansas City) as he appeared in 26 games and had 0-4 record . . . If you get to the park early enough, you can still catch him throwing batting practice . . . Born Sept. 22, 1927, in Norristown, Pa. . . . Walking into his office at Dodger Stadium is like walking into a photo gallery of the rich and famous.

ALL-TIME DODGER SEASON RECORDS

BATTING: Babe Herman, .393, 1930
HRs: Duke Snider, 43, 1956
RBI: Tommy Davis, 153, 1962
STEALS: Maury Wills, 104, 1962
WINS: Joe McGinnity, 29, 1900
STRIKEOUTS: Sandy Koufax, 382, 1965

SAN DIEGO PADRES

TEAM DIRECTORY: Chairman: Tom Werner; Vice Chairmen: Russell Goldsmith, Art Engel, Art Rivkin; Pres.: Dick Freeman; Exec. VP/GM: Joe McIlvaine; Dir. Minor Leagues: Ed Lynch; Dir. Scouting: Reggie Waller; Dir. Media Rel.: Jim Ferguson; Trav. Sec.: John Mattei; Mgr.: Jim Riggleman. Home: San Diego Jack Murphy Stadium (59,700). Field distances: 327, l.f. line; 405, c.f.; 327, r.f. line. Spring training: Yuma, Ariz.

SCOUTING REPORT

HITTING: Despite all their problems, the Padres still have three of the best hitters in baseball. Gary Sheffield (.330, 33, 100) is coming off a staggering year, winning the batting title in his first NL season. Fred McGriff (.286, 35, 104) is the best pure home-run hitter in the majors and four-time batting champ Tony Gwynn (.317, 6, 41) always hits .300.

That nuclear core enabled the Padres to finish third in the league in hitting at .255 and second in home runs with 135, only three back of the Braves. Six other teams, though, scored more runs than the Padres' 617. With the loss of Bip Roberts and Tony Fernandez, the Padres are hurting for table-setters.

Darrin Jackson (.249, 17, 70), who has hit 38 homers the last two seasons, will probably leadoff and left-handed-hitting Phil Plantier (.246, 7, 30 with the Red Sox) will bat behind McGriff. Catcher Dan Walters (.251, 4, 22) will have to take over Benito Santiago's role. Infielder Kurt Stillwell (.227, 2, 24) is coming off an embarrassing season and second base is wide open.

PITCHING: This could get ugly. GM Joe McIlvaine came to the Padres with the reputation of being able to build a great pitching staff, but so far all he has done is weaken the Padres' pitching, which finished eighth in the league in ERA at 3.56 in 1992.

A replacement is needed for Randy Myers, who saved a career-high 38 games, then left as a free agent. Youngster Jeremy Hernandez (1-4, 4.17) will be given the chance to win the job. Newcomers like ex-Met Wally Whitehurst (3-9, 3.62) and ex-Pirate Roger Mason (5-7, 4.09, 8 saves) aren't closers.

Among the starters, emerging star Andy Benes (13-14, 3.35) will win 20 if he gets offensive help. Greg Harris (4-8, 4.12) is coming off his second straight disappointing season and Bruce Hurst (14-9, 3.85), the Padres' top starter the last four seasons

Gary Sheffield just missed triple crown in Padre debut.

and a double-figure winner in each of the last 10 seasons, is coming off shoulder surgery. This staff is too inexperienced to succeed.

FIELDING: This is the year the Padres find out how valuable the four-time All-Star catcher Santiago was to their defense. Santiago did not allow a passed ball last season and the threat of his golden arm kept opponents from running.

The Padres will have a different catcher, second baseman and shortstop in '93, leaving major questions about their up-the-middle defense. Stillwell couldn't play second and now he's at short. At second, the Roberto Alomar trade continues to haunt this team. Only three teams finished with a better fielding percentage than the Padres' .982 last season, but that will change.

OUTLOOK: Jim Riggleman should have been made the manager at the start of last season, but Greg Riddoch wasted all that talent and was fired as the Padres finished a mediocre 82-80. This team has been diluted by ownership's lack of commitment to winning and some bad trades by McIlvaine. Instead of contending, the Padres will be lucky to finish fourth.

SAN DIEGO PADRES 1993 ROSTER

MANAGER Jim Rigglemann
Coaches—Bruce Bochy, Rob Picciolo, Dan Radison, Merv Rettenmund, Mike Roarke

PITCHERS

No.	Name	1992 Club	W-L	IP	SO	ERA	B-T	Ht.	Wt.	Born
40	Benes, Andy	San Diego	13-14	231	169	3.35	R-R	6-6	240	8/20/67 Evansville, IN
49	Brocail, Doug	Las Vegas	10-10	172	103	3.97	L-R	6-5	220	5/16/67 Clearfield, PA
		San Diego	0-0	14	15	6.43				
39	Bross, Terry	Las Vegas	7-3	86	42	3.26	R-R	6-9	230	3/30/66 El Paso, TX
—	Gomez, Pat	Greenville	7-0	48	38	1.13	L-L	5-11	185	3/17/68 Roseville, TX
		Richmond	3-5	71	48	5.45				
33	Harris, Gene	Seattle	0-0	9	6	7.00	R-R	5-11	190	12/5/64 Sebring, FL
		Las Vegas	0-2	34	35	3.67				
		San Diego	0-2	21	19	2.95				
46	Harris, Greg	High Desert	0-0	5	5	0.00	R-R	6-2	187	12/1/63 Greensboro, NC
		Las Vegas	2-0	16	15	0.56				
		San Diego	4-8	118	66	4.12				
50	Hernandez, Jeremy	Las Vegas	2-4	56	38	2.91	R-R	6-5	195	7/6/66 Burbank, CA
		San Diego	1-4	37	25	4.17				
47	Hurst, Bruce	San Diego	14-9	217	131	3.85	L-L	6-3	215	3/24/58 St. George, UT
—	Mason, Roger	Pittsburgh	5-7	88	56	4.09	R-R	6-6	220	9/18/58 Bellaire, MI
42	Rodriguez, Rich	San Diego	6-3	91	64	2.37	R-L	6-0	200	3/1/63 Downey, CA
27	Sanders, Scott	Wichita	7-5	88	95	3.49	R-R	6-4	210	3/25/69 Thibodaux, LA
		Las Vegas	3-6	72	51	5.50				
52	Schullstrom, Erik	Hagerstown	5-9	127	128	3.61	R-R	6-5	220	3/25/69 San Diego, CA
		Las Vegas	1-0	5	6	0.00				
54	Scott, Tim	Las Vegas	1-2	28	28	2.25	R-R	6-2	205	11/16/66 Hanford, CA
		San Diego	4-1	38	30	5.26				
44	Seminara, Frank	Las Vegas	6-4	81	48	4.13	R-R	6-2	205	5/15/67 Brooklyn, NY
		San Diego	9-4	100	61	3.68				
41	Whitehurst, Wally	New York (NL)	3-9	97	70	3.62	R-R	6-3	185	4/11/64 Shreveport, LA
58	Worrell, Tim	Wichita	8-6	126	109	2.86	R-R	6-2	200	7/5/67 Arcadia, CA
		Las Vegas	4-2	63	32	4.26				

CATCHERS

No.	Name	1992 Club	H	HR	RBI	Pct.	B-T	Ht.	Wt.	Born
55	Johnson, Brian	Wichita	71	3	26	.290	R-R	6-2	195	1/8/68 Oakland, CA
25	Lampkin, Tom	Las Vegas	104	3	48	.306	L-R	5-11	185	3/4/64 Cincinnati, OH
		San Diego	4	0	0	.235				
11	Walters, Dan	Las Vegas	50	2	25	.394	R-R	6-4	230	8/15/66 Brunswick, ME
		San Diego	45	4	22	.251				

INFIELDERS

No.	Name	1992 Club	H	HR	RBI	Pct.	B-T	Ht.	Wt.	Born
23	Faries, Paul	Las Vegas	134	1	40	.293	R-R	5-10	170	2/20/65 Berkeley, CA
		San Diego	5	0	1	.455				
31	Gainer, Jay	Wichita	98	23	67	.261	L-L	6-0	190	10/8/66 Panama City, FL
12	Gardner, Jeff	Las Vegas	147	1	51	.335	L-R	5-11	175	2/4/64 Newport Beach, CA
		San Diego	2	0	0	.105				
7	Gutierrez, Ricky	Rochester	109	0	41	.253	R-R	6-1	175	5/23/70 Miami, FL
		Las Vegas	1	0	1	.167				
53	Holbert, Ray	Wichita	86	2	23	.283	R-R	6-0	170	9/25/70 Torrance, CA
14	Lopez, Luis	Las Vegas	92	1	31	.233	S-R	5-11	175	9/4/70 Puerto Rico
29	McGriff, Fred	San Diego	152	35	104	.286	L-L	6-3	215	10/31/63 Tampa, FL
10	Sheffield, Gary	San Diego	184	33	100	.330	R-R	5-11	190	11/18/68 Tampa, FL
18	Shipley, Craig	San Diego	26	0	7	.248	R-R	6-1	190	1/7/63 Australia
15	Stillwell, Kurt	San Diego	86	2	24	.227	S-R	5-11	175	6/4/65 Glendale, CA
20	Teufel, Tim	San Diego	55	6	25	.224	R-R	6-0	175	7/7/58 Greenwich, CT
21	Velasquez, Guillermo	Las Vegas	158	7	99	.309	L-L	6-3	225	4/23/68 Mexico
		San Diego	7	1	5	.304				

OUTFIELDERS

No.	Name	1992 Club	H	HR	RBI	Pct.	B-T	Ht.	Wt.	Born
28	Dozier, D.J.	Tidewater	42	7	25	.225	R-R	6-0	205	9/21/65 Norfolk, VA
		New York (NL)	9	0	2	.191				
19	Gwynn, Tony	San Diego	165	6	41	.317	L-L	5-11	222	5/9/60 Los Angeles, CA
4	Jackson, Darrin	San Diego	146	17	70	.249	R-R	6-0	187	8/22/63 Los Angeles, CA
9	Pegues, Steve	Las Vegas	99	9	56	.263	R-R	6-2	190	5/21/68 Pontotoc, MS
—	Plantier, Phil	Boston	86	7	30	.246	L-R	5-11	195	1/27/69 Manchester, NH
		Pawtucket	17	5	14	.425				
3	Sherman, Darrell	Wichita	73	6	25	.332	L-L	5-7	160	12/4/67 Los Angeles, CA
		Las Vegas	77	3	22	.286				
26	Staton, Dave	Las Vegas	94	19	76	.281	R-R	6-5	215	4/12/68 Seattle, WA
2	Vatcher, Jim	Las Vegas	77	8	35	.275	R-R	5-9	175	5/27/66 Santa Monica, CA
		San Diego	4	0	2	.250				

PADRE PROFILES

GARY SHEFFIELD 24 5-11 190 Bats R Throws R

Wrists of lightning enabled former Brewer to make terrific run at triple crown in first season as a Padre, but a fractured right index finger ended his quest six games short of season's end . . . Became only second Padre to win the batting title and youngest NL batting champ since Tommy Davis won at 23 in 1962 . . . Finished third in NL in homers and fifth in RBI . . . Ranked second in slugging percentage (.580) . . . Set Padres record for RBI and homers by third baseman . . . Was fifth-hardest hitter to strike out in NL, fanning just once per 15.5 plate appearances . . . Came from Brewers for Ricky Bones, Jose Valentin and Matt Mieske just before start of last season . . . Perceived as an angry young man in Milwaukee, but was model citizen in San Diego . . . Born Nov. 18, 1968, in Tampa . . . Brewers chose him sixth overall in 1986 draft . . . Made $700,000 in 1992 . . . May be more famous than his uncle, Dwight Gooden.

Year	Club	Pos.	G	AB	R	H	2B	3B	HR	RBI	SB	Avg.
1988	Milwaukee	SS	24	80	12	19	1	0	4	12	3	.238
1989	Milwaukee	SS–3B	95	368	34	91	18	0	5	32	10	.247
1990	Milwaukee	3B	125	487	67	143	30	1	10	67	25	.294
1991	Milwaukee	3B	50	175	25	34	12	2	2	22	5	.194
1992	San Diego	3B	146	557	87	184	34	3	33	100	5	.330
	Totals		440	1667	225	471	95	6	54	233	48	.283

FRED McGRIFF 29 6-3 215 Bats L Throws L

NL home-run king is most consistent power hitter in baseball . . . Became first Padre to lead league and first player in major-league history to win home-run titles in both leagues . . . Captured AL title in 1989 for Toronto . . . Crushed longest homer in majors last season, too, a 473-foot shot against Pirates Aug. 28 . . . His Will Clark-type swing has enabled him to hit 30-plus homers for five straight years, the longest streak in the majors since Mike Schmidt did it nine years in a row (1979-87) . . . First baseman was acquired from Blue Jays with Tony Fernandez for Joe Carter and Roberto Alomar in blockbuster prior to

1991 season . . . Yanks' ninth-round pick in 1981 draft has matured as a hitter and can now hit left-handers, too . . . Led Padres in RBI . . . Ranked second in NL with 96 walks . . . Born Oct. 31, 1963, in Tampa . . . Hard to believe he and Cecil Fielder once platooned with Blue Jays. The two hit 70 homers last year and have bashed 145 over last two seasons.

Year	Club	Pos.	G	AB	R	H	2B	3B	HR	RBI	SB	Avg.
1986	Toronto	1B	3	5	1	1	0	0	0	0	0	.200
1987	Toronto	1B	107	295	58	73	16	0	20	43	3	.247
1988	Toronto	1B	154	536	100	151	35	4	34	82	6	.282
1989	Toronto	1B	161	551	98	148	27	3	36	92	7	.269
1990	Toronto	1B	153	557	91	167	21	1	35	88	5	.300
1991	San Diego	1B	153	528	84	147	19	1	31	106	4	.278
1992	San Diego	1B	152	531	79	152	30	4	35	104	8	.286
	Totals		883	3003	511	839	148	13	191	515	33	.279

TONY GWYNN 32 5-11 222 — Bats L Throws L

For third straight year, his season ended prematurely . . . Played in just four innings after Sept. 8 because of knee injury . . . Had post-season surgery on the knee for second straight year . . . Finished fifth in batting with same average as 1991 . . . Some critics maintain weight is more of a problem than opposing pitchers . . . Right fielder has hit .300 or better for the past decade . . . Suffered most embarrassing injury of the year when he broke the tip of his right middle finger by slamming it in the car door of his Porsche as he rushed to the bank May 18 . . . Was hitting .369 at that point . . . Born May 9, 1960, in Los Angeles . . . Was hardest batter in the majors to strike out once again, with one per 35.6 at-bats . . . Third-round pick in 1981 draft out of San Diego State, where he starred in basketball . . . Made $2 million last year and salary will double this season.

Year	Club	Pos.	G	AB	R	H	2B	3B	HR	RBI	SB	Avg.
1982	San Diego	OF	54	190	33	55	12	2	1	17	8	.289
1983	San Diego	OF	86	304	34	94	12	2	1	37	7	.309
1984	San Diego	OF	158	606	88	213	21	10	5	71	33	.351
1985	San Diego	OF	154	622	90	197	29	5	6	46	14	.317
1986	San Diego	OF	160	642	107	211	33	7	14	59	37	.329
1987	San Diego	OF	157	589	119	218	36	13	7	54	56	.370
1988	San Diego	OF	133	521	64	163	22	5	7	70	26	.313
1989	San Diego	OF	158	604	82	203	27	7	4	62	40	.336
1990	San Diego	OF	141	573	79	177	29	10	4	72	17	.309
1991	San Diego	OF	134	530	69	168	27	11	4	62	8	.317
1992	San Diego	OF	128	520	77	165	27	3	6	41	3	.317
	Totals		1463	5701	842	1864	275	75	59	591	249	.327

DARRIN JACKSON 29 6-0 187 Bats R Throws R

Proved that 1991 wasn't a fluke by setting career highs in RBI and games played . . . One of the best defensive center fielders around, he committed just two errors in 455 total chances to rank second among NL outfielders with a .996 fielding percentage. That established a club record for outfielders . . . Led majors in assists with 18 . . . Started the year feeling the pressure and batted just .221, then started career-best 13-game hitting streak . . . Intelligent hitter, he waits for the pitcher to make a mistake and jumps on it . . . Made $805,000 last season . . . Acquired from Cubs with Calvin Schiraldi and Phil Stephenson for Luis Salazar and Marvell Wynne during 1989 season . . . Born Aug. 22, 1963, in Los Angeles . . . Has beaten testicular cancer to make it to the majors . . . Cubs chose him in the second round of 1981 draft.

Year	Club	Pos.	G	AB	R	H	2B	3B	HR	RBI	SB	Avg.
1985	Chicago (NL) . .	OF	5	11	0	1	0	0	0	0	0	.091
1987	Chicago (NL) . .	OF	7	5	2	4	1	0	0	0	0	.800
1988	Chicago (NL) . .	OF	100	188	29	50	11	3	6	20	4	.266
1989	Chi. (NL)-S.D.	OF	70	170	17	37	7	0	4	20	1	.218
1990	San Diego	OF	58	113	10	29	3	0	3	9	3	.257
1991	San Diego	OF	122	359	51	94	12	1	21	49	5	.262
1992	San Diego	OF	155	587	72	146	23	5	17	70	14	.249
	Totals		517	1433	181	361	57	9	51	168	27	.252

KURT STILLWELL 27 5-11 175 Bats S Throws R

Padres signed ex-Royal as a free agent prior to last season, expecting they had solved their second-base problems . . . Experiment did not work out and now switch-hitter will be shifted back to his original position, taking over for traded Tony Fernandez at shortstop . . . Came to team with injury-prone reputation and lived up to it by playing in just 114 games due to assorted ailments . . . Was batting .285 into June before injuries took their toll . . . Finally went on the DL Aug. 31 with back problems and saw limited action the rest of the way . . . His 24 RBI marked the first time in five years he did not reach the 50 mark . . . Born June 4, 1965, in Glendale, Cal. . . . Reds selected him in first round of 1983 draft . . . Pulled down $1.75 million last season and will make the same this year.

Year	Club	Pos.	G	AB	R	H	2B	3B	HR	RBI	SB	Avg.
1986	Cincinnati	SS	104	279	31	64	6	1	0	26	6	.229
1987	Cincinnati	SS-2B-3B	131	395	54	102	20	7	4	33	4	.258
1988	Kansas City . . .	SS	128	459	63	115	28	5	10	53	6	.251
1989	Kansas City . . .	SS	130	463	52	121	20	7	7	54	9	.261
1990	Kansas City . . .	SS	144	506	60	126	35	4	3	51	0	.249
1991	Kansas City . . .	SS	122	385	44	102	17	1	6	51	3	.265
1992	San Diego	2B	114	379	35	86	15	3	2	24	4	.227
	Totals		873	2866	339	716	141	28	32	292	32	.250

PHIL PLANTIER 24 5-11 175 Bats L Throws R

A few years ago, outfielder was Red Sox' biggest power hope for the future . . . Slowed last year by elbow injury, he fell out of favor with manager Butch Hobson and became expendable . . . Traded to Padres last winter for reliever Jose Melendez and will be given the left-field job . . . Will bat behind Fred McGriff when a right-hander is on the mound . . . Hit 11 homers in just 148 at-bats two years ago for the Red Sox, but managed only seven last year . . . Led Pawtucket (AAA) with 33 homers in 1990 . . . Padres hope he follows in the footsteps of Jeff Bagwell, who starred for Red Sox' New Britain club the same year and developed into solid player with Astros . . . Lives just 15 miles north of Jack Murphy Stadium in Rancho Bernardo . . . Born Jan. 27, 1969, in Manchester, N.H. . . . Selected by Red Sox in 11th round of 1987 draft . . . Earned $109,000 last season.

Year	Club	Pos.	G	AB	R	H	2B	3B	HR	RBI	SB	Avg.
1990	Boston	OF	14	15	1	2	1	0	0	3	0	.133
1991	Boston	OF	53	148	27	49	7	1	11	35	1	.331
1992	Boston	OF	108	349	46	86	19	0	7	30	2	.246
	Totals		175	512	74	137	27	1	18	68	3	.264

DAN WALTERS 26 6-4 225 Bats R Throws R

Padres' Walter Mitty . . . Was a non-roster invitee to spring training, then started the year at Triple-A Las Vegas where he batted .394 before being called up May 31 because of injury to Benito Santiago . . . Catcher hit .318 while Santiago was on DL . . . Born Aug. 15, 1966, in Brunswick, Me. . . . Spent his high school years in San Diego and Terry Kennedy was his hero . . . Acquired from Astros prior to the 1989 season for pitcher Ed

Vosberg . . . Batted .317 for Las Vegas in 1991 . . . Astros chose him in fifth round in 1984 . . . Still learning how to call a game . . . Threw out 25 percent of base-runners attempting to steal.

Year	Club	Pos.	G	AB	R	H	2B	3B	HR	RBI	SB	Avg.
1992	San Diego	C	57	179	14	45	11	1	4	22	1	.251

ANDY BENES 25 6-6 240 Bats R Throws R

May be the unluckiest pitcher in baseball . . . After terrific 1991 finish, he was expected to carry the load last year but wound up with two less wins than previous year . . . Padres scored two runs or less in 18 of his 34 starts . . . Has double-digit victories in each of his three full seasons in majors . . . Dangerous in daytime, posting 6-1 mark . . . Ranked seventh in NL in innings and strikeouts while finishing in a tie for ninth with 6.6 Ks per nine innings . . . Struck out 11 April 19 vs. Houston and Sept. 22 against the Giants . . . On the cusp of becoming one of dominant pitchers in the majors . . . Had only 21 games of minor league experience before being called to majors in 1989 . . . Born Aug. 20, 1967, in Evansville, Ind. . . . First player selected in 1988 draft . . . Earned $475,000 last season.

Year	Club	G	IP	W	L	Pct.	SO	BB	H	ERA
1989	San Diego	10	66⅔	6	3	.667	66	31	51	3.51
1990	San Diego	32	192⅓	10	11	.476	140	69	177	3.60
1991	San Diego	33	223	15	11	.577	167	59	194	3.03
1992	San Diego	34	231⅓	13	14	.481	169	61	230	3.35
	Totals	109	713⅓	44	39	.530	542	220	652	3.33

BRUCE HURST 35 6-3 215 Bats L Throws L

Underwent shoulder surgery after 1992 season . . . Last season marked his 10th straight with double-digit victories, longest streak among active pitchers . . . After not having any shutouts in 1991 for the first time in nine years, he threw four last season . . . Three of those shutouts came against the Mets, including one-hitter May 13. He is 9-1 lifetime against them . . . Came into the season with .098 career batting average, but collected a career-high 11 hits . . . Boston's first pick in 1976 draft . . . Recorded two of Boston's three wins in 1986 World Series . . . Born March 24, 1958, in St. George, Utah . . . Made $2.75 million last year . . . Signed with the Padres as free agent prior to

1989 season . . . Has one of the best pickoff moves in majors . . . Has thrown 200-plus innings eight of last nine seasons.

Year	Club	G	IP	W	L	Pct.	SO	BB	H	ERA
1980	Boston	12	31	2	2	.500	16	16	39	9.00
1981	Boston	5	23	2	0	1.000	11	12	23	4.30
1982	Boston	28	117	3	7	.300	53	40	161	5.77
1983	Boston	33	211⅓	12	12	.500	115	62	241	4.09
1984	Boston	33	218	12	12	.500	136	88	232	3.92
1985	Boston	35	229⅓	11	13	.458	189	70	243	4.51
1986	Boston	25	174⅓	13	8	.619	167	50	169	2.99
1987	Boston	33	238⅔	15	13	.536	190	76	239	4.41
1988	Boston	33	216⅔	18	6	.750	166	65	222	3.66
1989	San Diego	33	244⅔	15	11	.577	179	66	214	2.69
1990	San Diego	33	223⅔	11	9	.550	162	63	188	3.14
1991	San Diego	31	221⅔	15	8	.652	141	59	201	3.29
1992	San Diego	32	217⅓	14	9	.609	131	51	223	3.85
	Totals.	366	2366⅔	143	110	.565	1656	718	2395	3.84

GREG HARRIS 29 6-2 187 **Bats R Throws R**

Durability is a question because he has made just 20 starts each of last two seasons . . . Spent two stints on DL with back problems and a broken finger . . . Velocity slipped dramatically last season . . . Possesses soap-opera-star good looks and one of the nastiest curves in majors . . . Led club in ERA in 1991 . . . Shifted from bullpen to rotation two years ago and paid the price early with elbow problems that forced him to miss more than two months of the season . . . Made $1 million last season and will double that this year . . . Born Dec. 1, 1963, in Greensboro, N.C. . . . Owns lifetime 24-13 mark vs. NL West teams . . . Selected in 10th round of 1985 draft . . . Has perfect offseason occupation for modern-day ballplayer: banking.

Year	Club	G	IP	W	L	Pct.	SO	BB	H	ERA
1988	San Diego	3	18	2	0	1.000	15	3	13	1.50
1989	San Diego	56	135	8	9	.471	106	52	106	2.60
1990	San Diego	73	117⅓	8	8	.500	97	49	92	2.30
1991	San Diego	20	133	9	5	.643	95	27	116	2.23
1992	San Diego	20	118	4	8	.333	66	35	113	4.12
	Totals.	172	521⅓	31	30	.508	379	166	440	2.74

TOP PROSPECTS

JEREMY HERNANDEZ 26 6-5 195 **Bats R Throws R**

Expected to take over closer's role . . . Fastball has been clocked in the 90's and has movement . . . A converted starter, so his problem is getting proper mindset . . . Bounced back and forth between Las Vegas (AAA) and San Diego last year, posting 1-4 mark and 4.17 ERA and one save with Padres and going 2-4 with 2.91 ERA and 11 saves for Vegas . . . Acquired from Cards for Randall Byers, April 24, 1989 . . . Born July 6, 1966, in Burbank, Cal. . . . How's this for bad luck: he had two cars stolen last year . . . Cards' second-round pick in 1987 draft.

RAY McDAVID 21 6-3 190 Bats L Throws R

Some scouts believe this outfielder has Barry Bonds-type potential . . . Has speed and power, but must improve on contact . . . Hit 24 homers and drove in 94 runs at High Desert (A) . . . Stole 43 bases, but struck out 126 times . . . Didn't play much baseball in high school and is still learning . . . Born July 20, 1971, in San Diego . . . Selected in ninth round of 1990 draft.

TIM WORRELL 25 6-2 200 Bats L Throws R

Little brother of Cards' Todd was 4-2 with 4.26 ERA for Las Vegas (AAA) and 8-6, 2.86 for Wichita (AA) . . . Born July 5, 1967, in Arcadia, Cal. . . . Selected in 20th round of 1989 draft . . . Was 13-6 in 1991 for Waterloo (A) and High Desert (A) . . . Averaged more than one strikeout per inning that season, but struck out only 32 in 63⅓ innings for Las Vegas.

JOEY HAMILTON 22 6-4 218 Bats R Throws R

Last year was his first in organization . . . Arm problems and late signing kept Padres' top pick in 1991 draft sidelined that year . . . Started last season at Charleston (A), where he was 2-2 with 3.38 ERA, then went to High Desert (A), where he posted 4-3 mark and 2.76 ERA . . . Finished at Wichita (AA), registering 3-0 record with 2.86 ERA . . . First-round pick in 1991 draft, out of Georgia Southern University . . . Born Sept. 9, 1970, in Statesboro, Ga.

DARRELL SHERMAN 25 5-7 160 Bats L Throws L

This waterbug of an outfielder impressed Padres with his defense and speed . . . Hit .286 for Las Vegas (AAA) with 26 walks in 71 games . . . At Wichita (AA), he batted .332 over 64 games with 26 stolen bases . . . One of those guys who refused to give up despite long odds and could find himself in the majors . . . Born Dec. 4, 1967, in Los Angeles . . . Orioles took him from the Padres in Rule V draft in 1991, but returned him prior to start of last season.

MANAGER JIM RIGGLEMAN: Replaced Greg Riddoch Sept. 28 . . . Should have taken over in June, when Riddoch lost control of the club . . . Recorded 4-8 record as Padres' manager and club finished 82-80 . . . Spent the last two-and-a-half seasons managing Las Vegas (AAA) . . . Stars posted a 200-194 record during that time . . . Believes in Whitey Herzog style of baseball . . . Treats his players like men and expects professional attitude in return . . . Spent nine years in St. Louis organization as a coach, including the final two seasons as Cards' first-base coach under Herzog . . . Born Nov. 9, 1952, in Fort Dix, N.J. and lives in Readington Shores, Fla. . . . Started his managerial career at St. Petersburg (A) from 1982-84 and then served in same capacity with Arkansas (AA) from 1985-88 before being named the Cards' director of player development in June 1988 . . . Dodgers' fourth-round draft pick in 1974, he was traded to Cardinals in 1976 . . . Spent eight seasons in Cardinals' system as infielder-outfielder before being named coach . . . Graduated from Frostburg (Md.) State College.

ALL-TIME PADRE SEASON RECORDS

BATTING: Tony Gwynn, .370, 1987
HRs: Fred McGriff, 35, 1992
RBI: Dave Winfield, 118, 1979
STEALS: Alan Wiggins, 70, 1984
WINS: Randy Jones, 22, 1976
STRIKEOUTS: Clay Kirby, 231, 1971

SAN FRANCISCO GIANTS

TEAM DIRECTORY: Pres./Managing General Partner: Peter Magowan; Sr. VP/Gen. Mgr.: Bob Quinn; Exec. VP: Larry Baer; Sr. VP-Business Oper.: Pat Gallagher; VP-Scouting and Player Pers.: Brian Sabean; VP-Baseball Adm. and Oper.: Tony Siegle; Dir. Media Rel.: Matt Fischer; Trav. Sec.: Dirk Smith; Mgr.: Dusty Baker. Home: Candlestick Park (62,000). Field distances: 335, l.f. line; 365, l.c.; 400, c.f.; 365, l.c.; 335, r.f. line. Spring training: Scottsdale, Ariz.

SCOUTING REPORT

HITTING: The Giants' new owners made an incredible splash when they made free agent Barry Bonds (.311, 34, 103 with the Pirates) the best-paid player in baseball during the winter meetings. The two-time NL MVP joins consistent Will Clark (.300, 16, 73) to give the Giants fearsome back-to-back left-handed punch. The Giants needed the jolt, because they finished next-to-last in hitting

Bill Swift was Giant asset when shoulder allowed.

in the NL with a .244 mark and next-to-last in runs at 574 in 1992, as they never got over losing Kevin Mitchell's potent bat.

Third baseman Matt Williams (.277, 20, 66) must rebound from a dreadful season. Williams batted just .213 from the seventh inning on and .135 with two strikes last year. If your idea of excitement is a high chopper, Willie McGee (.297, 1, 36) is your man. Second baseman Robby Thompson (.260, 14, 49) keeps plugging along despite series of back problems. Free agent Dave Martinez (.254, 3, 31 with the Reds) was signed to bolster the outfield depth in the wake of the departures of Cory Snyder and Mike Felder via free agency.

PITCHING: The Giants finished ninth in the NL with a 3.61 ERA as their arms gave up the most homers (128) and balks (22) in the NL.

Bill Swift (10-4, 2.08) was off to a tremendous start before being saddled with shoulder problems. The sinkerballer, who came over from Seattle in the Mitchell deal, captured the NL ERA title despite his physical problems. Left-hander Bud Black (10-12, 3.97) started slow because of a back injury. Trevor Wilson had rib surgery in spring training and finished with an 8-14 mark and 4.21 ERA. Now that Roger Craig is gone, it will be interesting to see if Giant hurlers are as injury-prone as in the past few years.

A bright spot in the rotation is John Burkett (13-9, 3.84), who has emerged as a solid starter. In the bullpen, condo-sized Rod Beck (3-3, 1.76) established himself as a closer and dominated in the final weeks of the season as he led the Giants with 17 saves. Beck's emergence means that Jeff Brantley (7-7, 2.95, 7 saves) could wind up a starter.

FIELDING: Williams had a rotten year in the field, too, leading NL third baseman in errors with 23. The normally reliable Thompson tied for second among NL second baseman with 15 errors. Both of them figure to bounce back this season. Despite those setbacks, only three teams finished with a higher fielding percentage than the Giants' .982 mark. Clark (.993 fielding percentage) is the best defensive first baseman in the majors.

OUTLOOK: After finishing 72-90 in 1992, this is a team that needed mondo change. There are new owners, a new star in Bonds, a new general manager in Bob Quinn, a new manager in Dusty Baker. If the pitching comes around, the Giants might surprise. A few months ago, San Francisco fans didn't think they would have a team. Now they just might have a contender.

1993 SAN FRANCISCO GIANTS ROSTER

MANAGER Dusty Baker

Coaches—Bobby Bonds, Bob Brenly, Wendell Kim, Bob Lillis, Dick Pole

PITCHERS

No.	Name	1992 Club	W-L	IP	SO	ERA	B-T	Ht.	Wt.	Born
64	Ard, Johnny	Phoenix	5-8	113	56	4.46	R-R	6-5	220	6/1/67 Las Vegas, NV
47	Beck, Rod	San Francisco	3-3	92	87	1.76	R-R	6-1	238	8/3/68 Burbank, CA
40	Black, Bud	San Francisco	10-12	177	82	3.97	L-L	6-2	185	6/30/57 San Mateo, CA
49	Brantley, Jeff	San Francisco	7-7	92	86	2.95	R-R	5-11	180	9/5/63 Florence, AL
34	Burba, Dave	San Francisco	2-7	71	47	4.97	R-R	6-4	240	7/7/66 Dayton, OH
		Phoenix	5-5	74	44	4.72				
33	Burkett, John	San Francisco	13-9	190	107	3.84	R-R	6-3	205	11/28/64 New Brighton, PA
—	Carlson, Dan	Shreveport	15-9	186	157	3.19	R-R	6-1	185	1/26/70 Portland, OR
52	Carter, Larry	Phoenix	11-6	185	126	4.37	R-R	6-5	196	5/22/65 Charleston, WV
		San Francisco	1-5	33	21	4.64				
60	Hancock, Chris	San Jose	7-4	111	80	4.04	L-L	6-3	175	9/12/69 Lynwood, CA
		Shreveport	2-4	49	30	3.10				
41	Hickerson, Bryan	San Francisco	5-3	87	68	3.09	L-L	6-2	203	10/13/63 Bemidji, MN
—	Huisman, Rick	Shreveport	7-4	103	100	2.35	R-R	6-3	200	5/17/69 Oak Park, IL
		Phoenix	3-2	56	44	2.41				
42	Jackson, Mike	San Francisco	6-6	82	80	3.73	R-R	6-2	223	12/22/64 Houston, TX
—	McGehee, Kevin	Shreveport	9-7	158	140	2.96	R-R	6-0	190	1/18/69 Alexandria, LA
31	Pena, Jim	Phoenix	7-3	39	27	4.15	L-L	6-0	187	9/17/64 Los Angeles, CA
		San Francisco	1-1	44	32	3.48				
19	Righetti, Dave	San Francisco	2-7	78	47	5.06	L-L	6-4	219	11/28/58 San Jose, CA
21	Rogers, Kevin	Shreveport	8-5	101	110	2.58	S-L	6-2	198	8/20/68 Cleveland, MS
		Phoenix	3-3	70	62	4.00				
		San Francisco	0-2	34	26	4.24				
26	Swift, Bill	San Francisco	10-4	165	77	2.08	R-R	6-0	180	10/27/61 S. Portland, ME
32	Wilson, Trevor	San Francisco	8-14	154	88	4.21	L-L	6-0	204	6/7/66 Torrance, CA

CATCHERS

No.	Name	1992 Club	H	HR	RBI	Pct.	B-T	Ht.	Wt.	Born
46	Colbert, Craig	San Francisco	29	1	16	.230	R-R	6-0	214	2/13/65 Iowa City, IA
		Phoenix	45	1	21	.321				
—	Christopherson, Eric	Shreveport	68	6	34	.252	R-R	6-0	195	4/25/69 Long Beach, CA
8	Manwaring, Kirt	San Francisco	85	4	26	.244	R-R	5-11	203	7/15/65 Elmira, NY

INFIELDERS

No.	Name	1992 Club	H	HR	RBI	Pct.	B-T	Ht.	Wt.	Born
18	Benjamin, Mike	Phoenix	33	0	17	.306	R-R	6-0	169	11/22/65 Euclid, OH
		San Francisco	13	1	3	.173				
22	Clark, Will	San Francisco	154	16	73	.300	L-L	6-1	190	3/13/64 New Orleans, LA
10	Clayton, Royce	San Francisco	72	4	24	.224	R-R	6-0	183	1/2/70 Burbank, CA
		Phoenix	46	3	18	.240				
7	Patterson, John	San Francisco	19	0	4	.184	S-R	5-9	160	2/11/67 Key West, FL
		Phoenix	109	2	37	.301				
—	Phillips, J. R.	Midland	118	14	77	.237	L-L	6-1	185	4/29/70 West Covina, CA
56	Santana, Andres	San Francisco		Injured			S-R	5-9	150	3/19/68 Dominican Republic
6	Thompson, Robby	San Francisco	115	14	49	.260	R-R	5-11	170	5/10/62 West Palm Beach, FL
9	Williams, Matt	San Francisco	120	20	66	.227	R-R	6-2	205	11/28/65 Bishop, CA

OUTFIELDERS

No.	Name	1992 Club	H	HR	RBI	Pct.	B-T	Ht.	Wt.	Born
25	Bonds, Barry	Pittsburgh	147	34	103	.311	L-L	6-1	185	7/24/64 Riverside, CA
29	Hosey, Steve	Phoenix	132	10	65	.286	R-R	6-3	225	4/2/69 Oakland, CA
		San Francisco	14	1	6	.250				
—	*James, Chris	San Francisco	60	5	32	.242	R-R	6-1	195	10/4/62 Rusk, TX
1	Leonard, Mark	San Francisco	30	4	16	.234	L-R	6-0	212	8/14/64 Mountain View, CA
		Phoenix	47	5	25	.338				
2	Lewis, Darren	San Francisco	74	1	18	.231	R-R	6-0	189	8/28/67 Berkeley, CA
		Phoenix	36	0	6	.228				
—	Martinez, Dave	Cincinnati	100	3	31	.254	L-L	5-10	180	9/26/64 New York, NY
51	McGee, Willie	San Francisco	141	1	36	.297	S-R	6-1	195	11/2/58 San Francisco, CA
39	Wood, Ted	Phoenix	127	7	63	.304	L-L	6-2	187	1/4/67 Mansfield, OH
		San Francisco	12	1	3	.207				

*Free agent offered arbitration

GIANT PROFILES

BARRY BONDS 28 6-1 185 Bats L Throws L

Arguably the best player in baseball, he converted another NL MVP season and free agency into six-year, $43.75-million contract with Giants in December . . . Pirates' three-time Gold Glove left fielder finished second in home runs, tied for sixth in batting, was fourth in RBI, ninth in doubles and stolen bases, and first in slugging percentage (.624), on-base average (.456), runs and walks (127) . . . Carried Pirates in September, batting .402 with nine homers and 25 RBI while also walking 33 times for on-base percentage of .556 . . . Became first Pirate to post three consecutive 100-RBI seasons since Willie Stargell (1971-73) . . . Partially erased past playoff failures with key double and homer in Games 5 and 6 of NLCS . . . Overall, he went 6-for-23 in playoffs, but had just two RBI . . . Missed 18 games in June with pulled muscle in side and Pirates were 8-10 without him . . . Born July 24, 1964, in Riverside, Cal. . . . Pirates' first pick in 1985 draft and sixth player taken overall, out of Arizona State . . . Named NL MVP in 1990 . . . Earned $4.7 million in 1992 . . . Father is former 30-30 man Bobby Bonds.

Year	Club	Pos.	G	AB	R	H	2B	3B	HR	RBI	SB	Avg.
1986	Pittsburgh	OF	113	413	72	92	26	3	16	48	36	.223
1987	Pittsburgh	OF	150	551	99	144	34	9	25	59	32	.261
1988	Pittsburgh	OF	144	538	97	152	30	5	24	58	17	.283
1989	Pittsburgh	OF	159	580	96	144	34	6	19	58	32	.248
1990	Pittsburgh	OF	151	519	104	156	32	3	33	114	52	.301
1991	Pittsburgh	OF	153	510	95	149	28	5	25	116	43	.292
1992	Pittsburgh	OF	140	473	109	147	36	5	34	103	39	.311
	Totals		1010	3584	672	984	220	36	176	556	251	.275

WILL CLARK 29 6-1 190 Bats L Throws L

Another down year for the Giants, another up year for "The Thrill" . . . Ranked in tie for second in NL in doubles and intentional walks (23) . . . Was ninth in slugging percentage (.476), eighth in on-base percentage (.384), second in sacrifice flies (11) and eighth in batting with men in scoring position (.330) . . . Picked up his 1,000th career hit with an RBI double off Reds' Tom Browning April 18th . . . His double against Atlanta July 1 was the 200th of his career, making him just the fourth SF player to reach that mark. Other three were Willie Mays, Willie McCovey and Orlando Cepeda . . . Peerless first baseman made his fifth consecutive All-Star Game appearance and hit three-run homer off Rick Aguilera, becoming first Giant to hit All-Star homer since Bobby Bonds in 1973 . . . Groin injury limited him to 144 games, his lowest total since 1986 . . . Batted .489 in 1989 NLCS with 11 RBI . . . Earned $4,250,000 last year . . . Born March 13, 1964, in New Orleans . . . Giants made him second player taken in 1985 draft, out of Mississippi State.

Year	Club	Pos.	G	AB	R	H	2B	3B	HR	RBI	SB	Avg.
1986	San Francisco	1B	111	408	66	117	27	2	11	41	4	.287
1987	San Francisco	1B	150	529	89	163	29	5	35	91	5	.308
1988	San Francisco	1B	162	575	102	162	31	6	29	109	9	.282
1989	San Francisco	1B	159	588	104	196	38	9	23	111	8	.333
1990	San Francisco	1B	154	600	91	177	25	5	19	95	8	.295
1991	San Francisco	1B	148	565	84	170	32	7	29	116	4	.301
1992	San Francisco	1B	144	513	69	154	40	1	16	73	12	.300
	Totals		1028	3778	605	1139	222	35	162	636	50	.301

MATT WILLIAMS 27 6-2 205 Bats R Throws R

Another Chris Brown? . . . After leading team in home runs (34) in 1991, he slumped badly last year in every category . . . Dropped 41 points in average, hit 14 fewer home runs, 11 fewer doubles and drove in 32 fewer runs . . . Took a big cut and paid the price with 109 strikeouts, third-highest mark in NL . . . In 682 major league games, he has 556 strikeouts . . . Falls into mechanical ruts at the plate . . . Hit just .165 through his first 21 games . . . Hit a pair of home runs off Kyle Abbott at Philadelphia May 13, becoming just the 37th player to reach upper deck since The Vet opened in 1971 . . . Fielding also fell apart . . . In 1991, he ranked fourth among NL third basemen in fielding percentage (.964). But last year he piled up the most errors (23) at that position . . . Made $2 million in 1992 . . . Attended Nevada-Las Vegas and Giants made him third pick in 1986 draft . . . Born Nov. 28, 1965, in Bishop, Cal.

Year	Club	Pos.	G	AB	R	H	2B	3B	HR	RBI	SB	Avg.
1987	San Francisco	SS-3B	84	245	28	46	9	2	8	21	4	.188
1988	San Francisco	3B-SS	52	156	17	32	6	1	8	19	0	.205
1989	San Francisco	3B-SS	84	292	31	59	18	1	18	50	1	.202
1990	San Francisco	3B	159	617	87	171	27	2	33	122	7	.277
1991	San Francisco	3B-SS	157	589	72	158	24	5	34	98	5	.268
1992	San Francisco	3B	146	529	58	120	13	5	20	66	7	.227
	Totals		682	2428	293	586	97	16	121	376	24	.241

ROBBY THOMPSON 30 5-11 170 Bats R Throws R

Has hung around a long time for a man with a bad back . . . Started his seventh consecutive opener at second base and you have go back 76 years to Larry Doyle to find another Giant who has done that . . . Strained rib cage muscle landed him on the DL at the end of April . . . Hit just .164 over his first 38 games back . . . Five of his homers either tied the game or gave the Giants the lead . . . His three-run shot Aug. 21 handed Pirates rookie knuckleballer Tim Wakefield his only loss . . . Owns SF record for homers by a second baseman with 19 in 1991 . . . Birthday basher . . . In 1991, he homered on his birthday, his wife's birthday and his daughter's birthday. Last year, he celebrated his twins' third birthday with a homer . . . Born May 10, 1962, in West Palm Beach, Fla. . . . Giants' first-round selection in secondary phase in 1983 draft, out of Florida. . . . Earned $1,600,000 last season.

Year	Club	Pos.	G	AB	R	H	2B	3B	HR	RBI	SB	Avg.
1986	San Francisco	2B-SS	149	549	73	149	27	3	7	47	12	.271
1987	San Francisco	2B	132	420	62	110	26	5	10	44	16	.262
1988	San Francisco	2B	138	477	66	126	24	6	7	48	14	.264
1989	San Francisco	2B	148	547	91	132	26	11	13	50	12	.241
1990	San Francisco	2B	144	498	67	122	22	3	15	56	14	.245
1991	San Francisco	2B	144	492	74	129	24	5	19	48	14	.262
1992	San Francisco	2B	128	443	54	115	25	1	14	49	5	.260
	Totals		983	3426	487	883	174	34	85	342	87	.258

WILLIE McGEE 34 6-1 195 Bats S Throw R

Needs to play on artificial turf . . . Center fielder uses his speed by putting the ball on the ground . . . Hits nearly four grounders for every fly . . . Finished under .300 for the first time in three years . . . Hit .337 with runners in scoring position and .351 with men on base, the best mark in NL . . . Led team with 38 infield hits . . . Signed as a free agent prior to the 1991 season . . . Made $3,562,500 last season . . . Won NL batting title in 1990 while in exile with Athletics . . . Traded to A's from Cardinals for Felix Jose, Stan Royer and Daryl Green, Aug. 29, 1990 . . . Born Nov. 2, 1958, in San Francisco . . . Played at Diablo Valley College . . . Another Yankee prospect who got away . . . New York's first-round pick in January 1977.

Year	Club	Pos.	G	AB	R	H	2B	3B	HR	RBI	SB	Avg.
1982	St. Louis	OF	123	422	43	125	12	8	4	56	24	.296
1983	St. Louis	OF	147	601	75	172	22	8	5	75	39	.286
1984	St. Louis	OF	145	571	82	166	19	11	6	50	43	.291
1985	St. Louis	OF	152	612	114	216	26	18	10	82	56	.353
1986	St. Louis	OF	124	497	65	127	22	7	7	48	19	.256
1987	St. Louis	OF-SS	153	620	76	177	37	11	11	105	16	.285
1988	St. Louis	OF	137	562	73	164	24	6	3	50	41	.292
1989	St. Louis	OF	58	199	23	47	10	2	3	17	8	.236
1990	St. Louis	OF	125	501	76	168	32	5	3	62	28	.335
1990	Oakland	OF	29	113	23	31	3	2	0	15	3	.274
1991	San Francisco	OF	131	497	67	155	30	3	4	43	17	.312
1992	San Francisco	OF	138	474	56	141	20	2	1	36	13	.297
	Totals		1462	5669	773	1689	257	83	57	639	307	.298

BUD BLACK 35 6-2 185 Bats L Throws L

Has lost 28 games the last two seasons . . . In third year of four-year, $10-million contract signed as free agent . . . Earned $2.75 million last year . . . Bothered by lower back injury and did not make his first start until May 7 . . . Was hammered that game, but went on to win nine of his next 11 decisions . . . Season ended with six straight losses, matching his career high, and defeats in nine of his last 10 decisions . . . ERA was third-highest in NL among title qualifiers and he surrendered league-high 23 homers . . . An excellent fielder, he has not committed an error since May 7, 1990 . . . Tied Trevor Wilson for NL lead in balks with seven . . . Born June 30, 1957, in San Mateo, Cal. . . . Selected by Mariners in 17th round of 1979 draft . . . Traded to Royals for Manny Castillo before 1982 season . . . Dealt to Indians for Pat Tabler June 3, 1988, then moved on to Blue Jays, Sept. 17, 1990.

Year	Club	G	IP	W	L	Pct.	SO	BB	H	ERA
1981	Seattle	2	1	0	0	.000	0	3	2	0.00
1982	Kansas City	22	88⅓	4	6	.400	40	34	92	4.58
1983	Kansas City	24	161⅓	10	7	.588	58	43	159	3.79
1984	Kansas City	35	257	17	12	.586	140	64	226	3.12
1985	Kansas City	33	205⅔	10	15	.400	122	59	216	4.33
1986	Kansas City	56	121	5	10	.333	68	43	100	3.20
1987	Kansas City	29	122⅓	8	6	.571	61	35	126	3.60
1988	K.C.-Clev.	33	81	4	4	.500	63	34	82	5.00
1989	Cleveland	33	222⅓	12	11	.522	88	52	213	3.36
1990	Clev.-Tor.	32	206⅔	13	11	.542	106	61	181	3.57
1991	San Francisco	34	214⅓	12	16	.429	104	71	201	3.99
1992	San Francisco	28	177	10	12	.455	82	59	178	3.97
	Totals.	361	1858	105	110	.488	932	558	1776	3.76

BILL SWIFT 31 6-0 180 Bats R Throws R

Biggest plus out of Kevin Mitchell deal . . . After coming over from Mariners with Mike Jackson and Dave Burba, he posted lowest ERA in NL . . . His 2.08 mark was lowest since Dwight Gooden registered 1.53 in 1985 and was second-lowest Giant mark ever. Bob Bolin had 1.98 ERA in 1968 . . . Started season 6-0, then went on the DL May 23 with shoulder problems . . . Giants fell apart without him, going 8-18 . . . He is made for tall grass of Candlestick, because his groundball-to-flyball ratio was 2.62-to-1 . . . Allowed just one homer every 27.4 innings . . . Earned $2,316,667 last season . . . Member of the 1984 Olympic team . . . Mariners made him second player chosen in 1984 draft . . . Born Oct. 27, 1961, in South Portland, Me. . . . Had to be swift at the dinner table if he wanted to eat, because he comes from family of 15 children.

Year	Club	G	IP	W	L	Pct.	SO	BB	H	ERA
1985	Seattle	23	120⅔	6	10	.375	55	48	131	4.77
1986	Seattle	29	115⅓	2	9	.182	55	55	148	5.46
1988	Seattle	38	174⅔	8	12	.400	47	65	199	4.59
1989	Seattle	37	130	7	3	.700	45	38	140	4.43
1990	Seattle	55	128	6	4	.600	42	21	135	2.39
1991	Seattle	71	90⅓	1	2	.333	48	26	74	1.99
1992	San Francisco	30	164⅔	10	4	.714	77	43	144	2.08
	Totals	283	923⅔	40	44	.476	369	296	971	3.69

ROD BECK 24 6-1 238 Bats R Throws R

Big man developed into excellent closer by end of the year and led team with 17 saves in 23 opportunities . . . Ranked second in NL in relief ERA with 1.76 mark and batting average allowed to left-handed hitters (.178) . . . Ranked among relief top 10 in seven categories . . . Started strong, finished strong . . . Retired 26 straight batters over five games in May . . . Allowed just one earned run in his last 28⅓ innings over his last 22 appearances . . . Converted into reliever in 1991 . . . Earned $120,000 . . . Acquired from the A's for Charlie Corbell before the 1988 season, he knocked around minors until 1991 . . . Born Aug. 3, 1968, in Burbank, Cal. . . . A's chose him in 13th round of 1986 draft.

Year	Club	G	IP	W	L	Pct.	SO	BB	H	ERA
1991	San Francisco	31	52⅓	1	1	.500	38	13	53	3.78
1992	San Francisco	65	92	3	3	.500	87	15	62	1.76
	Totals	96	144⅓	4	4	.500	125	28	115	2.49

JEFF BRANTLEY 29 5-11 180 Bats R Throws R

After collecting 34 saves previous two seasons, he picked up just seven last year . . . Shifted to starter toward end of the season and allowed only one run over 20⅓ innings in that role . . . Opponents hit .207 against him overall . . . Has lowered that mark every year in the majors (.275 in '88, .271 in '89, .240 in '90 and .225 in '91) . . . Particularly tough against lefties (.181), the fourth-lowest mark in NL . . . Opponents were 1-for-14 against him with bases loaded and, over his career, they are hitting .088 against him with the bases loaded, the lowest mark in majors over past 17 years . . . Was the losing pitcher in 1990 All-Star Game . . . Born Sept. 5, 1963, in Florence, Ala. . . . Giants' sixth-round selection in 1985 draft . . . Earned $375,000 last season . . . Will Clark's teammate at Mississippi State.

Year	Club	G	IP	W	L	Pct.	SO	BB	H	ERA
1988	San Francisco	9	20⅔	0	1	.000	11	6	22	5.66
1989	San Francisco	59	97⅓	7	1	.875	69	37	101	4.07
1990	San Francisco	55	86⅔	5	3	.625	61	33	77	1.56
1991	San Francisco	67	95⅓	5	2	.714	81	52	78	2.45
1992	San Francisco	56	91⅔	7	7	.500	86	45	67	2.95
	Totals.	246	391⅔	24	14	.632	308	173	345	2.94

JOHN BURKETT 28 6-3 205 Bats R Throws R

Determined youngster led club in wins, innings pitched and strikeouts . . . Run support of 4.7 per nine innings ranked fifth among NL pitchers . . . Won 14 games in 1990, his rookie year, after seven years in the minors, and wound up being Opening Night starter in '91 . . . One of the worst hitters in history . . . Batting average of .018 (1-for-55) was eighth lowest all-time among players with 50 or more at-bats and lowest since Bill Hands went 1-for-57 (.018) for the 1972 Cubs . . . Only hit was an RBI double off Jose DeLeon April 30 . . . Loves to bowl and wants to become a professional when baseball career is over . . . Has bowled three perfect games, but has yet to pitch one . . . Earned $375,000 last year . . . Born Nov. 28, 1964, in New Brighton, Pa. . . . Selected by Giants in sixth round of 1983 draft.

Year	Club	G	IP	W	L	Pct.	SO	BB	H	ERA
1987	San Francisco	3	6	0	0	.000	5	3	7	4.50
1990	San Francisco	33	204	14	7	.667	118	61	201	3.79
1991	San Francisco	36	206⅔	12	11	.522	131	60	223	4.18
1992	San Francisco	32	189⅔	13	9	.591	107	45	194	3.84
	Totals.	104	606⅓	39	27	.591	361	169	625	3.95

TREVOR WILSON 26 6-0 175 Bats L Throws L

Suffered through year of hell right from the start, when he had to undergo surgery in spring training to remove a benign growth from his rib . . . Ended the year with nerve problems in his elbow and did not pitch in September or October . . . Record and ERA were major disappointments, after he had paced Giants in wins and strikeouts in 1991 . . . Started beanball war with Padres when he hit Fred McGriff after Gary Sheffield grand slam June 18 . . . Was suspended for four games as result—and McGriff got even by belting home run off him the next time they met . . . Received just 29 runs of support in his 14 losses . . . Run support of 2.81 per nine innings would have been the worst in the NL, but he was eight innings short of qualifying . . . Born June 7, 1966, in Torrance, Cal. . . . Earned $400,000 last season . . . Giants' eighth-round selection in 1985 draft.

Year	Club	G	IP	W	L	Pct.	SO	BB	H	ERA
1988	San Francisco	4	22	0	2	.000	15	8	25	4.09
1989	San Francisco	14	39⅓	2	3	.400	22	24	28	4.35
1990	San Francisco	27	110⅓	8	7	.533	66	49	87	4.00
1991	San Francisco	44	202	13	11	.542	139	77	173	3.56
1992	San Francisco	26	154	8	14	.364	88	64	152	4.21
	Totals	115	527⅔	31	37	.456	330	222	465	3.92

TOP PROSPECTS

STEVE HOSEY 24 6-3 225 Bats R Throws R

Outfielder led Phoenix (AAA) in at-bats (462), hits (132) and doubles (28) and tied for team league in triples (7) and homers (10) . . . Needs to work on his defense . . . Led PCL outfielders with 12 errors . . . Impressed brass during 21-game callup to Giants, batting .286 in his 14 starts . . . Hit his first major league home run off Greg Swindell Sept. 26 . . . Giants' No. 1 selection in 1989 draft . . . Born April 2, 1969, in Oakland, Cal. . . . Rated by *Baseball America* as No. 7 collegiate prospect in his draft.

KEVIN ROGERS 24 6-2 198 Bats S Throws L

After posting 8-5 mark at Shreveport (AA), he was promoted to Phoenix (AAA), where he went 3-3 with 4.00 ERA . . . Injuries forced late-season callup . . . Was 0-2 in six starts with 4.24 ERA for Giants . . . His first pitch in majors became a home run by St. Louis' Geronimo Pena . . . During one stretch at Shreveport, he

John Burkett has emerged as solid starter.

did not allow a run over 29 innings . . . Selected in 11th round of 1988 draft . . . Born Aug. 20, 1968, in Cleveland, Miss. . . . Don't ask why, but he eats a baked potato the night before every start and spaghetti on the night he pitches.

JOHN PATTERSON 26 5-9 160 Bats S Throws R

Missed 1989 season with rotation-cuff surgery and injured the shoulder again in October and had to undergo surgery . . . Second baseman was shifted to the outfield and had the chance to be starting center fielder for Giants until latest surgery . . . His foul ball nearly killed A's pitcher Matt Keough in spring training . . . Batted .301 with 20 doubles, two homers, 37 RBI and 22 steals over 94 games for Phoenix (AAA) . . . Struggled with the Giants during 34-game stint, batting .184 . . . Born Feb. 11, 1967, in Key West, Fla. . . . Selected in 23rd round of 1988 draft, out of Grand Canyon College in Phoenix.

MANAGER DUSTY BAKER: Will try to make Giants contenders again after three straight disappointing seasons. . . . Former slugging outfielder was named to the position Dec. 16, replacing the fired Roger Craig and becoming the sixth minority manager in the majors . . . Spent nearly 16 years as a player with Braves, Dodgers, Giants and A's, compiling a .278 average, 242 home runs, and 1,013 RBI before retiring after 1986 season. . . . Hit .320 in 1981, helping Dodgers to World Championship. . . . After retiring, he worked for a year as an investment broker. . . . Has been a coach with Giants for the last five seasons, acting as hitting instructor. . . . Extremely popular with players and fans. . . . Believes communication is key to success. . . . His only mangerial experience came this winter in the Arizona Fall League . . . Will manage with his heart as well as his head . . . "As a hitter, Hank Aaron taught me you have to go with your feelings," he said. "I'm going to manage the same way." . . . Born June 15, 1949, in Riverside, Cal. . . . Boyhood friend of Bobby Bonds, who will be his hitting coach.

Will Clark is still The Thrill in Candlestick chill.

ALL-TIME GIANT SEASON RECORDS

BATTING: Bill Terry, .401, 1930
HRs: Willie Mays, 52, 1965
RBI: Mel Ott, 151, 1929
STEALS: George Burns, 62, 1914
WINS: Christy Mathewson, 37, 1908
STRIKEOUTS: Christy Mathewson, 267, 1903

INSIDE THE AMERICAN LEAGUE

By TONY DeMARCO and TOM PEDULLA
Ft. Worth Star Telegram — *Gannett Newspapers*

PREDICTED ORDER OF FINISH	*East*	*West*
	Baltimore Orioles	Minnesota Twins
	Toronto Blue Jays	Chicago White Sox
	Milwaukee Brewers	Oakland Athletics
	New York Yankees	Kansas City Royals
	Cleveland Indians	Texas Rangers
	Boston Red Sox	Seattle Mariners
	Detroit Tigers	California Angels

Playoff Winner: Minnesota

EAST DIVISION

	Team	Owner / Colors	1992	Morning Line Manager
1	**ORIOLES** Primed for upset	Lawrence Lucchino — Black & orange	W 89 L 73	2-1 John Oates
2	**BLUE JAYS** Can't repeat	P.N.T. Widdrington — Blue & white	W 96 L 66	5-2 Cito Gaston
3	**BREWERS** Speed to spare	Bud Selig — Blue, gold & white	W 92 L 70	4-1 Phil Garner
4	**YANKEES** Could surprise	George Steinbrenner III — Navy blue pinstripes	W 76 L 86	7-1 Buck Showalter
5	**INDIANS** Better days ahead	Richard Jacobs — Black & orange	W 76 L 86	30-1 Mike Hargrove
6	**RED SOX** Jockey in trouble	J. Harrington/H. Sullivan — Red, white & blue	W 73 L 89	40-1 Butch Hobson
7	**TIGERS** Can see them all	Michael Ilitch — Navy, orange & white	W 85 L 87	50-1 Sparky Anderson

ORIOLES set pace all the way and nip fast-closing, defending champion **BLUE JAYS** at the wire. **BREWERS** best the rest, edging **YANKEES** for show. **INDIANS** falter at midway mark. **RED SOX** are never in it and **TIGERS** barely make it out of the barn.

Metrodome Stakes

93rd Running. American League Race. Distance: 162 games plus playoff. Payoff (based on '92): $114,962.16 per winning player, World Series; $84,259.13 per losing player, World Series. A field of 14 entered in two divisions.

Track Record: 111 wins—Cleveland, 1954

WEST DIVISION		Owner		Morning Line Manager
1	**TWINS** Returns to the top	Carl Pohlad Scarlet, white & black	1992 W 90 L 72	4-1 Tom Kelly
2	**WHITE SOX** One pitcher short	J. Reinsdorf/E. Einhorn Navy, white & scarlet	1992 W 86 L 76	7-1 Gene Lamont
3	**ATHLETICS** Not like they were	Walter A. Haas Jr. Forest green, gold & white	1992 W 96 L 66	8-1 Tony La Russa
4	**ROYALS** Not enough punch	Ewing Kaufmann Royal blue & white	1992 W 72 L 90	15-1 Hal McRae
5	**RANGERS** Same old story	G. Bush/E. Rose Red, white & blue	1992 W 77 L 85	20-1 Kevin Kennedy
6	**MARINERS** A trifle improved	John Ellis Blue, gold & white	1992 W 64 L 98	25-1 Lou Piniella
7	**ANGELS** Not a prayer	Gene Autry Red, white & navy	1992 W 72 L 90	50-1 Buck Rodgers

Experienced **TWINS** pound it out as charging **WHITE SOX** make a bold but losing bid in the stretch. **ATHLETICS, ROYALS, RANGERS** and **MARINERS** are middle-of-the-pack, with youthful **ANGELS** trailing the field.

BALTIMORE ORIOLES

TEAM DIRECTORY: Pres.: Lawrence Lucchino; Exec. VP/GM: Roland Hemond; VP-Adm. Pers.: Calvin Hill; VP: Robert Aylward; Asst. GM-Player Dev. Dir.: Doug Melvin; Dir. Pub. Rel.: Rick Vaughn; Trav. Sec.: Philip Itzoe; Mgr.: John Oates. Home: Oriole Park (48,000). Field distances: 335, l.f. line; 410, l.c.; 400, c.f.; 386, r.c.; 318, r.f. line. Spring training: Sarasota, Fla.

SCOUTING REPORT

HITTING: The Orioles must flex more well-timed muscle than they did last year, when they produced only one three-run home run and no grand slams after July 21. Cal Ripken Jr., as always, holds the key to his club's fortunes. He must rebound from a very disappointing season in which he batted .251 with 14 home runs and 72 RBI and approach his MVP form of 1991.

Mike Devereaux (.276, 24, 107) has quietly developed into an offensive force, pacing the club in 10 offensive categories. The Orioles believe Glenn Davis (.276, 13, 48) can supply more power than he has shown in his first two injury-marred seasons with them. Leo Gomez (.265, 17, 64) also can provide some clout.

Brady Anderson (.271, 21, 80) reached safely in 138 of 158 games as a leadoff hitter, scored 100 runs and recorded 53 stolen bases, the second-highest total in club history. Free-agent signee Harold Reynolds, a .260 career hitter in 10 years as a Mariner, is another solid table-setter. And the Orioles added left-handed hitting in the trade for Oakland outfielder-DH Harold Baines (.253, 16, 76).

PITCHING: The Orioles worked hard in recent years to end their pitching woes and have succeeded. The Orioles' 3.79 ERA last season ranked fifth in the AL and was their lowest mark since 1984.

Ace Mike Mussina (18-5, 2.54 in his first full major league season) has a Cy Young award in his future, maybe even this year. The precocious 23-year-old with the poise of a 15-year veteran sports the best ERA in the AL since Sept. 1, 1991, at 2.39.

Ben McDonald (13-13, 4.24) should learn from last year, when he served up 32 home runs, the second-highest total in the majors. Re-signed Rick Sutcliffe (16-15, 4.47) is an unflappable veteran who helps stabilize the rotation. Arthur Rhodes (7-5, 3.63), the only left-hander in the top four, appears to be at a similar stage as McDonald—which is to say on the verge of becoming a big winner.

Dodger dumpee Mike Devereaux drove in 107 runs for O's.

Gregg Olson (1-5, 2.05, 36 saves) anchors an excellent bullpen that placed second in the AL with a 3.30 ERA to go with a 23-14 record.

FIELDING: No one does it better than Baltimore. The Orioles are aiming for their fifth consecutive season with fewer than 100 errors. No other club in major league history has accomplished that for more than two straight seasons.

The omnipresent Ripken Jr. (1,735 consecutive games, 395 games shy of Lou Gehrig) is a steadying influence at shortstop and should provide an outstanding keystone combination when paired with Reynolds. Devereaux and Anderson are outstanding outfielders.

OUTLOOK: Last season, Baltimore made a remarkable 22-game improvement from 1991 to finish 89-73, the fourth-best record in major league history for a team coming off a season in which it had lost 95-plus games. And there was nothing fluky about it. Pitching and defense spell winning and Johnny Oates' Orioles are very strong in both areas.

Baltimore and eventual world champion Toronto were within one game of each other from May 1 through July 3 last year. This season, look for the Orioles to go right to the wire with the defending world champions in a hotly-contested AL East race.

BALTIMORE ORIOLES 1993 ROSTER

MANAGER Johnny Oates
Coaches—Greg Biagini, Dick Bosman, Mike Ferraro, Elrod Hendricks, Davey Lopes, Jerry Narron

PITCHERS

No.	Name	1992 Club	W-L	IP	SO	ERA	B-T	Ht.	Wt.	Born
49	Frohwirth, Todd	Baltimore	4-3	106	58	2.46	R-R	6-4	211	9/28/62 Milwaukee, WI
19	McDonald, Ben	Baltimore	13-13	227	158	4.24	R-R	6-7	214	11/24/67 Baton Rouge, LA
75	Mills, Alan	Rochester	0-1	5	8	5.40	S-R	6-1	192	10/18/66 Lakeland, FL
		Baltimore	10-4	103	60	2.61				
35	Mussina, Mike	Baltimore	18-5	241	130	2.54	R-R	6-2	185	12/8/68 Williamsport, PA
—	O'Donoghue, John	Hagerstown	7-4	112	86	2.24	L-L	6-6	198	5/26/69 Wilmington, DE
		Rochester	5-4	70	47	3.50				
30	Olson, Gregg	Baltimore	1-5	61	58	2.05	R-R	6-4	206	10/11/66 Omaha, NE
56	Oquist, Mike	Rochester	10-12	153	111	4.11	R-R	6-2	170	5/30/68 La Junta, CO
47	Pennington, Brad	Frederick	1-0	9	16	2.00	L-L	6-5	205	4/14/69 Salem, IN
		Hagerstown	1-2	28	32	2.54				
		Rochester	1-3	39	56	2.08				
45	Poole, Jim	Hagerstown	0-1	13	4	2.77	L-L	6-2	203	4/28/66 Rochester, NY
		Rochester	1-6	42	30	5.31				
		Baltimore	0-0	3	3	0.00				
53	Rhodes, Arthur	Rochester	6-6	102	115	3.72	L-L	6-2	190	10/24/69 Waco, TX
		Baltimore	7-5	94	77	3.63				
40	Sutcliffe, Rick	Baltimore	16-15	237	109	4.47	L-R	6-7	215	6/21/56 Independence, MO
50	Telford, Anthony	Rochester	12-7	181	129	4.18	R-R	6-0	189	3/6/66 San Jose, CA
—	Williams, Jeff	Hagerstown	8-10	123	81	4.83	R-R	6-4	230	4/16/69 Salina, KS

CATCHERS

No.	Name	1992 Club	H	HR	RBI	Pct.	B-T	Ht.	Wt.	Born
59	Devarez, Cesar	Hagerstown	72	2	31	.226	R-R	5-10	175	9/22/69 Dominican Republic
23	Hoiles, Chris	Baltimore	85	20	40	.274	R-R	6-0	213	3/20/65 Bowling Green, OH
		Hagerstown	11	1	5	.458				
27	Parent, Mark	Rochester	102	17	69	.287	R-R	6-5	220	9/16/61 Ashland, OR
		Baltimore	8	2	4	.235				
41	Tackett, Jeff	Baltimore	43	5	24	.240	R-R	6-2	205	12/1/65 Fresno, CA

INFIELDERS

No.	Name	1992 Club	H	HR	RBI	Pct.	B-T	Ht.	Wt.	Born
48	Alexander, Manny	Hagerstown	129	2	41	.259	R-R	5-10	150	3/20/71 Dominican Republic
		Rochester	7	0	3	.292				
		Baltimore	1	0	0	.200				
—	Carey, Paul	Frederick	41	9	26	.301	R-L	6-4	230	1/8/68 Weymouth, MA
		Rochester	20	1	7	.230				
		Hagerstown	44	4	18	.270				
37	Davis, Glenn	Baltimore	110	13	48	.276	R-R	6-3	212	3/28/61 Jacksonville, FL
10	Gomez, Leo	Baltimore	124	17	64	.265	R-R	6-0	180	3/2/67 Puerto Rico
36	Hulett, Tim	Baltimore	41	2	21	.289	R-R	6-0	200	1/12/60 Springfield, IL
—	Jennings, Doug	Rochester	109	14	76	.275	L-L	5-10	175	9/30/64 Atlanta, GA
—	Lewis, T.R.	Kane County	40	2	22	.301	R-R	6-0	180	4/17/71 Jacksonville, FL
		Frederick	96	7	54	.307				
—	Reynolds, Harold	Seattle	113	3	33	.247	S-R	5-11	165	11/26/60 Eugene, OR
8	Ripken, Cal	Baltimore	160	14	72	.251	R-R	6-4	224	8/24/60 Havre de Grace, MD
43	Scarsone, Steve	S/WB-Roch.	110	12	60	.270	R-R	6-2	191	4/11/66 Anaheim, CA
		Philadelphia	2	0	0	.154				
		Baltimore	3	0	0	.176				
21	Segui, David	Baltimore	44	1	17	.233	S-R	6-1	202	7/19/66 Kansas City, KS

OUTFIELDERS

No.	Name	1992 Club	H	HR	RBI	Pct.	B-T	Ht.	Wt.	Born
9	Anderson, Brady	Baltimore	169	21	80	.271	L-L	6-1	185	1/18/64 Silver Springs, MD
3	Baines, Harold	Oakland	121	16	76	.253	L-L	6-2	195	3/15/59 Easton, MD
—	Buford, Damon	Hagerstown	89	1	30	.239	R-R	5-10	170	6/12/70 Baltimore, MD
		Rochester	44	1	12	.284				
12	Devereaux, Mike	Baltimore	180	24	107	.276	R-R	6-0	195	4/10/63 Casper, WY
14	Martinez, Chito	Baltimore	53	5	25	.268	L-L	5-10	185	12/19/65 Central America
11	Mercedes, Luis	Rochester	128	3	29	.313	R-R	6-3	193	2/20/68 Dominican Republic
		Baltimore	7	0	4	.140				
28	Voigt, Jack	Rochester	126	16	64	.284	R-R	6-1	175	5/17/66 Sarasota, FL
		Baltimore	0	0	0	.000				

ORIOLE PROFILES

CAL RIPKEN Jr. 32 6-4 224 Bats R Throws R

May be feeling strain of 1,735 consecutive game streak . . . He is only 395 games shy of Lou Gehrig's record . . . Went from career highs in home runs, RBI and extra-base hits as AL MVP in 1991 to career lows in those categories last season . . . String of 20-homer seasons ended at 10 . . . Endured career-high drought of 73 games without a home run, from June 24-Sept. 13 . . . Led league in double plays (119) and putouts (288) for sixth time, duplicating feat of Hall of Fame shortstop Walter Maranville . . . Needs 29 home runs to pass Ernie Banks for most homers by a major league shortstop . . . Has played 15,659 of a possible 15,787 innings during streak . . . Since streak began, 2,708 major league players have been disabled . . . AL Rookie of the Year in 1982 . . . Born Aug. 24, 1960, in Havre de Grace, Md. . . . Orioles' second-round pick in 1978 draft . . . Earned $2.1 million in 1992 . . . Signed five-year, $30.5-million contract to remain with Orioles . . . Won another Gold Glove in 1992.

Year	Club	Pos.	G	AB	R	H	2B	3B	HR	RBI	SB	Avg.
1981	Baltimore	SS-3B	23	39	1	5	0	0	0	0	0	.128
1982	Baltimore	SS-3B	160	598	90	158	32	5	28	93	3	.264
1983	Baltimore	SS	162	663	121	211	47	2	27	102	0	.318
1984	Baltimore	SS	162	641	103	195	37	7	27	86	2	.304
1985	Baltimore	SS	161	642	116	181	32	5	26	110	2	.282
1986	Baltimore	SS	162	627	98	177	35	1	25	81	4	.282
1987	Baltimore	SS	162	624	97	157	28	3	27	98	3	.252
1988	Baltimore	SS	161	575	87	152	25	1	23	81	2	.264
1989	Baltimore	SS	162	646	80	166	30	0	21	93	3	.257
1990	Baltimore	SS	161	600	78	150	28	4	21	84	3	.250
1991	Baltimore	SS	162	650	99	210	46	5	34	114	6	.323
1992	Baltimore	SS	162	637	73	160	29	1	14	72	4	.251
	Totals		1800	6942	1043	1922	369	34	273	1014	32	.277

BRADY ANDERSON 29 6-1 185 Bats L Throws L

Late bloomer has emerged as an All-Star . . . His average was 52 points higher than career mark coming into 1992 . . . His .449 slugging mark was 190 points higher than previous lifetime mark . . . Made 158 starts as leadoff hitter and reached safely in 138 of them . . . Became sixth player in Orioles' history to score 100 runs in a season . . . Finished third in AL in stolen bases, with second-highest total in club history and more than Orioles' team total in 1991 . . . Orioles were 68-33 in games in which he either drove in a run or scored one . . . Batted .305 when club won and .229 when it lost . . . Superb outfielder . . . Born Jan. 18, 1964, in Silver Springs, Md. . . . Acquired from Red Sox with Curt Schilling for Mike Boddicker, July 30, 1988 . . . Boston's 10th-round selection in 1985 draft, out of Cal-Irvine . . . Made $345,000 in 1992.

Year	Club	Pos.	G	AB	R	H	2B	3B	HR	RBI	SB	Avg.
1988	Bos-Balt.	OF	94	325	31	69	13	4	1	21	10	.212
1989	Baltimore	OF	94	266	44	55	12	2	4	16	16	.207
1990	Baltimore	OF	89	234	24	54	5	2	3	24	15	.231
1991	Baltimore	OF	113	256	40	59	12	3	2	27	12	.230
1992	Baltimore	OF	159	623	100	169	28	10	21	80	53	.271
	Totals		549	1704	239	406	70	21	31	168	106	.238

MIKE DEVEREAUX 30 6-0 195 Bats R Throws R

Will try to provide encore after outstanding season . . . Honored with Most Valuable Oriole award after finishing in top 10 in AL in RBI, hits, total bases (303), triples and extra-base hits (64) . . . Paced club in 10 offensive categories . . . Feasted on left-handed pitching for .351 average . . . He, Brady Anderson and Pirates' Andy Van Slyke were only players to reach double figures in doubles, triples and homers . . . Not afraid to go deep into counts . . . Produced major league-high 81 hits with two strikes . . . Plays a dazzling center field . . . His 436 successful total chances ranked third among AL outfielders . . . Born April 10, 1963, in Casper, Wy. . . . Acquired from Dodgers for Mike Morgan prior to 1989 season . . . Dodgers' fifth-round pick in 1985 draft, out of Arizona State . . . Earned $1 million in 1992.

Year	Club	Pos.	G	AB	R	H	2B	3B	HR	RBI	SB	Avg.
1987	Los Angeles . . .	OF	19	54	7	12	3	0	0	4	3	.222
1988	Los Angeles . . .	OF	30	43	4	5	1	0	0	2	0	.116
1989	Baltimore	OF	122	391	55	104	14	3	8	46	22	.266
1990	Baltimore	OF	108	367	48	88	18	1	12	49	13	.240
1991	Baltimore	OF	149	608	82	158	27	10	19	59	16	.260
1992	Baltimore	OF	156	653	76	180	29	11	24	107	10	.276
	Totals		584	2116	272	547	92	25	63	267	64	.259

GLENN DAVIS 32 6-3 211 Bats R Throws R

Has yet to meet expectations since acquisition from Astros for Pete Harnisch, Curt Schilling and Steve Finley prior to 1991 season . . . Missed 128 of first 186 games as an Oriole, including 105 games in 1991 after hurting spinal accessory nerve in his neck . . . Has not provided consistent source of power as Orioles had hoped . . . Averaged 28 home runs per year in NL, but has hit just 23 in two years in Baltimore . . . Batted .290 after All-Star break, but supplied only seven homers in 68 games . . . Connected once in 37 games from Aug. 14-Sept. 29 . . . Astros selected him in secondary phase of January 1981 draft, out of University of Georgia . . . Born March 28, 1961, in Jacksonville, Fla. . . . First baseman's salary was $2,865,000 in 1992.

Year	Club	Pos.	G	AB	R	H	2B	3B	HR	RBI	SB	Avg.
1984	Houston.	1B	18	61	6	13	5	0	2	8	0	.213
1985	Houston.	1B-OF	100	350	51	95	11	0	20	64	0	.271
1986	Houston.	1B	158	574	91	152	32	3	31	101	3	.265
1987	Houston.	1B	151	578	70	145	35	2	27	93	4	.251
1988	Houston.	1B	152	561	78	152	26	0	30	99	4	.271
1989	Houston.	1B	158	581	87	156	26	1	34	89	4	.269
1990	Houston.	1B	93	327	44	82	15	4	22	64	8	.251
1991	Baltimore	1B	49	176	29	40	9	1	10	28	4	.227
1992	Baltimore	1B	106	398	46	110	15	2	13	48	1	.276
	Totals		985	3606	502	945	174	13	189	594	28	.262

LEO GOMEZ 26 6-0 180 Bats R Throws R

Must rebound following poor finish . . . Ranked among league leaders with .316 average June 5, but hit just .241 the rest of the season . . . Guilty of only two errors in first 56 games, but made 13 in final 81 games . . . Did finish with most home runs by Oriole third baseman since Wayne Gross' 22 in 1984 . . . Clubbed 11 of his homers on the road . . . Closed with .425 slugging average, third-highest among AL third basemen, behind Seattle's Edgar Martinez (.544) and Chicago's Robin Ventura (.431) . . . Orioles' organization Player of the Year in 1987 and 1990 . . . Topped International League with 97 runs and 97 RBI for Rochester (AAA) in 1990 . . . Born March 2, 1967, in Canovanas, P.R.

... Signed by Baltimore as free agent in December 1985 ... Earned $150,000 in 1992.

Year	Club	Pos.	G	AB	R	H	2B	3B	HR	RBI	SB	Avg.
1990	Baltimore	3B	12	39	3	9	0	0	0	1	0	.231
1991	Baltimore	3B-1B	118	391	40	91	17	2	16	45	1	.233
1992	Baltimore	3B	137	468	62	124	24	0	17	64	2	.265
	Totals		267	898	105	224	41	2	33	110	3	.249

MIKE MUSSINA 24 6-2 185 Bats R Throws R

Has achieved stardom at tender age ... Led majors in winning percentage and was Orioles' youngest 18-game winner since Wally Bunker won 19 in 1964 ... Bullpen blew four possible victories for him ... Ranked third in AL in ERA, first in fewest base-runners per nine innings (9.8) and second in fewest walks per nine innings (1.8) ... Thrives on pressure ... Limited opponents to .175 average with men in scoring position ... Held opposition to .239 average overall ... Permitted two runs or fewer in 20 of 32 starts ... Worked into seventh inning or later in 26 starts ... Named to All-Star staff for first time and threw one perfect inning ... Compiled 25-12 record in three years at Stanford, where he earned economics ... Born Dec. 8, 1968, in Williamsport, Pa. ... Great bargain at a salary of $137,500 in 1992.

Year	Club	G	IP	W	L	Pct.	SO	BB	H	ERA
1991	Baltimore	12	87⅔	4	5	.444	52	21	77	2.87
1992	Baltimore	32	241	18	5	.783	130	48	212	2.54
	Totals	44	328⅔	22	10	.688	182	69	289	2.63

GREGG OLSON 26 6-4 206 Bats R Throws R

Closer depends on great curve for continued success ... Became youngest to reach 100 saves May 3 and finished season with 131 ... Became club's all-time saves leader when he recorded No. 106 to surpass Tippy Martinez May 30 at Oakland ... Converted 36 of 44 save chances for third straight 30-save season ... Permitted just 5 of 31 inherited runners to score ... Made good on 19 consecutive saves after missing on first try of season April 10 at Toronto ... Was particularly tough on left-handed hitters, holding them to .195 average ... Born Oct. 11,

1966, in Omaha, Neb. . . . Orioles made him fourth player picked overall in 1988 draft . . . Received All-America honors final two years at Auburn . . . Earned $1.45 million in 1992.

Year	Club	G	IP	W	L	Pct.	SO	BB	H	ERA
1988	Baltimore	10	11	1	1	.500	9	10	10	3.27
1989	Baltimore	64	85	5	2	.714	90	46	57	1.69
1990	Baltimore	64	74⅓	6	5	.545	74	31	57	2.42
1991	Baltimore	72	73⅔	4	6	.400	72	29	74	3.18
1992	Baltimore	60	61⅓	1	5	.167	58	24	46	2.05
	Totals.	270	305⅓	17	19	.472	303	140	244	2.36

BEN McDONALD 25 6-7 214 Bats R Throws R

Must get back on winning track after poor finish . . . Won first five decisions and was 7-2 June 1 . . . Won only six times in 24 starts after that, however, going 6-11 with 4.67 ERA . . . Often a victim of poor offensive support . . . Orioles scored only 29 runs in his final 10 starts . . . Gets in trouble when he makes mistakes with his fastball . . . Surrendered 32 home runs, second-highest total in majors behind Tigers' Bill Gullickson (35) . . . Didn't take to Camden Yards, amassing fat 4.90 ERA there . . . Orioles made him first player taken in 1989 draft . . . Fashioned 29-14 record in three years at LSU, including 14-4 as a senior . . . Fanned 373 in 308⅓ collegiate innings . . . Born Nov. 24, 1967, in Baton Rouge, La. . . . Earned $355,000 in 1992.

Year	Club	G	IP	W	L	Pct.	SO	BB	H	ERA
1989	Baltimore	6	7⅓	1	0	1.000	3	4	8	8.59
1990	Baltimore	21	118⅔	8	5	.615	65	35	88	2.43
1991	Baltimore	21	126⅓	6	8	.429	85	43	126	4.84
1992	Baltimore	35	227	13	13	.500	158	74	213	4.24
	Totals.	83	479⅓	28	26	.519	311	156	435	4.02

RICK SUTCLIFFE 36 6-7 215 Bats L Throws R

Very durable performer despite age . . . Tied for major league lead with career-high 36 starts . . . Last non-knuckleball pitcher to top that category at 36 years old or older was Walter Johnson in 1924 . . . Labored into seventh inning and beyond in 28 of 36 starts . . . Permitted two or fewer runs on 17 occasions . . . Did not yield a run before the seventh inning 11 times . . .

Missed most of 1990 and part of 1991 season with shoulder problems . . . Born June 21, 1956, in Independence, Mo. . . . Dodgers' first-round pick in 1974 . . . NL Rookie of the Year in 1979 . . . Won NL Cy Young Award in 1984 and came close to winning honor again three years later . . . Earned $1.2 million in 1992.

Year	Club	G	IP	W	L	Pct.	SO	BB	H	ERA
1976	Los Angeles.	1	5	0	0	.000	3	1	2	0.00
1978	Los Angeles.	2	2	0	0	.000	0	1	2	0.00
1979	Los Angeles.	39	242	17	10	.630	117	97	217	3.46
1980	Los Angeles.	42	110	3	9	.250	59	55	122	5.56
1981	Los Angeles.	14	47	2	2	.500	16	20	41	4.02
1982	Cleveland	34	216	14	8	.636	142	98	174	2.96
1983	Cleveland	36	243⅓	17	11	.607	160	102	251	4.29
1984	Cleveland	15	94⅓	4	5	.444	58	46	111	5.15
1984	Chicago (NL)	20	150⅓	16	1	.941	155	39	123	2.69
1985	Chicago (NL)	20	130	8	8	.500	102	44	119	3.18
1986	Chicago (NL)	28	176⅔	5	14	.263	122	96	166	4.64
1987	Chicago (NL)	34	237⅓	18	10	.643	174	106	223	3.68
1988	Chicago (NL)	32	226	13	14	.481	144	70	232	3.86
1989	Chicago (NL)	35	229	16	11	.593	153	69	202	3.66
1990	Chicago (NL)	5	21⅔	0	2	.000	7	12	25	5.82
1991	Chicago (NL)	19	96⅔	6	5	.545	52	45	96	4.10
1992	Baltimore	36	237⅓	16	15	.516	109	74	251	4.47
	Totals.	412	2464⅔	155	125	.554	1573	975	2357	3.90

ARTHUR RHODES 23 6-2 190 — Bats L Throws L

Orioles have high expectations for this hard thrower . . . Frequently compared to Vida Blue . . . Gave Orioles a lift after his July 8 recall from Rochester (AAA) . . . Club went 10-5 in his starts . . . Finished third among AL rookies with 77 strikeouts . . . When he defeated Twins July 9, it marked first win by Oriole left-hander since Jeff Ballard won, July 15, 1991 . . . Ran off victories in his first four decisions, then dropped four straight starts before finishing strong . . . Went 3-1 with 2.35 ERA in last six starts . . . Taken by Orioles in second round of 1988 draft . . . Born Oct. 24, 1969, in Waco, Tex. . . . Earned $109,000 in 1992.

Year	Club	G	IP	W	L	Pct.	SO	BB	H	ERA
1991	Baltimore	8	36	0	3	.000	23	23	47	8.00
1992	Baltimore	15	94⅓	7	5	.583	77	38	87	3.63
	Totals.	23	130⅓	7	8	.467	100	61	134	4.83

TOP PROSPECTS

MANNY ALEXANDER 22 5-10 150 Bats R Throws R
Excellent shortstop prospect ready to take final minor league step with full season at Triple-A . . . Batted .259 with two home runs, 41 RBI and team-leading 70 runs at Hagerstown (AA) last season . . . Ranked third in league with 43 steals and tied for second with eight triples . . . Named to midseason Eastern League All-Star team . . . Did well in brief stint at Rochester, batting .292 with three runs and three RBI in six games there . . . Born March 20, 1971, in San Pedro de Macoris, D.R. . . . Signed as free agent in February 1988.

BRAD PENNINGTON 23 6-5 205 Bats L Throws L
Should compete for bullpen job in spring . . . Moved rapidly last year, making three minor league stops . . . Opened at Frederick (A), going 1-0 with 2.00 ERA and two saves in eight appearances . . . Was 1-2, 2.54 with seven saves in 19 games at Hagerstown (AA) . . . Was 1-3 with 2.08 ERA and five saves in 29 appearances at Rochester (AAA) . . . Composite record was 3-5, 2.24 with 14 saves in 56 games . . . Fanned 104 in 76⅓ innings . . . Has potential to eventually succeed Gregg Olson as closer . . . Born April 14, 1969, in Salem, Ind. . . . Orioles' 12th-round choice in 1989 draft.

MARK SMITH 22 6-2 195 Bats R Throws R
Outfielder takes next step after strong season at Double-A level . . . Ranked fifth in Eastern League with .288 average for Hagerstown . . . Led league with 32 doubles and had four home runs and 62 RBI . . . Has more muscle than he showed in tough home-run park . . . Named to Eastern League All-Star team at end of season . . . Born May 7, 1970, in Pasadena, Cal. . . . Orioles' first-round pick in 1991 draft and ninth player taken overall.

JEFFREY HAMMONDS 22 6-0 185 Bats R Throws R
Fourth player picked in 1992 is regarded by many as that draft's best talent . . . His $975,000 signing bonus reflects how much outfielder is valued . . . Batted .380 with six home runs, 50 RBI and 33 stolen bases in final year at Stanford . . . Hit .353 with 27 home runs, 151 RBI and 102 steals in three-year career there . . . Missed first year in pro ball to play on U.S. Olympic team . . . Named first-team All-America by *Baseball America* in 1992 . . . Born March 5, 1971, in Scotch Plains, N.J.

MANAGER JOHNNY OATES: Deserves great deal of credit for Orioles' dramatic 22-game improvement to 89-73 in 1992 . . . Kept Birds close to Toronto most of the way, even though he had considerably less talent . . . Was team's first-base coach before he replaced Frank Robinson as manager in May 1991, taking over 13-24 club . . . Successful minor league manager who led all three of his teams to postseason play and two to league titles . . . Captured Southern League championship with Nashville (AA) in 1982 . . . Took regular-season title with Columbus (AAA) in 1983 . . . Spent next four years as major league coach with Cubs before returning to Orioles' organization after 16-year absence to manage Rochester (AAA) . . . Took Red Wings to first league championship since 1974 and gained International League Manager of the Year honors . . . Began catching career as Orioles' first-round choice in January 1967 draft . . . Also played for Braves, Phillies, Dodgers and Yankees in 10-year major league career . . . Known primarily for intelligence he showed behind the plate . . . Born Jan. 21, 1946, in Sylva, Va. . . . Career managerial mark in majors is 143-144.

ALL-TIME ORIOLE SEASON RECORDS

BATTING: Ken Singleton, .328, 1977
HRs: Frank Robinson, 49, 1966
RBI: Jim Gentile, 141, 1961
STEALS: Luis Aparicio, 57, 1964
WINS: Steve Stone, 25, 1980
STRIKEOUTS: Dave McNally, 202, 1968

BOSTON RED SOX

TEAM DIRECTORY: Owners and General Partners: JRY Corp. (John Harrington) and Haywood C. Sullivan; Sr. VP/GM: Lou Gorman; VP-Baseball Dev.: Edward Kasko; Dir. Scouting: Wayne Britton; Dir. Minor League Oper.: Edward P. Kenney; VP-Pub. Rel.: Dick Bresciani; Dir. Baseball Inf.: Jim Samia; Trav. Sec.: Steve August; Mgr.: Butch Hobson. Home: Fenway Park (34,171). Field distances: 315, l.f. line; 379, l.c.; 390, c.f.; 420, deep c.f.; 380, deep r.f.; 302, r.f. line. Spring training: Fort Myers, Fla.

SCOUTING REPORT

HITTING: Not long ago, Boston featured an imposing lineup. Not any more. The 1992 Red Sox were next-to-last in the AL with a .246 average, next-to-last in runs with 599 and third from the bottom with 84 home runs. Seven AL players surpassed the Red Sox' total of 44 stolen bases last year.

The Red Sox have bolstered their offense by signing free agent Andre Dawson (.277, 22, 90), the former Cub, and by acquiring injury-plagued Ivan Calderon (.265, 3, 24) from Montreal. Mo

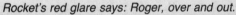

Rocket's red glare says: Roger, over and out.

Vaughn (.234, 13, 57), Bob Zupcic (.276, 3, 43), and Scott Cooper (.276, 5, 33) are some of the youngsters the Sox will build around now that Wade Boggs will be eating his chicken in New York.

Mike Greenwell (.233, 2, 18) figures to bounce back from an injury-marred 1992 season in which he played only 49 games. Is it possible once-powerful Jack Clark (.210, 5, 33) can go through another whole summer without connecting for a homer at cozy Fenway Park?

PITCHING: Boston possesses a powerful one-two punch in the incomparable Roger Clemens (18-11, 2.41, 208 Ks) and the crafty Frank Viola (13-12, 3.44). Clemens, 30, shows no sign of slowing down as he aims to lead the league in ERA for the fourth straight year and pursues his fourth Cy Young award. Viola still ranks among the best left-handers in the AL.

There's a great deal of uncertainty after the top two. Can Joe Hesketh (8-9, 4.36) or John Dopson (7-11, 4.08) be winning pitchers?

The bullpen picture also is muddled. Ex-Red Scott Bankhead (10-4, 2.93) was signed as a free agent to help in middle relief and an even greater lift should come from Jose Melendez (6-7, 2.92 with the Padres), acquired in a deal for underachieving outfielder Phil Plantier. Ken Ryan (0-0, 6.43, 1 save) may develop into a closer. Danny Darwin (9-9, 3.96) is helpful because he can start or relieve. Greg Harris (4-9, 2.51) is a useful veteran reliever.

FIELDING: This is an area that will undoubtedly be emphasized after Boston committed the third-highest error total in the AL with 139 last season. The Red Sox allowed second baseman Jody Reed to leave through the expansion draft and will try a new middle infield of John Valentin at shortstop and Tim Naehring at second base, with free-agent addition Scott Fletcher (.275, 3, 51 with the Brewers) as insurance. Veteran Tony Pena ranks among the better catchers in the AL and is a stabilizing influence behind the plate.

OUTLOOK: Clemens' indomitable presence is the chief source of encouragement for the Red Sox, whose long-suffering fans endured much pain in 1992: a 73-89 record and a finish at the bottom of the standings for the first time since 1932. While manager Butch Hobson is hardly responsible for the franchise's plunge, he will probably be a casualty of it in his second season. What is needed more than anything, though, is a patient rebuilding program.

BOSTON RED SOX 1993 ROSTER

MANAGER Butch Hobson
Coaches—Gary Allenson, Al Bumbry, Rick Burleson, Mike Easler, Rich Gale

PITCHERS

No.	Name	1992 Club	W-L	IP	SO	ERA	B-T	Ht.	Wt.	Born
—	Bankhead, Scott	Cincinnati	10-4	71	53	2.93	R-R	5-10	185	7/31/63 Raleigh, NC
21	Clemens, Roger	Boston	18-11	247	208	2.41	R-R	6-4	220	8/4/62 Dayton, OH
—	Conroy, Brian	New Britain	4-6	75	40	3.82	S-R	6-2	180	8/29/68 Needham, MA
		Pawtucket	7-5	86	57	4.62				
44	Darwin, Danny	Boston	9-9	161	124	3.96	R-R	6-3	195	10/25/55 Bonham, TX
40	Dopson, John	Pawtucket	1-2	38	23	2.37	R-R	6-4	235	7/14/63 Baltimore, MD
		Boston	7-11	141	55	4.08				
27	Harris, Greg	Boston	4-9	108	73	2.51	S-R	6-0	175	11/2/55 Lymwood, CA
55	Hesketh, Joe	Boston	8-9	149	104	4.36	L-L	6-2	173	2/15/59 Lackawanna, NY
59	Irvine, Daryl	Pawtucket	4-1	41	25	1.54	R-R	6-3	210	11/15/64 Harrisonburg, VA
		Boston	3-4	28	10	6.11				
—	Livernois, Derek	New Britain	11-7	121	86	3.63	L-R	6-1	185	4/17/67 Inglewood, CA
		Pawtucket	3-2	38	32	4.26				
—	Melendez, Jose	San Diego	6-7	89	82	2.92	R-R	6-2	180	9/2/65 Puerto Rico
—	Minchey, Nate	Greenville	13-6	172	115	2.30	R-R	6-7	210	8/3169 Austin, TX
		Pawtucket	2-0	7	4	0.00				
49	Quantrill, Paul	Pawtucket	6-8	119	56	4.46	L-R	6-1	185	11/3/68 Canada
		Boston	2-3	49	24	2.19				
50	Ryan, Ken	New Britain	1-4	51	51	1.95	R-R	6-3	200	10/24/68 Pawtucket, RI
		Pawtucket	2-0	9	6	2.08				
		Boston	0-0	7	5	6.43				
56	Taylor, Scott	Pawtucket	9-11	162	91	3.67	L-L	6-1	185	8/2/67 Defiance, OH
		Boston	1-1	15	7	4.91				
16	Viola, Frank	Boston	13-12	238	121	3.44	L-L	6-4	210	4/19/60 East Meadow, NY
30	Young, Matt	Boston	0-4	71	57	4.58	L-L	6-3	210	8/9/58 Pasadena, CA

CATCHERS

No.	Name	1992 Club	H	HR	RBI	Pct.	B-T	Ht.	Wt.	Born
15	Flaherty, John	Pawtucket	26	0	7	.250	R-R	6-1	195	10/21/67 New York, NY
		Boston	13	0	2	.197				
20	Marzano, John	Pawtucket	18	2	12	.290	R-R	5-11	195	2/14/63 Philadelphia, PA
		Boston	4	0	1	.080				
—	Melvin, Bob	Kansas City	22	0	6	.314	R-R	6-4	207	10/28/61 Palo Alto, CA
6	Pena, Tony	Boston	99	1	38	.241	R-R	6-0	185	6/4/57 Dominican Republic

INFIELDERS

—	Byrd, Jim	Winter Haven	19	0	1	.268	R-R	6-1	185	10/3/68 WeWahitchca, FL
		New Britain	14	0	6	.222				
		Pawtucket	55	2	18	.224				
25	Clark, Jack	Boston	54	5	33	.210	R-R	6-3	210	11/10/55 New Brighton, PA
45	Cooper, Scott	Boston	93	5	33	.276	L-R	6-3	205	10/13/67 St. Louis, MO
—	Fletcher, Scott	Milwaukee	106	3	51	.275	R-R	5-11	173	7/30/68 Fort Walton Beach, FL
—	Garcia, Cheo	Orlando	126	4	44	.258	R-R	5-11	165	4/27/68 Venezuela
		Portland	2	0	0	.333				
11	Naehring, Tim	Pawtucket	10	2	5	.294	R-R	6-2	205	2/1/67 Cincinnati, OH
		Boston	43	3	14	.231				
18	Quintana, Carlos	Boston		Injured			R-R	6-2	220	8/26/65 Venezuela
2	Rivera, Luis	Boston	62	0	29	.215	R-R	5-9	175	1/3/64 Puerto Rico
13	Valentin, John	Pawtucket	86	9	29	.260	R-R	6-0	180	2/18/67 Jersey City, NJ
		Boston	51	5	25	.276				
42	Vaughn, Mo	Boston	83	13	57	.234	L-R	6-1	230	12/15/67 Norwalk, CT
		Pawstucket	42	6	28	.282				

OUTFIELDERS

—	Blosser, Greg	New Britain	105	22	71	.242	L-L	6-3	200	6/26/71 Bradenton, FL
		Pawtucket	0	0	0	.000				
—	Calderon, Ivan	Montreal	45	3	24	.265	R-R	6-1	221	3/19/62 Puerto Rico
		W. Palm Beach	3	0	2	.115				
—	Dawson, Andre	Chicago (NL)	150	22	90	.277	R-R	6-3	197	7/10/54 Miami, FL
39	Greenwell, Mike	Boston	42	2	18	.233	L-R	6-0	205	7/18/63 Louisville, KY
22	Hatcher, Billy	Cincinnati	27	2	10	.287	R-R	5-10	190	10/4/60 Williams, AZ
		Boston	75	1	23	.238				
58	McNeely, Jeff	New Britain	57	2	11	.218	R-R	6-2	190	10/18/69 Monroe, NC
—	Ross, Sean	Rich.-Paw.	95	10	48	.244	L-L	6-2	185	10/21/67 Wilmington, NC
28	Zupcic, Bob	Pawtucket	8	2	5	.320	R-R	6-4	225	8/18/66 Pittsburgh, PA
		Boston	108	3	43	.276				

RED SOX PROFILES

IVAN CALDERON 31 6-1 221 Bats R Throws R

Came to Red Sox from Expos in December deal for Mike Gardiner and Terry Powers . . . Plagued by injuries during both years with Expos . . . Three stints on disabled list ruined his 1992 season . . . Left fielder was sidelined at various times in April by tender right elbow, sprained right wrist and pulled muscle in rib cage . . . Disabled from April 30-May 19 with muscle pull . . . Four days later, he bruised left shoulder in slide at plate and returned to DL . . . Underwent arthroscopic shoulder surgery after being disabled for third time June 14 . . . Finally was activated Sept. 3 and, six days later, went 3-for-3 against Cardinals . . . Batted .319 in first 47 at-bats after his return with three doubles, triple, homer and five RBI . . . Had four-RBI game against Mets April 12 . . . Born March 19, 1962, in Fajardo, P.R. . . . Signed with Mariners as free agent in 1979 . . . Traded to White Sox in 1986 and dealt to Expos following 1990 season . . . Shoulder surgery also cut short 1991 season . . . Earned $2.6 million in 1992.

Year	Club	Pos.	G	AB	R	H	2B	3B	HR	RBI	SB	Avg.
1984	Seattle	OF	11	24	2	5	1	0	1	1	1	.208
1985	Seattle	OF-1B	67	210	37	60	16	4	8	28	4	.286
1986	Sea.-Chi. (AL)	OF	50	164	16	41	7	1	2	15	3	.250
1987	Chicago (AL)	OF	144	542	93	159	38	2	28	83	10	.293
1988	Chicago (AL)	OF	73	264	40	56	14	0	14	35	4	.212
1989	Chicago (AL)	OF-1B	157	622	83	178	34	9	14	87	7	.286
1990	Chicago (AL)	OF-1B	158	607	85	166	44	2	14	74	32	.273
1991	Montreal	OF-1B	134	470	69	141	22	3	19	75	31	.300
1992	Montreal	OF	48	170	19	45	14	2	3	24	1	.265
	Totals		842	3073	444	851	190	23	103	422	93	.277

TONY PENA 35 6-0 185 Bats R Throws R

Experienced catcher whose greatest contribution is his defense . . . Hard-nosed player who started 122 games . . . Red Sox were 63-59 when he started and 10-30 when he didn't . . . Guilty of only six errors and seven passed balls . . . Adept at handling balls in the dirt . . . Has pitchers' confidence . . . Has slipped offensively, but still knows how to execute . . .

Ranked third in AL with 13 sacrifices . . . Signed one-year, $2.5-million contract to remain in Boston in 1993 . . . Born June 4, 1957, in Monte Cristi, D.R. . . . Began career as free-agent signee with Pittsburgh in July 1975 . . . Pirates dealt him to Cards in April 1987 and he helped Cardinals reach World Series, where he hit .409 . . . Joined Boston as free agent . . . Earned $2.4 million in 1992.

Year	Club	Pos.	G	AB	R	H	2B	3B	HR	RBI	SB	Avg.
1980	Pittsburgh	C	8	21	1	9	1	1	0	1	0	.429
1981	Pittsburgh	C	66	210	16	63	9	1	2	17	1	.300
1982	Pittsburgh	C	138	497	53	147	28	4	11	63	2	.296
1983	Pittsburgh	C	151	542	51	163	22	3	15	70	6	.301
1984	Pittsburgh	C	147	546	77	156	27	2	15	78	12	.286
1985	Pittsburgh	C-1B	147	546	53	136	27	2	10	59	12	.249
1986	Pittsburgh	C-1B	144	510	56	147	26	2	10	52	9	.288
1987	St. Louis	C-1B-OF	116	384	40	82	13	4	5	44	6	.214
1988	St. Louis	C-1B	149	505	55	133	23	1	10	51	6	.263
1989	St. Louis	C-OF	141	424	36	110	17	2	4	37	5	.259
1990	Boston	C-1B	143	491	62	129	19	1	7	56	8	.263
1991	Boston	C	141	464	45	107	23	2	5	48	8	.231
1992	Boston	C	133	410	39	99	21	1	1	38	3	.241
	Totals		1624	5550	584	1481	256	26	95	614	78	.267

MO VAUGHN 25 6-1 230 — Bats L Throws R

Bulky first baseman hasn't met lofty expectations so far . . . Floundered with .185 average in 23 games with Red Sox at start of last season and was demoted to Pawtucket (AAA), where he remained from May 11-June 22 . . . Did show significant improvement after recall to Boston . . . Batted .267 in final 65 games to boost average 48 points from .186 . . . Totaled 11 home runs and 46 RBI in 90 games after recall from Pawtucket . . . Enjoys hitting in big situations . . . Collected 26 of 57 RBI after two were out . . . Born Dec. 15, 1967, in Norwalk, Conn. . . . Red Sox' second pick in 1989 draft . . . Batted .417 with school-record 57 homers and 218 RBI in three-year career at Seton Hall . . . Earned $155,000 in 1992.

Year	Club	Pos.	G	AB	R	H	2B	3B	HR	RBI	SB	Avg.
1991	Boston	1B	74	219	21	57	12	0	4	32	2	.260
1992	Boston	1B	113	355	42	83	16	2	13	57	3	.234
	Totals		187	574	63	140	28	2	17	89	5	.244

JACK CLARK 37 6-3 210 Bats R Throws R

May be reaching the end . . . Power hitter suddenly lost his home-run stroke in 1992 . . . Produced only five home runs after slugging 25 or more each of previous five years . . . Designated hitter went through whole season without connecting at Fenway . . . Last Fenway homer was Oct. 6, 1991, against Milwaukee . . . Played only 81 games, his lowest total since 1986 . . . Went 3-for-6 with one RBI as pinch-hitter . . . Has developed reputation as being difficult to please . . . Born Nov. 10, 1955, in New Brighton, Pa. . . . Giants' 13th-round pick in 1973 draft . . . Was forced to declare bankruptcy during course of last season, despite $2.9-million salary in 1992.

Year	Club	Pos.	G	AB	R	H	2B	3B	HR	RBI	SB	Avg.
1975	San Francisco	OF-3B	8	17	3	4	0	0	0	2	1	.235
1976	San Francisco	OF	26	102	14	23	6	2	2	10	6	.225
1977	San Francisco	OF	136	413	64	104	17	4	13	51	12	.252
1978	San Francisco	OF	156	592	90	181	46	8	25	98	15	.306
1979	San Francisco	OF-3B	143	527	84	144	25	2	26	86	11	.273
1980	San Francisco	OF	127	437	77	124	20	8	22	82	2	.284
1981	San Francisco	OF	99	385	60	103	19	2	17	53	1	.268
1982	San Francisco	OF	157	563	90	154	30	3	27	103	6	.274
1983	San Francisco	OF-1B	135	492	82	132	25	0	20	66	5	.268
1984	San Francisco	OF-1B	57	203	33	65	9	1	11	44	1	.320
1985	St. Louis	1B-OF	126	442	71	124	26	3	22	87	1	.281
1986	St. Louis	1B	65	232	34	55	12	2	9	23	1	.237
1987	St. Louis	1B-OF	131	419	93	120	23	1	35	106	1	.286
1988	New York (AL)	OF-1B	150	496	81	120	14	0	27	93	3	.242
1989	San Diego	1B-OF	142	455	76	110	19	1	26	94	6	.242
1990	San Diego	1B	115	334	59	89	12	1	25	62	4	.266
1991	Boston	DH	140	481	75	120	18	1	28	87	0	.249
1992	Boston	1B	81	257	32	54	11	0	5	33	1	.210
	Totals		1994	6847	1118	1826	332	39	340	1180	77	.267

ANDRE DAWSON 38 6-3 197 Bats R Throws R

Cub free agent now batting at Fenway with two-year, $9.3-million contract . . . Always a class act, "Hawk" discovered Fountain of Youth playing mostly day baseball last six seasons on Wrigley's natural turf . . . Recorded 2,500th career hit Sept. 21 in New York . . . Hit 399th homer Oct. 4 to tie Al Kaline for 25th place on all-time list . . . Despite bad knees, right fielder has hit at least 20 homers in seven straight years . . . Recorded fifth career five-hit game Sept. 4 against Padres . . . Batted

.429 during 22-game stretch in September . . . Joined Hank Aaron and Stan Musial as only players with at least 45 extra-base hits in 16 consecutive seasons . . . Born July 10, 1954, in Miami . . . Expos' 11th choice in 1975 draft . . . Runnerup to Mike Schmidt in 1981 NL MVP voting and second to Dale Murphy in 1983 . . . Expos' all-time home-run leader with 225 . . . Signed with Cubs as free agent in 1987 and became first player to win NL MVP with last-place club that season . . . Led majors in batting in 1990 . . . Earned $3.3 million in 1992.

Year	Club	Pos.	G	AB	R	H	2B	3B	HR	RBI	SB	Avg.
1976	Montreal	OF	24	85	9	20	4	1	0	7	1	.235
1977	Montreal	OF	139	525	64	148	26	9	19	65	21	.282
1978	Montreal	OF	157	609	84	154	24	8	25	72	28	.253
1979	Montreal	OF	155	639	90	176	24	12	25	92	35	.275
1980	Montreal	OF	151	577	96	178	41	7	17	87	34	.308
1981	Montreal	OF	103	394	71	119	21	3	24	64	26	.302
1982	Montreal	OF	148	608	107	183	37	7	23	83	39	.301
1983	Montreal	OF	159	633	104	189	36	10	32	113	25	.299
1984	Montreal	OF	138	533	73	132	23	6	17	86	13	.248
1985	Montreal	OF	139	529	65	135	27	2	23	91	13	.255
1986	Montreal	OF	130	496	65	141	32	2	20	78	18	.284
1987	Chicago (NL) . .	OF	153	621	90	178	24	2	49	137	11	.287
1988	Chicago (NL) . .	OF	157	591	78	179	31	8	24	79	12	.303
1989	Chicago (NL) . .	OF	118	416	62	105	18	6	21	77	8	.252
1990	Chicago (NL) . .	OF	147	529	72	164	28	5	27	100	16	.310
1991	Chicago (NL) . .	OF	149	563	69	153	21	4	31	104	4	.272
1992	Chicago (NL) . .	OF	143	542	60	150	27	2	22	90	6	.277
	Totals		2310	8890	1259	2504	444	94	399	1425	310	.282

ROGER CLEMENS 30 6-4 220 Bats R Throws R

Taking aim at becoming first pitcher in AL history to win four Cy Young awards . . . Had shot at it last year before late-season groin strain cost him final two or three starts . . . Still topped AL in ERA, the third straight year he has led in that category and fourth time overall . . . Also recorded AL-high five shutouts, tied for fourth in victories, tied for second in complete games (11) and finished third in strikeouts . . . Limited opponents to .224 average, fourth-lowest among AL pitchers . . . In 1986, he became only pitcher to gain league MVP, Cy Young and All-Star Game MVP honors in same season . . . Repeated as Cy Young winner in 1987 to join Sandy Koufax (1965-66) and Jim Palmer (1975-76) as only consecutive winners . . . Added a third Cy Young award in 1991 . . . Holds club single-season strikeout record of 291, set in 1988 . . . Rare talent because he's a power pitcher with control . . . Born Aug. 4, 1962, in Dayton, Ohio . . . Boston's first pick in 1983 draft, out of University of Texas . . . Franchise player earned $4,555,250 in 1992.

Year	Club	G	IP	W	L	Pct.	SO	BB	H	ERA
1984	Boston	21	133⅓	9	4	.692	126	29	146	4.32
1985	Boston	15	98⅓	7	5	.583	74	37	83	3.29
1986	Boston	33	254	24	4	.857	238	67	179	2.48
1987	Boston	36	281⅔	20	9	.690	256	83	248	2.97
1988	Boston	35	264	18	12	.600	291	62	217	2.93
1989	Boston	35	253⅓	17	11	.607	230	93	215	3.13
1990	Boston	31	228⅓	21	6	.778	209	54	193	1.93
1991	Boston	35	271⅓	18	10	.643	241	65	219	2.62
1992	Boston	32	246⅔	18	11	.621	208	62	203	2.41
	Totals	273	2031	152	72	.679	1873	552	1703	2.80

DANNY DARWIN 37 6-3 195 Bats R Throws R

Hopes to give Red Sox a better return . . . Signed four-year contract as free agent prior to 1991 season . . . Missed bulk of 1991 and was out for most of May last year with pneumonia and shoulder tendinitis . . . Disabled from July 7 until end of season with sore right shoulder that required surgery . . . Did make 51 appearances for Red Sox last year, including 15 starts, and ranked third on poor staff in victories and innings pitched . . . Still has good stuff . . . Versatile pitcher throughout career . . . Led NL in ERA in 1990 . . . Born Oct. 25, 1955, in Bonham, Tex. . . . Earned $3.25 million in 1992.

Year	Club	G	IP	W	L	Pct.	SO	BB	H	ERA
1978	Texas	3	9	1	0	1.000	8	1	11	4.00
1979	Texas	20	78	4	4	.500	58	30	50	4.04
1980	Texas	53	110	13	4	.765	104	50	98	2.62
1981	Texas	22	146	9	9	.500	98	57	115	3.64
1982	Texas	56	89	10	8	.556	61	37	95	3.44
1983	Texas	28	183	8	13	.381	92	62	175	3.49
1984	Texas	35	223⅔	8	12	.400	123	54	249	3.94
1985	Milwaukee	39	217⅔	8	18	.308	125	65	212	3.80
1986	Milwaukee	27	130⅓	6	8	.429	80	35	120	3.52
1986	Houston	12	54⅓	5	2	.714	40	9	50	2.32
1987	Houston	33	195⅔	9	10	.474	134	69	184	3.59
1988	Houston	44	192	8	13	.381	129	48	189	3.84
1989	Houston	68	122	11	4	.733	104	33	92	2.36
1990	Houston	48	162⅔	11	4	.733	109	31	136	2.21
1991	Boston	12	68	3	6	.333	42	15	71	5.16
1992	Boston	51	161⅓	9	9	.500	124	53	159	3.96
	Totals	551	2142⅔	123	124	.498	1431	649	2006	3.49

FRANK VIOLA 32 6-4 210 **Bats L Throws L**

Durable left-hander pursuing double figures in victories for ninth straight season . . . Ex-Met joined Red Sox as free agent, signing a three-year, $13.9-million contract prior to 1992 season . . . Pitched better than record would indicate in first year in Boston . . . Held opponents to .242 average, 10th-lowest mark in AL . . . Has made at least 35 starts every year since 1983 and worked no fewer than 210 innings in any of those seasons . . . Most effective pitch is his change-up . . . Was MVP of 1987 World Series for Twins, with 2-1 record and 3.72 ERA in three starts . . . Gained AL Cy Young award with Minnesota in 1988 . . . Born April 19, 1960, in East Meadow, N.Y. . . . Earned $4,733,333 in 1992.

Year	Club	G	IP	W	L	Pct.	SO	BB	H	ERA
1982	Minnesota	22	126	4	10	.286	84	38	152	5.21
1983	Minnesota	35	210	7	15	.318	127	92	242	5.49
1984	Minnesota	35	257⅔	18	12	.600	149	73	225	3.21
1985	Minnesota	36	250⅔	18	14	.563	135	68	262	4.09
1986	Minnesota	37	245⅔	16	13	.552	191	83	257	4.51
1987	Minnesota	36	251⅔	17	10	.630	197	66	230	2.90
1988	Minnesota	35	255⅓	24	7	.774	193	54	236	2.64
1989	Minnesota	24	175⅔	8	12	.400	138	47	171	3.79
1989	New York (NL)	12	85⅓	5	5	.500	73	27	75	3.38
1990	New York (NL)	35	249⅔	20	12	.625	182	60	227	2.67
1991	New York (NL)	35	231⅓	13	15	.464	132	54	259	3.97
1992	Boston	35	238	13	12	.520	121	89	214	3.44
	Totals	377	2577	163	137	.543	1722	751	2550	3.70

JOHN DOPSON 29 6-4 235 **Bats R Throws R**

Must prove he can still pitch effectively . . . Stumbled to 1-6 record with six no-decisions and 4.73 ERA in final 13 starts . . . Dropped last four starts while compiling 8.79 ERA . . . Didn't win after beating Athletics Sept. 5 . . . Unable to win at Fenway Park after July 11 triumph over White Sox . . . Opened season by making six starts on rehabilitation assignment at Pawtucket (AAA) . . . Red Sox activated him May 17 . . . Spent most of 1991 recovering from elbow surgery performed in August 1990 . . . Born July 14, 1963, in Baltimore . . . Acquired from Expos with Luis Rivera for Spike Owen and Dan Gakeler prior to

1989 season . . . Expos' first selection in 1982 draft . . . Owns racehorses . . . Made $265,000 in 1992.

Year	Club	G	IP	W	L	Pct.	SO	BB	H	ERA
1985	Montreal	4	13	0	2	.000	4	4	25	11.08
1988	Montreal	26	168⅔	3	11	.214	101	58	150	3.04
1989	Boston	29	169⅓	12	8	.600	95	69	166	3.99
1990	Boston	4	17⅔	0	0	.000	9	9	13	2.04
1991	Boston	1	1	0	0	.000	0	1	2	18.00
1992	Boston	25	141⅓	7	11	.389	55	38	159	4.08
	Totals	89	511	22	32	.407	264	179	515	3.84

JOE HESKETH 34 6-2 173 — Bats L Throws L

Hopes to make better showing after mediocre season . . . Tied career high by making 25 starts, but was able to pitch into seventh inning in only 11 of them . . . Did not make it past sixth inning in seven of final 10 starts . . . Red Sox tallied three runs or fewer in seven of his nine defeats . . . Left with lead in four of eight no-decisions . . . Has good control . . . Permitted two walks or fewer in 17 starts . . . Five relief appearances included first AL save, when he recorded final two outs Sept. 7 at Texas . . . Expos picked him in second round in 1980 draft . . . Born Feb. 15, 1959, in Lackawanna, N.Y. . . . Made $1,775,000 in 1992.

Year	Club	G	IP	W	L	Pct.	SO	BB	H	ERA
1984	Montreal	11	45	2	2	.500	32	15	38	1.80
1985	Montreal	25	155⅓	10	5	.667	113	45	125	2.49
1986	Montreal	15	82⅔	6	5	.545	67	31	92	5.01
1987	Montreal	18	28⅔	0	0	.000	31	15	23	3.14
1988	Montreal	60	72⅔	4	3	.571	64	35	63	2.85
1989	Montreal	43	48⅓	6	4	.600	44	26	54	5.77
1990	Mont.-Atl.	33	34	1	2	.333	24	14	32	5.29
1990	Boston	12	25⅔	0	4	.000	26	11	37	3.51
1991	Boston	39	153⅓	12	4	.750	104	53	142	3.29
1992	Boston	30	148⅔	8	9	.471	104	58	162	4.36
	Totals	286	794⅓	49	38	.563	609	303	768	3.63

TOP PROSPECTS

JEFF McNEELY 22 6-2 190 — Bats R Throws R

Must rebound from injury to right shoulder that limited him to 85 games at New Britain (AA) . . . Struggled when he played, batting .218 with two home runs, 11 RBI and 10 stolen bases . . . Missed time early in season with broken finger suffered in spring training . . . Fine center fielder with great speed . . . Born Oct. 18, 1970, in Monroe, N.C. . . . Red Sox' fourth pick in 1989 draft . . . Was 1989 Junior College All-American at Spartanburg Methodist College in Spartanburg, S.C. . . . Batted .322 with 38 stolen bases at Lynchburg (A) in 1991.

FRANK RODRIGUEZ 20 6-0 175 Bats R Throws R

Made successful conversion from shortstop to starting pitcher at urging of Red Sox . . . Took 12 of 19 decisions with 3.09 ERA for Lynchburg (A) . . . Used lively fastball to strike out 129 batters in 148⅔ innings . . . Born Dec. 11, 1972, in Brooklyn, N.Y. . . . Taken in second round of 1990 draft . . . Hit .271 with six home runs and 31 RBI as shortstop for Elmira (A) in first year in pro ball.

KEN RYAN 24 6-3 200 Bats R Throws R

Overlooked high school prospect has chance to land job as closer . . . Signed by Red Sox as free agent in June 1986 . . . Made jump from New Britain (AA) to majors during last season . . . Was 1-4 with 1.95 ERA and 22 saves in 44 appearances for New Britain . . . Earned seven saves and two victories in nine appearances for Pawtucket (AAA) . . . Compiled 6.43 ERA with one save in seven appearances for Red Sox, but showed good stuff as he held opponents to .174 average . . . Must improve control . . . Fortunes improved dramatically when he was converted from starter into reliever in 1991 . . . Born Oct. 24, 1968, in Pawtucket, R.I.

SCOTT TAYLOR 25 6-1 185 Bats L Throws L

Will compete for spot on Red Sox staff . . . Was 9-11 with 3.67 ERA for Pawtucket (AAA), making 26 starts there . . . Went 1-1 with 4.91 ERA in 14⅔ innings with Boston . . . Gained first major league victory by tossing 6⅔ scoreless innings of one-hit ball against Yankees Oct. 3 . . . Possesses varied repertoire and mixes his pitches well . . . Born Aug. 2, 1967, in Defiance, Ohio . . . Red Sox' 28th-round choice in 1988 draft, out of Bowling Green.

MANAGER BUTCH HOBSON: Has much to prove after

rookie managerial season produced dismal 73-89 record . . . Opened himself to repeated second-guessing with various moves . . . Job is on the line if Red Sox don't show swift improvement . . . Succeeded successful unorthodox Joe Morgan . . . Red Sox were eager to keep their former third baseman from being hired by other organizations interested in him . . . Was hot candidate after guiding Pawtucket to 79-64 record in 1991, his only year managing at Triple-A level . . . Began minor league managerial career with Mets organization, handling Columbia (A) of South Atlantic League in 1987 and 1988 . . . Rejoined Red Sox organization as manager of New Britain (AA) in 1989 and club made 13-game improvement in first season under him . . . Piloted New Britain to final round of Eastern League playoffs in 1990 . . . Born Aug. 17, 1951, in Tuscaloosa, Ala. . . . Played baseball and football at University of Alabama, the latter under legendary coach Paul ''Bear'' Bryant . . . Boston's eighth pick in 1973 draft . . . Became important run producer who wasn't afraid to get his uniform dirty . . . Full name is Clell Lavern Hobson.

ALL-TIME RED SOX SEASON RECORDS

BATTING: Ted Williams, .406, 1941
HRs: Jimmie Foxx, 50, 1938
RBI: Jimmie Foxx, 175, 1938
STEALS: Tommy Harper, 54, 1973
WINS: Joe Wood, 34, 1912
STRIKEOUTS: Roger Clemens, 291, 1988

CLEVELAND INDIANS

TEAM DIRECTORY: Owner: Richard Jacobs; GM: John Hart; Dir. Baseball Oper./Asst. GM: Dam O'Dowd; VP-Pub. Rel: Bob DiBiasio: Mgr. Pub. Rel: John Maroon; Trav. Sec.: Mike Seghi; Mgr.: Mike Hargrove. Home: Cleveland Stadium (74,483). Field distances: 320, l.f. line; 377, l.c.; 400, c.f.; 395, r.c.; 320, r.f. line. Spring training: Tucson, Ariz.

SCOUTING REPORT

HITTING: Cleveland will again rely heavily on Albert Belle, bidding to lead the Indians in home runs and RBI for the third straight year after notching 34 home runs and 112 RBI in 1992.

Carlos Baerga (.312, 20, 105) is another fine young talent who

Indians have no reservations about Carlos Baerga.

has blossomed. Last year, he became the only second baseman in history to bat .300 with 200 hits, 20 home runs and 100 RBI. Kenny Lofton, who scored a team-leading 96 runs and set an AL rookie record with his league-leading 66 steals last summer, is a great catalyst.

Sandy Alomar Jr. (.251, 2, 26) hopes to make a much greater contribution after two straight injury-filled seasons. Paul Sorrento (.269, 18, 60) is a useful left-handed hitter.

PITCHING: Cleveland needs to develop more pitching in order to contend. The Indians ranked 11th among the 14 AL teams with a 4.11 ERA in 1992 and significant improvement seems unlikely.

Ace Charles Nagy (17-10, 2.96) is one of the premier right-handers in the league, even though he receives little attention. He won the most games by an Indian right-hander since Bert Blyleven's 19 victories in 1984.

The Indians bolstered their rotation somewhat by signing free-agent left-hander Bob Ojeda (6-9, 3.63 with the Dodgers) and free-agent right-hander Mike Bidecki (2-4, 2.57 with the Braves). Starting candidates include Jose Mesa (7-12, 4.59), Dennis Cook (5-7, 3.82), and Scott Scudder (6-10, 5.28). Steve Olin (8-5, 2.34, 29 saves) is a capable closer who gets help from Derek Lilliquist (5-3, 1.75 in 71 appearances), Ted Power (3-3, 2.54) and Kevin Wickander (2-0, 3.07).

FIELDING: Cleveland's pitching problems are amplified by poor defense as the Indians committed 141 errors last season. Only Texas, with 154 errors, was guilty of more mistakes.

A full season from Alomar behind the plate is critical. He ranked third in the AL by throwing out 41.1 percent of potential base-stealers and the team's ERA was 3.81 with him, compared to 4.41 when others caught. The Indians do have strong arms in the outfield in Lofton and Mark Whiten, who tied for second in the AL with 14 outfield assists, and a solid glove at shortstop with Felix Fermin.

OUTLOOK: It has been a long time coming, but Cleveland is finally heading in the right direction, under Mike Hargrove. The Indians made a 19-game improvement from 1991 to a 76-86 record last year, the second-best improvement in the majors after Baltimore's 22-game reversal. The Indians closed 62-54 after a 14-30 start and should pick up where they left off. It probably won't be until next season, though, that they can make a serious run at their first pennant since 1954.

CLEVELAND INDIANS 1993 ROSTER

MANAGER Mike Hargrove
Coaches—Rick Adair, Ken Bolek, Dom Chiti, Ron Clark, Jose Morales, Dave Nelson, Jeff Newman

PITCHERS

No.	Name	1992 Club	W-L	IP	SO	ERA	B-T	Ht.	Wt.	Born
—	Bielecky, Mike	Atlanta	2-4	81	62	2.57	R-R	6-3	195	7/31/59 Baltimore, MD
—	Bryant, Shawn	Kinston	10-8	168	121	3.81	R-L	6-2	190	6/10/69 Oklahoma City, OK
32	Christopher, Mike	Colorado Springs	4-4	59	39	2.91	R-R	6-5	205	11/3/63 Petersburg, VA
		Cleveland	0-0	18	13	3.00				
39	Cook, Dennis	Cleveland	5-7	158	96	3.82	L-L	6-3	185	10/4/62 Lamarque, TX
45	DiPoto, Jerry	Colorado Springs	9-9	122	62	4.94	R-R	6-2	203	5/24/68 Jersey City, NJ
56	Embree, Alan	Kinston	10-5	101	115	3.30	L-L	6-2	185	1/23/70 Vancouver, WA
		Canton-Akron	7-2	79	56	2.28				
		Cleveland	0-2	18	12	7.00				
64	Kramer, Tom	Colorado Springs	8-3	76	72	4.88	S-R	6-0	190	1/9/68 Cincinnati, OH
28	Lilliquist, Derek	Cleveland	5-3	62	47	1.75	L-L	6-0	214	2/20/66 Winter Park, FL
49	Mesa, Jose	Balt.-Clev.	7-12	161	62	4.59	R-R	6-3	219	5/22/66 Dominican Republic
36	Mlicki, Dave	Canton-Akron	11-9	173	146	3.60	R-R	6-4	185	6/8/68 Cleveland, OH
		Cleveland	0-2	22	16	4.98				
50	Mutis, Jeff	Colorado Springs	9-9	145	77	5.08	L-L	6-2	185	12/20/66 Allentown, PA
41	Nagy, Charles	Cleveland	17-10	252	169	2.96	L-R	6-3	200	5/5/67 Fairfield, CT
—	Ojeda, Bob	Los Angeles	6-9	166	94	3.63	L-L	6-1	195	12/17/57 Los Angeles, CA
31	Olin, Steve	Cleveland	8-5	88	47	2.34	R-R	6-2	190	10/4/65 Portland, OR
38	Plunk, Eric	Canton-Akron	1-2	16	19	1.72	R-R	6-5	217	9/3/63 Wilmington, CA
		Cleveland	9-6	72	50	3.64				
48	Power, Ted	Cleveland	3-3	99	51	2.54	R-R	6-4	220	1/31/55 Guthrie, OK
47	Scudder, Scott	Cleveland	6-10	109	66	5.28	R-R	6-2	185	2/14/68 Paris, TX
		Colorado Springs	0-1	3	1	6.00				
—	Shinall, Zak	Albuquerque	13-5	82	46	3.29	R-R	6-2	212	10/14/68 St. Louis, MO
—	Wertz, Bill	Canton-Akron	8-4	97	67	1.20	R-R	6-6	220	1/15/67 Cleveland, OH
53	Wickander, Kevin	Colorado Springs	0-0	11	18	1.64	L-L	6-3	200	1/4/65 Fort Dodge, IA
		Cleveland	2-0	41	38	3.07				

CATCHERS

No.	Name	1992 Club	H	HR	RBI	Pct.	B-T	Ht.	Wt.	Born
15	Alomar, Sandy	Cleveland	75	2	26	.251	R-R	6-5	215	6/18/66 Puerto Rico
14	Levis, Jesse	Colorado Springs	92	6	44	.364	L-R	5-9	180	4/14/68 Philadelphia, PA
		Cleveland	12	1	3	.279				
4	Skinner, Joel	Canton-Akron	6	1	5	.300	R-R	6-4	204	2/21/61 LaJolla, CA
—	Ortiz, Junior	Cleveland	61	0	24	.250	R-R	5-11	176	10/24/59 Puerto Rico

INFIELDERS

No.	Name	1992 Club	H	HR	RBI	Pct.	B-T	Ht.	Wt.	Born
9	Baerga, Carlos	Cleveland	205	20	105	.312	S-R	5-11	165	11/4/68 Puerto Rico
—	Espinoza, Alvaro	Colorado Springs	145	9	79	.300	R-R	6-0	190	2/19/62 Venezuela
16	Fermin, Felix	Cleveland	58	0	13	.270	R-R	5-11	170	10/9/63 Dominican Republic
2	Hernandez, Jose	Canton-Akron	103	3	46	.255	R-R	6-1	180	7/14/69 Puerto Rico
		Cleveland	0	0	0	.000				
44	Jefferson, Reggie	Colorado Springs	68	11	44	.312	S-L	6-4	210	9/25/68 Tallahassee, FL
		Cleveland	30	1	6	.337				
10	Lewis, Mark	Cleveland	109	5	30	.264	R-R	6-1	190	11/30/69 Hamilton, OH
42	Martinez, Carlos	Colorado Springs	10	0	5	.313	R-R	6-5	175	8/11/65 Venezuela
		Cleveland	60	5	35	.263				
11	Sorrento, Paul	Cleveland	123	18	60	.269	L-R	6-2	210	11/17/65 Somerville, MA
25	Thome, Jim	Canton-Akron	36	1	14	.336	L-R	6-4	215	8/27/70 Peoria, IL
		Cleveland	24	2	12	.205				
—	Treadway, Jeff	Atlanta	28	0	5	.222	L-R	5-11	170	1/22/63 Columbus, GA
		Greenville	5	0	1	.455				

OUTFIELDERS

No.	Name	1992 Club	H	HR	RBI	Pct.	B-T	Ht.	Wt.	Born
8	Belle, Albert	Cleveland	152	34	112	.260	R-R	6-2	200	8/25/66 Shreveport, LA
1	Hill, Glenallen	Cleveland	89	18	49	.241	R-R	6-2	210	3/22/65 Santa Cruz, CA
		Canton-Akron	1	0	1	.111				
33	Howard, Thomas	San Diego	1	0	0	.333	S-R	6-2	205	12/11/64 Middletown, OH
		Cleveland	99	2	32	.277				
35	Kirby, Wayne	Colorado Springs	162	11	74	.345	L-R	5-10	185	1/22/64 Williamsburg, VA
		Cleveland	3	1	1	.167				
7	Lofton, Kenny	Cleveland	164	5	42	.285	L-L	6-0	180	5/31/67 East Chicago, IL
—	Ramos, Ken	Canton-Akron	150	5	42	.339	L-L	6-0	168	6/8/67 Pueblo, CO
—	Sanders, Tracy	Canton-Akron	92	21	88	.241	L-R	6-1	200	7/26/69 Dallas, NC
23	Whiten, Mark	Cleveland	129	9	43	.254	S-R	6-3	215	11/25/66 Pensacola, FL

INDIAN PROFILES

ALBERT BELLE 26 6-2 200 Bats R Throws R

Temperamental performer, but has star credentials . . . Tied for fourth in AL in home runs and RBI . . . His 34 homers marked the second-highest total by an Indians player since Rocky Colavito's 42 in 1959. Joe Carter had 35 in 1989 . . . Led Tribe in homers and RBI for second straight year . . . Enjoyed five multi-homer games overall . . . Mediocre outfielder . . . Frequently fails to run out ground balls . . . Difficult to manage because of hot temper . . . Suspended for three games for charging Kansas City's Neal Heaton after two close pitches . . . Treated for alcoholism at Cleveland Clinic during 1990 season . . . Born Aug. 25, 1966, in Shreveport, La. . . . Selected by Cleveland in second round of 1987 draft after stellar career at LSU . . . Earned $175,000 in 1992.

Year	Club	Pos.	G	AB	R	H	2B	3B	HR	RBI	SB	Avg.
1989	Cleveland	OF	62	218	22	49	8	4	7	37	2	.225
1990	Cleveland	OF	9	23	1	4	0	0	1	3	0	.174
1991	Cleveland	OF	123	461	60	130	31	2	28	95	3	.282
1992	Cleveland	OF	153	585	81	152	23	1	34	112	8	.260
	Totals		347	1287	164	335	62	7	70	247	13	.260

KENNY LOFTON 25 6-0 180 Bats L Throws L

Second to Pat Listach in AL Rookie of the Year voting . . . Set AL rookie record and club record in steals, leading the league . . . Previous club mark was 61 by Miguel Dilone in 1980 . . . First rookie to lead AL in steals since Luis Aparicio (21) in 1956 and first Indian to top league in that category since George Case (28) in 1946 . . . Left-handed hitter who is more effective against lefties . . . Outstanding bunter with 31 bunt hits . . . Strong-armed center fielder recorded 14 outfield assists . . . Tribe did extremely well in acquiring him from Houston with Dave Rhode for Willie Blair and Eddie Taubensee prior to last season . . . Born May 31, 1967, in East Chicago, Ind. . . . Began career as Astros' 17th-round choice in 1988 draft . . . Will receive substantial raise after making only $110,000 in 1992.

Year	Club	Pos.	G	AB	R	H	2B	3B	HR	RBI	SB	Avg.
1991	Houston.	OF	20	74	9	15	1	0	0	0	2	.203
1992	Cleveland	OF	148	576	96	164	15	8	5	42	66	.285
	Totals		168	650	105	179	16	8	5	42	68	.275

CARLOS BAERGA 24 5-11 165 Bats S Throws R

First-time All-Star should be a force for many years . . . Joined Albert Belle to give Cleveland two 100-RBI men in same season for only time since Al Rosen and Larry Doby in 1954, the last year Indians won a pennant . . . His RBI total was most by AL second baseman since 1950, when Boston's Bobby Doerr had 120 . . . Set Indian records for homers and RBI by switch-hitter . . . Became only Indian second baseman with 200 hits since John Hodapp in 1930 . . . Placed second in AL with 205 hits, five behind Kirby Puckett . . . Member of major league All-Star team that toured Japan after the season . . . Underrated second baseman who turns double play extremely well and has strong arm . . . Acquired with Chris James and Sandy Alomar Jr. from San Diego for Joe Carter prior to 1990 season . . . Born Nov. 4, 1968, in San Juan, P.R. . . . Originally signed as free agent by Padres . . . Earned $500,000 in 1992.

Year	Club	Pos.	G	AB	R	H	2B	3B	HR	RBI	SB	Avg.
1990	Cleveland	3B-SS-2B	108	312	46	81	17	2	7	47	0	.260
1991	Cleveland	3B-2B-SS	158	593	80	171	28	2	11	69	3	.288
1992	Cleveland	2B	161	657	92	205	32	1	20	105	10	.312
	Totals		427	1562	218	457	77	5	38	221	13	.293

PAUL SORRENTO 27 6-2 210 Bats L Throws R

Proving to be a valuable addition . . . Was acquired from Minnesota for minor league pitchers Curtis Leskanic and Oscar Munoz just prior to last season . . . Clubbed 14 of 18 home runs as first baseman, most by a left-handed-hitting Indian first baseman since Boog Powell's 27 in 1975 . . . Hit ninth homer of season July 4, matching his career total entering the year . . . Recorded first hit at Baltimore's Camden Yards with second-inning single off Rick Sutcliffe . . . Also notched first home run there, in second game played . . . Beat Toronto with eighth-inning, two-run pinch-homer June 28 . . . Was fourth pinch-homer of career . . . Ideally a platoon player, because he struggles against lefties . . . Hit only .156 off southpaws last year . . . Born Nov. 17, 1965, in Somerville, Mass. . . . Earned $137,500 in 1992.

Year	Club	Pos.	G	AB	R	H	2B	3B	HR	RBI	SB	Avg.
1989	Minnesota	1B	14	21	2	5	0	0	0	1	0	.238
1990	Minnesota	1B	41	121	11	25	4	1	5	13	1	.207
1991	Minnesota	1B	26	47	6	12	2	0	4	13	0	.255
1992	Cleveland	1B	140	458	52	123	24	1	18	60	0	.269
	Totals		221	647	71	165	30	2	27	87	1	.255

SANDY ALOMAR Jr. 26 6-5 215 Bats R Throws R

Three-time All-Star catcher looks to stay healthy after two straight injury-plagued seasons . . . Was on disabled list from May 1-18 after tearing web between right middle and ring finger while blocking a pitch in the dirt . . . Tore cartilage in left knee while sliding into third Aug. 16 and injury required surgery Sept. 22 . . . Had two stints on DL in 1991, first time with inflamed right rotator cuff and second time with straight right hip flexor . . . Missed 111 games in 1991 . . . Threw out 29 of 67 potential base-stealers (43 percent) . . . *Baseball America*'s Minor League Player of the Year in 1988 and 1989 . . . Born June 18, 1966, in Salinas, P.R. . . . Signed with Padres as 17-year-old free agent in October 1983 . . . Father, Sandy Sr., enjoyed 15-year major league career . . . Earned $500,000 in 1992.

Year	Club	Pos.	G	AB	R	H	2B	3B	HR	RBI	SB	Avg.
1988	San Diego	PH	1	1	0	0	0	0	0	0	0	.000
1989	San Diego	C	7	19	1	4	1	0	1	6	0	.211
1990	Cleveland	C	132	445	60	129	26	2	9	66	4	.290
1991	Cleveland	C	51	184	10	40	9	0	0	7	0	.217
1992	Cleveland	C	89	299	22	75	16	0	2	26	3	.251
	Totals		280	948	93	248	52	2	12	105	7	.262

STEVE OLIN 27 6-2 190 Bats R Throws R

Sixteenth-round choice in 1987 draft has far exceeded expectations . . . Recorded 29 saves in 36 opportunities in first full season as closer . . . Already ranks third on Indians' all-time list with 48 career saves . . . His 72 appearances were most by an Indians pitcher since lefty Sid Monge's club-record 76 in 1979 . . . No right-hander has ever worked more often for Cleveland than this guy . . . Posted best results on road, fashioning 0.21 ERA in 35 games covering 43 innings . . . Sidearm style provides immediate advantage against right-handers, because they struggle to locate his release point . . . Has great difficulty retiring lefties, however, and they feasted on him for a .324 average last year . . . Played at Portland State . . . Born Oct. 4, 1965, in Portland . . . Salary was $300,000 in 1992.

Year	Club	G	IP	W	L	Pct.	SO	BB	H	ERA
1989	Cleveland	25	36	1	4	.200	24	14	35	3.75
1990	Cleveland	50	92⅓	4	4	.500	64	26	96	3.41
1991	Cleveland	48	56⅓	3	6	.333	38	23	61	3.36
1992	Cleveland	72	88⅓	8	5	.615	47	27	80	2.34
	Totals.	195	273	16	19	.457	173	90	272	3.10

CHARLES NAGY 25 6-3 200 **Bats L Throws R**

Ranks among game's finest starting pitchers . . . Achieved highest victory total by an Indian since Greg Swindell in 1988 . . . Won most games by an Indian right-hander since Bert Blyleven won 19 in 1984 . . . Excels at Cleveland Stadium . . . Owned 8-4 mark with 2.34 ERA in 17 starts there, compared to 9-6 with 3.67 in 16 starts on road . . . Was much more effective in first half of season with 11-4, 2.40 before All-Star break compared to 6-6 with 3.65 ERA after it . . . Surpassed 200 innings for second straight season . . . Named to All-Star staff for first time. Tossed one perfect inning and also recorded first hit by AL pitcher since Ken McBride in 1962 . . . Taken 17th overall by Cleveland in 1988 draft . . . Member of gold medal-winning team at 1988 Olympics . . . Born May 5, 1967, in Fairfield, Conn. . . . Starred for two years at University of Connecticut . . . Salary was $358,333 in 1992.

Year	Club	G	IP	W	L	Pct.	SO	BB	H	ERA
1990	Cleveland	9	45⅔	2	4	.333	26	21	58	5.91
1991	Cleveland	33	211⅓	10	15	.400	109	66	228	4.13
1992	Cleveland	33	252	17	10	.630	169	57	245	2.96
	Totals.	75	509	29	29	.500	304	144	531	3.71

DENNIS COOK 30 6-3 185 **Bats L Throws L**

A useful arm . . . Acquired from Los Angeles with right-hander Mike Christopher for right-hander Rudy Seanez . . . Indians went 15-10 in his 25 starts . . . Started year 1-4 with 5.91 ERA and was demoted to bullpen . . . Returned to rotation June 28 and was 4-2 with 3.43 ERA in next 16 starts . . . Vulnerable to long ball, allowing 29 home runs in 32 appearances . . . Tends to leave fastball up in zone . . . Recorded first AL victory April 26 against Milwaukee . . . Born Oct. 4, 1962, in Lamarque, Tex. . . . Was All-Conference outfielder for two seasons for University of Texas . . . His 1992 salary was $375,000.

Year	Club	G	IP	W	L	Pct.	SO	BB	H	ERA
1988	San Francisco	4	22	2	1	.667	13	11	9	2.86
1989	S.F.-Phil.	23	121	7	8	.467	67	38	110	3.72
1990	Phil.-LA	47	156	9	4	.692	64	56	155	3.92
1991	Los Angeles.	20	17⅔	1	0	1.000	8	7	12	0.51
1992	Cleveland	32	158	5	7	.417	96	50	156	3.82
	Totals.	126	474⅔	24	20	.545	248	162	442	3.66

BOB OJEDA 35 6-1 195 **Bats L Throws L**

Free-agent veteran signed one-year, $1.7-million contract with Indians, who are still awaiting development of their own pitchers . . . Comes off first losing season since 1987, when ulna-nerve surgery limited him to 10 appearances . . . Indians hope he'll benefit from return to AL, where he last pitched in 1985 . . . Far more effective against left-handed hitters throughout career . . . Intelligent pitcher known for outgoing personality . . . Born Dec. 17, 1957, in Los Angeles . . . Has been surprising critics since Boston signed him as free agent on May 20, 1978, to begin pro career . . . Earned $1.6 million as a Dodger in 1992.

Year	Club	G	IP	W	L	Pct.	SO	BB	H	ERA
1980	Boston	7	26	1	1	.500	12	14	39	6.92
1981	Boston	10	66	6	2	.750	28	25	50	3.14
1982	Boston	22	78⅓	4	6	.400	52	29	95	5.63
1983	Boston	29	173⅔	12	7	.632	94	73	173	4.04
1984	Boston	33	216⅔	12	12	.500	137	96	211	3.99
1985	Boston	39	157⅔	9	11	.450	102	48	166	4.00
1986	New York (NL)	32	217⅓	18	5	.783	148	52	185	2.57
1987	New York (NL)	10	46⅓	3	5	.375	21	10	45	3.88
1988	New York (NL)	29	190⅓	10	13	.435	133	33	158	2.88
1989	New York (NL)	31	192	13	11	.542	95	78	179	3.47
1990	New York (NL)	38	118	7	6	.538	62	40	123	3.66
1991	Los Angeles	31	189⅓	12	9	.571	120	70	181	3.18
1992	Los Angeles	29	166⅓	6	9	.400	94	81	169	3.63
	Totals	340	1838	113	97	.538	1098	649	1774	3.60

JOSE MESA 26 6-3 219 **Bats R Throws R**

Erratic righty still looking to establish himself . . . Acquired July 14 from Baltimore for Kyle Washington . . . Went 3-8 with 5.19 ERA in 13 games with Orioles, 12 of them starts . . . Made Indian debut July 16, dropping 3-2 decision to Kansas City . . . Gained first win as an Indian July 21 at Minnesota . . . Went 4-2 with 2.87 ERA in first 12 starts with Indians before fortunes plunged in last few starts . . . Best game of year was Sept. 14, when he beat Toronto and David Cone, 2-1 . . . Typically clocks in low 90's . . . Must work to reduce walk total . . . Walked seven at Baltimore Aug. 7 . . . Yielded Robin Yount's 3,000th hit

Sept. 9 at Milwaukee . . . Born May 22, 1966, in Azua, D.R. . . . Salary was $135,000 in 1992.

Year	Club	G	IP	W	L	Pct.	SO	BB	H	ERA
1987	Baltimore	6	31⅓	1	3	.250	17	15	38	6.03
1990	Baltimore	7	46⅔	3	2	.600	24	27	37	3.86
1991	Baltimore	23	123⅔	6	11	.353	64	62	151	5.97
1992	Balt.-Clev.	28	160⅔	7	12	.368	62	70	169	4.59
	Totals.	64	362⅓	17	28	.378	167	174	395	5.09

TOP PROSPECTS

JIM THOME 22 6-4 215 — Bats L Throws R

Should emerge as Tribe's third baseman, despite 1992 season wrecked by injuries . . . Hurt left wrist on checked swing during spring training and opened season on disabled list . . . Was activated May 18, only to be disabled 11 days later by a strained shoulder . . . Never got untracked after that and batted only .205 in 117 at-bats with Indians before being farmed out . . . Front office has not lost any faith in him . . . Born Aug. 27, 1970, in Peoria, Ill. . . . Cleveland's 13th selection in 1989 draft.

ALAN EMBREE 23 6-2 185 — Bats L Throws L

Fifth-round pick in 1989 draft has advanced swiftly . . . Reached majors last September after beginning year at Kinston (A) . . . Was 10-5, 3.30 in 15 starts at Kinston, then went 7-2 with a 2.28 ERA in 12 starts at Canton-Akron (AA) . . . Used low-90's fastball to strike out 171 in 180 minor league innings . . . Showed lack of readiness during brief major league trial, dropping his only two decisions with a 7.00 ERA . . . All he lacks is experience . . . Born Jan. 23, 1970, in Vancouver, Wash.

CHAD OGEA 22 6-2 200 — Bats R Throws R

Could bid for a spot in big league rotation very soon . . . Made huge impression in first year in organization . . . Went 13-3, 3.49 in 21 starts for Kinston (A) . . . Was even more convincing at Canton-Akron (AA), where he was 6-1, 2.20 . . . Gutsy competitor also won two playoff games for Canton, making him the victor in 21 games for the year . . . Born Nov. 9, 1970, in Lake Charles, La. . . . Starred for LSU in 1991 and helped Tigers win College World Series title . . . Third-round selection in 1991 missed first pro season due to late signing.

MANNY RAMIREZ 20 6-0 190 Bats R Throws R
First-round choice in 1991 draft is on course for standout career . . . Left fielder was batting .278 with 13 homers, 63 RBI in 81 games for Kinston (A) before suffering a season-ending injury to left hand July 4 . . . Known for extremely quick bat . . . Must reduce strikeouts, however, after fanning 74 times in 291 at-bats . . . Born May 30, 1972, in Santiago, D.R. . . . Raised in Bronx, N.Y.

MANAGER MIKE HARGROVE: Very capable manager has

Indians pointed in right direction after 76-86 finish last year . . . Has shown necessary patience in living with young players' mistakes and is beginning to reap rewards . . . Was serving as Indians' first-base coach when he was named to take over 26-52 club from John McNamara, July 6, 1991 . . . Built impressive credentials as minor league manager with 219-202 record . . . Coached at Batavia of New York-Penn League in 1986 . . . Honored as Carolina League Manager of the Year the following season with runnerup Kinston (A) . . . After year at Williamsport (AA), he was named Triple-A Manager of the Year in 1989, when he guided Colorado Springs to first-half championship of Pacific Coast League . . . Former first baseman spent six-plus seasons with Cleveland during 12-year major league career . . . Also played for Texas and San Diego . . . Named AL Rookie of the Year in 1974 . . . Led AL in walks in 1976 and 1978 . . . Boasted .400 career on-base percentage . . . Jokingly referred to as ''Human Rain Delay'' due to deliberate style of hitting . . . Born Oct. 26, 1949, in Perryton, Tex. . . . Wife, Sharon, co-authored ''Safe at Home,'' book about life of a baseball wife . . . Owns 108-137 major league managerial record.

ALL-TIME INDIAN SEASON RECORDS

BATTING: Joe Jackson, .408, 1911
HRs: Al Rosen, 43, 1953
RBI: Hal Trosky, 162, 1936
STEALS: Kenny Lofton, 66, 1992
WINS: Jim Bagby, 31, 1920
STRIKEOUTS: Bob Feller, 348, 1946

DETROIT TIGERS

TEAM DIRECTORY: Owner: Michael Ilitch; Chief Fin. Off.: Jerry Pasternak; GM: Jerry Walker; Asst. GM: Gary Vitto; Sr. Dir. Pub. Rel.: Dan Ewald; Dir. Pub. Rel.: Greg Shea; Trav. Sec.: Bill Brown; Mgr.: Sparky Anderson. Home: Tiger Stadium (52,416). Field distances: 340, l.f. line; 365, l.c.; 440, c.f.; 370, r.c.; 325, r.f. line. Spring training: Lakeland, Fla.

SCOUTING REPORT

HITTING: No team matches Detroit's clout. The Tigers will be attempting to pace the AL in home runs for the fourth consecutive season after slugging 182 last year, when they led the majors with 791 runs.

Hefty Cecil Fielder (.244, 35, 124) will be attempting to head the majors in RBI for the fourth consecutive season. He and Babe Ruth (1919-21) are the only players in history to do it for three years in a row. Rob Deer (.247, 32, 64) and Mickey Tettleton

Cecil Fielder is home office for RBI with 389 since '90.

(.238, 32, 83) give the Tigers two more 30-home-run men, although they combined for 268 strikeouts a year ago and contributed greatly to a staggering team total of 1,055 Ks.

Travis Fryman (.266, 20, 96) is a great young talent. Tony Phillips (.276, 10, 64) drew 114 walks last season and scored a major league-leading 114 runs. Lou Whitaker (.278, 19, 71) was retained as a free agent and Alan Trammell (.275, 1, 11) was re-signed, too, even though injuries limited the fading veteran to 29 games.

PITCHING: Detroit's offense puts runs on the board quickly, but its pitching gives them up at an even greater pace. The Tigers yielded 794 runs last year, marking only the second time in history that a team with the major league-leading offense generated fewer runs than its pitching allowed.

Detroit's rotation must be almost entirely rebuilt. Re-signing Bill Gullickson (14-13, 4.34) and signing free agents Mike Moore (17-12, 4.12), the former A's stalwart, and Bill Krueger (10-6, 4.30 with the Twins, 0-2, 6.75 with the Expos) represented a good start. Other help will have to come from the development of such young starters John Doherty (7-4, 3.88), David Haas (5-3, 3.94) and Greg Gohr (8-10, 3.99 for Triple-A Toledo). One of the assets of Mark Leiter (8-5, 4.18) is his versatility.

The bullpen is much more stable than the starting pitching. Mike Henneman (2-6, 3.96, 24 saves) will be trying for his fifth 20-save season. John Kiely (4-2, 2.13) and and Kurt Knudsen (2-3, 4.58) provide support from the right side. Mike Munoz (1-2, 3.00) has value from the left side.

FIELDING: Phillips is the Tigers' most significant defensive player because of his versatility. He started in the field at five different positions, starting 50 games at second base, 28 in right, 19 in center, 14 in left and 12 at third base. Tettleton has more going for him than his booming bat. He led AL catchers with a .996 fielding percentage, making only two errors in 524 total chances.

OUTLOOK: Neither Sparky Anderson nor Detroit is accustomed to losing. The Tigers' 75-87 record last year represented only their third season below .500 in the last 15 years. Their sixth-place finish marked only the second time since 1983 that they sank below third. But Tigers fans may have to become accustomed to tough times, because the pitching is still in tatters and the farm system is barren for the most part.

DETROIT TIGERS 1993 ROSTER

MANAGER Sparky Anderson

Coaches—Billy Consolo, Larry Herndon, Billy Muffett, Gene Roof, Dick Tracewski, Dan Whitmer

PITCHERS

No.	Name	1992 Club	W-L	IP	SO	ERA	B-T	Ht.	Wt.	Born
—	Bolton, Tom	Boston	1-2	29	23	3.41	L-L	6-3	185	5/6/62 Nashville, TN
		Cincinnati	3-3	46	27	5.24				
41	DeSilva, John	London	2-4	52	53	4.13	R-R	6-0	193	9/30/67 Fort Bragg, CA
		Toledo	0-3	19	21	8.53				
44	Doherty, John	Detroit	7-4	116	37	3.88	R-R	6-4	190	6/11/67 Bronx, NY
34	Gohr, Greg	Toledo	8-10	131	94	3.99	R-R	6-3	205	10/29/67 Santa Clara, CA
—	Gonzales, Frank	London	5-4	66	37	3.02	R-L	6-0	185	3/12/68 La Junta, CO
		Toledo	4-6	98	65	4.30				
42	Groom, Buddy	Toledo	7-7	109	71	2.80	L-L	6-2	200	7/10/65 Dallas, TX
		Detroit	0-5	39	15	5.82				
36	Gullickson, Bill	Detroit	14-13	222	64	4.34	R-R	6-3	220	2/20/59 Marshall, MN
16	Haas, David	Toledo	9-8	149	112	4.18	R-R	6-1	200	10/19/65 Independence, MO
		Detroit	5-3	62	16	3.94				
39	Henneman, Mike	Detroit	2-6	77	58	3.96	R-R	6-4	195	12/11/61 St. Charles, MO
46	Kiely, John	Toledo	1-1	32	31	2.84	R-R	6-3	215	10/4/64 Boston, MA
		Detroit	4-2	55	18	2.13				
27	Knudsen, Kurt	Toledo	3-1	22	19	2.08	R-R	6-3	200	2/20/67 Arlington Heights, IL
		Detroit	2-3	71	51	4.58				
—	Krueger, Bill	Minnesota	10-6	161	86	4.30	L-L	6-5	205	4/24/58 Waukegan, IL
		Montreal	0-2	17	13	6.75				
23	Leiter, Mark	Detroit	8-5	112	75	4.18	R-R	6-3	210	4/13/63 Joliet, IL
—	Lumley, Mike	London	8-3	75	51	2.52	R-R	6-1	185	1/29/67 Canada
—	Moore, Mike	Oakland	17-12	223	117	4.12	R-R	6-4	205	11/26/59 Eakly, OK
32	Munoz, Mike	Detroit	1-2	48	23	3.00	L-L	6-2	200	7/12/65 Baldwin Park, CA

CATCHERS

No.	Name	1992 Club	H	HR	RBI	Pct.	B-T	Ht.	Wt.	Born
19	Krueter, Chad	Detroit	48	2	16	.253	R-R	6-2	195	8/26/64 Greenbrae, CA
12	Rowland, Rich	Toledo	111	25	82	.235	R-R	6-1	215	2/25/67 Cloverdale, CA
		Detroit	3	0	0	.214				
20	Tettleton, Mickey	Detroit	125	32	83	.238	S-R	6-2	212	9/16/60 Oklahoma City, OK

INFIELDERS

9	Barnes, Skeeter	Detroit	45	3	25	.273	R-R	5-10	180	3/7/57 Cincinnati, OH
13	Brogna, Rico	Toledo	101	10	58	.261	L-L	6-2	202	4/18/70 Turner Falls, MA
		Detroit	5	1	3	.192				
—	Cruz, Ivan	London	144	14	104	.275	L-L	6-3	210	5/3/68 Puerto Rico
45	Fielder, Cecil	Detroit	145	35	124	.244	R-R	6-3	240	9/21/63 Los Angeles, CA
24	Fryman, Travis	Detroit	175	20	96	.266	R-R	6-1	180	4/25/69 Lexington, KY
7	Livingstone, Scott	Detroit	100	4	46	.282	L-R	6-0	198	7/15/65 Dallas, TX
4	Phillips, Tony	Detroit	167	10	64	.276	S-R	5-10	175	4/25/59 Atlanta, GA
3	Trammell, Alan	Detroit	28	1	11	.275	R-R	6-0	175	2/21/58 Garden Grove, CA
1	Whitaker, Lou	Detroit	126	19	71	.278	L-R	5-11	180	5/12/57 Brooklyn, NY

OUTFIELDERS

—	Bautista, Danny	Fayetteville	121	5	51	.268	R-R	5-11	170	5/24/72 Dominican Republic
40	Clark, Phil	Toledo	76	10	39	.280	R-R	6-0	180	5/6/68 Crockett, TX
		Detroit	22	1	5	.407				
22	Cuyler, Milt	Detroit	70	3	28	.241	S-R	5-10	185	10/7/68 Macon, GA
28	Deer, Rob	Detroit	97	32	64	.247	R-R	6-3	225	9/29/60 Orange, CA
32	Gladden, Dan	Detroit	106	7	42	.254	R-R	5-11	184	7/7/57 San Jose, CA
25	Hare, Shawn	Toledo	67	5	34	.330	L-L	6-1	200	3/26/67 St. Louis, MO
		Detroit	3	0	5	.115				
21	Hurst, Jody	Toledo	27	3	17	.186	R-L	6-4	185	3/11/67 Meridian, MS
		London	85	11	52	.316				
17	Ingram, Ricardo	Toledo	103	8	41	.251	R-R	6-0	198	9/10/66 Douglas, GA

TIGER PROFILES

CECIL FIELDER 29 6-3 240 Bats R Throws R

Slugger produces runs with machine-like consistency . . . Became second player to lead majors in RBI for three consecutive years, joining Babe Ruth (1919-21) . . . First Tiger to drive in at least 120 runs for three consecutive seasons and also first to slam 35 or more home runs in three straight seasons . . . His 389 RBI over last three years are most in majors in any three-year period since George Foster had 390 for Reds from 1976-78 . . . His 130 homers since 1990 are most in majors over three-year span since Frank Howard's 136 from 1968-70 . . . Averaged one home run per 17 at-bats last year, sixth-best ratio in AL . . . Only real flaw is penchant for strikeouts . . . Fanned 151 times, second-highest total in AL . . . Beefy first baseman gained Detroit's attention by slamming 38 home runs in 1989 for Hanshin Tigers, who had purchased him from Toronto after the 1988 season . . . Retains huge following in Japan . . . Royals' fourth-round pick in 1982 draft . . . Born Sept. 21, 1963, in Los Angeles . . . He earned $4.5 million in 1992 and signed a five-year, $36-million contract in January. This includes a record $10-million signing bonus, exceeding David Cone's $9 million for signing with the Royals in December.

Year	Club	Pos.	G	AB	R	H	2B	3B	HR	RBI	SB	Avg.
1985	Toronto	1B	30	74	6	23	4	0	4	16	0	.311
1986	Toronto	1B-3B-OF	34	83	7	13	2	0	4	13	0	.157
1987	Toronto	1B-3B	82	175	30	47	7	1	14	32	0	.269
1988	Toronto	1B-3B-2B	74	174	24	40	6	1	9	23	0	.230
1990	Detroit.	1B	159	573	104	159	25	1	51	132	0	.277
1991	Detroit.	1B	162	624	102	163	25	0	44	133	0	.261
1992	Detroit.	1B	155	594	80	145	22	0	35	124	0	.244
	Totals		696	2297	353	590	91	3	161	473	0	.257

TRAVIS FRYMAN 23 6-1 180 Bats R Throws R

Young star with tremendous future . . . Was Detroit's lone representative in All-Star Game, producing a hit in only at-bat . . . Led Tigers in hits, total bases (274), games and at-bats . . . Opened season at third base . . . Shifted to shortstop, his natural position, May 15, because Alan Trammell fractured an ankle . . . Did not miss a start at shortstop after Trammell went down . . . Also took over third position in batting order . . . Erupted for 25 RBI in July . . . Needs to reduce strikeouts after fanning 144 times, fourth-highest total in league . . . Born April 25, 1969, in Lexington, Ky. . . . Detroit's third selection in 1987 draft . . . A bargain at a salary of $300,000 in 1992.

Year	Club	Pos.	G	AB	R	H	2B	3B	HR	RBI	SB	Avg.
1990	Detroit.......	3B-SS	66	232	32	69	11	1	9	27	3	.297
1991	Detroit.......	3B-SS	149	557	65	144	36	3	21	91	12	.259
1992	Detroit.......	SS-3B	161	659	87	175	31	4	20	96	8	.266
	Totals.......		376	1448	184	388	78	8	50	214	23	.268

LOU WHITAKER 35 5-11 180 Bats L Throws R

Has had distinguished career and is still going strong . . . Joined Joe Morgan as only second basemen in history with 2,000 games, 2,000 hits and 200 home runs . . . Produced 2,000th hit June 6 off Yankees' Scott Kamieniecki . . . Smashed 200th homer off Seattle's Jeff Nelson July 3 . . . Ranks among Tigers elite with 2,095 games (fifth), 2,088 hits (fifth), 353 doubles (seventh), 209 home runs (seventh), 930 RBI (10th), 7,616 at-bats (fifth) and 1,211 runs (fifth) . . . Only knock on him is occasional absence from lineup with minor ailments . . . AL Rookie of the Year in 1978 . . . Born May 12, 1957, in Brooklyn, N.Y. . . . Detroit's fifth-round choice in 1975 draft . . . Earned $2.2 million in 1992, then became free agent and re-signed three-year, $10-million pact.

Year	Club	Pos.	G	AB	R	H	2B	3B	HR	RBI	SB	Avg.
1977	Detroit.......	2B	11	32	5	8	1	0	0	2	2	.250
1978	Detroit.......	2B	139	484	71	138	12	7	3	58	7	.285
1979	Detroit.......	2B	127	423	75	121	14	8	3	42	20	.286
1980	Detroit.......	2B	145	477	68	111	19	1	1	45	8	.233
1981	Detroit.......	2B	109	335	48	88	14	4	5	36	5	.263
1982	Detroit.......	2B	152	560	76	160	22	8	15	65	11	.286
1983	Detroit.......	2B	161	643	94	206	40	6	12	72	17	.320
1984	Detroit.......	2B	143	558	90	161	25	1	13	56	6	.289
1985	Detroit.......	2B	152	609	102	170	29	8	21	73	6	.279
1986	Detroit.......	2B	144	584	95	157	26	6	20	73	13	.269
1987	Detroit.......	2B	149	604	110	160	38	6	16	59	13	.265
1988	Detroit.......	2B	115	403	54	111	18	2	12	55	2	.275
1989	Detroit.......	2B	148	509	77	128	21	1	28	85	6	.251
1990	Detroit.......	2B	132	472	75	112	22	2	18	60	8	.237
1991	Detroit.......	2B	138	470	94	131	26	2	23	78	4	.279
1992	Detroit.......	2B	130	453	77	126	26	0	19	71	6	.278
	Totals.......		2095	7616	1211	2088	353	62	209	930	134	.274

TONY PHILLIPS 33 5-10 175 Bats S Throws R

Tremendous asset to Tigers . . . Became first Tiger with 100 runs and 100 walks in same season since 1961, when Norm Cash and Rocky Colavito did it . . . First Tiger to pace majors in runs since Ron LeFlore scored 126 in 1978 . . . Drew 114 walks, fourth-highest total in majors . . . Started at six different positions: 50 games at second base, 34 at DH, 28 in right field, 19 in center, 14 in left and 12 at third . . . Comes off career bests in games, at-bats, runs, hits, doubles and walks . . . Frequently praised for his solid makeup . . . Significant member of A's World Series teams in 1988 and 1989 . . . Played every position except pitcher and catcher with A's . . . Signed with Detroit as free agent prior to 1990 season . . . Born April 25, 1959, in Atlanta . . . Expos' first-round pick in January 1978 . . . Earned $1,566,667 in 1992.

Year	Club	Pos.	G	AB	R	H	2B	3B	HR	RBI	SB	Avg.
1982	Oakland	SS	40	81	11	17	2	2	0	8	2	.210
1983	Oakland	SS-2B-3B	148	412	54	102	12	3	4	35	16	.248
1984	Oakland	SS-2B-OF	154	451	62	120	24	3	4	37	10	.266
1985	Oakland	3B-2B	42	161	23	45	12	2	4	17	3	.280
1986	Oakland	SS-2B-3B	118	441	76	113	14	5	5	52	15	.256
1987	Oakland	2B-3B-SS-OF	111	379	48	91	20	0	10	46	7	.240
1988	Oakland	INF-OF	79	212	32	43	8	4	2	17	0	.203
1989	Oakland	INF-OF	143	451	48	118	15	6	4	47	3	.262
1990	Detroit	3B-2B-SS-OF	152	573	97	144	23	5	8	55	19	.251
1991	Detroit	OF-3B-2B-SS	146	564	87	160	28	4	17	72	10	.284
1992	Detroit	OF-2B-3B-SS	159	606	114	167	32	3	10	64	12	.276
	Totals		1292	4331	652	1120	190	37	68	450	97	.259

MICKEY TETTLETON 32 6-2 212 Bats S Throws R

Packs more clout than any other catcher . . . He and Cecil Fielder became only Tigers to enjoy consecutive 30-home-run seasons since Hank Greenberg . . . Patient hitter who tied with White Sox' Frank Thomas for AL lead in walks with 122 . . . Has drawn 100 walks in three consecutive seasons, but also is a 100-plus strikeout man . . . Did bulk of damage before All-Star break, with 19 homers and 52 RBI . . . Topped AL catchers with .996 fielding percentage . . . Made only two errors in 524 total chances . . . Obtained from Orioles for Jeff Robinson prior to 1991 season . . . Born Sept. 16, 1960, in Oklahoma City, Okla. . . . Athletics' fifth selection in 1981 draft . . . Salvaged career after release by A's just prior to 1988 season . . . Earned $3.3 million in 1992.

Year	Club	Pos.	G	AB	R	H	2B	3B	HR	RBI	SB	Avg.
1984	Oakland	C	33	76	10	20	2	1	1	5	0	.263
1985	Oakland	C	78	211	23	53	12	0	3	15	2	.251
1986	Oakland	C	90	211	26	43	9	0	10	35	7	.204
1987	Oakland	C-1B	82	211	19	41	3	0	8	26	1	.194
1988	Baltimore	C	86	283	31	74	11	1	11	37	0	.261
1989	Baltimore	C	117	411	72	106	21	2	26	65	3	.258
1990	Baltimore	C-1B-OF	135	444	68	99	21	2	15	51	2	.223
1991	Detroit.	C-OF-1B	154	501	85	132	17	2	31	89	3	.263
1992	Detroit.	C-1B-OF	157	525	82	125	25	0	32	83	0	.238
	Totals		932	2873	416	693	121	8	137	406	18	.241

ROB DEER 32 6-3 225 Bats R Throws R

Must continue to improve batting average while retaining power . . . His batting average was his highest since 1988 . . . Batted .293 from Aug. 21 to end of season . . . Has delivered 20 or more home runs for seven consecutive seasons . . . Only Andre Dawson owns a longer active streak, with eight . . . Enjoyed five two-homer games . . . Connected against every AL club . . . Quality outfielder with strong arm . . . Giants' fourth-round choice in 1978 draft . . . Born Sept. 29, 1960, in Orange, Cal. . . . Earned $2,016,667 in 1992.

Year	Club	Pos.	G	AB	R	H	2B	3B	HR	RBI	SB	Avg.
1984	San Francisco	OF	13	24	5	4	0	0	3	3	1	.167
1985	San Francisco	OF-1B	78	162	22	30	5	1	8	20	0	.185
1986	Milwaukee	OF-1B	134	466	75	108	17	3	33	86	5	.232
1987	Milwaukee	OF-1B	134	474	71	113	15	2	28	80	12	.238
1988	Milwaukee	OF	135	492	71	124	24	0	23	85	9	.252
1989	Milwaukee	OF	130	466	72	98	18	2	26	65	4	.210
1990	Milwaukee	OF-1B	134	440	57	92	15	1	27	69	2	.209
1991	Detroit.	OF	134	448	64	80	14	2	25	64	1	.179
1992	Detroit.	OF	110	393	66	97	20	1	32	64	4	.247
	Totals		1002	3365	503	746	128	12	205	536	38	.222

BILL GULLICKSON 34 6-3 220 Bats R Throws R

Must rebound after alarming late-season slump . . . Was staff ace through early August with 13-7 record and 3.56 ERA in 24 starts . . . Then went 1-6 with 6.45 ERA in last 10 starts . . . Went winless in last six starts, dropping five of them . . . Biggest problem was home-run ball . . . Surrendered league-high 35 home runs, including 13 in final six starts . . . May not be able to sustain velocity over full season any longer . . . Still led Tigers in victories, innings pitched, starts and complete games (4) for second straight year . . . Major league career appeared to be over some time ago . . . Spent 1988 and 1989 seasons with Japan's Yomiuri Giants . . . Born Feb. 20, 1959, in Marshall, Minn. . . . Expos made him second player taken overall, behind Harold Baines, in 1977 draft . . . Earned $1,925,000 in 1992, became free agent and then re-signed two-year, $4.6-million contract.

Year	Club	G	IP	W	L	Pct.	SO	BB	H	ERA
1979	Montreal	1	1	0	0	.000	0	0	2	0.00
1980	Montreal	24	141	10	5	.667	120	50	127	3.00
1981	Montreal	22	157	7	9	.438	115	34	142	2.81
1982	Montreal	34	236⅔	12	14	.462	155	61	231	3.57
1983	Montreal	34	242⅓	17	12	.586	120	59	230	3.75
1984	Montreal	32	226⅔	12	9	.571	100	37	230	3.61
1985	Montreal	29	181⅓	14	12	.538	68	47	187	3.52
1986	Cincinnati	37	244⅔	15	12	.556	121	60	245	3.38
1987	Cincinnati	27	165	10	11	.476	89	39	172	4.85
1987	New York (AL)	8	48	4	2	.667	28	11	46	4.88
1990	Houston	32	193⅓	10	14	.417	73	61	221	3.82
1991	Detroit	35	226⅓	20	9	.690	91	44	256	3.90
1992	Detroit	34	221⅔	14	13	.519	64	50	228	4.34
	Totals	349	2285	145	122	.543	1144	553	2317	3.73

MIKE HENNEMAN 31 6-4 195 Bats R Throws R

Difficult workload through years may be taking toll . . . Floundered from June 30 until end of season, posting worrisome 5.08 ERA in that span . . . Paced Tigers with 24 saves, in 28 tries, but overall ERA was career high . . . Was required to pitch two innings for eight of his saves . . . Stands ninth on all-time club list with 369 appearances . . . Ranks third with 104 career saves, 16 behind Willie Hernandez and 21 behind John Hiller . . . First Tiger to post 20 saves in four different seasons . . . Born Dec. 11, 1961, in St. Charles, Mo. . . . Tigers' third-round pick in 1984 draft . . . Helped Oklahoma State reach College World Series in 1983 and 1984 . . . Highest-paid Tiger pitcher in 1992 with $2,437,500 salary.

Year	Club	G	IP	W	L	Pct.	SO	BB	H	ERA
1987	Detroit	55	96⅔	11	3	.786	75	30	86	2.98
1988	Detroit	65	91⅓	9	6	.600	58	24	72	1.87
1989	Detroit	60	90	11	4	.733	69	51	84	3.70
1990	Detroit	69	94⅓	8	6	.571	50	33	90	3.05
1991	Detroit	60	84⅓	10	2	.833	61	34	81	2.88
1992	Detroit	60	77⅓	2	6	.250	58	20	75	3.96
	Totals	369	534	51	27	.654	371	192	488	3.05

MIKE MOORE 33 6-4 205 Bats R Throws R

Free agent became a Tiger with three-year, $10-million pact in December . . . Led A's in wins and innings and did not miss a turn . . . For third time in four years, he won at least 17 and pitched more than 200 innings . . . Has started 30 or more games last nine seasons . . . Up-and-down season included four wins and 1.51 ERA in April, 3-7 record and 6.52 ERA in May and June . . . Went 10-5 in final 19 starts . . . Went 66-46 with Oakland after going 66-96 as Mariner . . . Lost two ALCS games and posted 7.45 postseason ERA last year . . . Had been 4-1 with 1.88 ERA in five previous postseason starts . . . Earned $3.5 million in 1992 . . . Signed with Athletics as a free agent before 1989 season, after six years with Mariners . . . First pick overall by Mariners in 1981 draft . . . Born Nov. 26, 1959, in Eakly, Okla.

Year	Club	G	IP	W	L	Pct.	SO	BB	H	ERA
1982	Seattle	28	144⅓	7	14	.333	73	79	159	5.36
1983	Seattle	22	128	6	8	.429	108	60	130	4.71
1984	Seattle	34	212	7	17	.292	158	85	236	4.97
1985	Seattle	35	247	17	10	.630	155	70	230	3.46
1986	Seattle	38	266	11	13	.458	146	94	279	4.30
1987	Seattle	33	231	9	19	.321	115	84	268	4.71
1988	Seattle	37	228⅔	9	15	.375	182	63	196	3.78
1989	Oakland	35	241⅔	19	11	.633	172	83	193	2.61
1990	Oakland	33	199⅓	13	15	.464	73	84	204	4.65
1991	Oakland	33	210	17	8	.680	153	105	176	2.96
1992	Oakland	36	223	17	12	.586	117	103	229	4.12
	Totals	364	2331	132	142	.482	1452	910	2300	4.07

JOHN DOHERTY 25 6-4 190 Bats R Throws R

Surprising performer has chance to be a fixture in Tigers' rotation . . . Made club in spring training despite absence of Triple-A experience . . . Threw 12⅓ scoreless innings during exhibition season . . . Earned spot in bullpen and went 2-2 with 4.12 ERA and three saves in 36 appearances . . . Convinced Tigers he should be a starter when he worked five scoreless innings as long man in July 31 game at Cleveland . . . Did not pitch in relief again . . . Made 11 starts from Aug. 5 to end of season, going 5-2 with 3.82 ERA . . . Best asset is outstanding control . . . Walked only nine batters in 61⅓ innings as a starter . . . Born June 11, 1967, in Bronx, N.Y. . . . Detroit's 19th pick in 1989 draft . . . Earned minimum of $109,000 in 1992.

Year	Club	G	IP	W	L	Pct.	SO	BB	H	ERA
1992	Detroit	47	116	7	4	.636	37	25	131	3.88

TOP PROSPECTS

RICHARD ROWLAND 26 6-1 215 — Bats R Throws R

International League All-Star needs to continue defensive improvement to break into big leagues . . . Has excellent arm, but is still learning many elements of catching . . . Pull hitter with outstanding power hit .235 with 25 home runs and 82 RBI for Toledo (AAA) . . . Has made surprising rise since becoming Detroit's 17th pick in 1988 draft . . . Born Feb. 25, 1967, in Cloverdale, Cal.

GREG GOHR 25 6-3 205 — Bats R Throws R

Good velocity and mental makeup give him chance to succeed in big leagues . . . Went 8-10 with 3.99 ERA in 22 games for Toledo (AAA), including 20 starts . . . Missed last three weeks with pulled muscle behind rib cage . . . Still learning to pitch . . . Detroit's first pick in 1989 draft, out of Santa Clara University . . . Born Oct. 29, 1967, in Santa Clara, Cal. . . . Topped Lakeland (A) in victories with 13-5 record in 1990.

RICO BROGNA 22 6-2 202 — Bats L Throws L

Should make significant contribution to Tigers this year . . . Batted .261 with 10 homers and 58 RBI in 121 games for Toledo (AAA) . . . Outstanding first baseman . . . Learning to pull ball more . . . Possesses decent but not exceptional power . . . Tigers' first-round pick in 1988 . . . Born April 18, 1970, in Turner Falls, Mass. . . . Heavily recruited as a tight end by Clemson.

SEAN BERGMAN 22 6-4 205 — Bats R Throws R

On fast track to big leagues . . . Split second pro season between Lakeland (A) and London (AA) . . . Was 5-2 with 2.49 ERA in 13 starts for Lakeland and went 4-7 with 4.28 ERA in 14 starts for London . . . Sixth-round pick in 1991, out of Southern Illinois University . . . Born April 11, 1970, in Joliet, Ill.

MANAGER SPARKY ANDERSON: May have to prove himself to new ownership after rare poor finish at 75-87 . . . Has chance to win if he's given any material . . . Understands better than most managers the importance of team chemistry . . . Refuses to keep problem players on club . . . Track record is impeccable . . . First manager to win World Series in both leagues . . . Named Manager of the Year in both leagues . . . Led world champion 1984 Tigers to club-record 104 victories . . . Has won 18 League Championship Series games . . . First major league manager to win 700 games with two different teams . . . Boasts 21-year record of 1,996-1,611 . . . Record with Detroit stands at 1,133-1,025 . . . Became Tigers' manager in June 1979 . . . Big Red Machine won five NL West titles, four pennants and two World Series under him . . . Born Feb. 22, 1934, in Bridgewater, S.D. . . . Played in minors for six seasons as infielder . . . Played for Philadelphia in 1959, his lone year as major leaguer . . . Only Dodgers' Tommy Lasorda boasts longer continuous service among major league managers.

ALL-TIME TIGER SEASON RECORDS

BATTING: Ty Cobb, .420, 1911
HRs: Hank Greenberg, 58, 1938
RBI: Hank Greenberg, 183, 1937
STEALS: Ty Cobb, 96, 1915
WINS: Denny McLain, 31, 1968
STRIKEOUTS: Mickey Lolich, 308, 1971

MILWAUKEE BREWERS

TEAM DIRECTORY: Pres./CEO: Allan (Bud) Selig; Sr. VP-Baseball Oper.: Sal Bando; Sr. VP: Harry Dalton; Asst. VP-Baseball Oper.: Bruce Manno; Dir. Player Dev.: Fred Stanley; Dir. Communications: Laurel Prieb; Dir. Media Rel.: Tom Skibosh; Dir. Publications: Mario Ziino; Trav. Sec.: Steve Ethier; Mgr.: Phil Garner. Home: Milwaukee County Stadium (53,192). Field distances: 315, l.f. line; 362, l.f.; 392, l.c.; 402, c.f.; 392, r.c.; 362, r.f.; 315, r.f. line. Spring training: Chandler, Ariz.

SCOUTING REPORT

HITTING: The Brewers can hit their way aboard as well as almost any team, and what follows that is very predictable. They will run, run, run.

The Brewers embraced rookie manager Phil Garner's aggressive style last year and thrived. They recorded a major league-leading 256 stolen bases and became the first AL East team in history to surpass 200 steals in a season. Rookie of the Year Pat Listach (.290, 93 runs) returns to head the running game after registering a club-record 54 stolen bases.

Robin Yount (.264, 8, 77) picked up a Hall of Fame credential when he produced his 3,000th hit last September. Another big year is needed from powerful Greg Vaughn (.228, 23, 78). The Brewers finished with only 82 home runs last year and hope the acquisition of former Ranger Kevin Reimer (.267, 16, 58) will supply power from the left side. The Brewers suffered a huge blow when the virtually irreplaceable Paul Molitor (.320, 12, 89) signed with division rival Toronto last winter.

PITCHING: Milwaukee topped the AL with a 3.43 ERA last year and the staff might even be deep enough to withstand the loss of 16-game-winner Chris Bosio to Seattle as a free agent.

There are great expectations for Cal Eldred, who won 11 of 13 decisions and posted a 1.79 ERA after being recalled from Denver last July. Jaime Navarro (17-11, 3.33) is another excellent starter. Bill Wegman (13-14, 3.20 in 261⅔ innings) pitches quality innings in bunches. Ricky Bones (9-10, 4.57) also figures to receive an opportunity to start.

Doug Henry (1-4, 4.02) converted 29 saves in 33 opportunities in his first full season as closer, proving his dependability in that role. Mike Fetters (5-1, 1.87) and James Austin (5-2, 1.85) are

Rookie of the Year Pat Listach adds spice to Brew.

two other quality relievers, so the Brewers aren't likely to miss free-agent defector Dan Plesac.

FIELDING: Defense helped make a difference for Milwaukee last year and should do so again. The Brewers recorded a major league-leading .986 fielding percentage and set a club record by committing only 89 errors, 29 fewer than in 1991.

OUTLOOK: Milwaukee posted a 92-70 finish last season as the final club eliminated from the race. The Brewers, who did not bow out until the next-to-last day of the regular season, should be formidable again in 1993. However, they will not be as lightly regarded this time around and opponents should be much better prepared to control their running game.

MILWAUKEE BREWERS 1993 ROSTER

MANAGER Phil Garner

Coaches—Bill Castro, Duffy Dyer, Tim Foli, Don Rowe

PITCHERS

No.	Name	1992 Club	W-L	IP	SO	ERA	B-T	Ht.	Wt.	Born
42	Austin, James	Milwaukee	5-2	58	30	1.85	R-R	6-2	200	12/7/63 Farmville, VA
25	Bones, Ricky	Milwaukee	9-10	163	65	4.57	R-R	6-0	190	4/7/69 Puerto Rico
—	Boze, Marshall	Beloit	13-7	146	126	2.83	R-R	6-1	212	5/23/71 San Manuel, AZ
—	Corbin, Archie	Memphis	7-8	112	100	4.73	R-R	6-4	215	11/24/67 Cedar Rapids, IA
		Harrisburg	0-0	3	3	0.00				
21	Eldred, Cal	Denver	10-6	141	99	3.00	R-R	6-4	215	11/24/67 Cedar Rapids, IA
		Milwaukee	11-2	100	62	1.79				
36	Fetters, Mike	Milwaukee	5-1	63	43	1.87	R-R	6-4	212	12/19/64 Van Nuys, CA
—	Gamez, Francisco	Stockton	9-5	134	95	3.63	R-R	6-2	185	4/2/70 Mexico
—	George, Chris	Denver	2-3	43	20	4.64	R-R	6-2	200	9/24/66 Pittsburgh, PA
—	Green, Otis	Denver	11-8	152	114	4.61	L-L	6-2	192	3/11/64 Miami, FL
28	Henry, Doug	Milwaukee	1-4	65	52	4.02	R-R	6-4	185	12/10/63 Sacramento, CA
49	Higuera, Ted	Beloit	1-0	11	11	3.27	S-L	5-10	178	11/9/58 Mexico
		El Paso	0-1	5	3	3.60				
		Denver	1-0	9	4	4.15				
—	Ignasiak, Mike	Denver	7-4	92	64	2.93	S-R	5-11	175	3/12/66 Anchorville, MI
—	Kiefer, Mark	Denver	7-13	163	145	4.59	R-R	6-4	175	11/13/68 Orange, CA
—	Maldonado, Carlos	Omaha	7-4	75	60	3.60	R-R	6-1	215	10/18/66 Panama
—	Manzanillo, Josias	Omaha	7-10	136	114	4.36	R-R	6-0	190	10/16/67 Dominican Republic
		Memphis	0-2	7	8	7.36				
—	Miranda, Angel	Denver	6-12	160	122	4.77	L-L	6-1	160	11/9/69 Puerto Rico
31	Navarro, Jaime	Milwaukee	17-11	246	100	3.33	R-R	6-4	210	3/27/67 Puerto Rico
—	Novoa, Rafael	El Paso	10-7	146	124	3.26	L-L	6-1	180	10/26/67 New York, NY
47	Orosco, Jesse	Milwaukee	3-1	39	40	3.23	R-L	6-2	185	4/21/57 Santa Barbara, CA
33	Robinson, Ron	Stockton	1-1	23	11	3.57	R-R	6-4	235	3/24/62 Woodlake, CA
		Milwaukee	1-4	35	12	5.86				
46	Wegman, Bill	Milwaukee	13-14	262	127	3.20	R-R	6-5	220	12/19/62 Cincinnati, OH
—	Wishnevski, Rob	El Paso	1-0	17	16	1.04	R-R	6-1	215	1/2/67 Hammond, IN
		Denver	9-6	77	64	5.03				

CATCHERS

No.	Name	1992 Club	H	HR	RBI	Pct.	B-T	Ht.	Wt.	Born
27	Kmak, Joe	Denver	70	3	31	.311	R-R	6-0	185	5/3/63 Napa, CA
26	McIntosh, Tim	Milwaukee	14	0	6	.182	R-R	5-11	195	3/21/65 Minneapolis, MN
11	Nilsson, Dave	Denver	76	3	39	.317	L-R	6-3	185	12/14/69 Australia
		Milwaukee	38	4	25	.232				
5	Surhoff, B.J.	Milwaukee	121	4	62	.252	L-R	6-1	200	8/4/64 Bronx, NY

INFIELDERS

No.	Name	1992 Club	H	HR	RBI	Pct.	B-T	Ht.	Wt.	Born
32	Jaha, John	Denver	88	18	69	.321	R-R	6-1	195	5/27/66 Portland, OR
		Milwaukee	30	2	10	.226				
16	Listach, Pat	Milwaukee	168	1	47	.290	S-R	5-9	170	9/12/67 Natchitoches, LA
9	Spiers, Bill	Beloit	13	0	7	.236	L-R	6-2	190	6/5/66 Orangeburg, SC
		Milwaukee	5	0	2	.313				
0	Stubbs, Franklin	Milwaukee	66	9	42	.229	L-L	6-2	209	10/21/60 Laurinburg, NC
2	Suero, William	Denver	71	1	25	.257	R-R	5-9	175	11/7/66 Dominican Republic
		Milwaukee	3	0	0	.188				
54	Valentin, Jose	Denver	118	3	45	.240	S-R	5-10	175	10/12/69 Puerto Rico
		Milwaukee	0	0	1	.000				

OUTFIELDERS

No.	Name	1992 Club	H	HR	RBI	Pct.	B-T	Ht.	Wt.	Born
18	Diaz, Alex	Denver	122	1	41	.268	S-R	5-11	175	10/5/68 Brooklyn, NY
		Milwaukee	1	0	1	.111				
24	Hamilton, Darryl	Milwaukee	140	5	62	.298	L-R	6-1	180	12/3/64 Baton Rouge, LA
—	Maldonado, Candy	Toronto	133	20	66	.272	R-R	6-0	195	9/5/60 Puerto Rico
—	Mieske, Matt	Denver	140	19	77	.267	R-R	6-0	185	2/13/68 Midland, MI
—	O'Leary, Troy	El Paso	169	5	79	.334	L-L	6–0	175	8/4/69 Compton, CA
—	Reimer, Kevin	Texas	132	16	58	.267	L-R	6-2	225	6/28/64 Macon, GA
23	Vaughn, Greg	Milwaukee	114	23	78	.228	R-R	6-0	193	7/3/65 Sacramento, CA
19	Yount, Robin	Milwaukee	147	8	77	.264	R-R	6-0	180	9/16/55 Danville, IL

BREWER PROFILES

PAT LISTACH 25 5-9 170 Bats S Throws R

AL Rookie of the Year capitalized on unexpected opportunity to gain recognition . . . Sent to Denver (AAA) to open season, but did not play a game there . . . Was instead recalled by Brewers April 7 to replace disabled shortstop Bill Spiers . . . Went on to break club rookie records for hits, runs and stolen bases . . . Recorded first major league hit in first at-bat, April 12 off California's Mark Langston . . . Switch-hitter who is a much tougher out from right side (.345) than from left (.271) . . . Placed second in AL in stolen bases as he became first Brewer to register 50 steals in a season . . . Made 24 errors at shortstop, but just nine after All-Star break . . . Had 17-game hitting streak from Aug. 31-Sept. 18 . . . Born Sept. 12, 1967, in Natchitoches, La. . . . Second-round pick in 1988 draft . . . A great bargain at $109,000 in 1992.

Year	Club	Pos.	G	AB	R	H	2B	3B	HR	RBI	SB	Avg.
1992	Milwaukee	SS-2B-OF	149	579	93	168	19	6	1	47	54	.290

ROBIN YOUNT 37 6-0 180 Bats R Throws R

Brilliant veteran will continue climb on all-time hit list . . . Achieved 3,000-hit plateau Sept. 9, with seventh-inning single off Cleveland's Jose Mesa . . . Became 17th player to reach that level and third youngest, behind Ty Cobb and Hank Aaron . . . Cracked first hit at age 18, off Baltimore's Dave McNally in April 1974 . . . Ranks 14th all-time with 3,025 hits . . . Has lost some offensive skills, however . . . Has hit .264 or lower each of last three years . . . Failed to reach double figures in home runs for first time in six years . . . Center fielder did generate his highest total of doubles since 1983 . . . Two-time AL MVP honoree, receiving award in 1982 and '89 . . . Born Sept. 16, 1955, in Danville, Ill. . . . Selected in first round of 1973 draft . . . Earned $3.2 million in 1992.

Year	Club	Pos.	G	AB	R	H	2B	3B	HR	RBI	SB	Avg.
1974	Milwaukee	SS	107	344	48	86	14	5	3	26	7	.250
1975	Milwaukee	SS	147	558	67	149	28	2	8	52	12	.267
1976	Milwaukee	SS-OF	161	638	59	161	19	3	2	54	16	.252
1977	Milwaukee	SS	154	605	66	174	34	4	4	49	16	.288
1978	Milwaukee	SS	127	502	66	147	23	9	9	71	16	.293
1979	Milwaukee	SS	149	577	72	154	26	5	8	51	11	.267
1980	Milwaukee	SS	143	611	121	179	49	10	23	87	20	.293
1981	Milwaukee	SS	96	377	50	103	15	5	10	49	4	.273
1982	Milwaukee	SS	156	635	129	210	46	12	29	114	14	.331
1983	Milwaukee	SS	149	578	102	178	42	10	17	80	12	.308
1984	Milwaukee	SS	160	624	105	186	27	7	16	80	14	.298
1985	Milwaukee	OF-1B	122	466	76	129	26	3	15	68	10	.277
1986	Milwaukee	OF-1B	140	522	82	163	31	7	9	46	14	.312
1987	Milwaukee	OF	158	635	99	198	25	9	21	103	19	.312
1988	Milwaukee	OF	162	621	92	190	38	11	13	91	22	.306
1989	Milwaukee	OF	160	614	101	195	38	9	21	103	19	.318
1990	Milwaukee	OF	158	587	98	145	17	5	17	77	15	.247
1991	Milwaukee	OF	130	503	66	131	20	4	10	77	6	.260
1992	Milwaukee	OF	150	557	71	147	40	3	8	77	15	.264
	Totals		2729	10554	1570	3025	558	123	243	1355	262	.287

KEVIN REIMER 28 6-2 225 Bats L Throws R

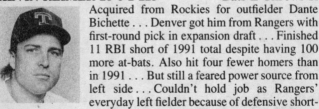

Acquired from Rockies for outfielder Dante Bichette . . . Denver got him from Rangers with first-round pick in expansion draft . . . Finished 11 RBI short of 1991 total despite having 100 more at-bats. Also hit four fewer homers than in 1991 . . . But still a feared power source from left side . . . Couldn't hold job as Rangers' everyday left fielder because of defensive shortcomings . . . Committed 11 errors, showed limited range and weak throwing arm . . . Not likely to play much defense any more, he could become a DH . . . Hard worker and hard-nosed player who was a defenseman in his days as an amateur hockey player . . . Earned $210,000 in 1992 . . . Born June 28, 1964, in Macon, Ga., but raised in British Columbia . . . Rangers' 11th-round draft pick in 1985.

Year	Club	Pos.	G	AB	R	H	2B	3B	HR	RBI	SB	Avg.
1988	Texas	OF	12	25	2	3	0	0	1	2	0	.120
1989	Texas	DH	3	5	0	0	0	0	0	0	0	.000
1990	Texas	OF	64	100	5	26	9	1	2	15	0	.260
1991	Texas	OF	136	394	46	106	22	0	20	69	0	.269
1992	Texas	OF	148	494	56	132	32	2	16	58	2	.267
	Totals		363	1018	109	267	63	3	39	144	2	.262

GREG VAUGHN 27 6-0 193 **Bats R Throws R**

Outfielder must make adjustments if he is to fulfill offensive potential . . . Led club in home runs for second straight year, but RBI total and average were both disappointing . . . Must reduce strikeouts to become a more effective run producer . . . Will try to pick up where he left off . . . Batted .306 with six home runs and 23 RBI in final month . . . Late flurry included 11-game hitting streak from Sept. 18-29 during which he batted .359 . . . Recorded career high in stolen bases . . . Loves to face Oakland, former hometown team, and owns 15 career homers against the Athletics . . . Born July 3, 1965, in Sacramento, Cal. . . . Brewers' first-round pick in 1986 draft, out of the University of Miami . . . Earned $500,000 in 1992.

Year	Club	Pos.	G	AB	R	H	2B	3B	HR	RBI	SB	Avg.
1989	Milwaukee	OF	38	113	18	30	3	0	5	23	4	.265
1990	Milwaukee	OF	120	382	51	84	26	2	17	61	7	.220
1991	Milwaukee	OF	145	542	81	132	24	5	27	98	2	.244
1992	Milwaukee	OF	141	501	77	114	18	2	23	78	15	.228
	Totals		444	1538	227	360	71	9	72	260	28	.234

KEVIN SEITZER 31 5-11 190 **Bats R Throws R**

Received second chance from Milwaukee after being released by Kansas City March 31 and made most of it . . . Was Brewers' Opening Day third baseman . . . Also played second base for new club . . . Fashioned 11-game hitting streak from May 10-23, batting .435 in that stretch . . . Enjoyed two-homer game July 17 at Chicago . . . Tied club record by scoring four runs in Aug. 28 game at Toronto . . . Placed second to Oakland's Mark McGwire in AL Rookie of the Year balloting in 1987 . . . Became first rookie in Royals history to record 200 hits . . . Born March 26, 1962, in Springfield, Ill. . . . Began career as Kansas City's 11th-round pick in 1983 draft . . . Earned just $109,000 in 1992, then became free agent last winter.

Year	Club	Pos.	G	AB	R	H	2B	3B	HR	RBI	SB	Avg.
1986	Kansas City . . .	1B-OF-3B	28	96	16	31	4	1	2	11	0	.323
1987	Kansas City . . .	3B-OF-1B	161	641	105	207	33	8	15	83	12	.323
1988	Kansas City . . .	3B-OF	149	559	90	170	32	5	5	60	10	.304
1989	Kansas City . . .	3B-SS-OF-1B	160	597	78	168	17	2	4	48	17	.281
1990	Kansas City . . .	3B-2B	158	622	91	171	31	5	6	38	7	.275
1991	Kansas City . . .	3B	85	234	28	62	11	3	1	25	4	.265
1992	Milwaukee	3B	148	540	74	146	35	1	5	71	13	.270
	Totals		889	3289	482	955	163	25	38	336	63	.290

JAIME NAVARRO 26 6-4 210 Bats R Throws R

Quality starting pitcher who provides good innings in bunches . . . Led club with most victories by a Brewer right-hander since Pete Vuckovich won 17 in 1982 . . . First Brewer to record 15 or more victories in consecutive seasons since Ted Higuera in 1987 and 1988 . . . Counted three shutouts among his successes . . . Ranked seventh in AL in innings pitched . . . Born March 27, 1967, in Bayamon, P.R. . . . Brewers' third-round pick in 1987 draft, out of Miami Dade Center College . . . Father, Julio, pitched in majors from 1962-70 . . . Earned $400,000 in 1992.

Year	Club	G	IP	W	L	Pct.	SO	BB	H	ERA
1989	Milwaukee	19	109⅔	7	8	.467	56	32	119	3.12
1990	Milwaukee	32	149⅓	8	7	.533	75	41	176	4.46
1991	Milwaukee	34	234	15	12	.556	114	73	237	3.92
1992	Milwaukee	34	246	17	11	.607	100	64	224	3.33
	Totals	119	739	47	38	.553	345	210	756	3.71

What a rousing season for rookie Cal Eldred!

DOUG HENRY 29 6-4 185 **Bats R Throws R**

Capable closer proved he could fill role in first full season on the job . . . Converted 29 saves in 33 opportunities, an 88 percent success rate . . . Save total was highest by Brewer right-hander since Rollie Fingers had that many in 1982 . . . Like many closers, he pitches better when save is at stake . . . Owned 3.16 ERA in save situations, including glittering 1.48 in last 25 chances . . . Tied for seventh in AL with 68 appearances . . . Lost virtually all of 1989 season to elbow injury that required surgery . . . Born Dec. 10, 1963, in Sacramento, Cal. . . . Taken in eighth round of 1985 draft, out of Arizona State . . . Earned just $125,000 in 1992.

Year	Club	G	IP	W	L	Pct.	SO	BB	H	ERA
1991	Milwaukee.	32	36	2	1	.667	28	14	16	1.00
1992	Milwaukee.	68	65	1	4	.200	52	24	64	4.02
	Totals.	100	101	3	5	.375	80	38	80	2.94

BILL WEGMAN 30 6-5 220 **Bats R Throws R**

Turned in yeoman's effort for Brewers . . . Racked up second-most innings in AL with 261⅔, four behind Texas' Kevin Brown . . . Last Brewer to supply that many innings was Teddy Higuera with identical total in 1987 . . . Topped Brewers with seven complete games . . . Consistent performer has won 12 or more games last four full seasons . . . Is vulnerable to long ball, surrendering 28 homers . . . Ranked third in AL in ERA in 1991 after missing most of previous two seasons with arm miseries . . . Born Dec. 19, 1962, in Cincinnati . . . Milwaukee's fifth-round selection in 1981 draft . . . Earned $2,375,000 in 1992.

Year	Club	G	IP	W	L	Pct.	SO	BB	H	ERA
1985	Milwaukee.	3	17⅔	2	0	1.000	6	3	17	3.57
1986	Milwaukee.	35	198⅓	5	12	.294	82	43	217	5.13
1987	Milwaukee.	34	225	12	11	.522	102	53	229	4.24
1988	Milwaukee.	32	199	13	13	.500	84	50	207	4.12
1989	Milwaukee.	11	51	2	6	.250	27	21	69	6.71
1990	Milwaukee.	8	29⅔	2	2	.500	20	6	37	4.85
1991	Milwaukee.	28	193⅓	15	7	.682	89	40	176	2.84
1992	Milwaukee.	35	261⅔	13	14	.481	127	55	251	3.20
	Totals.	186	1175⅔	64	65	.496	537	271	1203	4.02

CAL ELDRED 25 6-4 215 **Bats R Throws R**

Should develop into big winner if rousing rookie season is any indication . . . Won 11 of 13 decisions with 1.79 ERA after being recalled from Denver (AAA) in July . . . Went 10-6 with 3.00 ERA for Denver to earn promotion . . . Tied a club record by taking 10 straight decisions from Aug. 8-Sept. 29 . . . Possesses the poise of a veteran . . . Frequently has overpowering stuff . . . Limited opponents to .207 batting average . . . Notched season-high 12 strikeouts Sept. 13 at Baltimore . . . First-round selection in 1989 draft . . . Born Nov. 24, 1967, in Cedar Rapids, Iowa . . . Earned $109,000 in 1992.

Year	Club	G	IP	W	L	Pct.	SO	BB	H	ERA
1991	Milwaukee..........	3	16	2	0	1.000	10	6	20	4.50
1992	Milwaukee..........	14	100⅓	11	2	.846	62	23	76	1.79
	Totals.............	17	116⅓	13	2	.867	72	29	96	2.17

TOP PROSPECTS

MARK KIEFER 24 6-4 175 **Bats R Throws R**

Mainstay in rotation at Denver (AAA) may be ready to help Brewers . . . Possesses greater promise than 7-13 record with 4.59 ERA would indicate . . . Fanned 145 batters in 112⅔ innings . . . Born Nov. 13, 1968, in Orange, Cal. . . . Brewers' 21st-round pick in 1987 draft . . . Brother, Steve, was a former Brewers infielder.

MATT MIESKE 25 6-0 185 **Bats R Throws**

Highly rated outfielder bears watching . . . Led American Association with 49 extra-base hits . . . Very good defensive player who registered 21 assists at Denver (AAA) . . . Topped California League with .341 average in 1991 . . . Born Feb. 13, 1968, in Midland, Mich. . . . Acquired from San Diego with shortstop Jose Valentin and right-hander Ricky Bones in trade that sent third baseman Gary Sheffield to Padres prior to last season.

JOSE VALENTIN 23 5-10 175 **Bats S Throws R**

Shortstop will probably spend more time in American Association, because he is blocked at big league level by Pat Listach . . . Has some power . . . Placed second in American Association with 11 triples . . . Clouted 17 home runs for Wichita (AA) in 1991 . . . Has extremely strong throwing arm . . . Born Oct. 12, 1969, in

Manati, P.R. . . . Part of package with Matt Mieske and Ricky Bones in deal that sent Sheffield to San Diego prior to 1992.

TYRONE HILL 21 6-6 195 **Bats L Throws L**

First-round selection in 1991 draft shows great promise . . . Went 9-5 with 3.25 ERA for Beloit (A) of the Midwest League . . . Notched 133 strikeouts in 113⅔ innings . . . Averaged 10.5 strikeouts per nine innings . . . Size makes him imposing figure on mound . . . Born March 7, 1972, in Yucaipa, Cal.

MANAGER PHIL GARNER: Was runnerup to AL Manager of the Year Tony La Russa after piloting Brewers to startling 92-70 record despite lack of any previous major league experience . . . Players thrived on his aggressive style . . . Loves to turn base-runners loose and force mistakes . . . Not afraid of scrutiny if a move backfires . . . Served for three seasons as Astros coach after retirement as player in 1988 . . . Brewers GM Sal Bando cited his managerial potential in giving him three-year contract to succeed Tom Trebelhorn, whose dismissal was controversial . . . Earned nickname "Scrap Iron" during playing career for toughness he displayed as member of Pirates in late 1970's . . . Enjoyed 14-year major league career with Oakland, Pittsburgh, Houston, Los Angeles and San Francisco . . . Recognized as All-Star in 1976, 1980 and 1981 . . . Excelled in 1979 postseason for Pittsburgh, batting .417 in playoffs and tying seven-game World Series record with .500 average . . . Born April 30, 1949, in Jefferson City, Tenn. . . . Was an All-American at University of Tennessee.

ALL-TIME BREWER SEASON RECORDS

BATTING: Paul Molitor, .353, 1987
HRs: Gorman Thomas, 45, 1979
RBI: Cecil Cooper, 126, 1983
STEALS: Pat Listach, 54, 1992
WINS: Mike Caldwell, 22, 1978
STRIKEOUTS: Ted Higuera, 240, 1987

NEW YORK YANKEES

TEAM DIRECTORY: Principal Owner: George Steinbrenner III; Managing General Partner: Joseph Malloy; VP/GM: Gene Michael; VP-Player Dev. and Scouting: Bill Livesey; Scouting Coordinator: Kevin Elfering; Sr. VP: Arthur Richman; Dir. Media Rel.: Jeff Idelson; Trav. Sec.: David Szen; Mgr.: Buck Showalter. Home: Yankee Stadium (57,545). Field distances: 312, l.f. line; 379, l.f.; 411, l.c.; 410, c.f.; 385, r.c.; 310, r.f. line. Spring training: Fort Lauderdale, Fla.

SCOUTING REPORT

HITTING: Much depends on whether Danny Tartabull can stay healthy. The slugger has a long history of injuries and went on the disabled list twice last year. Despite playing only 123 games, he still reminded everyone of how potent his bat can be by pounding a team-leading 25 home runs to go with 85 RBI and a .266 average.

The Yankees expect another productive season from Don Mattingly (.288, 14, 86), the first Yankee to lead the club in RBI in six seasons since Yogi Berra (1949-55). Matt Nokes (.224, 22, 59), free-agent signee Wade Boggs (.259, 7.50 with the Red Sox) and Paul O'Neill (.246, 14, 66), acquired from Cincinnati for Roberto Kelly, join Mattingly in providing so much strength from the left side that Mel Hall was allowed to go to Japan.

Young Bernie Williams (.280, 5, 26), the switch-hitter who reached safely in 56 of 60 games after being recalled from Columbus last July 31, is developing into a fine leadoff hitter.

PITCHING: After posting a 4.21 staff ERA in 1991, the Yankees concentrated on improving their starting pitching during the offseason, acquiring left-handers Jim Abbott and Jimmy Key. Abbott's 2.77 ERA was a much better indicator of how well he pitched for the Angels last year than his 7-15 record. Key, a free-agent signee, has at least 12 wins in each of his last eight seasons, including a 13-13 mark with a 3.53 ERA for the Blue Jays last year.

Melido Perez is another fine starter whose 13-16 record last season did not begin to show how well he pitched. Perez compiled a 2.87 ERA—Abbott and Perez were fifth and sixth in the AL respectively—and placed second in the league with 218 strikeouts.

Scott Kamieniecki (6-14, 4.36) and Sam Militello (3-3, 3.45) are other starting candidates. Steve Farr (2-2, 1.56, 30 saves) is

Can Wade Boggs recapture old glory at Yankee Stadium?

complemented by the unbanned Steve Howe (3-0, 2.45, 6 saves) in the bullpen. John Habyan (5-6, 3.84) and Rich Monteleone (7-3, 3.30) are other capable relievers.

FIELDING: Mattingly is one of the greatest first basemen in history. He has won seven Gold Gloves in the last eight years, with his only miss occurring in 1990, when back problems held him to 102 games. The Yankees believe they solidified the shortstop position by signing free agent Spike Owen, the former Expo. However, the Yankees remain very weak at the all-important catching position as Nokes threw out only 19 percent of potential base-stealers last year. Plus, Charlie Hayes was allowed to get away to the Rockies in the expansion draft and his stabilizing glove at third base will be missed.

OUTLOOK: The Yankees have shown improvement each of the last two years and are continuing to move in the right direction. But, under Buck Showalter, they finished tied with Cleveland for fourth last season at 76-86, 20 games behind Toronto, and still have a long way to go. Sorry, George, but the Yankees still are not ready to contend in a division they have not won since 1981.

NEW YORK YANKEES 1993 ROSTER

MANAGER Buck Showalter
Coaches—Clete Boyer, Tony Cloninger, Mark Connor, Rick Down, Frank Howard, Ed Napoleon

PITCHERS

No.	Name	1992 Club	W-L	IP	SO	ERA	B-T	Ht.	Wt.	Born
—	Abbott, Jim	California	7-15	211	130	2.77	L-L	6-3	210	9/19/67 Flint, MI
—	Cook, Andy	Columbus	7-5	100	58	3.16	R-R	6-5	205	8/30/67 Memphis, TN
26	Farr, Steve	New York (AL)	2-2	52	37	1.56	R-R	5-11	206	12/12/56 Cheverly, MD
42	Habyan, John	New York (AL)	5-6	73	44	3.84	R-R	6-2	191	1/29/64 Bayshore, NY
54	Hitchcock, Sterling	Albany	6-9	147	156	2.58	L-L	6-1	192	5/20/69 Fayetteville, NC
		New York (AL)	0-2	13	6	8.31				
57	Howe, Steve	New York (AL)	3-0	22	12	2.45	L-L	5-11	198	3/10/58 Pontiac, MI
—	Hutton, Mark	Albany	13-7	165	128	3.59	R-R	6-6	225	2/6/70 Australia
		Columbus	0-1	5	4	5.40				
—	Jean, Domingo	Ft. Lauderdale	6-11	159	172	2.61	R-R	6-2	175	1/9/69 Dominican Republic
		Albany	0-0	4	6	2.25				
49	Johnson, Jeff	Columbus	2-1	58	38	2.17	R-L	6-3	195	8/4/66 Durham, NC
		New York (AL)	2-3	53	14	6.66				
22	Kamieniecki, Scott	Ft. Lauderdale	1-0	7	3	1.29	R-R	6-0	195	4/19/64 Mt. Clemens, MI
		Columbus	1-0	13	12	0.69				
		New York (AL)	6-14	188	88	4.36				
—	Key, Jimmy	Toronto	13-13	217	117	3.53	R-L	6-1	185	4/22/61 Huntsville, AL
—	Martel, Ed	Columbus	10-9	151	94	5.56	R-R	6-1	200	3/2/69 Mt. Clemens, MI
43	Militello, Sam	Columbus	12-2	141	152	2.29	R-R	6-3	200	11/26/69 Tampa, FL
		New York (AL)	3-3	60	42	3.45				
55	Monteleone, Rich	New York (AL)	7-3	93	62	3.30	R-R	6-2	235	3/22/63 Tampa, FL
—	Munoz, Bobby	Albany	7-5	112	66	3.28	R-R	6-7	237	3/3/68 Puerto Rico
33	Perez, Melido	New York (AL)	13-16	248	218	2.87	R-R	6-4	210	2/15/66 Dominican Republic
—	Rivera, Mariano	Ft. Lauderdale	5-3	59	42	2.28	R-R	6-4	168	11/29/69 Panama
31	Wickman, Bob	Columbus	12-5	157	108	2.92	R-R	6-1	212	2/6/69 Green Bay, WI
		New York (AL)	6-1	50	21	4.11				
39	Witt, Mike	Tampa	1-0	12	13	0.00	R-R	6-7	208	7/20/60 Fullerton, CA

CATCHERS

No.	Name	1992 Club	H	HR	RBI	Pct.	B-T	Ht.	Wt.	Born
12	Leyritz, Jim	New York (AL)	37	7	26	.257	R-R	6-0	195	12/27/63 Lakewood, OH
38	Nokes, Matt	New York (AL)	86	22	59	.224	L-R	6-1	210	10/31/63 San Diego, CA
20	Stanley, Mike	New York (AL)	43	8	27	.249	R-R	6-0	192	6/25/63 Ft. Lauderdale, Fl

INFIELDERS

No.	Name	1992 Club	H	HR	RBI	Pct.	B-T	Ht.	Wt.	Born
—	Boggs, Wade	Boston	133	7	50	.259	R-L	6-2	197	6/15/58 Omaha, NE
—	Davis, Russ	Albany	140	22	71	.285	R-R	6-0	170	9/13/69 Birmingham, AL
—	Eenhoorn, Robert	Ft. Lauderdale	62	4	33	.305	R-R	6-3	170	2/9/68 Netherlands
		Albany	46	1	23	.235				
2	Gallego, Mike	Ft. Lauderdale	2	0	2	.200	R-R	5-8	175	10/31/60 Whittier, CA
		New York (AL)	44	3	14	.254				
14	Kelly, Pat	Albany	0	0	0	.000	R-R	6-0	180	10/14/67 Philadelphia, PA
		New York (AL)	72	7	27	.226				
24	Maas, Kevin	New York (AL)	71	11	35	.248	L-L	6-3	204	1/20/65 Castro Valley, CA
23	Mattingly, Don	New York (AL)	184	14	86	.288	L-L	6-0	192	4/20/61 Evansville, IN
59	Meulens, Hensley	Columbus	147	26	100	.275	R-R	6-3	210	6/23/67 Curacao
		New York (AL)	3	1	1	.600				
—	Owen, Spike	Montreal	104	7	40	.269	S-R	5-10	170	4/19/61 Cleburne, TX
56	Silvestri, Dave	Columbus	117	13	73	.279	R-R	6-0	196	9/29/67 St. Louis, MO
		New York (AL)	4	0	1	.308				
17	Stankiewicz, Andy	New York (AL)	107	2	25	.268	R-R	5-9	165	8/10/64 Inglewood, CA
18	Velarde, Randy	New York (AL)	112	7	46	.272	R-R	6-0	192	11/24/62 Midland, TX

OUTFIELDERS

No.	Name	1992 Club	H	HR	RBI	Pct.	B-T	Ht.	Wt.	Born
—	Humphreys, Mike	Columbus	115	6	46	.282	R-R	6-0	195	4/10/67 Dallas, TX
		New York (AL)	1	0	0	.100				
19	James, Dion	New York (AL)	38	3	17	.262	L-L	6-1	185	11/9/62 Philadelphia, PA
21	O'Neill, Paul	Cincinnati	122	14	66	.246	L-L	6-4	210	2/25/63 Columbus, OH
45	Tartabull, Danny	New York (AL)	112	25	85	.266	R-R	6-1	210	10/30/62 Miami, FL
51	Williams, Bernie	Columbus	111	8	50	.306	S-R	6-2	195	9/13/68 Puerto Rico
		New York (AL)	73	5	26	.280				
13	Williams, Gerald	Columbus	156	16	86	.285	R-R	6-2	190	8/10/66 New Orleans, LA
		New York (AL)	8	3	6	.296				

YANKEE PROFILES

DON MATTINGLY 31 6-0 192 Bats L Throws L

Learning to overcome back problems that robbed him of superstar status . . . Home-run total matched previous two seasons combined . . . Topped Yankees in batting average, hits, doubles, runs and RBI . . . Posted his highest total of doubles since 1986 and ranks fourth on club's all-time list in that category . . . Did fail to hit .300 for third consecutive year after six straight seasons above that mark . . . Peerless first baseman added a seventh to collection of Gold Gloves . . . Set Hall of Fame pace early in career . . . Captured batting title with .343 average in 1984 . . . Earned AL MVP honors the following season by knocking in 145 runs, most by a Yankee since Joe DiMaggio's 155 in 1948 . . . Set club marks with 238 hits and 53 doubles in 1986 . . . Set major league mark with six grand slams in 1987 and tied another standard by homering in eight consecutive games . . . Born April 20, 1961, in Evansville, Ind. . . . Not chosen until 19th round of 1979 draft . . . Earned $3.62 million in 1992.

Year	Club	Pos.	G	AB	R	H	2B	3B	HR	RBI	SB	Avg.
1982	New York (AL)	OF-1B	7	12	0	2	0	0	0	1	0	.167
1983	New York (AL)	OF-1B-2B	91	279	34	79	15	4	4	32	0	.283
1984	New York (AL)	1B-OF	153	603	91	207	44	2	23	110	1	.343
1985	New York (AL)	1B	159	652	107	211	48	3	35	145	2	.324
1986	New York (AL)	1B-3B	162	677	117	238	53	2	31	113	0	.352
1987	New York (AL)	1B	141	569	93	186	38	2	30	115	1	.327
1988	New York (AL)	1B-OF	144	599	94	186	37	0	18	88	1	.311
1989	New York (AL)	1B-OF	158	631	79	191	37	2	23	113	3	.303
1990	New York (AL)	1B-OF	102	394	40	101	16	0	5	42	1	.256
1991	New York (AL)	1B	152	587	64	169	35	0	9	68	2	.288
1992	New York (AL)	1B	157	640	89	184	40	0	14	86	3	.288
	Totals		1426	5643	808	1754	363	15	192	913	14	.311

WADE BOGGS 34 6-2 197 Bats L Throws R

Signed to three-year, $11-million contract, Red Sox free agent must show he hasn't lost skills after career took sudden nosedive . . . Career-low batting average was 86 points below his lifetime mark entering 1992 season . . . Had never batted below .302 in 10 previous seasons . . . His hit total represented his fewest since rookie year . . . Struggled mightily in leadoff position, compiling .222 average in 55 games there compared to .287 mark in the 78 games in which he batted third . . . Opposing managers still respect him, because he drew a league-leading 19 intentional walks . . . Was still third-toughest in AL to strike out, fanning once per 19.3 at-bats . . . Never embraced by Red Sox fans even though he captured five AL batting titles from 1983-88, missing only in 1984 . . . Branded by some as a selfish player because of his preoccupation with his statistics . . . Born June 15, 1958, in Omaha, Neb. . . . Red Sox' seventh-round pick in 1976 draft . . . Third baseman made $2.7 million in 1992.

Year	Club	Pos.	G	AB	R	H	2B	3B	HR	RBI	SB	Avg.
1982	Boston	1B-3B-OF	104	338	51	118	14	1	5	44	1	.349
1983	Boston	3B	153	582	100	210	44	7	5	74	3	.361
1984	Boston	3B	158	625	109	203	31	4	6	55	3	.325
1985	Boston	3B	161	653	107	240	42	3	8	78	2	.368
1986	Boston	3B	149	580	107	207	47	2	8	71	0	.357
1987	Boston	3B-1B	147	551	108	200	40	6	24	89	1	.363
1988	Boston	3B	155	584	128	214	45	6	5	58	2	.366
1989	Boston	3B	156	621	113	205	51	7	3	54	2	.330
1990	Boston	3B	155	619	89	187	44	5	6	63	0	.302
1991	Boston	3B	144	546	93	181	42	2	8	51	1	.332
1992	Boston	3B	143	514	62	133	22	4	7	50	1	.259
	Totals		1625	6213	1067	2098	422	47	85	687	16	.338

PAUL O'NEILL 30 6-4 210 — Bats L Throws L

Did not play up to capabilities last year after getting huge raise and was dealt by Reds to Yanks for Roberto Kelly last winter . . . Former manager Lou Piniella always expected more from him and was often at odds with right fielder . . . Home-run production was cut in half from 1991, but his total of 14 was good enough to lead Reds . . . Led Reds in games and walks (a career-high 70) . . . Started hot, batting .319 with seven homers and 31 RBI over first two months of season . . . Ranked third in NL in outfield assists with 12 and led NL outfielders with .997 fielding percentage . . . Made one error in 304 chances . . . Batted .471 in 1990 NLCS . . . Born Feb. 25, 1963, in Columbus, Ohio . . . A pitcher in high school, he was Reds' fourth pick in 1981 . . . Made $2,333,333 last season.

Year	Club	Pos.	G	AB	R	H	2B	3B	HR	RBI	SB	Avg.
1985	Cincinnati.....	OF	5	12	1	4	1	0	0	1	0	.333
1986	Cincinnati.....	PH	3	2	0	0	0	0	0	0	0	.000
1987	Cincinnati.....	OF-1B-P	84	160	24	41	14	1	7	28	2	.256
1988	Cincinnati.....	OF-1B	145	485	58	122	25	3	16	73	8	.252
1989	Cincinnati.....	OF	117	428	49	118	24	2	15	74	20	.276
1990	Cincinnati.....	OF	145	503	59	136	28	0	16	78	13	.270
1991	Cincinnati.....	OF	152	532	71	136	36	0	28	91	12	.256
1992	Cincinnati.....	OF	148	496	59	122	19	1	14	66	6	.246
	Totals		799	2618	321	679	147	7	96	411	61	.259

DANNY TARTABULL 30 6-1 210 Bats R Throws R

Right fielder possesses superstar ability, if he could only stay healthy . . . Led Yankees in homers and placed second in RBI despite missing 38 games with injuries . . . Was disabled from April 24-May 8 with strained left hamstring . . . Disabled again from July 31-Aug. 14 with persistent muscle spasms in lower back . . . Critics question his desire to play with aches and pains . . . Showcased talent by erupting for nine RBI Sept. 8 at Baltimore, most by a Yankee since Tony Lazzeri's AL-record 11 in 1936 . . . Selective hitter drew 103 walks and placed second in AL in on-base percentage (.409) . . . Son of former major league outfielder Jose . . . Born Oct. 30, 1962, in Miami . . . Third-round pick of Reds in 1980 draft . . . Earned $5.3 million in 1992 after leaving Royals to sign with Yanks as free agent.

Year	Club	Pos.	G	AB	R	H	2B	3B	HR	RBI	SB	Avg.
1984	Seattle.......	SS-2B	10	20	3	6	1	0	2	7	0	.300
1985	Seattle.......	SS-3B	19	61	8	20	7	1	1	7	1	.328
1986	Seattle.......	OF-2B-3B	137	511	76	138	25	6	25	96	4	.270
1987	Kansas City ...	OF	158	582	95	180	27	3	34	101	9	.309
1988	Kansas City ...	OF	146	507	80	139	38	3	26	102	8	.274
1989	Kansas City ...	OF	133	441	54	118	22	0	18	62	4	.268
1990	Kansas City ...	OF	88	313	41	84	19	0	15	60	1	.268
1991	Kansas City ...	OF	132	484	78	153	35	3	31	100	6	.316
1992	New York (AL)	OF	123	421	72	112	19	0	25	85	2	.266
	Totals		946	3340	507	950	193	16	177	620	35	.284

BERNIE WILLIAMS 24 6-2 196 Bats S Throws R

Graceful center fielder has star potential . . . Established himself at big league level after July 31 recall from Columbus (AAA) . . . Patient leadoff hitter made 60 consecutive starts after recall and reached safely in 56 of them . . . Switch-hitter batted .328 in final 29 games and reached base safely in each of those . . . Flashed power with 445-foot home run in Detroit Aug. 10 . . . Has blazing speed once he is underway, but has poor instincts on bases . . . Needs great deal of work on base-stealing skills . . . Won Carolina League (AA) batting title with .338 average in 1988 and was heralded prospect throughout fine minor league career . . . Born Sept. 13, 1968, in San Juan, P.R. . . . Signed by the Yankees as free agent in September 1985 . . . Earned $125,000 in 1992.

Year	Club	Pos.	G	AB	R	H	2B	3B	HR	RBI	SB	Avg.
1991	New York (AL)	OF	85	320	43	76	19	4	3	34	10	.238
1992	New York (AL)	OF	62	261	39	73	14	2	5	26	7	.280
	Totals		147	581	82	149	33	6	8	60	17	.256

PAT KELLY 25 6-0 180 — Bats R Throws R

Should make stronger showing after injury-plagued first full season in big leagues . . . Was disabled from April 21-May 7 with sprained ligament in left thumb . . . Started only once in final 15 games due to inflammation in right knee . . . Did ease doubts about his offense by batting .254 in 56 games after All-Star break . . . Batted .271 from July 24 on . . . Excellent second baseman . . . Has great range . . . Turns double play extremely well . . . Born Oct. 14, 1967, in Philadelphia . . . Yankees' ninth-round choice in 1988 draft . . . Earned $147,500 in 1992.

Year	Club	Pos.	G	AB	R	H	2B	3B	HR	RBI	SB	Avg.
1991	New York (AL)	3B–2B	96	298	35	72	12	4	3	23	12	.242
1992	New York (AL)	2B	106	318	38	72	22	2	7	27	8	.226
	Totals		202	616	73	144	34	6	10	50	20	.234

JIM ABBOTT 25 6-3 210 — Bats L Throws L

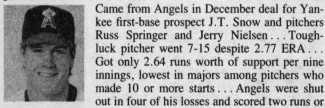

Came from Angels in December deal for Yankee first-base prospect J.T. Snow and pitchers Russ Springer and Jerry Nielsen . . . Tough-luck pitcher went 7-15 despite 2.77 ERA . . . Got only 2.64 runs worth of support per nine innings, lowest in majors among pitchers who made 10 or more starts . . . Angels were shut out in four of his losses and scored two runs or fewer in 17 of his 29 starts . . . In addition, bullpen blew two of his leads . . . ERA was lower than in 18-11 season of 1991 . . . Topped 200-inning mark for third time in four years . . . Career mark dropped below .500 . . . Eligible for free agency after 1993 season . . . Earned $1,850,000 in 1992 . . . Angels made him eighth pick overall in 1988 draft after inspiring amateur career capped by Sullivan Award and gold medal at 1988 Olympics . . . No one thinks about his birth defect any more . . . Born Sept. 19, 1957, in Flint, Mich.

Year	Club	G	IP	W	L	Pct.	SO	BB	H	ERA
1989	California	29	181⅓	12	12	.500	115	74	190	3.92
1990	California	33	211⅔	10	14	.417	105	72	246	4.51
1991	California	34	243	18	11	.621	158	73	222	2.89
1992	California	29	211	7	15	.318	130	68	208	2.77
	Totals.............	125	847	47	52	.475	508	287	866	3.49

MELIDO PEREZ 27 6-4 180 Bats R Throws R

Has chance to rank with best right-handers in league . . . Acquired from White Sox with Bob Wickman and Domingo Jean for Steve Sax and cash prior to last season and gave Yanks much more than they had hoped . . . Used nasty split-finger fastball to rank second in AL in strike-outs, 23 behind Seattle's Randy Johnson . . . Was first Yankee right-hander to strike out 200 batters in a season since Bob Turley (210) in 1955 . . . Strikeout total also was third-highest in Yankee history, trailing only Ron Guidry (248 in 1978) and Jack Chesbro (239 in 1904) . . . Ranked sixth in AL in ERA and in opponents' batting average (.235) . . . Finished fifth in innings pitched and tied for fourth with 10 complete games . . . Only apparent flaw is tendency toward early-inning trouble . . . Born Feb. 15, 1966, in San Cristobal, D.R. . . . Began career with Royals as free agent signee in July 1983 . . . A bargain at $1.165 million in 1992.

Year	Club	G	IP	W	L	Pct.	SO	BB	H	ERA
1987	Kansas City	3	10⅓	1	1	.500	5	5	18	7.84
1988	Chicago (AL)	32	197	12	10	.545	138	72	186	3.79
1989	Chicago (AL)	31	183⅓	11	14	.440	141	90	187	5.01
1990	Chicago (AL)	35	197	13	14	.481	161	86	177	4.61
1991	Chicago (AL)	49	135⅔	8	7	.533	128	52	111	3.12
1992	New York (AL)......	33	247⅔	13	16	.448	218	93	212	2.87
	Totals............	183	971	58	62	.483	791	398	891	3.90

JIMMY KEY 31 6-1 185 Bats R Throws L

Yanks put the lock on Blue Jay free agent, signing him to four-year, $17-million contract in December . . . He and Frank Viola are only two major league pitchers to post 12 or more victories in each of last eight seasons . . . Ranks third on Blue Jays' all-time victory list with 116 . . . Surpassed 200 innings for sixth time . . . Selected to All-Star staff in 1985 and 1991 . . . Was dropped from rotation for playoffs, but capitalized on start in World Series Game 4 by holding Atlanta to one run and five hits in 7⅔ innings . . . Poised veteran who responds to challenges . . . Won ERA title in 1987 and placed second to Roger Clemens in Cy Young voting . . . Born April 22, 1961, in Huntsville, Ala. . . . Toronto's third-round choice in 1982 draft . . . Earned $2,275,000 in 1992.

Year	Club	G	IP	W	L	Pct.	SO	BB	H	ERA
1984	Toronto	63	62	4	5	.444	44	32	70	4.65
1985	Toronto	35	212⅔	14	6	.700	85	50	188	3.00
1986	Toronto	36	232	14	11	.560	141	74	222	3.57
1987	Toronto	36	261	17	8	.680	161	66	210	2.76
1988	Toronto	21	131⅓	12	5	.706	65	30	127	3.29
1989	Toronto	33	216	13	14	.481	118	27	226	3.88
1990	Toronto	27	154⅔	13	7	.650	88	22	169	4.25
1991	Toronto	33	209⅓	16	12	.571	125	44	207	3.05
1992	Toronto	33	216⅔	13	13	.500	117	59	205	3.53
	Totals	317	1695⅔	116	81	.589	944	404	1124	3.42

STEVE HOWE 35 5-11 198 Bats L Throws L

Seven-time drug offender hopes to capitalize on another chance . . . Career has appeared over on numerous occasions, as recently as last summer when then-commissioner Fay Vincent made him first baseball player banned for life as a result of a cocaine-possession charge . . . Howe contested and arbitrator George Nicolau overturned ruling . . . Yankees re-signed him to two-year, $4.2-million contract . . . Hard thrower remains extremely effective . . . Held opponents to .122 average last season, including .093 by right-handed hitters . . . Boasts 1.92 ERA in two seasons with Yankees . . . Born March 10, 1958, in Pontiac, Mich. . . . Began career as Los Angeles' first-round selection in 1979 . . . NL Rookie of the Year in 1980, when he saved 17 games for the Dodgers . . . Off-field woes surfaced shortly thereafter.

Year	Club	G	IP	W	L	Pct.	SO	BB	H	ERA
1980	Los Angeles	59	85	7	9	.438	39	22	83	2.65
1981	Los Angeles	41	54	5	3	.625	32	18	51	2.50
1982	Los Angeles	66	99⅓	7	5	.583	49	17	87	2.08
1983	Los Angeles	46	68⅔	4	7	.364	52	12	55	1.44
1985	Los Angeles	19	22	1	1	.500	11	5	30	4.91
1985	Minnesota	13	19	2	3	.400	10	7	28	6.61
1987	Texas	24	31⅓	3	3	.500	19	8	33	4.31
1991	New York (AL)	37	48⅓	3	1	.750	34	7	39	1.68
1992	New York (AL)	20	22	3	0	1.000	12	3	9	2.45
	Totals	325	449⅔	35	32	.522	255	99	415	2.58

JOHN HABYAN 29 6-2 191 Bats R Throws R

Eager to rebound after terrible second half . . . Struggled to 8.22 ERA in second half, surrendering 21 runs and 42 hits in 23 innings . . . Was 3-2 with six saves and glittering 1.54 ERA as late as July 9, but had already made 35 appearances in 84 games to that point . . . Was used every other day for six straight appearances from July 1-11 . . . Finished with team-high 56 appearances . . . Back problem and tired arm doomed him after break . . . Outstanding set-up man when at full strength . . . Requires careful monitoring after undergoing shoulder surgery in 1989 . . . Born Jan. 29, 1964, in Bayshore, N.Y. . . . Acquired from Orioles for Stanley Jefferson, July 20, 1989 . . . Spent parts of nine seasons in minors . . . Earned $500,000 in 1992.

Year	Club	G	IP	W	L	Pct.	SO	BB	H	ERA
1985	Baltimore	2	2⅔	1	0	1.000	2	0	3	0.00
1986	Baltimore	6	26⅓	1	3	.250	14	18	24	4.44
1987	Baltimore	27	16⅓	6	7	.462	64	40	110	4.80
1988	Baltimore	7	14⅔	1	0	1	4	4	22	4.30
1990	New York (AL)	6	8⅔	0	0	.000	4	2	10	2.08
1991	New York (AL)	66	90	4	2	.667	70	20	73	2.30
1992	New York (AL)	56	72⅔	5	6	.455	44	21	84	3.84
	Totals	170	331⅓	18	18	.500	202	105	326	3.75

STEVE FARR 36 5-11 206 Bats R Throws R

Continues to do job, despite advancing age and lack of big fastball . . . Established career high with 30 saves, seven better than mark he set year before . . . Converted 30 of 36 tries and each of last 12 opportunities . . . Recorded first 30-save season by Yankee right-hander since Rich Gossage achieved that total in 1982 . . . His 1.59 ERA was lowest by Yankee reliever in full season since Steve Hamilton (1.40) in 1965 . . . Limited opponents to .186 batting average . . . Began career as undrafted free agent with Pirates and pitched seven-plus seasons in minors before breaking in with Cleveland in 1984 . . . Born Dec. 12, 1956, in Cheverly, Md. . . . Earned $2.4 million in 1992.

Year	Club	G	IP	W	L	Pct.	SO	BB	H	ERA
1984	Cleveland	31	116	3	11	.214	83	46	106	4.58
1985	Kansas City	16	37⅔	2	1	.667	36	20	34	3.11
1986	Kansas City	56	109⅓	8	4	.667	83	39	90	3.13
1987	Kansas City	47	91	4	3	.571	88	44	97	4.15
1988	Kansas City	62	82⅔	5	4	.556	72	30	74	2.50
1989	Kansas City	51	63⅓	2	5	.286	56	22	75	4.12
1990	Kansas City	57	127	13	7	.650	94	48	99	1.98
1991	New York (AL)	60	70	5	5	.500	60	20	57	2.19
1992	New York (AL)	50	52	2	2	.500	37	19	34	1.56
	Totals	430	749	44	42	.512	609	288	666	3.10

TOP PROSPECTS

SAM MILITELLO 23 6-3 200 Bats R Throws R

Has good chance to develop into quality starter . . . Won first three decisions with Yankees . . . International League Pitcher of the Year with 12-2 record and 2.29 ERA for Columbus (AAA) . . . Unusual motion makes him especially tough on right-handers . . . Has great slider and deceptive fastball . . . Needs to improve location with fastball . . . Boasts 34-8 minor league record with 1.76 ERA . . . Never lost more than two games at any stop . . . Yankees' sixth-round pick in 1990 draft . . . Was Division II Player of the Year at University of Tampa that season . . . Born Nov. 26, 1969, in Tampa.

BRIEN TAYLOR 21 6-3 205 Bats L Throws L

First player picked in 1991 draft lived up to expectations in first full pro season . . . Fashioned 2.57 ERA in 27 starts for Fort Lauderdale (A) . . . Used fastball clocked as high as 99 miles per hour to fan 187 batters in 161⅓ innings . . . Only negative was 6-8 record, but club finished 17 games under .500 . . . Should be ready for Yankee Stadium unveiling in 1994 . . . Became instant millionaire when he received a record $1.55-million minor league contract after protracted negotiations . . . Born Dec. 26, 1971, in Beaufort, N.C.

MANAGER BUCK SHOWALTER: Holds one of the most

difficult jobs in baseball as manager for demanding, returning George Steinbrenner . . . Extremely hard worker who is popular with players and media . . . Club met expectations by showing five-game improvement with 76-86 record in his first season . . . Received three-year contract extension through 1995, but does not have much security given Steinbrenner's history of abruptly changing managers . . . Became youngest manager in majors when he was given original one-year contract . . . Selected under bizarre set of circumstances typical of Yankees, he was named 22 days after GM Gene Michael had ruled him out, citing absence of major league managerial experience . . . Had been Yankees' third-base coach since June 1990 and had grown extremely popular among players . . . Built reputation as bright baseball mind while compiling 360-207 record in five minor league seasons . . . Won championships in New York-Penn League (1985), Florida State League (1987) and Eastern League (1989) . . . Played in Yankees' minor league system from 1977-83, but never played major league game . . . Born May 23, 1956, in DeFuniak Springs, Fla.

ALL-TIME YANKEE SEASON RECORDS

BATTING: Babe Ruth, .393, 1923
HRs: Roger Maris, 61, 1961
RBI: Lou Gehrig, 184, 1931
STEALS: Rickey Henderson, 93, 1988
WINS: Jack Chesbro, 41, 1904
STRIKEOUTS: Ron Guidry, 248, 1978

TORONTO BLUE JAYS

TEAM DIRECTORY: Chairman: P.N.T. Widdrington; Pres./CEO: Paul Beeston; Exec. VP-Baseball: Pat Gillick; VP-Baseball: Al LaMacchia, Bob Mattick; Dir. Pub. Rel.: Howard Starkman; Trav. Sec.: John Brioux; Mgr.: Cito Gaston. Home: Skydome (50,300). Field distances: 330, l.f. line; 375, l.c.; 400, c.f.; 375, r.c.; 330, r.f. line. Spring training: Dunedin, Fla.

SCOUTING REPORT

HITTING: Toronto, which placed second to Detroit with 780 runs last season, did well to re-sign free agent Joe Carter (.264, 34, 119). He has developed into one of the game's steadiest run producers, driving in at least 100 runs six times in the last seven years.

Devon White (.248, 17, 60) and Roberto Alomar (.310, 8, 76) give the Blue Jays two more formidable hitters with speed as they combined to score 203 runs and steal 86 bases in 1992. Still speedy Paul Molitor (.320, 12, 89, 31 steals), the veteran sparkplug for Milwaukee for so many years, was an outstanding free-agent acquisition.

John Olerud (.284, 16, 66) continues to improve. Pat Borders (.242, 13, 53), the World Series MVP, is another hitter with punch. The discarded Kelly Gruber is in decline, but will Dave Winfield's 26 homers, 108 RBI and leadership be missed, along with the punch provided by Candy Maldonado?

PITCHING: Great things are expected of 26-year-old right-hander Juan Guzman, who won 12 of his first 14 decisions before being forced to leave a start last July 23 with a shoulder injury. Guzman finished 16-5 with a 2.64 ERA and sparkled in the post-season.

Jack Morris (21-6, 4.04) and free-agent addition Dave Stewart (12-10, 3.66), the former Oakland ace, give Toronto two proven veterans who thrive in big-game situations. Todd Stottlemyre (12-11, 4.50) is an adequate starter with experience.

The departure of long-time relief ace Tom Henke to the Rangers via free agency puts the closer's role in the capable hands of Duane Ward (7-4, 1.95, 12 saves). He was primarily a setup man for Henke before this, but still strung together five consecutive seasons with double figures in saves.

Blue Jays finally have the White stuff in center field.

FIELDING: White, a Gold Glove winner each of the last four years, is a superb center fielder who possesses great range and catches what he reaches. Alomar has few, if any equals at second base. He made only five errors last season, just two after June 27. The durable Borders led AL catchers with 136 games last season. The postseason exposed him as a catcher teams can run against, however. Luis Sojo brings his second baseman's glove (and a promising bat) in the deal that sent Gruber to California.

OUTLOOK: Toronto GM Pat Gillick was anything but apathetic in the offseason, after his Blue Jays had finished 96-66 and had given Canada its first World Series championship. Within hours of losing free-agent defector David Cone to the Royals, for instance, he replaced him with Stewart. The Molitor acquisition deeply wounded division rival Milwaukee while boosting the Blue Jays. Toronto will be very difficult to stop as it chases a third straight AL East title under the steady hand of Cito Gaston.

TORONTO BLUE JAYS 1993 ROSTER

MANAGER Cito Gaston
Coaches—Bob Bailor, Galen Cisco, Rich Hacker, Larry Hisle, John Sullivan, Gene Tenace

PITCHERS

No.	Name	1992 Club	W-L	IP	SO	ERA	B-T	Ht.	Wt.	Born
—	Brow, Scott	Dunedin	14-2	171	107	2.43	R-R	6-3	200	3/17/69 Butte, MT
—	Cox, Danny	Phil.-Pitt.	5-3	63	48	4.60	R-R	6-4	225	9/21/59 England
		Buffalo	1-1	42	30	1.70				
—	*Eichhorn, Mark	Cal.-Tor.	4-4	88	61	3.08	R-R	6-3	210	11/21/60 San Jose, CA
—	Flener, Huck	Dunedin	7-3	112	93	2.24	S-L	5-11	185	2/25/69 Austin, TX
66	Guzman, Juan	Toronto	16-5	181	165	2.64	R-R	5-11	190	10/28/66 Dominican Republic
		Syracuse	0-0	3	3	6.00				
41	Hentgen, Pat	Syracuse	1-2	20	17	2.66	R-R	6-2	200	11/13/68 Detroit, MI
		Toronto	5-2	50	39	5.36				
28	Leiter, Al	Syracuse	8-9	163	108	3.86	L-L	6-3	215	10/23/65 Toms River, NJ
		Toronto	0-0	1	0	9.00				
26	Linton, Doug	Syracuse	12-10	171	126	3.69	R-R	6-1	190	9/2/65 Santa Ana, CA
		Toronto	1-3	24	16	8.63				
45	MacDonald, Bob	Syracuse	2-3	23	14	4.63	L-L	6-3	208	4/27/65 East Orange, NJ
		Toronto	1-0	47	26	4.37				
—	Menhart, Paul	Knoxville	10-11	178	104	3.85	R-R	6-2	190	3/25/69 St. Louis, MO
47	Morris, Jack	Toronto	21-6	241	132	4.04	R-R	6-3	200	5/16/55 St. Paul, MN
—	Small, Aaron	Knoxville	5-12	135	79	5.27	R-R	6-5	195	11/23/71 Oxnard, CA
—	Steed, Rick	Dunedin	6-6	104	57	3.81	R-R	6-3	185	9/8/70 Mt. Shasta, CA
—	Stewart, Dave	Oakland	12-10	199	130	3.66	R-R	6-2	200	2/19/57 Oakland, CA
30	Stottlemyre, Todd	Toronto	12-11	174	98	4.50	L-R	6-3	195	5/20/65 Yakima, WA
40	Timlin, Mike	Dunedin	0-0	10	7	0.90	R-R	6-4	210	3/10/66 Midland, TX
		Syracuse	0-1	11	7	8.74				
		Toronto	0-2	44	35	4.12				
35	Trlicek, Rick	Syracuse	1-1	43	35	4.36	R-R	6-3	200	4/26/69 Houston, TX
		Toronto	0-0	2	1	10.80				
31	Ward, Duane	Toronto	7-4	101	103	1.95	R-R	6-4	220	5/28/64 Parkview, NM
36	Wells, David	Toronto	7-9	120	62	5.40	L-L	6-4	225	5/20/63 Torrance, CA

CATCHERS

No.	Name	1992 Club	H	HR	RBI	Pct.	B-T	Ht.	Wt.	Born
10	Borders, Pat	Toronto	116	13	53	.242	R-R	6-2	195	5/14/63 Columbus, OH
—	Delgado, Carlos	Dunedin	157	30	100	.324	L-R	6-3	206	6/25/72 Puerto Rico
27	Knorr, Randy	Syracuse	62	11	27	.272	R-R	6-2	218	11/12/68 San Gabriel, CA
		Toronto	5	1	2	.263				
—	O'Halloran, Greg	Knoxville	111	2	34	.271	L-R	6-1	190	5/21/68 Canada
33	Sprague, Ed	Syracuse	102	16	50	.276	R-R	6-2	210	7/25/67 Castro Valley, CA
		Toronto	11	1	7	.234				

INFIELDERS

No.	Name	1992 Club	H	HR	RBI	Pct.	B-T	Ht.	Wt.	Born
12	Alomar, Roberto	Toronto	177	8	76	.310	S-R	6-0	185	2/5/68 Puerto Rico
—	Coles, Darnell	Nashville	24	6	16	.296	R-R	6-1	185	6/2/62 San Bernardino, CA
		Cincinnati	44	3	18	.312				
—	*Griffin, Alfredo	Toronto	35	0	10	.233	S-R	5-11	165	3/6/57 Dominican Republic
19	Martinez, Domingo	Syracuse	120	21	62	.274	R-R	6-2	215	8/4/67 Dominican Republic
		Toronto	5	1	3	.625				
—	Molitor, Paul	Milwaukee	195	12	89	.320	R-R	6-0	185	8/22/56 St. Paul, MN
9	Olerud, John	Toronto	130	16	66	.284	L-L	6-5	210	8/5/68 Seattle, WA
16	Quinlan, Tom	Syracuse	75	6	36	.215	R-R	6-3	215	3/27/68 St. Paul, MN
		Toronto	1	0	2	.067				
—	Sojo, Luis	California	100	7	43	.272	R-R	5-11	175	1/3/66 Venezuela
1	Zosky, Eddie	Syracuse	79	4	38	.231	R-R	6-0	175	2/10/68 Whittier, CA
		Toronto	2	0	1	.286				

OUTFIELDERS

No.	Name	1992 Club	H	HR	RBI	Pct.	B-T	Ht.	Wt.	Born
14	Bell, Derek	Toronto	39	2	15	.242	R-R	6-2	205	12/11/68 Tampa, FL
		Dunedin	6	0	4	.240				
—	Bowers, Brent	Dunedin	133	3	46	.254	L-R	6-3	190	5/2/71 Oak Lawn, IL
29	Carter, Joe	Toronto	164	34	119	.264	R-R	6-3	220	3/7/60 Oklahoma City, OK
—	De La Rosa, Juan	Knoxville	167	12	53	.329	R-R	6-1	180	12/1/68 Dominican Republic
—	Perez, Robert	Knoxville	137	9	59	.260	R-R	6-3	210	6/4/69 Venezuela
24	Ward, Turner	Syracuse	67	10	29	.239	S-R	6-2	200	4/11/65 Orlando, FL
		Toronto	10	1	3	.345				
25	White, Devon	Toronto	159	17	60	.248	S-R	6-2	180	12/29/62 Jamaica

*Free agent offered arbitration

BLUE JAY PROFILES

JOE CARTER 33 6-3 220 Bats R Throws R

Free agent re-signed three-year, $19.5-million contract that could go to $25 million for four seasons . . . One of game's most dependable run producers . . . Will be bidding for seventh 100-RBI season in eight years . . . Comes off fourth season with 30-plus home runs . . . Tied for second in AL in RBI, tied for fourth in home runs, was second in total bases (310) and extra-base hits (71) and ranked sixth in slugging percentage (.498) . . . Named to All-Star team for second consecutive season and started in place of injured Jose Canseco . . . Had woeful .192 average in ALCS, but crashed two-run homer to trigger rout in Game 6 clincher against Oakland . . . Hit .273 with two homers, three RBI in World Series . . . Fine right fielder who can fill in adequately at first . . . Came from Padres with Roberto Alomar for Fred McGriff and Tony Fernandez prior to 1991 season . . . Born March 7, 1960, in Oklahoma City, Okla. . . . Earned $3,666,667 in 1992.

Year	Club	Pos.	G	AB	R	H	2B	3B	HR	RBI	SB	Avg.
1983	Chicago (NL) . .	OF	23	51	6	9	1	1	0	1	1	.176
1984	Cleveland	OF-1B	66	244	32	67	6	1	13	41	2	.275
1985	Cleveland	OF-1B-2B-3B	143	489	64	128	27	0	15	59	24	.262
1986	Cleveland	OF-1B	162	663	108	200	36	9	29	121	29	.302
1987	Cleveland	OF-1B	149	588	83	155	27	2	32	106	31	.264
1988	Cleveland	OF	157	621	85	168	36	6	27	98	27	.271
1989	Cleveland	OF-1B	162	651	84	158	32	4	35	105	13	.243
1990	San Diego	OF-1B	162	634	79	147	27	1	24	115	22	.232
1991	Toronto	OF	162	638	89	174	42	3	33	108	20	.273
1992	Toronto	OF-1B	158	622	97	164	30	7	34	119	12	.264
	Totals		1344	5201	727	1370	264	34	242	873	181	.263

ROBERTO ALOMAR 25 6-0 185 Bats S Throws R

Young second baseman is regarded as franchise player . . . Led Blue Jays to first pennant by batting .423 with two home runs, four RBI in six playoff games to become youngest MVP in LCS history . . . Was hampered by elbow injury during World Series and batted only .208 . . . Clutch player in regular season, he batted .354 with runners in scoring position . . . Ranked third in AL in runs and on-base average (.405), fifth in stolen bases and seventh in batting average . . . Reached safely in 128 of 152 games . . . Voted to All-Star Game and set a record with two steals in one inning . . . Literally lived at ballpark last season, staying at SkyDome hotel . . . Brother Sandy is standout catcher with Indians . . . Born Feb. 5, 1968, in Salinas, P.R. . . . A bargain at $2,833,333 in 1992.

Year	Club	Pos.	G	AB	R	H	2B	3B	HR	RBI	SB	Avg.
1988	San Diego	2B	143	545	84	145	24	6	9	41	24	.266
1989	San Diego	2B	158	623	82	184	27	1	7	56	42	.295
1990	San Diego	2B-SS	147	586	80	168	27	5	6	60	24	.287
1991	Toronto	2B	161	637	88	188	41	11	9	69	53	.295
1992	Toronto	2B	152	571	105	177	27	8	8	76	49	.310
	Totals		761	2962	439	862	146	31	39	302	192	.291

PAUL MOLITOR 36 6-0 185 Bats R Throws R

Free agent flew to Blue Jays after 15 Brewer seasons for guaranteed $13 million over three years and $3-million option year . . . Veteran continues to be outstanding offensive player . . . Topped AL with 62 multi-hit games . . . Ranked fourth in batting average and sixth in on-base percentage (.389) . . . Batted .327 with men on base . . . Five-time All-Star stroked his first All-Star hit, a single off Atlanta's John Smoltz . . . Used at first base and as DH . . . Brewers were 34-15 when he started at first and he batted .377 in those games . . . Stole home for ninth time in career April 14 at Minnesota . . . Belying history of injuries, he was able to stay healthy for second straight year . . . His 39-game hitting streak in 1987 was AL's longest since Joe DiMaggio's record 56-gamer in 1941 . . . Born Aug. 22, 1956, in St. Paul, Minn. . . . Selected in first round of 1977 draft . . . Earned $3,433,334 in 1992.

Year	Club	Pos.	G	AB	R	H	2B	3B	HR	RBI	SB	Avg.
1978	Milwaukee	2B-SS-3B	125	521	73	142	26	4	6	45	30	.273
1979	Milwaukee	2B-SS	140	584	88	188	27	16	9	62	33	.322
1980	Milwaukee	2B-SS-3B	111	450	81	137	29	2	9	37	34	.304
1981	Milwaukee	OF	64	251	45	67	11	0	2	19	10	.267
1982	Milwaukee	3B-SS	160	666	136	201	26	8	19	71	41	.302
1983	Milwaukee	3B	152	608	95	164	28	6	15	47	41	.269
1984	Milwaukee	3B	13	46	3	10	1	0	0	6	1	.217
1985	Milwaukee	3B	140	576	93	171	28	3	10	48	21	.297
1986	Milwaukee	3B-OF	105	437	62	123	24	6	9	55	20	.281
1987	Milwaukee	3B-2B	118	465	114	164	41	5	16	75	45	.353
1988	Milwaukee	3B-2B	154	609	115	190	34	6	13	60	41	.312
1989	Milwaukee	3B-2B	155	615	84	194	35	4	11	56	27	.315
1990	Milwaukee	2B-1B-3B	103	418	64	119	27	6	12	45	18	.285
1991	Milwaukee	1B	158	665	133	216	32	13	17	75	19	.325
1992	Milwaukee	1B	158	609	89	195	36	7	12	89	31	.320
	Totals		1856	7520	1275	2281	405	86	160	790	412	.303

PAT BORDERS 29 6-2 195 **Bats R Throws R**

Enters new season with distinction of being World Series MVP . . . Batted .450 (9-for–20) with one home run, three RBI in six Series games . . . Also sizzled in ALCS with .318 average, one homer, three RBI . . . On negative side, catcher has difficulty stopping running game . . . Braves converted 14 of 17 stolen-base tries and he made numerous poor throws . . . Very durable . . . Caught more games in regular season (136) than any other AL catcher . . . Set career highs in games, walks (33), hits, at-bats, runs and doubles . . . Connected for all of his home runs against right-handed pitching . . . Born May 14, 1963, in Columbus, Ohio . . . Toronto's sixth-round selection in 1982 draft . . . Earned $950,000 in 1992.

Year	Club	Pos.	G	AB	R	H	2B	3B	HR	RBI	SB	Avg.
1988	Toronto	C–2B–3B	56	154	15	42	6	3	5	21	0	.273
1989	Toronto	C	94	241	22	62	11	1	3	29	2	.257
1990	Toronto	C	125	346	36	99	24	2	15	49	0	.286
1991	Toronto	C	105	291	22	71	17	0	5	36	0	.244
1992	Toronto	C	138	480	47	116	26	2	13	53	1	.242
	Totals		518	1512	142	390	84	8	41	188	3	.258

JOHN OLERUD 24 6-5 210 **Bats L Throws L**

One of five players in major league history who never spent time in minors . . . Shows improvement each season . . . Got off to slow start and was batting .225 May 9 . . . Reached safely in 91 of 108 games after that . . . Swung hot bat in ALCS with .348 average and hit .308 in World Series . . . Steady first baseman committed only two errors after May 20 . . . Will always be remembered for dramatic recovery he made following surgery for removal of aneurysm at base of brain . . . Collapsed after workout at Washington State in January 1989 . . . Still wears a batting helmet when he plays the field as a precaution . . . Born Aug. 5, 1968, in Seattle . . . Earned $387,500 in 1992.

Year	Club	Pos.	G	AB	R	H	2B	3B	HR	RBI	SB	Avg.
1989	Toronto	1B	6	8	2	3	0	0	0	0	0	.375
1990	Toronto	1B	111	358	43	95	15	1	14	48	0	.265
1991	Toronto	1B	139	454	64	116	30	1	17	68	0	.256
1992	Toronto	1B	138	458	68	130	28	0	16	66	1	.284
	Totals		394	1278	177	344	73	2	47	182	1	.269

DEVON WHITE 30 6-2 180 Bats S Throws R

Key member of world champions because of speed he provides at top of lineup and Gold Glove defense he offers in center field . . . Made tremendous grab against wall to start near-triple play in World Series Game 3 . . . Has now won four consecutive Gold Glove awards . . . Excelled in ALCS with .348 average . . . Had 13 straight successful stolen-base attempts from May 16-July 12 . . . His string of 188 games without an error ended June 9 in New York . . . Acquired from Angels with Willie Fraser and Marcus Moore for Junior Felix, Luis Sojo and Ken Rivers prior to 1991 season . . . Born Dec. 29, 1962, in Kingston, Jamaica . . . Earned $2,333,333 in 1992.

Year	Club	Pos.	G	AB	R	H	2B	3B	HR	RBI	SB	Avg.
1985	California	OF	21	7	7	1	0	0	0	0	3	.143
1986	California	OF	29	51	8	12	1	1	1	3	6	.235
1987	California	OF	159	639	103	168	33	5	24	87	32	.263
1988	California	OF	122	455	76	118	22	2	11	51	17	.259
1989	California	OF	156	636	86	156	18	13	12	56	44	.245
1990	California	OF	125	443	57	96	17	3	11	44	21	.217
1991	Toronto	OF	156	642	110	181	40	10	17	60	33	.282
1992	Toronto	OF	153	641	98	159	26	7	17	60	37	.248
	Totals		921	3514	545	891	157	41	93	361	193	.254

LUIS SOJO 27 5-11 175 Bats R Throws R

Second baseman continued to develop in second full season, then Angels sent him back to Blue Jays for Kelly Gruber last winter . . . Improved in most offensive categories . . . Free swinger . . . Walked only 14 times in 368 at-bats . . . Stole only seven bases in 18 attempts . . . Hit .221 against lefties and .289 against righties . . . Made 95 appearances at second, nine at third and five at short . . . Won Venezuelan Winter League batting title in 1990 . . . Earned $180,000 in 1992 . . . Blue Jays signed him originally as free agent in 1987 . . . Yet another Latin player discovered by Blue Jays' scout Epy Guerrero . . . Born Jan. 3, 1966, in Barquisimeto, Venezuela.

Year	Club	Pos.	G	AB	R	H	2B	3B	HR	RBI	SB	Avg.
1990	Toronto	2B-SS-OF–3B	33	80	14	18	3	0	1	9	1	.225
1991	California	2B-SS–3B-OF	113	364	38	94	14	1	3	20	4	.258
1992	California	2B–3B-SS	106	368	37	100	12	3	7	43	7	.272
	Totals		252	812	89	212	29	4	11	72	12	.261

JACK MORRIS 37 6-3 200 **Bats R Throws R**

Free-agent signee gave Blue Jays substantial boost, despite postseason woes . . . Tied for first in AL in victories and was first 20-game winner in franchise history . . . Placed second in league in winning percentage . . . Team was 25-9 in his starts . . . Set major league record with 13th consecutive Opening Day start, at Detroit April 6 . . . Was significantly better pitcher at SkyDome (11-2, 3.09) than on road (10-4, 5.11) . . . This 1991 World Series MVP secured crown for Twins by blanking Atlanta for 10 innings in 1-0 Game 7 triumph . . . Flopped in World Series last year, dropping both of his decisions and amassing 8.44 ERA . . . Was disappointing in ALCS as well, going 0-1 with a 6.57 ERA in two starts . . . Born May 16, 1955, in St. Paul, Minn. . . . Signed as free agent by Blue Jays prior to last season . . . Earned $4,425,000 in 1992.

Year	Club	G	IP	W	L	Pct.	SO	BB	H	ERA
1977	Detroit	7	46	1	1	.500	28	23	38	3.72
1978	Detroit	28	106	3	5	.375	48	49	107	4.33
1979	Detroit	27	198	17	7	.708	113	59	179	3.27
1980	Detroit	36	250	16	15	.516	112	87	252	4.18
1981	Detroit	25	198	14	7	.667	97	78	153	3.05
1982	Detroit	37	266⅓	17	16	.515	135	96	247	4.06
1983	Detroit	37	293⅔	20	13	.606	232	83	257	3.34
1984	Detroit	35	240⅓	19	11	.633	148	87	221	3.60
1985	Detroit	35	257	16	11	.593	191	110	212	3.33
1986	Detroit	35	267	21	8	.724	223	82	229	3.27
1987	Detroit	34	266	18	11	.621	208	93	227	3.38
1988	Detroit	34	235	15	13	.536	168	83	225	3.94
1989	Detroit	24	170⅓	6	14	.300	115	59	189	4.86
1990	Detroit	36	249⅔	15	18	.455	162	97	231	4.51
1991	Minnesota	35	246⅔	18	12	.600	163	92	226	3.43
1992	Toronto	34	240⅔	21	6	.778	132	80	222	4.04
	Totals	499	3530⅔	237	168	.585	2275	1258	3215	3.73

DAVE STEWART 36 6-2 200 **Bats R Throws R**

A's free agent signed two-year, $8.5-million contract with Blue Jays . . . Days of 20-win seasons are gone, but he is still dependable . . . Started 30-plus games for sixth consecutive season . . . Just missed sixth straight 200-inning campaign . . . Cut ERA by nearly 1.50 from subpar 1991 season . . . Outdueled Blue Jays' Jack Morris in Game 1 of ALCS for his record sixth LCS win . . . Has won 107 games since 1987, second only to Roger Clemens' 112, and had won only 39 in seven previous seasons . . . Made his fifth consecutive Opening Day start . . . Spent most of July on disabled list with elbow strain . . . Has 116 wins as member of Athletics, trailing only Jim Hunter and Vida Blue . . . Earned $3.5 million in 1992 . . . Born Feb. 19, 1957, in Oakland . . . Dodgers' 16th-round pick in 1975 draft . . . Went to Athletics after Phillies released him in 1986.

Year	Club	G	IP	W	L	Pct.	SO	BB	H	ERA
1978	Los Angeles	1	2	0	0	.000	1	0	1	0.00
1981	Los Angeles	32	43	4	3	.571	29	14	40	2.51
1982	Los Angeles	45	146⅓	9	8	.529	80	49	137	3.81
1983	Los Angeles	46	76	5	2	.714	54	33	67	2.96
1983	Texas	8	59	5	2	.714	24	17	50	2.14
1984	Texas	32	192⅓	7	14	.333	119	87	193	4.73
1985	Texas	42	81⅓	0	6	.000	64	37	86	5.42
1985	Philadelphia	4	4⅓	0	0	.000	2	4	5	6.23
1986	Philadelphia	8	12⅓	0	0	.000	9	4	15	6.57
1986	Oakland	29	149⅓	9	5	.643	102	65	137	3.74
1987	Oakland	37	261⅓	20	13	.606	205	105	224	3.68
1988	Oakland	37	275⅔	21	12	.636	192	110	240	3.23
1989	Oakland	36	257⅔	21	9	.700	155	69	260	3.32
1990	Oakland	36	267	22	11	.667	166	83	226	2.56
1991	Oakland	35	226	11	11	.500	144	105	245	5.18
1992	Oakland	31	199⅓	12	10	.545	130	79	175	3.66
	Totals	459	2253	146	106	.579	1476	861	2101	3.70

TODD STOTTLEMYRE 27 6-3 195 Bats L Throws R

Hasn't developed into big winner Blue Jays once thought he could be . . . Has won in double figures each of last three seasons . . . Worked six or more innings in 19 of 27 starts . . . Walked two men or fewer in 16 starts . . . Was sidelined from June 20-July 20 with sore right knee . . . Shows occasional flashes of brilliance . . . Sustained no-hit bid for 7⅓ innings at Chicago Aug. 26 before Dan Pasqua doubled and he settled for one-hitter . . . Finished with six complete games, one more than career total entering year . . . Known for losing temper on mound and was ejected twice last year, for hitting Milwaukee's Paul Molitor May 27 and later for bumping umpire Jim Joyce. Latter action cost him five games . . . Has hit 22 batters in last two seasons . . . Used in relief in postseason and pitched well . . . Born May 20, 1965, in Yakima, Wash. . . . Was third player picked overall in

1985 draft . . . Son of former Yankees pitcher and current Mets pitching coach Mel . . . Earned $1.2 million in 1992.

Year	Club	G	IP	W	L	Pct.	SO	BB	H	ERA
1988	Toronto	28	98	4	8	.333	67	46	109	5.69
1989	Toronto	27	127⅔	7	7	.500	63	44	137	3.88
1990	Toronto	33	203	13	17	.433	115	69	214	4.34
1991	Toronto	34	219	15	8	.652	116	75	194	3.78
1992	Toronto	28	174	12	11	.522	98	63	175	4.50
	Totals.	150	821⅔	51	51	.500	459	297	829	4.32

JUAN GUZMAN 26 5-11 190 Bats R Throws R

Rapidly emerging as one of best right-handers in either league . . . Enjoyed sizzling start and was 11-2 with AL-leading 2.11 ERA at All-Star break . . . Made first All-Star Game appearance, working a scoreless inning in relief . . . Second half marred by injury . . . Forced out of July 23 start in third inning with sore right shoulder . . . Was disabled from Aug. 4-29 and brought back slowly after that . . . Finished fourth in AL in ERA, third in winning percentage and second in opponents' batting average (.207) . . . Pitched extremely well in postseason with 2-0 record and 2.08 ERA in ALCS . . . Excelled in his lone World Series start, limiting Atlanta to one earned run in eight innings although he did not receive a decision in Game 3 . . . Born Oct. 28, 1966, in Santo Domingo, D.R. . . . Acquired from Dodgers for Mike Sharperson, Sept. 22, 1987 . . . Due for substantial raise after making only $220,000 in 1992.

Year	Club	G	IP	W	L	Pct.	SO	BB	H	ERA
1991	Toronto	23	138⅔	10	3	.769	123	66	98	2.99
1992	Toronto	28	180⅔	16	5	.762	165	72	135	2.64
	Totals.	51	319⅓	26	8	.765	288	138	233	2.79

DUANE WARD 28 6-4 220 Bats R Throws R

Formidable weapon as set-up man or closer . . . Had 12 saves last season . . . Has achieved double figures in saves each of last five seasons, despite secondary role to Tom Henke, and has 76 career saves . . . Extremely durable . . . Only reliever in majors to pitch at least 100 innings in each of last five seasons . . . Limited opponents to .207 average for second straight year . . . Ranked second in AL in appearances and third in relief innings

. . . Retired first batter he faced on 55 of 78 occasions (70.8 percent) . . . Saved AL East clincher against Detroit Oct. 3, registering final out with bases loaded . . . Gained two victories in World Series . . . Did not receive a save opportunity in postseason . . . Born May 28, 1964, in Parkview, N.M. . . . Acquired from Braves for Doyle Alexander, July 6, 1986 . . . Earned $2,425,000 in 1992.

Year	Club	G	IP	W	L	Pct.	SO	BB	H	ERA
1986	Atlanta	10	16	0	1	.000	8	8	22	7.31
1986	Toronto	2	2	0	1	.000	1	4	2	13.50
1987	Toronto	12	11⅔	1	0	1.000	10	12	14	6.94
1988	Toronto	64	111⅔	9	3	.750	91	60	101	3.30
1989	Toronto	66	114⅔	4	10	.286	122	58	94	3.77
1990	Toronto	73	127⅔	2	8	.200	112	42	101	3.45
1991	Toronto	81	107⅓	7	6	.538	132	33	80	2.77
1992	Toronto	79	101⅓	7	4	.636	103	39	76	1.95
	Totals	387	592⅓	30	33	.476	579	256	491	3.31

TOP PROSPECTS

CARLOS DELGADO 20 6-3 206 Bats L Throws R

Honored as *USA Today's* Minor League Player of the Year after eye-popping season at Dunedin (A) . . . Batted .324 with 30 home runs and 100 RBI . . . Home-run total was stunning because Florida State League is known for its big parks . . . Learning to use all fields . . . Must answer questions about his catching ability as he advances to higher levels . . . Born June 25, 1972, in Aquadilla, P.R. . . . Signed as a free agent in October 1988.

GRAEME LLOYD 25 6-7 215 Bats L Throws L

Australian is making impressive progress . . . Went 4-8 for Knoxville (AA) club that finished 32 games below .500, but fashioned 1.96 ERA to go with 14 saves . . . Fanned 65 batters in 92 innings and walked only 25 . . . Graduated in 1983 from Geelong Technical School, where he played baseball, Australian rules football and cricket . . . Born April 9, 1967, in Victoria, Australia . . . Signed as a free agent by Toronto in January 1988.

STEVE KARSAY 21 6-3 185 Bats R Throws R

First-round choice in 1990 continues to show promise . . . Posted 6-3 record with 2.73 ERA in 16 starts at Dunedin (A) . . . Struck out 87 batters in 85⅔ innings while walking 29 . . . Permitted only 56 hits . . . Born March 24, 1972, in Flushing, N.Y.

MANAGER CITO GASTON: Answered his critics by becoming first black manager to lead his team into World Series, after 96-66 finish . . . Took over club in May 1989 and Blue Jays went on to win first of three AL East crowns in four years . . . Described as players' manager and he agrees with that tag . . . Generally takes hands-off approach to players, trusting them to be professionals . . . Critics are uncomfortable with his soft-spoken, unemotional approach . . . Does not wish to be a long-term manager, citing desire to spend more time with family and have a more regular schedule . . . Originally signed as player by Milwaukee Braves . . . Selected by San Diego in 1969 NL expansion draft, beginning 10-year major league career . . . Represented San Diego in 1970 All-Star Game . . . Traded by Padres to Atlanta following 1974 season . . . Made coaching debut as Braves' minor league batting instructor in 1981 . . . Born March 17, 1944, in San Antonio . . . Owns 331-248 major league managerial record, a .573 winning percentage.

ALL-TIME BLUE JAY SEASON RECORDS

BATTING: Tony Fernandez, .322, 1987
HRs: George Bell, 47, 1987
RBI: George Bell, 134, 1987
STEALS: Damaso Garcia, 54, 1982
WINS: Jack Morris, 21, 1992
STRIKEOUTS: Dave Stieb, 198, 1984

CALIFORNIA ANGELS

TEAM DIRECTORY: Chairman: Gene Autry; Pres./CEO: Richard Brown; Exec. VP: Jackie Autry; Sr. VP-Dir. Player Pers.: Whitey Herzog; Sr. VP-Baseball Oper.: Daniel O'Brien; Dir. Minor League Oper.: Bill Bavasi; VP-Pub. Rel. and Broadcasting: Tom Seeberg; Dir. Media Rel.: Tim Mead; Trav. Sec.: Frank Sims; Mgr. Buck Rodgers. Home: Anaheim Stadium (65,158). Field distances: 333, l.f. line; 386, l.c.; 404, c.f.; 386, r.c.; 333, r.f. line. Spring training: Tempe, Ariz.

SCOUTING REPORT

HITTING: Not much to get excited about here. The Angels finished last in the AL in batting average (.243), runs (579), RBI (537), slugging percentage (.338) and on-base percentage (.301) in 1992, and did little to improve themselves.

Luis Polonia (.286, 51 steals) is one of the league's best leadoff hitters, but it goes downhill quickly from there. Chad Curtis (.259, 10, 46, 18 steals) had a surprisingly good rookie season in 1992, and the Angels are hoping minor league sluggers Tim Salmon and J.T. Snow can do the same in the bigs this year. Each has a job to lose: Salmon in right field and the ex-Yankee prospect Snow at first base, where he displaces last year's rookie flop, Lee Stevens.

Kelly Gruber (.229, 11, 43), acquired from the Blue Jays for Luis Sojo, is coming off his worst season, but he hasn't faded as badly as Gary Gaetti (.226, 12, 48). Free-agent signee Chili Davis (.288, 12, 66) is back from Minnesota as the designated hitter. But, it isn't hard to figure why Jim Abbott went 7-15 despite a 2.77 ERA for these punchless Angels last year.

PITCHING: More glum news here as Buck Rodgers will have to manage without the traded Abbott, closer Bryan Harvey (lost to the Marlins in the expansion draft) and highly regarded pitching coach Marcel Lachemann.

Other than 1991, Mark Langston (13-14, 3.66) hasn't measured up to a four-year, $16-million contract. Chuck Finley (7-12, 3.96) appears to be regaining arm strength after his elbow woes of 1991. Julio Valera (8-11, 3.73) is promising, but prospects for the fourth and fifth rotation spots aren't.

Joe Grahe (5-6, 3.52, 21 saves) took over when Harvey went down with elbow problems. Now the closer's job is his, at least

Luis Polonia has swiped 99 bases the last two seasons.

until hard-throwing rookie Troy Percival can take it away. The rest of the bullpen is a mediocre cast including Steve Frey, Scott Lewis, Chuck Crim and ex-Yankee prospects Jerry Nielsen and Russ Springer.

FIELDING: It used to be that the Angels could beat you with pitching and defense, but standout defensive players such as Wally Joyner, Devon White and Dickie Schofield are long gone and the Angels finished 10th in fielding percentage (.979) in 1992.

Gruber is a big improvement at third base. Shortstop Gary DiSarcina tied for the league lead with 25 errors, but figures to get better. Left fielder Polonia has improved, but hardly is a Gold Glove threat and Curtis probably is better suited for left field than center. Catcher Greg Myers threw out only 23 percent of would-be base-stealers. An addition by subtraction was the loss of the erratic Junior Felix to the Marlins in the expansion draft.

OUTLOOK: It was supposed to be a winning combination: owner Gene Autry's money and GM Whitey Herzog's expertise. But with The Cowboy bowing to the fiscal conservatism of wife and co-owner Jackie, Herzog has been hamstrung in his efforts to build a winner.

The dealing of Abbott, one of the most popular Angels, to the Yankees won't help in the standings or at the box office. There is little chance of this young, inexperienced team staying out of last place after a 72-90 finish a year ago.

CALIFORNIA ANGELS 1993 ROSTER

MANAGER Buck Rodgers
Coaches—Rod Carew, Chuck Hernandez, Bobby Knoop, Ken Macha, Jimmie Reese, Rick Turner, John Wathan

PITCHERS

No.	Name	1992 Club	W-L	IP	SO	ERA	B-T	Ht.	Wt.	Born
23	Butcher, Michael	Edmonton	5-2	29	32	3.07	R-R	6-1	200	5/10/65 Davenport, IA
		California	2-2	28	24	3.25				
32	Crim, Chuck	California	7-6	87	30	5.17	R-R	6-0	185	7/23/61 Van Nuys, CA
38	Farrell, John	California		Injured			R-R	6-4	210	8/4/62 Neptune, NJ
31	Finley, Chuck	California	7-12	204	124	3.96	L-L	6-6	215	11/26/62 Monroe, LA
40	Fortugno, Tim	Edmonton	6-4	73	82	3.56	L-L	6-0	185	4/11/62 Clinton, MA
		California	1-1	42	31	5.18				
41	Frey, Steve	California	4-2	45	24	3.57	L-L	5-9	170	7/29/63 Southampton, PA
19	Grahe, Joe	California	5-6	95	39	3.52	R-R	6-2	200	8/14/67 W. Palm Beach, FL
		Edmonton	1-0	20	12	3.20				
48	Hathaway, Hilly	Palm Springs	2-1	24	17	1.50	L-L	6-4	195	9/12/69 Jacksonville, FL
		Midland	7-2	96	69	3.21				
		California	0-0	6	1	7.94				
42	Holzemer, Mark	Palm Springs	3-2	30	32	3.00	L-R	6-0	165	8/20/69 Littleton, CO
		Midland	2-5	45	36	3.83				
		Edmonton	5-7	89	49	6.67				
12	Langston, Mark	California	13-14	229	174	3.66	R-L	6-2	185	8/20/60 San Diego, CA
18	Lewis, Scott	California	4-0	38	18	3.99	R-R	6-3	178	12/5/65 Grants Pass, OR
		Edmonton	10-6	147	88	4.17				
45	Mussett, Jose	Quad City	8-2	72	104	2.39	R-R	6-3	173	9/18/66 Dominican Republic
—	Nielsen, Jerry	Albany	3-5	53	59	1.19	L-L	6-3	188	8/5/66 Sacramento, CA
		Columbus	0-0	5	5	1.80				
		New York (AL)	1-0	20	12	4.58				
34	Percival, Troy	Palm Springs	1-1	11	16	5.06	R-R	6-3	200	8/9/69 Fontana, CA
		Midland	3-0	19	21	2.37				
43	Scott, Darryl	Midland	1-1	30	36	1.82	R-R	6-1	185	8/6/88 Fresno, CA
		Edmonton	0-2	36	48	5.20				
51	Silverio, Victor	Palm Springs	2-5	52	32	7.22	R-R	6-4	186	9/20/68 Dominican Republic
		Quad City	5-2	78	76	2.53				
—	Springer, Russ	Columbus	8-5	124	95	2.69	R-R	6-4	205	11/7/68 Alexandria, LA
		New York (AL)	0-0	16	12	6.19				
35	Swingle, Paul	Midland	8-10	150	104	4.75	R-R	6-0	185	12/21/66 Inglewood, CA
36	Watson, Ron	Quad City	8-5	70	69	1.29	L-R	6-5	240	9/12/68 Newton, MA
44	Valera, Julio	Tidewater	1-0	6	7	0.00	R-R	6-2	215	10/13/68 Puerto Rico
		California	8-11	188	113	3.73				
46	Vasquez, Julian	Binghamton	2-1	27	24	1.35	R-R	6-3	185	5/24/68 Dominican Republic
		Tidewater	1-4	23	22	5.56				

CATCHERS

No.	Name	1992 Club	H	HR	RBI	Pct.	B-T	Ht.	Wt.	Born
21	Myers, Greg	Tor.-Cal.	18	1	13	.231	L-R	6-2	208	4/14/66 Riverside, CA
14	Orton, John	Edmonton	38	3	25	.255	R-R	6-1	192	12/8/65 Santa Cruz, CA
		California	25	2	12	.219				
24	Tingley, Ron	California	25	3	8	.197	R-R	6-2	194	5/27/59 Presque Isle, ME

INFIELDERS

No.	Name	1992 Club	H	HR	RBI	Pct.	B-T	Ht.	Wt.	Born
5	Correia, Rod	Midland	140	6	56	.290	R-R	5-11	170	9/13/67 Providence, RI
33	DiSarcina, Gary	California	128	3	42	.247	R-R	6-1	180	11/19/67 Malden, MA
1	Easley, Damion	Edmonton	124	3	44	.289	R-R	5-11	155	11/11/69 New York, NY
		California	39	1	12	.258				
6	Flora, Kevin	Edmonton	55	3	19	.324	R-R	6-0	180	6/10/69 Fontana, CA
3	Gaetti, Gary	California	103	12	48	.226	R-R	6-2	200	8/19/58 Centralia, IL
—	Gonzales, Rene	California	91	7	38	.277	R-R	6-3	201	9/3/61 Austin, TX
—	Gruber, Kelly	Toronto	102	11	43	.229	R-R	6-0	185	2/26/62 Houston, TX
10	Lovullo, Torey	Columbus	138	19	89	.295	S-R	6-0	185	7/25/65 Santa Monica, CA
—	Snow, J.T.	Columbus	154	15	78	.313	S-L	6-2	202	2/26/68 Long Beach, CA
		New York (AL)	2	0	2	.143				
9	Stevens, Lee	California	69	7	37	.221	L-L	6-4	219	7/10/67 Kansas City, MO
20	Van Burkleo, Ty	Edmonton	125	19	88	.273	L-L	6-5	225	10/7/63 Oakland, CA

OUTFIELDERS

No.	Name	1992 Club	H	HR	RBI	Pct.	B-T	Ht.	Wt.	Born
17	Curtis, Chad	California	114	10	46	.259	R-R	5-10	175	11/6/68 Marion, IN
—	Davis, Chili	Minnesota	128	12	66	.288	S-R	6-3	210	1/17/60 Jamaica
16	Edmonds, Jim	Midland	77	8	32	.313	L-L	6-1	190	6/27/70 Fullerton, CA
		Edmonton	58	6	36	.299				
22	Polonia, Luis	California	165	0	35	.286	L-L	5-8	150	10/12/64 Dominican Republic
15	Salmon, Tim	Edmonton	142	29	105	.347	R-R	6-3	200	8/24/68 Long Beach, CA
		California	14	2	6	.177				
11	Williams, Reggie	Edmonton	141	3	64	.272	S-R	6-1	180	5/5/66 Laurene, SC
		California	6	0	2	.231				

ANGEL PROFILES

LUIS POLONIA 28 5-8 150 **Bats L Throws L**

One of Angels' few weapons in 1992 . . . Led Angels in average, runs and hits . . . Led in total bases, despite the fact he had only 21 extra-base hits and no home runs . . . Average slipped for second consecutive year since .335 mark in 1990 . . . One of AL's better leadoff hitters despite low walk total (41) . . . Outfielder finished fourth in AL in steals with 51 . . . Was caught 21 times . . . Started 99 games in left field and 47 at DH . . . Earned $1,650,000 in 1992 . . . Angels got him from Yanks for Claudell Washington and Rich Monteleone, April 29, 1990 . . . Spent time in jail between 1990 and 1991 seasons after arrest in Milwaukee for having sex with a 15-year-old girl . . . Originally signed as free agent by A's in January 1984 . . . Born Oct. 12, 1964, in Santiago City, D.R.

Year	Club	Pos.	G	AB	R	H	2B	3B	HR	RBI	SB	Avg.
1987	Oakland	OF	125	435	78	125	16	10	4	49	29	.287
1988	Oakland	OF	84	288	51	84	11	4	2	27	24	.292
1989	Oak.-NY (AL) . .	OF	125	433	70	130	17	6	3	46	22	.300
1990	NY (AL)-Cal. . . .	OF	120	403	52	135	7	9	2	35	21	.335
1991	California	OF	150	604	92	179	28	8	2	50	48	.296
1992	California	OF	149	577	83	165	17	4	0	35	51	.286
	Totals		753	2740	426	818	96	41	13	242	195	.299

GARY DiSARCINA 25 6-1 180 **Bats R Throws R**

Solid shortstop in the Greg Gagne mold . . . Tied for AL lead with 25 errors in first full season, but led league in assists and was second in putouts . . . Started 155 games, second-most in AL . . . On the night this Massachusetts native changed number from 11 to 33 in honor of boyhood hero Larry Bird, he won the game with an RBI hit . . . Should improve offensively . . . Hit .310 in final year at Edmonton (AAA) . . . Earned $117,500 in 1992 . . . Angels' sixth-round pick in 1988 draft . . . Born Nov. 19, 1967, in Malden, Mass.

Year	Club	Pos.	G	AB	R	H	2B	3B	HR	RBI	SB	Avg.
1990	California	SS–2B	18	57	8	8	1	1	0	0	1	.140
1991	California	SS–2B–3B	18	57	5	12	2	0	0	3	0	.211
1992	California	SS	157	518	48	128	19	0	3	42	9	.247
	Totals		193	632	61	148	22	1	3	45	10	.234

GARY GAETTI 34 6-0 200 **Bats R Throws R**

Veteran in decline . . . Posted career lows in average, runs and RBI . . . Played 67 games at third and 44 at first base . . . Walked only 21 times in 456 at-bats . . . Hit just .191 on the road and .217 against right-handers . . . Committed 17 errors . . . One of game's most potent third basemen from 1986-88, when he averaged 31 homers and 102 RBI . . . Hit career-high .301 in 1988 . . . Earned $2,700,000 in 1992, second year of four-year deal signed as new-look free agent . . . Twins' first-round pick in 1978 draft . . . Left Minnesota in part because of clubhouse problems resulting from conversion from hell-raiser to born-again Christian . . . Born Aug. 19, 1958, in Centralia, Ill.

Year	Club	Pos.	G	AB	R	H	2B	3B	HR	RBI	SB	Avg.
1981	Minnesota	3B	9	26	4	5	0	0	2	3	0	.192
1982	Minnesota	3B-SS	145	508	59	117	25	4	25	84	0	.230
1983	Minnesota	3B-SS	157	584	81	143	30	3	21	78	7	.245
1984	Minnesota	3B-OF-SS	162	588	55	154	29	4	5	65	11	.262
1985	Minnesota	3B-OF-1B	160	560	71	138	31	0	20	63	13	.246
1986	Minnesota	3B-SS-OF-2B	157	596	91	171	34	1	34	108	14	.287
1987	Minnesota	3B	154	584	95	150	36	2	31	109	10	.257
1988	Minnesota	3B-SS	133	468	66	141	29	2	28	88	7	.301
1989	Minnesota	3B-1B	130	498	63	125	11	4	19	75	6	.251
1990	Minnesota	3B-1B-SS-OF	154	577	61	132	27	5	16	85	6	.229
1991	California	3B	152	586	58	144	22	1	18	66	5	.246
1992	California	3B-1B	130	456	41	103	13	2	12	48	3	.226
	Totals		1643	6031	745	1523	287	28	231	872	82	.253

CHILI DAVIS 33 6-3 210 **Bats B Throws R**

Suffered severe power drop after renaissance season in 1991, then returned to Angels as free-agent defector from Twins . . . Dropped from 29 homers to 12 and 93 RBI to 66 . . . Did raise his average 11 points, however . . . Between his slump and Kent Hrbek's injuries, the Twins were left without any left-handed power, a major reason for their late fade . . . Down year continued good-season, bad-season pattern that started with 1989, when he was Angels' MVP . . . Fell into Doug Rader's doghouse in 1990, when he hit only 12 homers and 58 RBI . . . Signed with Twins as a new-look free agent . . . Designated hitter plays outfield only in emergencies . . . Real name is Charles Theodore . . . Earned $2.8 million in 1992 . . . Giants' 11th-round pick in 1977 draft . . .

Born Jan. 17, 1960, in Kingston, Jamaica . . . Became free agent last winter.

Year	Club	Pos.	G	AB	R	H	2B	3B	HR	RBI	SB	Avg.
1981	San Francisco	OF	8	15	1	2	0	0	0	0	2	.133
1982	San Francisco	OF	154	641	86	167	27	6	19	76	24	.261
1983	San Francisco	OF	137	486	54	113	21	2	11	59	10	.233
1984	San Francisco	OF	137	499	87	157	21	6	21	81	12	.315
1985	San Francisco	OF	136	481	53	130	25	2	13	56	15	.270
1986	San Francisco	OF	153	526	71	146	28	3	13	70	16	.278
1987	San Francisco	OF	149	500	80	125	22	1	24	76	16	.250
1988	California	OF	158	600	81	161	29	3	21	93	9	.268
1989	California	OF	154	560	81	152	24	1	22	90	3	.271
1990	California	OF	113	412	58	109	17	1	12	58	1	.265
1991	Minnesota	OF	153	534	84	148	34	1	29	93	5	.277
1992	Minnesota	OF-1B	138	444	63	128	27	2	12	66	4	.288
	Totals		1590	5698	799	1538	275	28	197	818	117	.270

CHAD CURTIS 24 5-10 175 Bats R Throws R

Overshadowed by very strong AL rookie class, but nonetheless put together a solid first season . . . Stole 43 bases in 61 attempts, ranking eighth in AL . . . One of only two Angels to hit double figures in home runs . . . Could develop into valuable bench player, if he doesn't become an everyday outfielder . . . Played all three outfield positions . . . Earned minimum of $109,000 in 1992 . . . Most Valuable Player of 1991 Venezuelan Winter League, when he hit .338 to win the batting title . . . Hit .316 and stole 46 bases for Edmonton (AAA) in 1991 . . . Classic overachiever . . . Picked by Angels in 45th round in 1989 draft . . . Born Nov. 6, 1968, in Marion, Ind.

Year	Club	Pos.	G	AB	R	H	2B	3B	HR	RBI	SB	Avg.
1992	California	OF	139	441	59	114	16	2	10	46	43	.259

KELLY GRUBER 31 6-0 185 Bats R Throws R

Salary dumping by Blue Jays put veteran third baseman in new uniform . . . Angels sent Luis Sojo to Toronto and got cash along with this former offensive force last winter . . . Coming off worst season, in which he hit .229 with 11 homers and 43 RBI . . . Things were so bad he was booed lustily by normally reserved SkyDome fans . . . Spent seven seasons in Toronto, his best being 1990, when he hit 31 homers and drove in

118 runs . . . Two-time all-star . . . Blue Jays drafted him out of Indians organization in 1983 Rule 5 draft . . . Earned $3,633,333 in 1992 . . . Born Feb. 26, 1962, in Bellaire, Tex.

Year	Club	Pos.	G	AB	R	H	2B	3B	HR	RBI	SB	Avg.
1984	Toronto	3B-OF-SS	15	16	1	1	0	0	1	2	0	.063
1985	Toronto	3B-2B	5	13	0	3	0	0	0	1	0	.231
1986	Toronto	3B-2B-OF-SS	87	143	20	28	4	1	5	15	2	.196
1987	Toronto	3B-SS-2B-OF	138	341	50	80	14	3	12	36	12	.235
1988	Toronto	3B-SS-2B-OF	158	569	75	158	33	5	16	81	23	.278
1989	Toronto	3B-OF-SS	135	545	83	158	24	4	18	73	10	.290
1990	Toronto	3B-OF	150	592	92	162	36	6	31	118	14	.274
1991	Toronto	3B	113	429	58	108	18	2	20	65	12	.252
1992	Toronto	3B	120	446	42	102	16	3	11	43	7	.229
	Totals		921	3094	421	800	145	24	114	134	80	.259

MARK LANGSTON 32 6-2 185 Bats R Throws L

Finished below .500 for second time in three years since signing four-year, $16-million deal . . . Angels have received 42-39 record for their huge investment . . . Led staff in starts and innings . . . Pitched eight complete games and two shutouts . . . Second in AL with five pickoffs . . . Has pitched 200 or more innings in seven of last eight years . . . Two-time All-Star . . . Had 12-3 record at 1991 All-Star break . . . Combined with Mike Witt for a no-hitter against Seattle, April 11, 1990 . . . Won fourth Gold Glove in 1992 . . . Earned $3,550,000 in 1992 . . . Signed with Angels as free agent prior to 1990 season . . . Spent six years as Mariner . . . Born Aug. 20, 1960, in San Diego.

Year	Club	G	IP	W	L	Pct.	SO	BB	H	ERA
1984	Seattle	35	225	17	10	.630	204	118	188	3.40
1985	Seattle	24	126⅔	7	14	.333	72	91	122	5.47
1986	Seattle	37	239⅓	12	14	.462	245	123	234	4.85
1987	Seattle	35	272	19	13	.594	262	114	242	3.84
1988	Seattle	35	261⅓	15	11	.577	235	110	222	3.34
1989	Seattle	10	73⅓	4	5	.444	60	19	60	3.56
1989	Montreal	24	176⅔	12	9	.571	175	93	138	2.39
1990	California	33	223	10	17	.370	195	104	215	4.40
1991	California	34	246⅓	19	8	.704	183	96	190	3.00
1992	California	32	229	13	14	.481	174	74	206	3.66
	Totals.	299	2072⅔	128	115	.527	1805	942	1817	3.75

CHUCK FINLEY 30 6-6 215 Bats L Throws L

Decline continued as elbow trouble struck . . . Started season on disabled list . . . Made first of 31 starts April 22 . . . Won only seven games after logging 52 victories in previous three seasons . . . ERA was his highest since 1988 . . . Alarming strikeout-to-walk ratio and 24 home runs allowed were at root of his troubles . . . Surrendered more hits than innings pitched for first time since 1987 . . . The few lefties who faced him hit an amazing .402 in 1992 . . . Earned $4,375,000 in 1992, first year of four-year, $18.5-million deal . . . Two-time All-Star . . . Angels' first-round pick in January 1985 draft . . . Born Nov. 16, 1962, in Monroe, La.

Year	Club	G	IP	W	L	Pct.	SO	BB	H	ERA
1986	California	25	46⅓	3	1	.750	37	23	40	3.30
1987	California	35	90⅔	2	7	.222	63	43	102	4.67
1988	California	31	194⅓	9	15	.375	111	82	191	4.17
1989	California	29	199⅔	16	9	.640	156	82	171	2.57
1990	California	32	236	18	9	.667	177	81	210	2.40
1991	California	34	227⅓	18	9	.667	171	101	205	3.80
1992	California	31	204⅓	7	12	.368	124	98	212	3.96
	Totals.	217	1198⅔	73	62	.541	839	510	1131	3.45

JOE GRAHE 25 6-0 200 Bats R Throws R

Began season in starting rotation and ended it as Angels' closer . . . Spent three weeks at Edmonton (AAA) in between . . . Moved to bullpen in June, when Bryan Harvey suffered elbow injury . . . Recorded 21 saves in 24 opportunities, the fourth-best conversion rate in AL . . . Allowed only 85 hits in 94⅔ innings, but walked exactly as many as he struck out . . . Was 2-3 with a 5.70 ERA as starter . . . Right-handers hit only .212 against him . . . Earned $125,000 in 1992 . . . Angels' second-round pick in 1989 after successful career at the University of Miami . . . Born Aug. 14, 1967, in West Palm Beach, Fla.

Year	Club	G	IP	W	L	Pct.	SO	BB	H	ERA
1990	California	8	43⅓	3	4	.429	25	23	51	4.98
1991	California	18	73	3	7	.300	40	33	84	4.81
1992	California	46	94⅔	5	6	.455	39	39	85	3.52
	Totals.	72	211	11	17	.393	104	95	220	4.27

TOP PROSPECTS

TIM SALMON 24 6-3 200 Bats R Throws R

Was headed for Triple Crown in Pacific Coast League when recalled Aug. 20 . . . Hit .347 with 29 homers and 105 RBI for Edmonton (AAA) . . . Struggled to .177 mark in 79 at-bats with Angels . . . Angels' third-round pick in 1989 draft . . . Born Aug. 24, 1968, in Long Beach, Cal.

J.T. SNOW 25 6-2 202 Bats S Throws L

Came on strong in fourth pro season to win International League batting crown with .313 average, then Yankees packaged him with Russ Springer and Jerry Nielsen in deal that cost Angels Jim Abbott last winter . . . Also produced 15 homers and 78 RBI for Columbus (AAA) . . . Excellent-fielding first baseman . . . Switch-hitter needs more work from right side . . . Compiled .333 average in three-year career for University of Arizona . . . Born Feb. 26, 1968, in Long Beach, Cal. . . . Father, Jack, was standout receiver at Notre Dame and later with Los Angeles Rams.

DAMION EASLEY 23 5-11 155 Bats R Throws R

Made strong late-season showing . . . Hit .258 and stole nine bases in 47 games at third base for Angels . . . Played shortstop in minors, where he hit .289 with 26 steals for Edmonton (AAA) in 1992 . . . Angels' 30th-round pick in 1988 draft . . . Born Nov. 11, 1969, in New York, N.Y.

HILLARY HATHAWAY 23 6-4 195 Bats L Throws L

Made first major league start Oct. 3 . . . Lasted 4⅔ innings, allowing two runs against Texas . . . Was 7-2 with 3.21 ERA for Midland (AA) . . . Control pitcher . . . Walked only 10 in 95 innings . . . Angels' 35th-round pick in 1989 draft . . . Born Sept. 12, 1969, in Jacksonville, Fla.

TROY PERCIVAL 23 6-3 200 Bats R Throws R

Could get shot at closer's role now that Bryan Harvey was lost to Florida in draft . . . His fastball is clocked in 92-95-mph range . . . Had 37 strikeouts in 30 innings for Palm Springs (A) and Midland (AA) . . . Went 1-1 with 5.06 ERA for Palm Springs, 3-0 with 2.37 ERA for Midland . . . Had 63 strikeouts in 38 innings for Boise (Rookie) in 1991 . . . Angels' sixth-round pick in 1990 draft . . . Born Aug. 9, 1969, in Fontana, Cal.

MANAGER BUCK RODGERS: Tough season was interrupted by near-tragic bus accident on May 21 . . . He suffered a broken knee cap, rib and elbow . . . Returned for final month, with interim skipper John Wathan returning to coaching role . . . Team was 19-20 at time of crash . . . Finished 18 games below .500 . . . Under Rodgers, Angels were 33-44, bringing his career mark to 697-655 . . . Fired by Montreal in middle of 1991 season . . . Replaced Doug Rader as Angels' manager on Aug. 26, 1991, when Angels were 61-64. Finished 20-17 . . . Highly regarded for getting most out of talent he's given . . . NL Manager of the Year in 1987, when he led Expos to 91-77 record and third-place finish . . . Best job might have been in 1990, when Expos finished 85-77 despite massive free-agent exodus . . . His teams have never finished higher than third or lower than fifth . . . Fired by Brewers after 23-24 start in 1982, when club went on to win pennant for Harvey Kuenn . . . Three-time minor league Manager of the Year . . . Born Aug. 16, 1938, in Delaware, Ohio.

ALL-TIME ANGEL SEASON RECORDS

BATTING: Rod Carew, .339, 1983
HRs: Reggie Jackson, 39, 1982
RBI: Don Baylor, 139, 1979
STEALS: Mickey Rivers, 70, 1975
WINS: Clyde Wright, 22, 1970
Nolan Ryan, 22, 1974
STRIKEOUTS: Nolan Ryan, 383, 1973

CHICAGO WHITE SOX

TEAM DIRECTORY: Chairman: Jerry Reinsdorf; Vice Chairman: Eddie Einhorn; Exec. VP: Howard Pizer; Sr. VP-Baseball: Jack Gould; Sr. VP-Major League Oper.: Ron Schueler; VP-Scouting and Minor League Oper.: Larry Monroe; Dir. Baseball Oper.: Dan Evans; Dir. Pub. Rel./Community Affairs: Doug Abel; Trav. Sec.: Glen Rosenbaum; Mgr.: Gene Lamont. Home: Comiskey Park (44,229). Field distances: 347, l.f. line; 375, l.c.; 400, c.f.; 375, r.c., 347, r.f. line. Spring training: Sarasota, Fla.

SCOUTING REPORT

HITTING: The pieces all seem to be there, but the whole is uninspiring. Frank Thomas (.323, 24, 115) arguably is the AL's best offensive player. Robin Ventura (.282, 16, 93) and George Bell (.255, 25, 112) are potent forces. Tim Raines (.294, 45 steals) and Lance Johnson (.279, 41 steals) get on base and have speed. However, the entire home-run output of the outfield was 19 and Steve Sax' average dropped precipitously to .236. The end result was middle-of-the-pack finishes for the White Sox in average (.261), runs (738) and homers (110).

The White Sox attempted to address the outfield power shortage by signing Red Sox free agent Ellis Burks (.255, 8, 30) and hope his back woes are over. Bo Jackson's hip has improved, but even if he can return, it will be only as a designated hitter. Ron Karkovice (.237, 13, 50) is developing as a power threat, so Carlton Fisk's role has been reduced.

PITCHING: Ace Jack McDowell (20-10, 3.18) is a quality pitcher, but the same can't be said for the rest of the rotation. Instead of signing one of the many front-line free-agent starters, the White Sox settled for injury-plagued ex-Blue Jay Dave Stieb (4-6, 5.04) and didn't bring back Charlie Hough. It's up to veteran Kirk McCaskill (12-13, 4.18) and youngsters Alex Fernandez (8-11, 4.27) and Wilson Alvarez (5-3, 5.20) to improve now that Greg Hibbard has been lost in the expansion draft.

Roberto Hernandez (7-3, 1.65, 12 saves) made a stirring comeback from a blood-clotting problem that threatened his career and displaced struggling Bobby Thigpen (1-3, 4.75, 22 saves) as the closer. Scott Radinsky (3-7, 2.73, 15 saves) is as tough as any left-handed reliever, but too inconsistent. Terry Leach and Donn Pall fill out one of the league's deepest bullpens.

There's no doubting the power and the eye of Frank Thomas.

FIELDING: The good news is that shortstop Ozzie Guillen is expected to return after missing almost all of last season following knee surgery. Beyond his Gold Glove abilities, Guillen is a positive clubhouse force. Ventura won a Gold Glove at third, but the right side of the infield has the unreliable Sax at second and first baseman Thomas, whose shoulder trouble and aversion to defense make him best-suited for a DH role.

Lance Johnson is perhaps the game's most underrated defensive center fielder. The strong-armed Karkovice threw out 32 percent of would-be base-stealers and is one of the game's best at blocking balls in the dirt and handling pitchers.

OUTLOOK: With the breakup of the A's and the Twins' loss of John Smiley and Greg Gagne, some folks see the White Sox—86-76 in 1992—as AL West favorites this season. It would have been a lot easier to see them that way if they had added an offensive threat in right field and a quality No. 2 starter. Gene Lamont's White Sox have holes, just like everybody else in a division that no longer appears as strong as it used to be. Can they win a division title for the first time since Tony La Russa went west? They certainly could.

CHICAGO WHITE SOX 1993 ROSTER

MANAGER Gene Lamont
Coaches—Terry Bevington, Jackie Brown, Walt Hriniak, Doug Mansolino, Joe Nossek, Dewey Robinson

PITCHERS

No.	Name	1992 Club	W-L	IP	SO	ERA	B-T	Ht.	Wt.	Born
40	Alvarez, Wilson	Chicago (AL)	5-3	100	66	5.20	L-L	6-1	235	3/24/70 Venezuela
—	Bere, Jason	Sarasota (FSL)	7-2	116	106	2.41	R-R	6-3	185	5/26/71 Cambridge, MA
		Birmingham	4-4	54	45	3.00				
		Vancouver	0-0	1	2	0.00				
—	Bolton, Rodney	Vancouver	11-9	187	111	2.93	R-R	6-2	190	9/23/68 Chattanooga, TN
50	Drahman, Brian	Vancouver	2-4	58	34	2.01	R-R	6-3	231	11/7/66 Kenton, KY
		Chicago (AL)	0-0	7	1	2.57				
54	Dunne, Michael	Vancouver	10-6	133	78	2.78	L-R	6-4	212	10/27/62 South Bend, IN
		Chicago (AL)	2-0	13	6	4.26				
—	Ellis, Robert	Sarasota (GCL)	1-0	5	4	10.80	R-R	6-5	215	12/25/70 Baton Rouge, LA
		South Bend	6-5	123	97	2.34				
32	Fernandez, Alex	Chicago (AL)	8-11	188	95	4.27	R-R	6-1	210	8/13/69 Miami Beach, FL
		Vancouver	2-1	29	27	0.94				
43	Garcia, Ramon	Vancouver	9-11	170	79	3.71	R-R	6-2	200	12/9/69 Venezuela
39	Hernandez, Roberto	Vancouver	3-3	21	23	2.61	R-R	6-4	235	11/11/64 Puerto Rico
		Chicago (AL)	7-3	71	68	1.65				
34	Leach, Terry	Chicago (AL)	6-5	74	22	1.95	R-R	6-0	194	3/13/54 Selma, AL
25	McCaskill, Kirk	Chicago (AL)	12-13	209	109	4.18	R-R	6-1	205	4/9/61 Canada
29	McDowell, Jack	Chicago (AL)	20-10	261	178	3.18	R-R	6-5	180	1/16/66 Van Nuys, CA
22	Pall, Donn	Chicago (AL)	5-2	73	27	4.93	R-R	6-1	180	1/11/62 Chicago, IL
31	Radinsky, Scott	Chicago (AL)	3-7	59	48	2.73	L-L	6-3	204	3/3/68 Glendale, CA
47	Ruffin, Johnny	Birmingham	0-7	48	44	6.04	R-R	6-3	172	7/29/71 Butler, AL
		Sarasota (FSL)	3-7	63	61	5.89				
—	Schwarz, Jeff	Birmingham	2-1	39	53	1.16	R-R	6-5	190	5/20/64 Ft. Pierce, FL
		Vancouver	1-3	36	42	3.00				
—	Stieb, Dave	Toronto	4-6	96	45	5.04	R-R	6-1	195	7/22/57 Santa Ana, CA
37	Thigpen, Bobby	Chicago (AL)	1-3	55	45	4.75	R-R	6-3	222	7/17/63 Tallahassee, FL

CATCHERS

No.	Name	1992 Club	H	HR	RBI	Pct.	B-T	Ht.	Wt.	Born
72	Fisk, Carlton	South Bend	1	1	3	.500	R-R	6-2	225	12/26/47 Bellows Falls, VT
		Sarasota (FSL)	3	1	2	.120				
		Chicago (AL)	43	3	21	.229				
36	Hemond, Scott	Tacoma	8	0	3	.242	R-R	6-0	215	11/18/65 Taunton, MA
		Oak.-Chi. (AL)	9	0	2	.225				
20	Karkovice, Ron	Chicago (AL)	81	13	50	.237	R-R	6-1	219	8/8/63 Union, NJ
5	Merullo, Matt	Chicago (AL)	9	0	3	.180	L-R	6-2	200	8/4/65 Ridgefield, CT
		Vancouver	8	1	4	.178				

INFIELDERS

38	Beltre, Esteban	Vancouver	43	0	16	.267	R-R	5-10	172	12/26/67 Dominican Republic
		Chicago (AL)	21	1	10	.191				
28	Cora, Joey	Chicago (AL)	30	0	9	.246	S-R	5-8	155	5/14/65 Puerto Rico
57	Cron, Chris	Vancouver	139	16	81	.278	R-R	6-2	207	3/31/64 Albuquerque, NM
		Chicago (AL)	0	0	0	.000				
—	Gilbert, Shawn	Portland	109	3	52	.245	R-R	5-9	170	3/12/65 Camden, NJ
14	Grebeck, Craig	Chicago (AL)	77	3	35	.268	R-R	5-7	148	12/29/64 Johnstown, PA
13	Guillen, Ozzie	Chicago (AL)	8	0	7	.200	L-R	5-11	160	1/20/64 Venezuela
—	Martin, Norberto	Vancouver	143	0	29	.288	S-R	5-10	164	12/10/66 Dominican Republic
7	Sax, Steve	Chicago (AL)	134	4	47	.236	R-R	6-0	185	1/29/60 Sacramento, CA
35	Thomas, Frank	Chicago (AL)	185	24	115	.323	R-R	6-5	240	5/27/68 Columbus, GA
23	Ventura, Robin	Chicago (AL)	167	16	93	.282	L-R	6-1	192	7/14/67 Santa Maria, CA
—	Wilson, Brandon	Sarasota (FSL)	118	4	54	.296	R-R	6-1	170	2/26/69 Owensboro, KY
		Birmingham	29	0	4	.271				

OUTFIELDERS

45	Abner, Shawn	Vancouver	21	0	2	.266	R-R	6-1	196	6/17/66 Hamilton, OH
		Chicago (AL)	58	1	16	.279				
21	Bell, George	Chicago (AL)	160	25	112	.255	R-R	6-1	205	10/21/59 Dominican Republic
—	Burks, Ellis	Boston	60	8	30	.255	R-R	6-2	202	9/11/64 Vicksburg, MS
12	Huff, Michael	Chicago (AL)	24	0	8	.209	R-R	6-1	190	8/11/63 Honolulu, HI
		Vancouver	1	0	0	.250				
		South Bend	15	1	5	.375				
8	Jackson, Bo	Chicago (AL)		Injured			R-R	6-1	228	11/30/62 Bessemer, AL
1	Johnson, Lance	Chicago (AL)	158	3	47	.279	L-L	5-11	160	7/6/63 Cincinnati, OH
24	Newson, Warren	Chicago (AL)	30	1	11	.221	L-L	5-7	202	7/3/64 Newman, GA
		Vancouver	15	0	9	.254				
44	Pasqua, Dan	Chicago (AL)	56	6	33	.211	L-L	6-0	218	10/17/61 Yonkers, NY
		Birmingham	1	0	0	.125				
30	Raines, Tim	Chicago (AL)	162	7	54	.294	S-R	5-8	185	9/16/59 Sanford, FL

WHITE SOX PROFILES

FRANK THOMAS 24 6-5 240 Bats R Throws R

They call him "The Big Hurt" and few players hurt opponents more with the bat . . . Drew AL MVP consideration for finishing first in AL in doubles, on-base percentage (.439) and walks (122), second in runs, third in average, RBI and slugging percentage (.536), fourth in total bases (307) and fifth in hits . . . First baseman built upon outstanding first full season in 1991, when he hit .318 with 32 homers and 109 RBI and led majors in walks (138) and on-base percentage (.453) . . . Former Auburn football teammate of Bo Jackson . . . Eighth pick overall in 1989 draft . . . Named Minor League Player of the Year by *Baseball America* in 1990 . . . Born May 27, 1968, in Columbus, Ga. . . . Earned $600,000 in 1992 and that figure will climb much higher.

Year	Club	Pos.	G	AB	R	H	2B	3B	HR	RBI	SB	Avg.
1990	Chicago (AL) . .	1B	60	191	39	63	11	3	7	31	0	.330
1991	Chicago (AL) . .	1B	158	559	104	178	31	2	32	109	1	.318
1992	Chicago (AL) . .	1B	160	573	108	185	46	2	24	115	6	.323
	Totals		378	1323	251	426	88	7	63	255	7	.322

ROBIN VENTURA 25 6-1 192 Bats L Throws R

Third full year was almost a duplicate of outstanding 1991 season . . . Fell off in home runs from 23 in 1991 to 16, but batting average, runs and RBI were on par . . . Hard to believe this guy suffered through an 0-for-41 slump in 1990 . . . Third baseman's error total jumped from 18 in 1991 to 23, but he won second straight Gold Glove nonetheless . . . Member of 1988 U.S. Olympic team . . . Was 10th player selected in 1988 draft . . . Was one of college baseball's all-time great hitters at Oklahoma State . . . Earned $600,000 in 1992 . . . Born July 14, 1967, in Santa Maria, Cal.

Year	Club	Pos.	G	AB	R	H	2B	3B	HR	RBI	SB	Avg.
1989	Chicago (AL) . .	3B	16	45	5	8	3	0	0	7	0	.178
1990	Chicago (AL) . .	3B-1B	150	493	48	123	17	1	5	54	1	.249
1991	Chicago (AL) . .	3B-1B	157	606	92	172	25	1	23	100	2	.284
1992	Chicago (AL) . .	3B-1B	157	592	85	167	38	1	16	93	2	.282
	Totals		480	1736	230	470	83	3	44	254	5	.271

GEORGE BELL 33 6-1 205 Bats R Throws R

Went crosstown in late-spring trade, then had another productive season . . . Traded by Cubs for Sammy Sosa and Ken Patterson, he played for his third team in as many seasons . . . His RBI total was his best since 1987 MVP season . . . Home run total matched 1991, which also was his most in six seasons . . . Hit career-low .255 and just .239 against right-handed pitching . . . DH started only 15 games in left field . . . Went to Cubs as free agent before 1991 season after seven full years and parts of two others in Toronto . . . Blue Jays plucked him out of Phillies organization in Rule V draft in 1980 . . . Signed originally as free agent by Philadelphia in 1978 . . . Born Oct. 21, 1959, in San Pedro de Macoris, D.R. . . . Earned $3.6 million in 1992.

Year	Club	Pos.	G	AB	R	H	2B	3B	HR	RBI	SB	Avg.
1981	Toronto	OF	60	163	19	38	2	1	5	12	3	.233
1983	Toronto	OF	39	112	5	30	5	4	2	17	1	.268
1984	Toronto	OF-3B	159	606	85	177	39	4	26	87	11	.292
1985	Toronto	OF-1B	157	607	87	167	28	6	28	95	21	.275
1986	Toronto	OF-3B	159	641	101	198	38	6	31	108	7	.309
1987	Toronto	OF-2B-3B	156	610	111	188	32	4	47	134	5	.308
1988	Toronto	OF	156	614	78	165	27	5	24	97	4	.269
1989	Toronto	OF	153	613	88	182	41	2	18	104	4	.297
1990	Toronto	OF	142	562	67	149	25	0	21	86	3	.265
1991	Chicago (NL) . .	OF	149	558	63	159	27	0	25	86	2	.285
1992	Chicago (AL) . .	OF	155	627	74	160	27	0	25	112	5	.255
	Totals		1485	5713	778	1613	291	32	252	938	66	.282

TIM RAINES 33 5-8 185 Bats S Throws R

Strong second half showed he still has something left . . . Raised average 42 points after All-Star break . . . September power burst brought homer total to seven after he had two entering the month . . . Pushed career stolen-base total to 730 . . . Acquired from Expos with Jeff Carter for Ivan Calderon and Barry Jones prior to 1991 season . . . Topped 40-steal mark for 11th time in 12 years . . . Has averaged 49 steals over last four years . . . Was caught stealing only six times in 1992 . . . Equalled 1991 run total with 102 . . . Made only two errors in 125 starts in left field . . . Earned $3.5 million in 1992 . . . Born Sept. 16, 1959, in Samford, Fla.

Year	Club	Pos.	G	AB	R	H	2B	3B	HR	RBI	SB	Avg.
1979	Montreal	PR	6	0	3	0	0	0	0	0	2	.000
1980	Montreal	2B-OF	15	20	5	1	0	0	0	0	5	.050
1981	Montreal	OF-2B	88	313	61	95	13	7	5	37	71	.304
1982	Montreal	OF-2B	156	647	90	179	32	8	4	43	78	.277
1983	Montreal	OF-2B	156	615	133	183	32	8	11	71	90	.298
1984	Montreal	OF-2B	160	622	106	192	38	9	8	60	75	.309
1985	Montreal	OF	150	575	115	184	30	13	11	41	70	.320
1986	Montreal	OF	151	580	91	194	35	10	9	62	70	.334
1987	Montreal	OF	139	530	123	175	34	8	18	68	50	.330
1988	Montreal	OF	109	429	66	116	19	7	12	48	33	.270
1989	Montreal	OF	145	517	76	148	29	6	9	60	41	.286
1990	Montreal	OF	130	457	65	131	11	5	9	62	49	.287
1991	Chicago (AL) . .	OF	155	609	102	163	20	6	5	50	51	.268
1992	Chicago (AL) . .	OF	144	551	102	162	22	9	7	54	45	.294
	Totals		1704	6465	1138	1923	315	96	108	656	730	.297

OZZIE GUILLEN 29 5-11 160 Bats L Throws R

Many think club's 1992 title chances were shot by shortstop's season-ending knee injury . . . Played only 12 games and had only 40 at-bats when injury occurred in outfield collision with Tim Raines . . . Underwent surgery and was back taking ground balls and batting practice by end of last season . . . AL Rookie of the Year in 1985 . . . Won Gold Glove in 1990 . . . Once an offensive liability, but average topped .270 in each of last four full seasons . . . Came up in Padres' system . . . Acquired in deal for Lamarr Hoyt after 1984 season . . . Earned $1.9 million in 1992 . . . Follows Chico Carrasquel and Luis Aparicio in long line of quality White Sox shortstops from Venezuela . . . Born Jan. 20, 1964, in Oculare del Tuy, Venezuela.

Year	Club	Pos.	G	AB	R	H	2B	3B	HR	RBI	SB	Avg.
1985	Chicago (AL) . .	SS	150	491	71	134	21	9	1	33	7	.273
1986	Chicago (AL) . .	SS	159	547	58	137	19	4	2	47	8	.250
1987	Chicago (AL) . .	SS	149	560	64	156	22	7	2	51	25	.279
1988	Chicago (AL) . .	SS	156	566	58	148	16	7	0	39	25	.261
1989	Chicago (AL) . .	SS	155	597	63	151	20	8	1	54	36	.253
1990	Chicago (AL) . .	SS	160	516	61	144	21	4	1	58	13	.279
1991	Chicago (AL) . .	SS	154	524	52	143	20	3	3	49	21	.273
1992	Chicago (AL) . .	SS	12	40	5	8	4	0	0	7	1	.200
	Totals		1095	3841	432	1021	143	42	10	338	136	.266

STEVE SAX 33 6-0 185 Bats R Throws R

Couldn't repeat outstanding 1991 season . . . Instead, he fell to his worst numbers in 11 full seasons . . . White Sox traded Melido Perez, Domingo Jean and Bob Wickman to Yanks for him in anticipation of top-of-the-order production that never materialized . . . Has three years left on mega-contract extension bestowed upon him by Yankees . . . Earned $3,575,000 in 1992 . . . Signed with Yankees as free agent after 1989 season . . . Batted .304 and led Yanks in six offensive categories in 1991 . . . Hit .300 in 1988 World Series, when Dodgers upset Athletics . . . Has hit .300 or better three times . . . NL Rookie of the Year in 1982 . . . Dodgers' ninth-round pick in 1978 draft . . . Born Jan. 29, 1960, in West Sacramento, Cal.

Year	Club	Pos.	G	AB	R	H	2B	3B	HR	RBI	SB	Avg.
1981	Los Angeles . . .	2B	31	119	15	33	2	0	2	9	5	.277
1982	Los Angeles . . .	2B	150	638	88	180	23	7	4	47	49	.282
1983	Los Angeles . . .	2B	155	623	94	175	18	5	5	41	58	.281
1984	Los Angeles . . .	2B	145	569	70	138	24	4	1	35	34	.243
1985	Los Angeles . . .	2B-3B	136	488	62	136	8	4	1	42	27	.279
1986	Los Angeles . . .	2B	157	633	91	210	43	4	6	56	40	.332
1987	Los Angeles . . .	2B-OF-3B	157	610	84	171	22	7	6	46	37	.280
1988	Los Angeles . . .	2B	160	632	70	175	19	4	5	57	42	.277
1989	New York (AL)	2B	158	651	88	205	26	3	5	63	43	.315
1990	New York (AL)	2B	155	615	70	160	24	2	4	42	43	.260
1991	New York (AL)	2B-3B	158	652	85	198	38	2	10	56	31	.304
1992	Chicago (AL) . .	2B	143	567	74	134	26	4	4	47	30	.236
	Totals		1705	6797	891	1915	273	46	53	541	439	.282

CARLTON FISK 45 6-2 225 Bats R Throws R

Future Hall of Famer should set mark for most games caught this season . . . Already has most homers by a catcher, with 355 . . . Needs 25 homers to reach 400 for career . . . Injuries limited him to 62 games and 188 at-bats, his fewest since 1974 . . . Posted career lows in average, home runs and RBI . . . Career hit total is 2,346 despite loss of almost three full seasons due to various injuries . . . Has played 21 full seasons and parts of two others and the last 12 have been with White Sox . . . Has played 1,396 games for White Sox and 1,078 with Red Sox, the team he will forever remain linked with because of memorable 1975 World Series Game 6 homer . . . Earned $1 million in 1992 . . .

Red Sox drafted him fourth overall in 1967 . . . Born Dec. 26, 1947, in Bellows Falls, Vt.

Year	Club	Pos.	G	AB	R	H	2B	3B	HR	RBI	SB	Avg.
1969	Boston	C	2	5	0	0	0	0	0	0	0	.000
1971	Boston	C	14	48	7	15	2	1	2	6	0	.313
1972	Boston	C	131	457	74	134	28	9	22	61	5	.293
1973	Boston	C	135	508	65	125	21	0	26	71	7	.246
1974	Boston	C	52	187	36	56	12	1	11	26	5	.299
1975	Boston	C	79	263	47	87	14	4	10	52	4	.331
1976	Boston	C	134	487	76	124	17	5	17	58	12	.255
1977	Boston	C	152	536	106	169	26	3	26	102	7	.315
1978	Boston	C-OF	157	571	94	162	39	5	20	88	7	.284
1979	Boston	C-OF	91	320	49	87	23	2	10	42	3	.272
1980	Boston	C-OF-1B-3B	131	478	73	138	25	3	18	62	11	.289
1981	Chicago (AL) ..	C-1B-3B-OF	96	338	44	89	12	0	7	45	3	.263
1982	Chicago (AL) ..	C-1B	135	476	66	127	17	3	14	65	17	.267
1983	Chicago (AL) ..	C	138	488	85	141	26	4	26	86	9	.289
1984	Chicago (AL) ..	C	102	359	54	83	20	1	21	43	6	.231
1985	Chicago (AL) ..	C	153	543	85	129	23	1	37	107	17	.238
1986	Chicago (AL) ..	OF-C	125	457	42	101	11	0	14	63	2	.221
1987	Chicago (AL) ..	C-1B-OF	135	454	68	116	22	1	23	71	1	.256
1988	Chicago (AL) ..	C	76	253	37	70	8	1	19	50	0	.277
1989	Chicago (AL) ..	C	103	375	47	110	25	2	13	68	1	.293
1990	Chicago (AL) ..	C	137	452	65	129	21	0	18	65	7	.285
1991	Chicago (AL) ..	C-1B	134	460	42	111	25	0	18	74	1	.241
1992	Chicago (AL) ..	C	62	188	12	43	4	1	3	21	3	.229
	Totals		2474	8703	1274	2346	421	47	375	1326	128	.270

JACK McDOWELL 27 6-5 180 Bats R Throws R

"Black Jack" definitely is White Sox' ace . . . Won 20 games for the first time and earned serious Cy Young Award consideration for second consecutive year . . . Two-year record is 37-20 . . . Led AL with 13 complete games . . . Ranked second in AL in wins, third in innings, fifth in winning percentage and strikeouts and eighth in ERA . . . Looks more like rock poet and band leader than dominating ace pitcher . . . Is lead singer and guitarist for modern rock group V.I.E.W. Teammate Scott Radinsky is group's drummer . . . Earned $1.6 million in 1991 . . . White Sox drafted him fifth overall in 1987, out of Stanford . . . Born Jan. 16, 1966, in Van Nuys, Cal.

Year	Club	G	IP	W	L	Pct.	SO	BB	H	ERA
1987	Chicago (AL)	4	28	3	0	1.000	15	6	16	1.93
1988	Chicago (AL)	26	158⅔	5	10	.333	84	68	147	3.97
1990	Chicago (AL)	33	205	14	9	.609	165	77	189	3.82
1991	Chicago (AL)	35	253⅔	17	10	.630	191	82	212	3.41
1992	Chicago (AL)	34	260⅔	20	10	.667	178	75	247	3.18
	Totals...........	132	906	59	39	.602	633	308	811	3.49

KIRK McCASKILL 31 6-1 205 Bats R Throws R

Improved from horrible 1991 season, but still finished below .500 . . . Signed a three-year, $6.7-million deal after going 10-19 in 1991 . . . Was second on staff in starts and innings . . . Walked almost as many as he struck out . . . ERA was above 4.00 for second consecutive year . . . Went 78-74 in seven seasons with Angels . . . Has had recurring elbow troubles and was operated on in 1990 . . . Angels' fourth-round pick in 1982, one year after he became first collegian picked in NHL draft, by Winnipeg . . . Didn't give up hockey until 1984, the year before he emerged in Angels' rotation . . . Born April 9, 1961, in Kapuskasing, Ont.

Year	Club	G	IP	W	L	Pct.	SO	BB	H	ERA
1985	California	30	189⅔	12	12	.500	102	64	189	4.70
1986	California	34	246⅓	17	10	.630	202	92	207	3.36
1987	California	14	74⅔	4	6	.400	56	34	84	5.67
1988	California	23	146⅓	8	6	.571	98	61	155	4.31
1989	California	32	212	15	10	.600	107	59	202	2.93
1990	California	29	174⅓	12	11	.522	78	72	161	3.25
1991	California	30	177⅔	10	19	.345	71	66	193	4.26
1992	Chicago (AL)	34	209	12	13	.480	109	95	193	4.18
	Totals	226	1430	90	87	.508	823	543	1384	3.91

ALEX FERNANDEZ 23 6-1 210 Bats R Throws R

Still hasn't fulfilled potential, but few don't expect him to develop into a big winner . . . Flashed brilliance in one-hit, complete-game victory over Milwaukee May 4 . . . Pitched four complete games in 29 starts . . . Sent down to Vancouver (AAA) June 22 to straighten out problems, returned after All-Star break . . . Went 5-4 after coming back and was much improved over 3-7 start . . . First-round pick of Brewers in 1988, out of high school, but decided to attend University of Miami . . . White Sox picked him fourth overall in 1990 draft, the fourth in a string of first-round successes that also includes Jack McDowell, Frank Thomas and Robin Ventura . . . Born Aug. 13, 1969, in Miami Beach, Fla. . . . Earned $160,000 in 1992.

Year	Club	G	IP	W	L	Pct.	SO	BB	H	ERA
1990	Chicago (AL)	13	87⅔	5	5	.500	61	34	89	3.80
1991	Chicago (AL)	34	191⅔	9	13	.409	145	88	186	4.51
1992	Chicago (AL)	29	187⅔	8	11	.421	95	50	199	4.27
	Totals	76	467	22	29	.431	301	172	474	4.28

TOP ROOKIES

WILSON ALVAREZ 23 6-1 175 Bats L Throws L
Expected to step into rotation . . . Winter of overuse left him drained, especially early in 1992 season . . . Went 5-3 with 5.20 ERA for White Sox . . . Made nine starts and 25 relief appearances, totalling 100 innings . . . Must improve control . . . Walked one fewer than he struck out (66) . . . Came from Rangers with Sammy Sosa and Scott Fletcher for Harold Baines in July 1989 deal . . . Originally signed at age 16 as free agent by Rangers . . . Born March 24, 1970, in Maracaibo, Venezuela.

ESTEBAN BELTRE 25 5-10 172 Bats R Throws R
Another shortstop from the Dominican . . . Slick fielder in mold of Atlanta's Rafael Belliard . . . Has strong but erratic arm . . . Hit .191 in 100 at-bats with White Sox after both Ozzie Guillen and Craig Grebeck went down with injuries . . . Did hit his first major-league home run and scored 21 runs . . . Hit .267 with no homers and 16 RBI for Vancouver (AAA) in 1992 . . . Born Dec. 26, 1967, in Ingenio Quisfuella, D.R.

MANAGER GENE LAMONT: Soft-spoken skipper came under some heat when club didn't perform as well as expected in 86-76 rookie season . . . Problems were not of his making as Ozzie Guillen went down, Carlton Fisk played little and Bobby Thigpen lost effectiveness . . . Isn't a dynamic personality, but has players' respect . . . Spent six years as Jim Leyland's third-base coach in Pittsburgh . . . Also handled the club's defensive alignment and outfield instruction . . . Managed eight years in Royals' system, twice reaching Southern League (AA) championship series . . . A former catcher, he hit .223 in 159 major league at-bats spread over five seasons with Detroit . . . Only had one full season in majors as a player (1974) . . . Tigers' chose him 11th overall in 1965 draft . . . Born Christmas Day, 1946, in Rockford, Ill.

Cool mound musician Jack McDowell hit 20-win high note.

ALL-TIME WHITE SOX SEASON RECORDS

BATTING: Luke Appling, .388, 1936
HRs: Dick Allen, 37, 1972
Carlton Fisk, 37, 1985
RBI: Zeke Bonura, 138, 1936
STEALS: Rudy Law, 77, 1983
WINS: Ed Walsh, 40, 1908
STRIKEOUTS: Ed Walsh, 269, 1908

KANSAS CITY ROYALS

TEAM DIRECTORY: Chairman: Ewing Kauffman; Exec. VP/GM: Herk Robinson; VP-Adm.: Dennis Cryder; Dir. Scouting: Art Stewart; Dir. Minor League Oper.: Bob Hegman; VP-Pub. Rel.: Dean Vogelaar; Trav. Sec.: Dave Witty; Mgr.: Hal McRae. Home: Royals Stadium (40,625). Field distances: 330, l.f. line; 385, l.c.; 410, c.f.; 385, r.c.; 330, r.f. line. Spring training: Baseball City Stadium, Orlando, Fla.

SCOUTING REPORT

HITTING: Royals Stadium dictates an offense built around speed and line-drive hitters. But a little power also is a necessity—and that's what the Royals are missing. Having failed to enlist Kansas City resident Joe Carter, they will have to settle for much the same attack that finished 12th in runs (610) last season.

It would help if the manager's son, Brian McRae (.223, 4, 52) developed into a top-of-the-lineup force to join Gregg Jefferies (.285, 10, 75). However, Wally Joyner (.269, 9, 66) and Kevin McReynolds (.247, 13, 49) also must put up bigger numbers in the middle. George Brett (.285, 7, 61), who got caught up in the chase for his 3,000th hit, is due for a reduced role. Mike Macfarlane (.234, 17, 48) is a needed power source, and free-agent

David Cone: From World Champions to Royal debut.

signee Greg Gagne (.246, 7, 39) will add a bat at the bottom of the order.

PITCHING: The Royals righted a past wrong by signing David Cone (17-10, 2.81, a major league-leading 261 Ks), a product of their farm system who had been foolishly dealt to the Mets. Put him with Kevin Appier (15-8, 2.46) and that's a strong one-two combination. Mark Gubicza (7-6, 3.72) will try to overcome arm trouble that cut his season in half. Mark Gardner (12-10, 4.36) was imported from the Expos to fill another rotation spot.

Four more right-handers—Hector Pichardo (9-6, 3.95), Tom Gordon (6-10, 4.59), Luis Aquino (3-6, 4.52) and Rick Reed (3-7, 3.68)—can start or relieve. Left-handers Chris Haney (2-3, 3.86), Ed Pierce (0-0, 3.38) and Mike Magnante (4-9, 4.94) provide more depth in front of closer Jeff Montgomery (1-6, 2.18, 39 saves) and setup man Rusty Meacham (10-4, 2.74).

FIELDING: The Royals won't be giving away as many games as they did last year with ex-Pirate Jose Lind and ex-Twin Gagne as the new double-play combination. Lind finally won a Gold Glove at second base and Gagne is a dependable turf shortstop with a strong arm. McRae is a human highlight film in center and, when Brent Mayne plays behind the plate, few teams will be better up the middle.

The first baseman Joyner also is an excellent defensive player, but the same can't be said for Jefferies, who committed 25 errors at third base. McReynolds doesn't have the range he used to, but is reliable in right. Keith Miller could pop in at any number of positions, but most likely he'll be in left. Overall, the Royals figure to improve on their middle-of-the-pack fielding percentage (.980) in 1993.

OUTLOOK: Royals owner Ewing Kauffman once again has pinned his hopes on free agents. It's the only way to go now that the Royals' once-vaunted farm system has stopped producing. The failures of Mark Davis and Storm Davis, Kirk Gibson and Mike Boddicker are fresh in the memory of Royals' fans, but Cone and Gagne appear to be wise signings. Lind cost only two prospects, because the Pirates wanted to dump his salary.

After two sixth-place finishes and one fifth-place tie, Hal McRae's Royals should move up a bit in a weakened AL West, but everything would have to go right for them to contend after finishing 72-90 in 1992.

KANSAS CITY ROYALS 1993 ROSTER

MANAGER Hal McRae

Coaches—Steve Boros, Glenn Ezell, Guy Hansen, Bruce Kison, Lee May

PITCHERS

No.	Name	1992 Club	W-L	IP	SO	ERA	B-T	Ht.	Wt.	Born
55	Appier, Kevin	Kansas City	15-8	208	150	2.46	R-R	6-2	200	12/6/67 Lancaster, CA
27	Aquino, Luis	Kansas City	3-6	68	11	4.52	R-R	6-1	195	5/19/65 Puerto Rico
		Omaha	0-0	10	3	2.61				
52	Boddicker, Mike	Kansas City	1-4	87	47	4.98	R-R	5-11	185	8/23/57 Cedar Rapids, IA
—	Cone, David	New York (NL)	13-7	197	214	2.88	R-L	6-1	190	1/2/63 Kansas City, MO
		Toronto	4-3	53	47	2.55				
—	Gardner, Mark	Montreal	12-10	180	132	4.36	R-R	6-1	200	3/1/62 Los Angeles, CA
36	Gordon, Tom	Kansas City	6-10	118	98	4.59	R-R	5-9	180	11/18/67 Sebring, FL
23	Gubicza, Mark	Kansas City	7-6	111	81	3.72	R-R	6-5	225	8/14/62 Philadelphia, PA
33	Haney, Chris	Montreal	2-3	38	27	5.45	L-L	6-3	185	11/16/68 Baltimore, MD
		Indianapolis	5-2	84	61	5.14				
		Kansas City	2-3	42	27	3.86				
—	Harris, Doug	Baseball City	0-2	29	22	2.15	R-R	6-4	190	9/27/69 Carlisle, PA
57	Magnante, Mike	Kansas City	4-9	89	31	4.94	L-L	6-1	180	6/17/65 Glendale, CA
28	Meacham, Rusty	Kansas City	10-4	102	64	2.74	R-R	6-2	165	1/27/68 Stuart, FL
21	Montgomery, Jeff	Kansas City	1-6	83	69	2.18	R-R	5-11	180	1/7/62 Wellston, OH
—	Morton, Kevin	Pawtucket	2-12	154	131	5.45	R-L	6-2	185	8/3/68 Norwalk, CT
58	Pichardo, Hipolito	Memphis	0-0	14	10	0.64	R-R	6-1	160	8/22/69 Dominican Republic
		Kansas City	9-6	144	59	3.95				
54	Pierce, Ed	Memphis	10-10	154	131	3.81	L-L	6-1	185	10/6/68 Arcadia, CA
		Kansas City	0-0	5	3	3.38				
47	Rasmussen, Dennis	Rochester	0-7	46	33	5.57	L-L	6-7	235	4/18/59 Los Angeles, CA
		Iowa-Omaha	4-4	62	50	2.03				
		Chicago (NL)	0-0	5	0	10.80				
		Kansas City	4-1	38	12	1.43				
38	Reed, Rick	Omaha	5-4	62	35	4.35	R-R	6-0	210	8/16/64 Huntington, WV
		Kansas City	3-7	100	49	3.68				
50	Sampen, Bill	Montreal	1-4	63	23	3.13	R-R	6-2	195	1/18/63 Lincoln, IL
		Indianapolis	1-1	3	4	6.00				
		Kansas City	0-2	20	14	3.66				
49	Shifflett, Steve	Omaha	3-2	44	19	1.65	R-R	6-1	205	1/5/66 Kansas City, MO
		Kansas City	1-4	52	25	2.60				

CATCHERS

No.	Name	1992 Club	H	HR	RBI	Pct.	B-T	Ht.	Wt.	Born
—	Jennings, Lance	Baseball City	45	7	24	.259	R-R	6-0	190	10/3/71 Redlands, CA
		Memphis	21	1	8	.145				
15	Macfarlane, Mike	Kansas City	94	17	48	.234	R-R	6-1	205	4/12/64 Stockton, CA
24	Mayne, Brent	Kansas City	48	0	18	.225	L-R	6-1	190	4/19/68 Loma Linda, CA

INFIELDERS

No.	Name	1992 Club	H	HR	RBI	Pct.	B-T	Ht.	Wt.	Born
5	Brett, George	Kansas City	169	7	61	.285	L-R	6-0	210	5/15/53 Glen Dale, WV
—	Gagne, Greg	Minnesota	108	7	39	.246	R-R	5-11	175	11/12/61 Fall River, MA
—	Hamelin, Bob	Baseball City	12	1	6	.273	L-L	6-0	230	11/29/67 Elizabeth, NJ
		Memphis	40	6	22	.333				
		Omaha	19	5	15	.200				
—	Hiatt, Phil	Memphis	119	27	83	.244	R-R	6-3	190	5/1/69 Pensacola, FL
		Omaha	3	2	4	.214				
13	Howard, David	Kansas City	49	1	18	.224	S-R	6-0	165	2/26/67 Sarasota, FL
		Baseball City	4	0	0	.444				
		Omaha	8	0	5	.118				
9	Jefferies, Gregg	Kansas City	172	10	75	.285	S-R	5-10	190	8/1/67 Burlingame, CA
12	Joyner, Wally	Kansas City	154	9	66	.269	L-L	6-2	205	6/16/62 Atlanta, GA
—	Lind, Jose	Pittsburgh	110	0	39	.235	R-R	5-11	170	5/1/64 Puerto Rico
16	Miller, Keith	Kansas City	118	4	38	.284	R-R	5-11	185	6/12/63 Midland, MI
32	Rossy, Rico	Omaha	55	4	17	.316	R-R	5-10	175	2/16/64 Puerto Rico
		Kansas City	32	1	12	.215				
3	Shumpert, Terry	Kansas City	14	1	11	.149	R-R	5-11	190	8/16/66 Paducah, KY
		Omaha	42	1	14	.200				
—	Wilkerson, Curtis	Kansas City	74	2	29	.250	S-R	5-9	173	4/26/61 Petersburg, VA

OUTFIELDERS

No.	Name	1992 Club	H	HR	RBI	Pct.	B-T	Ht.	Wt.	Born
29	Gwynn, Chris	Kansas City	24	1	7	.286	L-L	6-0	210	10/13/64 Los Angeles, CA
40	Koslofski, Kevin	Omaha	87	4	32	.311	L-R	5-8	165	9/24/66 Decatur, IL
		Kansas City	33	3	13	.248				
56	McRae, Brian	Kansas City	119	4	52	.223	S-R	6-0	185	8/27/67 Bradenton, FL
22	McReynolds, Kevin	Kansas City	92	13	49	.247	R-R	6-1	220	10/16/59 Little Rock, AR
51	Pulliam, Harvey	Omaha	97	16	60	.270	R-R	6-0	210	10/20/67 San Francisco, CA
		Kansas City	1	0	0	.200				
25	Thurman, Gary	Kansas City	49	0	20	.245	R-R	5-10	175	11/12/64 Indianapolis, IN

ROYAL PROFILES

GREG GAGNE 31 5-11 175 Bats R Throws R

Twins' free agent opted for three-year, $10.7-million pact with Royals . . . Shortstop's usually rangy and reliable defense suffered somewhat . . . Error total rose from nine in 1991 to 18 last year and fielding percentage dropped from .984 to .973 . . . His defensive slump was one of many reasons Twins fell apart in August . . . Offense just about equalled his typical output for last four seasons, which is to say it was adequate at best . . . Hit game-winning homer in Game 2 of 1991 World Series . . . Yanks' fourth-round pick in 1979 draft . . . Salary was $1,933,334 in 1992 . . . Acquired from Yankees in deal involving Roy Smalley, April 10, 1982 . . . Born Nov. 12, 1961, in Fall River, Mass.

Year	Club	Pos.	G	AB	R	H	2B	3B	HR	RBI	SB	Avg.
1983	Minnesota	SS	10	27	2	3	1	0	0	3	0	.111
1984	Minnesota	PR-PH	2	1	0	0	0	0	0	0	0	.000
1985	Minnesota	SS	114	293	37	66	15	3	2	23	10	.225
1986	Minnesota	SS-2B	156	472	63	118	22	6	12	54	12	.250
1987	Minnesota	SS-OF-2B	137	437	68	116	28	7	10	40	6	.265
1988	Minnesota	SS-OF-2B-3B	149	461	70	109	20	6	14	48	15	.236
1989	Minnesota	SS-OF	149	460	69	125	29	7	9	48	11	.272
1990	Minnesota	SS-OF	138	388	38	91	22	3	7	38	8	.235
1991	Minnesota	SS-3B	139	408	52	108	23	3	8	42	11	.265
1992	Minnesota	SS	146	439	53	108	23	0	7	39	6	.246
	Totals		1140	3386	452	844	183	35	69	335	79	.249

GEORGE BRETT 39 6-0 210 Bats L Throws R

Became only 18th player to reach 3,000-hit plateau . . . Got there with a flourish Sept. 30, going 4-for-5, including milestone single off Angels' Tim Fortugno . . . He and Brewers' Robin Yount became fifth twosome to reach 3,000 in same season . . . And to think he pondered quitting after he and Royals got off to disastrous starts in 1992 . . . Posted career-low totals in homers and RBI, excluding strike-shortened 1981 season . . . Has hit .300 or better 11 times, including .390 mark in 1980, when he flirted with .400 into September . . . Only player to win batting titles in three decades (1976, 1980, 1990) . . . Moved to first base in 1987 after 12 years at third . . . Almost exclusively a DH now

. . . Royals' second-round pick in 1971 draft . . . Made $3.1 million in 1992 . . . Born May 15, 1953, in Glen Dale, W. Va.

Year	Club	Pos.	G	AB	R	H	2B	3B	HR	RBI	SB	Avg.
1973	Kansas City . . .	3B	13	40	2	5	2	0	0	0	0	.125
1974	Kansas City . . .	3B-SS	133	457	49	129	21	5	2	47	8	.282
1975	Kansas City . . .	3B-SS	159	634	84	195	35	13	11	89	13	.308
1976	Kansas City . . .	3B-SS	159	645	94	215	34	14	7	67	21	.333
1977	Kansas City . . .	3B-SS	139	564	105	176	32	13	22	88	14	.312
1978	Kansas City . . .	3B-SS	128	510	79	150	45	8	9	62	23	.294
1979	Kansas City . . .	3B-1B	154	645	119	212	42	20	23	107	17	.329
1980	Kansas City . . .	3B-1B	117	449	87	175	33	9	24	118	15	.390
1981	Kansas City . . .	3B	89	347	42	109	27	7	6	43	14	.314
1982	Kansas City . . .	3B-OF	144	552	101	166	32	9	21	82	6	.301
1983	Kansas City . . .	3B-1B-OF	123	464	90	144	38	2	25	93	0	.310
1984	Kansas City . . .	3B	104	377	42	107	21	3	13	69	0	.284
1985	Kansas City . . .	3B	155	550	108	184	38	5	30	112	9	.335
1986	Kansas City . . .	3B-SS	124	441	70	128	28	4	16	73	1	.290
1987	Kansas City . . .	1B-3B	115	427	71	124	18	2	22	78	6	.290
1988	Kansas City . . .	1B-SS	157	589	90	180	42	3	24	103	14	.306
1989	Kansas City . . .	1B-OF	124	457	67	129	26	3	12	80	14	.282
1990	Kansas City . . .	1B-OF-3B	142	544	82	179	45	7	14	87	9	.329
1991	Kansas City . . .	1B	131	505	77	129	40	2	10	61	2	.255
1992	Kansas City . . .	1B-3B	152	592	55	169	35	5	7	61	8	.285
	Totals		2562	9789	1514	3005	634	134	298	1520	194	.307

WALLY JOYNER 30 6-2 205 Bats L Throws L

First baseman's first year in Kansas City was his worst in majors, except for injury-shortened 1990 . . . Made an emotional departure from Angels as free agent after six years, because of bitter contract negotiation . . . Sobbed at press conference announcing one-year, $4.2-million deal he signed with Royals . . . Wisely accepted Royals' offer of four-year, $16-million extension during middle of 1992 season . . . Spacious Royals Stadium cut into his power . . . Did steal a career-high 11 bases . . . Has topped 16 homers and 85 RBI only once in last five seasons . . . That's quite a comedown from career-high 34 homers and 117 RBI in 1987 . . . Angels' third-round pick in 1983, out of Brigham Young . . . Born June 16, 1962, in Atlanta.

Year	Club	Pos.	G	AB	R	H	2B	3B	HR	RBI	SB	Avg.
1986	California	1B	154	593	82	172	27	3	22	100	5	.290
1987	California	1B	149	564	100	161	33	1	34	117	8	.285
1988	California	1B	158	597	81	176	31	2	13	85	8	.295
1989	California	1B	159	593	78	167	30	2	16	79	3	.282
1990	California	1B	83	310	35	83	15	0	8	41	2	.268
1991	California	1B	143	551	79	166	34	3	21	96	2	.301
1992	Kansas City . . .	1B	149	572	66	154	36	2	9	66	11	.269
	Totals		995	3780	521	1079	206	13	123	584	39	.285

KEVIN McREYNOLDS 33 6-1 220 Bats R Throws R

Career continued its downward curve in first season with Royals after five with Mets . . . Finished with career lows in home runs, RBI and runs . . . Batting average was 22 points below career mark entering 1992 . . . Separated shoulder sidelined left fielder from Aug. 5-Sept. 4 . . . Another intended target of manager Hal McRae's postseason criticism of overweight players . . . Between 1986-90, he averaged 26 homers and 91 RBI . . . Finished third in 1988 NL MVP voting . . . Slowing down in field, as well . . . Traded to Mets by Padres in eight-player deal involving Kevin Mitchell after 1986 season . . . Padres' first-round pick in 1981 draft . . . Made $3,416,667 in 1992 . . . Born Oct. 16, 1969, in Little Rock, Ark.

Year	Club	Pos.	G	AB	R	H	2B	3B	HR	RBI	SB	Avg.
1983	San Diego	OF	39	140	15	31	3	1	4	14	2	.221
1984	San Diego	OF	147	525	68	146	26	6	20	75	3	.278
1985	San Diego	OF	152	564	61	132	24	4	15	75	4	.234
1986	San Diego	OF	158	560	89	161	31	6	26	96	8	.288
1987	New York (NL)	OF	151	590	86	163	32	5	29	95	14	.276
1988	New York (NL)	OF	147	552	82	159	30	2	27	99	21	.288
1989	New York (NL)	OF	148	545	74	148	25	3	22	85	15	.272
1990	New York (NL)	OF	147	521	75	140	23	1	24	82	9	.269
1991	New York (NL)	OF	143	522	65	135	32	1	16	74	6	.259
1992	Kansas City . . .	OF	109	373	45	92	25	0	13	49	7	.247
	Totals		1341	4892	660	1307	251	29	196	744	89	.267

JOSE LIND 28 5-11 170 Bats R Throws R

Traded in November by Pirates for Royal pitchers Joel Johnston and Dennis Moeller . . . Gold Glove second baseman was goat in NLCS when his ninth-inning error in Game 7 paved way for Braves' winning rally . . . Overall, "Chico" went 6-for-27 in playoffs with two doubles, triple, homer and team-high five RBI and five runs . . . Broke up John Smoltz's no-hitter in Game 1 with fifth-inning single and later homered for Pirates' only run. It was his lone homer of 1992 . . . NL's fourth-toughest batter to strike out in 1992, whiffing just once per 17.4 plate appearances . . . Finished regular season with 24 straight errorless games . . . A fast finisher, he has career regular season September-October batting average of .295 with 55 RBI . . . Born May 1, 1964, in Toabaja, P.R. . . . Signed by Pirates as non-drafted free agent in

1982 . . . Made major league debut Aug. 28, 1987 and became Pirates' everyday second baseman after Johnny Ray was traded to Angels . . . Earned $2 million in 1992.

Year	Club	Pos.	G	AB	R	H	2B	3B	HR	RBI	SB	Avg.
1987	Pittsburgh	2B	35	143	21	46	8	4	0	11	2	.322
1988	Pittsburgh	2B	154	611	82	160	24	4	2	49	15	.262
1989	Pittsburgh	2B	153	578	52	134	21	3	2	48	15	.232
1990	Pittsburgh	2B	152	514	46	134	28	5	1	48	8	.261
1991	Pittsburgh	2B	150	502	53	133	16	6	3	54	7	.265
1992	Pittsburgh	2B	135	468	38	110	14	1	0	39	3	.235
	Totals		779	2816	292	717	111	23	8	249	50	.255

MIKE MacFARLANE 28 6-1 205 Bats R Throws R

His batting average declined, but he hit a career high in homers . . . Binged in final two months, when he went deep 11 times . . . Played in 129 games after bouncing back from knee injury that cut his 1991 season in half . . . Posted career best in runs . . . Started 97 games behind the plate . . . Threw out 29 percent of would-be base-stealers, an improvement for him . . . In third year as a regular, he held off challenge from young Brett Mayne . . . Had 13 homers by July 16 in 1991, then underwent knee surgery that limited him to 84 games that season . . . Earned $740,000 in 1992 . . . Royals' first-round pick in 1985 draft . . . Born April 12, 1964, in Stockton, Cal.

Year	Club	Pos.	G	AB	R	H	2B	3B	HR	RBI	SB	Avg.
1987	Kansas City . . .	C	8	19	0	4	1	0	0	3	0	.211
1988	Kansas City . . .	C	70	211	25	56	15	0	4	26	0	.265
1989	Kansas City . . .	C	69	157	13	35	6	0	2	19	0	.223
1990	Kansas City . . .	C	124	400	37	102	24	4	6	58	1	.255
1991	Kansas City . . .	C	84	267	34	74	18	2	13	41	1	.277
1992	Kansas City . . .	C	129	402	51	94	28	3	17	48	1	.234
	Totals		484	1456	160	365	92	9	42	195	3	.251

GREGG JEFFERIES 25 5-10 190 Bats S Throws R

Set career highs in batting average and RBI in first year with Royals, but still wasn't the player many envision he can be . . . Left Mets along with Kevin McReynolds and Keith Miller in blockbuster winter deal for Bret Saberhagen and Bill Pecota prior to last season . . . Named Minor League Player of the 1980s by *Baseball America* . . . Has never hit .300 in a full season or scored 100 runs and his defense is sub-standard . . . Led majors with 26 errors as an everyday third baseman . . . Could steal more bases if he shed the extra 10-15 pounds he is carrying . . . Had problems gaining acceptance from Mets teammates, but fit in with Royals . . . New teammates nicknamed him "Puggsly" after the chubby Addams Family youth . . . Earned $1,115,000 in 1992 . . . Mets' first-round pick in 1985 draft . . . Born Aug. 1, 1967, in Burlingame, Cal.

Year	Club	Pos.	G	AB	R	H	2B	3B	HR	RBI	SB	Avg.
1987	New York (NL)	PH	6	6	0	3	1	0	0	2	0	.500
1988	New York (NL)	3B-2B	29	109	19	35	8	2	6	17	5	.321
1989	New York (NL)	2B-3B	141	508	72	131	28	2	12	56	21	.258
1990	New York (NL)	2B-3B	153	604	96	171	40	3	15	68	11	.283
1991	New York (NL)	2B-3B	136	486	59	132	19	2	9	62	26	.272
1992	Kansas City . . .	3B-2B	152	604	66	172	36	3	10	75	19	.285
	Totals		617	2317	312	644	132	12	52	280	82	.278

RUSTY MEACHAM 25 6-2 165 Bats R Throws R

Pleasant surprise after being claimed on waivers from pitching-poor Tigers in October 1991 . . . Second on staff in wins from middle relief spot . . . Walked only 21 in 101⅔ innings . . . His gangly body and sinking fastball remind many of Mark Fidrych . . . Lefties hit only .188 against him, righties .261 . . . Did blow four save opportunities, but none resulted in him earning cheap victories . . . Promoted April 13, after Luis Aquino suffered a strained shoulder . . . Tigers' 33rd-round choice in 1987 draft . . . Debuted with Tigers in 1991 after four impressive minor league seasons . . . Earned $120,000 in 1992 . . . Born Jan. 27, 1968, in Stuart, Fla.

Year	Club	G	IP	W	L	Pct.	SO	BB	H	ERA
1991	Detroit	10	27⅔	2	1	.667	14	11	35	5.20
1992	Kansas City	64	101⅔	10	4	.714	64	21	88	2.74
	Totals.	74	129⅓	12	5	.706	78	32	123	3.27

DAVID CONE 30 6-1 190 Bats L Throws R

Blue Jay free agent returned home to Kansas City with three-year, $18-million contract . . . Has never experienced losing season in majors . . . Struck out a combined 261 batters with the Mets and Toronto to pace majors . . . His 13-7 record with Mets included five shutouts . . . Named to All-Star staff for second time . . . Enjoyed eight-game winning streak from June 16-Aug. 2 . . . Sent from Mets to Blue Jays for Jeff Kent and Ryan

Thompson Aug. 27 . . . Pitched well down stretch . . . Held Oakland to one run in eight innings to win Game 2 of ALCS . . . Struggled in next two postseason starts . . . Pitched well when Blue Jays clinched Series in Game 6, checking Atlanta on one run in six innings and outpitching Steve Avery . . . Fine repertoire includes a back-door slider . . . Willing to challenge hitters in big situations . . . Born Jan. 2, 1963, in Kansas City, Mo. . . . Royals' third-round choice in 1981 draft . . . Earned $4,250,000 last season.

Year	Club	G	IP	W	L	Pct.	SO	BB	H	ERA
1986	Kansas City	11	22⅔	0	0	.000	21	13	29	5.56
1987	New York (NL)	21	99⅓	5	6	.455	68	44	87	3.71
1988	New York (NL)	35	231⅓	20	3	.870	213	80	178	2.22
1989	New York (NL)	34	219⅔	14	8	.636	190	74	183	3.52
1990	New York (NL)	31	211⅔	14	10	.583	233	65	177	3.23
1991	New York (NL)	34	232⅔	14	14	.500	241	73	204	3.29
1992	New York (NL)	27	196⅔	13	7	.650	214	82	162	2.88
1992	Toronto	8	53	4	3	.571	47	29	39	2.55
	Totals	201	1267	84	51	.622	1227	460	1059	3.10

MARK GUBICZA 30 6-5 225 Bats R Throws R

Didn't pitch after July 10 because of forearm and shoulder problems . . . Had made nice recovery from rotator-cuff surgery in August 1990 . . . Made 18 starts, including two complete games and one shutout . . . ERA in 1992 almost matched career mark . . . Has gone 20-25 over last three injury-filled seasons . . . Was 35-19 with a sub-3.00 in 1988 and 1989, when he pitched a combined total of 525⅓ innings . . . Earned career victory No. 100 May 11, a four-hit shutout of Cleveland . . . Earned $2,950,000 in 1992 . . . Two-time All-Star . . . Won a game in 1985 ALCS . . . Royals' second-round pick in 1981 draft . . . Born Aug. 14, 1962, in Philadelphia . . . Became free agent last winter and re-signed for one year at $1.25 million.

Year	Club	G	IP	W	L	Pct.	SO	BB	H	ERA
1984	Kansas City	29	189	10	14	.417	111	75	172	4.05
1985	Kansas City	29	177⅓	14	10	583	99	77	160	4.06
1986	Kansas City	35	180⅔	12	6	.667	118	84	155	3.64
1987	Kansas City	35	241⅔	13	18	.419	166	120	231	3.98
1988	Kansas City	35	269⅔	20	8	.714	183	83	237	2.70
1989	Kansas City	36	255	15	11	.577	173	63	252	3.04
1990	Kansas City	16	94	4	7	.364	71	38	101	4.50
1991	Kansas City	26	133	9	12	.429	89	42	168	5.68
1992	Kansas City	18	111⅓	7	6	.538	81	36	110	3.72
	Totals	259	1651⅔	104	92	.531	1091	618	1586	3.75

KEVIN APPIER 25 6-2 200 Bats R Throws R

Keeps getting better . . . Royals traded Bret Saberhagen and kept this guy and were rewarded with 15 victories and a 2.46 ERA . . . Finished second in AL in ERA, just behind Red Sox' Roger Clemens . . . Missed last month due to arm trouble and finished with 208⅓ innings pitched . . . His across-his-body delivery has some scouts insisting he's a serious injury waiting to happen . . . Has gone 40-26 over last three seasons . . . AL Rookie Pitcher of the Year in 1990, when he also finished third in Rookie of the Year balloting . . . Royals' first-round pick in 1987 draft . . . Salary was $390,000 in 1992, but he is due for big raise . . . Born Dec. 6, 1967, in Lancaster, Cal.

Year	Club	G	IP	W	L	Pct.	SO	BB	H	ERA
1989	Kansas City	6	21⅔	1	4	.200	10	12	34	9.14
1990	Kansas City	32	185⅔	12	8	.600	127	54	179	2.76
1991	Kansas City	34	207⅔	13	10	.565	158	61	205	3.42
1992	Kansas City	30	208⅓	15	8	.652	150	68	167	2.46
	Totals	102	623⅓	41	30	.577	445	195	585	3.10

JEFF MONTGOMERY 31 5-11 180 Bats R Throws R

A bright spot in an otherwise miserable season for Royals . . . Finished with career-high 39 saves . . . Missed final two chances at 40th save and finished with seven blown saves . . . Also lost six games, but three of those came in first month of season . . . ERA was second-best of career . . . First batters he faced hit only .143 against him . . . A busy closer . . . Pitched 82⅔ innings . . . Both lefties and righties hit .205 against him . . . Held opponents to .155 average on road . . . Reds' ninth-round pick in 1983 draft . . . Was acquired for outfielder Van Snider prior to 1988 season. Where is Snider now? . . . Earned $2,410,000 in 1992 . . . Born Jan. 7, 1962, in Wellston, Ohio.

Year	Club	G	IP	W	L	Pct.	SO	BB	H	ERA
1987	Cincinnati	14	19⅓	2	2	.500	13	9	25	6.52
1988	Kansas City	45	62⅔	7	2	.778	47	30	54	3.45
1989	Kansas City	63	92	7	3	.700	94	25	66	1.37
1990	Kansas City	73	94⅓	6	5	.545	94	34	81	2.39
1991	Kansas City	67	90	4	4	.500	77	28	83	2.90
1992	Kansas City	65	82⅔	1	6	.143	69	27	61	2.18
	Totals	327	441	27	22	.551	394	153	370	2.57

TOP PROSPECT

KEVIN KOSLOFSKI 26 5-8 165 Bats L Throws R
Played far more than expected with Royals and showed ability as a fourth-outfielder type . . . Homered off Nolan Ryan Sept. 1 . . . Finished at .248 with three homers and 13 RBI in 133 at-bats . . . Has stolen as many as 41 bases in a minor league season . . . Royals' 20th-round pick in 1984 draft . . . Born Sept. 24, 1966, in Decatur, Ill.

MANAGER HAL McRAE: Team got off to disastrous 1-16 start, but went 71-74 after that in 1992 . . . Obviously, he didn't have team ready coming out of spring training . . . Received a one-year extension late in season . . . Replaced former teammate John Wathan, May 24, 1991 and Royals finished 66-56 under him that season . . . Has rare opportunity to manage his son, Brian . . . Fifth black manager in major league history, following Frank Robinson, Larry Doby, Maury Wills and Cito Gaston . . . Left job as Expos' hitting instructor to manage . . . Was minor-league hitting instructor for Pirates in 1988 and 1989 . . . Batted .290 in 18 major league seasons, the last 15 with Royals . . . Hit .300 or better six times, including career-high .332 in 1976 . . . Played in eight League Championship Series and four World Series . . . Born July 10, 1945, in Avon Park, Fla. . . . Overall managerial record is 138-146.

ALL-TIME ROYAL SEASON RECORDS

BATTING: George Brett, .390, 1980
HRs: Steve Balboni, 36, 1985
RBI: Hal McRae, 133, 1982
STEALS: Willie Wilson, 83, 1979
WINS: Bret Saberhagen, 23, 1989
STRIKEOUTS: Dennis Leonard, 244, 1977

MINNESOTA TWINS

TEAM DIRECTORY: Owner: Carl Pohlad; Pres.: Jerry Bell; Exec. VP/GM: Andy MacPhail; VP-Player Pers.: Terry Ryan; Dir. Media Rel.: Rob Antony; Trav. Sec.: Remzi Kiratli; Mgr.: Tom Kelly. Home: Hubert H. Humphrey Metrodome (55,883). Field distances: 343, l.f. line; 408, c.f.; 327, r.f. line. Spring training: Fort Myers, Fla.

SCOUTING REPORT

HITTING: Two of the best things you can say about the Twins' winter are that Kirby Puckett (.329, 19, 110) stayed and Dave Winfield (.290, 26, 108 with the Blue Jays) arrived. Those two offensive forces should go a long way toward softening the loss of Chili Davis and Greg Gagne to free agency.

Last season, the Twins led the majors in hitting by a good margin (.277) and were third in the AL in runs (747). And they did it with their best power hitter, Kent Hrbek (.244, 15, 58), on the shelf for 50 games.

One through four, it's hard to top Shane Mack (.315, 16, 75, 26 steals), Chuck Knoblauch (.297, 104 runs, 34 steals), Puckett and a healthy Hrbek. Brian Harper (.307, 9, 73) is an excellent-hitting catcher and right fielder Pedro Munoz (.270, 12, 71) figures to improve under hitting guru Terry Crowley. Scott Leius (.249) can match Gagne's output, but a left-handed bat is needed.

PITCHING: Budgetary restrictions once again cost the Twins a key starting pitcher. This time, it was John Smiley, who defected to the Reds. That leaves a young but potentially strong rotation headed by right-handers Kevin Tapani (16-11, 3.97) and Scott Erickson (13-12, 3.40). Both are capable of better seasons than they had in 1992.

Manager Tom Kelly would prefer to keep Mark Guthrie (2-3, 2.88) in the bullpen, but won't have the luxury of doing so unless young right-handers Pat Mahomes (3-4, 5.04), Mike Trombley (3-2, 3.30) and Willie Banks (4-4, 5.70) develop.

Rick Aguilera (2-6, 2.84, 41 saves) is one of the league's top closers and setup man Carl Willis (7-3, 2.72) has revived his fading career with two solid seasons. An unnoticed but valuable pickup was Mike Hartley (7-6, 3.44 for the Phils). He will replace Tom Edens, who was lost in the expansion draft. Larry Casian and Paul Abbott can be effective.

Kirby Puckett needs 188 hits to join the 2,000 Club.

FIELDING: This is always a Twins strength—and 1992 was no exception as they finished .001 off the AL lead in fielding percentage at .985. However, Gagne's loss will be felt at shortstop. Leius is dependable, but few can match Gagne's arm and range. Third base is a question mark now that Leius has slid over to short and Mike Pagliarulo wasn't re-signed.

Knoblauch and Hrbek are strong on the right side. Harper's throwing percentage improved with the help of the pitching staff paying closer attention to holding runners. Puckett keeps winning Gold Gloves in center, but Mack is the superior outfielder. Munoz is only adequate.

OUTLOOK: The loss of Smiley and Gagne will be felt, but the dropoff won't be significant if Winfield continues to hit like a youngster and if the young talent emerges. Tom Kelly's Twins won 90 games last season and finished only six games behind the A's, who lost more from their division title-winning roster.

With the right acquisition here and there—something GM Andy MacPhail always seems to be able to find—this team could be back on top.

MINNESOTA TWINS 1993 ROSTER

MANAGER Tom Kelly
Coaches—Terry Crowley, Ron Gardenhire, Rick Stelmaszek, Dick Such, Wayne Terwilliger

PITCHERS

No.	Name	1992 Club	W-L	IP	SO	ERA	B-T	Ht.	Wt.	Born
37	Abbott, Paul	Portland	4-1	46	46	2.33	R-R	6-3	194	9/15/67 Van Nuys, CA
		Minnesota	0-0	11	13	3.27				
38	Aguilera, Rick	Minnesota	2-6	67	52	2.84	R-R	6-5	205	12/31/61 San Gabriel, CA
23	Banks, Willie	Portland	6-1	75	41	1.92	R-R	6-1	190	2/27/69 Jersey City, NJ
		Minnesota	4-4	71	37	5.70				
—	Best, Jayson	Ft. Myers	0-6	51	50	4.09	R-R	6-0	170	9/9/68 Lafayette, IN
		Orlando	0-0	11	12	0.79				
48	Casian, Larry	Portland	4-0	62	43	2.32	R-L	6-0	170	10/28/65 Lynwood, CA
		Minnesota	1-0	7	2	2.70				
—	Deshaies, Jim	San Diego	4-7	96	46	3.28	L-L	6-4	222	6/23/60 Massena, NY
19	Erickson, Scott	Minnesota	13-12	212	101	3.40	R-R	6-4	224	2/2/68 Long Beach, CA
41	Garces, Richard	Orlando	3-3	73	72	4.54	R-R	6-0	215	5/18/71 Venezuela
53	Guthrie, Mark	Minnesota	2-3	75	76	2.88	S-L	6-4	206	9/22/65 Buffalo, NY
—	Hartley, Mike	Philadelphia	7-6	55	53	3.44	R-R	6-1	195	8/31/61 Hawthorne, CA
		Scranton	1-2	11	10	4.09				
20	Mahomes, Pat	Minnesota	3-4	70	44	5.04	R-R	6-1	175	8/9/70 Bryan, TX
		Portland	9-5	111	87	3.41				
—	Munoz, Oscar	Orlando	3-5	68	74	5.05	R-R	6-2	205	9/25/69 Hialeah, FL
54	Newman, Alan	Orlando	4-8	102	86	4.15	L-L	6-6	212	10/2/69 La Habra, CA
36	Tapani, Kevin	Minnesota	16-11	220	138	3.97	R-R	6-0	187	2/18/64 Des Moines, IA
21	Trombley, Mike	Portland	10-8	165	138	3.65	R-R	6-2	200	4/14/67 Springfield, MA
		Minnesota	3-2	46	38	3.30				
30	Tsamis, George	Portland	13-4	164	71	3.90	R-L	6-2	175	6/14/87 Campbell, CA
47	Wayne, Gary	Portland	0-1	23	20	2.35	L-L	6-3	193	11/30/62 Dearborn, MI
		Minnesota	3-3	48	29	2.63				
51	Willis, Carl	Minnesota	7-3	79	45	2.72	L-R	6-4	215	12/28/60 Danville, VA

CATCHERS

No.	Name	1992 Club	H	HR	RBI	Pct.	B-T	Ht.	Wt.	Born
12	Harper, Brian	Minnesota	154	9	73	.307	R-R	6-2	206	10/16/59 Los Angeles, CA
—	Maksudian, Mike	Syracuse	95	13	58	.281	L-R	5-11	220	5/28/66 Belleville, IL
		Toronto	0	0	0	.000				
16	Parks, Derek	Portland	61	12	49	.245	R-R	6-0	205	9/29/68 Covina, CA
		Minnesota	2	0	0	.333				
15	Webster, Lenny	Minnesota	33	1	13	.280	R-R	5-9	191	2/10/65 New Orleans, LA

INFIELDERS

No.	Name	1992 Club	H	HR	RBI	Pct.	B-T	Ht.	Wt.	Born
—	Dunn, Steve	Visalia	150	26	113	.305	L-L	6-4	205	4/18/70 Champaign, IL
—	Hocking, Dennis	Visalia	182	7	81	.331	S-R	5-10	165	4/2/70 Torrance, CA
14	Hrbek, Kent	Minnesota	96	15	58	.244	L-R	6-4	252	5/21/60 Minneapolis, MN
27	Jorgensen, Terry	Portland	149	14	71	.295	R-R	6-4	213	9/2/66 Kewaunee, WI
		Minnesota	18	0	5	.310				
11	Knoblauch, Chuck	Minnesota	178	2	56	.297	R-R	5-9	180	7/7/68 Houston, TX
9	Larkin, Gene	Minnesota	83	6	42	.246	S-R	6-3	205	10/24/62 Astoria, NY
31	Leius, Scott	Minnesota	102	2	35	.249	R-R	6-3	195	9/24/65 Yonkers, NY
—	Meares, Pat	Orlando	76	3	23	.253	R-R	5-11	185	9/6/68 Salina, KS
17	Reboulet, Jeff	Portland	46	2	21	.286	R-R	6-0	170	4/30/64 Dayton, OH
		Minnesota	26	1	16	.190				
—	Russo, Paul	Orlando	107	22	74	.255	R-R	6-0	215	8/26/69 Tampa, FL

OUTFIELDERS

No.	Name	1992 Club	H	HR	RBI	Pct.	B-T	Ht.	Wt.	Born
26	Bruett, J.T.	Portland	70	0	17	.250	L-L	5-11	175	10/8/67 Milwaukee, WI
		Minnesota	19	0	2	.250				
25	*Bush, Randy	Minnesota	39	2	22	.214	L-L	6-1	190	10/5/58 Dover, DE
—	Cordova, Marty	Visalia	175	28	131	.341	R-R	6-0	195	7/10/69 Las Vegas, NV
—	Howell, Patrick	Tidewater	99	1	22	.244	S-R	5-11	155	8/31/68 Mobile, AL
		New York (NL)	14	0	1	.187				
—	Lee, Derek	Vancouver	104	7	50	.273	L-R	6-0	195	7/28/66 Chicago, IL
24	Mack, Shane	Minnesota	189	16	75	.315	R-R	6-0	190	12/7/63 Los Angeles, CA
5	Munoz, Pedro	Minnesota	113	12	71	.270	R-R	5-10	207	9/19/68 Puerto Rico
34	Puckett, Kirby	Minnesota	104	19	110	.329	R-R	5-8	216	3/14/61 Chicago, IL
32	Winfield, Dave	Toronto	169	26	108	.290	R-R	6-6	246	10/3/51 St. Paul, MN

*Free agent offered arbitration

TWIN PROFILES

KIRBY PUCKETT 32 5-8 216 Bats R Throws R

Another brilliant season in face of pending free agency created outpouring of emotion from usually reserved Twins fans who wanted him re-signed . . . Result: A five-year, $30-million contract . . . And he could have made more elsewhere . . . Put up best numbers since 1988 last year . . . Has hit .300 or better in eight of 10 major league seasons and one of his misses was .298 in 1991 . . . RBI total was his second-highest, topped only by 124 in 1988 . . . Has made seven consecutive AL All-Star teams . . . Currently just 188 hits away from 2,000 plateau . . . Center fielder's defense has slipped only slightly from standard established by five-time Gold Glove winner . . . On top of all that, he comes to the park with a smile on his face and rarely misses a game . . . Played third base, shortstop and second base in same game last year . . . Earned $2,966,667 in 1992 . . . Twins' first-round pick in January 1982 draft . . . Born March 14, 1961, in Chicago.

Year	Club	Pos.	G	AB	R	H	2B	3B	HR	RBI	SB	Avg.
1984	Minnesota	OF	128	557	63	165	12	5	0	31	14	.296
1985	Minnesota	OF	161	691	80	199	29	13	4	74	21	.288
1986	Minnesota	OF	161	680	119	223	37	6	31	96	20	.328
1987	Minnesota	OF	157	624	96	207	32	5	28	99	12	.332
1988	Minnesota	OF	158	657	109	234	42	5	24	121	6	.356
1989	Minnesota	OF	159	635	75	215	45	4	9	85	11	.339
1990	Minnesota	OF-2B-SS-3B	146	551	82	164	40	3	12	80	5	.298
1991	Minnesota	OF	152	611	92	195	29	6	15	89	11	.319
1992	Minnesota	OF-2B-3B-SS	160	639	104	210	38	4	19	110	17	.329
	Totals		1382	5645	820	1812	304	51	142	785	117	.321

DAVE WINFIELD 41 6-6 245 Bats R Throws R

Designated hitter shed "Mr. May" tag with one swing, lashing two-run, 11th-inning double to win World Series Game 6 clincher for Blue Jays . . . Was 5-for-43 in World Series play overall before that decisive bullet past third base . . . Remains an offensive force despite his age . . . Became oldest player to reach 100 RBI in a season and it was eighth time in career he achieved century mark . . . Also has 13 seasons with 20 or more homers . . . Leads all active players in career homers . . . Played in 156 games and Pete Rose, Honus Wagner and Darrell Evans are only other players to appear in that many at age 40 . . . Born Oct. 3, 1951, in St. Paul, Minn. . . . Was selected in baseball, football and basketball drafts, out of Minnesota, and joined Padres in 1973 without ever playing in minors . . . Earned $2.3 million in 1992, became free agent and signed two-year, $5.2-million Twins contract.

Year	Club	Pos.	G	AB	R	H	2B	3B	HR	RBI	SB	Avg.
1973	San Diego	OF-1B	56	141	9	39	4	1	3	12	0	.277
1974	San Diego	OF	145	498	57	132	18	4	20	75	9	.265
1975	San Diego	OF	143	509	74	136	20	2	15	76	23	.267
1976	San Diego	OF	137	492	81	139	26	4	13	69	26	.283
1977	San Diego	OF	157	615	104	169	29	7	25	92	16	.275
1978	San Diego	OF-1B	158	587	88	181	30	5	24	97	21	.308
1979	San Diego	OF	159	597	97	184	27	10	34	118	15	.308
1980	San Diego	OF	162	558	89	154	25	6	20	87	23	.276
1981	New York (AL)	OF	105	388	52	114	25	1	13	68	11	.294
1982	New York (AL)	OF	140	539	84	151	24	8	37	106	5	.280
1983	New York (AL)	OF	152	598	99	169	26	8	32	116	15	.283
1984	New York (AL)	OF	141	567	106	193	34	4	19	100	6	.340
1985	New York (AL)	OF	155	633	105	174	34	6	26	114	19	.275
1986	New York (AL)	OF-3B	154	565	90	148	31	5	24	104	6	.262
1987	New York (AL)	OF	156	575	83	158	22	1	27	97	5	.275
1988	New York (AL)	OF	149	559	96	180	37	2	25	107	9	.322
1989	New York (AL)				Injured							
1990	NY (AL)-Cal. . . .	OF	132	475	70	127	21	2	21	78	0	.267
1991	California	OF	150	568	75	149	27	4	28	86	7	.262
1992	Toronto	OF	156	583	92	169	33	3	26	108	2	.290
	Totals		2707	10047	1551	2866	493	83	432	1710	218	.285

SHANE MACK 29 6-0 190 **Bats R Throws R**

Quietly has become one of AL's most complete outfielders . . . Established career highs in runs, home runs, RBI and stolen bases for second consecutive year . . . Besides that, he's a superb defensive outfielder . . . One of three Twins to score more than 100 runs . . . Fourth in AL in hits . . . Fifth in league in batting . . . On-base percentage of .394 was fifth-best in AL . . . Had 22-game hitting streak from July 26-Aug. 18, the second-longest in AL . . . Stolen by Twins from Padres in December 1989 minor league draft . . . Padres made him 11th pick overall in 1984 draft . . . Did stint with U.S. Olympic Team that summer . . . Earned $1.075 million in 1992 . . . Born Dec. 7, 1963, in Los Angeles.

Year	Club	Pos.	G	AB	R	H	2B	3B	HR	RBI	SB	Avg.
1987	San Diego	OF	105	238	28	57	11	3	4	25	4	.239
1988	San Diego	OF	56	119	13	29	3	0	0	12	5	.244
1990	Minnesota	OF	125	313	50	102	10	4	8	44	13	.326
1991	Minnesota	OF	143	442	79	137	27	8	18	74	13	.310
1992	Minnesota	OF	156	600	101	189	31	6	16	75	26	.315
	Totals		585	1712	271	514	82	21	46	230	61	.300

KENT HRBEK 32 6-4 255 Bats L Throws R

Shoulder trouble led to worst season in 11-year career of hometown hero . . . Average and power totals were lowest of his career . . . Batting average was 45 points below career mark entering 1992 . . . Had averaged 23 homers and 82 RBI over previous four seasons . . . Injury woes began in spring training and nagged him throughout season . . . Played in only 119 games before undergoing surgery . . . For someone who aspires to wrestle under the name "Tyrannasaurus Rex," he has been quite nimble around first base . . . Earned $3.1 million in 1992 . . . Was Twins' seventh-round draft choice in 1978 . . . Born May 21, 1960, in Minneapolis, and grew up in shadow of old Metropolitan Stadium.

Year	Club	Pos.	G	AB	R	H	2B	3B	HR	RBI	SB	Avg.
1981	Minnesota	1B	24	67	5	16	5	0	1	7	0	.239
1982	Minnesota	1B	140	532	82	160	21	4	23	92	3	.301
1983	Minnesota	1B	141	515	75	153	41	5	16	84	4	.297
1984	Minnesota	1B	149	559	80	174	31	3	27	107	1	.311
1985	Minnesota	1B	158	593	78	165	31	2	21	93	1	.278
1986	Minnesota	1B	149	550	85	147	27	1	29	91	2	.267
1987	Minnesota	1B	143	477	85	136	20	1	34	90	5	.285
1988	Minnesota	1B	143	510	75	159	31	0	25	76	0	.312
1989	Minnesota	1B	109	375	59	102	17	0	25	84	3	.272
1990	Minnesota	1B-3B	143	492	61	141	26	0	22	79	5	.287
1991	Minnesota	1B	132	462	72	131	20	1	20	89	4	.284
1992	Minnesota	1B	112	394	52	96	20	0	15	58	5	.244
	Totals		1543	5526	809	1580	290	17	258	950	33	.286

BRIAN HARPER 33 6-2 205 Bats R Throws R

No better hitter for average among AL's catchers . . . Topped .300 for the third time in four years . . . Only time he didn't hit .300 was 1990, when he batted .294 . . . Established new career high in RBI . . . Finished one short of tying best homer output . . . Struck out only 22 times in 502 at-bats . . . Played in career-high 140 games, 128 behind the plate. Only three catchers started more games . . . With help of Twins' staff, he showed marked improvement in throwing out base-stealers, from 18 percent in 1991 to 31 percent last season . . . Signed by Twins as a free agent prior to 1988 season . . . Earned $2.5 million in 1992 . . . Angels' fourth-round pick in 1977 draft . . . First appeared in majors in 1979, but didn't log more than 131 big league at-bats in any year until 1988 . . . Born Oct. 16, 1959, in Los Angeles.

Year	Club	Pos.	G	AB	R	H	2B	3B	HR	RBI	SB	Avg.
1979	California	DH	1	2	0	0	0	0	0	0	0	.000
1981	California	OF	4	11	1	3	0	0	0	1	1	.273
1982	Pittsburgh	OF	20	29	4	8	1	0	2	4	0	.276
1983	Pittsburgh	OF–1B	61	131	16	29	4	1	7	20	0	.221
1984	Pittsburgh	OF-C	46	112	4	29	4	0	2	11	0	.259
1985	St. Louis	OF–3B-C–1B	43	52	5	13	4	0	0	8	0	.250
1986	Detroit	OF–1B-C	19	36	2	5	1	0	0	3	0	.139
1987	Oakland	OF	11	17	1	4	1	0	0	3	0	.235
1988	Minnesota	C–3B	60	166	15	49	11	1	3	20	0	.295
1989	Minnesota	C-OF–1B–3B	126	385	43	125	24	0	8	57	2	.325
1990	Minnesota	C–3B–1B	134	479	61	141	42	3	6	54	3	.294
1991	Minnesota	C-1B-OF	123	441	54	137	28	1	10	69	1	.311
1992	Minnesota	C	140	502	58	154	25	0	9	73	0	.307
	Totals		788	2363	264	697	145	6	47	323	7	.295

CHUCK KNOBLAUCH 24 5-9 180 Bats R Throws R

Second baseman showed his rookie season was no fluke . . . Improved in every facet . . . Made AL All-Star team for first time . . . Cut error total from 18 in 1991 to six last year . . . Was at or above .300 mark most of season . . . Ranked third on team and fifth in AL with 52 multi-hit games . . . Tied with Kirby Puckett for fourth in AL in runs . . . Was ninth in hits and 10th in walks (88) . . . Stole nine more bases than in 1991 . . . Capped AL Rookie of Year season in 1991 with 15 postseason hits, a record for first-year players . . . Hit .308 with two RBI in World Series . . . Earned $325,000 in 1992 . . . Twins' first pick in 1989 draft, after stellar career at Texas A&M . . . Born July 7, 1968, in Houston.

Year	Club	Pos.	G	AB	R	H	2B	3B	HR	RBI	SB	Avg.
1991	Minnesota	2B-SS	151	565	78	159	24	6	1	50	25	.281
1992	Minnesota	2B-SS	155	600	104	178	19	6	2	56	34	.297
	Totals		306	1165	182	337	43	12	3	106	59	.289

KEVIN TAPANI 29 6-0 187 Bats R Throws R

Matched his 1991 victory total, but ERA rose almost a full run . . . Issued only 48 walks in 220 innings . . . Very slow start hurt final numbers . . . Was 6-4 with a 5.52 ERA in first 13 starts . . . Won four of next five decisions to become a 10-game winner before All-Star break . . . Was 0-6 in May 1991, before rebounding to go 11-2 after 1991 All-Star break . . . Won

Game 2 of 1991 World Series after two poor ALCS outings . . . Earned $485,000 in 1992 . . . Big part of payoff from Mets in Frank Viola trade, July 31, 1989 . . . Born Feb. 18, 1964, in Des Moines, Iowa . . . Athletics' second-round pick in 1986 draft.

Year	Club	G	IP	W	L	Pct.	SO	BB	H	ERA
1989	New York (NL)	3	7⅓	0	0	.000	2	4	5	3.68
1989	Minnesota	5	32⅔	2	2	.500	21	8	34	3.86
1990	Minnesota	28	159⅓	12	8	.600	101	29	164	4.07
1991	Minnesota	34	244	16	9	.640	135	40	225	2.99
1992	Minnesota	34	220	16	11	.593	138	48	226	3.97
	Totals	104	663⅓	46	30	.605	397	129	654	3.62

SCOTT ERICKSON 25 6-4 225 Bats R Throws R

Dramatic fall last year for 20-game winner in 1991 . . . Has been slightly better than .500 pitcher since 1991 All-Star break . . . Did pitch three shutouts, so talent is still there, even if consistency isn't . . . Walked alarmingly high total of 83 while striking out 101 . . . Was 3-5 with a 5.13 ERA in mid-June . . . In contrast, he was 12-3 at 1991 All-Star break, before elbow strain cut into his velocity and command . . . Had scoreless streak of 30⅓ innings that season . . . Had 5.06 ERA in two 1991 World Series starts . . . Earned $425,000 in 1992 . . . Twins' fourth-round pick in 1981 draft, out of University of Arizona . . . Born Feb. 2, 1968, in Long Beach, Cal.

Year	Club	G	IP	W	L	Pct.	SO	BB	H	ERA
1990	Minnesota	19	113	8	4	.667	53	51	108	2.87
1991	Minnesota	32	204	20	8	.714	108	71	189	3.18
1992	Minnesota	32	212	13	12	.520	101	83	197	3.40
	Totals	83	529	41	24	.631	262	205	494	3.20

RICK AGUILERA 31 6-5 205 Bats R Throws R

Converted 41 of 48 save opportunities in 1992 . . . Only Athletics' Dennis Eckersley saved more in the AL . . . Save total was one short of his 1991 mark, which tied Jeff Reardon's club record . . . Has 115 saves over last three seasons . . . Allowed seven homers in 66⅔ innings, including game-deciding, three-run blast by Oakland's Eric Fox July 26 that capped an A's sweep in the Metrodome . . . Had 17 saves by mid-June and 26 saves by All-Star break . . . Earned $2,133,333 in 1992 . . . Saved two games and earned a victory in another in 1991 World Series

. . . Another key part of the package Twins received from Mets for Frank Viola, July 31, 1989 . . . Born Dec. 31, 1961, in San Gabriel, Cal. . . . Mets' third-round pick in 1983 draft.

Year	Club	G	IP	W	L	Pct.	SO	BB	H	ERA
1985	New York (NL)	21	122⅓	10	7	.588	74	37	118	3.24
1986	New York (NL)	28	141⅔	10	7	.588	104	36	145	3.88
1987	New York (NL)	18	115	11	3	.786	77	33	124	3.60
1988	New York (NL)	11	24⅔	0	4	.000	16	10	29	6.93
1989	New York (NL)	36	69⅓	6	6	.500	80	21	59	2.34
1989	Minnesota	11	75⅔	3	5	.375	57	17	71	3.21
1990	Minnesota	56	65⅓	5	3	.625	61	19	55	2.76
1991	Minnesota	63	69	4	5	.444	61	30	44	2.35
1992	Minnesota	64	66⅔	2	6	.250	52	17	60	2.84
	Totals	308	749⅔	51	46	.526	582	220	705	3.29

CARL WILLIS 32 6-4 215 — Bats R Throws R

Put together a near duplicate of his 1991 season, when he was a back-from-the-dead success story . . . In two seasons as setup man, he is 15-6 with 2.67 ERA and three saves . . . Key is throwing strikes . . . Has walked 30 while striking out 98 as a Twin . . . Issued only 11 free passes in 79⅓ innings last season . . . Bounced through four organizations before Twins signed him as a free agent in December 1990 . . . Was 2-6 with a 5.88 ERA in parts of five big-league seasons at that point and had pitched only 12 big-league innings in his previous four seasons . . . Earned $325,000 in 1992 . . . Tigers' 23rd-round pick in June 1983 draft . . . Born Dec. 28, 1960, in Danville, Va.

Year	Club	G	IP	W	L	Pct.	SO	BB	H	ERA
1984	Detroit	10	16	0	2	.000	4	5	25	7.31
1984	Cincinnati	7	9⅔	0	1	.000	3	2	8	3.72
1985	Cincinnati	11	13⅔	1	0	1.000	6	5	21	9.22
1986	Cincinnati	29	52⅓	1	3	.250	24	32	54	4.47
1988	Chicago (AL)	6	12	0	0	.000	6	7	17	8.25
1991	Minnesota	40	89	8	3	.727	53	19	76	2.63
1992	Minnesota	59	79⅓	7	3	.700	45	11	73	2.72
	Totals	162	272	17	12	.587	141	81	274	3.90

TOP PROSPECTS

MIKE TROMBLEY 25 6-2 200 — Bats R Throws R

Expected to step into rotation after impressive late-season showing . . . Was 3-2 with 3.30 ERA in seven starts with Twins . . . Received only 3.5 runs of support per start, so record could have been better . . . Went 10-8 with 3.65 ERA in 25 starts for Portland (AAA) . . . Chosen in 14th round of 1989 draft . . . Born April 14, 1967, in Springfield, Mass.

PAT MAHOMES 22 6-1 175 Bats R Throws R
Another likely member of Twins' rotation, especially if he captures command of great stuff . . . Was 3-4 with 5.04 ERA in 13 starts with Twins . . . Sent down in midseason and returned in September . . . Was 9-5 with 3.41 ERA for Portland (AAA) . . . In 1991, he was 8-5 with 1.78 ERA and 136 strikeouts in 116 innings for Orlando (AA) . . . Picked in sixth round of 1988 draft . . . Born Aug. 9, 1970, in Bryan, Tex.

MANAGER TOM KELLY: Despite Twins' late-season fade to 90-72, he is regarded as one of game's best managers . . . Players swear by him and love to play for him . . . Gets the most out of roster, adeptly handling pitching staff and pressing right buttons with role players . . . Has 527-468 career record after seven seasons in Minnesota . . . Won second world championship and AL Manager of the Year honors in 1991, after starting the season amidst questions about his longevity . . . Has lightened up with media since once challenging a Twins beat writer to a fight . . . Replaced Ray Miller, Sept. 12, 1986 . . . Wasn't given job permanently until before 1987 season, when Twins won first of their two world championships in last six seasons . . . Was Twins' third-base coach from 1983 until replacing Miller . . . Three-time Manager of the Year in minors from 1979-81 . . . Spent all but 49 games of 11-year playing career in minors . . . Hit .181 in 127 at-bats as Twin toward end of 1975 season and never got another chance . . . Born Aug. 15, 1950, in Graceville, Minn.

ALL-TIME TWIN SEASON RECORDS

BATTING: Rod Carew, .388, 1977
HRs: Harmon Killebrew, 49, 1964, 1969
RBI: Harmon Killebrew, 140, 1969
STEALS: Rod Carew, 49, 1976
WINS: Jim Kaat, 25, 1966
STRIKEOUTS: Bert Blyleven, 258, 1973

OAKLAND ATHLETICS

TEAM DIRECTORY: Chairman: Walter J. Haas; Pres./GM: Sandy Alderson; Exec. VP: Andy Dolich; Dir. Player Dev.: Keith Lieppman; Dir. Scouting: Dick Bogard; Dir. Media Rel.: Kathy Jacobson; Dir. Baseball Inf.: Jay Alves; Trav. Sec.: Mickey Morabito; Mgr.: Tony La Russa. Home: Oakland Coliseum (47,313). Field distances: 330, l.f. line; 375, l.c.; 400, c.f.; 375, r.c.; 330, r.l. line. Spring training: Phoenix, Ariz.

SCOUTING REPORT

HITTING: The Bash Brothers are a thing of the past, but the Athletics chose to allocate their dollar resources with an eye toward re-signing sluggers Mark McGwire (.268, 42, 104), Terry Steinbach (.279, 12, 53) and Ruben Sierra (.278, 17, 87). Those three rejoin a Rickey Henderson (.283, 15, 46, 48 steals) who is playing for a new contract, a healthy Dave Henderson and the blossoming Mike Bordick (.300, 3, 48), so there remains a potentially potent offense.

The Athletics were ninth in batting average (.258), but fourth in runs (745) and fifth in stolen bases (143) a year ago, despite being without Dave Henderson for most of the year and dealing Jose Canseco to Texas Aug. 31. With Tony La Russa picking their spots, Jerry Browne (.287, 3, 40) and Lance Blankenship (.241, 3, 34, 21 steals) were very productive part-time players and their roles figure to increase.

PITCHING: The Athletics waved goodbye to free agents Dave Stewart, Mike Moore, and Kelly Downs (a combined 80 starts) and brought in only former Oriole Storm Davis (7-3, 3.43) as a free agent to replace them.

Who's left, you ask? Well, there's Bob Welch (11-7, 3.27), Ron Darling (15-10, 3.66), Bobby Witt (10-14, 4.29) and Joe Slusarsky (5-5, 5.45). Rookie Todd Van Poppel might be in the picture if he is healthy. They're counting on pitching coach Dave Duncan to work his magic, but he'll have to be an amazing magician to get this group to match the club's recent rotations.

Most Valuable Player and Cy Young Award winner Dennis Eckersley (7-1, 1.91, 51 saves) will be around for the ninth inning. Getting to him won't be as easy without Jeff Russell and Jim Corsi, but Vince Horsman (2-1, 2.49), Rick Honeycutt (1-4, 3.69) and Goose Gossage (0-2, 2.84) are useful arms.

Re-signed Ron Darling gives A's 15-game winner.

FIELDING: An unheralded part of the Athletics' success has been defense, but the roster purge took its toll here, too. Carney Lansford retired and Walt Weiss was dealt to the Marlins, two moves that will weaken the left side of the infield. Bordick played well at both second base and shortstop, but he doesn't have Weiss' range.

The return of Dave Henderson would be a plus in center field. Steinbach caught 44 percent of would-be base-stealers, one of the AL's best percentages. McGwire is surprisingly adept around first base. Blankenship and Browne are versatile, but are better employed as utility men, not in the regular roles which they may have to assume.

OUTLOOK: We learned last year never to count out a La Russa team. Despite a series of major injuries, the Athletics put together one last hurrah with a 96-66 finish. But payroll considerations have torn apart the starting rotation and few teams can win a division title without an effective one. The Athletics won't fall apart, but they probably will fall short of winning their fifth division title in six years.

OAKLAND ATHLETICS 1993 ROSTER

MANAGER Tony La Russa

Coaches—Dave Duncan, Art Kusnyer, Dave McKay, Tommie Reynolds

PITCHERS

No.	Name	1992 Club	W-L	IP	SO	ERA	B-T	Ht.	Wt.	Born
—	Baker, Scott	St. Petersburg	10-9	152	125	1.96	L-L	6-2	175	5/18/70 San Jose, CA
—	Darling, Ron	Oakland	15-10	206	99	3.66	R-R	6-3	195	8/19/60 Honolulu, HI
—	Davis, Storm	Baltimore	7-3	89	53	3.43	R-R	6-4	225	12/26/6 Dallas, TX
—	Downs, Kelly	San Francisco	1-2	62	33	3.47	R-R	6-4	205	10/25/60 Ogden, UT
		Oakland	5-5	82	38	3.29				
43	Eckersley, Dennis	Oakland	7-1	80	93	1.91	R-R	6-2	195	10/3/54 Oakland, CA
—	Erwin, Scott	Huntsville	3-5	36	39	3.28	R-R	6-1	215	8/21/67 Tampa, FL
—	Gossage, Rich	Oakland	0-2	38	26	2.84	R-R	6-3	225	7/5/51 Colorado Springs, CO
41	Guzman, Johnny	Huntsville	8-2	90	55	3.71	R-L	5-10	155	1/21/71 Dominican Republic
		Tacoma	3-6	69	45	5.11				
		Oakland	0-0	3	0	12.00				
57	Hillegas, Shawn	Ft. Lauderdale	1-0	6	2	0.00	R-R	6-2	223	8/21/64 Dos Palos, CA
		Columbus	2-0	27	20	3.29				
		NY (AL)-Oak.	1-8	86	49	5.23				
40	Honeycutt, Rick	Oakland	1-4	39	32	3.69	L-L	6-1	191	6/29/54 Chattanooga, TN
26	Horsman, Vince	Oakland	2-1	43	18	2.49	R-L	6-2	180	3/9/67 Canada
—	Mohler, Mike	Huntsville	3-8	80	56	3.59	R-L	6-2	195	7/26/68 Dayton, OH
—	Osteen, Gavin	Huntsville	5-5	102	56	3.61	R-L	6-0	195	11/27/69 Orange City, DE
		Tacoma	0-2	14	7	10.06				
56	Revenig, Todd	Huntsville	1-1	64	49	1.70	R-R	6-1	185	6/28/69 Brainerd, MN
		Oakland	0-0	2	1	0.00				
—	Shaw, Curtis	Modesto	13-4	177	154	3.05	L-L	6-1	190	8/16/69 Charlotte, NC
37	Slusarski, Joe	Tacoma	2-4	57	26	3.77	R-R	6-4	195	12/19/66 Indianapolis, IN
		Oakland	5-5	76	38	5.45				
—	Sturtze, Tanyon	Modesto	7-11	151	126	3.75	R-R	6-5	190	10/12/70 Worcester, MA
—	Van Poppel, Todd	Tacoma	4-2	45	29	3.97	R-R	6-5	205	12/9/71 Hinsdale, IL
35	Welch, Bob	Oakland	11-7	124	47	3.27	R-R	6-3	198	11/3/56 Detroit, MI
32	Witt, Bobby	Tex.-Oak.	10-14	193	125	4.29	R-R	6-2	205	5/11/64 Arlington, VA
—	Young, Curt	Kansas City-NY (AL)	4-2	68	20	3.99	R-L	6-1	180	4/16/60 Saginaw, MI
—	Zancanaro, David	Tacoma	2-11	106	47	4.26	S-L	6-1	170	1/8/69 Carmichael, CA

CATCHERS

No.	Name	1992 Club	H	HR	RBI	Pct.	B-T	Ht.	Wt.	Born
—	Helfand, Eric	Modesto	72	10	44	.289	L-R	6-0	195	3/25/89 Erie, PA
		Huntsville	26	2	9	.228				
39	Mercedes, Henry	Tacoma	57	0	20	.232	R-R	5-11	185	7/23/69 Dominican Republic
		Oakland	4	0	1	.800				
—	Molina, Islay	Reno	113	10	75	.259	R-R	6-1	200	6/3/71 New York, NY
		Tacoma	7	0	5	.194				
36	Steinbach, Terry	Oakland	122	12	53	.279	R-R	6-1	200	3/2/62 New Ulm, MN

INFIELDERS

12	Blankenship, Lance	Tacoma	3	1	5	.158	R-R	6-0	185	12/6/63 Portland, OR
		Oakland	84	3	34	.241				
14	Bordick, Mike	Oakland	151	3	48	.300	R-R	5-11	175	7/21/65 Marquette, MI
2	Brosius, Scott	Tacoma	56	9	31	.237	R-R	6-1	185	8/15/66 Hillsboro, OR
		Oakland	19	4	13	.218				
30	Browne, Jerry	Tacoma	7	0	3	.412	S-R	5-10	170	2/3/66 Virgin Islands
		Oakland	93	3	40	.287				
25	McGwire, Mark	Oakland	125	42	104	.268	R-R	6-5	225	10/1/63 Pomona, CA
—	Paquette, Craig	Huntsville	116	17	71	.258	R-R	6-0	190	3/28/69 Long Beach, CA
		Tacoma	18	2	11	.273				

OUTFIELDERS

—	Armas, Marcos	Huntsville	144	17	85	.283	R-R	6-5	190	8/5/69 Venezuela
42	Henderson, Dave	Modesto	4	1	2	.308	R-R	6-2	220	7/21/58 Dos Palos, CA
		Tacoma	2	0	1	.182				
		Oakland	9	0	2	.143				
24	Henderson, Rickey	Oakland	112	15	46	.283	R-L	5-10	190	12/25/58 Chicago, IL
—	Lydy, Scott	Reno	49	2	27	.395	R-R	6-5	190	10/26/68 Mesa, AZ
		Huntsville	118	9	65	.305				
16	Neel, Troy	Tacoma	139	17	74	.351	L-R	6-4	210	9/14/65 Freeport, TX
		Oakland	14	3	9	.264				
—	Sierra, Ruben	Tex.-Oak.	167	17	87	.278	S-R	6-1	200	10/6/65 Puerto Rico

ATHLETIC PROFILES

MARK McGWIRE 29 6-5 225 Bats R Throws R

Returned to form in big way and turned free agency into five-year, 28-million pact with his only team . . . Just missed winning AL homer title, finishing one behind Rangers' Juan Gonzalez . . . Lost three weeks due to rib cage injury . . . Went deep once per 11.1 at-bats, best ratio in majors . . . Led league with .585 slugging percentage . . . Tied for sixth with 64 extra-base hits . . . Walked 90 times, bringing on-base average to .385, 10th-best mark in AL . . . Earned $2,650,000 in 1992, when he took a slight cut from previous year . . . Bottomed out at .201 with 22 homers in 1991 . . . Already has 220 homers in just six full seasons . . . Set major league rookie record with 49 homers in 1987 . . . Athletics drafted him 10th overall in 1984 . . . Was member of U.S. Olympic Team that summer . . . Born Oct. 1, 1963, in Pomona, Cal.

Year	Club	Pos.	G	AB	R	H	2B	3B	HR	RBI	SB	Avg.
1986	Oakland	3B	18	53	10	10	1	0	3	9	0	.189
1987	Oakland	1B-3B-OF	151	557	97	161	28	4	49	118	1	.289
1988	Oakland	1B-OF	155	550	87	143	22	1	32	99	0	.260
1989	Oakland	1B	143	490	74	113	17	0	33	95	1	.231
1990	Oakland	1B	156	523	87	123	16	0	39	108	2	.235
1991	Oakland	1B	154	483	62	97	22	0	22	75	2	.201
1992	Oakland	1B	139	467	87	125	22	0	42	104	0	.268
	Totals		916	3123	504	772	128	5	220	608	6	.247

RUBEN SIERRA 27 6-1 200 Bats S Throws R

Right fielder found himself on division winner following Aug. 31 blockbuster that sent him west along with Bobby Witt and Jeff Russell for Jose Canseco . . . Otherwise, 1992 was a disappointment . . . Trouble started with failure to sign a deal with Texas that would have kept him out of free agency . . . Contracted chicken pox just prior to trade and missed 11 games . . . Due for big season, if his good-great pattern continues . . . Has averaged .292, 28 homers and 115 RBI in odd-numbered years and .270, 19 homers and 91 RBI in even-numbered years . . . Won $5-million salary for 1992 in arbitration hearing . . . Signed originally as free agent by Rangers in November 1982 . . . Born Oct. 6, 1965, in Rio Piedras, P.R. . . . Declared free agency last winter, then re-signed for five-years at close to $30 million.

Year	Club	Pos.	G	AB	R	H	2B	3B	HR	RBI	SB	Avg.
1986	Texas	OF	113	382	50	101	13	10	16	55	7	.264
1987	Texas	OF	158	643	97	169	35	4	30	109	16	.263
1988	Texas	OF	156	615	77	156	32	2	23	91	18	.254
1989	Texas	OF	162	634	101	194	35	14	29	119	8	.306
1990	Texas	OF	159	608	70	170	37	2	16	96	9	.280
1991	Texas	OF	161	661	110	203	44	5	25	116	16	.307
1992	Tex.-Oak......	OF	151	601	83	167	34	7	17	87	14	.278
	Totals		1060	4144	588	1160	230	44	156	673	88	.280

TERRY STEINBACH 31 6-1 200 Bats R Throws R

One of the AL's best behind the plate . . . Had best offensive numbers since rookie season . . . Also caught most games of his career (124) and threw out 50 of 118 would-be base-stealers, the third-best percentage in majors . . . Staff had 3.49 ERA when he was behind plate, 3.73 overall . . . Missed 14 games in April due to hairline fracture of left wrist . . . Hit .326 on the road, fourth-best mark in AL . . . Was Athletics' best clutch hitter, posting .337 average with runners in scoring position last season . . . Two-time all-star, including MVP performance in 1988 game . . . Earned $2,050,000 in 1992 . . . Oakland's ninth-round pick in 1983 draft . . . Born March 2, 1962, in New Ulm, Minn. . . . Opted for free agency, but chose to stay put with a four-year, $14-million contract.

Year	Club	Pos.	G	AB	R	H	2B	3B	HR	RBI	SB	Avg.
1986	Oakland......	C	6	15	3	5	0	0	2	4	0	.333
1987	Oakland......	C-3B-1B	122	391	66	111	16	3	16	56	1	.284
1988	Oakland......	C-3B-1B-OF	104	351	42	93	19	1	9	51	3	.265
1989	Oakland......	C-OF-1B-3B	130	454	37	124	13	1	7	42	1	.273
1990	Oakland......	C-1B	114	379	32	95	15	2	9	57	0	.251
1991	Oakland......	C-1B	129	456	50	125	31	1	6	67	2	.274
1992	Oakland......	C-1B	128	438	48	122	20	1	12	53	2	.279
	Totals		733	2484	278	675	114	9	61	330	9	.272

RICKEY HENDERSON 34 5-10 190 Bats R Throws L

Left fielder missed 45 games due to variety of injuries . . . Couldn't avoid further questioning of his attitude . . . Became first player to reach 1,000 stolen bases with steal of third May 1 at Detroit . . . Didn't win AL stolen-base title for first time since 1987 . . . Stole fewer than 50 bases for only second time in 13 full seasons, but pushed career total to 1,042 . . . Got 2,000th hit on final at-bat of regular season, a single off Milwaukee's Cal Eldred . . . Earned $3,250,000 in 1992 . . . Athletics drafted him in fourth round in 1976 . . . A's got him back after 4½ seasons in

New York for Greg Cadaret, Luis Polonia and Eric Plunk, June 20, 1989 . . . Born Christmas Day, 1958 in Chicago, but was raised in Oakland.

Year	Club	Pos.	G	AB	R	H	2B	3B	HR	RBI	SB	Avg.
1979	Oakland	OF	89	351	49	96	13	3	1	26	33	.274
1980	Oakland	OF	158	591	111	179	22	4	9	53	100	.303
1981	Oakland	OF	108	423	89	135	18	7	6	35	56	.319
1982	Oakland	OF	149	536	119	143	24	4	10	51	130	.267
1983	Oakland	OF	145	513	105	150	25	7	9	48	108	.292
1984	Oakland	OF	142	502	113	147	27	4	16	58	66	.293
1985	New York (AL)	OF	143	547	146	172	28	5	24	72	80	.314
1986	New York (AL)	OF	153	608	130	160	31	5	28	74	87	.263
1987	New York (AL)	OF	95	358	78	104	17	3	17	37	41	.291
1988	New York (AL)	OF	140	554	118	169	30	2	6	50	93	.305
1989	NY (AL)-Oak. . .	OF	150	541	113	148	26	3	12	57	77	.274
1990	Oakland	OF	136	489	119	159	33	3	28	61	65	.325
1991	Oakland	OF	134	470	105	126	17	1	18	57	58	.268
1992	Oakland	OF	117	396	77	112	18	3	15	46	48	.283
	Totals		1859	6879	1472	2000	329	54	199	725	1042	.291

DAVE HENDERSON 34 6-2 220 Bats R Throws R

Coming off lost season . . . Strained right calf and pulled right hamstring cost "Hendu" all but 20 games . . . Got only 63 at-bats and wasn't fully healthy for those . . . Hasn't been healthy since first half of 1991, when he was on his way to best season before injuries struck . . . Had .298 average, 18 homers and 50 RBI at 1991 All-Star break . . . Averaged .275 with 21 homers and 80 RBI in first four seasons in Oakland . . . Has been on division winner in six of last seven seasons . . . Hit memorable pennant-winning homer for Boston in 1986 ALCS against California . . . Earned $2.6 million in 1992 . . . Signed with Athletics as free agent before 1988 season . . . Mariners' first-round pick in 1977 draft . . . Born July 21, 1958, in Dos Palos, Cal.

Year	Club	Pos.	G	AB	R	H	2B	3B	HR	RBI	SB	Avg.
1981	Seattle.	OF	59	126	17	21	3	0	6	13	2	.167
1982	Seattle.	OF	104	324	47	82	17	1	14	48	2	.253
1983	Seattle.	OF	137	484	50	130	24	5	17	55	9	.269
1984	Seattle.	OF	112	350	42	98	23	0	14	43	5	.280
1985	Seattle.	OF	139	502	70	121	28	2	14	68	6	.241
1986	Sea.-Bos	OF	139	388	59	103	22	4	15	47	2	.265
1987	Boston	OF	75	184	30	43	10	0	8	25	1	.234
1987	San Francisco	OF	15	21	2	5	2	0	0	1	2	.238
1988	Oakland	OF	146	507	100	154	38	1	24	94	2	.304
1989	Oakland	OF	152	579	77	145	24	3	15	80	8	.250
1990	Oakland	OF	127	450	65	122	28	0	20	63	3	.271
1991	Oakland	OF-2B	150	572	86	158	33	0	25	85	6	.276
1992	Oakland	OF	20	63	1	9	1	0	0	2	0	.143
	Totals		1375	4550	646	1191	253	16	172	624	48	.262

RON DARLING 32 6-3 195 Bats R Throws R

Coming off best season since 1988 . . . Second on staff in wins, innings and starts . . . Fully recovered from 1990 elbow surgery . . . Had no-hitters through six innings in five outings . . . Twice took no-hitters into the eighth inning . . . Pitched three two-hit shutouts . . . Finished strong, going 7-3 with a 2.90 ERA after All-Star break . . . Was 99-70 in seven-plus seasons with Mets, including five consecutive winning records from 1984-88 . . . Yale product is one of game's best interviews . . . Another Athletics steal as they sent Russ Cormier and Matt Grott to Expos to get him in July 1991 . . . Earned $2.1 million in 1992 . . . Rangers drafted him ninth overall in 1981, then dealt him to Mets in ill-fated trade for Lee Mazzilli . . . Born Aug. 19, 1960, in Honolulu . . . Re-signed three-year contract as free agent last winter.

Year	Club	G	IP	W	L	Pct.	SO	BB	H	ERA
1983	New York (NL)	5	35⅓	1	3	.250	23	17	31	2.80
1984	New York (NL)	33	205⅔	12	9	.571	136	104	179	3.81
1985	New York (NL)	36	248	16	6	.727	167	114	214	2.90
1986	New York (NL)	34	237	15	6	.714	184	81	203	2.81
1987	New York (NL)	32	207⅔	12	8	.600	167	96	183	4.29
1988	New York (NL)	34	240⅔	17	9	.654	161	60	218	3.25
1989	New York (NL)	33	217⅓	14	14	.500	153	70	214	3.52
1990	New York (NL)	33	126	7	9	.438	99	44	135	4.50
1991	NY (NL)-Mont.	20	119⅓	5	8	.385	69	33	121	4.37
1991	Oakland	12	75	3	7	.300	60	38	64	4.08
1992	Oakland	33	206⅓	15	10	.600	99	72	198	3.66
	Totals	305	1918⅓	117	89	.568	1318	729	1760	3.57

DENNIS ECKERSLEY 38 6-2 195 Bats R Throws R

Simply put, there is none better . . . Another amazing season included 51 saves in 54 opportunities, a Cy Young Award and AL MVP recognition . . . Became ninth player to win Cy and MVP in same season and fourth reliever to win MVP, joining Jim Konstanty (1950), Rollie Fingers (1981) and Willie Hernandez (1984) . . . Had streak of 36 saves in a row . . . Did not blow a save opportunity until Aug. 8 . . . Athletics won 65 of the 69 games in which he appeared . . . Since 1988, he has saved 220 in 246 opportunities (89 percent) . . . Only pitcher in history to save 40 or more games four times . . . Save total of 239 is AL record and ranks him eighth all-time . . . Also has pitched a no-hitter, has been a 20-game winner and has posted 181 victories in certain Hall of Fame career . . . Signed two-year, $7.8-million extension July 19 of last season . . . Indians' third-round pick in 1982 draft . . . Stolen by Athletics from Cubs just before start of 1987 season, for forgettable trio of Dave Wilder, Brian Guinn and Mark Leonette . . . Born Oct. 3, 1954, in Oakland.

Year	Club	G	IP	W	L	Pct.	SO	BB	H	ERA
1975	Cleveland	34	187	13	7	.650	152	90	147	2.60
1976	Cleveland	36	199	13	12	.520	200	75	155	3.44
1977	Cleveland	33	247	14	13	.519	191	54	214	3.53
1978	Boston	35	268	20	8	.714	162	71	258	2.99
1979	Boston	33	247	17	10	.630	150	59	234	2.99
1980	Boston	30	198	12	14	.462	121	44	188	4.27
1981	Boston	23	154	9	8	.529	79	35	160	4.27
1982	Boston	33	224⅓	13	13	.500	127	43	228	3.73
1983	Boston	28	176⅓	9	13	.409	77	39	223	5.61
1984	Boston	9	64⅔	4	4	.500	33	13	71	[illegible]
1984	Chicago (NL)	24	160⅓	10	8	.556	81	36	152	[illegible]
1985	Chicago (NL)	25	169⅓	11	7	.611	117	19	145	3.08
1986	Chicago (NL)	33	201	6	11	.353	137	43	226	4.57
1987	Oakland	54	115⅔	6	8	.429	113	17	99	3.03
1988	Oakland	60	72⅔	4	2	.667	70	11	52	2.35
1989	Oakland	51	57⅔	4	0	1.000	55	3	32	1.56
1990	Oakland	63	73⅓	4	2	.667	73	4	41	0.61
1991	Oakland	67	76	5	4	.556	87	9	60	2.96
1992	Oakland	69	80	7	1	.875	93	11	62	1.91
	Totals	740	2971⅓	181	145	.555	2118	679	2747	3.43

BOB WELCH 36 6-3 198 — Bats R Throws R

Won 10-plus games for sixth consecutive season, despite three stints on disabled list . . . Made only 20 starts . . . Bothered by right shoulder tendinitis, strained back, sore left knee and sore right elbow . . . Next victory will be his 200th . . . Loves Oakland Coliseum . . . Has gone 49-18 with 2.75 ERA there in five seasons, as opposed to 35-25 with 4.36 ERA on road . . . Pitched seven strong innings in Game 4 of ALCS, but no-decision left him at 3-3 in 10 postseason appearances, including memorable whiff of Reggie Jackson in 1978 World Series . . . Was AL Cy Young Award winner in 1990 . . . Earned $3,450,000 in 1992, the second year of four-year, $13.8-million deal . . . Dodgers' first-round pick in 1977 draft went to Athletics in three-team, eight-player deal prior to 1988 season . . . Born Nov. 3, 1956, in Detroit.

Year	Club	G	IP	W	L	Pct.	SO	BB	H	ERA
1978	Los Angeles.	23	111	7	4	.636	66	26	92	2.03
1979	Los Angeles.	25	81	5	6	.455	64	32	82	4.00
1980	Los Angeles.	32	214	14	9	.609	141	79	190	3.28
1981	Los Angeles.	23	141	9	5	.643	88	41	141	3.45
1982	Los Angeles.	36	235⅔	16	11	.593	176	81	199	3.36
1983	Los Angeles.	31	204	15	12	.556	156	72	164	2.65
1984	Los Angeles.	31	178⅔	13	13	.500	126	58	191	3.78
1985	Los Angeles.	23	167⅓	14	4	.778	96	35	141	2.31
1986	Los Angeles.	33	235⅔	7	13	.350	183	55	227	3.28
1987	Los Angeles.	35	251⅔	15	9	.625	196	86	204	3.22
1988	Oakland	36	244⅔	17	9	.654	158	81	237	3.64
1989	Oakland	33	209⅔	17	8	.680	137	78	191	3.00
1990	Oakland	35	238	27	6	.818	127	77	214	2.95
1991	Oakland	35	220	12	13	.480	101	91	220	4.58
1992	Oakland	20	123⅔	11	7	.611	47	43	114	3.27
	Totals.	451	2856	199	129	.607	1862	935	2607	3.27

BOBBY WITT 28 6-2 205 Bats R Throws R

Maybe Athletics pitching coach Dave Duncan can do what Tom House in Texas couldn't—get this talented right-hander to fulfill his potential . . . Went to Oakland along with Ruben Sierra and Jeff Russell for Jose Canseco Aug. 31 . . . Made five starts with Athletics, splitting two decisions . . . Finished 10-14, dropping career record to 69-73 . . . Has had only one winning season, a brilliant 17-10 effort in 1990, when he won 12 consecutive decisions . . . Not the power pitcher he used to be . . . Relies more on sharp slider as arm trouble has cut into velocity of former 95-mph fastball . . . Earned $2,833,333 in 1992 . . . Rangers' first pick and third player taken overall in 1985 draft . . . Member of 1984 U.S. Olympic Team . . . Born May 11, 1964, in Arlington, Va.

Year	Club	G	IP	W	L	Pct.	SO	BB	H	ERA
1986	Texas	31	157⅔	11	9	.550	174	143	130	5.48
1987	Texas	26	143	8	10	.444	160	140	114	4.91
1988	Texas	22	174⅓	8	10	.444	148	101	134	3.92
1989	Texas	31	194⅓	12	13	.480	166	114	182	5.14
1990	Texas	33	222	17	10	.630	221	110	197	3.36
1991	Texas	17	88⅔	3	7	.300	82	74	84	6.09
1992	Texas-Oak.	31	193	10	14	.417	125	114	183	4.29
	Totals.	191	1173	69	73	.486	1076	796	1024	4.57

STORM DAVIS 31 6-4 225 **Bats R Throws R**

Back for second turn with A's. . . . Signed two-year, free-agent deal for $1.8 million . . . Will return to rotation after two years almost exclusively in relief . . . Spent two-plus seasons in Oakland, including 19-win season in 1989 . . . A's pitching coach Dave Duncan was the key to reviving then-fading career. So Dave and Storm try it again . . . Hailed as big-money free agent in Kansas City after leaving A's in 1990 . . . Bounced back last year with Orioles, his original team . . . Has played with five teams in 11 years, including four since 1987 . . . Seventh-round pick of Baltimore in 1979 . . . Born Dec. 26, 1961, in Dallas . . . Earned $2,466,667 in 1992.

Year	Club	G	IP	W	L	Pct.	SO	BB	H	ERA
1982	Baltimore	29	100⅔	8	4	.667	67	28	96	3.49
1983	Baltimore	34	200⅓	13	7	.650	125	64	180	3.59
1984	Baltimore	35	225	14	9	.609	105	71	205	3.12
1985	Baltimore	31	175	10	8	.556	93	70	172	4.53
1986	Baltimore	25	154	9	12	.429	96	49	166	3.62
1987	San Diego	21	62⅔	2	7	.222	37	36	70	6.18
1987	Oakland	5	30⅓	1	1	.500	28	11	28	3.26
1988	Oakland	33	201⅔	16	7	.696	127	91	211	3.70
1989	Oakland	31	169⅓	19	7	.731	91	68	187	4.36
1990	Kansas City	21	112	7	10	.412	62	35	129	4.74
1991	Kansas City	51	114⅓	3	9	.250	53	46	140	4.96
1992	Baltimore	48	89⅓	7	3	.700	53	36	79	3.43
	Totals	364	1634⅔	109	84	.565	937	605	1663	3.98

TOP PROSPECTS

TODD VAN POPPEL 21 6-5 205 **Bats R Throws R**

Shoulder trouble interrupted progress of perhaps the game's best pitching prospect . . . Went 4-2 with 3.97 ERA in nine starts for Tacoma (AAA) before being shut down . . . Made major league debut Sept. 11, 1991, only 14 months after graduating from high school, and struck out six White Sox in 4⅔ innings . . . Received then-record $1.2-million deal that included a major league contract after Athletics picked him 14th overall in 1990 draft . . . Born Dec. 9, 1971, in Hinsdale, Ill.

TROY NEEL 27 6-4 210 **Bats L Throws R**

Outfielder led Pacific Coast League with .351 mark and was second in slugging percentage and on-base percentage with Tacoma

(AAA) . . . Had 16 homers and 70 RBI . . . Had three homers and nine RBI in 53 at-bats for Athletics . . . Acquired from Indians for Larry Arndt prior to 1991 season . . . Born Sept. 14, 1965, in Freeport, Tex.

SCOTT BROSIUS 26 6-1 185 **Bats R Throws R**
Versatile player who should stick . . . Has spent parts of last two seasons in Oakland . . . Can play anywhere in infield, as well as left and right . . . Hit .231 with nine homers and 31 RBI for Tacoma (AAA) in 1992 . . . Has .226 average, six homers and 17 RBI in 155 big-league at-bats after last year's .218 showing with four homers and 13 RBI . . . Born Aug. 15, 1966 in Hillsboro, Ore. . . . Athletics' 20th-round pick in 1987 draft.

MANAGER TONY La RUSSA: Won another AL Manager of the Year award for brilliant handling of injury-riddled team that used the disabled list 22 times . . . Consistently plugged the right guy into the right spot . . . In 1992, his Athletics were never lower than second place, took over first Aug. 5 and weren't challenged down the stretch en route to 96-66 finish . . . Has won four division titles in last five seasons and five division titles in all . . . Athletics' record under him since start of 1987 is 486-324 . . . Took over July 7, 1986, shortly after being fired by White Sox, where he spent seven years . . . Career record is sparkling 1,134-949 . . . Was an Athletics bonus baby in 1962, when he was drafted out of high school . . . Hit only .199 with no homers and seven RBI in 176 big league at-bats . . . One of five lawyer-managers in baseball history . . . Played youth baseball with Mariners' manager Lou Piniella in Tampa . . . Born Oct. 4, 1944, in Tampa.

ALL-TIME A's SEASON RECORDS

BATTING: Napoleon Lajoie, .422, 1901
HRs: Jimmie Foxx, 58, 1932
RBI: Jimmie Foxx, 169, 1932
STEALS: Rickey Henderson, 130, 1982
WINS: John Coombs, 31, 1910
Lefty Grove, 31, 1931
STRIKEOUTS: Rube Waddell, 349, 1904

SEATTLE MARINERS

TEAM DIRECTORY: Chairman: John Ellis; Pres.: Chuck Armstrong; VP-Baseball Oper.: Woody Woodward; VP-Scouting and Player Dev.: Roger Jongewaard; Dir. Baseball Adm.: Lee Pelekoudas; Farm Dir.: Jim Beattie; Dir. Pub. Rel.: David Aust; Trav. Sec.: Craig Detwiler; Mgr.: Lou Piniella. Home: Kingdome (59,702). Field distances: 331, l.f. line; 376, l.c.; 405, c.f.; 352, r.c.; 314, r.f. line. Spring training: Peoria, Ariz.

SCOUTING REPORT

HITTING: Any lineup that contains the defending batting champion and an emerging superstar can't be all bad. Edgar Martinez (.343, 18, 73) shed his cloak of anonymity with his runaway win in the batting race and everybody knows Ken Griffey Jr. (.308, 27, 103) hasn't even come close to reaching his potential yet.

There will be some new faces, however. Popular free-agent defector Harold Reynolds has been replaced by Bret Boone (.194) and, in place of the grievously disappointing Kevin Mitchell, free-

Edgar Martinez wore AL crown at a Boggsian .343.

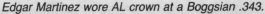

agent signee Mike Felder (.286, 29 steals), another ex-Giant, will play left and likely hit leadoff.

The Mariners finished tied for fourth in average (.263), but were ninth in runs (679) in 1992. That means Jay Buhner (.243, 25, 79) will have to become a more consistent threat in the middle of the lineup. So will Tino Martinez (.257, 16, 66), who established himself in the second half. Omar Vizquel (.294) is prepared to help, too, now that he has become more than a good-field, no-hit shortstop.

PITCHING: New manager Lou Piniella made it his mission to improve the league's worst staff and he succeeded. Ex-Brewer Chris Bosio (16-6, 3.62) was signed as a free agent and he joins Randy Johnson (12-14, 3.77) and Dave Fleming (17-10, 3.39) to form a very good trio of starters. If Erik Hanson (8-17, 4.82) can put it back together and Brian Holman can rebound from surgery, the rotation would be drastically better. If not, Tim Leary (8-10, 5.36) and Rich DeLucia (3-6, 5.49) must improve.

Norm Charlton (4-2, 2.99, 26 saves for the Reds), obtained in the Kevin Mitchell deal, gives the Mariners a reliable closer for the first time since Mike Schooler (2-7, 4.70, 13 saves) was healthy. Schooler could share the role or be a setup man. Lefty Russ Swan (3-10, 4.74, 9 saves) and righty Jeff Nelson (1-7, 3.44, 6 saves) make this bullpen a decent one.

FIELDING: It's a mixed bag that resulted in the Mariners finishing fifth in fielding percentage (.982) and errors (112) last season. Griffey Jr. is a Gold Glove winner in center and Buhner has one of the best arms in the game. Vizquel led the league's shortstops in fielding percentage (.989) and tied for fewest errors (7).

Anything will be an improvement over the overweight Mitchell in left. But Boone is no Reynolds at second base, even the slowed-down version of Reynolds. Martinez has very limited range at third and tied for fifth in errors despite playing only 103 games.

OUTLOOK: Piniella didn't go to the Pacific Northwest with the intent to lose 90-plus games, as the Mariners did last year in finishing last at 64-98. He was promised the financial backing to improve this perennially sub-.500 team, and on paper, he has succeeded. Besides adding Charlton and Bosio, the club locked up Griffey for four more years, avoiding a potentially ugly free-agent departure. However, the best that can be hoped for here in 1993 is the franchise's second winning season in its history.

SEATTLE MARINERS 1993 ROSTER

MANAGER Lou Piniella

Coaches—Lee Elia, Sammy Ellis, Ken Griffey Sr., John McLaren, Sam Perlozzo

PITCHERS

No.	Name	1992 Club	W-L	IP	SO	ERA	B-T	Ht.	Wt.	Born
—	Bosio, Chris	Milwaukee	16-6	231	120	3.62	R-R	6-3	225	4/3/63 Carmichael, CA
—	Charlton, Norm	Cincinnati	4-2	81	90	2.99	S-L	6-3	200	1/6/63 Ft. Polk, LA
—	Coffman, Kevin	Greenville	6-0	38	33	2.13	R-R	6-3	206	1/19/65 Austin, TX
		Richmond	6-5	91	78	3.15				
—	Cummings, John	Peninsula	16-6	168	144	2.57	L-L	6-3	200	5/10/69 Torrance, CA
—	Darwin, Jeff	Peninsula	5-11	140	122	3.35	R-R	6-3	180	7/6/69 Sherman, TX
55	DeLucia, Rich	Seattle	3-6	84	66	5.49	R-R	6-0	185	10/7/64 Reading, PA
		Calgary	4-2	40	38	2.45				
35	Fleming, Dave	Seattle	17-10	228	112	3.39	L-L	6-3	200	11/7/69 Queens, NY
—	*Grant, Mark	Seattle	2-4	81	42	3.89	R-R	6-2	215	10/24/63 Aurora, IL
39	Hanson, Erik	Seattle	8-17	187	112	4.82	R-R	6-6	210	5/18/65 Kinnelon, NJ
36	Holman, Brian	Seattle		Injured			R-R	6-4	190	1/25/65 Denver, CO
51	Johnson, Randy	Seattle	12-14	210	241	3.77	R-L	6-10	225	9/10/63 Walnut Creek, CA
54	Leary, Tim	NY (AL)-Sea.	8-10	141	46	5.36	R-R	6-3	220	12/23/58 Santa Monica, CA
40	Nelson, Jeff	Seattle	1-7	81	46	3.44	R-R	6-8	235	11/17/66 Baltimore, MD
		Calgary	1-0	4	0	0.00				
—	Perez, Yorkis	Yomiuri	0-1	6	6	7.11	L-L	6-0	180	9/30/67 Dominican Republic
48	Powell, Dennis	Seattle	4-2	57	35	4.58	R-L	6-3	227	8/13/63 Moultrie, GA
18	Remlinger, Mike	Calgary	1-7	70	24	6.65	L-L	6-0	195	3/23/66 Middletown, NY
		Jacksonville	1-1	26	21	3.46				
—	Salkeld, Roger			Injured			R-R	6-5	215	3/6/71 Burbank, CA
29	Schooler, Mike	Seattle	2-7	52	33	4.70	R-R	6-3	220	8/10/62 Anaheim, CA
		Bellingham	0-0	3	3	0.00				
		Calgary	0-0	2	0	0.00				
37	Swan, Russ	Seattle	3-10	104	45	4.74	L-L	6-4	210	1/3/64 Fremont, CA
—	Wainhouse, Dave	Indianapolis	5-4	46	37	4.11	L-R	6-2	185	11/7/67 Canada
42	Woodson, Kerry	Jacksonville	5-4	68	55	3.57	R-R	6-2	190	5/18/69 Jacksonville, FL
		Calgary	1-4	21	9	3.43				
		Seattle	0-1	14	6	3.29				

CATCHERS

No.	Name	1992 Club	H	HR	RBI	Pct.	B-T	Ht.	Wt.	Born
—	Deak, Brian	Richmond	62	9	36	.261	R-R	6-0	183	10/25/67 Harrisburg, PA
15	Haselman, Bill	Oklahoma City	14	1	9	.241	R-R	6-3	215	5/25/66 Long Branch, NJ
		Calgary	77	19	53	.255				
		Seattle	5	0	0	.263				
10	Sasser, Mackey	New York (NL)	34	2	18	.241	L-R	6-1	210	8/3/62 Fort Gaines, GA
10	Valle, David	Seattle	88	9	30	.240	R-R	6-2	200	10/30/60 Bayside, NY

INFIELDERS

No.	Name	1992 Club	H	HR	RBI	Pct.	B-T	Ht.	Wt.	Born
8	Amaral, Rich	Calgary	128	0	21	.318	R-R	6-0	175	4/1/62 Visalia, CA
		Seattle	24	1	7	.240				
34	Boone, Bret	Calgary	138	13	73	.314	R-R	5-10	180	4/6/69 El Cajon, CA
		Seattle	25	4	15	.194				
11	Martinez, Edgar	Seattle	181	18	73	.343	R-R	5-11	180	1/2/63 New York, NY
23	Martinez, Tino	Seattle	118	16	66	.257	L-R	6-2	205	12/7/67 Tampa, FL
9	O'Brien, Pete	Seattle	88	14	52	.222	L-L	6-2	205	2/9/58 Santa Monica, CA
—	Pirkl, Greg	Jacksonville	66	10	29	.291	R-R	6-5	225	8/7/70 Long Beach, CA
		Calgary	76	6	32	.266				
13	Vizquel, Omar	Seattle	142	0	21	.294	S-R	5-9	165	4/24/67 Venezuela

OUTFIELDERS

No.	Name	1992 Club	H	HR	RBI	Pct.	B-T	Ht.	Wt.	Born
1	Briley, Greg	Seattle	55	5	12	.275	L-R	5-8	180	5/24/65 Greenville, NC
19	Buhner, Jay	Seattle	132	25	79	.243	R-R	6-3	205	8/13/64 Louisville, KY
28	Cotto, Henry	Seattle	76	5	27	.259	R-R	6-2	180	1/5/61 Bronx, NY
—	Felder, Mike	San Francisco	92	4	23	.286	S-R	5-9	175	11/18/62 Vallejo, CA
24	Griffey, Ken	Seattle	174	27	103	.308	L-L	6-3	195	11/21/69 Donora, PA
—	Tinsley, Lee	Colorado Springs	19	0	4	.235	S-R	5-10	185	3/4/69 Shelbyville, KY
		Canton-Akron	100	5	38	.287				

*Free agent offered arbitration

MARINER PROFILES

KEN GRIFFEY Jr. 23 6-3 195 Bats L Throws L

Franchise player was signed four-year, $24-million extension last winter as Mariners couldn't risk losing him after 1994 season . . . Set career highs in homers and RBI . . . Hit .300 or better for third consecutive season . . . Youngest player to drive in 100 runs since Al Kaline in 1956 . . . Missed 20 games because of sprained wrist . . . Didn't run as much as he stole only 10 bases . . . Didn't always run out ground balls, either . . . Won Gold Glove for outstanding play in center last season . . . Earned $2,000,000 in 1992 . . . Mariners made him first pick overall in 1987 draft, out of Moeller High in Cincinnati . . . Was big league regular two years later . . . Part of first simultaneous father-son player combo with Ken Sr., now a Mariner coach . . . Born Nov. 21, 1969, in Donora, Pa.

Year	Club	Pos.	G	AB	R	H	2B	3B	HR	RBI	SB	Avg.
1989	Seattle.......	OF	127	455	61	120	23	0	16	61	16	.264
1990	Seattle.......	OF	155	597	91	179	28	7	22	80	16	.300
1991	Seattle.......	OF	154	548	76	179	42	1	22	100	18	.327
1992	Seattle.......	OF	142	565	83	174	39	4	27	103	10	.308
	Totals.......		578	2165	311	652	132	12	87	344	60	.301

EDGAR MARTINEZ 30 5-11 180 Bats R Throws R

Emerged as AL batting champion after coming out of nowhere . . . His .343 average was 45 points above career mark entering 1992 season . . . Won title by comfortable 14-point margin over Twins' Kirby Puckett . . . Third baseman also established career highs in homers, RBI and runs . . . Second in league in doubles and slugging percentage (.544) . . . Fourth in on-base percentage (.404) . . . Missed final 18 games due to arthroscopic surgery on right shoulder . . . Earned just $500,000 in 1992 . . . Cousin of Carmelo Martinez . . . Originally signed as free agent by Mariners in 1962 . . . Played six minor league seasons before reaching majors to stay . . . Born Jan. 2, 1963, in New York.

Year	Club	Pos.	G	AB	R	H	2B	3B	HR	RBI	SB	Avg.
1987	Seattle.	3B	13	43	6	16	5	2	0	5	0	.372
1988	Seattle.	3B	14	32	0	9	4	0	0	5	0	.281
1989	Seattle.	3B	65	171	20	41	5	0	2	20	2	.240
1990	Seattle.	3B	144	487	71	147	27	2	11	49	1	.302
1991	Seattle.	3B	150	544	98	167	35	1	14	52	0	.307
1992	Seattle.	3B-1B	135	528	100	181	46	3	18	73	14	.343
	Totals		521	1805	295	561	112	8	45	204	17	.311

JAY BUHNER 28 6-3 205 Bats R Throws R

Consistent in his inconsistency . . . In last two seasons, he has hit .244 and .243, with 27 and 25 home runs and 77 and 79 RBI . . . Hits them a long way . . . Belted 479-foot blast in Yankee Stadium in 1991 . . . Has rocket arm in right field . . . Had 14 assists, tying for AL high . . . Committed only two errors . . . Went 0-for-6 in stolen-base attempts, making second year in a row he has been shut out in that category . . . Salary in 1992 was $1,445,000 . . . Seattle got him and two minor leaguers from Yankees for Ken Phelps, July 21, 1988 . . . Began career with Pirates as January 1984 secondary draft pick . . . Born Aug. 13, 1964, in Louisville, Ky.

Year	Club	Pos.	G	AB	R	H	2B	3B	HR	RBI	SB	Avg.
1987	New York (AL)	OF	7	22	0	5	2	0	0	1	0	.227
1988	NY (AL)-Sea. . .	OF	85	261	36	56	13	1	13	38	1	.215
1989	Seattle.	OF	58	204	27	56	15	1	9	33	1	.275
1990	Seattle.	OF	51	163	16	45	12	0	7	33	2	.276
1991	Seattle.	OF	137	406	64	99	14	4	27	77	0	.244
1992	Seattle.	OF	152	543	69	132	16	3	25	79	0	.243
	Totals		490	1599	212	393	72	9	81	261	4	.246

OMAR VIZQUEL 25 5-9 165 Bats R Throws R

Led regular AL shortstops in batting average, fielding percentage (.989) and tied for fewest errors (7) . . . Defense has always been outstanding. Set club fielding mark in 1991, which he broke last season . . . Has committed only nine errors since August 1991, a span of 212 games . . . Raised average 64 points over 1991 mark . . . Stole career-high 15 bases in 28 tries . . . It helps when you're on base much more often . . . Went on disabled list April 13 because of knee strain . . . Missed 26 games in all . . . Moved to second spot in order June 24 . . . Earned $360,000 in 1992 . . . Originally signed by Seattle as free agent in April 1984 . . . Born April 24, 1967, in Caracas, Venezuela.

Year	Club	Pos.	G	AB	R	H	2B	3B	HR	RBI	SB	Avg.
1989	Seattle.	SS	143	387	45	85	7	3	1	20	1	.220
1990	Seattle.	SS	81	255	19	63	3	2	2	18	4	.247
1991	Seattle.	SS-2B	142	426	42	98	16	4	1	41	7	.230
1992	Seattle.	SS	136	483	49	142	20	4	0	21	15	.294
	Totals		502	1551	155	388	46	13	4	100	27	.250

TINO MARTINEZ 25 6-2 205 Bats L Throws R

Established himself at first base, supplanting veteran Pete O'Brien . . . Appears ready to fulfill 20-homer, 80-RBI potential . . . Needs to improve against left-handers, against whom he hit only .228 . . . Made 74 starts at first base and 47 as DH . . . Earned $132,500 in 1992 . . . Began 1991 with Calgary (AAA), where he was Pacific Coast League MVP and All-Star . . . Member of 1988 U.S. Olympic Team . . . MVP of World Amateur Championships in 1988 . . . Mariners' first-round pick in 1988 draft . . . Three-time All-American at University of Tampa . . . Born Dec. 7, 1967, in Tampa, and is product of same high school that produced Fred McGriff.

Year	Club	Pos.	G	AB	R	H	2B	3B	HR	RBI	SB	Avg.
1990	Seattle.	1B	24	68	4	15	4	0	0	5	0	.221
1991	Seattle.	1B	36	112	11	23	2	0	4	9	0	.205
1992	Seattle.	1B	136	460	53	118	19	2	16	66	2	.257
	Totals		196	640	68	156	25	2	20	80	2	.244

DAVE VALLE 32 6-2 200 Bats R Throws R

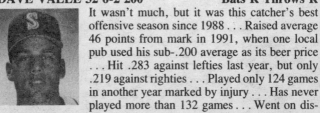

It wasn't much, but it was this catcher's best offensive season since 1988 . . . Raised average 46 points from mark in 1991, when one local pub used his sub-.200 average as its beer price . . . Hit .283 against lefties last year, but only .219 against righties . . . Played only 124 games in another year marked by injury . . . Has never played more than 132 games . . . Went on disabled list May 10, making 12th time he has been there since 1979 . . . Threw out 32.3 percent of would-be base-stealers . . . Earned $1,366,667 in 1992 . . . Mariners' second-round pick in 1978 draft

. . . Spent eight years in minors before sticking with Mariners . . . Born Oct. 30, 1960, in Bayside, N.Y.

Year	Club	Pos.	G	AB	R	H	2B	3B	HR	RBI	SB	Avg.
1984	Seattle.	C	13	27	4	8	1	0	1	4	0	.296
1985	Seattle.	C	31	70	2	11	1	0	0	4	0	.157
1986	Seattle.	C-1B	22	53	10	18	3	0	5	15	0	.340
1987	Seattle.	C-1B-OF	95	324	40	83	16	3	12	53	2	.256
1988	Seattle.	C-1B	93	290	29	67	15	2	10	50	0	.231
1989	Seattle.	C	94	316	32	75	10	3	7	34	0	.237
1990	Seattle.	C-1B	107	308	37	66	15	0	7	33	1	.214
1991	Seattle.	C-1B	132	324	38	63	8	1	8	32	0	.194
1992	Seattle.	C	124	367	39	88	16	1	9	30	0	.240
	Totals		711	2079	231	479	85	10	59	255	3	.230

DAVE FLEMING 23 6-3 200 Bats L Throws L

Late-season losing streak cut into what still should be regarded as great rookie year . . . Went 17-10 for team that finished 34 games under .500 . . . Did it with average of 4.34 runs worth of support per game . . . Was 9-1 June 9, when Mariners were 23-34 . . . Shelled by Texas in his first start, then he ran off nine consecutive victories . . . Was 11-3 at All-Star break . . . Threw two-hit shutout against Cleveland Aug. 25 to raise record to 15-5 . . . Lost next five decisions before winning final two . . . Pitched four shutouts and seven complete games . . . Earned minimum $109,000 salary in 1992 . . . Mariners' third-round pick in 1990 draft, out of University of Georgia . . . Saved Bulldogs' College World Series clinching victory over Oklahoma State . . . Born Nov. 7, 1969, in Queens, N.Y.

Year	Club	G	IP	W	L	Pct.	SO	BB	H	ERA
1991	Seattle	9	17⅔	1	0	1.000	11	3	19	6.62
1992	Seattle	33	228⅓	17	10	.630	112	60	225	3.39
	Totals.	42	246	18	10	.643	123	63	244	3.62

RANDY JOHNSON 29 6-10 225 Bats R Throws L

Off-beat lefty slipped below .500 for first time in three seasons . . . Led AL in strikeouts, with 23 more than Yanks' Melido Perez . . . Also posted AL's lowest opponents' batting average, at .206 . . . Led AL in walks for third consecutive season with 144, 30 more than Bobby Witt . . . Only one other AL pitcher walked more than 100 batters . . . Threw no-hitter against Detroit in 1990 . . . Tallest player in major league history . . . Went to USC on baseball-basketball scholarship . . . Listens to rock music and plays drums on days when he pitches . . . A photography bug . . . Was highest-paid Mariner pitcher at $1,392,500 in 1992 . . . Mariners got him from Expos with Brian Holman and Gene Harris for Mark Langston, May 25, 1989 . . . Montreal's second-round pick in 1985 draft . . . Born Sept. 10, 1963, in Walnut Creek, Cal.

Year	Club	G	IP	W	L	Pct.	SO	BB	H	ERA
1988	Montreal	4	26	3	0	1.000	25	7	23	2.42
1989	Montreal	7	29⅔	0	4	.000	26	26	29	6.67
1989	Seattle	22	131	7	9	.438	104	70	118	4.40
1990	Seattle	33	219⅔	14	11	.560	194	120	174	3.65
1991	Seattle	33	201⅓	13	10	.565	228	152	151	3.98
1992	Seattle	31	210⅓	12	14	.462	241	144	154	3.77
	Totals	130	818	49	48	.505	818	519	649	3.95

ERIK HANSON 27 6-6 210 Bats R Throws R

Scouts shake their heads in disappointment at this guy . . . Had 90-plus-mph fastball and one of game's best curves . . . Won 18 games with 3.24 ERA and 211 strikeouts in 1990 . . . Has done nothing since . . . Elbow trouble interrupted 1991 season, but he had no such excuse last year . . . Has lost velocity and some say he doesn't have the proper makeup to be a winner . . . Allowed 209 hits in 186⅔ innings on way to 8-17 mark . . . Led majors in losses . . . Right-handers batted alarming .333 against him . . . Still has time on his side, however . . . Earned $1,345,000 in 1992 . . . Mariners' second-round pick in 1986 draft . . . Born May 18, 1965, in Kinnelon, N.J.

Year	Club	G	IP	W	L	Pct.	SO	BB	H	ERA
1988	Seattle	6	41⅔	2	3	.400	36	12	35	3.24
1989	Seattle	17	113⅓	9	5	.643	75	32	103	3.18
1990	Seattle	33	236	18	9	.667	211	68	205	3.24
1991	Seattle	27	174⅔	8	8	.500	143	56	182	3.81
1992	Seattle	31	186⅔	8	17	.320	112	57	209	4.82
	Totals	144	752⅓	45	42	.517	577	225	734	3.76

NORM CHARLTON 30 6-3 200 Bats S Throws L

Acquired from Reds at Mariner manager Lou Piniella's urging last winter in deal for Kevin Mitchell . . . Led Reds in saves (26) and games . . . Had only three career saves prior to last season . . . Began like a rocket and finished like a dud . . . Piled up 21 saves and 3-1 record before All-Star break . . . Spent two weeks on sidelines in September with shoulder tendinitis

. . . Earned $1.1 million last season . . . Born Jan. 6, 1963, in Ft. Polk, La. . . . Earned All-America honors at Rice, where he graduated with a triple major in political science, religion and physical education . . . Acquired by Reds from Montreal with Tim Barker for Wayne Krenchicki, prior to 1986 season . . . Expos' first-round pick in June 1984 draft.

Year	Club	G	IP	W	L	Pct.	SO	BB	H	ERA
1988	Cincinnati	10	61⅓	4	5	.444	39	20	60	3.96
1989	Cincinnati	69	95⅓	8	3	.727	98	40	67	2.93
1990	Cincinnati	56	154⅓	12	9	.571	117	70	131	2.74
1991	Cincinnati	39	108⅓	3	5	.375	77	34	92	2.91
1992	Cincinnati	64	81⅓	4	2	.667	90	26	79	2.99
	Totals.	238	500⅔	31	24	.564	421	190	429	3.00

MIKE SCHOOLER 30 6-3 220 Bats R Throws R

Hasn't been right since end of 1990 season, when shoulder troubles began . . . Another incomplete season has left future in question and prompted trade for Norm Charlton . . . Had all 13 of his saves by June 17, but had blown four opportunities and lost five games by then . . . Lost closer's role by All-Star break . . . Pitched only 16 innings in second half . . . Saved 30 games in 1989 and 33 games in 1990 . . . Set AL record for fastest ascent to 50 saves, getting there in 110 games . . . Earned $800,000 in 1992 . . . Mariners' second-round pick in 1985 draft . . . Born Aug. 10, 1962, in Anaheim, Cal.

Year	Club	G	IP	W	L	Pct.	SO	BB	H	ERA
1988	Seattle	40	48⅓	5	8	.385	54	24	45	3.54
1989	Seattle	67	77	1	7	.125	69	19	81	2.81
1990	Seattle	49	56	1	4	.200	45	16	47	2.25
1991	Seattle	34	34⅓	3	3	.500	31	10	25	3.67
1992	Seattle	53	51⅔	2	7	.222	33	24	55	4.70
	Totals.	243	267⅓	12	29	.293	232	93	253	3.30

CHRIS BOSIO 30 6-3 225 Bats R Throws R

Brewer free agent landed four-year, $15.25-million contract with Mariners . . . Will try to sustain success after huge second half . . . Was 6-5 at the All-Star break, 10-1 after that . . . Became first Brewer to win as many as 10 consecutive decisions, accomplishing that from July 25-Sept. 24, a feat matched five days later by Cal Eldred . . . Boasts 24-9 mark since 1991 All-Star break . . . Totaled 200-plus innings for third time in four years . . . Underwent two knee operations in 1990 . . . Must work to control his weight . . . Fast starter who boasts 18-5 career mark in April . . . Born April 3, 1963, in Carmichael, Cal. . . . Selected in second round of January 1982 draft . . . Made $2,287,000 in 1992.

Year	Club	G	IP	W	L	Pct.	SO	BB	H	ERA
1986	Milwaukee	10	34⅔	0	4	.000	29	13	41	7.01
1987	Milwaukee	46	170	11	8	.579	150	50	187	5.24
1988	Milwaukee	38	182	7	15	.318	84	38	190	3.36
1989	Milwaukee	33	234⅔	15	10	.600	173	48	225	2.95
1990	Milwaukee	20	132⅔	4	9	.308	76	38	131	4.00
1991	Milwaukee	32	204⅔	14	10	.583	117	58	187	3.25
1992	Milwaukee	33	231⅓	16	6	.727	120	44	223	3.62
	Totals	212	1190	67	62	.519	749	289	1184	3.76

TOP PROSPECTS

BRET BOONE 23 5-10 180 — Bats R Throws R

Youngest member of first three-generation big league baseball family . . . Grandfather is Ray and father is Bob . . . Second baseman is not your typical middle infielder . . . Free swinger with power . . . Hit .194 with four homers and 15 RBI for Mariners . . . Hit .314 with 13 homers and 73 RBI for Calgary (AAA) . . . Expected to replace longtime Mariner Harold Reynolds . . . Mariners' fifth-round pick in 1990 draft, out of USC . . . Born April 6, 1969, in El Cajon, Cal.

ROGER SALKELD 22 6-5 215 — Bats R Throws R

Great prospect will try to recover from serious shoulder surgery . . . Shut down after entering spring camp with chance to earn spot in Mariners' rotation . . . Rated third-best prospect in baseball by *Baseball America* . . . Third overall pick in 1989 draft, out of high school . . . Born March 6, 1971, in Burbank, Cal.

KERRY WOODSON 23 6-2 190 — Bats R Throws R

Made major league debut July 19 . . . Had 3.29 ERA in 13⅔ innings over eight appearances for Mariners, including one start . . . Went 1-4 with 3.43 ERA for Calgary (AAA) and 5-4 with 3.57 ERA for Jacksonville (AA) last year . . . From same high school that produced Mariners' first baseman Pete O'Brien . . . Mariners' 29th-round pick in 1988 draft . . . Born May 18, 1969, in Jacksonville, Fla.

BRENT KNACKERT 23 6-3 195 Bats R Throws R
Was picked up on waivers from Mets before 1990 season . . . Spent all of that year with Mariners, going 1-1 with 6.51 ERA . . . Missed almost all of 1991 because of elbow trouble . . . Went 7-8 with 4.08 ERA for Jacksonville (AA) last year . . . Needs more time, but big leagues are in his future . . . Born Aug. 1, 1969, in Los Angeles . . . White Sox drafted him in second round of 1987 draft.

MANAGER LOU PINIELLA: Color his parachute Mariners' blue and gold . . . Tired of Marge Schott's meddling, he left Reds after three seasons, turning his back on a new deal . . . Signed three-year, $2.5-million pact with Seattle, his third managerial stop . . . Has 434-376 mark in stints in New York and Cincinnati, where Reds won 1990 world championship by sweeping Oakland . . . Doubled salary after that season and remains one of baseball's highest-paid managers . . . Reds won 90 games last season despite a series of crippling injuries . . . Frustration boiled over in late-season clubhouse fight with temperamental reliever Rob Dibble . . . If Giants had left San Francisco for Tampa-St. Petersburg, this bio might be appearing with that team . . . Born and raised in Tampa, where he was a youth league teammate of A's manager Tony La Russa . . . Posted 179-145 record as Yankee manager in 1986 and 1987, but that wasn't good enough for owner George Steinbrenner, who shifted him to GM . . . Was back in the saddle by the following June, going 45-48 after replacing Billy Martin . . . Batted .291 in 16 seasons with Yankees and Royals . . . Taken in expansion draft by Mariners, then traded to Royals . . . Was AL Rookie of the Year in 1969 . . . Born Aug. 28, 1943.

ALL-TIME MARINER SEASON RECORDS

BATTING: Edgar Martinez, .343, 1992
HRs: Gorman Thomas, 32, 1985
RBI: Alvin Davis, 116, 1984
STEALS: Harold Reynolds, 60, 1987
WINS: Mark Langston, 19, 1987
STRIKEOUTS: Mark Langston, 262, 1987

TEXAS RANGERS

TEAM DIRECTORY: General Partners: George W. Bush, Edward W. (Rusty) Rose; Pres.: J. Thomas Schieffer; VP/GM: Tom Grieve; VP-Business Oper.: John McMichael; VP-Adm.: Charles Wangner; VP-Marketing: Marty Conway; Asst. GM-Player Pers./Scouting: Sandy Johnson; Dir. Player Dev.: Marty Scott; VP-Pub. Rel.: John Blake; Trav. Sec.: Dan Schimek; Mgr.: Kevin Kennedy. Home: Arlington Stadium (43,508). Field distances: 330, l.f. line; 380, l.c.; 400, c.f.; 380, r.c.; 330, r.f. line. Spring training: Port Charlotte, Fla.

SCOUTING REPORT

HITTING: Any chance the Rangers had of contending last season evaporated when what figured to be one of the AL's best offenses proved decidedly mediocre. How did that happen? Defending batting champion Julio Franco dropped from .341 to .234 as he was limited by knee trouble to 35 games. Ruben Sierra pouted about a contract dispute and had one of his worst seasons before being dealt to the Athletics. And Rafael Palmeiro fell from .332 to .268.

So what happens now? There is plenty of right-handed power—maybe too much, given the strikeout tendencies of AL home run champion Juan Gonzalez (.260, 43, 109), Jose Canseco (.244, 26, 87) and Dean Palmer (.229, 26, 72). Ivan Rodriguez (.260, 8, 37) is a threat near the bottom of the order. But Franco's health remains in question and there are questions about who will hit leadoff and who will play center. David Hulse (.304 in 92 at-bats) will get a shot at the latter and maybe the former.

PITCHING: A bad rotation got worse with the loss of 16-game-winner Jose Guzman to the Cubs via free agency. Newcomer Charlie Leibrandt (15-7, 3.36 for the Braves) replaces Guzman, but this team needed to add arms, not break even. Beyond ace Kevin Brown (21-11, 3.32) and Leibrandt, the rotation is filled with question marks, both young and old. Senior citizen Nolan Ryan (5-9, 3.72) is effective when healthy, but he was healthy enough to pitch only 157 innings in 1992. Roger Pavlik (4-4, 4.21), Todd Burns (3-5, 3.84), Dan Smith (0-3, 5.02) and Brian Bohanon (1-1, 6.31) all figure to get their shots.

The bullpen closing duties will be inherited by free-agent signee Tom Henke (3-2, 2.26, 34 saves with the Blue Jays). Supporting him will be Kenny Rogers (3-6, 3.09, 6 saves), ex-Pirate Bob

Kevin Brown finished what he started 11 times.

Patterson (6-3, 2.92, 9 saves for Pittsburgh) and Matt Whiteside (1-1, 1.93, 4 saves).

FIELDING: Even the Rangers' only Gold Glove Award winner is flawed. Rodriguez won on the strength of his powerful arm behind the plate, but he led the league in errors. He figures to improve with better concentration. The signing of free-agent second baseman Manny Lee from Toronto should help up the middle for a team that finished dead last in fielding percentage (.975) and errors (154). Even if he is healthy, Franco is likely to be limited to designated hitting.

Gonzalez will remain in left, rather than shuffling between there and center. Canseco can play solid right when he is so moved and Palmeiro is a solid first baseman. Palmer has a very strong arm and improved dramatically in his first full season at third.

OUTLOOK: New manager Kevin Kennedy, who inherits a 77-85 team, has been a success everywhere he has been, with a no-nonsense approach. But he is saddled with a Ranger team that, barring a dramatic transformation, will be plagued by the same shortcomings as in recent years: not enough pitching and defense.

TEXAS RANGERS 1993 ROSTER

MANAGER Kevin Kennedy
Coaches—Mickey Hatcher, Perry Hill, Jackie Moore, Dave Oliver, Claude Osteen, Willie Upshaw

PITCHERS

No.	Name	1992 Club	W-L	IP	SO	ERA	B-T	Ht.	Wt.	Born
45	Bohanon, Brian	Oklahoma City	4-2	56	24	2.73	L-L	6-2	220	8/1/68 Denton, TX
		Texas	1-1	46	29	6.31				
		Tulsa	2-1	28	25	1.27				
31	Bronkey, Jeff	Tulsa	2-7	71	58	2.55	R-R	6-3	210	9/18/65 Afghanistan
		Oklahoma City	0-1	16	10	7.47				
—	Bross, Terry	Las Vegas	7-3	86	42	3.26	R-R	6-9	230	3/30/66 El Paso, TX
41	Brown, Kevin	Texas	21-11	266	173	3.32	R-R	6-4	195	3/14/65 McIntyre, GA
28	Burns, Todd	Oklahoma City	3-2	42	16	2.55	R-R	6-2	195	7/6/63 Maywood, CA
		Texas	3-5	103	55	3.84				
35	Burrows, Terry	Charlotte	4-2	80	66	2.03	L-L	6-1	185	11/28/68 Lake Charles, LA
		Tulsa	6-3	76	59	2.13				
		Oklahoma City	1-0	8	0	1.13				
32	Fajardo, Hector	Gulf Coast	0-1	6	9	5.68	R-R	6-4	200	11/6/70 Mexico
		Charlotte	2-2	23	12	2.78				
		Tulsa	2-1	25	26	2.16				
		Oklahoma City	1-0	7	6	0.00				
—	Gomez, Pat	Greenville	7-0	48	38	1.13	L-L	5-11	185	3/17/68 Roseville, TX
		Richmond	3-5	71	48	5.45				
50	Henke, Tom	Toronto	3-2	56	46	2.26	R-R	6-5	225	12/21/57 Kansas City, MO
—	Leibrandt, Charlie	Atlanta	15-7	193	104	3.36	R-L	6-3	200	10/4/56 Chicago, IL
49	Leon, Danny	Charlotte	0-0	9	7	1.93	R-R	6-1	175	4/3/67 Venezuela
		Tulsa	5-0	30	34	0.60				
		Texas	1-1	18	15	5.89				
		Oklahoma City	1-0	5	4	0.00				
47	Manuel, Barry	Oklahoma City	1-8	27	11	5.27	R-R	5-11	185	8/12/65 Mamou, LA
		Texas	1-0	6	9	4.76				
		Tulsa	2-0	27	28	4.00				
48	Nen, Robb	Tulsa	1-1	25	20	2.16	R-R	6-4	200	11/28/69 San Pedro, CA
—	Patterson, Bob	Pittsburgh	6-3	65	43	2.92	R-L	6-2	192	5/16/59 Jacksonville, FL
59	Pavlik, Roger	Oklahoma City	7-5	118	104	2.98	R-R	6-2	220	10/4/67 Houston, TX
		Texas	4-4	62	45	4.21				
37	Rogers, Kenny	Texas	3-6	79	70	3.09	L-L	6-1	205	11/10/64 Savannah, GA
34	Ryan, Nolan	Texas	5-9	157	157	3.72	R-R	6-2	215	1/31/47 Refugio, TX
38	Smith, Dan	Tulsa	11-7	146	122	2.52	L-L	6-5	190	8/20/69 St. Paul, MN
		Texas	0-3	14	5	5.02				
46	Whiteside, Matt	Tulsa	0-1	34	30	2.41	R-R	6-0	185	8/8/67 Sikeston, MO
		Oklahoma City	1-0	11	13	0.79				
		Texas	1-1	28	13	1.93				

CATCHERS

No.	Name	1992 Club	H	HR	RBI	Pct.	B-T	Ht.	Wt.	Born
12	Petralli, Geno	Texas	38	1	18	.198	S-R	6-1	190	9/25/59 Sacramento, CA
7	Rodriguez, Ivan	Texas	109	8	37	.260	R-R	5-9	210	11/30/71 Puerto Rico
24	Stephens, Ray	Scranton	9	1	2	.205	R-R	6-0	190	9/22/62 Houston, TX
		Oklahoma City	58	6	32	.304				
		Texas	2	0	0	.154				

INFIELDERS

No.	Name	1992 Club	H	HR	RBI	Pct.	B-T	Ht.	Wt.	Born
54	Colon, Cris	Tulsa	109	1	44	.263	S-R	6-2	190	1/3/89 Venezuela
		Texas	6	0	1	.167				
14	Franco, Julio	Texas	25	2	8	.234	R-R	6-1	205	8/23/61 Dominican Republic
1	Frye, Jeff	Oklahoma City	101	2	28	.300	R-R	5-9	165	8/31/66 Oakland, CA
		Texas	51	1	12	.256				
9	Huson, Jeff	Texas	83	4	24	.261	L-R	6-3	180	8/15/64 Scottsdale, AZ
4	Lee, Manuel	Toronto	104	3	39	.263	S-R	5-9	166	6/17/65 Dominican Republic
39	Maurer, Rob	Oklahoma City	142	10	82	.288	L-L	6-3	210	1/7/67 Evansville, IN
		Texas	2	0	1	.222				
25	Palmeiro, Rafael	Texas	163	22	85	.268	L-L	6-0	190	9/24/64 Cuba
16	Palmer, Dean	Texas	124	26	72	.229	R-R	6-1	190	12/27/68 Tallahassee, FL
30	Shave, Jon	Tulsa	130	2	36	.287	R-R	6-0	185	11/4/67 Waycross, GA

OUTFIELDERS

No.	Name	1992 Club	H	HR	RBI	Pct.	B-T	Ht.	Wt.	Born
33	Canseco, Jose	Oak.-Tex.	107	26	87	.244	R-R	6-4	240	7/2/64 Cuba
—	Dascenzo, Doug	Chicago (NL)	96	0	20	.255	S-L	5-8	160	6/30/64 Cleveland, OH
19	Gonzalez, Juan	Texas	152	43	109	.260	R-R	6-3	220	10/16/69 Puerto Rico
18	Harris, Donald	Tulsa	77	11	39	.254	R-R	6-1	185	11/12/67 Waco, TX
		Texas	6	0	1	.182				
15	Hulse, David	Tulsa	101	3	20	.285	L-L	5-11	170	2/25/68 San Angelo, TX
		Oklahoma City	7	0	3	.233				
		Texas	28	0	2	.304				
17	Miller, Keith	Oklahoma City	118	7	56	.257	S-R	5-11	175	3/7/63 Dallas, TX
53	Peltier, Dan	Oklahoma City	133	7	53	.296	L-L	6-1	200	6/30/68 Clifton Park, NY
		Texas	4	0	2	.167				

RANGER PROFILES

JOSE CANSECO 28 6-4 240 **Bats R Throws R**

It took Ruben Sierra, Jeff Russell, Bobby Witt and $450,000 to bring one of game's icons to Texas from Oakland last Aug. 31 . . . Back and shoulder problems limited right fielder to 119 games in 1992 and his worst totals except for injury-filled 1989 season . . . His running days are over as he stole only six bases . . . Remains only 40-homer, 40-steal man in history . . . Earned $4.3 million in 1992, part of five-year, $23.5-million deal that extends through 1995 . . . He and Rafael Palmeiro are Cuban-born and Miami-reared Rangers . . . Born July 2, 1964, in Havana, a minute or so after twin brother Ozzie, an outfielder in the Cards organization . . . Oakland drafted him out of high school in 15th round in 1982.

Year	Club	Pos.	G	AB	R	H	2B	3B	HR	RBI	SB	Avg.
1985	Oakland	OF	29	96	16	29	3	0	5	13	1	.302
1986	Oakland	OF	157	600	85	144	29	1	33	117	15	.240
1987	Oakland	OF	159	630	81	162	35	3	31	113	15	.257
1988	Oakland	OF	158	610	120	187	34	0	42	124	40	.307
1989	Oakland	OF	65	227	40	61	9	1	17	57	6	.269
1990	Oakland	OF	131	481	83	132	14	2	37	101	19	.274
1991	Oakland	OF	154	572	115	152	32	1	44	122	26	.266
1992	Oak-Tex	OF	119	439	74	107	15	0	26	87	6	.244
	Totals		972	3655	614	974	171	8	235	734	128	.266

JUAN GONZALEZ 23 6-3 220 **Bats R Throws R**

Young slugger edged Athletics' Mark McGwire for AL homer title by going deep in season finale . . . Became only the sixth player 23 or younger to win a homer title . . . Also established career high in RBI, topping 100 for second consecutive year . . . Two years ago, he became only the 18th player to drive in 100 before his 22nd birthday . . . On the downside, he went through hitting slumps and took them into the outfield, where his defense suffered . . . Expected to play only left this season after splitting time between there and center in 1992 . . . Was pulled out of games twice for questionable effort on defense . . . Jewel of Rangers' long line of Latin standouts . . . Earned

$280,000 in 1992 . . . Born Oct. 16, 1969, in Vega Baja, P.R. . . . Signed as free agent in May 1986.

Year	Club	Pos.	G	AB	R	H	2B	3B	HR	RBI	SB	Avg.
1989	Texas	OF	24	60	6	9	3	0	1	7	0	.150
1990	Texas	OF	25	90	11	26	7	1	4	12	0	.289
1991	Texas	OF	142	545	78	144	34	1	27	102	4	.264
1992	Texas	OF	155	584	77	152	24	2	43	109	0	.260
	Totals		346	1279	172	331	68	4	75	230	4	.259

RAFAEL PALMEIRO 28 6-0 190 Bats L Throws L

Like many of his teammates, he suffered through disappointing offensive season . . . His career-low average was 34 points below his career mark entering 1992 season . . . Scored 31 fewer runs and hit 22 fewer doubles than in 1991, when he established club records in both categories . . . Finished strong and approached career-high numbers in homers and RBI . . . Improved defensively at first, committing only seven errors . . . Earned $3.8 million in 1992 after winning arbitration hearing . . . Played in Miami youth leagues with Jose Canseco . . . Born Sept. 24, 1964, in Havana, a few years before his family emigrated to Miami . . . Cubs' first-round pick in 1985 draft . . . Acquired in nine-player trade that sent Mitch Williams to Chicago after 1988 season.

Year	Club	Pos.	G	AB	R	H	2B	3B	HR	RBI	SB	Avg.
1986	Chicago (NL)	OF	22	73	9	18	4	0	3	12	1	.247
1987	Chicago (NL)	OF-1B	84	221	32	61	15	1	14	30	2	.276
1988	Chicago (NL)	OF-1B	152	580	75	178	41	5	8	53	12	.307
1989	Texas	1B	156	559	76	154	23	4	8	64	4	.275
1990	Texas	1B	154	598	72	191	35	6	14	89	3	.319
1991	Texas	1B	159	631	115	203	49	3	26	88	4	.322
1992	Texas	1B	159	608	84	163	27	4	22	85	2	.268
	Totals		886	3270	463	968	194	23	95	421	28	.296

IVAN RODRIGUEZ 21 5-9 210 Bats R Throws R

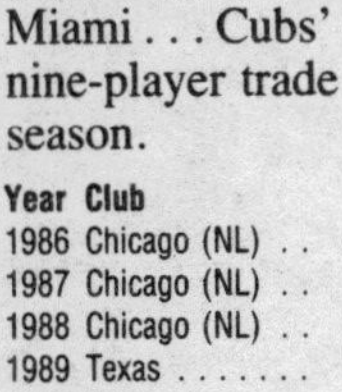

Catcher enhanced his reputation as one of the game's best throwers, leading majors in gunning down base-stealers and earning Gold Glove in his first full season . . . But inexperience and overaggressiveness led to league-high 15 errors . . . Was particularly sloppy in second half, after becoming AL's youngest All-Star . . . Showed power early in the season before series of nagging injuries cut into playing time . . . Walked 24 times in 420 at-bats after drawing only five in 280 at-bats in rookie season . . . Came to majors June 20, 1991, same day he was married at home plate of Drillers Stadium in Tulsa . . . Nicknamed "Pudge" in minors because of his stocky frame . . . Earned $135,000 in 1992 . . . Born Nov. 30, 1971, in Vega Baja, P.R., same town as teammate Juan Gonzalez . . . Signed as free agent in July 1988.

Year	Club	Pos.	G	AB	R	H	2B	3B	HR	RBI	SB	Avg.
1991	Texas	C	88	280	24	74	16	0	3	27	0	.264
1992	Texas	C	123	420	39	109	16	1	8	37	0	.260
	Totals		211	700	63	183	32	1	11	64	0	.261

DEAN PALMER 24 6-1 190 Bats R Throws R

Power-hitting third baseman enjoyed productive first full season . . . Improved batting average 42 points from 1991 to .229 and is expected to improve more as he cuts down on major league-leading strikeout total (154) . . . Promoted in June 1991, after hitting 22 homers in 70 games for Oklahoma City (AAA) . . . Regular spot at third was cleared for him with Aug. 30, 1991 trade of Steve Buechele to Pittsburgh . . . Committed 22 errors, but showed flashes of excellence with glove and possesses a powerful arm . . . Earned $135,000 in 1992 . . . Born Dec. 27, 1968, in Tallahassee, Fla. . . . Sleeper as Rangers' third-round pick in 1986 draft.

Year	Club	Pos.	G	AB	R	H	2B	3B	HR	RBI	SB	Avg.
1989	Texas	3B-SS-OF	16	19	0	2	2	0	0	1	0	.105
1991	Texas	3B-OF	81	268	38	50	9	2	15	37	0	.187
1992	Texas	3B	152	541	74	124	25	0	26	72	10	.229
	Totals		249	828	112	176	36	2	41	110	10	.213

JULIO FRANCO 31 6-1 205 Bats R Throws R

Suffered one of the biggest dropoffs ever for a defending batting champion as average dropped from .341 in 1991 to .234 last year . . . Patella tendinitis in right knee limited him to just 107 at-bats . . . Had surgery in September, but situation is believed to be chronic, leaving his status in doubt entering spring training . . . Injury could limit second baseman to designated hitter status . . . Hadn't hit below .286 in eight seasons prior to 1992 . . . Had topped .300 mark in five of six previous seasons . . . Was first Ranger batting champion and first AL second baseman to win one since Rod Carew in 1975 . . . Earned $2.45 million in 1992 and is signed through 1994 . . . Born Aug. 23, 1961, in

San Pedro de Macoris, D.R. . . . Phils signed him originally as free agent in 1978.

Year	Club	Pos.	G	AB	R	H	2B	3B	HR	RBI	SB	Avg.
1982	Philadelphia . . .	SS-3B	16	29	3	8	1	0	0	3	0	.276
1983	Cleveland	SS	149	560	68	153	24	8	8	80	32	.273
1984	Cleveland	SS	160	658	82	188	22	5	3	79	19	.286
1985	Cleveland	SS-2B	160	636	97	183	33	4	6	90	13	.288
1986	Cleveland	SS-2B	149	599	80	183	30	5	10	74	10	.306
1987	Cleveland	SS-2B	128	495	86	158	24	3	8	52	32	.319
1988	Cleveland	2B	152	613	88	186	23	6	10	54	25	.303
1989	Texas	2B	150	548	80	173	31	5	13	92	21	.316
1990	Texas	2B	157	582	96	172	27	1	11	69	31	.296
1991	Texas	2B	146	589	108	201	27	3	15	78	36	.341
1992	Texas	2B-OF	35	107	19	25	7	0	2	8	1	.234
	Totals		1402	5416	807	1630	249	40	86	679	220	.301

CHARLIE LEIBRANDT 36 6-3 200 Bats R Throws L

Braves sent him with Pat Gomez to Rangers for Jose Oliva in December . . . Sorry, Charlie . . . Even though only Tom Glavine won more games for Braves, lefty will be forever burdened by his two Game 6 relief performances in World Series the past two seasons . . . In 1991, he surrendered Kirby Puckett's game-winning homer in 11th inning. Last year, he gave up Dave Winfield's tie-breaking, two-run double in 11th . . . Is just not a reliever . . . Finished the regular season with 23 consecutive scoreless innings over his final three starts . . . Tied Phils' Terry Mulholland for NL lead with 15 pickoffs . . . Born Oct. 4, 1956, in Chicago . . . Selected by Reds in ninth round of 1978 draft . . . Acquired by Braves from Kansas City with Rick Luecken for Gerald Perry and Jim Lemasters prior to 1990 season . . . Earned $2,833,000.

Year	Club	G	IP	W	L	Pct.	SO	BB	H	ERA
1979	Cincinnati	3	4	0	0	.000	1	2	2	0.00
1980	Cincinnati	36	174	10	9	.526	62	54	200	4.24
1981	Cincinnati	7	30	1	1	.500	9	15	28	3.60
1982	Cincinnati	36	107⅔	5	7	.417	34	48	130	5.10
1984	Kansas City	23	143⅔	11	7	.611	53	38	158	3.63
1985	Kansas City	33	237⅔	17	9	.654	108	68	223	2.69
1986	Kansas City	35	231⅓	14	11	.560	108	63	238	4.09
1987	Kansas City	35	240⅓	16	11	.593	151	74	235	3.41
1988	Kansas City	35	243	13	12	.520	125	62	244	3.19
1989	Kansas City	33	161	5	11	.313	73	54	196	5.14
1990	Atlanta	24	162⅓	9	11	.450	76	35	164	3.16
1991	Atlanta	36	229⅔	15	13	.536	128	56	212	3.49
1992	Atlanta	32	193	15	7	.682	104	42	191	3.36
	Totals.	368	2157⅔	131	109	.546	1032	611	2221	3.65

KEVIN BROWN 28 6-4 195 **Bats R Throws R**

Finally fulfilled potential suggested by 90-plus-mph sinking fastball and sharp slider . . . Joined Ferguson Jenkins as only 20-game winners in Rangers' history . . . Victory total matched combined mark of previous two seasons . . . Made first All-Star Game appearance and earned victory with one scoreless inning . . . Also led league in innings and was tied for second in starts and complete games (11) . . . Was 14-3 at All-Star break . . . Best season followed step backward in 1991, when he went 9-12 with 4.40 ERA . . . Won 12 games in each of his first two seasons, both cut short by late-season arm trouble . . . Earned $1.2 million in 1992 . . . Engineering major at Georgia Tech . . . Rangers' first pick in 1986 draft . . . Born March 14, 1965, in McIntyre, Ga.

Year	Club	G	IP	W	L	Pct.	SO	BB	H	ERA
1986	Texas	1	5	1	0	1.000	4	0	6	3.60
1988	Texas	4	23⅓	1	1	.500	12	8	33	4.24
1989	Texas	28	191	12	9	.571	104	70	167	3.35
1990	Texas	26	180	12	10	.545	88	60	175	3.60
1991	Texas	33	210⅔	9	12	.429	96	90	233	4.40
1992	Texas	35	265⅔	21	11	.656	173	76	262	3.32
	Totals	127	875⅔	56	43	.566	477	304	876	3.67

NOLAN RYAN 46 6-2 215 **Bats R Throws R**

Sets yet another record with this season, his 27th. Nobody has played more than 26 . . . Holds 40-plus major league records, including seven no-hitters and 5,668 strikeouts . . . Last year, he suffered through first losing season since 1987. But like that year, he was victim of non-support as bullpen allowed six of his leads to slip away . . . Went winless in first 11 starts, but was 4-1 with 1.96 ERA in July . . . Struck out 157 in 157⅓ innings, a testimony to a fastball that still reaches 90-plus mph . . . Earned $4.2 million in 1991 . . . Has 10-year personal services deal with club following his retirement . . . Budding entrepreneur . . . Owns three ranches and two banks in South Texas . . . Signed as free agent by Rangers in 1989 . . . Son Reid pitches for Texas Christian . . . Born Jan. 31, 1947, in Refugio, Tex. . . . Mets drafted him in 10th round in 1965.

Year	Club	G	IP	W	L	Pct.	SO	BB	H	ERA
1966	New York (NL)	2	3	0	1	.000	6	3	5	15.00
1968	New York (NL)	21	134	6	9	.400	133	75	93	3.09
1969	New York (NL)	25	89	6	3	.667	92	53	60	3.54
1970	New York (NL)	27	132	7	11	.389	125	97	86	3.41
1971	New York (NL)	30	152	10	14	.417	137	116	125	3.97
1972	California	39	284	19	16	.543	329	157	166	2.28
1973	California	41	326	21	16	.568	383	162	238	2.87
1974	California	42	333	22	16	.578	367	202	221	2.89
1975	California	28	198	14	12	.538	186	132	152	3.45
1976	California	39	284	17	18	.486	327	183	193	3.36
1977	California	37	299	19	16	.543	341	204	198	2.77
1978	California	31	235	10	13	.435	260	148	183	3.71
1979	California	34	223	16	14	.533	223	114	169	3.59
1980	Houston	35	234	11	10	.524	200	98	205	3.35
1981	Houston	21	149	11	5	.688	140	68	99	1.69
1982	Houston	35	250⅓	16	12	.571	245	109	196	3.16
1983	Houston	29	196⅓	14	9	.609	183	101	134	2.98
1984	Houston	30	183⅔	12	11	.522	197	69	143	3.04
1985	Houston	35	232	10	12	.455	209	95	205	3.80
1986	Houston	30	178	12	8	.600	194	82	119	3.34
1987	Houston	34	211⅔	8	16	.333	270	87	154	2.76
1988	Houston	33	220	12	11	.522	228	87	186	3.52
1989	Texas	32	239⅓	16	10	.615	301	98	162	3.20
1990	Texas	30	204	13	9	.591	232	74	137	3.44
1991	Texas	27	173	12	6	.667	203	72	102	2.91
1992	Texas	27	157⅓	5	9	.357	157	69	138	3.72
	Totals	794	5320⅓	319	287	.526	5668	2755	3869	3.17

TOM HENKE 35 6-5 225 Bats R Throws R

Turned Blue Jay free agency into two-year, $8-million pact with Rangers . . . Consistent closer comes off another strong season . . . Matched career high with 34 saves, in 37 tries . . . Marked fourth time he saved 30 or more games . . . Owns seven consecutive seasons with 20-plus saves . . . Ranked fifth in AL in saves and eighth in games finished (50) . . . Very tough on both righties (.204) and lefties (.190) . . . Toronto's all-time leader in appearances with 410 . . . Earned three saves in ALCS and two more in World Series . . . Blew save in ninth inning of World Series Game 6, although Blue Jays went on to win . . . Born Dec. 21, 1957, in Kansas City, Mo. . . . Selected by Blue Jays from Texas as compensation for loss of Cliff Johnson prior to the 1985 season . . . Earned $3,366,667 in 1992.

Year	Club	G	IP	W	L	Pct.	SO	BB	H	ERA
1982	Texas	8	15⅔	1	0	1.000	9	8	14	1.15
1983	Texas	8	16	1	0	1.000	17	4	16	3.38
1984	Texas	25	28⅓	1	1	.500	25	20	36	6.35
1985	Toronto	28	40	3	3	.500	42	8	29	2.03
1986	Toronto	63	91⅓	9	5	.643	118	32	63	3.35
1987	Toronto	72	94	0	6	.000	128	25	62	2.49
1988	Toronto	52	68	4	4	.500	66	24	60	2.91
1989	Toronto	64	89	8	3	.727	116	25	66	1.92
1990	Toronto	61	74⅔	2	4	.333	75	19	58	2.17
1991	Toronto	49	50⅓	0	2	.000	53	11	33	2.32
1992	Toronto	57	55⅔	3	2	.600	46	22	40	2.26
	Totals	487	623	32	30	.516	695	198	477	2.64

KENNY ROGERS 28 6-1 205 Bats L Throws L

Finished last season as principal closer after departure of Jeff Russell . . . Earned six saves and posted team-leading 3.09 ERA . . . Stayed in bullpen entire season after a failed shot at the rotation in 1991 . . . Still hasn't captured consistent command of quality stuff . . . Throws fastball in low 90s, something you can't say about too many lefties these days . . . Very durable, he edged Blue Jays' Duane Ward for AL lead in appearances . . . Was also among league leaders in that category two years ago . . . Earned $620,000 in 1992 after losing an arbitration hearing . . . Thirty-seven rounds passed in 1982 draft before Rangers selected him . . . Battled arm trouble in minors . . . Grew up on strawberry farm in Plant City, Fla. . . . Born Nov. 10, 1964, in Savannah, Ga.

Year	Club	G	IP	W	L	Pct.	SO	BB	H	ERA
1989	Texas	73	73⅔	3	4	.429	63	42	60	2.93
1990	Texas	69	97⅔	10	6	.625	74	42	93	3.13
1991	Texas	63	109⅔	10	10	.500	73	61	121	5.42
1992	Texas	81	78⅔	3	6	.333	70	26	80	3.09
	Totals	286	359⅔	26	26	.500	280	171	354	3.78

TOP PROSPECTS

DAN SMITH 23 6-5 190 Bats L Throws L

Made two late-season starts following promotion from Tulsa (AA) . . . Named Texas League Pitcher of the Year and led that league with 2.52 ERA . . . Was second in league with 11 wins . . . Re-

HR king Juan Gonzalez is Rangers' latest Latin lovable.

bounded from dismal 4-17, 5.52 performance for Oklahoma City (AAA) in 1991 . . . Rangers' first choice in 1990 draft, out of Creighton University . . . Born Aug. 20, 1969, in Golden Valley, Minn.

ROB MAURER 26 6-3 210 Bats L Throws L
Highly regarded first baseman is blocked by Rafael Palmeiro . . . Hit .288 with 10 homers and 82 RBI in second year of Triple-A ball at Oklahoma City . . . Hit .222 in nine at-bats with Rangers . . . Rangers' sixth-round pick in 1988 draft, out of University of Evansville . . . Born Jan. 7, 1967, in Evansville, Ind.

CRIS COLON 24 6-2 190 Bats B Throws R
Finished season as Rangers' regular shortstop after injuries to Jeff Huson and Dickie Thon . . . Still probably a year away . . . Hit .263 with 44 RBI and seven steals for Tulsa (AA) . . . Switch-hitter who has shown ability to play second and third, too . . . Signed as free agent in October 1986 . . . Name translates to Christopher Columbus . . . Born Jan. 3, 1969, in LaGuaira, Venezuela.

DONALD HARRIS 25 6-1 185 Bats R Throws R
Has spent last two Septembers in big leagues, hitting .182 in 33 at-bats with Rangers in 1992 . . . Has great range defensively in outfield, but hasn't hit enough to stay . . . Batted .254 with 11 homers and 39 RBI for Tulsa (AA) . . . Left club in late summer for tryout with Cowboys, who picked him in 12th round in 1992 NFL draft . . . Former All-Southwest Conference defensive back at Texas Tech . . . Rangers' first pick in 1988 draft . . . Born Nov. 12, 1967, in Waco, Tex.

MANAGER KEVIN KENNEDY: Many said, "Kevin who?"

when he was hired. But those around the game who know him have earmarked this 38-year-old former minor league catcher for managerial success . . . Served as Felipe Alou's bench coach during the Expos' surprising second-place finish in 1992 . . . Had spent only six months as the Expos' director of minor league field operations before moving into the dugout . . . Enjoyed great success as manager in Dodger organization (533-373) before leaving because of lack of promotion opportunity . . . Also managed four years in winter ball . . . Received a two-year deal . . . Never spent a day in the majors before last season . . . Hit .238 in eight minor league seasons . . . Typical of his self-confidence, Kennedy said about his new role: "I don't think this is a dream come true. I believe I'm here by design, and I believe I'm here to win at the big league level." . . . Will be third-youngest major league manager this season . . . Was high school teammate of Milwaukee's Robin Yount . . . Born May 26, 1954, in Los Angeles.

ALL-TIME RANGER SEASON RECORDS

BATTING: Julio Franco, .341, 1991
HRs: Juan Gonzalez, 43, 1992
RBI: Ruben Sierra, 119, 1989
STEALS: Bump Wills, 52, 1987
WINS: Ferguson Jenkins, 25, 1974
STRIKEOUTS: Nolan Ryan, 301, 1989

MAJOR LEAGUE YEAR-BY-YEAR LEADERS

NATIONAL LEAGUE MVP

Year	Player, Club
1931	Frank Frisch, St. Louis Cardinals
1932	Chuck Klein, Philadelphia Phillies
1933	Carl Hubbell, New York Giants
1934	Dizzy Dean, St. Louis Cardinals
1935	Gabby Hartnett, Chicago Cubs
1936	Carl Hubbell, New York Giants
1937	Joe Medwick, St. Louis Cardinals
1938	Ernie Lombardi, Cincinnati Reds
1939	Bucky Walters, Cincinnati Reds
1940	Frank McCormick, Cincinnati Reds
1941	Dolph Camilli, Brooklyn Dodgers
1942	Mort Cooper, St. Louis Cardinals
1943	Stan Musial, St. Louis Cardinals
1944	Marty Marion, St. Louis Cardinals
1945	Phil Cavarretta, Chicago Cubs
1946	Stan Musial, St. Louis Cardinals
1947	Bob Elliott, Boston Braves
1948	Stan Musial, St. Louis Cardinals
1949	Jackie Robinson, Brooklyn Dodgers
1950	Jim Konstanty, Philadelphia Phillies
1951	Roy Campanella, Brooklyn Dodgers
1952	Hank Sauer, Chicago Cubs
1953	Roy Campanella, Brooklyn Dodgers
1954	Willie Mays, New York Giants
1955	Roy Campanella, Brooklyn Dodgers
1956	Don Newcombe, Brooklyn Dodgers
1957	Hank Aaron, Milwaukee Braves
1958	Ernie Banks, Chicago Cubs
1959	Ernie Banks, Chicago Cubs
1960	Dick Groat, Pittsburgh Pirates

Year	Player, Club
1961	Frank Robinson, Cincinnati Reds
1962	Maury Wills, Los Angeles Dodgers
1963	Sandy Koufax, Los Angeles Dodgers
1964	Ken Boyer, St. Louis Cardinals
1965	Willie Mays, San Francisco Giants
1966	Roberto Clemente, Pittsburgh Pirates
1967	Orlando Cepeda, St. Louis Cardinals
1968	Bob Gibson, St. Louis Cardinals
1969	Willie McCovey, San Francisco Giants
1970	Johnny Bench, Cincinnati Reds
1971	Joe Torre, St. Louis Cardinals
1972	Johnny Bench, Cincinnati Reds
1973	Pete Rose, Cincinnati Reds
1974	Steve Garvey, Los Angeles Dodgers
1975	Joe Morgan, Cincinnati Reds
1976	Joe Morgan, Cincinnati Reds
1977	George Foster, Cincinnati Reds
1978	Dave Parker, Pittsburgh Pirates
1979	Keith Hernandez, St. Louis Cardinals
	Willie Stargell, Pittsburgh Pirates
1980	Mike Schmidt, Philadelphia Phillies
1981	Mike Schmidt, Philadelphia Phillies
1982	Dale Murphy, Atlanta Braves
1983	Dale Murphy, Atlanta Braves
1984	Ryne Sandberg, Chicago Cubs
1985	Willie McGee, St. Louis Cardinals
1986	Mike Schmidt, Philadelphia Phillies
1987	Andre Dawson, Chicago Cubs
1988	Kirk Gibson, Los Angeles Dodgers
1989	Kevin Mitchell, San Francisco Giants
1990	Barry Bonds, Pittsburgh Pirates
1991	Terry Pendleton, Atlanta Braves
1992	Barry Bonds, Pittsburgh Pirates

AMERICAN LEAGUE MVP

Year	Player, Club
1931	Lefty Grove, Philadelphia Athletics
1932	Jimmie Foxx, Philadelphia Athletics
1933	Jimmie Foxx, Philadelphia Athletics
1934	Mickey Cochrane, Detroit Tigers
1935	Hank Greenberg, Detroit Tigers
1936	Lou Gehrig, New York Yankees
1937	Charley Gehringer, Detroit Tigers

Year	Player, Club
1938	Jimmy Foxx, Boston Red Sox
1939	Joe DiMaggio, New York Yankees
1940	Hank Greenberg, Detroit Tigers
1941	Joe DiMaggio, New York Yankees
1942	Joe Gordon, New York Yankees
1943	Spud Chandler, New York Yankees
1944	Hal Newhouser, Detroit Tigers
1945	Hal Newhouser, Detroit Tigers
1946	Ted Williams, Boston Red Sox
1947	Joe DiMaggio, New York Yankees
1948	Lou Boudreau, Cleveland Indians
1949	Ted Williams, Boston Red Sox
1950	Phil Rizzuto, New York Yankees
1951	Yogi Berra, New York Yankees
1942	Bobby Shantz, Philadelphia Athletics
1953	Al Rosen, Cleveland Indians
1954	Yogi Berra, New York Yankees
1955	Yogi Berra, New York Yankees
1956	Mickey Mantle, New York Yankees
1957	Mickey Mantle, New York Yankees
1958	Jackie Jensen, Boston Red Sox
1959	Nellie Fox, Chicago White Sox
1960	Roger Maris, New York Yankees
1961	Roger Maris, New York Yankees
1962	Mickey Mantle, New York Yankees
1963	Elston Howard, New York Yankees
1964	Brooks Robinson, Baltimore Orioles
1965	Zoilo Versalles, Minnesota Twins
1966	Frank Robinson, Baltimore Orioles
1967	Carl Yastrzemski, Boston Red Sox
1968	Dennis McLain, Detroit Tigers
1969	Harmon Killebrew, Minnesota Twins
1970	Boog Powell, Baltimore Orioles
1971	Vida Blue, Oakland A's
1972	Dick Allen, Chicago White Sox
1973	Reggie Jackson, Oakland A's
1974	Jeff Burroughs, Texas Rangers
1975	Fred Lynn, Boston Red Sox
1976	Thurman Munson, New York Yankees
1977	Rod Carew, Minnesota Twins
1978	Jim Rice, Boston Red Sox
1979	Don Baylor, California Angels
1980	George Brett, Kansas City Royals

Year	Player, Club
1981	Rollie Fingers, Milwaukee Brewers
1982	Robin Yount, Milwaukee Brewers
1983	Cal Ripken Jr., Baltimore Orioles
1984	Willie Hernandez, Detroit Tigers
1985	Don Mattingly, New York Yankees
1986	Roger Clemens, Boston Red Sox
1987	George Bell, Toronto Blue Jays
1988	Jose Canseco, Oakland A's
1989	Robin Yount, Milwaukee Brewers
1990	Rickey Henderson, Oakland A's
1991	Cal Ripken Jr., Baltimore Orioles
1992	Dennis Eckersley, Oakland A's

AMERICAN LEAGUE
Batting Champions

Year	Player, Club	Avg.
1901	Napoleon Lajoie, Philadelphia Athletics	.422
1902	Ed Delahanty, Washington Senators	.376
1903	Napoleon Lajoie, Cleveland Indians	.355
1904	Napoleon Lajoie, Cleveland Indians	.381
1905	Elmer Flick, Cleveland Indians	.306
1906	George Stone, St. Louis Browns	.358
1907	Ty Cobb, Detroit Tigers	.350
1908	Ty Cobb, Detroit Tigers	.324
1909	Ty Cobb, Detroit Tigers	.377
1910	Ty Cobb, Detroit Tigers	.385
1911	Ty Cobb, Detroit Tigers	.420
1912	Ty Cobb, Detroit Tigers	.410
1913	Ty Cobb, Detroit Tigers	.390
1914	Ty Cobb, Detroit Tigers	.368
1915	Ty Cobb, Detroit Tigers	.370
1916	Tris Speaker, Cleveland Indians	.386
1917	Ty Cobb, Detroit Tigers	.383
1918	Ty Cobb, Detroit Tigers	.382
1919	Ty Cobb, Detroit Tigers	.384
1920	George Sisler, St. Louis Browns	.407
1921	Harry Heilmann, Detroit Tigers	.393
1922	George Sisler, St. Louis Browns	.420
1923	Harry Heilmann, Detroit Tigers	.398
1924	Babe Ruth, New York Yankees	.378
1925	Harry Heilmann, Detroit Tigers	.393

Year	Player, Club	Avg.
1926	Heinie Manush, Detroit Tigers	.377
1927	Harry Heilmann, Detroit Tigers	.398
1928	Goose Goslin, Washington Senators	.379
1929	Lew Fonseca, Cleveland Indians	.369
1930	Al Simmons, Philadelphia Athletics	.381
1931	Al Simmons, Philadelphia Athletics	.390
1932	David Alexander, Detroit Tigers-Boston Red Sox	.367
1933	Jimmie Foxx, Philadelphia Athletics	.356
1934	Lou Gehrig, New York Yankees	.365
1935	Buddy Myer, Washington Senators	.349
1936	Luke Appling, Chicago White Sox	.388
1937	Charlie Gehringer, Detroit Tigers	.371
1938	Jimmie Foxx, Boston Red Sox	.349
1939	Joe DiMaggio, New York Yankees	.381
1940	Joe DiMaggio, New York Yankees	.352
1941	Ted Williams, Boston Red Sox	.406
1942	Ted Williams, Boston Red Sox	.356
1943	Luke Appling, Chicago White Sox	.328
1944	Lou Boudreau, Cleveland Indians	.327
1945	Snuffy Stirnweiss, New York Yankees	.309
1946	Mickey Vernon, Washington Senators	.353
1947	Ted Williams, Boston Red Sox	.343
1948	Ted Williams, Boston Red Sox	.369
1949	George Kell, Detroit Tigers	.343
1950	Billy Goodman, Boston Red Sox	.354
1951	Ferris Fain, Philadelphia Athletics	.344
1952	Ferris Fain, Philadelphia Athletics	.327
1953	Mickey Vernon, Washington Senators	.337
1954	Bobby Avila, Cleveland Indians	.341
1955	Al Kaline, Detroit Tigers	.340
1956	Mickey Mantle, New York Yankees	.353
1957	Ted Williams, Boston Red Sox	.388
1958	Ted Williams, Boston Red Sox	.328
1959	Harvey Kuenn, Detroit Tigers	.353
1960	Pete Runnels, Boston Red Sox	.320
1961	Norm Cash, Detroit Tigers	.361
1962	Pete Runnels, Boston Red Sox	.326
1963	Carl Yastrzemski, Boston Red Sox	.321
1964	Tony Oliva, Minnesota Twins	.323
1965	Tony Oliva, Minnesota Twins	.321
1966	Frank Robinson, Baltimore Orioles	.316
1967	Carl Yastrzemski, Boston Red Sox	.326
1968	Carl Yastrzemski, Boston Red Sox	.301

Year	Player, Club	Avg.
1969	Rod Carew, Minnesota Twins	.332
1970	Alex Johnson, California Angels	.329
1971	Tony Oliva, Minnesota Twins	.337
1972	Rod Carew, Minnesota Twins	.318
1973	Rod Carew, Minnesota Twins	.350
1974	Rod Carew, Minnesota Twins	.364
1975	Rod Carew, Minnesota Twins	.359
1976	George Brett, Kansas City Royals	.333
1977	Rod Carew, Minnesota Twins	.388
1978	Rod Carew, Minnesota Twins	.333
1979	Fred Lynn, Boston Red Sox	.333
1980	George Brett, Kansas City Royals	.390
1981	Carney Lansford, Boston Red Sox	.336
1982	Willie Wilson, Kansas City Royals	.332
1983	Wade Boggs, Boston Red Sox	.361
1984	Don Mattingly, New York Yankees	.343
1985	Wade Boggs, Boston Red Sox	.368
1986	Wade Boggs, Boston Red Sox	.357
1987	Wade Boggs, Boston Red Sox	.363
1988	Wade Boggs, Boston Red Sox	.366
1989	Kirby Puckett, Minnesota Twins	.339
1990	George Brett, Kansas City Royals	.329
1991	Julio Franco, Texas Rangers	.341
1992	Edgar Martinez, Seattle Mariners	.343

NATIONAL LEAGUE
Batting Champions

Year	Player, Club	Avg.
1876	Roscoe Barnes, Chicago	.403
1877	James White, Boston	.385
1878	Abner Dalrymple, Milwaukee	.356
1879	Cap Anson, Chicago	.407
1880	George Gore, Chicago	.365
1881	Cap Anson, Chicago	.399
1882	Dan Brouthers, Buffalo	.367
1883	Dan Brouthers, Buffalo	.371
1884	Jim O'Rourke, Buffalo	.350
1885	Roger Connor, New York	.371
1886	Mike Kelly, Chicago	.388
1887	Cap Anson, Chicago	.421
1888	Cap Anson, Chicago	.343

Year	Player, Club	Avg.
1889	Dan Brouthers, Boston	.373
1890	Jack Glassock, New York	.336
1891	Billy Hamilton, Philadelphia	.338
1892	Cupid Childs, Cleveland	.335
	Dan Brouthers, Brooklyn	.335
1893	Hugh Duffy, Boston	.378
1894	Hugh Duffy, Boston	.438
1895	Jesse Burkett, Cleveland	.423
1896	Jesse Burkett, Cleveland	.410
1897	Willie Keeler, Baltimore	.432
1898	Willie Keeler, Baltimore	.379
1899	Ed Delahanty, Philadelphia	.408
1900	Honus Wagner, Pittsburgh	.380
1901	Jesse Burkett, St. Louis Cardinals	.382
1902	C.H. Beaumont, Pittsburgh Pirates	.357
1903	Honus Wagner, Pittsburgh Pirates	.355
1904	Honus Wagner, Pittsburgh Pirates	.349
1905	J. Bentley Seymour, Cincinnati Reds	.377
1906	Honus Wagner, Pittsburgh Pirates	.339
1907	Honus Wagner, Pittsburgh Pirates	.350
1908	Honus Wagner, Pittsburgh Pirates	.354
1909	Honus Wagner, Pittsburgh Pirates	.339
1910	Sherwood Magee, Philadelphia Phillies	.331
1911	Honus Wagner, Pittsburgh Pirates	.334
1912	Heinie Zimmerman, Chicago Cubs	.372
1913	Jake Daubert, Brooklyn Dodgers	.350
1914	Jake Daubert, Brooklyn Dodgers	.329
1915	Larry Doyle, New York Giants	.320
1916	Hal Chase, Cincinnati Reds	.339
1917	Edd Roush, Cincinnati Reds	.341
1918	Zack Wheat, Brooklyn Dodgers	.335
1919	Edd Roush, Cincinnati Reds	.321
1920	Rogers Hornsby, St. Louis Cardinals	.370
1921	Rogers Hornsby, St. Louis Cardinals	.397
1922	Rogers Hornsby, St. Louis Cardinals	.401
1923	Rogers Hornsby, St. Louis Cardinals	.384
1924	Rogers Hornsby, St. Louis Cardinals	.424
1925	Rogers Hornsby, St. Louis Cardinals	.403
1926	Bubbles Hargrave, Cincinnati Reds	.353
1927	Paul Waner, Pittsburgh Pirates	.380
1928	Rogers Hornsby, Boston Braves	.387
1929	Lefty O'Doul, Philadelphia Phillies	.398
1930	Bill Terry, New York Giants	.401

Year	Player, Club	Avg.
1931	Chick Hafey, St. Louis Cardinals	.349
1932	Lefty O'Doul, Brooklyn Dodgers	.368
1933	Chuck Klein, Philadelphia Phillies	.368
1934	Paul Waner, Pittsburgh Pirates	.362
1935	Arky Vaughan, Pittsburgh Pirates	.385
1936	Paul Waner, Pittsburgh Pirates	.373
1937	Joe Medwick, St. Louis Cardinals	.374
1938	Ernie Lombardi, Cincinnati Reds	.342
1939	Johnny Mize, St. Louis Cardinals	.349
1940	Debs Garms, Pittsburgh Pirates	.355
1941	Pete Reiser, Brooklyn Dodgers	.343
1942	Ernie Lombardi, Boston Braves	.330
1943	Stan Musial, St. Louis Cardinals	.330
1944	Dixie Walker, Brooklyn Dodgers	.357
1945	Phil Cavarretta, Chicago Cubs	.355
1946	Stan Musial, St. Louis Cardinals	.365
1947	Harry Walker, St. L. Cardinals-Phila. Phillies	.363
1948	Stan Musial, St. Louis Cardinals	.376
1949	Jackie Robinson, Brooklyn Dodgers	.342
1950	Stan Musial, St. Louis Cardinals	.346
1951	Stan Musial, St. Louis Cardinals	.355
1952	Stan Musial, St. Louis Cardinals	.336
1953	Carl Furillo, Brooklyn Dodgers	.344
1954	Willie Mays, New York Giants	.345
1955	Richie Ashburn, Philadelphia Phillies	.338
1956	Hank Aaron, Milwaukee Braves	.328
1957	Stan Musial, St. Louis Cardinals	.351
1958	Richie Ashburn, Philadelphia Phillies	.350
1959	Hank Aaron, Milwaukee Braves	.328
1960	Dick Groat, Pittsburgh Pirates	.325
1961	Roberto Clemente, Pittsburgh Pirates	.351
1962	Tommy Davis, Los Angeles Dodgers	.346
1963	Tommy Davis, Los Angeles Dodgers	.326
1964	Roberto Clemente, Pittsburgh Pirates	.339
1965	Roberto Clemente, Pittsburgh Pirates	.329
1966	Matty Alou, Pittsburgh Pirates	.342
1967	Roberto Clemente, Pittsburgh Pirates	.357
1968	Pete Rose, Cincinnati Reds	.335
1969	Pete Rose, Cincinnati Reds	.348
1970	Rico Carty, Atlanta Braves	.366
1971	Joe Torre, St. Louis Cardinals	.363
1972	Billy Williams, Chicago Cubs	.333
1973	Pete Rose, Cincinnati Reds	.338

Year	Player, Club	Avg.
1974	Ralph Garr, Atlanta Braves	.353
1975	Bill Madlock, Chicago Cubs	.354
1976	Bill Madlock, Chicago Cubs	.339
1977	Dave Parker, Pittsburgh Pirates	.338
1978	Dave Parker, Pittsburgh Pirates	.334
1979	Keith Hernandez, St. Louis Cardinals	.344
1980	Bill Buckner, Chicago Cubs	.324
1981	Bill Madlock, Pittsburgh Pirates	.341
1982	Al Oliver, Montreal Expos	.331
1983	Bill Madlock, Pittsburgh Pirates	.323
1984	Tony Gwynn, San Diego Padres	.351
1985	Willie McGee, St. Louis Cardinals	.353
1986	Tim Raines, Montreal Expos	.334
1987	Tony Gwynn, San Diego Padres	.370
1988	Tony Gwynn, San Diego Padres	.313
1989	Tony Gwynn, San Diego Padres	.336
1990	Willie McGee, St. Louis Cardinals	.335
1991	Terry Pendleton, Atlanta Braves	.319
1992	Gary Sheffield, San Diego Padres	.330

NATIONAL LEAGUE
Home Run Leaders

Year	Player, Club	HRs
1900	Herman Long, Boston Nationals	12
1901	Sam Crawford, Cincinnati Reds	16
1902	Tom Leach, Pittsburgh Pirates	6
1903	Jim Sheckard, Brooklyn Dodgers	9
1904	Harry Lumley, Brooklyn Dodgers	9
1905	Fred Odwell, Cincinnati Reds	9
1906	Tim Jordan, Brooklyn Dodgers	12
1907	Dave Brain, Boston Nationals	10
1908	Tim Jordan, Brooklyn Dodgers	12
1909	Jim Murray, New York Giants	7
1910	Fred Beck, Boston Nationals	10
	Frank Schulte, Chicago Cubs	10
1911	Frank Schulte, Chicago Cubs	21
1912	Heinie Zimmerman, Chicago Cubs	14
1913	Gavvy Cravath, Philadelphia Phillies	19
1914	Gavvy Cravath, Philadelphia Phillies	19
1915	Gavvy Cravath, Philadelphia Phillies	24

Year	Player, Club	HRs
1916	Dave Robertson, New York Giants	12
	Cy Williams, Chicago Cubs	12
1917	Gavvy Cravath, Philadelphia Phillies	12
	Dave Robertson, New York Giants	12
1918	Gavvy Cravath, Philadelphia Phillies	8
1919	Gavvy Cravath, Philadelphia Phillies	12
1920	Cy Williams, Philadelphia Phillies	15
1921	George Kelly, New York Giants	23
1922	Rogers Hornsby, St. Louis Cardinals	42
1923	Cy Williams, Philadelphia Phillies	41
1924	Jack Fournier, Brooklyn Dodgers	27
1925	Rogers Hornsby, St. Louis Cardinals	39
1926	Hack Wilson, Chicago Cubs	21
1927	Cy Williams, Philadelphia Phillies	30
	Hack Wilson, Chicago Cubs	30
1928	Jim Bottomley, St. Louis Cardinals	31
	Hack Wilson, Chicago Cubs	31
1929	Chuck Klein, Philadelphia Phillies	43
1930	Hack Wilson, Chicago Cubs	56
1931	Chuck Klein, Philadelphia Phillies	31
1932	Chuck Klein, Philadelphia Phillies	38
	Mel Ott, New York Giants	38
1933	Chuck Klein, Philadelphia Phillies	28
1934	Rip Collins, St. Louis Cardinals	35
	Mel Ott, New York Giants	35
1935	Wally Berger, Boston Braves	34
1936	Mel Ott, New York Giants	33
1937	Joe Medwick, St. Louis Cardinals	31
	Mel Ott, New York Giants	31
1938	Mel Ott, New York Giants	36
1939	Johnny Mize, St. Louis Cardinals	28
1940	Johnny Mize, St. Louis Cardinals	43
1941	Dolph Camilli, Brooklyn Dodgers	34
1942	Mel Ott, New York Giants	30
1943	Bill Nicholson, Chicago Cubs	29
1944	Bill Nicholson, Chicago Cubs	33
1945	Tommy Holmes, Boston Braves	28
1946	Ralph Kiner, Pittsburgh Pirates	23
1947	Ralph Kiner, Pittsburgh Pirates	51
	Johnny Mize, New York Giants	51
1948	Ralph Kiner, Pittsburgh Pirates	40
	Johnny Mize, New York Giants	40
1949	Ralph Kiner, Pittsburgh Pirates	54

Year	Player, Club	HRs
1950	Ralph Kiner, Pittsburgh Pirates	47
1951	Ralph Kiner, Pittsburgh Pirates	42
1952	Ralph Kiner, Pittsburgh Pirates	37
	Hank Sauer, Chicago Cubs	37
1953	Eddie Mathews, Milwaukee Braves	47
1954	Ted Kluszewski, Cincinnati Reds	49
1955	Willie Mays, New York Giants	51
1956	Duke Snider, Brooklyn Dodgers	43
1957	Hank Aaron, Milwaukee Braves	44
1958	Ernie Banks, Chicago Cubs	47
1959	Eddie Mathews, Milwaukee Braves	46
1960	Ernie Banks, Chicago Cubs	41
1961	Orlando Cepeda, San Francisco Giants	46
1962	Willie Mays, San Francisco Giants	49
1963	Hank Aaron, Milwaukee Braves	44
	Willie McCovey, San Francisco Giants	44
1964	Willie Mays, San Francisco Giants	47
1965	Willie Mays, San Francisco Giants	52
1966	Hank Aaron, Atlanta Braves	44
1967	Hank Aaron, Atlanta Braves	39
1968	Willie McCovey, San Francisco Giants	36
1969	Willie McCovey, San Francisco Giants	45
1970	Johnny Bench, Cincinnati Reds	45
1971	Willie Stargell, Pittsburgh Pirates	48
1972	Johnny Bench, Cincinnati Reds	40
1973	Willie Stargell, Pittsburgh Pirates	44
1974	Mike Schmidt, Philadelphia Phillies	36
1975	Mike Schmidt, Philadelphia Phillies	38
1976	Mike Schmidt, Philadelphia Phillies	38
1977	George Foster, Cincinnati Reds	52
1978	George Foster, Cincinnati Reds	40
1979	Dave Kingman, Chicago Cubs	48
1980	Mike Schmidt, Philadelphia Phillies	48
1981	Mike Schmidt, Philadelphia Phillies	31
1982	Dave Kingman, New York Mets	37
1983	Mike Schmidt, Philadelphia Phillies	40
1984	Mike Schmidt, Philadelphia Phillies	36
1984	Dale Murphy, Atlanta Braves	36
1985	Dale Murphy, Atlanta Braves	37
1986	Mike Schmidt, Philadelphia Phillies	37
1987	Andre Dawson, Chicago Cubs	49
1988	Darryl Strawberry, New York Mets	39
1989	Kevin Mitchell, San Francisco Giants	47

Year	Player, Club	HRs
1990	Ryne Sandberg, Chicago Cubs	40
1991	Howard Johnson, New York Mets	38
1992	Fred McGriff, San Diego Padres	35

AMERICAN LEAGUE
Home Run Leaders

Year	Player, Club	HRs
1901	Napoleon Lajoie, Philadelphia Athletics	13
1902	Ralph Seybold, Philadelphia Athletics	16
1903	John Freeman, Boston Pilgrims	13
1904	Harry Davis, Philadelphia Athletics	10
1905	Harry Davis, Philadelphia Athletics	8
1906	Harry Davis, Philadelphia Athletics	12
1907	Harry Davis, Philadelphia Athletics	8
1908	Sam Crawford, Detroit Tigers	7
1909	Ty Cobb, Detroit Tigers	9
1910	Garland Stahl, Boston Red Sox	10
1911	Frank (Home Run) Baker, Philadelphia Athletics	9
1912	Frank (Home Run) Baker, Philadelphia Athletics	10
1913	Frank (Home Run) Baker, Philadelphia Athletics	12
1914	Frank (Home Run) Baker, Philadelphia Athletics	8
	Sam Crawford, Detroit Tigers	8
1915	Bob Roth, Cleveland Indians	7
1916	Wally Pipp, New York Yankees	12
1917	Wally Pipp, New York Yankees	9
1918	Babe Ruth, Boston Red Sox	11
	Clarence Walker, Philadelphia Athletics	11
1919	Babe Ruth, Boston Red Sox	29
1920	Babe Ruth, New York Yankees	54
1921	Babe Ruth, New York Yankees	59
1922	Ken Williams, St. Louis Browns	39
1923	Babe Ruth, New York Yankees	41
1924	Babe Ruth, New York Yankees	46
1925	Bob Meusel, New York Yankees	33
1926	Babe Ruth, New York Yankees	47
1927	Babe Ruth, New York Yankees	60
1928	Babe Ruth, New York Yankees	54
1929	Babe Ruth, New York Yankees	46
1930	Babe Ruth, New York Yankees	49
1931	Babe Ruth, New York Yankees	46
	Lou Gehrig, New York Yankees	46

Year	Player, Club	HRs
1932	Jimmie Foxx, Philadelphia Athletics	58
1933	Jimmie Foxx, Philadelphia Athletics	48
1934	Lou Gehrig, New York Yankees	49
1935	Hank Greenberg, Detroit Tigers	36
	Jimmie Foxx, Philadelphia Athletics	36
1936	Lou Gehrig, New York Yankees	49
1937	Joe DiMaggio, New York Yankees	46
1938	Hank Greenberg, Detroit Tigers	58
1939	Jimmy Foxx, Boston Red Sox	35
1940	Hank Greenberg, Detroit Tigers	41
1941	Ted Williams, Boston Red Sox	37
1942	Ted Williams, Boston Red Sox	36
1943	Rudy York, Detroit Tigers	34
1944	Nick Etten, New York Yankees	22
1945	Vern Stephens, St. Louis Browns	24
1946	Hank Greenberg, Detroit Tigers	44
1947	Ted Williams, Boston Red Sox	32
1948	Joe DiMaggio, New York Yankees	39
1949	Ted Williams, Boston Red Sox	43
1950	Al Rosen, Cleveland Indians	37
1951	Gus Zernial, Philadelphia Athletics	33
1952	Larry Doby, Cleveland Indians	32
1953	Al Rosen, Cleveland Indians	43
1954	Larry Doby, Cleveland Indians	32
1955	Mickey Mantle, New York Yankees	37
1956	Mickey Mantle, New York Yankees	52
1957	Roy Sievers, Washington Senators	42
1958	Mickey Mantle, New York Yankees	42
1959	Rocky Colavito, Cleveland Indians	42
	Harmon Killebrew, Washington Senators	42
1960	Mickey Mantle, New York Yankees	40
1961	Roger Maris, New York Yankees	61
1962	Harmon Killebrew, Minnesota Twins	48
1963	Harmon Killebrew, Minnesota Twins	45
1964	Harmon Killebrew, Minnesota Twins	49
1965	Tony Conigliaro, Boston Red Sox	32
1966	Frank Robinson, Baltimore Orioles	49
1967	Carl Yastrzemski, Boston Red Sox	44
	Harmon Killebrew, Minnesota Twins	44
1968	Frank Howard, Washington Senators	44
1969	Harmon Killebrew, Minnesota Twins	49
1970	Frank Howard, Washington Senators	44
1971	Bill Melton, Chicago White Sox	33

Year	Player, Club	HRs
1972	Dick Allen, Chicago White Sox	37
1973	Reggie Jackson, Oakland A's	32
1974	Dick Allen, Chicago White Sox	32
1975	George Scott, Milwaukee Brewers	36
	Reggie Jackson, Oakland A's	36
1976	Graig Nettles, New York Yankees	32
1977	Jim Rice, Boston Red Sox	39
1978	Jim Rice, Boston Red Sox	46
1979	Gorman Thomas, Milwaukee Brewers	45
1980	Ben Oglivie, Milwaukee Brewers	41
	Reggie Jackson, New York Yankees	41
1981	Bobby Grich, California Angels	22
	Eddie Murray, Baltimore Orioles	22
	Dwight Evans, Boston Red Sox	22
	Tony Armas, Oakland A's	22
1982	Reggie Jackson, California Angels	39
	Gorman Thomas, Milwaukee Brewers	39
1983	Jim Rice, Boston Red Sox	39
1984	Tony Armas, Boston Red Sox	43
1985	Darrell Evans, Detroit Tigers	40
1986	Jesse Barfield, Toronto Blue Jays	40
1987	Mark McGwire, Oakland A's	49
1988	Jose Canseco, Oakland A's	42
1989	Fred McGriff, Toronto Blue Jays	36
1990	Cecil Fielder, Detroit Tigers	51
1991	Jose Canseco, Oakland A's	44
	Cecil Fielder, Detroit Tigers	44
1992	Juan Gonzalez, Texas Rangers	43

CY YOUNG AWARD WINNERS

(Prior to 1967 there was a single overall major league award.)

Year	Player, Club
1956	Don Newcombe, Brooklyn Dodgers
1957	Warren Spahn, Milwaukee Braves
1958	Bob Turley, New York Yankees
1959	Early Wynn, Chicago White Sox
1960	Vernon Law, Pittsburgh Pirates
1961	Whitey Ford, New York Yankees
1962	Don Drysdale, Los Angeles Dodgers
1963	Sandy Koufax, Los Angeles Dodgers
1964	Dean Chance, Los Angeles Angels

Year	Player, Club
1965	Sandy Koufax, Los Angeles Dodgers
1966	Sandy Koufax, Los Angeles Dodgers

AL CY YOUNG

Year	Player, Club
1967	Jim Lonborg, Boston Red Sox
1968	Dennis McLain, Detroit Tigers
1969	Mike Cuellar, Baltimore Orioles
	Dennis McLain, Detroit Tigers
1970	Jim Perry, Minnesota Twins
1971	Vida Blue, Oakland A's
1972	Gaylord Perry, Cleveland Indians
1973	Jim Palmer, Baltimore Orioles
1974	Jim Hunter, Oakland A's
1975	Jim Palmer, Baltimore Orioles
1976	Jim Palmer, Baltimore Orioles
1977	Sparky Lyle, New York Yankees
1978	Ron Guidry, New York Yankees
1979	Mike Flanagan, Baltimore Orioles
1980	Steve Stone, Baltimore Orioles
1981	Rollie Fingers, Milwaukee Brewers
1982	Pete Vuckovich, Milwaukee Brewers
1983	LaMarr Hoyt, Chicago White Sox
1984	Willie Hernandez, Detroit Tigers
1985	Bret Saberhagen, Kansas City Royals
1986	Roger Clemens, Boston Red Sox
1987	Roger Clemens, Boston Red Sox
1988	Frank Viola, Minnesota Twins
1989	Bret Saberhagen, Kansas City Royals
1990	Bob Welch, Oakland A's
1991	Roger Clemens, Boston Red Sox
1992	Dennis Eckersley, Oakland A's

NL CY YOUNG

Year	Player, Club
1967	Mike McCormick, San Francisco Giants
1968	Bob Gibson, St. Louis Cardinals
1969	Tom Seaver, New York Mets
1970	Bob Gibson, St. Louis Cardinals
1971	Ferguson Jenkins, Chicago Cubs
1972	Steve Carlton, Philadelphia Phillies

Year	Player, Club
1973	Tom Seaver, New York Mets
1974	Mike Marshall, Los Angeles Dodgers
1975	Tom Seaver, New York Mets
1976	Randy Jones, San Diego Padres
1977	Steve Carlton, Philadelphia Phillies
1978	Gaylord Perry, San Diego Padres
1979	Bruce Sutter, Chicago Cubs
1980	Steve Carlton, Philadelphia Phillies
1981	Fernando Valenzuela, Los Angeles Dodgers
1982	Steve Carlton, Philadelphia Phillies
1983	John Denny, Philadelphia Phillies
1984	Rick Sutcliffe, Chicago Cubs
1985	Dwight Gooden, New York Mets
1986	Mike Scott, Houston Astros
1987	Steve Bedrosian, Philadelphia Phillies
1988	Orel Hershiser, Los Angeles Dodgers
1989	Mark Davis, San Diego Padres
1990	Doug Drabek, Pittsburgh Pirates
1991	Tom Glavine, Atlanta Braves
1992	Greg Maddux, Chicago Cubs

NATIONAL LEAGUE
Rookie of Year

Year	Player, Club
1947	Jackie Robinson, Brooklyn Dodgers
1948	Al Dark, Boston Braves
1949	Don Newcombe, Brooklyn Dodgers
1950	Sam Jethroe, Boston Braves
1951	Willie Mays, New York Giants
1952	Joe Black, Brooklyn Dodgers
1953	Junior Gilliam, Brooklyn Dodgers
1954	Wally Moon, St. Louis Cardinals
1955	Bill Virdon, St. Louis Cardinals
1956	Frank Robinson, Cincinnati Reds
1957	Jack Sanford, Philadelphia Phillies
1958	Orlando Cepeda, San Francisco Giants
1959	Willie McCovey, San Francisco Giants
1960	Frank Howard, Los Angeles Dodgers
1961	Billy Williams, Chicago Cubs
1962	Kenny Hubbs, Chicago Cubs
1963	Pete Rose, Cincinnati Reds

Year	Player, Club
1964	Richie Allen, Philadelphia Phillies
1965	Jim Lefebvre, Los Angeles Dodgers
1966	Tommy Helms, Cincinnati Reds
1967	Tom Seaver, New York Mets
1968	Johnny Bench, Cincinnati Reds
1969	Ted Sizemore, Los Angeles Dodgers
1970	Carl Morton, Montreal Expos
1971	Earl Williams, Atlanta Braves
1972	Jon Matlack, New York Mets
1973	Gary Matthews, San Francisco Giants
1974	Bake McBride, St. Louis Cardinals
1975	John Montefusco, San Francisco Giants
1976	Pat Zachry, Cincinnati Reds
	Butch Metzger, San Diego Padres
1977	Andre Dawson, Montreal Expos
1978	Bob Horner, Atlanta Braves
1979	Rick Sutcliffe, Los Angeles Dodgers
1980	Steve Howe, Los Angeles Dodgers
1981	Fernando Valenzuela, Los Angeles Dodgers
1982	Steve Sax, Los Angeles Dodgers
1983	Darryl Strawberry, New York Mets
1984	Dwight Gooden, New York Mets
1985	Vince Coleman, St. Louis Cardinals
1986	Todd Worrell, St. Louis Cardinals
1987	Benito Santiago, San Diego Padres
1988	Chris Sabo, Cincinnati Reds
1989	Jerome Walton, Chicago Cubs
1990	Dave Justice, Atlanta Braves
1991	Jeff Bagwell, Houston Astros
1992	Eric Karros, Los Angeles Dodgers

AMERICAN LEAGUE
Rookie of Year

Year	Player, Club
1949	Roy Sievers, St. Louis Browns
1950	Walt Dropo, Boston Red Sox
1951	Gil McDougald, New York Yankees
1952	Harry Byrd, Philadelphia Athletics
1953	Harvey Kuenn, Detroit Tigers
1954	Bob Grim, New York Yankees
1955	Herb Score, Cleveland Indians

Year	Player, Club
1956	Luis Aparicio, Chicago White Sox
1957	Tony Kubek, New York Yankees
1958	Albie Pearson, Washington Senators
1959	Bob Allison, Washington Senators
1960	Ron Hansen, Baltimore Orioles
1961	Don Schwall, Boston Red Sox
1962	Tom Tresh, New York Yankees
1963	Gary Peters, Chicago White Sox
1964	Tony Oliva, Minnesota Twins
1965	Curt Blefary, Baltimore Orioles
1966	Tommie Agee, Chicago White Sox
1967	Rod Carew, Minnesota Twins
1968	Stan Bahnsen, New York Yankees
1969	Lou Piniella, Kansas City Royals
1970	Thurman Munson, New York Yankees
1971	Chris Chambliss, Cleveland Indians
1972	Carlton Fisk, Boston Red Sox
1973	Al Bumbry, Baltimore Orioles
1974	Mike Hargrove, Texas Rangers
1975	Fred Lynn, Boston Red Sox
1976	Mark Fidrych, Detroit Tigers
1977	Eddie Murray, Baltimore Orioles
1978	Lou Whitaker, Detroit Tigers
1979	John Castino, Minnesota Twins
	Alfredo Griffin, Toronto Blue Jays
1980	Joe Charboneau, Cleveland Indians
1981	Dave Righetti, New York Yankees
1982	Cal Ripken, Jr., Baltimore Orioles
1983	Ron Kittle, Chicago White Sox
1984	Alvin Davis, Seattle Mariners
1985	Ozzie Guillen, Chicago White Sox
1986	Jose Canseco, Oakland A's
1987	Mark McGwire, Oakland A's
1988	Walt Weiss, Oakland A's
1989	Gregg Olson, Baltimore Orioles
1990	Sandy Alomar Jr., Cleveland Indians
1991	Chuck Knoblauch, Minnesota Twins
1992	Pat Listach, Milwaukee Brewers

ALL-TIME MAJOR LEAGUE RECORDS

National	American
Batting (Season)	
Average	
.438 Hugh Duffy, Boston, 1894	.422 Napoleon Lajoie, Phila., 1901
.424 Rogers Hornsby, St. Louis, 1924	
At Bat	
701 Juan Samuel, Phila., 1984	705 Willie Wilson, Kansas City, 1980
Runs	
196 William Hamilton, Phila., 1894	177 Babe Ruth, New York, 1921
158 Chuck Klein, Phila., 1930	
Hits	
254 Frank J. O'Doul, Phila., 1929	257 George Sisler, St. Louis, 1920
254 Bill Terry, New York, 1930	
Doubles	
64 Joseph M. Medwick, St. L., 1936	67 Earl W. Webb, Boston, 1931
Triples	
36 J. Owen Wilson, Pitts., 1912	26 Joseph Jackson, Cleve., 1912
	26 Samuel Crawford, Detroit, 1914
Home Runs	
56 Hack Wilson, Chicago, 1930	61 Roger Maris, New York, 1961
Runs Batted In	
190 Hack Wilson, Chicago, 1930	184 Lou Gehrig, New York, 1931
Stolen Bases	
118 Lou Brock, St. Louis, 1974	130 Rickey Henderson, Oakland, 1982
Bases on Balls	
148 Eddie Stanky, Brooklyn, 1945	170 Babe Ruth, New York, 1923
148 Jim Wynn, Houston, 1969	
Strikeouts	
189 Bobby Bonds, S.F., 1970	186 Rob Deer, Milwaukee, 1987
Pitching (Season)	
Games	
106 Mike Marshall, L.A., 1974	88 Wilbur Wood, Chicago, 1968
Innings Pitched	
434 Joseph J. McGinnity, N.Y., 1903	464 Edward Walsh, Chicago, 1908
Victories	
37 Christy Mathewson, N.Y., 1908	41 Jack Chesbro, New York, 1904
Losses	
29 Victor Willis, Boston, 1905	26 John Townsend, Wash., 1904
	26 Robert Groom, Wash., 1909
Strikeouts	
(Left-hander)	
382 Sandy Koufax, Los Angeles, 1965	343 Rube Waddell, Phila., 1904
(Right-hander)	
313 J.R. Richard, Houston, 1979	383 Nolan Ryan, Cal., 1973
Bases on Balls	
185 Sam Jones, Chicago, 1955	208 Bob Feller, Cleveland, 1938
Earned-Run Average	
(Qualifiers)	
1.12 Bob Gibson, St. L., 1968	1.00 Hubert Leonard, Boston, 1914
Shutouts	
16 Grover C. Alexander, Phila., 1916	13 John W. Coombs, Phila., 1910

WORLD SERIES WINNERS

Year	A. L. Champion	N. L. Champion	World Series Winner
1903	Boston Red Sox	Pittsburgh Pirates	Boston, 5-3
1905	Philadelphia Athletics	New York Giants	New York, 4-1
1906	Chicago White Sox	Chicago Cubs	Chicago (AL), 4-2
1907	Detroit Tigers	Chicago Cubs	Chicago, 4-0-1
1908	Detroit Tigers	Chicago Cubs	Chicago, 4-1
1909	Detroit Tigers	Pittsburgh Pirates	Pittsburgh, 4-3
1910	Philadelphia Athletics	Chicago Cubs	Philadelphia, 4-1
1911	Philadelphia Athletics	New York Giants	Philadelphia, 4-2
1912	Boston Red Sox	New York Giants	Boston, 4-3-1
1913	Philadelphia Athletics	New York Giants	Philadelphia, 4-1
1914	Philadelphia Athletics	Boston Braves	Boston, 4-0
1915	Boston Red Sox	Philadelphia Phillies	Boston, 4-1
1916	Boston Red Sox	Brooklyn Dodgers	Boston, 4-1
1917	Chicago White Sox	New York Giants	Chicago, 4-2
1918	Boston Red Sox	Chicago Cubs	Boston, 4-2
1919	Chicago White Sox	Cincinnati Reds	Cincinnati, 5-3
1920	Cleveland Indians	Brooklyn Dodgers	Cleveland, 5-2
1921	New York Yankees	New York Giants	New York (NL), 5-3
1922	New York Yankees	New York Giants	New York (NL), 4-0-1
1923	New York Yankees	New York Giants	New York (AL), 4-2
1924	Washington Senators	New York Giants	Washington, 4-2
1925	Washington Senators	Pittsburgh Pirates	Pittsburgh, 4-3
1926	New York Yankees	St. Louis Cardinals	St. Louis, 4-3
1927	New York Yankees	Pittsburgh Pirates	New York, 4-0
1928	New York Yankees	St. Louis Cardinals	New York, 4-0
1929	Philadelphia Athletics	Chicago Cubs	Philadelphia, 4-2
1930	Philadelphia Athletics	St. Louis Cardinals	Philadelphia, 4-2
1931	Philadelphia Athletics	St. Louis Cardinals	St. Louis, 4-3
1932	New York Yankees	Chicago Cubs	New York, 4-0
1933	Washington Senators	New York Giants	New York, 4-1
1934	Detroit Tigers	St. Louis Cardinals	St. Louis, 4-3
1935	Detroit Tigers	Chicago Cubs	Detroit, 4-2
1936	New York Yankees	New York Giants	New York (AL), 4-2
1937	New York Yankees	New York Giants	New York (AL), 4-1
1938	New York Yankees	Chicago Cubs	New York, 4-0
1939	New York Yankees	Cincinnati Reds	New York, 4-0
1940	Detroit Tigers	Cincinnati Reds	Cincinnati, 4-3
1941	New York Yankees	Brooklyn Dodgers	New York, 4-1
1942	New York Yankees	St. Louis Cardinals	St. Louis, 4-1
1943	New York Yankees	St. Louis Cardinals	New York, 4-1
1944	St. Louis Browns	St. Louis Cardinals	St. Louis (NL), 4-2
1945	Detroit Tigers	Chicago Cubs	Detroit, 4-3
1946	Boston Red Sox	St. Louis Cardinals	St. Louis, 4-3
1947	New York Yankees	Brooklyn Dodgers	New York, 4-3
1948	Cleveland Indians	Boston Braves	Cleveland, 4-2
1949	New York Yankees	Brooklyn Dodgers	New York, 4-1
1950	New York Yankees	Philadelphia Phillies	New York, 4-0
1951	New York Yankees	New York Giants	New York (AL), 4-2
1952	New York Yankees	Brooklyn Dodgers	New York, 4-3
1953	New York Yankees	Brooklyn Dodgers	New York, 4-2

Who could have predicted Series MVP for Pat Borders?

Year	A. L. Champion	N. L. Champion	World Series Winner
1954	Cleveland Indians	New York Giants	New York, 4-0
1955	New York Yankees	Brooklyn Dodgers	Brooklyn, 4-3
1956	New York Yankees	Brooklyn Dodgers	New York, 4-3
1957	New York Yankees	Milwaukee Braves	Milwaukee, 4-3
1958	New York Yankees	Milwaukee Braves	New York, 4-3
1959	Chicago White Sox	Los Angeles Dodgers	Los Angeles, 4-2
1960	New York Yankees	Pittsburgh Pirates	Pittsburgh, 4-3
1961	New York Yankees	Cincinnati Reds	New York, 4-1
1962	New York Yankees	San Francisco Giants	New York, 4-3
1963	New York Yankees	Los Angeles Dodgers	Los Angeles, 4-0
1964	New York Yankees	St. Louis Cardinals	St. Louis, 4-3
1965	Minnesota Twins	Los Angeles Dodgers	Los Angeles, 4-3
1966	Baltimore Orioles	Los Angeles Dodgers	Baltimore, 4-0
1967	Boston Red Sox	St. Louis Cardinals	St. Louis, 4-3
1968	Detroit Tigers	St. Louis Cardinals	Detroit, 4-3
1969	Baltimore Orioles	New York Mets	New York, 4-1
1970	Baltimore Orioles	Cincinnati Reds	Baltimore, 4-1
1971	Baltimore Orioles	Pittsburgh Pirates	Pittsburgh, 4-3
1972	Oakland A's	Cincinnati Reds	Oakland, 4-3
1973	Oakland A's	New York Mets	Oakland, 4-3
1974	Oakland A's	Los Angeles Dodgers	Oakland, 4-1
1975	Boston Red Sox	Cincinnati Reds	Cincinnati, 4-3
1976	New York Yankees	Cincinnati Reds	Cincinnati, 4-0
1977	New York Yankees	Los Angeles Dodgers	New York, 4-2
1978	New York Yankees	Los Angeles Dodgers	New York, 4-2
1979	Baltimore Orioles	Pittsburgh Pirates	Pittsburgh, 4-3
1980	Kansas City Royals	Philadelphia Phillies	Philadelphia, 4-2
1981	New York Yankees	Los Angeles Dodgers	Los Angeles, 4-2
1982	Milwaukee Brewers	St. Louis Cardinals	St. Louis, 4-3
1983	Baltimore Orioles	Philadelphia Phillies	Baltimore, 4-1
1984	Detroit Tigers	San Diego Padres	Detroit, 4-1
1985	Kansas City Royals	St. Louis Cardinals	Kansas City, 4-3
1986	Boston Red Sox	New York Mets	New York, 4-3
1987	Minnesota Twins	St. Louis Cardinals	Minnesota, 4-3
1988	Oakland A's	Los Angeles Dodgers	Los Angeles, 4-1
1989	Oakland A's	San Francisco Giants	Oakland, 4-0
1990	Oakland A's	Cincinnati Reds	Cincinnati, 4-0
1991	Minnesota Twins	Atlanta Braves	Minnesota, 4-3
1992	Toronto Blue Jays	Atlanta Braves	Toronto, 4-2

1992 WORLD SERIES

TORONTO BLUE JAYS

PLAYER	AVG	G	AB	R	H	2B	3B	HR	RBI	SH	SF	HB	BB	SO	SB	CS	E
Alomar, R	.208	6	24	3	5	1	0	0	0	0	0	0	3	3	3	0	0
RIGHT	.188	-	16	-	3	0	0	0	0	0	0	0	1	3	-	-	-
LEFT	.250	-	8	-	2	1	0	0	0	0	0	0	2	0	-	-	-
Bell, D	.000	2	1	1	0	0	0	0	0	0	0	0	1	0	0	0	0
Borders, P	.450	6	20	2	9	3	0	1	3	0	0	0	2	1	0	0	1
Carter, J	.273	6	22	2	6	2	0	2	3	0	1	0	3	2	0	0	0
Griffin, A	.000	2	0	0	0	0	0	0	0	0	0	0	0	0	0	0	1
Gruber, K	.105	6	19	2	2	0	0	1	1	1	0	0	2	5	1	0	1
Lee, M	.105	6	19	1	2	0	0	0	0	0	0	0	1	2	0	0	1
RIGHT	.000	-	13	-	0	0	0	0	0	0	0	0	0	1	-	-	-
LEFT	.333	-	6	-	2	0	0	0	0	0	0	0	1	1	-	-	-
Maldonado, C	.158	6	19	1	3	0	0	1	2	0	0	0	2	5	0	0	0
Olerud, J	.308	4	13	2	4	0	0	0	0	0	0	0	0	4	0	0	0
Sprague, E	.500	3	2	1	1	0	0	1	2	0	0	0	1	0	0	0	0
Tabler, P	.000	2	2	0	0	0	0	0	0	0	0	0	0	0	0	0	0
White, D	.231	6	26	2	6	1	0	0	2	0	0	1	0	6	1	0	0
RIGHT	.294	-	17	-	5	1	0	0	1	0	0	1	0	3	-	-	-
LEFT	.111	-	9	-	1	0	0	0	1	0	0	0	0	3	-	-	-
Winfield, D	.227	6	22	0	5	1	0	0	3	1	0	0	2	3	0	0	0
Cone, D	.500	2	4	0	2	0	0	0	1	0	0	0	1	0	0	0	0
Key, J	.000	2	1	0	0	0	0	0	0	0	0	0	0	0	0	0	0
Morris, J	.000	2	2	0	0	0	0	0	0	0	0	0	0	2	0	0	0
DH	.200	6	10	0	2	0	0	0	0	1	0	0	1	2	0	0	0
PITCHERS	.286	6	7	0	2	0	0	0	1	0	0	0	1	2	0	0	0
BLUE JAYS	.230	6	196	17	45	8	0	6	17	2	1	1	18	33	5	0	4
BRAVES	.220	6	200	20	44	6	0	3	19	2	2	1	20	48	15	3	2

PITCHER		W	L	ERA	G	GS	CG	SHO	SV	IP	H	R	ER	HR	HB	BB	SO	WP
Cone, D	R	0	0	3.48	2	2	0	0	0	10.1	9	5	4	0	0	8	8	1
Eichhorn, M	R	0	0	0.00	1	0	0	0	0	1.0	0	0	0	0	0	0	1	0
Guzman, J	R	0	0	1.13	1	1	0	0	0	8.0	8	2	1	0	0	1	7	0
Henke, T	R	0	0	2.70	3	0	0	0	2	3.1	2	1	1	0	1	2	1	0
Key, J	L	2	0	1.00	2	1	0	0	0	9.0	6	2	1	0	0	0	6	0
Morris, J	R	0	2	8.44	2	2	0	0	0	10.2	13	10	10	3	0	6	12	1
Stottlemyre, T	R	0	0	0.00	4	0	0	0	0	3.2	4	0	0	0	0	0	4	0
Timlin, M	R	0	0	0.00	2	0	0	0	1	1.1	0	0	0	0	0	0	0	0
Ward, D	R	2	0	0.00	4	0	0	0	0	3.1	1	0	0	0	0	1	6	1
Wells, D	L	0	0	0.00	4	0	0	0	0	4.1	1	0	0	0	0	2	3	0
BLUE JAYS		4	2	2.78	6	6	0	0	3	55.0	44	20	17	3	1	20	48	3
BRAVES		2	4	2.65	6	6	2	0	1	54.1	45	17	16	6	1	18	33	2

Game 1
At ATLANTA
Saturday, October 17 (night)

Toronto	000	100	000	1 4 0
Atlanta	000	003	00x	3 4 0

MORRIS, Stottlemyre (7) and Wells (8)
GLAVINE
HR: Toronto (1)-Carter; Atlanta (1)-Berryhill
Time: 2:37
Att: 51,763

Game 2
At ATLANTA
Sunday, October 18 (night)

Toronto	000	020	012	5 9 2
Atlanta	010	120	000	4 5 1

Cone, Wells (5), Stottlemyre (7), WARD (8) and Henke (S) (9)
Smoltz, Stanton (8) and REARDON (8)
HR: Toronto (1)-Sprague
Time: 3:30
Att: 51,763

Game 3
At TORONTO
Tuesday, October 20 (night)

Atlanta	000	001	010	2 9 0
Toronto	000	100	011	3 6 1

AVERY, Wohlers (9), Stanton (9) and Reardon (9)
Guzman and WARD (9)
HR: Toronto (2)-Carter, Gruber
Time: 2:49
Att: 51,813

ATLANTA BRAVES

PLAYER	AVG	G	AB	R	H	2B	3B	HR	RBI	SH	SF	HB	BB	SO	SB	CS	E
Belliard, R	.000	4	0	0	0	0	0	0	0	1	0	0	0	0	0	0	0
Berryhill, D	.091	6	22	1	2	0	0	1	3	1	0	0	1	11	0	0	0
RIGHT	.143	-	7	-	1	0	0	0	0	0	0	0	0	3	-	-	-
LEFT	.067	-	15	-	1	0	0	1	3	1	0	0	1	8	-	-	-
Blauser, J	.250	6	24	2	6	0	0	0	0	0	0	0	1	9	2	1	0
Bream, S	.200	5	15	1	3	0	0	0	0	0	0	0	4	0	0	0	1
Cabrera, F	.000	1	1	0	0	0	0	0	0	0	0	0	0	0	0	0	0
Gant, R	.125	4	8	2	1	1	0	0	0	0	0	0	1	2	2	0	0
Hunter, B	.200	4	5	0	1	0	0	0	2	0	1	0	0	1	0	1	0
Justice, D	.158	6	19	4	3	0	0	1	3	0	0	0	6	5	1	0	1
Lemke, M	.211	6	19	0	4	0	0	0	2	0	0	0	1	3	0	0	0
RIGHT	.000	-	5	-	0	0	0	0	1	0	0	0	0	1	-	-	-
LEFT	.286	-	14	-	4	0	0	0	1	0	0	0	1	2	-	-	-
Nixon, O	.296	6	27	3	8	1	0	0	1	0	0	0	1	3	5	1	0
RIGHT	.400	-	5	-	2	0	0	0	0	0	0	0	0	0	-	-	-
LEFT	.273	-	22	-	6	1	0	0	1	0	0	0	1	3	-	-	-
Pendleton, T	.240	6	25	2	6	2	0	0	2	0	1	0	1	5	0	0	0
RIGHT	.000	-	3	-	0	0	0	0	0	0	0	0	0	0	-	-	-
LEFT	.273	-	22	-	6	2	0	0	2	0	1	0	1	5	-	-	-
Sanders, D	.533	4	15	4	8	2	0	0	1	0	0	0	2	1	5	0	0
Smith, L	.167	5	12	1	2	0	0	1	5	0	0	1	1	4	0	0	0
Treadway, J	.000	1	1	0	0	0	0	0	0	0	0	0	0	0	0	0	0
Avery, S	.000	2	1	0	0	0	0	0	0	0	0	0	0	1	0	0	0
Glavine, T	.000	2	2	0	0	0	0	0	0	0	0	0	1	0	0	0	0
Smith, P	.000	1	1	0	0	0	0	0	0	0	0	0	0	1	0	0	0
Smoltz, J	.000	3	3	0	0	0	0	0	0	0	0	0	0	2	0	0	0
DH	.167	6	12	1	2	0	0	1	5	0	0	0	0	4	0	0	0
BRAVES	.220	6	200	20	44	6	0	3	19	2	2	1	20	48	15	3	2
BLUE JAYS	.230	6	196	17	45	8	0	6	17	2	1	1	18	33	5	0	4

PITCHER		W	L	ERA	G	GS	CG	SHO	SV	IP	H	R	ER	HR	HB	BB	SO	WP
Avery, S	L	0	1	3.75	2	2	0	0	0	12.0	11	5	5	3	0	3	11	0
Freeman, M	R	0	0	---	0	0	0	0	0	0.0	0	0	0	0	0	0	0	0
Glavine, T	L	1	1	1.59	2	2	2	0	0	17.0	10	3	3	2	0	4	8	0
Leibrandt, C	L	0	1	9.00	1	0	0	0	0	2.0	3	2	2	0	1	0	0	0
Nied, D	R	0	0	---	0	0	0	0	0	0.0	0	0	0	0	0	0	0	0
Reardon, J	R	0	1	13.50	2	0	0	0	0	1.1	2	2	2	1	0	1	1	0
Smith, P	R	0	0	0.00	1	0	0	0	0	3.0	3	0	0	0	0	0	0	0
Smoltz, J	R	1	0	2.70	2	2	0	0	0	13.1	13	5	4	0	0	7	12	2
Stanton, M	L	0	0	0.00	4	0	0	0	1	5.0	3	0	0	0	0	2	1	0
Wohlers, M	R	0	0	0.00	2	0	0	0	0	0.2	0	0	0	0	0	1	0	0
BRAVES		2	4	2.65	6	6	2	0	1	54.1	45	17	16	6	1	18	33	2
BLUE JAYS		4	2	2.78	6	6	0	0	3	55.0	44	20	17	3	1	20	48	3

Game 4
At TORONTO
Wednesday, October 21 (night)

Atlanta	000 000 010	1 5 0
Toronto	001 000 10x	2 6 0

GLAVINE
KEY, Ward (8) and Henke (S) (9)
HR: Toronto (1)-Borders
Time: 2:21
Att: 52,090

Game 5
At TORONTO
Thursday, October 22 (night)

Atlanta	100 150 000	7 13 0
Toronto	010 100 000	2 6 0

SMOLTZ and Stanton (S) (7)
MORRIS, Wells (5), Timlin (7), Eichhorn (8) and Stottlemyre (9)
HR: Atlanta (2)-Justice, L. Smith
Time: 3:05
Att: 52,268

Game 6
At ATLANTA
Saturday, October 24 (night)

Toronto	100 100 000 02	4 14 1
Atlanta	001 000 001 01	3 8 1

Cone, Stottlemyre (7), Wells (7), Ward (8), Henke (9), KEY (10) and Timlin (S) (11)
Avery, P. Smith (5), Stanton (8), Wohlers (9) and LEIBRANDT (10)
HR: Toronto (1)-Maldonado
Time: 4:07
Att: 51,763

OFFICIAL 1992 NATIONAL LEAGUE RECORDS

COMPILED BY MLB-IBM BASEBALL INFORMATION SYSTEM
Official Statistician: ELIAS SPORTS BUREAU

FINAL STANDINGS

EASTERN DIVISION	W	L	PCT.	GB
PITTSBURGH	96	66	.593	
MONTREAL	87	75	.537	9.0
ST. LOUIS	83	79	.512	13.0
CHICAGO	78	84	.481	18.0
NEW YORK	72	90	.444	24.0
PHILADELPHIA	70	92	.432	26.0

WESTERN DIVISION	W	L	PCT.	GB
ATLANTA	98	64	.605	
CINCINNATI	90	72	.556	8.0
SAN DIEGO	82	80	.506	16.0
HOUSTON	81	81	.500	17.0
SAN FRANCISCO	72	90	.444	26.0
LOS ANGELES	63	99	.389	35.0

Championship Series: Atlanta defeated Pittsburgh, 4 games to 3

Batting

Individual Batting Leaders

Batting Average	.330	Sheffield	S.D.
Games	162	Bagwell	Hou.
		Biggio	Hou.
		Finley	Hou.
At Bats	653	Grissom	Mon.
Runs	109	Bonds	Pit.
Hits	199	Pendleton	Atl.
		Van Slyke	Pit.
Total Bases	323	Sheffield	S.D.
Singles	143	Butler	L.A.
Doubles	45	Van Slyke	Pit.
Triples	14	Sanders	Atl.
Home Runs	35	McGriff	S.D.
Runs Batted In	109	Daulton	Phi.
Sacrifice Hits	24	Butler	L.A.
Sacrifice Flies	13	Bagwell	Hou.
Hit by Pitch	19	Hollins	Phi.
Bases on Balls	127	Bonds	Pit.
Intentional Bases on Balls	32	Bonds	Pit.
Strikeouts	147	Lankford	St.L.
Stolen Bases	78	Grissom	Mon.
Caught Stealing	24	Lankford	St.L.
Grounded Into Double Play	21	Jackson	S.D.
Slugging Percentage	.624	Bonds	Pit.
On-Base Percentage	.456	Bonds	Pit.
Longest Batting Streak	22	Bell	Pit. (Aug. 24-Sept. 17)

TOP 15 QUALIFIERS FOR BATTING CHAMPIONSHIP

BATTER	TEAM	B	AVG	G	AB	R	H	TB	2B	3B	HR	RBI	SH	SF	HP	BB	IBB	SO	SB	CS	GI DP	SLG	OBP	E
Sheffield, G	SD	R	.330	146	557	87	184	323	34	3	33	100	0	7	6	48	5	40	5	6	19	.580	.385	16
Van Slyke, A	PIT	L	.324	154	614	103	199	310	45	12	14	89	0	9	4	58	4	99	12	3	9	.505	.381	5
Kruk, J	PHI	L	.323	144	507	86	164	232	30	4	10	70	0	7	1	92	8	88	3	5	11	.458	.423	8
Roberts, L	CIN	S	.323	147	532	92	172	230	34	6	4	45	1	4	2	62	4	54	44	16	7	.432	.393	7
Gwynn, T	SD	L	.317	128	520	77	165	216	27	3	6	41	0	3	0	46	12	16	3	6	12	.415	.371	5
Pendleton, T	ATL	S	.311	160	640	98	199	303	39	1	21	105	5	7	0	37	8	67	5	2	16	.473	.345	19
Bonds, B	PIT	L	.311	140	473	109	147	295	36	5	34	103	0	7	5	127	32	69	39	8	9	.624	.456	3
Butler, B	LA	L	.309	157	553	86	171	216	14	11	3	39	24	1	3	95	2	67	41	21	4	.391	.413	2
Grace, M	CHI	L	.307	158	603	72	185	259	37	5	9	79	2	8	4	72	8	36	6	1	14	.430	.380	4
Larkin, B	CIN	R	.304	140	533	76	162	242	32	6	12	78	2	7	4	63	8	58	15	4	13	.454	.377	11
Sandberg, R	CHI	R	.304	158	612	100	186	312	32	8	26	87	0	6	1	68	4	73	17	6	13	.510	.371	8
Walker, L	MON	L	.301	143	528	85	159	267	31	4	23	93	0	8	6	41	10	97	18	6	9	.506	.353	2
Clark, W	SF	L	.300	144	513	69	154	244	40	1	16	73	0	11	4	73	23	82	12	7	5	.476	.384	10
McGee, W	SF	S	.297	138	474	56	141	168	20	2	1	36	5	1	1	29	3	88	13	4	7	.354	.339	6
Smith, O	STL	S	.295	132	518	73	153	177	20	2	0	31	12	1	0	59	4	34	43	9	11	.342	.367	10

INDIVIDUAL BATTING

BATTER	TEAM	B	AVG	G	AB	R	H	TB	2B	3B	HR	RBI	SH	SF	HP	BB	IBB	SO	SB	CS	GI DP	SLG	OBP	E
Abbott, K	PHI	L	.069	31	29	1	2	3	1	0	0	2	6	0	0	1	0	18	0	0	0	.103	.100	0
Afenir, T	CIN	R	.176	16	34	3	6	11	1	2	0	4	1	0	0	5	0	12	0	0	0	.324	.282	0
Agosto, J	STL	L	.000	22	4	0	0	0	0	0	0	0	0	0	0	0	0	2	0	0	0	.000	.000	0
Alicea, L	STL	S	.245	85	265	26	65	102	9	11	2	32	2	4	4	27	1	40	2	5	5	.385	.320	7
Alou, M	MON	R	.282	115	341	53	96	155	28	2	9	56	5	5	1	25	0	46	16	2	5	.455	.328	4
Amaro, R	PHI	S	.219	126	374	43	82	130	15	6	7	34	4	2	9	37	1	54	11	5	11	.348	.303	2
Andersen, L	SD	R	.000	34	1	1	0	0	0	0	0	0	0	0	0	1	0	1	0	0	0	.000	.500	1
Anderson, D	LA	R	.286	51	84	10	24	37	4	0	3	8	1	2	0	4	0	11	0	4	3	.440	.311	4
Anthony, E	HOU	L	.239	137	440	45	105	179	15	1	19	80	0	4	1	38	5	98	5	4	7	.407	.298	5

BATTER	TEAM	B	AVG	G	AB	R	H	TB	2B	3B	HR	RBI	SH	SF	HP	BB	IBB	SO	SB	CS	GIDP	SLG	OBP	E
Arias, A	CHI	R	.293	32	99	14	29	35	6	0	0	7	1	0	2	11	0	13	0	0	4	.354	.375	4
Ashby, A	PHI	R	.091	10	11	0	1	2	1	0	0	1	2	0	0	0	0	7	0	0	0	.182	.091	0
Ashley, B	LA	R	.221	29	95	6	21	32	5	0	2	6	0	0	0	5	0	34	0	0	2	.337	.260	6
Assenmacher, P	CHI	L	.000	70	4	1	0	0	0	0	0	0	2	0	0	1	0	1	0	0	0	.000	.200	0
Astacio, P	LA	R	.125	11	24	2	3	3	0	0	0	1	5	0	0	0	0	14	0	0	0	.125	.125	2
Avery, S	ATL	L	.171	35	76	8	13	17	2	1	0	4	9	0	0	3	0	22	0	1	0	.224	.203	3
Ayala, R	CIN	R	.000	5	9	1	0	0	0	0	0	0	1	0	0	0	0	6	0	0	0	.000	.000	0
Azocar, O	SD	L	.190	99	168	15	32	38	6	0	0	8	4	1	0	9	1	12	1	0	3	.226	.230	4
Backman, W	PHI	L	.271	42	48	6	13	14	1	0	0	6	1	0	0	6	1	9	1	0	3	.292	.352	1
Baez, K	NY	R	.154	6	13	0	2	2	0	0	0	0	0	0	0	0	0	0	0	0	1	.154	.154	2
Bagwell, J	HOU	R	.273	162	586	87	160	260	34	6	18	96	2	13	12	84	13	97	10	6	17	.444	.368	7
Bailey, M	SF	S	.154	13	26	0	4	5	1	0	0	1	0	0	0	3	0	7	0	0	0	.192	.241	0
Bankhead, S	CIN	R	.222	54	9	0	2	2	0	0	0	0	2	0	0	0	0	7	0	0	0	.222	.222	2
Barberie, B	MON	S	.232	111	285	26	66	80	11	0	1	24	1	2	8	47	3	62	9	5	4	.281	.354	13
Barnes, B	MON	L	.276	21	29	1	8	8	0	0	0	1	6	0	0	1	0	15	0	0	0	.276	.300	0
Bass, K	SF-NY	S	.269	135	402	40	108	168	23	5	9	39	1	3	1	23	3	70	14	9	8	.418	.308	3
Batiste, K	PHI	R	.206	44	136	9	28	35	4	0	1	10	2	3	0	4	1	18	0	0	7	.257	.224	13
Beck, R	SF	R	.500	65	2	0	1	1	0	0	0	0	0	0	0	0	0	1	0	0	0	.500	.500	1
Belcher, T	CIN	R	.105	35	76	3	8	12	1	0	1	4	7	0	0	0	0	28	0	0	1	.158	.105	1
Belinda, S	PIT	R	.667	59	3	1	2	3	1	0	0	2	0	0	0	0	0	0	0	0	0	1.000	.667	0
Bell, J	PIT	R	.264	159	632	87	167	242	36	6	9	55	19	2	4	55	0	103	7	5	12	.383	.326	22
Bell, J	PHI	S	.204	46	147	12	30	38	3	1	1	8	0	2	1	18	5	29	5	0	1	.259	.292	6
Belliard, R	ATL	R	.211	144	285	20	60	68	6	1	0	14	13	0	3	14	4	43	0	1	6	.239	.255	14
Benavides, F	CIN	R	.231	74	173	14	40	55	10	1	1	17	2	0	1	10	4	34	0	1	3	.318	.277	6
Benes, A	SD	R	.149	34	67	3	10	15	2	0	1	5	5	1	0	5	0	29	0	0	1	.224	.205	1
Benjamin, M	SF	R	.173	40	75	4	13	20	2	1	1	3	3	0	0	4	1	15	1	0	1	.267	.215	1
Benzinger, T	LA	S	.239	121	293	24	70	102	16	2	4	31	0	5	0	15	1	54	2	4	6	.348	.272	1
Berenguer, J	ATL	R	.000	28	2	0	0	0	0	0	0	0	0	0	0	0	0	1	0	0	0	.000	.000	0
Berroa, G	CIN	R	.267	13	15	2	4	5	1	0	0	0	0	0	1	2	0	1	0	1	1	.333	.389	0
Berry, S	MON	R	.333	24	57	5	19	23	1	0	1	4	0	0	0	1	0	11	2	1	1	.404	.345	4
Berryhill, D	ATL	S	.228	101	307	21	70	118	16	1	10	43	0	3	1	17	4	67	0	2	4	.384	.268	1
Bielecki, M	ATL	R	.125	19	24	1	3	3	0	0	0	0	4	0	0	0	0	13	0	0	1	.125	.125	0
Biggio, C	HOU	R	.277	162	613	96	170	226	32	3	6	39	5	2	7	94	9	95	38	15	5	.369	.378	12
Bilardello, D	SD	R	.121	17	33	2	4	5	1	0	0	1	3	0	0	4	1	8	0	0	1	.152	.216	0

Birkbeck, M	NY	R	.000	1	2	0	0	0	0	0	0	0	0	0	0	0	0	0	0	0	0	.000	.000	1
Black, B	SF	L	.056	28	54	1	3	4	1	0	0	2	10	0	0	2	0	16	0	0	0	.074	.089	0
Blair, W	HOU	R	.059	29	17	0	1	1	0	0	0	0	1	0	0	1	0	14	0	0	0	.059	.111	2
Blauser, J	ATL	R	.262	123	343	61	90	157	19	3	14	46	7	3	4	46	2	82	5	5	2	.458	.354	14
Boever, J	HOU	R	.000	81	7	0	0	0	0	0	0	0	0	0	0	0	0	3	0	0	0	.000	.000	2
Bolton, T	CIN	L	.000	16	14	0	0	0	0	0	0	0	1	0	0	0	0	5	0	0	0	.000	.000	0
Bonds, B	PIT	L	.311	140	473	109	147	295	36	5	34	103	0	7	5	127	32	69	39	8	9	.624	.456	3
Bonilla, B	NY	S	.249	128	438	62	109	189	23	0	19	70	0	1	1	66	10	73	4	3	11	.432	.348	4
Boskie, S	CHI	R	.185	23	27	1	5	6	1	0	0	1	3	0	0	2	0	9	0	0	0	.222	.241	1
Boston, D	NY	L	.249	130	289	37	72	123	14	2	11	35	0	4	3	38	6	60	12	6	5	.426	.338	1
Bottenfield, K	MON	S	.375	10	8	1	3	3	0	0	0	0	1	0	0	0	0	3	0	0	0	.375	.375	0
Bournigal, R	LA	R	.150	10	20	1	3	4	1	0	0	0	0	0	1	1	0	2	0	0	0	.200	.227	1
Bowen, R	HOU	R	.111	15	9	1	1	1	0	0	0	0	0	0	0	0	0	3	0	1	0	.111	.111	0
Bradley, S	CIN	L	.400	5	5	1	2	2	0	0	0	1	0	0	0	1	0	0	0	0	0	.400	.500	0
Braggs, G	CIN	R	.237	92	266	40	63	109	16	3	8	38	1	2	2	36	5	48	3	1	10	.410	.330	6
Branson, J	CIN	L	.296	72	115	12	34	43	7	1	0	15	2	1	0	5	2	16	0	1	4	.374	.322	7
Brantley, C	PHI	R	.214	28	14	1	3	5	0	1	0	1	7	0	0	1	0	4	0	0	0	.357	.267	3
Brantley, J	SF	R	.111	56	9	2	1	1	0	0	0	0	0	0	0	1	0	2	0	0	0	.111	.200	0
Bream, S	ATL	L	.261	125	372	30	97	154	25	1	10	61	3	4	1	46	2	51	6	0	3	.414	.340	10
Brewer, R	STL	L	.301	29	103	11	31	37	6	0	0	10	0	1	1	8	0	12	0	1	1	.359	.354	0
Brink, B	PHI	R	.083	8	12	0	1	1	0	0	0	0	1	0	1	0	0	5	0	0	0	.083	.154	1
Brocail, D	SD	L	.200	3	5	0	1	1	0	0	0	0	0	0	0	0	0	0	0	0	0	.200	.200	1
Brown, K	CIN	S	.000	2	2	0	0	0	0	0	0	0	1	0	0	0	0	1	0	0	0	.000	.000	1
Browning, T	CIN	L	.226	16	31	4	7	8	1	0	0	2	2	1	0	1	0	6	0	0	1	.258	.242	1
Brumfield, J	CIN	R	.133	24	30	6	4	4	0	0	0	2	0	0	1	2	1	4	6	0	0	.133	.212	0
Buechele, S	PIT-CHI	R	.261	145	524	52	137	195	23	4	9	64	4	3	7	52	6	105	1	3	10	.372	.334	17
Bullinger, J	CHI	R	.250	39	20	3	5	8	0	0	1	2	1	0	0	1	0	7	1	0	0	.400	.286	0
Bullock, E	MON	L	.000	8	5	0	0	0	0	0	0	0	0	0	0	0	0	1	0	0	0	.000	.000	0
Burba, D	SF	R	.067	23	15	0	1	1	0	0	0	1	3	0	0	1	0	8	0	0	0	.067	.125	0
Burkett, J	SF	R	.018	32	55	2	1	2	1	0	0	2	8	0	0	4	0	24	0	0	1	.036	.085	1
Butler, B	LA	L	.309	157	553	86	171	216	14	11	3	39	24	1	3	95	2	67	41	21	4	.391	.413	2
Cabrera, F	ATL	R	.300	12	10	2	3	9	0	0	2	3	0	0	0	1	0	1	0	0	0	.900	.364	0
Calderon, I	MON	R	.265	48	170	19	45	72	14	2	3	24	0	1	1	14	1	22	1	2	4	.424	.323	1
Caminiti, K	HOU	S	.294	135	506	68	149	223	31	2	13	62	2	4	1	44	13	68	10	4	14	.441	.350	11
Candaele, C	HOU	S	.213	135	320	19	68	85	12	1	1	18	7	6	3	24	3	36	7	1	5	.266	.269	11
Candelaria, J	LA	R	.000	50	0	0	0	0	0	0	0	0	0	0	0	1	0	0	0	0	0	.000	1.000	0

BATTER	TEAM	B	AVG	G	AB	R	H	TB	2B	3B	HR	RBI	SH	SF	HP	BB	IBB	SO	SB	CS	GI DP	SLG	OBP	E
Candiotti, T	LA	R	.107	32	56	3	6	7	1	0	0	1	12	0	0	1	0	9	0	0	5	.125	.123	1
Canseco, O	STL	R	.276	9	29	7	8	13	5	0	0	3	0	0	0	7	0	4	0	0	1	.448	.417	1
Carpenter, C.........	STL	R	.333	73	3	0	1	1	0	0	0	2	1	0	0	0	0	1	0	0	0	.333	.333	0
Carr, C	STL	S	.219	22	64	8	14	17	3	0	0	3	3	0	0	9	0	6	10	2	0	.266	.315	0
Carter, G	MON	R	.218	95	285	24	62	97	18	1	5	29	1	4	2	33	4	37	0	4	4	.340	.299	6
Carter, L	SF	R	.200	6	10	1	2	2	0	0	0	0	1	0	1	0	0	5	0	0	0	.200	.273	0
Castilla, V	ATL	R	.250	9	16	1	4	5	1	0	0	1	0	0	1	1	1	4	0	0	0	.313	.333	1
Castillo, B.............	PHI	R	.197	28	76	12	15	26	3	1	2	7	1	0	0	4	0	15	1	0	1	.342	.238	2
Castillo, F.............	CHI	R	.092	33	65	3	6	6	0	0	0	1	5	0	0	3	0	21	0	0	2	.092	.132	1
Cedeno, A	HOU	R	.173	71	220	15	38	61	13	2	2	13	0	0	3	14	2	71	2	0	1	.277	.232	11
Cerone, R	MON	R	.270	33	63	10	17	24	4	0	1	7	1	0	1	3	0	5	1	2	0	.381	.313	0
Chamberlain, W ...	PHI	R	.258	76	275	26	71	116	18	0	9	41	1	2	1	10	2	55	4	0	7	.422	.285	4
Charlton, N...........	CIN	S	.200	64	5	0	1	1	0	0	0	0	2	0	0	0	0	3	0	0	0	.200	.200	3
Cianfrocco, A	MON	R	.241	86	232	25	56	83	5	2	6	30	1	2	1	11	0	66	3	0	2	.358	.276	8
Clark, D................	PIT	L	.212	23	33	3	7	13	0	0	2	7	0	1	0	6	0	8	0	0	0	.394	.325	0
Clark, J	SD	R	.242	146	496	45	120	190	22	6	12	58	1	3	4	22	3	97	3	0	7	.383	.278	3
Clark, M	STL	R	.139	20	36	0	5	5	0	0	0	1	4	0	0	0	0	18	0	0	0	.139	.139	1
Clark, W	SF	L	.300	144	513	69	154	244	40	1	16	73	0	11	4	73	23	82	12	7	5	.476	.384	10
Clayton, R	SF	R	.224	98	321	31	72	99	7	4	4	24	3	2	0	26	3	63	8	4	11	.308	.281	11
Clements, P..........	SD	R	.000	27	1	0	0	0	0	0	0	0	0	0	0	0	0	0	0	0	0	.000	.000	0
Colbert, C	SF	R	.230	49	126	10	29	41	5	2	1.	16	2	2	0	9		22	1	0	8	.325	.277	1
Colbrunn, G..........	MON	R	.268	52	168	12	45	59	8	0	2	18	0	4	2	6	1	34	3	2	1	.351	.294	3
Cole, A	PIT	L	.278	64	205	33	57	74	3	7	0	10	1	1	0	18	1	46	7	4	2	.361	.335	1
Cole, V	PIT	S	.000	8	4	0	0	0	0	0	0	0	1	0	0	0	0	0	0	0	0	.000	.000	0
Coleman, V...........	NY	S	.275	71	229	37	63	82	11	1	2	21	2	1	2	27	3	41	24	9	1	.358	.355	1
Coles, D................	CIN	R	.312	55	141	16	44	68	11	2	3	18	3	2	0	3	0	15	1	0	1	.482	.322	0
Combs, P	PHI	L	.125	4	8	1	1	2	1	0	0	2	1	0	0	1	0	1	0	0	0	.250	.222	0
Cone, D	NY	L	.092	27	65	5	6	7	1	0	0	4	7	0	0	3	0	19	0	0	1	.108	.132	2
Cooke, S	PIT	R	.333	11	3	0	1	1	0	0	0	1	2	0	0	0	0	0	0	0	0	.333	.333	0
Cordero, W	MON	R	.302	45	126	17	38	50	4	1	2	8	1	0	1	9	0	31	0	0	3	.397	.353	8
Cormier, R	STL	L	.102	31	59	3	6	8	2	0	0	2	10	0	0	0	0	13	0	0	0	.136	.102	0
Costo, T	CIN	R	.222	12	36	3	8	10	2	0	0	2	0	1	0	5	0	6	0	0	4	.278	.310	0
Cox, D	PHI-PIT	R	.071	25	14	0	1	1	0	0	0	1	0	0	0	0	0	8	0	0	0	.071	.071	2
Crews, T...............	LA	R	.286	49	7	1	2	2	0	0	0	0	0	0	0	0	0	4	0	0	0	.286	.286	1

Daniels, K	LA-CHI	L	.241	83	212	21	51	80	11	0	6	25	0	2	2	22	0	54	0	2	10	.377	.315	2
Dascenzo, D	CHI	S	.255	139	376	37	96	117	13	4	0	20	4	2	0	27	2	32	6	8	3	.311	.304	5
Daulton, D	PHI	L	.270	145	485	80	131	254	32	5	27	109	0	6	6	88	11	103	11	2	3	.524	.385	11
Davis, E	LA	R	.228	76	267	21	61	86	8	1	5	32	0	2	3	36	2	71	19	1	9	.322	.325	5
Davis, M	ATL	L	.000	14	1	0	0	0	0	0	0	0	0	0	0	0	0	1	0	0	0	.000	.000	1
Dawson, A	CHI	R	.277	143	542	60	150	247	27	2	22	90	0	6	4	30	8	70	6	2	13	.456	.316	2
Decker, S	SF	R	.163	15	43	3	7	8	1	0	0	1	0	0	1	6	0	7	0	0	0	.186	.280	0
DeLeon, J	STL-PHI	R	.115	32	26	4	3	3	0	0	0	1	5	0	0	2	0	9	0	0	0	.115	.179	0
Deshaies, J	SD	L	.207	15	29	3	6	6	0	0	0	0	5	0	0	1	0	9	0	0	0	.207	.233	0
DeShields, D	MON	L	.292	135	530	82	155	211	19	8	7	56	9	3	3	54	4	108	46	15	10	.398	.359	15
Dewey, M	NY	R	.000	20	1	0	0	0	0	0	0	0	0	0	0	0	0	1	0	0	0	.000	.000	0
Dibble, R	CIN	L	.400	63	5	0	2	2	0	0	0	1	0	0	0	0	0	0	0	0	0	.400	.400	1
DiPino, F	STL	L	1.000	9	1	0	1	1	0	0	0	0	0	0	0	0	0	0	0	0	0	1.000	1.000	0
Distefano, B	HOU	L	.233	52	60	4	14	18	0	2	0	7	0	0	1	5	1	14	0	0	1	.300	.303	0
Donnels, C	NY	L	.174	45	121	8	21	25	4	0	0	6	1	0	0	17	0	25	1	0	1	.207	.275	5
Doran, B	CIN	S	.235	132	387	48	91	135	16	2	8	47	3	2	0	64	9	40	7	4	11	.349	.342	5
Downs, K	SF	R	.000	19	14	0	0	0	0	0	0	0	2	0	0	0	0	5	0	0	0	.000	.000	0
Dozier, D	NY	R	.191	25	47	4	9	11	2	0	0	2	1	1	1	4	0	19	4	0	0	.234	.264	1
Drabek, D	PIT	R	.157	35	89	5	14	17	3	0	0	6	8	0	0	2	0	28	0	0	0	.191	.176	3
Duncan, M	PHI	R	.267	142	574	71	153	223	40	3	8	50	5	4	5	17	0	108	23	3	15	.389	.292	16
Dunston, S	CHI	R	.315	18	73	8	23	28	3	1	0	2	0	0	0	3	0	13	2	3	0	.384	.342	1
Dykstra, L	PHI	L	.301	85	345	53	104	140	18	0	6	39	0	4	3	40	4	32	30	5	1	.406	.375	3
Eiland, D	SD	R	.111	7	9	1	1	4	0	0	1	2	1	0	0	0	0	4	0	0	0	.444	.111	0
Elster, K	NY	R	.222	6	18	0	4	4	0	0	0	0	0	0	0	0	0	2	0	0	1	.222	.222	0
Espy, C	PIT	S	.258	112	194	21	50	66	7	3	1	20	1	1	0	15	2	40	6	3	3	.340	.310	4
Faries, P	SD	R	.455	10	11	3	5	6	1	0	0	1	0	0	0	1	0	2	0	0	0	.545	.500	0
Fassero, J	MON	L	.143	70	7	0	1	2	1	0	0	0	1	0	0	0	0	3	0	0	0	.286	.143	0
Felder, M	SF	S	.286	145	322	44	92	123	13	3	4	23	3	3	2	21	1	29	14	4	3	.382	.330	1
Fernandez, S	NY	L	.203	32	74	8	15	18	3	0	0	0	7	0	0	0	0	25	0	0	1	.243	.203	1
Fernandez, T	SD	S	.275	155	622	84	171	223	32	4	4	37	9	3	4	56	4	62	20	20	6	.359	.337	11
Figueroa, B	STL	R	.182	12	11	1	2	3	1	0	0	4	0	0	0	1	0	2	0	0	0	.273	.250	1
Filer, T	NY	R	.000	9	3	0	0	0	0	0	0	0	0	0	0	0	0	1	0	0	0	.000	.000	1
Finley, S	HOU	L	.292	162	607	84	177	247	29	13	5	55	16	2	3	58	6	63	44	9	10	.407	.355	3
Fletcher, D	MON	L	.243	83	222	13	54	74	10	2	2	26	2	4	2	14	3	28	0	2	8	.333	.289	2
Foley, T	MON	L	.174	72	115	7	20	25	3	1	0	5	3	2	1	8	2	21	3	0	6	.217	.230	5
Foster, S	CIN	R	.200	31	5	0	1	1	0	0	0	0	0	0	0	0	0	1	0	0	0	.200	.200	0

BATTER	TEAM	B	AVG	G	AB	R	H	TB	2B	3B	HR	RBI	SH	SF	HP	BB	IBB	SO	SB	CS	GIDP	SLG	OBP	E
Franco, J	NY	L	.000	31	1	0	0	0	0	0	0	0	0	0	0	0	0	1	0	0	0	.000	.000	0
Freeman, M	ATL	R	.500	58	4	0	2	2	0	0	0	0	0	0	0	0	0	2	0	0	0	.500	.500	2
Galarraga, A	STL	R	.243	95	325	38	79	127	14	2	10	39	0	3	8	11	0	69	5	4	8	.391	.282	8
Gallagher, D	NY	R	.240	98	175	20	42	58	11	1	1	21	3	7	1	19	0	16	4	5	7	.331	.307	2
Gant, R	ATL	R	.259	153	544	74	141	226	22	6	17	80	0	6	7	45	5	101	32	10	10	.415	.321	4
Garcia, C	PIT	R	.205	22	39	4	8	9	1	0	0	4	1	2	0	0	0	9	0	0	1	.231	.195	2
Gardner, J	SD	L	.105	15	19	0	2	2	0	0	0	0	0	0	0	1	0	8	0	0	0	.105	.150	0
Gardner, M	MON	R	.140	33	50	4	7	9	0	1	0	2	8	2	0	3	0	18	0	0	0	.180	.182	2
Gedman, R	STL	L	.219	41	105	5	23	30	4	0	1	8	0	1	0	11	1	22	0	0	0	.286	.291	3
Gibson, K	PIT	L	.196	16	56	6	11	17	0	0	2	5	1	0	0	3	0	12	3	1	1	.304	.237	0
Gibson, P	NY	R	.000	43	6	0	0	0	0	0	0	0	1	0	0	1	0	3	0	0	0	.000	.143	0
Gilkey, B	STL	R	.302	131	384	56	116	164	19	4	7	43	3	4	1	39	1	52	18	12	5	.427	.364	5
Girardi, J	CHI	R	.270	91	270	19	73	81	3	1	1	12	0	1	1	19	3	38	0	2	8	.300	.320	4
Glavine, T	ATL	L	.247	35	77	11	19	22	1	1	0	7	9	1	0	3	0	10	0	0	0	.286	.272	0
Gleaton, J	PIT	L	.000	23	2	0	0	0	0	0	0	0	1	0	0	1	0	1	0	0	0	.000	.333	0
Goff, J	MON	L	.000	3	3	0	0	0	0	0	0	0	0	0	0	0	0	3	0	0	0	.000	.000	0
Gonzalez, L	HOU	L	.243	122	387	40	94	149	19	3	10	55	1	2	2	24	3	52	7	7	6	.385	.289	2
Gooden, D	NY	R	.264	33	72	8	19	27	3	1	1	9	4	0	0	1	0	16	0	0	1	.375	.274	6
Goodwin, T	LA	L	.233	57	73	15	17	20	1	1	0	3	0	0	0	6	0	10	7	3	0	.274	.291	0
Gott, J	LA	R	.500	68	2	0	1	1	0	0	0	0	0	0	0	0	0	1	0	0	0	.500	.500	0
Grace, M	CHI	L	.307	158	603	72	185	259	37	5	9	79	2	8	4	72	8	36	6	1	14	.430	.380	4
Green, G	CIN	R	.333	8	12	3	4	5	1	0	0	0	0	0	0	0	0	2	0	0	0	.417	.333	0
Greene, T	PHI	R	.125	13	24	1	3	3	0	0	0	0	0	0	0	0	0	12	0	0	0	.125	.125	3
Greene, W	CIN	L	.269	29	93	10	25	40	5	2	2	13	0	1	0	10	0	23	0	2	1	.430	.337	3
Gregg, T	ATL	L	.263	18	19	1	5	8	0	0	1	1	0	0	0	1	0	7	1	0	1	.421	.300	0
Grissom, M	MON	R	.276	159	653	99	180	273	39	6	14	66	3	4	5	42	6	81	78	13	12	.418	.322	7
Gross, Ke	LA	R	.095	34	63	3	6	7	1	0	0	0	3	0	0	4	0	26	0	0	0	.111	.149	1
Gross, Ki	LA	R	1.000	16	2	1	2	2	0	0	0	1	1	0	0	0	0	0	0	0	0	1.000	1.000	0
Grotewold, J	PHI	L	.200	72	65	7	13	24	2	0	3	5	0	0	1	9	0	16	0	0	4	.369	.307	0
Guerrero, J	HOU	R	.200	79	125	8	25	36	4	2	1	14	1	2	1	10	2	32	1	0	0	.288	.261	2
Guerrero, P	STL	R	.219	43	146	10	32	43	6	1	1	16	0	2	0	11	3	25	2	2	4	.295	.270	4
Guetterman, L	NY	L	.000	43	2	0	0	0	0	0	0	0	0	0	0	0	0	2	0	0	0	.000	.000	0
Gwynn, T	SD	L	.317	128	520	77	165	216	27	3	6	41	0	3	0	46	12	16	3	6	12	.415	.371	5
Hammond, C	CIN	L	.136	30	44	7	6	10	1	0	1	4	3	1	0	6	0	20	0	0	0	.227	.235	2

Haney, C	MON	L	.222	10	9	1	2	2	0	0	0	3	1	0	0	0	0	1	0	0	0	.222	.222	0
Haney, T	MON	R	.300	7	10	0	3	4	1	0	0	1	1	0	0	0	0	0	0	0	1	.400	.300	0
Hansen, D	LA	L	.214	132	341	30	73	102	11	0	6	22	0	2	1	34	3	49	0	2	9	.299	.286	8
Harkey, M	CHI	R	.267	8	15	4	4	4	0	0	0	0	0	0	0	0	0	3	0	0	0	.267	.267	0
Harnisch, P	HOU	R	.164	34	67	7	11	16	5	0	0	8	5	0	0	2	0	12	0	1	1	.239	.188	2
Harris, Ge	SD	R	.333	15	3	0	1	1	0	0	0	0	0	0	0	0	0	1	0	0	0	.333	.333	1
Harris, Gr	SD	R	.129	20	31	1	4	5	1	0	0	1	5	0	0	5	0	13	0	0	0	.161	.250	5
Harris, L	LA	L	.271	135	347	28	94	105	11	0	0	30	6	2	1	24	3	24	19	7	10	.303	.318	27
Hartley, M	PHI	R	.000	47	4	0	0	0	0	0	0	0	0	0	0	0	0	1	0	0	0	.000	.000	1
Hartsock, J	CHI	R	.000	4	2	0	0	0	0	0	0	0	0	0	0	0	0	0	0	0	0	.000	.000	0
Hatcher, B	CIN	R	.287	43	94	10	27	36	3	0	2	10	0	3	0	5	0	11	0	2	2	.383	.314	1
Henry, B	HOU	L	.148	28	54	3	8	11	0	0	1	7	5	0	0	1	0	10	0	0	1	.204	.164	3
Henry, D	CIN	R	.250	60	4	1	1	1	0	0	0	0	0	0	0	0	0	3	0	0	0	.250	.250	2
Heredia, G	SF-MON	R	.111	20	9	0	1	1	0	0	0	0	1	0	0	0	0	1	0	0	0	.111	.111	0
Hernandez, C	CIN	R	.275	34	51	6	14	18	4	0	0	4	0	0	0	0	0	10	3	1	1	.353	.275	1
Hernandez, C	LA	R	.260	69	173	11	45	58	4	0	3	17	0	2	4	11	1	21	0	1	8	.335	.316	7
Hernandez, J	SD	R	.000	26	2	0	0	0	0	0	0	0	0	0	0	0	0	0	0	0	0	.000	.000	0
Hernandez, X	HOU	L	.000	77	9	1	0	0	0	0	0	0	0	0	0	0	0	5	0	0	0	.000	.000	1
Hershiser, O	LA	R	.221	35	68	6	15	20	5	0	0	5	6	1	0	1	0	10	1	0	0	.294	.229	3
Hickerson, B	SF	L	.000	61	4	0	0	0	0	0	0	0	0	0	0	0	0	3	0	0	0	.000	.000	0
Hill, K	MON	R	.177	33	62	10	11	19	3	1	1	4	10	0	0	8	0	13	0	0	0	.306	.271	4
Hillman, E	NY	L	.077	11	13	0	1	1	0	0	0	0	5	0	0	0	0	7	0	0	0	.077	.077	0
Hollins, D	PHI	S	.270	156	586	104	158	275	28	4	27	93	0	4	19	76	4	110	9	6	8	.469	.369	18
Hosey, S	SF	R	.250	21	56	6	14	18	1	0	1	6	0	2	0	0	0	15	1	1	1	.321	.241	1
Howard, T	SD	S	.333	5	3	1	1	1	0	0	0	0	1	0	0	0	0	0	0	0	0	.333	.333	0
Howell, P	NY	S	.187	31	75	9	14	15	1	0	0	1	1	0	1	2	0	15	4	2	0	.200	.218	0
Hudler, R	STL	R	.245	61	98	17	24	37	4	0	3	5	1	1	1	2	0	23	2	6	0	.378	.265	3
Hundley, T	NY	S	.209	123	358	32	75	113	17	0	7	32	7	2	4	19	4	76	3	0	8	.316	.256	3
Hunter, B	ATL	R	.239	102	238	34	57	116	13	2	14	41	1	8	0	21	3	50	1	2	2	.487	.292	4
Hurst, B	SD	L	.159	33	69	2	11	15	4	0	0	1	9	0	0	3	0	27	0	0	0	.217	.194	1
Hurst, J	MON	R	.000	3	4	0	0	0	0	0	0	0	2	0	0	0	0	2	0	0	0	.000	.000	0
Incaviglia, P	HOU	R	.266	113	349	31	93	150	22	1	11	44	0	2	3	25	2	99	2	2	6	.430	.319	6
Innis, J	NY	R	.000	76	2	0	0	0	0	0	0	0	0	0	0	0	0	0	0	0	0	.000	.000	0
Jackson, D	CHI-PIT	R	.083	34	60	2	5	5	0	0	0	2	9	0	0	1	0	31	0	1	0	.083	.098	8
Jackson, D	SD	R	.249	155	587	72	146	230	23	5	17	70	6	5	4	26	4	106	14	3	21	.392	.283	2
Jackson, M	SF	R	.000	67	2	0	0	0	0	0	0	0	0	0	0	0	0	0	0	0	0	.000	.000	1

BATTER	TEAM	B	AVG	G	AB	R	H	TB	2B	3B	HR	RBI	SH	SF	HP	BB	IBB	SO	SB	CS	GIDP	SLG	OBP	E
James, C	SF	R	.242	111	248	25	60	93	10	4	5	32	0	3	2	14	2	45	2	3	2	.375	.285	3
Javier, S	LA-PHI	S	.249	130	334	42	83	105	17	1	1	29	3	2	3	37	2	54	18	3	4	.314	.327	3
Johnson, H	NY	S	.223	100	350	48	78	118	19	0	7	43	0	3	2	55	5	79	22	5	7	.337	.329	4
Jones, B	PHI-NY	R	.000	61	2	0	0	0	0	0	0	0	0	0	0	0	0	1	0	0	0	.000	.000	0
Jones, C	HOU	R	.190	54	63	7	12	19	2	1	1	4	3	0	0	7	0	21	3	0	1	.302	.271	2
Jones, D	HOU	R	.000	80	4	0	0	0	0	0	0	0	0	0	0	0	0	2	0	0	0	.000	.000	2
Jones, J	HOU	R	.167	26	36	5	6	7	1	0	0	4	9	0	0	6	0	13	0	0	1	.194	.286	0
Jones, T	STL	L	.200	67	145	9	29	33	4	0	0	3	2	0	0	11	1	29	5	2	1	.228	.256	4
Jordan, B	STL	R	.207	55	193	17	40	72	9	4	5	22	0	0	1	10	1	48	7	2	6	.373	.250	1
Jordan, R	PHI	R	.304	94	276	33	84	115	19	0	4	34	0	3	0	5	0	44	3	0	8	.417	.313	2
Jose, F	STL	S	.295	131	509	62	150	220	22	3	14	75	0	1	1	40	8	100	28	12	9	.432	.347	6
Justice, D	ATL	L	.256	144	484	78	124	216	19	5	21	72	0	6	2	79	8	85	2	4	1	.446	.359	8
Karros, E	LA	R	.257	149	545	63	140	232	30	1	20	88	0	5	2	37	3	103	2	4	15	.426	.304	9
Kent, J	NY	R	.239	37	113	16	27	46	8	1	3	15	0	0	1	7	0	29	0	2	2	.407	.289	3
Kile, D	HOU	R	.156	22	32	2	5	5	0	0	0	2	5	0	0	3	0	15	0	0	0	.156	.229	5
King, J	PIT	R	.231	130	480	56	111	178	21	2	14	65	8	5	2	27	3	56	4	6	8	.371	.272	12
Klesko, R	ATL	L	.000	13	14	0	0	0	0	0	0	1	0	0	1	0	0	5	0	0	0	.000	.067	0
Krueger, B	MON	L	.000	9	3	0	0	0	0	0	0	0	1	0	0	0	0	2	0	0	0	.000	.000	0
Kruk, J	PHI	L	.323	144	507	86	164	232	30	4	10	70	0	7	1	92	8	88	3	5	11	.458	.423	8
Kunkel, J	CHI	R	.138	20	29	0	4	6	2	0	0	1	0	0	0	0	0	8	0	0	1	.207	.138	1
Lake, S	PHI	R	.245	20	53	3	13	18	2	0	1	2	0	1	0	1	0	8	0	0	1	.340	.255	2
Laker, T	MON	R	.217	28	46	8	10	13	3	0	0	4	0	0	0	2	0	14	1	1	1	.283	.250	1
Lamp, D	PIT	R	.000	21	1	0	0	0	0	0	0	0	0	0	0	0	0	0	0	0	0	.000	.000	0
Lampkin, T	SD	L	.235	9	17	3	4	4	0	0	0	0	0	0	1	6	0	1	2	0	0	.235	.458	0
Lankford, R	STL	L	.293	153	598	87	175	287	40	6	20	86	2	5	5	72	6	147	42	24	5	.480	.371	2
Larkin, B	CIN	R	.304	140	533	76	162	242	32	6	12	78	2	7	4	63	8	58	15	4	13	.454	.377	11
LaValliere, M	PIT	L	.256	95	293	22	75	96	13	1	2	29	0	5	1	44	14	21	0	3	8	.328	.350	3
Lefferts, C	SD	L	.077	27	52	0	4	4	0	0	0	0	9	0	0	0	0	21	0	0	0	.077	.077	1
Leibrandt, C	ATL	R	.121	32	58	1	7	8	1	0	0	4	8	1	0	1	0	12	0	0	1	.138	.133	3
Lemke, M	ATL	S	.227	155	427	38	97	130	7	4	6	26	12	2	0	50	11	39	0	3	9	.304	.307	9
Leonard, M	SF	L	.234	55	128	13	30	49	7	0	4	16	0	1	3	16	0	31	0	1	3	.383	.331	1
Lewis, D	SF	R	.231	100	320	38	74	87	8	1	1	18	10	2	1	29	0	46	28	8	3	.272	.295	0
Lind, J	PIT	R	.235	135	468	38	110	126	14	1	0	39	7	4	1	26	12	29	3	1	14	.269	.275	6
Lindeman, J	PHI	R	.256	29	39	6	10	14	1	0	1	6	0	0	0	3	0	11	0	0	1	.359	.310	0

Litton, G...............	SF	R	.229	68	140	9	32	49	5	0	4	15	3	0	0	11	0	33	0	1	2	.350	.285	4
Lopez, J.................	ATL	R	.375	9	16	3	6	8	2	0	0	2	0	0	0	0	0	1	0	0	0	.500	.375	0
Lyons, S	ATL-MON	L	.148	27	27	2	4	6	0	1	0	2	1	0	0	1	0	7	1	2	2	.222	.179	0
Maddux, G............	CHI	R	.170	35	88	6	15	21	3	0	1	8	13	0	0	1	0	22	0	0	1	.239	.180	3
Maddux, M	SD	L	.111	50	9	0	1	1	0	0	0	0	3	0	0	1	0	4	0	0	0	.111	.200	1
Magadan, D..........	NY	L	.283	99	321	33	91	111	9	1	3	28	2	0	0	56	3	44	1	0	6	.346	.390	11
Magrane, J	STL	R	.200	5	10	1	2	5	0	0	1	2	1	0	0	0	0	2	0	0	0	.500	.200	0
Mallicoat, R..........	HOU	L	.000	25	1	1	0	0	0	0	0	0	0	0	0	0	0	0	0	0	0	.000	.000	0
Manwaring, K	SF	R	.244	109	349	24	85	117	10	5	4	26	6	0	5	29	0	42	2	1	12	.335	.311	4
Marsh, T	PHI	R	.200	42	125	7	25	38	3	2	2	16	2	2	1	2	0	23	0	1	2	.304	.215	2
Martin, A	PIT	L	.167	12	12	1	2	4	0	1	0	2	0	1	0	0	0	5	0	0	0	.333	.154	0
Martinez, D	MON	R	.189	32	74	3	14	14	0	0	0	2	10	0	0	0	0	20	0	0	1	.189	.189	4
Martinez, D	CIN	L	.254	135	393	47	100	139	20	5	3	31	6	4	0	42	4	54	12	8	6	.354	.323	6
Martinez, P	LA	R	.000	2	2	0	0	0	0	0	0	0	0	0	0	0	0	0	0	0	0	.000	.000	0
Martinez, R	LA	L	.120	26	50	1	6	6	0	0	0	2	5	0	0	0	0	14	0	0	0	.120	.120	2
Mason, R	PIT	R	.000	65	10	0	0	0	0	0	0	0	0	0	0	1	0	5	0	0	1	.000	.091	1
Mathews, G	PHI	R	.000	14	14	0	0	0	0	0	0	0	2	0	0	1	0	8	0	0	0	.000	.067	0
May, D	CHI	L	.274	124	351	33	96	131	11	0	8	45	2	1	3	14	4	40	5	3	10	.373	.306	5
McClendon, L	PIT	R	.253	84	190	26	48	67	8	1	3	20	1	3	2	28	0	24	1	3	5	.353	.350	3
McCray, R	NY	S	1.000	18	1	3	1	1	0	0	0	1	0	0	0	0	0	0	2	0	0	1.000	1.000	0
McDowell, R	LA	R	.000	65	3	1	0	0	0	0	0	0	1	0	1	2	0	3	0	0	0	.000	.500	3
McElroy, C...........	CHI	L	.667	72	6	2	4	8	2	1	0	1	0	0	0	0	0	0	0	0	0	1.333	.667	1
McGee, W.............	SF	S	.297	138	474	56	141	168	20	2	1	36	5	1	1	29	3	88	13	4	7	.354	.339	6
McGriff, F............	SD	L	.286	152	531	79	152	295	30	4	35	104	0	4	1	96	23	108	8	6	14	.556	.394	12
McKnight, J	NY	S	.271	31	85	10	23	34	3	1	2	13	0	0	0	2	0	8	0	1	2	.400	.287	3
McNamara, J	SF	L	.216	30	74	6	16	20	1	0	1	9	2	0	0	6	2	25	0	0	1	.270	.275	1
Melendez, J	SD	R	.000	56	5	0	0	0	0	0	0	0	1	0	0	0	0	4	0	0	0	.000	.000	1
Merced, O	PIT	S	.247	134	405	50	100	156	28	5	6	60	1	5	2	52	8	63	5	4	6	.385	.332	5
Mercker, K...........	ATL	L	.000	53	5	0	0	0	0	0	0	0	0	0	0	0	0	5	0	0	0	.000	.000	0
Miller, P	PIT	R	.000	6	3	0	0	0	0	0	0	0	0	0	0	0	0	3	0	0	0	.000	.000	0
Millette, J............	PHI	R	.205	33	78	5	16	16	0	0	0	2	2	0	2	5	2	10	1	0	8	.205	.271	3
Morandini, M	PHI	L	.265	127	422	47	112	145	8	8	3	30	6	2	0	25	2	64	8	3	4	.344	.305	6
Morgan, M	CHI	R	.108	34	74	1	8	8	0	0	0	5	11	1	0	2	0	16	0	0	1	.108	.130	3
Morris, H..............	CIN	L	.271	115	395	41	107	152	21	3	6	53	2	2	2	45	8	53	6	6	12	.385	.347	1
Mulholland, T	PHI	R	.096	32	83	1	8	9	1	0	0	3	6	0	0	3	0	35	0	0	0	.108	.128	3
Murphy, D............	PHI	R	.161	18	62	5	10	17	1	0	2	7	0	0	0	1	0	13	0	0	3	.274	.175	1

BATTER	TEAM	B	AVG	G	AB	R	H	TB	2B	3B	HR	RBI	SH	SF	HP	BB	IBB	SO	SB	CS	GI DP	SLG	OBP	E
Murphy, R	HOU	L	.000	59	1	1	0	0	0	0	0	0	1	0	0	0	0	0	0	0	0	.000	.000	0
Murray, E	NY	S	.261	156	551	64	144	233	37	2	16	93	0	8	0	66	8	74	4	2	15	.423	.336	12
Myers, R	SD	L	.143	66	7	0	1	1	0	0	0	0	1	0	0	0	0	5	0	0	1	.143	.143	0
Nabholz, C	MON	L	.123	32	65	3	8	11	3	0	0	2	7	0	0	1	0	12	0	0	3	.169	.136	2
Natal, R	MON	R	.000	5	6	0	0	0	0	0	0	0	0	0	0	1	0	1	0	0	1	.000	.143	1
Neagle, D	PIT	L	.000	56	11	0	0	0	0	0	0	0	2	0	0	0	0	2	0	1	0	.000	.000	0
Nied, D	ATL	R	.286	6	7	1	2	2	0	0	0	0	0	0	0	0	0	2	0	0	0	.286	.286	0
Nieves, M	ATL	S	.211	12	19	0	4	5	1	0	0	1	0	0	0	2	0	7	0	0	0	.263	.286	3
Nixon, O	ATL	S	.294	120	456	79	134	158	14	2	2	22	5	2	0	39	0	54	41	18	4	.346	.348	3
Noboa, J	NY	R	.149	46	47	7	7	7	0	0	0	3	0	1	1	3	0	8	0	0	2	.149	.212	3
O'Brien, C	NY	R	.212	68	156	15	33	51	12	0	2	13	4	0	1	16	1	18	0	1	4	.327	.289	7
Offerman, J	LA	S	.260	149	534	67	139	178	20	8	1	30	5	2	0	57	4	98	23	16	5	.333	.331	42
Ojeda, B	LA	L	.102	29	49	1	5	7	0	1	0	3	5	0	0	1	0	11	0	0	1	.143	.120	2
Olivares, O	STL	R	.235	36	68	7	16	20	1	0	1	4	3	0	0	1	0	19	0	0	0	.294	.246	0
Oliver, J	CIN	R	.270	143	485	42	131	188	25	1	10	57	6	7	1	35	19	75	2	3	12	.388	.316	8
Oliveras, F	SF	R	.143	16	7	0	1	1	0	0	0	0	0	0	0	1	0	2	0	0	0	.143	.250	1
Olson, G	ATL	R	.238	95	302	27	72	99	14	2	3	27	1	2	1	34	4	31	2	1	8	.328	.316	1
O'Neill, P	CIN	L	.246	148	496	59	122	185	19	1	14	66	3	6	2	77	15	85	6	3	10	.373	.346	1
Oquendo, J	STL	S	.257	14	35	3	9	14	3	1	0	3	0	0	0	5	1	3	0	0	0	.400	.350	1
Osborne, D	STL	L	.121	34	58	4	7	9	0	1	0	0	2	0	0	0	0	21	0	0	0	.155	.121	2
Owen, S	MON	S	.269	122	386	52	104	147	16	3	7	40	4	6	0	50	3	30	9	4	10	.381	.348	9
Pagnozzi, T	STL	R	.249	139	485	33	121	174	26	3	7	44	6	3	1	28	9	64	2	5	15	.359	.290	1
Palacios, V	PIT	R	.071	20	14	0	1	1	0	0	0	0	2	0	0	0	0	6	0	0	0	.071	.071	1
Patterson, B	PIT	R	.333	60	6	1	2	3	1	0	0	4	0	0	0	1	0	3	0	0	0	.500	.429	0
Patterson, J	SF	S	.184	32	103	10	19	22	1	1	0	4	0	0	1	5	0	24	5	1	2	.214	.229	4
Patterson, K	CHI	L	.000	32	1	0	0	0	0	0	0	0	1	0	0	0	0	1	0	0	0	.000	.000	1
Pecota, B	NY	R	.227	117	269	28	61	80	13	0	2	26	5	2	1	25	3	40	9	3	7	.297	.293	12
Pedre, J	CHI	R	.000	4	4	0	0	0	0	0	0	0	0	0	0	0	0	1	0	0	0	.000	.000	0
Peguero, J	LA	S	.222	14	9	3	2	2	0	0	0	0	1	0	0	3	0	3	0	0	0	.222	.417	0
Pena, A	ATL	R	.000	41	2	0	0	0	0	0	0	0	0	0	0	0	0	2	0	0	0	.000	.000	0
Pena, G	STL	S	.305	62	203	31	62	97	12	1	7	31	0	4	5	24	0	37	13	8	1	.478	.386	5
Pena, J	SF	L	.200	25	5	0	1	1	0	0	0	0	3	0	0	0	0	2	0	0	0	.200	.200	3
Pendleton, T	ATL	S	.311	160	640	98	199	303	39	1	21	105	5	7	0	37	8	67	5	2	16	.473	.345	19
Pennyfeather, W	PIT	R	.222	15	9	2	2	2	0	0	0	0	1	0	0	0	0	0	0	0	1	.222	.222	0

Perez, M	STL	R	.000	77	4	0	0	0	0	0	0	0	2	0	0	0	0	2	0	0	1	.000	.000	0
Perry, G	STL	L	.238	87	143	13	34	45	8	0	1	18	0	2	1	15	4	23	3	6	3	.315	.311	3
Pettis, G	SD	S	.200	30	30	0	6	7	1	0	0	0	0	0	0	2	0	11	1	0	0	.233	.250	1
Piazza, M	LA	R	.232	21	69	5	16	22	3	0	1	7	0	0	1	4	0	12	0	0	1	.319	.284	1
Portugal, M	HOU	R	.107	18	28	1	3	3	0	0	0	0	6	0	0	0	0	12	0	0	0	.107	.107	3
Pratt, T	PHI	R	.283	16	46	6	13	20	1	0	2	10	0	0	0	4	0	12	0	0	2	.435	.340	2
Prince, T	PIT	R	.091	27	44	1	4	6	2	0	0	5	0	2	0	6	0	9	1	1	2	.136	.192	2
Pugh, T	CIN	R	.077	7	13	0	1	1	0	0	0	0	1	0	0	1	0	4	0	0	0	.077	.143	0
Ramirez, R	HOU	R	.250	73	176	17	44	53	6	0	1	13	1	0	1	7	1	24	0	0	5	.301	.283	7
Ramsey, F	CHI	R	.120	18	25	0	3	3	0	0	0	2	0	0	0	0	0	6	0	0	0	.120	.120	0
Randolph, W	NY	R	.252	90	286	29	72	91	11	1	2	15	6	0	4	40	1	34	1	3	6	.318	.352	8
Rapp, P	SF	R	.000	3	2	0	0	0	0	0	0	0	1	0	0	0	0	2	0	0	0	.000	.000	0
Rasmussen, D	CHI	L	.000	3	0	0	0	0	0	0	0	0	1	0	0	0	0	0	0	0	0	.000	.000	0
Redus, G	PIT	R	.256	76	176	26	45	67	7	3	3	12	0	0	0	17	0	25	11	4	1	.381	.321	1
Reed, D	MON	R	.173	42	81	10	14	31	2	0	5	10	0	0	1	6	2	23	0	0	3	.383	.239	0
Reed, J	CIN	L	.160	15	25	2	4	4	0	0	0	2	0	0	0	1	1	4	0	0	1	.160	.192	0
Reynolds, S	HOU	R	.500	8	4	1	2	3	1	0	0	0	2	0	0	0	0	0	0	0	0	.750	.500	1
Reynoso, A	ATL	R	.000	3	2	0	0	0	0	0	0	0	1	0	0	0	0	1	0	0	0	.000	.000	0
Rhodes, K	HOU	L	.000	5	4	0	0	0	0	0	0	0	0	0	0	0	0	2	0	0	0	.000	.000	0
Righetti, D	SF	L	.143	54	7	0	1	1	0	0	0	0	4	0	0	0	0	4	0	0	0	.143	.143	1
Rijo, J	CIN	R	.194	33	72	3	14	16	2	0	0	6	6	0	0	0	0	18	0	0	0	.222	.194	2
Riles, E	HOU	L	.262	39	61	5	16	20	1	0	1	4	0	1	0	2	0	11	1	0	0	.328	.281	1
Risley, B	MON	R	.000	1	2	0	0	0	0	0	0	0	0	0	0	0	0	0	0	0	0	.000	.000	0
Ritchie, W	PHI	L	.000	40	1	0	0	0	0	0	0	0	0	0	0	1	0	1	0	0	0	.000	.500	0
Rivera, B	ATL-PHI	R	.091	28	33	1	3	3	0	0	0	2	2	0	0	2	0	11	0	0	0	.091	.143	0
Roberts, L	CIN	S	.323	147	532	92	172	230	34	6	4	45	1	4	2	62	4	54	44	16	7	.432	.393	7
Robinson, D	PHI	R	.389	10	18	0	7	10	3	0	0	1	0	0	0	0	0	5	0	0	1	.556	.389	0
Robinson, J	CHI	R	.000	49	12	0	0	0	0	0	0	0	2	0	0	0	0	3	0	0	0	.000	.000	0
Robinson, J	PIT	R	.091	8	11	0	1	1	0	0	0	1	2	0	0	0	0	8	0	0	0	.091	.091	0
Rodriguez, H	LA	L	.219	53	146	11	32	48	7	0	3	14	1	1	0	8	0	30	0	0	2	.329	.258	3
Rodriguez, R	SD	L	.000	61	6	0	0	0	0	0	0	0	2	0	0	1	0	0	0	0	1	.000	.143	1
Rogers, K	SF	L	.222	6	9	0	2	2	0	0	0	0	3	0	0	0	0	6	0	0	1	.222	.222	0
Rojas, M	MON	R	.067	68	15	0	1	1	0	0	0	0	0	0	0	0	0	10	0	0	0	.067	.067	2
Royer, S	STL	R	.323	13	31	6	10	18	2	0	2	9	0	1	0	1	0	4	0	0	0	.581	.333	3
Ruskin, S	CIN	R	.000	57	3	0	0	0	0	0	0	0	2	0	0	0	0	3	0	0	0	.000	.000	0
Saberhagen, B	NY	R	.107	17	28	0	3	3	0	0	0	0	3	0	0	1	0	9	0	0	0	.107	.138	0

BATTER	TEAM	B	AVG	G	AB	R	H	TB	2B	3B	HR	RBI	SH	SF	HP	BB	IBB	SO	SB	CS	GIDP	SLG	OBP	E
Sabo, C.	CIN	R	.244	96	344	42	84	145	19	3	12	43	1	6	1	30	1	54	4	5	12	.422	.302	9
Salazar, L.	CHI	R	.208	98	255	20	53	79	7	2	5	25	3	4	0	11	2	34	1	1	10	.310	.237	6
Sampen, B.	MON	R	.000	44	6	0	0	0	0	0	0	0	1	0	0	0	0	5	0	0	0	.000	.000	0
Samuel, J.	LA	R	.262	47	122	7	32	37	3	1	0	15	4	2	1	7	3	22	2	2	0	.303	.303	5
Sanchez, R.	CHI	R	.251	74	255	24	64	87	14	3	1	19	5	2	3	10	1	17	2	1	7	.341	.285	9
Sandberg, R.	CHI	R	.304	158	612	100	186	312	32	8	26	87	0	6	1	68	4	73	17	6	13	.510	.371	8
Sanders, D.	ATL	L	.304	97	303	54	92	150	6	14	8	28	1	1	2	18	0	52	26	9	5	.495	.346	3
Sanders, R.	CIN	R	.270	116	385	62	104	178	26	6	12	36	0	1	4	48	2	98	16	7	6	.462	.356	6
Santiago, B.	SD	R	.251	106	386	37	97	148	21	0	10	42	0	4	0	21	1	52	2	5	14	.383	.287	12
Sasser, M.	NY	L	.241	92	141	7	34	46	6	0	2	18	0	5	0	3	0	10	0	0	4	.326	.248	1
Scanlan, B.	CHI	R	.000	69	4	1	0	0	0	0	0	0	0	0	0	0	0	1	0	0	0	.000	.000	2
Scarsone, S.	PHI	R	.154	7	13	1	2	2	0	0	0	0	0	0	0	1	0	6	0	0	0	.154	.214	0
Scheid, R.	HOU	L	.000	7	1	0	0	0	0	0	0	0	0	0	0	0	0	1	0	0	0	.000	.000	0
Schilling, C.	PHI	R	.156	42	64	3	10	11	1	0	0	3	8	0	0	1	0	22	0	0	0	.172	.169	3
Schofield, D.	NY	R	.205	142	420	52	86	120	18	2	4	36	10	3	5	60	4	82	11	4	11	.286	.309	7
Schourek, P.	NY	L	.048	23	42	0	2	2	0	0	0	1	2	1	0	0	0	13	0	0	0	.048	.047	0
Scioscia, M.	LA	L	.221	117	348	19	77	98	6	3	3	24	5	3	1	32	4	31	3	2	9	.282	.286	9
Scott, G.	CHI	R	.156	36	96	8	15	23	2	0	2	11	1	0	0	5	1	14	0	1	3	.240	.198	5
Seminara, F.	SD	R	.118	19	34	3	4	4	0	0	0	0	2	0	0	1	0	9	0	0	0	.118	.143	2
Servais, S.	HOU	R	.239	77	205	12	49	58	9	0	0	15	6	0	5	11	2	25	0	0	7	.283	.294	2
Service, S.	MON	R	.000	5	2	0	0	0	0	0	0	0	0	0	0	0	0	2	0	0	0	.000	.000	0
Sharperson, M.	LA	R	.300	128	317	48	95	125	21	0	3	36	5	3	0	47	1	33	2	2	9	.394	.387	13
Sheffield, G.	SD	R	.330	146	557	87	184	323	34	3	33	100	0	7	6	48	5	40	5	6	19	.580	.385	16
Shipley, C.	SD	R	.248	52	105	7	26	32	6	0	0	7	1	0	0	2	1	21	1	1	2	.305	.262	1
Simms, M.	HOU	R	.250	15	24	1	6	10	1	0	1	3	0	0	1	2	0	9	0	0	1	.417	.333	0
Slaught, D.	PIT	R	.345	87	255	26	88	123	17	3	4	37	6	5	2	17	5	23	2	2	6	.482	.384	5
Slocumb, H.	CHI	R	.000	30	4	0	0	0	0	0	0	0	0	0	0	0	0	3	0	0	0	.000	.000	2
Smith, B.	STL	R	.000	13	3	0	0	0	0	0	0	0	1	0	0	0	0	0	0	0	0	.000	.000	0
Smith, D.	CHI	L	.276	109	217	28	60	85	10	3	3	24	0	2	1	13	0	40	9	8	1	.392	.318	2
Smith, L.	ATL	R	.247	84	158	23	39	69	8	2	6	33	0	4	3	17	1	37	4	0	1	.437	.324	3
Smith, O.	STL	S	.295	132	518	73	153	177	20	2	0	31	12	1	0	59	4	34	43	9	11	.342	.367	10
Smith, P.	ATL	R	.038	12	26	1	1	1	0	0	0	2	3	0	0	2	0	11	0	0	0	.038	.107	1
Smith, Z.	PIT	L	.122	26	49	2	6	8	2	0	0	3	3	0	0	2	0	11	0	0	0	.163	.157	0
Smoltz, J.	ATL	R	.160	36	75	7	12	15	0	0	1	4	10	0	0	6	0	32	0	0	1	.200	.222	1

Snyder, C	SF	R	.269	124	390	48	105	173	22	2	14	57	2	3	2	23	2	96	4	4	10	.444	.311	6
Sosa, S	CHI	R	.260	67	262	41	68	103	7	2	8	25	4	2	4	19	1	63	15	7	4	.393	.317	6
Springer, S	NY	R	.400	4	5	0	2	3	1	0	0	0	0	0	0	0	0	1	0	0	0	.600	.400	0
Stairs, M	MON	L	.167	13	30	2	5	7	2	0	0	5	0	1	0	7	0	7	0	0	0	.233	.316	1
Stanton, M	ATL	L	.500	65	2	1	1	1	0	0	0	0	0	0	0	0	0	0	0	0	0	.500	.500	0
Stephenson, P	SD	L	.155	53	71	5	11	15	2	1	0	8	3	0	0	10	0	11	0	0	0	.211	.259	1
Stillwell, K	SD	S	.227	114	379	35	86	113	15	3	2	24	4	6	1	26	9	58	4	1	6	.298	.274	16
Strange, D	CHI	S	.160	52	94	7	15	19	1	0	1	5	2	0	0	10	2	15	1	0	2	.202	.240	6
Strawberry, D	LA	L	.237	43	156	20	37	60	8	0	5	25	0	1	1	19	4	34	3	1	2	.385	.322	1
Sveum, D	PHI	S	.178	54	135	13	24	34	4	0	2	16	0	2	0	16	4	39	0	0	5	.252	.261	8
Swift, B	SF	R	.157	34	51	3	8	11	3	0	0	3	5	0	0	1	0	18	0	0	0	.216	.173	1
Swindell, G	CIN	R	.125	31	80	2	10	12	2	0	0	4	5	1	0	1	0	15	0	0	0	.150	.134	1
Taubensee, E	HOU	L	.222	104	297	23	66	96	15	0	5	28	0	1	2	31	3	78	2	1	4	.323	.299	5
Teufel, T	SD	R	.224	101	246	23	55	83	10	0	6	25	0	1	1	31	3	45	2	1	7	.337	.312	7
Tewksbury, B	STL	R	.086	33	70	4	6	7	1	0	0	3	6	0	0	4	0	29	0	0	1	.100	.135	1
Thompson, M	STL	L	.293	109	208	31	61	84	9	1	4	17	0	0	2	16	3	39	18	6	3	.404	.350	2
Thompson, R	SF	R	.260	128	443	54	115	184	25	1	14	49	7	4	8	43	1	75	5	9	8	.415	.333	15
Thompson, R	NY	R	.222	30	108	15	24	42	7	1	3	10	0	1	0	8	0	24	2	2	2	.389	.274	1
Tomlin, R	PIT	L	.138	35	65	4	9	9	0	0	0	1	7	0	0	3	0	15	0	0	1	.138	.176	1
Treadway, J	ATL	L	.222	61	126	5	28	36	6	1	0	5	1	0	0	9	4	16	1	2	3	.286	.274	1
Tucker, E	HOU	R	.120	20	50	5	6	7	1	0	0	3	1	0	2	3	0	13	1	1	2	.140	.200	2
Uribe, J	SF	S	.241	66	162	24	39	56	9	1	2	13	4	1	0	14	3	25	2	2	3	.346	.299	7
Valdez, S	MON	R	.000	27	3	0	0	0	0	0	0	0	0	0	0	0	0	2	0	0	0	.000	.000	0
Vander Wal, J	MON	L	.239	105	213	21	51	75	8	2	4	20	0	0	0	24	2	36	3	0	2	.352	.316	2
Van Slyke, A	PIT	L	.324	154	614	103	199	310	45	12	14	89	0	9	4	58	4	99	12	3	9	.505	.381	5
Varsho, G	PIT	L	.222	103	162	22	36	60	6	3	4	22	0	1	0	10	1	32	5	2	2	.370	.266	1
Vatcher, J	SD	R	.250	13	16	1	4	5	1	0	0	2	1	0	0	3	0	6	0	0	0	.313	.368	0
Velasquez, G	SD	L	.304	15	23	1	7	10	0	0	1	5	0	0	0	1	0	7	0	0	0	.435	.333	1
Villanueva, H	CHI	R	.152	51	112	9	17	29	6	0	2	13	0	0	0	11	2	24	0	0	5	.259	.228	4
Vizcaino, J	CHI	S	.225	86	285	25	64	85	10	4	1	17	5	1	0	14	2	35	3	0	4	.298	.260	9
Wagner, P	PIT	R	.333	6	3	0	1	1	0	0	0	0	0	0	0	0	0	1	0	0	0	.333	.333	0
Wakefield, T	PIT	R	.071	14	28	0	2	2	0	0	0	0	4	0	0	1	0	9	0	0	0	.071	.103	0
Walk, B	PIT	R	.093	36	43	2	4	5	1	0	0	2	1	0	0	0	0	11	0	0	1	.116	.093	1
Walker, C	CHI-NY	S	.289	126	253	26	73	99	12	1	4	38	0	5	0	27	3	50	15	1	9	.391	.351	8
Walker, L	MON	L	.301	143	528	85	159	267	31	4	23	93	0	8	6	41	10	97	18	6	9	.506	.353	2
Wallach, T	MON	R	.223	150	537	53	120	178	29	1	9	59	0	7	8	50	2	90	2	2	10	.331	.296	15

BATTER	TEAM	B	AVG	G	AB	R	H	TB	2B	3B	HR	RBI	SH	SF	HP	BB	IBB	SO	SB	CS	GI DP	SLG	OBP	E
Walling, D	HOU	L	.333	3	3	1	1	1	0	0	0	0	0	0	0	0	0	0	0	0	0	.333	.333	0
Walters, D	SD	R	.251	57	179	14	45	70	11	1	4	22	1	2	2	10	0	28	1	0	3	.391	.295	3
Walton, J	CHI	R	.127	30	55	7	7	9	0	1	0	1	3	0	2	9	0	13	1	2	1	.164	.273	2
Ward, K	SD	R	.197	81	147	12	29	43	5	0	3	12	1	1	2	14	0	38	2	3	8	.293	.274	4
Webster, M	LA	S	.267	135	262	33	70	110	12	5	6	35	8	5	2	27	3	49	11	5	1	.420	.334	3
Wehner, J	PIT	R	.179	55	123	11	22	28	6	0	0	4	2	0	0	12	2	22	3	0	4	.228	.252	4
Weston, M	PHI	R	.000	1	2	0	0	0	0	0	0	0	0	0	0	0	0	2	0	0	0	.000	.000	0
Wetteland, J	MON	R	.200	67	5	0	1	1	0	0	0	0	1	0	0	0	0	4	0	0	0	.200	.200	1
Whitehurst, W	NY	R	.182	44	22	1	4	5	1	0	0	3	1	0	0	1	0	5	0	1	0	.227	.217	1
Wilkins, R	CHI	L	.270	83	244	20	66	101	9	1	8	22	1	1	0	28	7	53	0	2	6	.414	.344	3
Willard, J	ATL-MON	L	.229	47	48	2	11	18	1	0	2	8	0	0	0	2	1	10	0	0	5	.375	.260	1
Williams, B	HOU	R	.133	20	30	2	4	5	1	0	0	4	5	1	0	0	0	13	0	0	0	.167	.129	2
Williams, Mitch	PHI	L	.250	66	4	0	1	1	0	0	0	0	0	0	0	0	0	2	0	0	0	.250	.250	3
Williams, M	SF	R	.227	146	529	58	120	203	13	5	20	66	0	2	6	39	11	109	7	7	15	.384	.286	23
Williams, Mike	PHI	R	.400	5	10	1	4	4	0	0	0	2	1	0	0	0	0	4	0	0	0	.400	.400	0
Wilson, C	STL	R	.311	61	106	6	33	39	6	0	0	13	2	1	0	10	2	18	1	2	4	.368	.368	3
Wilson, D	CIN	R	.360	12	25	2	9	10	1	0	0	3	0	0	0	3	0	8	0	0	2	.400	.429	0
Wilson, S	LA	L	.333	60	3	0	1	1	0	0	0	0	0	0	0	0	0	2	0	0	0	.333	.333	1
Wilson, T	SF	L	.077	27	39	3	3	4	1	0	0	3	7	0	0	3	0	21	0	0	2	.103	.143	2
Wohlers, M	ATL	R	.000	32	2	0	0	0	0	0	0	0	0	0	0	0	0	2	0	0	0	.000	.000	0
Wood, T	SF	L	.207	24	58	5	12	17	2	0	1	3	2	0	1	6	0	15	0	0	4	.293	.292	1
Woodson, T	STL	R	.307	31	114	9	35	46	8	0	1	22	1	0	1	3	0	10	0	0	1	.404	.331	3
Wrona, R	CIN	R	.174	11	23	0	4	4	0	0	0	0	0	0	0	0	0	3	0	0	2	.174	.174	2
Yelding, E	HOU	R	.250	9	8	1	2	2	0	0	0	0	0	0	0	0	0	3	0	0	0	.250	.250	0
Young, A	NY	R	.111	52	27	2	3	3	0	0	0	0	2	0	0	1	0	13	0	0	0	.111	.143	2
Young, E	LA	R	.258	49	132	9	34	38	1	0	1	11	4	0	0	8	0	9	6	1	3	.288	.300	9
Young, G	HOU	S	.184	74	76	14	14	17	1	1	0	4	4	0	0	10	0	11	6	2	2	.224	.279	2
Young, K	PIT	R	.571	10	7	2	4	4	0	0	0	4	0	0	0	2	0	0	1	0	0	.571	.667	1
Zeile, T	STL	R	.257	126	439	51	113	160	18	4	7	48	0	7	0	68	4	70	7	10	11	.364	.352	13

CLUB BATTING

CLUB	AVG	G	AB	R	OR	H	TB	2B	3B	HR	GS	RBI	SH	SF	HP	BB	IBB	SO	SB	CS	GIDP	LOB	SHO	SLG	OBP
ST. LOUIS	.262	162	5594	631	604	1464	2096	262	44	94	3	599	68	41	32	495	49	996	208	118	96	1153	11	.375	.323
CINCINNATI	.260	162	5460	660	609	1418	2084	281	44	99	2	606	66	52	21	563	83	888	125	65	123	1181	10	.382	.328
PITTSBURGH......	.255	162	5527	693	595	1409	2107	272	54	106	4	656	89	56	25	569	88	872	110	53	102	1177	9	.381	.324
SAN DIEGO	.255	162	5476	617	636	1396	2116	255	30	135	4	576	78	41	26	453	67	864	69	52	126	1082	12	.386	.313
CHICAGO............	.254	162	5590	593	624	1420	2035	221	41	104	3	566	78	40	31	417	49	816	77	51	121	1148	20	.364	.307
ATLANTA...........	.254	162	5480	682	569	1391	2124	223	48	138	2	641	93	50	26	493	58	924	126	60	82	1132	8	.388	.316
PHILADELPHIA .	.253	162	5500	686	717	1392	2073	255	36	118	5	638	64	46	52	509	45	1059	127	31	111	1172	9	.377	.320
MONTREAL	.252	162	5477	648	581	1381	2024	263	37	102	1	601	82	55	43	463	43	976	196	63	104	1087	11	.370	.313
LOS ANGELES	.248	162	5368	548	636	1333	1818	201	34	72	2	499	102	40	24	503	36	899	142	78	111	1138	15	.339	.313
HOUSTON...........	.246	162	5480	608	668	1350	1969	255	38	96	2	582	88	40	48	506	65	1025	139	54	97	1162	18	.359	.313
SAN FRANCISCO	.244	162	5456	574	647	1330	1937	220	36	105	1	532	101	39	39	435	53	1067	112	64	111	1087	18	.355	.302
NEW YORK	.235	162	5340	599	653	1254	1826	259	17	93	3	564	74	45	28	572	53	956	129	52	117	1098	16	.342	.310

Pitching

Individual Pitching Leaders

Games Won	20	Glavine	Atl.
		Maddux	Chi.
Games Lost	15	Candiotti	L.A.
		Hershiser	L.A.
Won-Lost Percentage	.762	Tewksbury	St.L. (16-5)
Earned Run Average	2.08	Swift	S.F.
Games	81	Boever	Hou.
Games Started	35	Avery	Atl.
		Maddux	Chi.
		Smoltz	Atl.
Complete Games	12	Mulholland	Phi.
Games Finished	70	D. Jones	Hou.
Shutouts	5	Cone	N.Y.
		Glavine	Atl.
Saves	43	L. Smith	St.L.
Innings	268.0	Maddux	Chi.
Hits	230	Benes	S.D.
Batsmen Faced	1061	Maddux	Chi.
Runs	104	Belcher	Cin.
Earned Runs	99	Belcher	Cin.
Home Runs	23	Black	S.F.
Sacrifice Hits	20	Candiotti	L.A.
Sacrifice Flies	11	Belcher	Cin.
		Fernandez	N.Y.
Hit Batsmen	14	Maddux	Chi.
Bases on Balls	82	Cone	N.Y.
Intentional Bases on Balls	13	Gott	L.A.
		Hershiser	L.A.
		McDowell	L.A.
Strikeouts	215	Smoltz	Atl.
Wild Pitches	17	Smoltz	Atl.
Balks	7	Black	S.F.
		Wilson	S.F.
Games Won, Consecutive	13	Glavine	Atl. (May 27-Aug. 19)
Games Lost, Consecutive	14	Young	N.Y. (May 6-Sept. 29)

TOP 15 QUALIFIERS FOR EARNED RUN AVERAGE CHAMPIONSHIP

PITCHER	TEAM	T	W	L	ERA	G	GS	CG	SHO	GF	SV	IP	H	TBF	R	ER	HR	SH	SF	HB	BB	IBB	SO	WP	BK	OPP AVG
Swift, B	SF	R	10	4	2.08	30	22	3	2	2	1	164.2	144	655	41	38	6	5	2	3	43	3	77	0	1	.239
Tewksbury, B	STL	R	16	5	2.16	33	32	5	0	1	0	233.0	217	915	63	56	15	9	7	3	20	0	91	2	0	.248
Maddux, G	CHI	R	20	11	2.18	35	35	9	4	0	0	268.0	201	1061	68	65	7	15	3	14	70	7	199	5	0	.210
Schilling, C	PHI	R	14	11	2.35	42	26	10	4	10	2	226.1	165	895	67	59	11	7	8	1	59	4	147	4	0	.201
Martinez, D	MON	R	16	11	2.47	32	32	6	0	0	0	226.1	172	900	75	62	12	12	5	9	60	3	147	2	0	.211
Morgan, M	CHI	R	16	8	2.55	34	34	6	1	0	0	240.0	203	966	80	68	14	10	5	3	79	10	123	11	0	.234
Rijo, J	CIN	R	15	10	2.56	33	33	2	0	0	0	211.0	185	836	67	60	15	9	4	3	44	1	171	2	1	.238
Hill, K	MON	R	16	9	2.68	33	33	3	3	0	0	218.0	187	908	76	65	13	15	3	3	75	4	150	11	4	.230
Swindell, G	CIN	L	12	8	2.70	31	30	5	3	0	0	213.2	210	867	72	64	14	9	7	2	41	4	138	3	2	.260
Fernandez, S	NY	L	14	11	2.73	32	32	5	2	0	0	214.2	162	865	67	65	12	12	11	4	67	4	193	0	0	.210
Glavine, T	ATL	L	20	8	2.76	33	33	7	5	0	0	225.0	197	919	81	69	6	2	6	2	70	7	129	5	0	.235
Drabek, D	PIT	R	15	11	2.77	34	34	10	4	0	0	256.2	218	1021	84	79	17	8	8	6	54	8	177	11	1	.231
Smoltz, J	ATL	R	15	12	2.85	35	35	9	3	0	0	246.2	206	1021	90	78	17	7	8	5	80	5	215	17	1	.224
Cone, D	NY	R	13	7	2.88	27	27	7	5	0	0	196.2	162	831	75	63	12	6	6	9	82	5	214	9	1	.223
Candiotti, T	LA	R	11	15	3.01	32	30	6	2	1	0	203.2	177	839	78	68	13	20	6	3	63	5	152	9	2	.237

INDIVIDUAL PITCHING

PITCHER	TEAM	T	W	L	ERA	G	GS	CG	SHO	GF	SV	IP	H	TBF	R	ER	HR	SH	SF	HB	BB	IBB	SO	WP	BK	OPP AVG
Abbott, K	PHI	L	1	14	5.13	31	19	0	0	0	0	133.1	147	577	80	76	20	6	5	1	45	0	88	9	1	.283
Agosto, J	STL	L	2	4	6.25	22	0	0	0	10	0	31.2	39	143	24	22	2	3	3	3	9	2	13	2	0	.312
Andersen, L	SD	R	1	1	3.34	34	0	0	0	13	2	35.0	26	140	14	13	2	1	1	1	8	2	35	0	0	.202
Ashby, A	PHI	R	1	3	7.54	10	8	0	0	0	0	37.0	42	171	31	31	6	2	2	1	21	0	24	2	0	.290
Assenmacher, P	CHI	L	4	4	4.10	70	0	0	0	23	8	68.0	72	298	32	31	6	1	2	3	26	5	67	4	0	.271
Astacio, P	LA	R	5	5	1.98	11	11	4	4	0	0	82.0	80	341	23	18	1	3	2	2	20	4	43	1	0	.255
Avery, S	ATL	L	11	11	3.20	35	35	2	2	0	0	233.2	216	969	95	83	14	12	8	0	71	3	129	7	3	.246
Ayala, R	CIN	R	2	1	4.34	5	5	0	0	0	0	29.0	33	127	15	14	1	2	0	1	13	2	23	0	0	.297

PITCHER	TEAM	T	W	L	ERA	G	GS	CG	SHO	GF	SV	IP	H	TBF	R	ER	HR	SH	SF	HB	BB	IBB	SO	WP	BK	OPP AVG
Ayrault, B	PHI	R	2	2	3.12	30	0	0	0	7	0	43.1	32	178	16	15	0	4	3	1	17	1	27	0	0	.209
Baller, J	PHI	R	0	0	8.18	8	0	0	0	4	0	11.0	10	51	10	10	5	0	1	0	10	0	9	1	0	.250
Bankhead, S	CIN	R	10	4	2.93	54	0	0	0	10	1	70.2	57	299	26	23	4	3	3	3	29	5	53	6	0	.218
Barnes, B	MON	L	6	6	2.97	21	17	0	0	2	0	100.0	77	417	34	33	9	5	1	3	46	1	65	1	2	.213
Batista, M	PIT	R	0	0	9.00	1	0	0	0	1	0	2.0	4	13	2	2	1	0	0	0	3	0	1	0	0	.400
Beck, R	SF	R	3	3	1.76	65	0	0	0	42	17	92.0	62	352	20	18	4	6	2	2	15	2	87	5	2	.190
Belcher, T	CIN	R	15	14	3.91	35	34	2	1	1	0	227.2	201	949	104	99	17	12	11	3	80	2	149	3	1	.238
Belinda, S	PIT	R	6	4	3.15	59	0	0	0	42	18	71.1	58	299	26	25	8	4	6	0	29	5	57	1	0	.223
Benes, A	SD	R	13	14	3.35	34	34	2	2	0	0	231.1	230	961	90	86	14	19	6	5	61	6	169	1	1	.264
Berenguer, J	ATL	R	3	1	5.13	28	0	0	0	8	1	33.1	35	148	22	19	7	1	0	1	16	4	19	2	2	.269
Bielecki, M	ATL	R	2	4	2.57	19	14	1	1	0	0	80.2	77	336	27	23	2	3	2	1	27	1	62	4	0	.254
Birkbeck, M	NY	R	0	1	9.00	1	1	0	0	0	0	7.0	12	33	7	7	3	1	0	0	1	1	2	1	0	.387
Black, B	SF	L	10	12	3.97	28	28	2	1	0	0	177.0	178	749	88	78	23	8	4	1	59	11	82	3	7	.263
Blair, W	HOU	R	5	7	4.00	29	8	0	0	1	0	78.2	74	331	47	35	5	4	3	2	25	2	48	2	0	.249
Boever, J	HOU	R	3	6	2.51	81	0	0	0	26	2	111.1	103	479	38	31	3	10	4	4	45	9	67	4	0	.248
Bolton, T	CIN	L	3	3	5.24	16	8	0	0	3	0	46.1	52	210	28	27	9	1	1	2	23	2	27	3	1	.284
Borbon, P	ATL	L	0	1	6.75	2	0	0	0	2	0	1.1	2	7	1	1	0	0	0	0	1	1	1	0	0	.333
Boskie, S	CHI	R	5	11	5.01	23	18	0	0	2	0	91.2	96	393	55	51	14	9	6	4	36	3	39	5	1	.284
Bottenfield, K	MON	R	1	2	2.23	10	4	0	0	2	1	32.1	26	135	9	8	1	1	2	1	11	1	14	0	0	.217
Bowen, R	HOU	R	0	7	10.96	11	9	0	0	2	0	33.2	48	179	43	41	8	3	0	2	30	3	22	5	0	.333
Brantley, C	PHI	R	2	6	4.60	28	9	0	0	6	0	76.1	71	353	45	39	6	5	3	4	58	4	32	4	1	.251
Brantley, J	SF	R	7	7	2.95	56	4	0	0	32	7	91.2	67	381	32	30	8	7	3	3	45	5	86	3	1	.207
Brink, B	PHI	R	0	4	4.14	8	7	0	0	0	0	41.1	53	187	27	19	2	1	0	1	13	2	16	0	0	.308
Brocail, D	SD	R	0	0	6.43	3	3	0	0	0	0	14.0	17	64	10	10	2	2	0	0	5	0	15	0	0	.298
Brown, K	CIN	R	0	1	4.50	2	2	0	0	0	0	8.0	10	37	5	4	2	0	0	0	5	0	5	0	0	.313
Browning, T	CIN	L	6	5	5.07	16	16	0	0	0	0	87.0	108	386	49	49	6	5	4	2	28	7	33	3	1	.311
Bullinger, J	CHI	R	2	8	4.66	39	9	1	0	15	7	85.0	72	380	49	44	9	9	4	4	54	6	36	4	0	.233
Burba, D	SF	R	2	7	4.97	23	11	0	0	4	0	70.2	80	318	43	39	4	2	4	2	31	2	47	1	1	.287
Burke, T	NY	R	1	2	5.74	15	0	0	0	9	0	15.2	26	76	15	10	1	1	1	0	3	0	7	2	0	.371
Burkett, J	SF	R	13	9	3.84	32	32	3	1	0	0	189.2	194	799	96	81	13	11	4	4	45	6	107	0	0	.264

Candelaria, J	LA	L	2	5	2.84	50	0	0	0	11	5	25.1	20	108	9	8	1	2	2	0	13	3	23	1	0	.220
Candiotti, T	LA	R	11	15	3.00	32	30	6	2	1	0	203.2	177	839	78	68	13	20	6	3	63	5	152	9	2	.237
Carpenter, C.......	STL	R	5	4	2.97	73	0	0	0	21	1	88.0	69	355	29	29	10	8	3	4	27	8	46	5	0	.220
Carter, L	SF	R	1	5	4.64	6	6	0	0	0	0	33.0	34	147	17	17	6	2	1	0	18	0	21	2	0	.270
Castillo, F..........	CHI	R	10	11	3.46	33	33	0	0	0	0	205.1	179	856	91	79	19	11	5	6	63	6	135	11	0	.232
Chapin, D	PHI	R	0	0	9.00	1	0	0	0	0	0	2.0	2	8	2	2	1	0	0	0	0	0	1	1	0	.250
Charlton, N.........	CIN	L	4	2	2.99	64	0	0	0	46	26	81.1	79	341	39	27	7	7	3	3	26	4	90	8	0	.262
Clark, M	STL	R	3	10	4.45	20	20	1	1	0	0	113.1	117	488	59	56	12	7	4	0	36	2	44	4	0	.265
Clements, P........	SD	L	2	1	2.66	27	0	0	0	7	0	23.2	25	105	9	7	0	2	0	2	12	4	11	0	0	.281
Cole, V	PIT	R	0	2	5.48	8	4	0	0	2	0	23.0	23	104	14	14	1	1	1	0	14	0	12	1	0	.261
Combs, P	PHI	L	1	1	7.71	4	4	0	0	0	0	18.2	20	88	16	16	0	3	1	0	12	0	11	1	0	.278
Cone, D	NY	R	13	7	2.88	27	27	7	5	0	0	196.2	162	831	75	63	12	6	6	9	82	5	214	9	1	.223
Cooke, S	PIT	L	2	0	3.52	11	0	0	0	8	1	23.0	22	91	9	9	2	0	0	0	4	1	10	0	0	.253
Cormier, R	STL	L	10	10	3.68	31	30	3	0	1	0	186.0	194	772	83	76	15	11	3	5	33	2	117	4	2	.269
Cox, D	PHI-PIT	R	5	3	4.60	25	7	0	0	8	3	62.2	66	278	37	32	5	5	3	0	27	2	48	1	0	.272
Crews, T.............	LA	R	0	3	5.19	49	2	0	0	13	0	78.0	95	339	46	45	6	6	5	2	20	9	43	3	0	.310
Davis, M.............	ATL	L	1	0	7.02	14	0	0	0	7	0	16.2	22	85	13	13	3	0	1	1	13	2	15	4	1	.314
DeLeon, J...........	STL-PHI	R	2	8	4.37	32	18	0	0	3	0	117.1	111	506	63	57	7	6	6	2	48	1	79	3	0	.250
Deshaies, J	SD	L	4	7	3.28	15	15	0	0	0	0	96.0	92	395	40	35	6	3	2	1	33	2	46	1	2	.258
Dewey, M	NY	R	1	0	4.32	20	0	0	0	6	0	33.1	37	143	16	16	2	1	0	0	10	2	24	0	1	.280
Dibble, R	CIN	R	3	5	3.07	63	0	0	0	49	25	70.1	48	286	26	24	3	2	2	2	31	2	110	6	0	.193
DiPino, F............	STL	L	0	0	1.64	9	0	0	0	3	0	11.0	9	45	2	2	0	1	0	0	3	0	8	0	0	.220
Downs, K............	SF	R	1	2	3.47	19	7	0	0	5	0	62.1	65	272	27	24	4	7	2	3	24	0	33	4	0	.275
Drabek, D...........	PIT	R	15	11	2.77	34	34	10	4	0	0	256.2	218	1021	84	79	17	8	8	6	54	8	177	11	1	.231
Eiland, D............	SD	R	0	2	5.67	7	7	0	0	0	0	27.0	33	120	21	17	1	0	0	0	5	0	10	0	1	.287
Fassero, J	MON	L	8	7	2.84	70	0	0	0	22	1	85.2	81	368	35	27	1	5	2	2	34	6	63	7	1	.249
Fernandez, S	NY	L	14	11	2.73	32	32	5	2	0	0	214.2	162	865	67	65	12	12	11	4	67	4	193	0	0	.210
Filer, T...............	NY	R	0	1	2.05	9	1	0	0	1	0	22.0	18	88	8	5	2	1	0	0	6	2	9	1	0	.222
Foster, S	CIN	R	1	1	2.88	31	1	0	0	7	2	50.0	52	209	16	16	4	5	2	0	13	1	34	1	0	.275
Franco, J............	NY	L	6	2	1.64	31	0	0	0	30	15	33.0	24	128	6	6	1	0	2	0	11	2	20	0	0	.209
Freeman, M	ATL	R	7	5	3.22	58	0	0	0	15	3	64.1	61	276	26	23	7	2	1	1	29	7	41	4	0	.251
Gardner, M	MON	R	12	10	4.36	33	30	0	0	1	0	179.2	179	778	91	87	15	12	7	9	60	2	132	2	0	.259

PITCHER	TEAM	T	W	L	ERA	G	GS	CG	SHO	GF	SV	IP	H	TBF	R	ER	HR	SH	SF	HB	BB	IBB	SO	WP	BK	OPP AVG
Gibson, P.	NY	L	0	1	5.23	43	1	0	0	12	0	62.0	70	273	37	36	7	3	1	0	25	0	49	1	0	.287
Glavine, T	ATL	L	20	8	2.76	33	33	7	5	0	0	225.0	197	919	81	69	6	2	6	2	70	7	129	5	0	.235
Gleaton, J	PIT	L	1	0	4.26	23	0	0	0	6	0	31.2	34	142	16	15	4	2	1	0	19	3	18	1	0	.283
Gooden, D	NY	R	10	13	3.67	31	31	3	0	0	0	206.0	197	863	93	84	11	10	7	3	70	7	145	3	1	.255
Gott, J	LA	R	3	3	2.45	68	0	0	0	28	6	88.0	72	369	27	24	4	6	1	1	41	13	75	9	3	.225
Greene, T	PHI	R	3	3	5.32	13	12	0	0	0	0	64.1	75	298	39	38	5	4	2	0	34	2	39	1	0	.291
Gross, Ke	LA	R	8	13	3.17	34	30	4	3	0	0	204.2	182	856	82	72	11	14	6	3	77	10	158	4	2	.241
Gross, Ki	LA	R	1	1	4.18	16	1	0	0	7	0	23.2	32	109	14	11	1	0	0	0	10	1	14	1	1	.323
Guetterman, L	NY	L	3	4	5.82	43	0	0	0	15	2	43.1	57	196	28	28	5	2	3	1	14	5	15	3	0	.324
Hammond, C	CIN	L	7	10	4.21	28	26	0	0	1	0	147.1	149	627	75	69	13	5	3	3	55	6	79	6	0	.266
Haney, C.	MON	L	2	3	5.45	9	6	1	1	2	0	38.0	40	165	25	23	6	0	3	4	10	0	27	5	1	.270
Harkey, M	CHI	R	4	0	1.89	7	7	0	0	0	0	38.0	34	159	13	8	4	1	2	1	15	0	21	3	1	.243
Harnisch, P	HOU	R	9	10	3.70	34	34	0	0	0	0	206.2	182	859	92	85	18	5	5	5	64	3	164	4	1	.234
Harris, Ge	SD	R	0	2	2.95	14	1	0	0	2	0	21.1	15	90	8	7	0	3	0	1	9	0	19	1	1	.195
Harris, Gr	SD	R	4	8	4.12	20	20	1	0	0	0	118.0	113	496	62	54	13	8	3	2	35	2	66	2	1	.252
Hartley, M	PHI	R	7	6	3.44	46	0	0	0	15	0	55.0	54	243	23	21	5	5	1	2	23	6	53	4	0	.255
Hartsock, J	CHI	R	0	0	6.75	4	0	0	0	0	0	9.1	15	46	7	7	2	1	1	0	4	0	6	2	0	.375
Henry, B	HOU	L	6	9	4.02	28	28	2	1	0	0	165.2	185	710	81	74	16	12	7	1	41	7	96	2	2	.285
Henry, D	CIN	R	3	3	3.33	60	0	0	0	11	0	83.2	59	352	31	31	4	7	3	1	44	6	72	12	0	.199
Heredia, G	SF-MON	R	2	3	4.23	20	5	0	0	4	0	44.2	44	187	23	21	4	2	1	1	20	1	22	1	0	.270
Hernandez, J	SD	R	1	4	4.17	26	0	0	0	11	1	36.2	39	157	17	17	4	6	5	1	11	5	25	0	0	.291
Hernandez, X	HOU	R	9	1	2.11	77	0	0	0	25	7	111.0	81	454	31	26	5	3	2	3	42	7	96	5	0	.200
Hershiser, O	LA	R	10	15	3.67	33	33	1	0	0	0	210.2	209	910	101	86	15	15	6	8	69	13	130	10	0	.257
Hickerson, B	SF	L	5	3	3.09	61	1	0	0	8	0	87.1	74	345	31	30	7	4	5	1	21	2	68	4	1	.236
Hill, K.	MON	R	16	9	2.68	33	33	3	3	0	0	218.0	187	908	76	65	13	15	3	3	75	4	150	11	4	.230
Hill, M	CIN	R	0	0	3.15	14	0	0	0	5	1	20.0	15	80	9	7	1	2	1	1	5	2	10	0	0	.211
Hillman, E	NY	L	2	2	5.33	11	8	0	0	2	0	52.1	67	227	31	31	9	3	1	2	10	2	16	1	0	.318
Hollins, J	CHI	R	0	0	13.50	4	0	0	0	3	0	4.2	8	27	7	7	1	0	2	0	5	0	0	1	0	.400
Howell, J	LA	R	1	3	1.54	41	0	0	0	26	4	46.2	41	203	9	8	2	5	1	1	18	5	36	3	1	.230
Hurst, B	SD	L	14	9	3.85	32	32	6	4	0	0	217.1	223	902	96	93	22	12	4	0	51	3	131	4	3	.267

Hurst, J	MON	R	1	1	5.51	3	3	0	0	0	0	16.1	18	72	10	10	1	0	0	1	7	0	4	1	0	.281
Innis, J	NY	R	6	9	2.86	76	0	0	0	28	1	88.0	85	373	32	28	4	7	4	6	36	4	39	1	0	.266
Jackson, D	CHI-PIT	L	8	13	3.84	34	34	0	0	0	0	201.1	211	883	99	86	6	17	10	4	77	6	97	2	2	.272
Jackson, M	SF	R	6	6	3.73	67	0	0	0	24	2	82.0	76	346	35	34	7	5	2	4	33	10	80	1	0	.252
Jones, B	PHI-NY	R	7	6	5.68	61	0	0	0	17	1	69.2	85	319	46	44	3	3	3	2	35	7	30	2	2	.308
Jones, D	HOU	R	11	8	1.85	80	0	0	0	70	36	111.2	96	440	29	23	5	9	0	5	17	5	93	2	1	.235
Jones, J	HOU	R	10	6	4.07	25	23	0	0	1	0	139.1	135	579	64	63	13	7	4	5	39	3	69	4	1	.258
Kile, D	HOU	R	5	10	3.95	22	22	2	0	0	0	125.1	124	554	61	55	8	5	6	4	63	4	90	3	4	.261
Krueger, B	MON	L	0	2	6.75	9	2	0	0	3	0	17.1	23	81	13	13	0	0	0	1	7	0	13	1	0	.315
Lamp, D	PIT	R	1	1	5.14	21	0	0	0	2	0	28.0	33	125	16	16	3	1	0	2	9	4	15	0	1	.292
Landrum, B	MON	R	1	1	7.20	18	0	0	0	6	0	20.0	27	95	16	16	3	1	0	2	9	2	7	0	0	.325
Lefferts, C	SD	L	13	9	3.69	27	27	0	0	0	0	163.1	180	684	76	67	16	12	5	0	35	2	81	4	1	.285
Leibrandt, C	ATL	L	15	7	3.36	32	31	5	2	0	0	193.0	191	799	78	72	9	7	4	5	42	4	104	3	2	.258
Maddux, G	CHI	R	20	11	2.18	35	35	9	4	0	0	268.0	201	1061	68	65	7	15	3	14	70	7	199	5	0	.210
Maddux, M	SD	R	2	2	2.37	50	1	0	0	14	5	79.2	71	330	25	21	2	2	3	0	24	4	60	4	1	.236
Magrane, J	STL	L	1	2	4.02	5	5	0	0	0	0	31.1	34	143	15	14	2	3	1	2	15	0	20	4	0	.279
Mallicoat, R	HOU	L	0	0	7.23	23	0	0	0	6	0	23.2	26	120	19	19	2	3	1	5	19	2	20	2	0	.283
Martinez, D	MON	R	16	11	2.47	32	32	6	0	0	0	226.1	172	900	75	62	12	12	5	9	60	3	147	2	0	.211
Martinez, P	LA	R	0	1	2.25	2	1	0	0	1	0	8.0	6	31	2	2	0	0	0	0	1	0	8	0	0	.200
Martinez, R	LA	R	8	11	4.00	25	25	1	1	0	0	150.2	141	662	82	67	11	12	1	5	69	4	101	9	0	.245
Mason, R	PIT	R	5	7	4.09	65	0	0	0	26	8	88.0	80	374	41	40	11	8	4	4	33	8	56	3	0	.246
Mathews, G	PHI	L	2	3	5.16	14	7	0	0	1	0	52.1	54	228	31	30	7	2	1	1	24	2	27	1	2	.270
Maysey, M	MON	R	0	0	3.86	2	0	0	0	1	0	2.1	4	12	1	1	1	0	0	1	0	0	1	0	0	.364
McClure, B	STL	L	2	2	3.17	71	0	0	0	16	0	54.0	52	230	21	19	6	1	3	2	25	5	24	1	0	.261
McDowell, R	LA	R	6	10	4.09	65	0	0	0	39	14	83.2	103	393	46	38	3	10	3	1	42	13	50	4	1	.306
McElroy, C	CHI	L	4	7	3.55	72	0	0	0	30	6	83.2	73	369	40	33	5	5	5	0	51	10	83	3	0	.237
Melendez, J	SD	R	6	7	2.92	56	3	0	0	18	0	89.1	82	363	32	29	9	7	4	3	20	7	82	1	1	.249
Menendez, A	CIN	R	1	0	1.93	3	0	0	0	1	0	4.2	1	15	1	1	1	0	0	0	0	0	5	0	0	.067
Mercker, K	ATL	L	3	2	3.42	53	0	0	0	18	6	68.1	51	289	27	26	4	4	1	3	35	1	49	6	0	.207
Miller, P	PIT	R	1	0	2.38	6	0	0	0	1	0	11.1	11	46	3	3	0	1	1	0	1	0	5	1	0	.256
Minor, B	PIT	R	0	0	4.50	1	0	0	0	0	0	2.0	3	9	2	1	0	0	0	0	0	0	0	1	0	.333
Morgan, M	CHI	R	16	8	2.55	34	34	6	1	0	0	240.0	203	966	80	68	14	10	5	3	79	10	123	11	0	.234

PITCHER	TEAM	T	W	L	ERA	G	GS	CG	SHO	GF	SV	IP	H	TBF	R	ER	HR	SH	SF	HB	BB	IBB	SO	WP	BK	OPP AVG
Mulholland, T	PHI	L	13	11	3.81	32	32	12	2	0	0	229.0	227	937	101	97	14	10	7	3	46	3	125	3	0	.261
Murphy, R	HOU	L	3	1	4.04	59	0	0	0	6	0	55.2	56	242	28	25	2	3	3	0	21	4	42	4	0	.260
Myers, R	SD	L	3	6	4.29	66	0	0	0	57	38	79.2	84	348	38	38	7	7	5	1	34	3	66	5	0	.279
Nabholz, C	MON	L	11	12	3.32	32	32	1	1	0	0	195.0	176	812	80	72	11	7	4	5	74	2	130	5	1	.244
Neagle, D	PIT	L	4	6	4.48	55	6	0	0	8	2	86.1	81	380	46	43	9	4	3	2	43	8	77	3	2	.247
Nied, D	ATL	R	3	0	1.17	6	2	0	0	0	0	23.0	10	83	3	3	0	1	0	0	5	0	19	0	0	.130
Ojeda, B	LA	L	6	9	3.63	29	29	2	1	0	0	166.1	169	731	80	67	8	11	7	1	81	8	94	3	0	.268
Olivares, O	STL	R	9	9	3.84	32	30	1	0	1	0	197.0	189	818	84	84	20	8	7	4	63	5	124	2	0	.257
Oliveras, F	SF	R	0	3	3.63	16	7	0	0	3	0	44.2	41	179	19	18	11	2	2	1	10	2	17	0	0	.250
Osborne, D	STL	L	11	9	3.77	34	29	0	0	2	0	179.0	193	754	91	75	14	7	4	2	38	2	104	6	0	.275
Osuna, A	HOU	L	6	3	4.23	66	0	0	0	17	0	61.2	52	270	29	29	8	5	6	1	38	5	37	3	1	.236
Palacios, V	PIT	R	3	2	4.25	20	8	0	0	4	0	53.0	56	232	25	25	1	4	1	0	27	1	33	7	0	.280
Patterson, B	PIT	L	6	3	2.92	60	0	0	0	26	9	64.2	59	268	22	21	7	3	2	0	23	6	43	3	0	.246
Patterson, K	CHI	L	2	3	3.89	32	1	0	0	4	0	41.2	41	191	25	18	7	6	4	1	27	6	23	3	1	.268
Pecota, B	NY	R	0	0	9.00	1	0	0	0	1	0	1.0	1	4	1	1	1	0	0	0	0	0	0	0	0	.250
Pena, A	ATL	R	1	6	4.07	41	0	0	0	31	15	42.0	40	173	19	19	7	2	1	0	13	5	34	0	0	.255
Pena, J	SF	L	1	1	3.48	25	2	0	0	4	0	44.0	49	204	19	17	4	8	1	1	20	5	32	0	0	.282
Perez, M	STL	R	9	3	1.84	77	0	0	0	22	0	93.0	70	377	23	19	4	7	4	1	32	9	46	4	0	.210
Portugal, M	HOU	R	6	3	2.66	18	16	1	1	0	0	101.1	76	405	32	30	7	5	1	1	41	3	62	1	1	.213
Pugh, T	CIN	R	4	2	2.58	7	7	0	0	0	0	45.1	47	187	15	13	2	2	1	1	13	3	18	0	0	.276
Rapp, P	SF	R	0	2	7.20	3	2	0	0	1	0	10.0	8	43	8	8	0	2	0	1	6	1	3	0	0	.235
Rasmussen, D	CHI	L	0	0	10.80	3	1	0	0	1	0	5.0	7	24	6	6	2	0	1	1	2	1	0	0	0	.350
Reardon, J	ATL	R	3	0	1.15	14	0	0	0	11	3	15.2	14	62	2	2	0	1	0	1	2	1	7	0	0	.241
Reed, S	SF	R	1	0	2.30	18	0	0	0	2	0	15.2	13	63	5	4	2	0	0	1	3	0	11	0	0	.220
Reynolds, S	HOU	R	1	3	7.11	8	5	0	0	0	0	25.1	42	122	22	20	2	6	1	0	6	1	10	1	1	.385
Reynoso, A	ATL	R	1	0	4.70	3	1	0	0	1	1	7.2	11	32	4	4	2	1	0	1	2	1	2	0	0	.393
Righetti, D	SF	L	2	7	5.06	54	4	0	0	23	3	78.1	79	340	47	44	4	6	4	0	36	5	47	5	2	.269
Rijo, J	CIN	R	15	10	2.56	33	33	2	0	0	0	211.0	185	836	67	60	15	9	4	3	44	1	171	2	1	.238
Risley, B	MON	R	1	0	1.80	1	1	0	0	0	0	5.0	4	19	1	1	0	1	0	0	1	0	2	0	0	.235
Ritchie, W	PHI	L	2	1	3.00	40	0	0	0	13	1	39.0	44	174	17	13	3	4	0	0	17	3	19	0	0	.288

Rivera, B	ATL-PHI	R	7	4	3.07	28	14	4	1	7	0	117.1	99	487	40	40	9	5	2	4	45	4	77	5	0	.230
Robinson, D	PHI	R	1	4	6.18	8	8	0	0	0	0	43.2	49	183	32	30	6	3	6	1	4	0	17	0	0	.290
Robinson, J	CHI	R	4	3	3.00	49	5	0	0	12	1	78.0	76	335	29	26	5	2	2	2	40	7	46	8	1	.263
Robinson, J	PIT	R	3	1	4.46	8	7	0	0	0	0	36.1	33	152	18	18	2	0	1	1	15	0	14	0	0	.244
Rodriguez, R	SD	L	6	3	2.37	61	1	0	0	15	0	91.0	77	369	28	24	4	2	2	0	29	4	64	1	1	.229
Rogers, K	SF	L	0	2	4.24	6	6	0	0	0	0	34.0	37	148	17	16	4	2	0	1	13	1	26	2	0	.280
Rojas, M	MON	R	7	1	1.43	68	0	0	0	26	10	100.2	71	399	17	16	2	4	2	2	34	8	70	2	0	.199
Ruskin, S	CIN	L	4	3	5.03	57	0	0	0	19	0	53.2	56	234	31	30	6	7	2	1	20	4	43	1	0	.275
Saberhagen, B	NY	R	3	5	3.50	17	15	1	1	0	0	97.2	84	397	39	38	6	3	3	4	27	1	81	1	2	.233
St. Claire, R	ATL	R	0	0	5.87	10	0	0	0	1	0	15.1	17	68	11	10	1	0	0	0	8	3	7	0	0	.283
Sampen, B	MON	R	1	4	3.13	44	1	0	0	10	0	63.1	62	267	22	22	4	5	1	1	29	6	23	1	2	.268
Scanlan, B	CHI	R	3	6	2.89	69	0	0	0	41	14	87.1	76	360	32	28	4	4	2	1	30	6	42	6	4	.235
Scheid, R	HOU	L	0	1	6.00	7	1	0	0	3	0	12.0	14	56	8	8	2	0	0	0	6	1	8	1	1	.280
Schilling, C	PHI	R	14	11	2.35	42	26	10	4	10	2	226.1	165	895	67	59	11	7	8	1	59	4	147	4	0	.201
Schourek, P	NY	L	6	8	3.64	22	21	0	0	0	0	136.0	137	578	60	55	9	4	4	2	44	6	60	4	2	.261
Scott, T	SD	R	4	1	5.26	34	0	0	0	16	0	37.2	39	173	24	22	4	4	1	1	21	6	30	0	1	.267
Searcy, S	PHI	L	0	0	6.10	10	0	0	0	3	0	10.1	13	50	9	7	0	1	1	0	8	0	5	0	0	.325
Seminara, F	SD	R	9	4	3.68	19	18	0	0	0	0	100.1	98	435	46	41	5	3	2	3	46	3	61	1	1	.258
Service, S	MON	R	0	0	14.14	5	0	0	0	0	0	7.0	15	41	11	11	1	0	0	0	5	0	11	0	0	.417
Shepherd, K	PHI	R	1	1	3.27	12	0	0	0	6	2	22.0	19	91	10	8	0	4	3	0	6	1	10	1	0	.247
Simons, D	MON	L	0	0	23.63	7	0	0	0	2	0	5.1	15	35	14	14	3	1	1	1	2	0	6	1	0	.500
Slocumb, H	CHI	R	0	3	6.50	30	0	0	0	11	1	36.0	52	174	27	26	3	2	2	1	21	3	27	1	0	.351
Smith, B	STL	R	4	2	4.64	13	1	0	0	3	0	21.1	20	91	11	11	3	2	0	3	5	1	9	1	0	.247
Smith, D	CHI	R	0	0	2.51	11	0	0	0	4	0	14.1	15	61	4	4	0	1	1	0	4	2	3	0	1	.273
Smith, L	STL	R	4	9	3.12	70	0	0	0	55	43	75.0	62	310	28	26	4	2	1	0	26	4	60	2	0	.221
Smith, P	ATL	R	7	0	2.05	12	11	2	1	0	0	79.0	63	323	19	18	3	4	1	0	28	2	43	2	1	.217
Smith, Z	PIT	L	8	8	3.06	23	22	4	3	0	0	141.0	138	566	56	48	8	12	4	2	19	3	56	0	0	.261
Smoltz, J	ATL	R	15	12	2.85	35	35	9	3	0	0	246.2	206	1021	90	78	17	7	8	5	80	5	215	17	1	.224
Stanton, M	ATL	L	5	4	4.10	65	0	0	0	23	8	63.2	59	264	32	29	6	1	2	2	20	2	44	3	0	.247
Swift, B	SF	R	10	4	2.08	30	22	3	2	2	1	164.2	144	655	41	38	6	5	2	3	43	3	77	0	1	.239
Swindell, G	CIN	L	12	8	2.70	31	30	5	3	0	0	213.2	210	867	72	64	14	9	7	2	41	4	138	3	2	.260
Tewksbury, B	STL	R	16	5	2.16	33	32	5	0	1	0	233.0	217	915	63	56	15	9	7	3	20	0	91	2	0	.248

PITCHER	TEAM	T	W	L	ERA	G	GS	CG	SHO	GF	SV	IP	H	TBF	R	ER	HR	SH	SF	HB	BB	IBB	SO	WP	BK	OPP AVG
Tomlin, R	PIT	L	14	9	3.41	35	33	1	1	0	0	208.2	226	866	85	79	11	13	5	5	42	4	90	7	2	.282
Valdez, S	MON	R	0	2	2.41	27	0	0	0	9	0	37.1	25	148	12	10	2	1	0	0	12	1	32	4	0	.185
Vitko, J	NY	R	0	1	13.50	3	1	0	0	1	0	4.2	12	29	11	7	1	0	1	0	1	0	6	1	0	.444
Wagner, P	PIT	R	2	0	0.69	6	1	0	0	1	0	13.0	9	52	1	1	0	0	0	0	5	0	5	1	0	.191
Wakefield, T	PIT	R	8	1	2.15	13	13	4	1	0	0	92.0	76	373	26	22	3	6	4	1	35	1	51	3	1	.232
Walk, B	PIT	R	10	6	3.20	36	19	1	0	7	2	135.0	132	567	54	48	10	5	1	6	43	5	60	7	2	.258
Weston, M	PHI	R	0	1	12.27	1	1	0	0	0	0	3.2	7	19	5	5	1	0	0	1	1	0	0	0	0	.412
Wetteland, J	MON	R	4	4	2.92	67	0	0	0	58	37	83.1	64	347	27	27	6	5	1	4	36	3	99	4	0	.213
Whitehurst, W	NY	R	3	9	3.62	44	11	0	0	7	0	97.0	99	421	45	39	4	6	3	4	33	5	70	2	1	.264
Williams, B	HOU	R	7	6	3.92	16	16	0	0	0	0	96.1	92	413	44	42	10	7	3	0	42	1	54	2	1	.255
Williams, Mike	PHI	R	1	1	5.34	5	5	1	0	0	0	28.2	29	121	20	17	3	1	1	0	7	0	5	0	0	.259
Williams, Mitch	PHI	L	5	8	3.78	66	0	0	0	56	29	81.0	69	368	39	34	4	8	3	6	64	2	74	5	3	.240
Wilson, S	LA	L	2	5	4.19	60	0	0	0	18	0	66.2	74	301	37	31	6	5	4	1	29	7	54	7	0	.282
Wilson, T	SF	L	8	14	4.21	26	26	1	1	0	0	154.0	152	661	82	72	18	11	6	6	64	5	88	2	7	.265
Wohlers, M	ATL	R	1	2	2.55	32	0	0	0	16	4	35.1	28	140	11	10	0	5	1	1	14	4	17	1	0	.235
Worrell, T	STL	R	5	3	2.11	67	0	0	0	14	3	64.0	45	256	15	15	4	3	0	1	25	5	64	1	1	.198
Young, A	NY	R	2	14	4.17	52	13	1	0	26	15	121.0	134	517	66	56	8	11	4	1	31	5	64	3	1	.285
Young, P	MON	R	0	0	3.98	13	0	0	0	6	0	20.1	18	85	9	9	0	0	2	1	9	2	11	1	0	.247

CLUB PITCHING

CLUB	W	L	ERA	G	CG	SHO	REL	SV	IP	H	R	ER	HR	HB	BB	IBB	SO	WP	BK	OPP AVG
ATLANTA..........	98	64	3.14	162	26	24	338	41	1460.0	1321	569	510	89	26	489	55	948	58	10	.242
MONTREAL	87	75	3.25	162	11	14	349	49	1468.0	1296	581	530	92	50	525	41	1014	48	11	.238
PITTSBURGH....	96	66	3.35	162	20	20	354	43	1479.2	1410	595	551	101	30	455	61	844	52	9	.254
ST. LOUIS	83	79	3.38	162	10	9	424	47	1480.0	1405	604	556	118	32	400	46	842	41	3	.252
CHICAGO...........	78	84	3.39	162	16	11	372	37	1469.0	1337	624	554	107	44	575	75	901	68	11	.246
LOS ANGELES ..	63	99	3.41	162	18	13	353	29	1438.0	1401	636	545	82	28	553	95	981	64	10	.257
CINCINNATI	90	72	3.46	162	9	11	357	55	1449.2	1362	609	558	109	28	470	51	1060	54	6	.251
SAN DIEGO	82	80	3.56	162	9	11	363	46	1461.1	1444	636	578	111	21	439	53	971	25	15	.261
SAN FRANCISCO	72	90	3.61	162	9	12	386	30	1461.0	1385	647	586	128	35	502	61	927	33	22	.253
NEW YORK	72	90	3.66	162	17	13	333	34	1446.2	1404	653	588	98	36	482	54	1025	34	9	.256
HOUSTON..........	81	81	3.72	162	5	12	422	45	1459.1	1386	668	603	114	38	539	60	978	45	14	.252
PHILADELPHIA	70	92	4.11	162	27	7	323	34	1428.0	1387	717	652	113	27	549	37	851	43	9	.257

OFFICIAL 1992 AMERICAN LEAGUE RECORDS

COMPILED BY MLB-IBM BASEBALL INFORMATION SYSTEM
Official Statistician: ELIAS SPORTS BUREAU

FINAL STANDINGS

AMERICAN LEAGUE EAST

CLUB	WON	LOST	PCT.	GB
TORONTO	96	66	.593	
MILWAUKEE	92	70	.568	4.0
BALTIMORE	89	73	.549	7.0
CLEVELAND	76	86	.469	20.0
NEW YORK	76	86	.469	20.0
DETROIT	75	87	.463	21.0
BOSTON	73	89	.451	23.0

AMERICAN LEAGUE WEST

CLUB	WON	LOST	PCT.	GB
OAKLAND	96	66	.593	
MINNESOTA	90	72	.556	6.
CHICAGO	86	76	.531	10.
TEXAS	77	85	.475	19.
CALIFORNIA	72	90	.444	24.
KANSAS CITY	72	90	.444	24.
SEATTLE	64	98	.395	32.

Championship Series: Toronto defeated Oakland, 4 games to 2

Batting

INDIVIDUAL BATTING LEADERS

Batting Average	.343	E. Martinez	Sea.
Games	162	C. Ripken	Bal.
At Bats	659	Fryman	Det.
Runs	114	Phillips	Det.
Hits	210	Puckett	Min.
Total Bases	313	Puckett	Min.
Singles	152	Baerga	Cle.
Doubles	46	E. Martinez	Sea.
		Thomas	Chi.
Triples	12	Johnson	Chi.
Home Runs	43	Gonzalez	Tex.
Runs Batted In	124	Fielder	Det.
Sacrifice Hits	16	Browne	Oak.
Sacrifice Flies	13	Carter	Tor.
Hit by Pitch	15	Macfarlane	K.C.
		Mack	Min.
Bases on Balls	122	Tettleton	Det.
		Thomas	Chi.
Intentional Bases on Balls	19	Boggs	Bos.
Strikeouts	154	Palmer	Tex.
Stolen Bases	66	Lofton	Cle.
Caught Stealing	21	Polonia	Cal.
Grounded Into Double Play	29	Bell	Chi.
Slugging Percentage	.585	McGwire	Oak.
On-Base Percentage	.439	Thomas	Chi.
Longest Batting Streak	25	Johnson	Chi. (July 16-Aug. 11)

BATTER	TEAM	B	AVG	G	AB	R	H	TB	2B	3B	HR	RBI	SH	SF	HP	BB	IBB	SO	SB	CS	GI DP	SLG	OBP	E
Martinez, E	SEA	R	.343	135	528	100	181	287	46	3	18	73	1	5	4	54	2	61	14	4	15	.544	.404	17
Puckett, K	MIN	R	.329	160	639	104	210	313	38	4	19	110	1	6	6	44	13	97	17	7	17	.490	.374	3
Thomas, F	CHI	R	.323	160	573	108	185	307	46	2	24	115	0	11	5	122	6	88	6	3	19	.536	.439	13
Molitor, P	MIL	R	.320	158	609	89	195	281	36	7	12	89	4	11	3	73	12	66	31	6	13	.461	.389	2
Mack, S	MIN	R	.315	156	600	101	189	280	31	6	16	75	11	2	15	64	1	106	26	14	8	.467	.394	4
Baerga, C	CLE	S	.312	161	657	92	205	299	32	1	20	105	2	9	13	35	10	76	10	2	15	.455	.354	19
Alomar, R	TOR	S	.310	152	571	105	177	244	27	8	8	76	6	2	5	87	5	52	49	9	8	.427	.405	5
Griffey, K	SEA	L	.308	142	565	83	174	302	39	4	27	103	0	3	5	44	15	67	10	5	15	.535	.361	1
Harper, B	MIN	R	.307	140	502	58	154	206	25	0	9	73	1	10	7	26	7	22	0	1	15	.410	.343	13
Bordick, M	OAK	R	.300	154	504	62	151	187	19	4	3	48	14	5	9	40	2	59	12	6	10	.371	.358	16
Hamilton, D	MIL	L	.298	128	470	67	140	188	19	7	5	62	4	7	1	45	0	42	41	14	10	.400	.356	0
Knoblauch, C	MIN	R	.297	155	600	104	178	215	19	6	2	56	2	12	5	88	1	60	34	13	8	.358	.384	6
Raines, T	CHI	S	.294	144	551	102	162	223	22	9	7	54	4	8	0	81	4	48	45	6	5	.405	.380	2
Vizquel, O	SEA	S	.294	136	483	49	142	170	20	4	0	21	9	1	2	32	0	38	15	13	14	.352	.340	7
Listach, P	MIL	S	.290	149	579	93	168	202	19	6	1	47	12	2	1	55	0	124	54	18	3	.349	.352	24

INDIVIDUAL BATTING

BATTER	TEAM	B	AVG	G	AB	R	H	TB	2B	3B	HR	RBI	SH	SF	HP	BB	IBB	SO	SB	CS	GI DP	SLG	OBP	E
Abner, S	CHI	R	.279	97	208	21	58	73	10	1	1	16	2	3	3	12	2	35	1	2	3	.351	.323	0
Alexander, M	BAL	R	.200	4	5	1	1	1	0	0	0	0	0	0	0	0	0	3	0	0	0	.200	.200	0
Allanson, A	MIL	R	.320	9	25	6	8	9	1	0	0	0	2	0	0	1	0	2	3	1	1	.360	.346	2
Alomar, R	TOR	S	.310	152	571	105	177	244	27	8	8	76	6	2	5	87	5	52	49	9	8	.427	.405	5
Alomar, S	CLE	R	.251	89	299	22	75	97	16	0	2	26	3	0	5	13	3	32	3	3	7	.324	.293	2
Amaral, R	SEA	R	.240	35	100	9	24	30	3	0	1	7	4	0	0	5	0	16	4	2	4	.300	.276	3
Anderson, B	BAL	L	.271	159	623	100	169	280	28	10	21	80	10	9	9	98	14	98	53	16	2	.449	.373	8
Baerga, C	CLE	S	.312	161	657	92	205	299	32	1	20	105	2	9	13	35	10	76	10	2	15	.455	.354	19
Baines, H	OAK	L	.253	140	478	58	121	187	18	0	16	76	0	6	0	59	6	61	1	3	11	.391	.331	1
Barfield, J	NY	R	.137	30	95	8	13	21	2	0	2	7	0	1	0	9	2	27	1	1	5	.221	.210	2
Barnes, S	DET	R	.273	95	165	27	45	64	8	1	3	25	2	2	2	10	1	18	3	1	4	.388	.318	11

BATTER	TEAM	B	AVG	G	AB	R	H	TB	2B	3B	HR	RBI	SH	SF	HP	BB	IBB	SO	SB	CS	GI DP	SLG	OBP	E
Barrett, T	BOS	S	.000	4	3	1	0	0	0	0	0	0	1	0	0	2	0	0	0	0	0	.000	.400	0
Bell, D	TOR	R	.242	61	161	23	39	57	6	3	2	15	2	1	5	15	1	34	7	2	6	.354	.324	0
Bell, G	CHI	R	.255	155	627	74	160	262	27	0	25	112	0	6	6	31	8	97	5	2	29	.418	.294	1
Belle, A	CLE	R	.260	153	585	81	152	279	23	1	34	112	1	8	4	52	5	128	8	2	18	.477	.320	3
Beltre, E	CHI	R	.191	49	110	21	21	26	2	0	1	10	2	1	0	3	0	18	1	0	3	.236	.211	12
Bergman, D	DET	L	.232	87	181	17	42	48	3	0	1	10	1	2	0	20	1	19	1	0	4	.265	.305	5
Bichette, D	MIL	R	.287	112	387	37	111	157	27	2	5	41	2	3	3	16	3	74	18	7	13	.406	.318	2
Blankenship, L	OAK	R	.241	123	349	59	84	119	24	1	3	34	8	1	6	82	2	57	21	7	10	.341	.393	6
Blowers, M	SEA	R	.192	31	73	7	14	20	3	0	1	2	1	0	0	6	0	20	0	0	3	.274	.253	1
Boggs, W	BOS	L	.259	143	514	62	133	184	22	4	7	50	0	6	4	74	19	31	1	3	10	.358	.353	15
Boone, B	SEA	R	.194	33	129	15	25	41	4	0	4	15	1	0	1	4	0	34	1	1	4	.318	.224	6
Borders, P	TOR	R	.242	138	480	47	116	185	26	2	13	53	1	5	2	33	3	75	1	1	11	.385	.290	8
Bordick, M	OAK	R	.300	154	504	62	151	187	19	4	3	48	14	5	9	40	2	59	12	6	10	.371	.358	16
Bradley, S	SEA	L	.000	2	1	0	0	0	0	0	0	0	0	0	0	1	0	1	0	0	0	.000	.500	0
Brett, G	KC	L	.285	152	592	55	169	235	35	5	7	61	0	4	6	35	6	69	8	6	15	.397	.330	3
Briley, G	SEA	L	.275	86	200	18	55	80	10	0	5	12	0	2	1	4	0	31	9	2	4	.400	.290	4
Brito, B	MIN	R	.143	8	14	1	2	3	1	0	0	2	0	1	0	0	0	4	0	1	0	.214	.133	1
Brogna, R	DET	L	.192	9	26	3	5	9	1	0	1	3	0	0	0	3	0	5	0	0	0	.346	.276	1
Brooks, H	CAL	R	.216	82	306	28	66	103	13	0	8	36	0	1	1	12	3	46	3	3	10	.337	.247	1
Brosius, S	OAK	R	.218	38	87	13	19	33	2	0	4	13	0	1	2	3	1	13	3	0	0	.379	.258	1
Brown, J	MIN	R	.067	35	15	8	1	1	0	0	0	0	0	0	1	2	0	4	2	2	0	.067	.222	1
Browne, J	OAK	S	.287	111	324	43	93	118	12	2	3	40	16	6	4	40	0	40	3	3	7	.364	.366	5
Bruett, J	MIN	L	.250	56	76	7	19	23	4	0	0	2	1	0	1	6	1	12	6	3	0	.303	.313	1
Brumley, M	BOS	S	.000	2	1	0	0	0	0	0	0	0	0	0	0	0	0	0	0	0	0	.000	.000	0
Brunansky, T	BOS	R	.266	138	458	47	122	204	31	3	15	74	2	7	0	66	2	96	2	5	11	.445	.354	6
Buhner, J	SEA	R	.243	152	543	69	132	229	16	3	25	79	1	8	6	71	2	146	0	6	12	.422	.333	2
Burks, E	BOS	R	.255	66	235	35	60	98	8	3	8	30	0	2	1	25	2	48	5	2	5	.417	.327	2
Bush, R	MIN	L	.214	100	182	14	39	55	8	1	2	22	0	3	2	11	3	37	1	1	5	.302	.263	0
Cangelosi, J	TEX	S	.188	73	85	12	16	21	2	0	1	6	3	0	0	18	0	16	6	5	0	.247	.330	3
Canseco, J	OAK-TEX	R	.244	119	439	74	107	200	15	0	26	87	0	4	6	63	2	128	6	7	16	.456	.344	3
Carreon, M	DET	R	.232	101	336	34	78	121	11	1	10	41	1	4	1	22	2	57	3	1	12	.360	.278	4
Carter, J	TOR	R	.264	158	622	97	164	310	30	7	34	119	1	13	11	36	4	109	12	5	14	.498	.309	9
Clark, J	BOS	R	.210	81	257	32	54	80	11	0	5	33	0	5	2	56	3	87	1	1	4	.311	.350	1
Clark, P	DET	R	.407	23	54	3	22	29	4	0	1	5	1	0	0	6	1	9	1	0	2	.537	.467	2

Cochrane, D	SEA	S	.250	65	152	10	38	49	5	0	2	12	2	0	1	12	0	34	1	0	3	.322	.309	6
Cole, A	CLE	L	.206	41	97	11	20	21	1	0	0	5	0	1	1	10	0	21	9	2	2	.216	.284	1
Colon, C	TEX	S	.167	14	36	5	6	6	0	0	0	1	1	0	0	1	0	8	0	0	2	.167	.189	3
Conine, J	KC	R	.253	28	91	10	23	32	5	2	0	9	0	0	0	8	1	23	0	0	1	.352	.313	0
Cooper, S	BOS	L	.276	123	337	34	93	129	21	0	5	33	2	2	0	37	0	33	1	1	5	.383	.346	9
Cora, J	CHI	S	.246	68	122	27	30	39	7	1	0	9	2	3	4	22	1	13	10	3	2	.320	.371	3
Cotto, H	SEA	R	.259	108	294	42	76	104	11	1	5	27	3	1	1	14	3	49	23	2	2	.354	.294	0
Cron, C	CHI	R	.000	6	10	0	0	0	0	0	0	0	0	0	0	0	0	4	0	0	0	.000	.000	1
Curtis, C	CAL	R	.259	139	441	59	114	164	16	2	10	46	5	4	6	51	2	71	43	18	10	.372	.341	6
Cuyler, M	DET	S	.241	89	291	39	70	92	11	1	3	28	8	0	4	10	0	62	8	5	4	.316	.275	4
Daugherty, J	TEX	S	.205	59	127	13	26	35	9	0	0	9	0	2	1	16	1	21	2	1	3	.276	.295	2
Davis, A	CAL	L	.250	40	104	5	26	34	8	0	0	16	0	1	0	13	2	9	0	0	2	.327	.331	1
Davis, C	MIN	S	.288	138	444	63	128	195	27	2	12	66	0	9	3	73	11	76	4	5	11	.439	.386	0
Davis, D	TEX	R	1.000	1	1	0	1	1	0	0	0	0	0	0	0	0	0	0	0	0	0	1.000	1.000	0
Davis, G	BAL	R	.276	106	398	46	110	168	15	2	13	48	1	4	2	37	2	65	1	0	12	.422	.338	0
Deer, R	DET	R	.247	110	393	66	97	215	20	1	32	64	0	1	3	51	1	131	4	2	8	.547	.337	4
Dempsey, R	BAL	R	.111	8	9	2	1	1	0	0	0	0	0	0	0	2	0	1	0	0	1	.111	.273	0
Devereaux, M	BAL	R	.276	156	653	76	180	303	29	11	24	107	0	9	4	44	1	94	10	8	14	.464	.321	5
Diaz, A	MIL	S	.111	22	9	5	1	1	0	0	0	1	0	0	0	0	0	0	3	2	0	.111	.111	0
Diaz, M	TEX	R	.226	19	31	2	7	8	1	0	0	1	1	0	0	1	1	2	0	1	2	.258	.250	1
DiSarcina, G	CAL	R	.247	157	518	48	128	156	19	0	3	42	5	3	7	20	0	50	9	7	15	.301	.283	25
Downing, B	TEX	R	.278	107	320	53	89	137	18	0	10	39	0	1	8	62	2	58	1	0	7	.428	.407	0
Ducey, R	TOR-CAL	L	.188	54	80	7	15	19	4	0	0	2	0	1	0	5	0	22	2	4	1	.238	.233	2
Easley, D	CAL	R	.258	47	151	14	39	47	5	0	1	12	2	1	3	8	0	26	9	5	2	.311	.307	5
Eisenreich, J	KC	L	.269	113	353	31	95	120	13	3	2	28	0	3	0	24	4	36	11	6	6	.340	.313	1
Fariss, M	TEX	R	.217	67	166	13	36	54	7	1	3	21	2	0	2	17	0	51	0	2	3	.325	.297	0
Felix, J	CAL	S	.246	139	509	63	125	184	22	5	9	72	5	9	2	33	5	128	8	8	9	.361	.289	6
Fermin, F	CLE	R	.270	79	215	27	58	69	7	2	0	13	9	2	1	18	1	10	0	0	7	.321	.326	8
Fielder, C	DET	R	.244	155	594	80	145	272	22	0	35	124	0	7	2	73	8	151	0	0	14	.458	.325	10
Fisk, C	CHI	R	.229	62	188	12	43	58	4	1	3	21	0	2	1	23	5	38	3	0	2	.309	.313	2
Fitzgerald, M	CAL	R	.212	95	189	19	40	60	2	0	6	17	3	0	0	22	0	34	2	2	4	.317	.294	3
Flaherty, J	BOS	R	.197	35	66	3	13	15	2	0	0	2	1	1	0	3	0	7	0	0	0	.227	.229	2
Fletcher, S	MIL	R	.275	123	386	53	106	139	18	3	3	51	6	4	7	30	1	33	17	10	4	.360	.335	9
Fox, E	OAK	S	.238	51	143	24	34	52	5	2	3	13	6	1	0	13	0	29	3	4	1	.364	.299	1
Franco, J	TEX	R	.234	35	107	19	25	38	7	0	2	8	1	0	0	15	2	17	1	1	3	.355	.328	3
Frye, J	TEX	R	.256	67	199	24	51	65	9	1	1	12	11	1	3	16	0	27	1	3	2	.327	.320	7

BATTER	TEAM	B	AVG	G	AB	R	H	TB	2B	3B	HR	RBI	SH	SF	HP	BB	IBB	SO	SB	CS	GI DP	SLG	OBP	E
Fryman, T	DET	R	.266	161	659	87	175	274	31	4	20	96	5	6	6	45	1	144	8	4	13	.416	.316	22
Gaetti, G	CAL	R	.226	130	456	41	103	156	13	2	12	48	0	3	6	21	4	79	3	1	9	.342	.267	22
Gagne, G	MIN	R	.246	146	439	53	108	152	23	0	7	39	12	1	2	19	0	83	6	7	11	.346	.280	18
Gallego, M	NY	R	.254	53	173	24	44	62	7	1	3	14	3	1	4	20	0	22	0	1	5	.358	.343	6
Gantner, J	MIL	L	.246	101	256	22	63	80	12	1	1	18	3	2	0	12	2	17	6	2	9	.313	.278	3
Gladden, D	DET	R	.254	113	417	57	106	149	20	1	7	42	5	5	2	30	0	64	4	2	10	.357	.304	3
Gomez, L	BAL	R	.265	137	468	62	124	199	24	0	17	64	5	8	8	63	4	78	2	3	14	.425	.356	18
Gonzales, R	CAL	R	.277	104	329	47	91	131	17	1	7	38	5	1	4	41	1	46	7	4	17	.398	.363	9
Gonzalez, J	CAL	R	.182	33	55	4	10	12	2	0	0	2	1	1	0	7	1	20	0	1	2	.218	.270	0
Gonzalez, J	TEX	R	.260	155	584	77	152	309	24	2	43	109	0	8	5	35	1	143	0	1	16	.529	.304	10
Grebeck, C	CHI	R	.268	88	287	24	77	111	21	2	3	35	10	3	3	30	0	34	0	3	5	.387	.341	8
Greenwell, M	BOS	L	.233	49	180	16	42	50	2	0	2	18	0	2	2	18	1	19	2	3	8	.278	.307	0
Griffey, K	SEA	L	.308	142	565	83	174	302	39	4	27	103	0	3	5	44	15	67	10	5	15	.535	.361	1
Griffin, A	TOR	S	.233	63	150	21	35	42	7	0	0	10	3	2	0	9	0	19	3	1	3	.280	.273	7
Gruber, K	TOR	R	.229	120	446	42	102	157	16	3	11	43	1	4	4	26	3	72	7	7	14	.352	.275	17
Guillen, O	CHI	L	.200	12	40	5	8	12	4	0	0	7	1	1	0	1	0	5	1	0	1	.300	.214	0
Gwynn, C	KC	L	.286	34	84	10	24	34	3	2	1	7	1	2	0	3	0	10	0	0	1	.405	.303	0
Hall, M	NY	L	.280	152	583	67	163	250	36	3	15	81	0	9	1	29	4	53	4	2	13	.429	.310	3
Hamilton, D	MIL	L	.298	128	470	67	140	188	19	7	5	62	4	7	1	45	0	42	41	14	10	.400	.356	0
Hare, S	DET	L	.115	15	26	0	3	4	1	0	0	5	0	1	0	2	0	4	0	0	0	.154	.172	0
Harper, B	MIN	R	.307	140	502	58	154	206	25	0	9	73	1	10	7	26	7	22	0	1	15	.410	.343	13
Harris, D	TEX	R	.182	24	33	3	6	7	1	0	0	1	0	0	0	0	0	15	1	0	0	.212	.182	1
Haselman, B	SEA	R	.263	8	19	1	5	5	0	0	0	0	0	0	0	0	0	7	0	0	1	.263	.263	0
Hatcher, B	BOS	R	.238	75	315	37	75	98	16	2	1	23	6	1	3	17	1	41	4	6	9	.311	.283	5
Hayes, C	NY	R	.257	142	509	52	131	208	19	2	18	66	3	6	3	28	0	100	3	5	12	.409	.297	13
Hayes, V	CAL	L	.225	94	307	35	69	100	17	1	4	29	3	3	0	37	4	54	11	6	9	.326	.305	3
Heffernan, B	SEA	L	.091	8	11	0	1	2	1	0	0	1	0	0	0	0	0	1	0	0	1	.182	.091	0
Hemond, S	OAK-CHI	R	.225	25	40	8	9	11	2	0	0	2	0	1	0	4	0	13	1	0	2	.275	.289	1
Henderson, D	OAK	R	.143	20	63	1	9	10	1	0	0	2	0	0	0	2	0	16	0	0	0	.159	.169	1
Henderson, R	OAK	R	.283	117	396	77	112	181	18	3	15	46	0	3	6	95	5	56	48	11	5	.457	.426	4
Hernandez, J	CLE	R	.000	3	4	0	0	0	0	0	0	0	0	0	0	0	0	2	0	0	0	.000	.000	1
Hill, D	MIN	S	.294	25	51	7	15	18	3	0	0	2	2	0	1	5	0	6	0	0	0	.353	.368	3
Hill, G	CLE	R	.241	102	369	38	89	161	16	1	18	49	0	1	4	20	0	73	9	6	11	.436	.287	6
Hoiles, C	BAL	R	.274	96	310	49	85	157	10	1	20	40	1	3	2	55	2	60	0	2	8	.506	.384	3

Horn, S	BAL	L	.235	63	162	13	38	65	10	1	5	19	0	1	1	21	2	60	0	0	8	.401	.324	0
Howard, D	KC	S	.224	74	219	19	49	62	6	2	1	18	8	2	0	15	0	43	3	4	3	.283	.271	8
Howard, T	CLE	S	.277	117	358	36	99	124	15	2	2	32	10	2	0	17	1	60	15	8	4	.346	.308	2
Howitt, D	OAK-SEA	L	.188	35	85	7	16	28	4	1	2	10	1	3	0	8	1	9	1	1	6	.329	.250	2
Hrbek, K	MIN	L	.244	112	394	52	96	161	20	0	15	58	2	3	0	71	9	56	5	2	12	.409	.357	3
Huff, M	CHI	R	.209	60	115	13	24	29	5	0	0	8	2	2	1	10	1	24	1	2	2	.252	.273	0
Hulett, T	BAL	R	.289	57	142	11	41	58	7	2	2	21	0	0	1	10	1	31	0	1	7	.408	.340	7
Hulse, D	TEX	L	.304	32	92	14	28	32	4	0	0	2	2	0	0	3	0	18	3	1	0	.348	.326	1
Humphreys, M	NY	R	.100	4	10	0	1	1	0	0	0	0	0	0	0	0	0	1	0	0	2	.100	.100	0
Huson, J	TEX	L	.261	123	318	49	83	115	14	3	4	24	8	6	1	41	2	43	18	6	7	.362	.342	9
Jacoby, B	CLE	R	.261	120	291	30	76	95	7	0	4	36	3	4	1	28	2	54	0	3	13	.326	.324	10
Jaha, J	MIL	R	.226	47	133	17	30	41	3	1	2	10	1	4	2	12	1	30	10	0	1	.308	.291	0
James, D	NY	L	.262	67	145	24	38	55	8	0	3	17	0	2	1	22	0	15	1	0	3	.379	.359	0
Jefferies, G	KC	S	.285	152	604	66	172	244	36	3	10	75	0	9	1	43	4	29	19	9	24	.404	.329	26
Jefferson, R	CLE	S	.337	24	89	8	30	43	6	2	1	6	0	0	1	1	0	17	0	0	2	.483	.352	1
Jeter, S	CHI	L	.111	13	18	1	2	2	0	0	0	0	0	0	0	0	0	7	0	0	0	.111	.111	1
Johnson, L	CHI	L	.279	157	567	67	158	206	15	12	3	47	4	5	1	34	4	33	41	14	20	.363	.318	6
Jorgensen, T	MIN	R	.310	22	58	5	18	19	1	0	0	5	0	1	1	3	0	11	1	2	4	.328	.349	1
Joyner, W	KC	L	.269	149	572	66	154	221	36	2	9	66	0	2	4	55	4	50	11	5	19	.386	.336	10
Karkovice, R	CHI	R	.237	123	342	39	81	134	12	1	13	50	4	2	3	30	1	89	10	4	3	.392	.302	6
Kelly, P	NY	R	.226	106	318	38	72	119	22	2	7	27	6	3	10	25	1	72	8	5	6	.374	.301	11
Kelly, R	NY	R	.272	152	580	81	158	223	31	2	10	66	1	6	4	41	4	96	28	5	19	.384	.322	7
Kent, J	TOR	R	.240	65	192	36	46	85	13	1	8	35	0	4	6	20	0	47	2	1	3	.443	.324	11
Kingery, M	OAK	L	.107	12	28	3	3	3	0	0	0	1	0	0	0	1	0	3	0	0	1	.107	.138	0
Kirby, W	CLE	L	.167	21	18	9	3	7	1	0	1	1	0	0	0	3	0	2	0	3	1	.389	.286	0
Knoblauch, C	MIN	R	.297	155	600	104	178	215	19	6	2	56	2	12	5	88	1	60	34	13	8	.358	.384	6
Knorr, R	TOR	R	.263	8	19	1	5	8	0	0	1	2	0	0	0	1	1	5	0	0	0	.421	.300	0
Koslofski, K	KC	L	.248	55	133	20	33	46	0	2	3	13	3	1	1	12	0	23	2	1	2	.346	.313	1
Kreuter, C	DET	S	.253	67	190	22	48	63	9	0	2	16	3	2	0	20	1	38	0	1	8	.332	.321	5
Langston, M	CAL	R	.000	33	2	1	0	0	0	0	0	0	0	0	0	0	0	2	0	0	0	.000	.000	3
Lansford, C	OAK	R	.262	135	496	65	130	183	30	1	7	75	7	8	7	43	0	39	7	2	14	.369	.325	11
Larkin, G	MIN	S	.246	115	337	38	83	121	18	1	6	42	0	4	4	28	6	43	7	2	7	.359	.308	5
Lee, M	TOR	S	.263	128	396	49	104	125	10	1	3	39	8	3	0	50	0	73	6	2	8	.316	.343	7
Leius, S	MIN	R	.249	129	409	50	102	130	18	2	2	35	5	0	1	34	0	61	6	5	10	.318	.309	15
Lennon, P	SEA	R	.000	1	2	0	0	0	0	0	0	0	0	0	0	0	0	0	0	0	0	.000	.000	0
Levis, J	CLE	L	.279	28	43	2	12	19	4	0	1	3	0	0	0	0	0	5	0	0	1	.442	.279	1

BATTER	TEAM	B	AVG	G	AB	R	H	TB	2B	3B	HR	RBI	SH	SF	HP	BB	IBB	SO	SB	CS	GI DP	SLG	OBP	E
Lewis, M	CLE	R	.264	122	413	44	109	145	21	0	5	30	1	4	3	25	1	69	4	5	12	.351	.308	26
Leyritz, J	NY	R	.257	63	144	17	37	64	6	0	7	26	0	3	6	14	1	22	0	1	2	.444	.341	1
Listach, P	MIL	S	.290	149	579	93	168	202	19	6	1	47	12	2	1	55	0	124	54	18	3	.349	.352	24
Livingston, S	DET	L	.282	117	354	43	100	133	21	0	4	46	3	4	0	21	1	36	1	3	8	.376	.319	10
Lofton, K	CLE	L	.285	148	576	96	164	210	15	8	5	42	4	1	2	68	3	54	66	12	7	.365	.362	8
Lyons, S	BOS	L	.250	21	28	3	7	9	0	1	0	2	0	0	0	2	0	1	0	1	0	.321	.300	0
Maas, K	NY	L	.248	98	286	35	71	116	12	0	11	35	0	4	0	25	4	63	3	1	1	.406	.305	2
Macfarlane, M	KC	R	.234	129	402	51	94	179	28	3	17	48	1	2	15	30	2	89	1	5	8	.445	.310	4
Mack, S	MIN	R	.315	156	600	101	189	280	31	6	16	75	11	2	15	64	1	106	26	14	8	.467	.394	4
Maksudian, M	TOR	L	.000	3	3	0	0	0	0	0	0	0	0	0	0	0	0	0	0	0	0	.000	.000	0
Maldonado, C	TOR	R	.272	137	489	64	133	226	25	4	20	66	2	3	7	59	3	112	2	2	13	.462	.357	6
Martinez, C	BAL	L	.268	83	198	26	53	80	10	1	5	25	0	4	2	31	4	47	0	1	9	.404	.366	3
Martinez, C	CLE	R	.263	69	228	23	60	86	9	1	5	35	1	4	1	7	0	21	1	2	5	.377	.283	4
Martinez, D	TOR	R	.625	7	8	2	5	8	0	0	1	3	0	0	0	0	0	1	0	0	0	1.000	.625	0
Martinez, E	SEA	R	.343	135	528	100	181	287	46	3	18	73	1	5	4	54	2	61	14	4	15	.544	.404	17
Martinez, T	SEA	L	.257	136	460	53	118	189	19	2	16	66	1	8	2	42	9	77	2	1	24	.411	.316	4
Marzano, J	BOS	R	.080	19	50	4	4	8	2	1	0	1	1	0	1	2	0	12	0	0	0	.160	.132	3
Mattingly, D	NY	L	.288	157	640	89	184	266	40	0	14	86	0	6	1	39	7	43	3	0	11	.416	.327	4
Maurer, R	TEX	L	.222	8	9	1	2	2	0	0	0	1	0	0	0	1	0	2	0	0	0	.222	.300	0
Mayne, B	KC	L	.225	82	213	16	48	58	10	0	0	18	2	3	0	11	0	26	0	4	5	.272	.260	3
McGinnis, R	TEX	R	.242	14	33	2	8	12	4	0	0	4	0	0	0	3	0	7	0	0	1	.364	.306	0
McGwire, M	OAK	R	.268	139	467	87	125	273	22	0	42	104	0	9	5	90	12	105	0	1	10	.585	.385	6
McIntosh, T	MIL	R	.182	35	77	7	14	17	3	0	0	6	1	1	2	3	0	9	1	3	1	.221	.229	1
McLemore, M	BAL	S	.246	101	228	40	56	67	7	2	0	27	6	1	0	21	1	26	11	5	6	.294	.308	7
McRae, B	KC	S	.223	149	533	63	119	164	23	5	4	52	7	4	6	42	1	88	18	5	10	.308	.285	3
McReynolds, K	KC	R	.247	109	373	45	92	156	25	0	13	49	0	5	0	67	3	48	7	1	6	.418	.357	3
Melvin, B	KC	R	.314	32	70	5	22	27	5	0	0	6	0	2	0	5	0	13	0	0	3	.386	.351	1
Mercedes, H	OAK	R	.800	9	5	1	4	6	0	1	0	1	0	0	0	0	0	1	0	0	0	1.200	.800	1
Mercedes, L	BAL	R	.140	23	50	7	7	9	2	0	0	4	2	1	1	8	0	9	0	1	2	.180	.267	2
Merullo, M	CHI	L	.180	24	50	3	9	12	1	1	0	3	0	1	1	1	0	8	0	0	0	.240	.208	2
Meulens, H	NY	R	.600	2	5	1	3	6	0	0	1	1	0	0	0	1	0	0	0	0	1	1.200	.667	0
Miller, K	KC	R	.284	106	416	57	118	162	24	4	4	38	1	2	14	31	0	46	16	6	1	.389	.352	15
Milligan, R	BAL	R	.240	137	462	71	111	167	21	1	11	53	0	5	4	106	0	81	0	1	15	.361	.383	7
Mitchell, K	SEA	R	.286	99	360	48	103	154	24	0	9	67	0	4	3	35	4	46	0	2	4	.428	.351	0

[illegible]	[illegible]	[illegible]	[illegible]	[illegible]	[illegible]	[illegible]	[illegible]	[illegible]	30	7	12	[illegible]	4	11	3	73	12	66	31	6	13	.461	.389	2
Morris, J	CAL	L	.193	43	57	4	11	15	1	0	1	3	1	0	1	4	1	11	1	0	0	.263	.258	0
Moses, J	SEA	S	.136	21	22	3	3	4	1	0	0	1	2	0	0	5	0	4	0	0	0	.182	.296	0
Mulliniks, R	TOR	L	.500	3	2	1	1	1	0	0	0	0	0	0	0	1	0	0	0	0	0	.500	.667	0
Munoz, P	MIN	R	.270	127	418	44	113	171	16	3	12	71	0	3	1	17	1	90	4	5	18	.409	.298	3
Myers, G	TOR-CAL	L	.231	30	78	4	18	28	7	0	1	13	1	2	0	5	0	11	0	0	2	.359	.271	1
Naehring, T	BOS	R	.231	72	186	12	43	60	8	0	3	14	6	1	3	18	0	31	0	0	1	.323	.308	3
Neel, T	OAK	L	.264	24	53	8	14	26	3	0	3	9	0	0	1	5	0	15	0	1	1	.491	.339	3
Nelson, G	OAK	R	.000	29	0	1	0	0	0	0	0	0	0	0	0	0	0	0	0	0	0	.000	.000	0
Newman, A	TEX	S	.220	116	246	25	54	59	5	0	0	12	8	0	1	34	0	26	9	6	5	.240	.317	8
Newson, W	CHI	L	.221	63	136	19	30	36	3	0	1	11	0	0	0	37	2	38	3	0	4	.265	.387	0
Nilsson, D	MIL	L	.232	51	164	15	38	58	8	0	4	25	2	0	0	17	1	18	2	2	1	.354	.304	2
Nokes, M	NY	L	.224	121	384	42	86	163	9	1	22	59	0	6	3	37	11	62	0	1	13	.424	.293	4
Oberkfell, K	CAL	L	.264	41	91	6	24	25	1	0	0	10	0	2	0	8	2	5	0	1	2	.275	.317	1
O'Brien, P	SEA	L	.222	134	396	40	88	147	15	1	14	52	1	7	0	40	8	27	2	1	8	.371	.289	3
Olerud, J	TOR	L	.284	138	458	68	130	206	28	0	16	66	1	7	1	70	11	61	1	0	15	.450	.375	7
Orsulak, J	BAL	L	.289	117	391	45	113	149	18	3	4	39	4	1	4	28	5	34	5	4	3	.381	.342	4
Ortiz, J	CLE	R	.250	86	244	20	61	68	7	0	0	24	2	0	4	12	0	23	1	3	7	.279	.296	5
Orton, J	CAL	R	.219	43	114	11	25	34	3	0	2	12	2	0	2	7	0	32	1	1	1	.298	.276	5
Pagliarulo, M	MIN	L	.200	42	105	10	21	25	4	0	0	9	0	1	1	1	0	17	1	0	1	.238	.213	3
Palmeiro, R	TEX	L	.268	159	608	84	163	264	27	4	22	85	5	6	10	72	8	83	2	3	10	.434	.352	7
Palmer, D	TEX	R	.229	152	541	74	124	227	25	0	26	72	2	4	4	62	2	154	10	4	9	.420	.311	22
Parent, M	BAL	R	.235	17	34	4	8	15	1	0	2	4	2	0	1	3	0	7	0	0	0	.441	.316	1
Parks, D	MIN	R	.333	7	6	1	2	2	0	0	0	0	0	0	1	1	0	1	0	0	0	.333	.500	0
Parrish, L	CAL-SEA	R	.233	93	275	26	64	115	13	1	12	32	1	3	1	24	3	70	1	1	7	.418	.294	6
Pasqua, D	CHI	L	.211	93	265	26	56	92	16	1	6	33	1	3	1	36	1	57	0	1	4	.347	.305	6
Peltier, D	TEX	L	.167	12	24	1	4	4	0	0	0	2	0	0	0	0	0	3	0	0	0	.167	.167	1
Pena, T	BOS	R	.241	133	410	39	99	125	21	1	1	38	13	2	1	24	0	61	3	2	11	.305	.284	6
Perezchica, T	CLE	R	.100	18	20	2	2	3	1	0	0	1	2	0	0	2	0	6	0	0	0	.150	.182	2
Petralli, G	TEX	L	.198	94	192	11	38	53	12	0	1	18	1	0	0	20	2	34	0	0	8	.276	.274	4
Pettis, G	DET	S	.202	48	129	27	26	39	4	3	1	12	3	1	0	27	0	34	13	4	3	.302	.338	1
Phillips, T	DET	S	.276	159	606	114	167	235	32	3	10	64	5	7	1	114	2	93	12	10	13	.388	.387	11
Plantier, P	BOS	L	.246	108	349	46	86	126	19	0	7	30	2	2	2	44	8	83	2	3	9	.361	.332	4
Polonia, L	CAL	L	.286	149	577	83	165	190	17	4	0	35	8	4	1	45	6	64	51	21	18	.329	.337	4
Puckett, K	MIN	R	.329	160	639	104	210	313	38	4	19	110	1	6	6	44	13	97	17	7	17	.490	.374	3
Pulliam, H	KC	R	.200	4	5	2	1	2	1	0	0	0	0	0	0	1	0	3	0	0	0	.400	.333	0

BATTER	TEAM	B	AVG	G	AB	R	H	TB	2B	3B	HR	RBI	SH	SF	HP	BB	IBB	SO	SB	CS	GIDP	SLG	OBP	E
Quinlan, T	TOR	R	.067	13	15	2	1	2	1	0	0	2	0	0	0	2	0	9	0	0	0	.133	.176	1
Quinones, L	MIN	S	.200	3	5	0	1	1	0	0	0	1	0	1	0	0	0	0	0	0	0	.200	.167	2
Quirk, J	OAK	L	.220	78	177	13	39	54	7	1	2	11	5	1	3	16	3	28	0	0	4	.305	.294	8
Raines, T	CHI	S	.294	144	551	102	162	223	22	9	7	54	4	8	0	81	4	48	45	6	5	.405	.380	2
Ready, R	OAK	R	.200	61	125	17	25	36	2	0	3	17	2	2	0	25	1	23	1	0	1	.288	.329	5
Reboulet, J	MIN	R	.190	73	137	15	26	38	7	1	1	16	7	0	1	23	0	26	3	2	0	.277	.311	5
Reed, D	MIN	R	.182	14	33	2	6	8	2	0	0	4	0	2	0	2	0	11	0	0	0	.242	.216	0
Reed, J	BOS	R	.247	143	550	64	136	174	27	1	3	40	10	4	0	62	2	44	7	8	17	.316	.321	14
Reimer, K	TEX	L	.267	148	494	56	132	216	32	2	16	58	0	1	10	42	5	103	2	4	10	.437	.336	11
Reynolds, H	SEA	S	.247	140	458	55	113	151	23	3	3	33	11	4	3	45	1	41	15	12	12	.330	.316	12
Ripken, C	BAL	R	.251	162	637	73	160	233	29	1	14	72	0	7	7	64	14	50	4	3	13	.366	.323	12
Ripken, B	BAL	R	.230	111	330	35	76	103	15	0	4	36	10	2	3	18	1	26	2	3	10	.312	.275	4
Rivera, L	BOS	R	.215	102	288	17	62	75	11	1	0	29	5	0	3	26	0	56	4	3	5	.260	.287	14
Rodriguez, I	TEX	R	.260	123	420	39	109	151	16	1	8	37	7	2	1	24	2	73	0	0	15	.360	.300	15
Rohde, D	CLE	S	.000	5	7	0	0	0	0	0	0	0	0	0	0	2	1	3	0	0	0	.000	.222	1
Rose, B	CAL	R	.214	30	84	10	18	29	5	0	2	10	1	1	2	8	1	9	1	1	2	.345	.295	7
Rossy, R	KC	R	.215	59	149	21	32	45	8	1	1	12	7	1	1	20	1	20	0	3	6	.302	.310	10
Rowland, R	DET	R	.214	6	14	2	3	3	0	0	0	0	0	0	0	3	0	3	0	0	1	.214	.353	0
Russell, J	TEX	R	.100	7	10	1	1	1	0	0	0	2	0	1	1	1	0	4	0	0	0	.100	.231	1
Salmon, T	CAL	R	.177	23	79	8	14	21	1	0	2	6	0	1	1	11	1	23	1	1	1	.266	.283	2
Samuel, J	KC	R	.284	29	102	15	29	40	5	3	0	8	0	0	1	7	1	27	6	1	2	.392	.336	6
Santovenia, N	CHI	R	.333	2	3	1	1	4	0	0	1	2	0	0	0	0	0	0	0	0	0	1.333	.333	0
Sax, S	CHI	R	.236	143	567	74	134	180	26	4	4	47	12	6	2	43	4	42	30	12	17	.317	.290	20
Scarsone, S	BAL	R	.176	11	17	2	3	3	0	0	0	0	1	0	0	1	0	6	0	0	0	.176	.222	2
Schaefer, J	SEA	R	.114	65	70	5	8	13	2	0	1	3	6	0	0	2	0	10	0	1	2	.186	.139	9
Schofield, D	CAL	R	.333	1	3	0	1	1	0	0	0	0	0	0	0	1	0	0	0	0	0	.333	.500	0
Segui, D	BAL	S	.233	115	189	21	44	56	9	0	1	17	2	0	0	20	3	23	1	0	4	.296	.306	1
Seitzer, K	MIL	R	.270	148	540	74	146	198	35	1	5	71	7	9	2	57	4	44	13	11	16	.367	.337	12
Shumpert, T	KC	R	.149	36	94	6	14	24	5	1	1	11	2	0	0	3	0	17	2	2	2	.255	.175	4
Sierra, R	TEX-OAK	S	.278	151	601	83	167	266	34	7	17	87	0	10	0	45	12	68	14	4	11	.443	.323	7
Silvestri, D	NY	R	.308	7	13	3	4	8	0	2	0	1	0	0	0	0	0	3	0	0	1	.615	.308	2
Sinatro, M	SEA	R	.107	18	28	0	3	3	0	0	0	0	0	0	0	0	0	5	0	0	1	.107	.107	0
Snow, J	NY	S	.143	7	14	1	2	3	1	0	0	2	0	0	0	5	1	5	0	0	0	.214	.368	0
Sojo, L	CAL	R	.272	106	368	37	100	139	12	3	7	43	7	1	1	14	0	24	7	11	14	.378	.299	9

Sorrento, P	CLE	L	.269	140	458	52	123	203	24	1	18	60	1	3	1	51	7	89	0	3	13	.443	.341	8
Spiers, B	MIL	L	.313	12	16	2	5	7	2	0	0	2	1	0	0	1	0	4	1	1	0	.438	.353	0
Sprague, E	TOR	R	.234	22	47	6	11	16	2	0	1	7	0	0	0	3	0	7	0	0	0	.340	.280	1
Stankiewicz, A	NY	R	.268	116	400	52	107	139	22	2	2	25	7	1	5	38	0	42	9	5	13	.348	.338	12
Stanley, M	NY	R	.249	68	173	24	43	74	7	0	8	27	0	0	1	33	0	45	0	0	6	.428	.372	6
Steinbach, T	OAK	R	.279	128	438	48	122	180	20	1	12	53	0	3	1	45	3	58	2	3	20	.411	.345	10
Stephens, R	TEX	R	.154	8	13	0	2	2	0	0	0	0	1	0	0	0	0	5	0	0	0	.154	.154	0
Stevens, L	CAL	L	.221	106	312	25	69	109	19	0	7	37	1	2	1	29	6	64	1	4	4	.349	.288	4
Stubbs, F	MIL	L	.229	92	288	37	66	106	11	1	9	42	5	1	1	27	3	68	11	8	2	.368	.297	8
Suero, W	MIL	R	.188	18	16	4	3	4	1	0	0	0	0	0	1	2	0	1	1	1	2	.250	.316	1
Surhoff, B	MIL	L	.252	139	480	63	121	154	19	1	4	62	5	10	2	46	8	41	14	8	9	.321	.314	6
Sveum, D	CHI	S	.219	40	114	15	25	40	9	0	2	12	2	3	0	12	0	29	1	1	1	.351	.287	8
Tabler, P	TOR	R	.252	49	135	11	34	39	5	0	0	16	0	1	0	11	0	14	0	0	6	.289	.306	0
Tackett, J	BAL	R	.240	65	179	21	43	68	8	1	5	24	6	4	2	17	1	28	0	0	11	.380	.307	1
Tartabull, D	NY	R	.266	123	421	72	112	206	19	0	25	85	0	2	0	103	14	115	2	2	7	.489	.409	3
Tatum, J	MIL	R	.125	5	8	0	1	1	0	0	0	0	0	0	0	1	0	2	0	0	0	.125	.222	0
Tettleton, M	DET	S	.238	157	525	82	125	246	25	0	32	83	0	6	1	122	18	137	0	6	5	.469	.379	2
Thomas, F	CHI	R	.323	160	573	108	185	307	46	2	24	115	0	11	5	122	6	88	6	3	19	.536	.439	13
Thome, J	CLE	L	.205	40	117	8	24	35	3	1	2	12	0	2	2	10	2	34	2	0	3	.299	.275	11
Thon, D	TEX	R	.247	95	275	30	68	101	15	3	4	37	3	5	0	20	1	40	12	2	2	.367	.293	15
Thurman, G	KC	R	.245	88	200	25	49	61	6	3	0	20	6	0	1	9	0	34	9	6	3	.305	.281	2
Tingley, R	CAL	R	.197	71	127	15	25	38	2	1	3	8	5	0	2	13	0	35	0	1	4	.299	.282	4
Trammell, A	DET	R	.275	29	102	11	28	40	7	1	1	11	1	1	1	15	0	4	2	2	6	.392	.370	3
Turner, S	SEA	L	.270	34	74	8	20	25	5	0	0	5	2	2	0	9	0	15	2	1	4	.338	.341	5
Valentin, J	BOS	R	.276	58	185	21	51	79	13	0	5	25	4	1	2	20	0	17	1	0	5	.427	.351	10
Valentin, J	MIL	S	.000	4	3	1	0	0	0	0	0	1	0	1	0	0	0	0	0	0	0	.000	.000	1
Valle, D	SEA	R	.240	124	367	39	88	133	16	1	9	30	7	1	8	27	1	58	0	0	7	.362	.305	7
Vaughn, G	MIL	R	.228	141	501	77	114	205	18	2	23	78	2	5	5	60	1	123	15	15	8	.409	.313	3
Vaughn, M	BOS	L	.234	113	355	42	83	142	16	2	13	57	0	3	3	47	7	67	3	3	9	.400	.326	15
Velarde, R	NY	R	.272	121	412	57	112	159	24	1	7	46	4	5	2	38	1	78	7	2	13	.386	.333	15
Ventura, R	CHI	L	.282	157	592	85	167	255	38	1	16	93	1	8	0	93	9	71	2	4	14	.431	.375	23
Vizquel, O	SEA	S	.294	136	483	49	142	170	20	4	0	21	9	1	2	32	0	38	15	13	14	.352	.340	7
Ward, T	TOR	S	.345	18	29	7	10	16	3	0	1	3	0	0	0	4	0	4	0	1	1	.552	.424	0
Webster, L	MIN	R	.280	53	118	10	33	48	10	1	1	13	2	0	0	9	0	11	0	2	3	.407	.331	1
Wedge, E	BOS	R	.250	27	68	11	17	34	2	0	5	11	0	0	0	13	0	18	0	0	0	.500	.370	0
Weiss, W	OAK	S	.212	103	316	36	67	76	5	2	0	21	11	4	1	43	1	39	6	3	10	.241	.305	19

BATTER	TEAM	B	AVG	G	AB	R	H	TB	2B	3B	HR	RBI	SH	SF	HP	BB	IBB	SO	SB	CS	GIDP	SLG	OBP	E
Whitaker, L	DET	L	.278	130	453	77	126	209	26	0	19	71	5	4	1	81	5	46	6	4	9	.461	.386	9
White, D	TOR	S	.248	153	641	98	159	250	26	7	17	60	0	3	5	47	0	133	37	4	9	.390	.303	7
Whiten, M.............	CLE	S	.254	148	508	73	129	183	19	4	9	43	3	3	2	72	10	102	16	12	12	.360	.347	7
Wilkerson, C.........	KC	S	.250	111	296	27	74	92	10	1	2	29	7	4	1	18	3	47	18	7	4	.311	.292	10
Williams, B...........	NY	S	.280	62	261	39	73	106	14	2	5	26	2	0	1	29	1	36	7	6	5	.406	.354	1
Williams, G	NY	R	.296	15	27	7	8	19	2	0	3	6	0	0	0	0	0	3	2	0	0	.704	.296	2
Williams, R	CAL	S	.231	14	26	5	6	9	1	1	0	2	0	0	0	1	0	10	0	2	0	.346	.259	0
Wilson, W	OAK	S	.270	132	396	38	107	132	15	5	0	37	2	3	1	35	2	65	28	8	11	.333	.329	7
Winfield, D	TOR	R	.290	156	583	92	169	286	33	3	26	108	1	3	1	82	10	89	2	3	10	.491	.377	0
Winningham, H	BOS	L	.235	105	234	27	55	68	8	1	1	14	0	0	0	10	0	53	6	5	3	.291	.266	3
Worthington, C.....	CLE	R	.167	9	24	0	4	4	0	0	0	2	0	0	0	2	0	4	0	1	0	.167	.231	4
Yount, R...............	MIL	R	.264	150	557	71	147	217	40	3	8	77	4	12	3	53	9	81	15	6	9	.390	.325	2
Zosky, E	TOR	R	.286	8	7	1	2	4	0	1	0	1	0	1	0	0	0	2	0	0	0	.571	.250	1
Zupcic, R	BOS	R	.276	124	392	46	108	138	19	1	3	43	7	4	4	25	1	60	2	2	6	.352	.322	6

TOP 15 DESIGNATED HITTERS
(Minimum: 100 At-Bats)

BATTER	TEAM	B	AVG	G	AB	R	H	TB	2B	3B	HR	RBI	SH	SF	HP	BB	IBB	SO	SB	CS	GIDP	SLG	OBP
Martinez, E	SEA	R	.392	28	120	22	47	68	9	0	4	17	0	1	0	10	0	9	5	0	5	.567	.435
Polonia, L.............	CAL	L	.314	47	188	30	59	71	8	2	0	12	3	1	1	12	2	20	15	9	7	.378	.356
Canseco, J	OAK-TEX	R	.312	28	109	23	34	60	5	0	7	29	0	1	1	14	0	29	2	2	5	.550	.392
Mitchell, K	SEA	R	.304	26	102	17	31	49	6	0	4	27	0	1	1	11	1	22	0	1	1	.480	.374
Molitor, P.............	MIL	R	.298	108	413	53	123	176	20	3	9	57	2	8	2	56	9	53	24	3	9	.426	.378
Tettleton, M	DET	S	.295	40	139	19	41	73	5	0	9	25	0	0	0	37	6	35	0	1	1	.525	.443
Downing, B	TEX	R	.285	93	309	53	88	136	18	0	10	38	0	1	7	60	1	52	1	0	7	.440	.411

Brett, G	KC	L	.282	132	521	54	147	202	26	4	7	53	0	4	6	30	5	62	8	6	12	.388	.326
Davis, C	MIN	S	.280	125	428	59	120	182	25	2	11	60	0	8	3	72	11	73	4	5	11	.425	.382
Winfield, D	TOR	R	.278	130	490	75	136	234	27	1	23	91	1	3	1	67	9	81	1	2	8	.478	.364
Davis, G	BAL	R	.276	103	392	45	108	166	15	2	13	48	1	4	2	36	2	64	1	0	11	.423	.336
Tartabull, D	NY	R	.270	53	185	28	50	80	9	0	7	33	0	0	0	38	3	51	0	2	4	.432	.395
Belle, A	CLE	R	.258	100	380	52	98	171	14	1	19	75	1	8	3	39	4	95	5	1	14	.450	.326
Martinez, T	SEA	L	.249	48	169	20	42	76	13	0	7	25	1	3	0	13	3	23	2	0	7	.450	.297
Bell, G	CHI	R	.247	140	570	59	141	230	23	0	22	98	0	5	6	26	8	90	2	2	27	.404	.285

CLUB BATTING

CLUB	AVG	G	AB	R	OR	H	TB	2B	3B	HR	GS	RBI	SH	SF	HP	BB	IBB	SO	SB	CS	GI DP	LOB	SHO	SLG	OBP
MINNESOTA	.277	162	5582	747	653	1544	2185	275	27	104	5	701	46	59	53	527	53	834	123	74	130	1183	8	.391	.341
MILWAUKEE	.268	162	5504	740	604	1477	2065	272	35	82	2	683	61	72	33	511	45	779	256	115	102	1101	5	.375	.330
CLEVELAND	.266	162	5620	674	746	1495	2151	227	24	127	4	637	42	44	45	448	46	885	144	67	140	1105	11	.383	.323
SEATTLE	.263	162	5564	679	799	1466	2239	278	24	149	5	638	52	51	38	474	47	841	100	55	148	1120	14	.402	.323
TORONTO	.263	162	5536	780	682	1458	2292	265	40	163	2	737	26	54	47	561	41	933	129	39	123	1159	10	.414	.333
NEW YORK	.261	162	5593	733	746	1462	2268	281	18	163	4	703	26	55	42	536	51	903	78	37	138	1157	8	.406	.328
CHICAGO	.261	162	5498	738	690	1434	2105	269	36	110	4	686	47	69	31	622	48	784	160	57	134	1174	11	.383	.336
BALTIMORE	.259	162	5485	705	656	1423	2182	243	36	148	5	680	50	59	51	647	55	827	89	48	139	1218	6	.398	.340
OAKLAND	.258	162	5387	745	672	1389	2082	219	24	142	4	693	72	59	49	707	46	831	143	59	139	1225	6	.386	.346
KANSAS CITY	.256	162	5501	610	667	1411	2004	284	42	75	1	568	45	46	51	439	30	741	131	71	121	1106	13	.364	.315
DETROIT	.256	162	5515	791	794	1411	2245	256	16	182	5	746	43	53	24	675	42	1055	66	45	124	1188	9	.407	.337
TEXAS	.250	162	5537	682	753	1387	2176	266	23	159	3	646	56	45	50	550	36	1036	81	44	115	1172	14	.393	.321
BOSTON	.246	162	5461	599	669	1343	1896	259	21	84	7	567	60	43	31	591	46	865	44	48	118	1215	11	.347	.321
CALIFORNIA	.243	162	5364	579	671	1306	1812	202	20	88	1	537	56	40	40	416	40	882	160	101	137	975	15	.338	.301

Pitching

Individual Pitching Leaders

Games Won	21	Brown	Tex.
		Morris	Tor.
Games Lost	17	Hanson	Sea.
Won-Lost Percentage	.783	Mussina	Bal. (18-5)
Earned Run Average	2.41	Clemens	Bos.
Games	81	Rogers	Tex.
Games Started	36	Moore	Oak.
		Sutcliffe	Bal.
Complete Games	13	McDowell	Chi.
Games Finished	65	Eckersley	Oak.
Shutouts	5	Clemens	Bos.
Saves	51	Eckersley	Oak.
Innings	265.2	Brown	Tex.
Hits	262	Brown	Tex.
Batsmen Faced	1108	Brown	Tex.
Runs	123	Sutcliffe	Bal.
Earned Runs	118	Sutcliffe	Bal.
Home Runs	35	Gullickson	Det.
Sacrifice Hits	13	Mussina	Bal.
Sacrifice Flies	13	Navarro	Mil.
Hit Batsmen	18	Johnson	Sea.
Bases on Balls	144	Johnson	Sea.
Intentional Bases on Balls	12	Lancaster	Det.
		Nelson	Sea.
Strikeouts	241	Johnson	Sea.
Wild Pitches	22	Moore	Oak.
Balks	5	Cook	Cle.
Games Won, Consecutive	10	Bosio	Mil. (July 25-Sept. 24)
		Eldred	Mil. (Aug. 8-Sept. 29)
Games Lost, Consecutive	9	Gardiner	Bos. (May 24-July 16)

Wunderkind Mike Mussina went 18-5 as baby Bird.

TOP 15 QUALIFIERS FOR EARNED RUN AVERAGE CHAMPIONSHIP

PITCHER	TEAM	T	W	L	ERA	G	GS	CG	SHO	GF	SV	IP	H	TBF	R	ER	HR	SH	SF	HB	BB	IBB	SO	WP	BK	OPP AVG
Clemens, R	BOS	R	18	11	2.41	32	32	11	5	0	0	246.2	203	989	80	66	11	5	5	9	62	5	208	3	0	.224
Appier, K	KC	R	15	8	2.46	30	30	3	0	0	0	208.1	167	852	59	57	10	8	3	2	68	5	150	4	0	.217
Mussina, M	BAL	R	18	5	2.54	32	32	8	4	0	0	241.0	212	957	70	68	16	13	6	2	48	2	130	6	0	.239
Guzman, J	TOR	R	16	5	2.64	28	28	1	0	0	0	180.2	135	733	56	53	6	5	3	1	72	2	165	14	2	.207
Abbott, J	CAL	L	7	15	2.77	29	29	7	0	0	0	211.0	208	874	73	65	12	8	4	4	68	3	130	2	0	.263
Perez, M	NY	R	13	16	2.87	33	33	10	1	0	0	247.2	212	1013	94	79	16	6	8	5	93	5	218	13	0	.235
Nagy, C	CLE	R	17	10	2.96	33	33	10	3	0	0	252.0	245	1018	91	83	11	6	9	2	57	1	169	7	0	.260
McDowell, J	CHI	R	20	10	3.18	34	34	13	1	0	0	260.2	247	1079	95	92	21	8	6	7	75	9	178	6	0	.251
Wegman, B	MIL	R	13	14	3.20	35	35	7	0	0	0	261.2	251	1079	104	93	28	7	4	9	55	3	127	1	2	.250
Smiley, J	MIN	L	16	9	3.21	34	34	5	2	0	0	241.0	205	970	93	86	17	4	9	6	65	0	163	4	0	.231
Brown, K	TEX	R	21	11	3.32	35	35	11	1	0	0	265.2	262	1108	117	98	11	7	8	10	76	2	173	8	2	.260
Navarro, J	MIL	R	17	11	3.33	34	34	5	3	0	0	246.0	224	1004	98	91	14	9	13	6	64	4	100	6	0	.246
Fleming, D	SEA	L	17	10	3.39	33	33	7	4	0	0	228.1	225	946	95	86	13	3	2	4	60	3	112	8	1	.257
Erickson, S	MIN	R	13	12	3.40	32	32	5	3	0	0	212.0	197	888	86	80	18	9	7	8	83	3	101	6	1	.252
Viola, F	BOS	L	13	12	3.44	35	35	6	1	0	0	238.0	214	999	99	91	13	7	10	7	89	4	121	12	2	.242

INDIVIDUAL PITCHING

PITCHER	TEAM	T	W	L	ERA	G	GS	CG	SHO	GF	SV	IP	H	TBF	R	ER	HR	SH	SF	HB	BB	IBB	SO	WP	BK	OPP AVG
Abbott, J	CAL	L	7	15	2.77	29	29	7	0	0	0	211.0	208	874	73	65	12	8	4	4	68	3	130	2	0	.263
Abbott, P	MIN	R	0	0	3.27	6	0	0	0	5	0	11.0	12	50	4	4	1	0	1	1	5	0	13	1	0	.279
Acker, J	SEA	R	0	0	5.28	17	0	0	0	3	0	30.2	45	148	19	18	4	1	2	0	12	1	11	1	0	.338
Agosto, J	SEA	L	0	0	5.89	17	1	0	0	2	0	18.1	27	84	12	12	0	2	1	0	3	0	12	0	0	.346
Aguilera, R	MIN	R	2	6	2.84	64	0	0	0	61	41	66.2	60	273	28	21	7	1	2	1	17	4	52	5	0	.238
Aldred, S	DET	L	3	8	6.78	16	13	0	0	0	0	65.0	80	304	51	49	12	4	3	3	33	4	34	1	0	.307
Alexander, G	TEX	R	1	0	27.00	3	0	0	0	1	0	1.2	5	12	5	5	1	0	1	0	1	0	1	0	0	.500

Alvarez, W	CHI	L	5	3	5.20	34	9	0	0	4	1	100.1	103	455	64	58	12	3	4	4	65	2	66	2	0	.272
Appier, K	KC	R	15	8	2.46	30	30	3	0	0	0	208.1	167	852	59	57	10	8	3	2	68	5	150	4	0	.217
Aquino, L	KC	R	3	6	4.52	15	13	0	0	1	0	67.2	81	293	35	34	5	2	3	1	20	1	11	1	1	.303
Armstrong, J	CLE	R	6	15	4.64	35	23	1	0	5	0	166.2	176	735	100	86	23	6	5	3	67	0	114	6	3	.269
Arnsberg, B	CLE	R	0	0	11.81	8	0	0	0	1	0	10.2	13	54	14	14	6	0	0	2	11	0	5	2	0	.317
Austin, J	MIL	R	5	2	1.85	47	0	0	0	12	0	58.1	38	235	13	12	2	1	1	2	32	6	30	1	0	.191
Bailes, S	CAL	L	3	1	7.45	32	0	0	0	10	0	38.2	59	200	34	32	7	1	2	1	28	4	25	2	1	.351
Banks, W	MIN	R	4	4	5.70	16	12	0	0	2	0	71.0	80	324	46	45	6	2	5	2	37	0	37	5	1	.288
Bannister, F	TEX	L	1	1	6.32	36	0	0	0	8	0	37.0	39	173	27	26	3	3	7	3	21	6	30	3	0	.281
Barton, S	SEA	L	0	1	2.92	14	0	0	0	2	0	12.1	10	50	5	4	1	1	0	0	7	2	4	2	0	.238
Bell, E	CLE	L	0	2	7.63	7	1	0	0	2	0	15.1	22	75	13	13	1	1	1	1	9	0	10	1	0	.349
Berenguer, J	KC	R	1	4	5.64	19	2	0	0	2	0	44.2	42	195	30	28	3	1	3	1	20	3	26	2	1	.247
Blyleven, B	CAL	R	8	12	4.74	25	24	1	0	0	0	133.0	150	568	76	70	17	3	5	5	29	2	70	3	1	.285
Boddicker, M	KC	R	1	4	4.98	29	8	0	0	8	3	86.2	92	392	50	48	5	2	3	8	37	3	47	2	0	.270
Bohanon, B	TEX	L	1	1	6.31	18	7	0	0	3	0	45.2	57	220	38	32	7	0	2	1	25	0	29	2	0	.297
Bolton, T	BOS	L	1	2	3.41	21	1	0	0	6	0	29.0	34	135	11	11	0	0	0	2	14	1	23	2	1	.286
Bones, R	MIL	R	9	10	4.57	31	28	0	0	0	0	163.1	169	705	90	83	27	2	5	9	48	0	65	3	2	.264
Bosio, C	MIL	R	16	6	3.62	33	33	4	2	0	0	231.1	223	937	100	93	21	6	5	4	44	1	120	8	2	.254
Boucher, D	CLE	L	2	2	6.37	8	7	0	0	0	0	41.0	48	184	29	29	9	1	3	1	20	0	17	1	0	.302
Briscoe, J	OAK	R	0	1	6.43	2	2	0	0	0	0	7.0	12	40	6	5	0	1	0	0	9	0	4	2	0	.400
Brown, K	TEX	R	21	11	3.32	35	35	11	1	0	0	265.2	262	1108	117	98	11	7	8	10	76	2	173	8	2	.260
Brown, K	SEA	L	0	0	9.00	2	0	0	0	0	0	3.0	4	15	3	3	1	0	0	0	3	0	2	0	0	.333
Burke, T	NY	R	2	2	3.25	23	0	0	0	10	0	27.2	26	122	14	10	2	2	0	1	15	4	8	2	0	.250
Burns, T	TEX	R	3	5	3.84	35	10	0	0	9	1	103.0	97	433	54	44	8	2	4	4	32	1	55	5	0	.249
Butcher, M	CAL	R	2	2	3.25	19	0	0	0	6	0	27.2	29	125	11	10	3	0	0	2	13	1	24	0	0	.264
Cadaret, G	NY	L	4	8	4.25	46	11	1	1	9	1	103.2	104	471	53	49	12	3	3	2	74	7	73	5	1	.267
Campbell, K	OAK	R	2	3	5.12	32	5	0	0	6	1	65.0	66	297	39	37	4	3	2	0	45	3	38	2	0	.267
Campbell, M	TEX	R	0	1	9.82	1	0	0	0	0	0	3.2	3	15	4	4	1	0	0	0	2	0	2	0	0	.231
Carman, D	TEX	L	0	0	7.71	2	0	0	0	1	0	2.1	4	11	3	2	0	0	0	0	0	0	2	0	0	.364
Casian, L	MIN	L	1	0	2.70	6	0	0	0	1	0	6.2	7	28	2	2	0	0	0	0	1	0	2	0	0	.259
Chiamparino, S	TEX	R	0	4	3.55	4	4	0	0	0	0	25.1	25	102	11	10	2	0	1	0	5	0	13	1	0	.260
Christopher, M	CLE	R	0	0	3.00	10	0	0	0	4	0	18.0	17	79	8	6	2	1	1	0	10	1	13	2	0	.254
Clemens, R	BOS	R	18	11	2.41	32	32	11	5	0	0	246.2	203	989	80	66	11	5	5	9	62	5	208	3	0	.224
Clements, P	BAL	L	2	0	3.28	23	0	0	0	4	0	24.2	23	105	10	9	0	2	1	2	11	0	9	1	0	.258

PITCHER	TEAM	T	W	L	ERA	G	GS	CG	SHO	GF	SV	IP	H	TBF	R	ER	HR	SH	SF	HB	BB	IBB	SO	WP	BK	OPP AVG
Cone, D	TOR	R	4	3	2.55	8	7	0	0	0	0	53.0	39	224	16	15	3	0	3	3	29	2	47	3	0	.207
Cook, D	CLE	L	5	7	3.82	32	25	1	0	1	0	158.0	156	669	79	67	29	3	3	2	50	2	96	4	5	.255
Corsi, J	OAK	R	4	2	1.43	32	0	0	0	16	0	44.0	44	185	12	7	2	4	2	0	18	2	19	0	0	.275
Crim, C	CAL	R	7	6	5.17	57	0	0	0	16	1	87.0	100	383	56	50	11	3	4	6	29	6	30	4	0	.293
Darling, R	OAK	R	15	10	3.66	33	33	4	3	0	0	206.1	198	866	98	84	15	4	3	4	72	5	99	13	0	.253
Darwin, D	BOS	R	9	9	3.96	51	15	2	0	21	3	161.1	159	688	76	71	11	7	5	5	53	9	124	5	0	.257
Davis, M	KC	L	1	3	7.18	13	6	0	0	4	0	36.1	42	176	31	29	6	1	4	0	28	0	19	1	0	.294
Davis, S	BAL	R	7	3	3.43	48	2	0	0	24	4	89.1	79	372	35	34	5	6	4	2	36	6	53	4	0	.244
DeLucia, R	SEA	R	3	6	5.49	30	11	0	0	6	1	83.2	100	382	55	51	13	2	2	2	35	1	66	1	0	.293
Doherty, J	DET	R	7	4	3.88	47	11	0	0	9	3	116.0	131	491	61	50	4	3	2	4	25	5	37	5	0	.287
Dopson, J	BOS	R	7	11	4.08	25	25	0	0	0	0	141.1	159	598	78	64	17	2	2	2	38	2	55	3	3	.287
Downs, K	OAK	R	5	5	3.29	18	13	0	0	2	0	82.0	72	364	36	30	4	6	4	4	46	3	38	3	1	.237
Drahman, B	CHI	R	0	0	2.57	5	0	0	0	2	0	7.0	6	29	3	2	0	0	0	0	2	0	1	1	0	.222
Dunne, M	CHI	R	2	0	4.26	4	1	0	0	0	0	12.2	12	54	7	6	0	0	0	1	6	1	6	0	0	.255
Eckersley, D	OAK	R	7	1	1.91	69	0	0	0	65	51	80.0	62	309	17	17	5	3	0	1	11	6	93	0	0	.211
Edens, T	MIN	R	6	3	2.83	52	0	0	0	14	3	76.1	65	317	26	24	1	4	0	2	36	3	57	5	0	.236
Eichhorn, M	CAL-TOR	R	4	4	3.08	65	0	0	0	26	2	87.2	86	372	34	30	3	3	5	2	25	8	61	9	1	.255
Eldred, C	MIL	R	11	2	1.79	14	14	2	1	0	0	100.1	76	394	21	20	4	1	0	2	23	0	62	3	0	.207
Embree, A	CLE	L	0	2	7.00	4	4	0	0	0	0	18.0	19	81	14	14	3	0	2	1	8	0	12	1	1	.271
Erickson, S	MIN	R	13	12	3.40	32	32	5	3	0	0	212.0	197	888	86	80	18	9	7	8	83	3	101	6	1	.252
Farr, S	NY	R	2	2	1.56	50	0	0	0	42	30	52.0	34	207	10	9	2	1	2	2	19	0	37	0	0	.186
Fernandez, A	CHI	R	8	11	4.27	29	29	4	2	0	0	187.2	199	804	100	89	21	6	4	8	50	3	95	3	0	.270
Fetters, M	MIL	R	5	1	1.87	50	0	0	0	11	2	62.2	38	243	15	13	3	5	2	7	24	2	43	4	1	.185
Finley, C	CAL	L	7	12	3.96	31	31	4	1	0	0	204.1	212	885	99	90	24	10	10	3	98	2	124	6	0	.278
Fireovid, S	TEX	R	1	0	4.05	3	0	0	0	0	0	6.2	10	31	5	3	0	0	0	0	4	2	0	0	0	.370
Fisher, B	SEA	R	4	3	4.53	22	14	0	0	2	1	91.1	80	394	49	46	9	1	3	1	47	2	26	3	1	.234
Flanagan, M	BAL	L	0	0	8.05	42	0	0	0	15	0	34.2	50	180	34	31	3	2	2	5	23	1	17	4	0	.338
Fleming, D	SEA	L	17	10	3.39	33	33	7	4	0	0	228.1	225	946	95	86	13	3	2	4	60	3	112	8	1	.257
Fortugno, T	CAL	L	1	1	5.18	14	5	1	1	5	1	41.2	37	177	24	24	5	0	1	0	19	0	31	2	1	.236
Fossas, T	BOS	L	1	2	2.43	60	0	0	0	17	2	29.2	31	129	9	8	1	3	0	1	14	3	19	0	0	.279
Frey, S	CAL	L	4	2	3.57	51	0	0	0	20	4	45.1	39	193	18	18	6	2	3	2	22	3	24	1	0	.238
Frohwirth, T	BAL	R	4	3	2.46	65	0	0	0	23	4	106.0	97	444	33	29	4	7	1	3	41	4	58	1	0	.247

Gardiner, M	BOS	R	4	10	4.75	28	18	0	0	3	0	130.2	126	566	78	69	12	3	5	2	58	2	79	8	0	.253
Gordon, T	KC	R	6	10	4.59	40	11	0	0	13	0	117.2	116	516	67	60	9	2	6	4	55	4	98	5	2	.258
Gossage, R	OAK	R	0	2	2.84	30	0	0	0	13	0	38.0	32	163	13	12	5	1	2	2	19	4	26	0	0	.230
Gozzo, M	MIN	R	0	0	27.00	2	0	0	0	0	0	1.2	7	12	5	5	2	0	0	0	0	0	1	1	0	.583
Grahe, J	CAL	R	5	6	3.52	46	7	0	0	31	21	94.2	85	399	37	37	5	4	4	6	39	2	39	3	0	.246
Grant, M	SEA	R	2	4	3.89	23	10	0	0	4	0	81.0	100	352	39	35	6	5	1	2	22	2	42	2	0	.311
Groom, B............	DET	L	0	5	5.82	12	7	0	0	3	1	38.2	48	177	28	25	4	3	2	0	22	4	15	0	1	.320
Gubicza, M	KC	R	7	6	3.72	18	18	2	1	0	0	111.1	110	470	47	46	8	5	3	1	36	3	81	5	1	.259
Guetterman, L ...	NY	L	1	1	9.53	15	0	0	0	7	0	22.2	35	114	24	24	5	0	2	0	13	3	5	1	0	.354
Gullickson, B......	DET	R	14	13	4.34	34	34	4	1	0	0	221.2	228	919	109	107	35	7	9	0	50	5	64	6	0	.267
Gunderson, E	SEA	L	2	1	8.68	9	0	0	0	4	0	9.1	12	45	12	9	1	0	2	1	5	3	2	0	2	.324
Guthrie, M	MIN	L	2	3	2.88	54	0	0	0	15	5	75.0	59	303	27	24	7	4	2	0	23	7	76	2	0	.215
Guzman, J	TEX	R	16	11	3.66	33	33	5	0	0	0	224.0	229	947	103	91	17	9	7	4	73	0	179	6	0	.268
Guzman, J	TOR	R	16	5	2.64	28	28	1	0	0	0	180.2	135	733	56	53	6	5	3	1	72	2	165	14	2	.207
Guzman, J	OAK	L	0	0	12.00	2	0	0	0	2	0	3.0	8	18	4	4	0	0	0	1	0	0	0	0	0	.471
Haas, D	DET	R	5	3	3.94	12	11	1	1	1	0	61.2	68	264	30	27	8	1	0	1	16	1	29	2	0	.276
Habyan, J	NY	R	5	6	3.84	56	0	0	0	20	7	72.2	84	316	32	31	6	5	3	2	21	5	44	2	1	.295
Haney, C.............	KC	L	2	3	3.86	7	7	1	1	0	0	42.0	35	174	18	18	5	0	3	0	16	2	27	0	0	.226
Hanson, E...........	SEA	R	8	17	4.82	31	30	6	1	0	0	186.2	209	809	110	100	14	8	9	7	57	1	112	6	0	.287
Harris, G	BOS	R	4	9	2.51	70	2	1	0	22	4	107.2	82	459	38	30	6	8	5	4	60	11	73	5	0	.215
Harris, G	SEA	R	0	0	7.00	8	0	0	0	2	0	9.0	8	40	7	7	3	0	0	0	6	0	6	0	1	.235
Harvey, B	CAL	R	0	4	2.83	25	0	0	0	22	13	28.2	22	122	12	9	4	2	3	0	11	1	34	4	0	.208
Hathaway, H	CAL	L	0	0	7.94	2	1	0	0	0	0	5.2	8	29	5	5	1	1	1	0	3	0	1	0	0	.333
Heaton, N	KC-MIL	L	3	1	4.07	32	0	0	0	9	0	42.0	43	189	21	19	5	2	3	1	23	2	31	3	1	.269
Henke, T.............	TOR	R	3	2	2.26	57	0	0	0	50	34	55.2	40	228	19	14	5	0	3	0	22	2	46	4	0	.197
Henneman, M.....	DET	R	2	6	3.96	60	0	0	0	53	24	77.1	75	321	36	34	6	3	5	0	20	10	58	7	0	.256
Henry, D	MIL	R	1	4	4.02	68	0	0	0	56	29	65.0	64	277	34	29	6	1	2	0	24	4	52	4	0	.256
Hentgen, P	TOR	R	5	2	5.36	28	2	0	0	10	0	50.1	49	229	30	30	7	2	2	0	32	5	39	2	1	.254
Hernandez, R	CHI	R	7	3	1.65	43	0	0	0	27	12	71.0	45	277	15	13	4	0	3	4	20	1	68	2	0	.180
Hesketh, J	BOS	L	8	9	4.36	30	25	1	0	1	1	148.2	162	659	84	72	15	5	6	2	58	9	104	6	0	.276
Hibbard, G..........	CHI	L	10	7	4.40	31	28	0	0	2	1	176.0	187	755	92	86	17	10	6	7	57	2	69	1	1	.277
Hillegas, S	NY-OAK	R	1	8	5.23	26	9	1	1	6	0	86.0	104	385	57	50	13	2	3	0	37	2	49	2	0	.303
Hitchcock, S	NY	L	0	2	8.31	3	3	0	0	0	0	13.0	23	68	12	12	2	0	0	1	6	0	6	0	0	.377
Holmes, D	MIL	R	4	4	2.55	41	0	0	0	25	6	42.1	35	173	12	12	1	4	0	2	11	4	31	0	0	.224

PITCHER	TEAM	T	W	L	ERA	G	GS	CG	SHO	GF	SV	IP	H	TBF	R	ER	HR	SH	SF	HB	BB	IBB	SO	WP	BK	OPP AVG
Honeycutt, R	OAK	L	1	4	3.69	54	0	0	0	7	3	39.0	41	169	19	16	2	4	1	3	10	3	32	2	0	.272
Horsman, V	OAK	L	2	1	2.49	58	0	0	0	9	1	43.1	39	180	13	12	3	3	1	0	21	4	18	1	0	.252
Hough, C	CHI	R	7	12	3.93	27	27	4	0	0	0	176.1	160	751	88	77	19	2	6	7	66	2	76	10	1	.239
Howe, S	NY	L	3	0	2.45	20	0	0	0	10	6	22.0	9	79	7	6	1	1	1	0	3	1	12	1	0	.122
Hoy, P	BOS	R	0	0	7.36	5	0	0	0	2	0	3.2	8	19	3	3	0	0	0	0	2	1	2	0	0	.471
Irvine, D	BOS	R	3	4	6.11	21	0	0	0	8	0	28.0	31	128	20	19	1	1	3	2	14	2	10	3	0	.287
Jeffcoat, M	TEX	L	0	1	7.32	6	3	0	0	2	0	19.2	28	89	17	16	2	2	2	0	5	0	6	0	0	.350
Johnson, J	NY	L	2	3	6.66	13	8	0	0	3	0	52.2	71	245	44	39	4	2	2	2	23	0	14	1	0	.329
Johnson, R	SEA	L	12	14	3.77	31	31	6	2	0	0	210.1	154	922	104	88	13	3	8	18	144	1	241	13	1	.206
Johnston, J	KC	R	0	0	13.50	5	0	0	0	1	0	2.2	3	13	4	4	2	0	0	0	2	0	0	1	0	.273
Jones, C	SEA	R	3	5	5.69	38	1	0	0	14	0	61.2	50	275	39	39	8	1	4	2	47	1	49	10	0	.226
Kamieniecki, S	NY	R	6	14	4.36	28	28	4	0	0	0	188.0	193	804	100	91	13	3	5	5	74	9	88	9	1	.269
Key, J	TOR	L	13	13	3.53	33	33	4	2	0	0	216.2	205	900	88	85	24	2	7	4	59	0	117	5	0	.248
Kiely, J	DET	R	4	2	2.13	39	0	0	0	20	0	55.0	44	231	14	13	2	4	3	0	28	3	18	0	0	.224
King, E	DET	R	4	6	5.22	17	14	0	0	2	1	79.1	90	348	47	46	12	1	2	1	28	1	45	3	0	.285
Kipper, B	MIN	L	3	3	4.42	25	0	0	0	12	0	38.2	40	168	23	19	8	2	0	3	14	3	22	1	0	.268
Knudsen, K	DET	R	2	3	4.58	48	1	0	0	14	5	70.2	70	313	39	36	9	4	2	1	41	9	51	5	0	.264
Kramer, R	SEA	R	0	1	7.71	4	4	0	0	0	0	16.1	30	84	14	14	2	1	0	1	7	0	6	0	0	.400
Krueger, B	MIN	L	10	6	4.30	27	27	2	2	0	0	161.1	166	684	82	77	18	4	1	3	46	2	86	11	0	.263
Lancaster, L	DET	R	3	4	6.33	41	1	0	0	17	0	86.2	101	404	66	61	11	2	4	3	51	12	35	2	0	.294
Langston, M	CAL	L	13	14	3.66	32	32	9	2	0	0	229.0	206	941	103	93	14	4	5	6	74	2	174	5	0	.242
Leach, T	CHI	R	6	5	1.95	51	0	0	0	21	0	73.2	57	292	17	16	2	2	1	4	20	5	22	0	0	.215
Leary, T	NY-SEA	R	8	10	5.36	26	23	3	0	2	0	141.0	131	624	89	84	12	6	11	9	87	5	46	9	0	.256
Lefferts, C	BAL	L	1	3	4.09	5	5	1	0	0	0	33.0	34	136	19	15	3	2	1	0	6	0	23	1	0	.268
Leiter, A	TOR	L	0	0	9.00	1	0	0	0	0	0	1.0	1	7	1	1	0	0	0	0	2	0	0	0	0	.200
Leiter, M	DET	R	8	5	4.18	35	14	1	0	7	0	112.0	116	475	57	52	9	2	8	3	43	5	75	3	0	.277
Leon, D	TEX	R	1	1	5.89	15	0	0	0	3	0	18.1	18	84	14	12	5	0	0	3	10	0	15	0	0	.254
Lewis, R	BAL	R	1	1	10.80	2	2	0	0	0	0	6.2	13	40	8	8	1	0	1	0	7	0	4	0	0	.406
Lewis, S	CAL	R	4	0	3.99	21	2	0	0	7	0	38.1	36	160	18	17	3	0	3	2	14	1	18	1	1	.255
Lilliquist, D	CLE	L	5	3	1.75	71	0	0	0	22	6	61.2	39	239	13	12	5	5	4	2	18	6	47	2	0	.187
Linton, D	TOR	R	1	3	8.63	8	3	0	0	2	0	24.0	31	116	23	23	5	1	2	0	17	0	16	2	0	.323
MacDonald, B	TOR	L	1	0	4.37	27	0	0	0	9	0	47.1	50	204	24	23	4	1	1	1	16	3	26	0	0	.270

Magnante, M	KC	L	4	9	4.94	44	12	0	0	11	0	89.1	115	403	53	49	5	5	7	2	35	5	31	2	0	.325
Mahomes, P	MIN	R	3	4	5.04	14	13	0	0	1	0	69.2	73	302	41	39	5	0	3	0	37	0	44	2	1	.279
Manuel, B	TEX	R	1	0	4.76	3	0	0	0	0	0	5.2	6	25	3	3	2	0	0	1	1	0	9	0	0	.261
Mathews, T	TEX	R	2	4	5.95	40	0	0	0	11	0	42.1	48	199	29	28	4	1	3	1	31	3	26	2	1	.294
McCaskill, K	CHI	R	12	13	4.18	34	34	0	0	0	0	209.0	193	911	116	97	11	7	7	6	95	5	109	6	2	.242
McCullers, L	TEX	R	1	0	5.40	5	0	0	0	1	0	5.0	1	23	4	3	0	0	0	0	8	0	3	0	0	.067
McDonald, B	BAL	R	13	13	4.24	35	35	4	2	0	0	227.0	213	958	113	107	32	6	6	9	74	5	158	3	2	.247
McDowell, J	CHI	R	20	10	3.18	34	34	13	1	0	0	260.2	247	1079	95	92	21	8	6	7	75	9	178	6	0	.251
Meacham, R	KC	R	10	4	2.74	64	0	0	0	20	2	101.2	88	412	39	31	5	3	9	1	21	5	64	4	0	.233
Mesa, J	BAL-CLE	R	7	12	4.59	28	27	1	1	1	0	160.2	169	700	86	82	14	2	5	4	70	1	62	2	0	.273
Milacki, B	BAL	R	6	8	5.84	23	20	0	0	1	1	115.2	140	525	78	75	16	3	3	2	44	2	51	7	1	.297
Militello, S	NY	R	3	3	3.45	9	9	0	0	0	0	60.0	43	255	24	23	6	0	0	2	32	1	42	1	0	.195
Mills, A	BAL	R	10	4	2.61	35	3	0	0	12	2	103.1	78	428	33	30	5	6	5	1	54	10	60	2	0	.215
Mlicki, D	CLE	R	0	2	4.98	4	4	0	0	0	0	21.2	23	101	14	12	3	2	0	1	16	0	16	1	0	.280
Moeller, D	KC	L	0	3	7.00	5	4	0	0	1	0	18.0	24	89	17	14	5	3	3	0	11	2	6	1	1	.333
Monteleone, R	NY	R	7	3	3.30	47	0	0	0	15	0	92.2	82	380	35	34	7	3	1	0	27	3	62	0	3	.235
Montgomery, J	KC	R	1	6	2.18	65	0	0	0	62	39	82.2	61	333	23	20	5	4	2	3	27	2	69	2	0	.205
Moore, M	OAK	R	17	12	4.12	36	36	2	0	0	0	223.0	229	982	113	102	20	7	11	8	103	5	117	22	0	.269
Morris, J	TOR	R	21	6	4.04	34	34	6	1	0	0	240.2	222	1005	114	108	18	4	7	10	80	2	132	9	2	.246
Munoz, M	DET	L	1	2	3.00	65	0	0	0	15	2	48.0	44	210	16	16	3	4	2	0	25	6	23	2	0	.246
Mussina, M	BAL	R	18	5	2.54	32	32	8	4	0	0	241.0	212	957	70	68	16	13	6	2	48	2	130	6	0	.239
Mutis, J	CLE	L	0	2	9.53	3	2	0	0	0	0	11.1	24	64	14	12	4	0	2	0	6	0	8	2	0	.429
Nagy, C	CLE	R	17	10	2.96	33	33	10	3	0	0	252.0	245	1018	91	83	11	6	9	2	57	1	169	7	0	.260
Navarro, J	MIL	R	17	11	3.33	34	34	5	3	0	0	246.0	224	1004	98	91	14	9	13	6	64	4	100	6	0	.246
Nelson, G	OAK	R	3	1	6.45	28	2	0	0	8	0	51.2	68	234	37	37	5	4	5	0	22	5	23	2	0	.335
Nelson, J	SEA	R	1	7	3.44	66	0	0	0	27	6	81.0	71	352	34	31	7	9	3	6	44	12	46	2	0	.245
Nichols, R	CLE	R	4	3	4.53	30	9	0	0	5	0	105.1	114	456	58	53	13	1	5	2	31	1	56	3	0	.273
Nielsen, G	NY	L	1	0	4.58	20	0	0	0	12	0	19.2	17	90	10	10	1	1	1	0	18	2	12	1	0	.243
Nunez, E	MIL-TEX	R	1	3	4.85	49	0	0	0	16	3	59.1	63	263	34	32	6	0	4	2	22	0	49	5	0	.268
Olin, S	CLE	R	8	5	2.34	72	0	0	0	62	29	88.1	80	360	25	23	8	5	2	4	27	6	47	1	1	.249
Olson, G	BAL	R	1	5	2.05	60	0	0	0	56	36	61.1	46	244	14	14	3	0	2	0	24	0	58	4	0	.211
Orosco, J	MIL	L	3	1	3.23	59	0	0	0	14	1	39.0	33	158	15	14	5	0	2	1	13	1	40	2	0	.232
Otto, D	CLE	L	5	9	7.06	18	16	0	0	0	0	80.1	110	368	64	63	12	3	1	1	33	0	32	5	0	.333
Pall, D	CHI	R	5	2	4.93	39	0	0	0	12	1	73.0	79	323	43	40	9	1	3	2	27	8	27	1	2	.272

PITCHER	TEAM	T	W	L	ERA	G	GS	CG	SHO	GF	SV	IP	H	TBF	R	ER	HR	SH	SF	HB	BB	IBB	SO	WP	BK	OPP AVG
Parker, C	SEA	R	0	2	7.56	8	6	0	0	1	0	33.1	47	154	28	28	6	0	2	2	11	0	20	1	0	.338
Parrett, J	OAK	R	9	1	3.02	66	0	0	0	14	0	98.1	81	410	35	33	7	4	4	2	42	3	78	13	0	.226
Pavlik, R	TEX	R	4	4	4.21	13	12	1	0	0	0	62.0	66	275	32	29	3	0	2	3	34	0	45	9	0	.280
Perez, M	NY	R	13	16	2.87	33	33	10	1	0	0	247.2	212	1013	94	79	16	6	8	5	93	5	218	13	0	.235
Pichardo, H	KC	R	9	6	3.95	31	24	1	1	0	0	143.2	148	615	71	63	9	4	5	3	49	1	59	3	1	.267
Pierce, E	KC	L	0	0	3.38	2	1	0	0	0	0	5.1	9	26	2	2	1	0	1	0	4	0	3	0	0	.429
Plesac, D	MIL	L	5	4	2.96	44	4	0	0	13	1	79.0	64	330	28	26	5	8	4	3	35	5	54	3	1	.229
Plunk, E	CLE	R	9	6	3.64	58	0	0	0	20	4	71.2	61	309	31	29	5	3	2	0	38	2	50	5	0	.229
Poole, J	BAL	L	0	0	0.00	6	0	0	0	1	0	3.1	3	14	3	0	0	0	0	0	1	0	3	0	0	.231
Powell, D	SEA	L	4	2	4.58	49	0	0	0	11	0	57.0	49	243	30	29	5	5	0	3	29	2	35	2	0	.238
Power, T	CLE	R	3	3	2.54	64	0	0	0	16	6	99.1	88	409	33	28	7	7	8	4	35	9	51	2	1	.248
Quantrill, P	BOS	R	2	3	2.19	27	0	0	0	10	1	49.1	55	213	18	12	1	4	2	1	15	5	24	1	0	.288
Raczka, M	OAK	L	0	0	8.53	8	0	0	0	1	0	6.1	8	33	7	6	0	0	2	0	5	0	2	0	0	.308
Radinsky, S	CHI	L	3	7	2.73	68	0	0	0	33	15	59.1	54	261	21	18	3	2	1	2	34	5	48	3	0	.243
Rasmussen, D	KC	L	4	1	1.43	5	5	1	1	0	0	37.2	25	134	7	6	0	1	0	0	6	0	12	3	0	.197
Reardon, J	BOS	R	2	2	4.25	46	0	0	0	39	27	42.1	53	183	20	20	6	1	2	1	7	0	32	0	0	.308
Reed, R	KC	R	3	7	3.68	19	18	1	1	0	0	100.1	105	419	47	41	10	2	5	5	20	3	49	0	0	.271
Revenig, T	OAK	R	0	0	0.00	2	0	0	0	2	0	2.0	2	7	0	0	0	0	0	0	0	0	1	0	0	.286
Rhodes, A	BAL	L	7	5	3.63	15	15	2	1	0	0	94.1	87	394	39	38	6	5	1	1	38	2	77	2	1	.250
Ritz, K	DET	R	2	5	5.60	23	11	0	0	4	0	80.1	88	368	52	50	4	1	4	3	44	4	57	7	1	.278
Robinson, D	CAL	R	1	0	2.20	3	3	0	0	0	0	16.1	19	69	4	4	1	1	0	0	3	0	9	1	0	.292
Robinson, J	TEX	R	4	4	5.72	16	4	0	0	2	0	45.2	50	203	30	29	6	1	3	0	21	1	18	6	1	.281
Robinson, R	MIL	R	1	4	5.86	8	8	0	0	0	0	35.1	51	171	26	23	3	0	1	2	14	0	12	0	0	.331
Rogers, K	TEX	L	3	6	3.09	81	0	0	0	38	6	78.2	80	337	32	27	7	4	1	0	26	8	70	4	1	.261
Rosenthal, W	TEX	R	0	0	7.71	6	0	0	0	2	0	4.2	7	24	4	4	1	1	0	0	2	0	1	1	0	.333
Ruffin, B	MIL	L	1	6	6.67	25	6	1	0	6	0	58.0	66	272	43	43	7	3	3	0	41	3	45	2	0	.293
Russell, J	TEX-OAK	R	4	3	1.63	59	0	0	0	46	30	66.1	55	276	14	12	3	1	2	2	25	3	48	3	0	.224
Ryan, K	BOS	R	0	0	6.43	7	0	0	0	6	1	7.0	4	30	5	5	2	1	1	0	5	0	5	0	0	.174
Ryan, N	TEX	R	5	9	3.72	27	27	2	0	0	0	157.1	138	675	75	65	9	6	7	12	69	0	157	9	0	.238
Sampen, B	KC	R	0	2	3.66	8	1	0	0	3	0	19.2	21	81	10	8	0	1	2	3	3	1	14	1	0	.292
Sanderson, S	NY	R	12	11	4.93	33	33	2	1	0	0	193.1	220	851	116	106	28	3	11	4	64	5	104	4	1	.286
Sauveur, R	KC	L	0	1	4.40	8	0	0	0	2	0	14.1	15	65	7	7	1	0	0	2	8	1	7	0	1	.273

Schmidt, D	SEA	R	0	0	18.90	3	0	0	0	0	0	3.1	7	19	7	7	1	0	0	0	3	0	1	0	0	.438
Schooler, M	SEA	R	2	7	4.70	53	0	0	0	36	13	51.2	55	232	29	27	7	4	3	1	24	6	33	0	0	.275
Scudder, S	CLE	R	6	10	5.28	23	22	0	0	0	0	109.0	134	509	80	64	10	6	4	2	55	0	66	7	0	.303
Shaw, J	CLE	R	0	1	8.22	2	1	0	0	1	0	7.2	7	33	7	7	2	2	0	0	4	0	3	0	0	.259
Shifflett, S	KC	R	1	4	2.60	34	0	0	0	15	0	52.0	55	221	15	15	6	4	1	2	17	6	25	2	1	.279
Slusarski, J	OAK	R	5	5	5.45	15	14	0	0	1	0	76.0	85	338	52	46	15	1	5	6	27	0	38	0	1	.284
Smiley, J	MIN	L	16	9	3.21	34	34	5	2	0	0	241.0	205	970	93	86	17	4	9	6	65	0	163	4	0	.231
Smith, D	TEX	L	0	3	5.02	4	2	0	0	1	0	14.1	18	67	8	8	1	2	1	0	8	1	5	0	0	.321
Springer, R	NY	R	0	0	6.19	14	0	0	0	5	0	16.0	18	75	11	11	0	0	0	1	10	0	12	0	0	.281
Stewart, D	OAK	R	12	10	3.66	31	31	2	0	0	0	199.1	175	838	96	81	25	5	8	8	79	1	130	3	1	.237
Stieb, D	TOR	R	4	6	5.04	21	14	1	0	3	0	96.1	98	415	58	54	9	6	5	4	43	3	45	4	0	.275
Stottlemyre, T	TOR	R	12	11	4.50	28	27	6	2	0	0	174.0	175	755	99	87	20	2	11	10	63	4	98	7	0	.262
Sutcliffe, R	BAL	R	16	15	4.47	36	36	5	2	0	0	237.1	251	1018	123	118	20	6	11	7	74	4	109	7	2	.273
Swan, R	SEA	L	3	10	4.74	55	9	1	0	26	9	104.1	104	457	60	55	8	7	5	3	45	7	45	6	0	.262
Tanana, F	DET	L	13	11	4.39	32	31	3	0	0	0	186.2	188	818	102	91	22	7	10	7	90	9	91	11	1	.267
Tapani, K	MIN	R	16	11	3.97	34	34	4	1	0	0	220.0	226	911	103	97	17	8	11	5	48	2	138	4	0	.269
Taylor, S	BOS	L	1	1	4.91	4	1	0	0	1	0	14.2	13	57	8	8	4	0	0	0	4	0	7	0	0	.245
Terrell, W	DET	R	7	10	5.20	36	14	1	0	7	0	136.2	163	611	86	79	14	6	7	3	48	10	61	3	0	.298
Thigpen, B	CHI	R	1	3	4.75	55	0	0	0	40	22	55.0	58	253	29	29	4	2	4	3	33	5	45	0	0	.275
Timlin, M	TOR	R	0	2	4.12	26	0	0	0	14	1	43.2	45	190	23	20	0	2	1	1	20	5	35	0	0	.271
Trlicek, R	TOR	R	0	0	10.80	2	0	0	0	0	0	1.2	2	9	2	2	0	0	0	0	2	0	1	0	0	.286
Trombley, M	MIN	R	3	2	3.30	10	7	0	0	0	0	46.1	43	194	20	17	5	2	0	1	17	0	38	0	0	.247
Valera, J	CAL	R	8	11	3.73	30	28	4	2	0	0	188.0	188	792	82	78	15	6	2	2	64	5	113	5	0	.262
Viola, F	BOS	L	13	12	3.44	35	35	6	1	0	0	238.0	214	999	99	91	13	7	10	7	89	4	121	12	2	.242
Walker, M	SEA	R	0	3	7.36	5	3	0	0	1	0	14.2	21	74	14	12	4	1	1	0	9	3	5	1	0	.333
Walton, B	OAK	R	0	0	9.90	7	0	0	0	2	0	10.0	17	49	11	11	1	0	1	0	3	0	7	0	1	.378
Ward, D	TOR	R	7	4	1.95	79	0	0	0	35	12	101.1	76	414	27	22	5	3	4	1	39	3	103	7	0	.207
Wayne, G	MIN	L	3	3	2.63	41	0	0	0	13	0	48.0	46	210	18	14	2	8	3	3	19	5	29	1	1	.260
Weathers, D	TOR	R	0	0	8.10	2	0	0	0	0	0	3.1	5	15	3	3	1	0	0	0	2	0	3	0	0	.385
Wegman, B	MIL	R	13	14	3.20	35	35	7	0	0	0	261.2	251	1079	104	93	28	7	4	9	55	3	127	1	2	.250
Welch, B	OAK	R	11	7	3.27	20	20	0	0	0	0	123.2	114	513	47	45	13	3	3	2	43	0	47	1	0	.247
Wells, D	TOR	L	7	9	5.40	41	14	0	0	14	2	120.0	138	529	84	72	16	3	4	8	36	6	62	3	1	.289
West, D	MIN	L	1	3	6.99	9	3	0	0	1	0	28.1	32	139	24	22	3	0	2	1	20	0	19	2	0	.276
Whiteside, M	TEX	R	1	1	1.93	20	0	0	0	8	4	28.0	26	118	8	6	1	0	1	0	11	2	13	2	0	.245

Mariners' Randy Johnson led majors in strikeouts.

PITCHER	TEAM	T	W	L	ERA	G	GS	CG	SHO	GF	SV	IP	H	TBF	R	ER	HR	SH	SF	HB	BB	IBB	SO	WP	BK	OPP AVG
Wickander, K	CLE	L	2	0	3.07	44	0	0	0	10	1	41.0	39	187	14	14	1	2	2	4	28	3	38	1	1	.260
Wickman, B........	NY	R	6	1	4.11	8	8	0	0	0	0	50.1	51	213	25	23	2	1	3	2	20	0	21	3	0	.273
Williamson, M	BAL	R	0	0	0.96	12	0	0	0	5	1	18.2	16	78	3	2	1	1	0	0	10	1	14	1	0	.239
Willis, C.............	MIN	R	7	3	2.72	59	0	0	0	21	1	79.1	73	313	25	24	4	2	3	0	11	1	45	2	1	.246
Witt, B	TEX-OAK	R	10	14	4.29	31	31	0	0	0	0	193.0	183	848	99	92	16	7	10	2	114	2	125	9	1	.256
Woodson, K	SEA	R	0	1	3.29	8	1	0	0	0	0	13.2	12	62	7	5	0	0	0	2	11	0	6	1	0	.245
Young, C	KC-NY	L	4	2	3.99	23	7	0	0	5	0	67.2	80	295	35	30	2	3	3	2	17	2	20	0	0	.296
Young, M	BOS	L	0	4	4.58	28	8	1	0	4	0	70.2	69	321	42	36	7	4	3	3	42	2	57	2	0	.257

CLUB PITCHING

CLUB	W	L	ERA	G	CG	SHO	REL	SV	IP	H	R	ER	HR	HB	BB	IBB	SO	WP	BK	OPP AVG
MILWAUKEE	92	70	3.43	162	19	14	338	39	1457.0	1344	604	556	127	47	435	33	793	37	8	.246
BOSTON	73	89	3.58	162	22	13	328	39	1448.2	1403	669	577	107	41	535	56	943	50	6	.255
MINNESOTA	90	72	3.70	162	16	13	323	50	1453.0	1391	653	598	121	36	479	30	923	52	5	.254
OAKLAND	96	66	3.73	162	8	9	400	58	1447.0	1396	672	599	129	41	601	46	843	67	4	.256
BALTIMORE	89	73	3.79	162	20	16	290	48	1464.0	1419	656	616	124	36	518	38	846	45	6	.257
KANSAS CITY ...	72	90	3.81	162	9	12	340	44	1447.1	1426	667	613	106	39	512	50	834	42	10	.259
CHICAGO...........	86	76	3.82	162	21	5	292	52	1461.2	1400	690	621	123	55	550	48	810	35	6	.252
CALIFORNIA	72	90	3.84	162	26	13	297	42	1446.0	1449	671	617	130	39	532	40	888	42	5	.264
TORONTO	96	66	3.91	162	18	14	284	49	1440.2	1346	682	626	124	45	541	37	954	66	6	.248
TEXAS...............	77	85	4.09	162	19	3	359	42	1460.1	1471	753	663	113	48	598	30	1034	72	6	.264
CLEVELAND	76	86	4.11	162	13	7	379	46	1470.0	1507	746	671	159	34	566	31	890	53	12	.268
NEW YORK	76	86	4.21	162	20	9	308	44	1452.2	1453	746	679	129	35	612	49	851	52	7	.263
SEATTLE	64	98	4.55	162	21	9	372	30	1445.0	1467	799	730	129	60	661	50	894	61	6	.266
DETROIT	75	87	4.60	162	10	4	355	36	1435.2	1534	794	733	155	29	564	88	693	57	3	.277

OFFICIAL 1993 AMERICAN LEAGUE SCHEDULE

BOLD = SUNDAY ( ) = HOLIDAY * = NIGHT GAME (2) DOUBLEHEADER

	AT SEATTLE	AT OAKLAND	AT CALIFORNIA	AT TEXAS	AT KANSAS CITY	AT MINNESOTA	AT CHICAGO
SEATTLE		May 14*,15,**16** Aug. 3*,4,5	June 11*,12*,**13** Sept. 13*,14*,15*	May 17*,18*,19*,20* Aug. 6*,7*,**8***	May 21*,22*,**23*** Aug. 9*,10*,11*	June 28*,29*,30* July 1 Oct. 1*,2,3	June 25*,26*,**27** Sept. 27*,28*,29*,30*
OAKLAND	June 21*,22*,23*,24 Sept. 24*,25*,**26**		May 7*,8*,**9** July 26*,27*,28*,29*	June 25*,26*,**27*** Sept. 28*,29*,30*	May 18*,19*,20* Aug. 6*,7*,**8**	June 11*,12*,**13** Sept. 13*,14*,15*,16*	May 21*,22 ,**23** Aug. 9*,10*,11
CALIFORNIA	May 24*,25*,26*,27* Aug. 13*,14*,**15**	June 29*,30 July 1 Oct. 1*,2,3		May 21*,22,**23** Aug. 10*,11*,12*	June 21*,22*,23*,24 Sept. 24*,25*,**26**	June 25*,26*,**27** Sept. 27*,28*,29*,30	May 17*,18*,19* Aug. 6*,7*,**8**
TEXAS	June 18*,19*,**20** Sept. 20*,21*,22*	May 10*,11*,12*,13 July 30*,31 Aug. **1**	June 14*,15*,16*,17* Sept. 17*,18*,**19**		May 7*,8*,**9** July 26*,27*,28*,29	May (31) June 1*,2* Sept. 3*,4*,5*	June 21*,22,23 Sept. 24*,25*,**26**
KANSAS CITY	June 14*,15*,16* Sept. 16*,17*,18*,**19**	June 18,19,**20** Sept. 20*,21*,22*,23	May 14*,15*,**16** Aug. 3*,4*,5	June 28*,29*,30* Oct. 1*,2*,**3**		April 16*,17,**18** Aug. 17*,18*,19	May 25*,26*,27 Aug. 12*,13*,14*,**15**
MINNESOTA	May 7*,8*,**9** July 27*,28*,29*	May 25*,26,27 Aug. 13*,14,**15**	May 10*,11*,12 July 30*,31* Aug. **1**	June 7*,8*,9*,10* Sept. 10*,11*,**12**	April 9*,10,11 Aug. 23*,24*,25*,26*		April 12*,13*,14* Aug. 27*,28*,**29***,30*
CHICAGO	May 10*,11*,12 July 30,31* Aug. **1**	June 14*,15*,16,17 Sept. 17*,18,**19**	June 18*,19*,**20** Sept. 20*,21*,22*,23	May 14*,15*,**16** Aug. 2*,3*,4*,5*	June 11*,12*,**13** Sept. 13*,14*,15*	April 6*,7*,8 Aug. 20*,21*,**22**	

MILWAUKEE	June 1*,2 Sept. 2*,3*,4*,5	April 9*,10,11 Aug. 16*,17*,18	April 6,7* Aug. 19*,20*,21*,22	April 30* May 1,2,3* July 19*,20*	June 3*,4*,5*,6 Sept. (6),8*	April 20*,21*,22 July 2*,3,(4)	April 28*,29 July 22*,23*,24*,25
DETROIT	May 28*,29*,30 Aug. 30*,31* Sept. 1	April 5*,7*,8 Aug. 27*,28,29	April 9*,10*,11 Aug. 16*,17*,18*	April 28*,29* July 15*,16*,17*,18*	April 26*,27* July 8*,9*,10*,11	April 23*,24*,25 July 5*,6*,7	June 7*,8*,9* Sept. 10*,11*,12
CLEVELAND	April 26*,27*,28* July 9*,10*,11	April 23*,24,25 July 5,6*,7	April 20*,21*,22* July 2*,3*,(4*)	June 11*,12*,13* Sept. 13*,14*,15*	July 30*,31* Aug. 1 Sept. 27*,28*,29*	May 28*,29*,30 Aug. 31* Sept. 1*,2*	May 7*,8*,9 July 26*,27*,28
TORONTO	April 6*,7 Aug. 26*,27*,28*,29	May 28*,29,30 Aug. 30*,31* Sept. 1	May (31) June 1*,2* Sept. 3*,4*,5	May 4*,5* July 22*,23*,24*,25*	April 20*,21*,22* July 2*,3*,(4*)	June 14*,15*,16 Sept. 17*,18,19	April 30* May 1*,2 July 19*,20*,21*
BALTIMORE	April 9*,10*,11 Aug. 16*,17*,18	May (31) June 1*,2 Sept. 3*,4,5	May 28*,29*,30 Aug. 31* Sept. 1*,2*	April 12*,13*,14* Aug. 27*,28*,29	April 23*,24,25 July 5*,6*,7*	May 4*,5 July 22*,23*,24,25	April 26*,27* July 1*,2*,3*,(4)
NEW YORK	April 23*,24*,25 July 5*,6*,7	April 20*,21*,22 July 2*,3,(4*)	April 27*,28* July 8*,9*,10*,11	June 4*,5*,6* Sept. (6*),7*,8*	June 7*,8*,9* Sept. 10*,11*,12	May 17*,18*,19 Aug. 6*,7*,8	April 9,10*,11 Aug. 23*,24*,25*
BOSTON	April 20*,21*,22* July 2*,3*,(4)	April 27*,28 July 8,9*,10,11	April 23*,24*,25 July 5*,6*,7	April 9*,10*,11 Aug. 24*,25*,26*	April 5,7*,8* Aug. 27*,28,29	May 14*,15,16 Aug. 3*,4*,5	June 4*,5*,6 Sept. (6*),7*,8*

JULY 13 - ALL - STAR GAME AT BALTIMORE

OFFICIAL 1993 AMERICAN LEAGUE SCHEDULE

BOLD = SUNDAY ( ) = HOLIDAY * = NIGHT GAME (2) DOUBLEHEADER

	AT MILWAUKEE	AT DETROIT	AT CLEVELAND	AT TORONTO	AT BALTIMORE	AT NEW YORK	AT BOSTON
SEATTLE	June 7*,8*,9 Sept. 10*,11,12	April 16*,17,18,19 Aug. 24*,25	May 5*,6 July 22*,23*,24*,25	April 13*,14*,15 Aug. 20*,21,22	June 4*,5*,6 Sept. (6*),7*,8*	April 30* May 1,2 July 19*,20*,21	May 3*,4* July 15*,16*,17,18
OAKLAND	April 16*,17,18 Aug. 24*,25*,26	April 13,15 Aug. 20*,21,22,23*	April 30* May 1,2 July 19*,20*,21*	June 4*,5,6 Sept. 7*,8*,9*	June 7*,8*,9* Sept. 10*,11*,12*	May 3*,4* July 15*,16*,17,18*	May 5*,6 July 22*,23*,24,25
CALIFORNIA	April 12,14*,15 Aug. 27*,28,29	June 4*,5,6 Sept. 7*,8*,9*	May 3*,4* July 15*,16*,17,18	June 7*,8*,9* Sept. 10*,11,12	April 16*,17,18 Aug. 24*,25*,26	May 5*,6 July 22*,23*,24,25	April 30* May 1,2 July 19*,20*,21
TEXAS	April 23*,24,25 July 5,6*,7	April 20*,21 July 1*,2*,3,(4)	May 24*,25*,26* Aug. 13*,14*,15	April 26*,27* July 8*,9*,10,11	April 5,7* Aug. 20*,21*,22,23*	April 16*,17,18 Aug. 16*,17*,18	May 28*,29,30 Aug. 30*,31* Sept. 1*
KANSAS CITY	May 28*,29*,30 Aug. 30*,31* Sept. 1	May 4*,5 July 22*,23*,24,25	May 11*,12*,13 June 25*,26*,27*	April 28*,29 July 15*,16*,17,18	April 30* May 1*,2 July 19*,20*,21	April 12,14,15* Aug. 20*,21,22	May (31*) June 1*,2* Sept. 3*,4,5
MINNESOTA	April 26*,27 July 8*,9*,10*,11	April 30* May 1,2 July 19*,20*,21	June 4*,5,6 Sept. 7*,8*,9*	May 21*,22,23 Aug. 10*,11*,12	April 28*,29* July 15*,16*,17*,18	June 17*,18*,19,20 Sept. 21*,22*	June 21*,22*,23* Sept. 24*,25,26
CHICAGO	May 4*,5 July 15*,16*,17*,18	June 1*,2*,3* Sept. 3*,4,5	June 28*,29*,30* Oct. 1*,2,3	April 23*,24,25 July 5*,6*,7*	April 20*,21* July 8*,9*,10,11	May 28*, 29,30 Aug. 31* Sept. 1*,2*	April 16*,17,18,19 Aug. 17*,18*

MILWAUKEE		June 18*,19,20 Sept. 20*,21*,22	June 21*,22*,23*,24* Sept. 24*,25,26	May 24,25*,26*,27 Aug. 6*,7,8*	May 21*,22*,23 Aug. 2*,3*,4*,5*	May 11*,12*,13* July 30*,31 Aug. 1	June 28*,29*,30* Oct. 1*,2,3
DETROIT	May 17*,18*,19*,20 Aug. 13*,14*,15		May 21*,22,23 Aug. 3*,4*,5	May 11*,12*,13* July 29*,30*,31 Aug. 1	June 22*,23*,24* Sept. 24*,25*,26	June 28*,29*,30 Oct. 1*,2,3	June 25*,26,27 Sept. 27*,28*,29*,30*
CLEVELAND	May 14*,15,16 Aug. 10*,11*,12	June 14*,15*,16*,17 Sept. 17*,18,19		April 9,10,11 Aug. 23*,24*,25	May 17*,18*,19*,20 Aug. 6*,7*,8	May (31) June 1*,2* Sept. 3*,4,5	April 12,14,15* Aug. 19*,20*,21,22
TORONTO	June 25*,26*,27 Sept. 27*,28*,29*	June 10*,11*,12*,13 Sept. 14*,15*	April 16*,17,18,19 Aug. 16*,17*,18*		June 28*,29*,30* Sept. 30* Oct. 1*,2*,3	May 14*,15,16 Aug. 2*,3*,4*,5	May 17*,18*,19* Aug. 13*,14,15
BALTIMORE	June 14*,15*,16 Sept. 17*,18*,19	May 14*,15,16 Aug. 9*,10*,11*,12	June 18*,19,20 Sept. 20*,21*,22*	May 6*,7*,8,9 July 27*,28*		May 24*,25*,26*,27* Aug. 13*,14,15	June 10*,11*,12,13 Sept. 13*,14*,15*
NEW YORK	June 10*,11*,12*,13* Sept. 13*,14*,15	May 7*,8*,9,10* July 26*,27*,28	April 5,7*,8* Aug. 26*,27*,28,29	June 22*,23*,24* Sept. 24*,25,26	June 25*,26*,27 Sept. 27*,28*,29*		May 21*,22,23* Aug. 10*,11*,12*
BOSTON	May 7*,8,9 July 26*,27*,28*,29	May 24*,25*,26 Aug. 6*,7,8	June 7*,8*,9* Sept. 10*,11,12	June 17*,18*,19,20 Sept. 21*,22*,23*	May 10*,11*,12* July 30*,31* Aug. 1	June 14*,15*,16* Sept. 16*,17*,18,19	

JULY 13 - ALL - STAR GAME AT BALTIMORE

OFFICIAL 1993

EAST

	AT FLORIDA	AT MONTREAL	AT NEW YORK
Florida		May 11*,12*,13* July 30*,31*, Aug. 1	May 7*,8,9,10* July 27*,28*,29
Montreal	June 25*,26*,27* Sept. 27*,28*,29*,30*		June 21*,22*,23 Sept. 24*,25*,26
New York	June 29*,30*,July 1* Oct. 1*,2*,3	May 14*,15,16 Aug. 2*,3*,4*,5	
Philadelphia	May 17*,18*,19* Aug. 6*,7*,8*	June 14*,15*,16* Sept. 17*,18*,19	June 10*,11*,12*,13 Sept. 13*,14*,15*
Pittsburgh	June 10*,11*,12*,13* Sept. 14*,15*,16*	June 28*,29*,30*, July 1 Oct. 1*,2,3	May 17*,18*,19* Aug. 6*,7,8
Chicago	May 21*,22*,23 Aug. 9*,10*,11*,12*	June 3*,4*,5*,6* Aug. 23*,24*,25*	June 7*,8*,9* Sept. 10*,11,12
St. Louis	June 21*,22*,23* Sept. 24*,25*,26	May 24*,25*,26* Aug. 13*,14*,15	June 25*,26,27 Sept. 27*,28*,29*,30*
Atlanta	April 20*,21*,22 July 9*,10*,11*	June 18*,19*,20 Sept. 21*,22*,23*	May 21*,22,23 Aug. 10*,11*,12*
Cincinnati	May 4*,5* July 22*,23*,24*,25*	June 7*,8*,9* Sept. 10*,11*,12	May 28*,29,30 Aug. 23*,24*,25
Houston	May 28*,29*,30 Aug. 24*,25*,26	April 13,14*,15 Aug. 27*,28*,29	April 9*,10,11 Aug. 30*,31*,Sept. 1
Colorado	April 30*,May 1*,2* July 19*,20*,21*	April 16*,17,18 Sept. 6,7*,8*	April 5,7 Aug. 26*,27*,28*,29
Los Angeles	April 5,6*,7* Sept. 3*,4*,5	April 20*,21*,22* July 2*,3*,4	April 26*,27 July 8*,9*,10,11*
San Diego	April 9*,10*,11 Aug. 31*,Sept. 1*,2*	May 4*,5* July 8*,9*,10*,11	April 23*,24,25 July 5*,6*,7
San Francisco	May 31, June 1*,2* Aug. 27*,29*,30*	April 23*,24,25 July 5*,6*,7*	April 20*,21*,22* July 2*,3*,4

* NIGHT GAME
NIGHT GAMES: Any game starting after 5:00 P.M.
(dh) Doubleheader (tn) Twi-Night Doubleheader

BOLD BLACK FIGURES DENOTE SUNDAYS

NATIONAL LEAGUE SCHEDULE

EAST

AT PHILADELPHIA	AT PITTSBURGH	AT CHICAGO	AT ST. LOUIS
June 17*,18*,19*,20 Sept. 20*,21*,22*	May 25*,26*,27* Aug. 13*,14*,15	June 14*,15,16 Sept. 17,18,19	May 14*,15*,16 Aug. 2*,3*,4*,5*
May 20*,21*,22*,23 Aug. 10*,11*,12	May 7*,8*,9 July 27*,28*,29*	May 28,29,30 Aug. 17,18,19*	June 10*,11*,12*,13 Sept. 14*,15*,16*
May 24*,25*,26* Aug. 13*,14*,15	June 17*,18*,19*,20* Sept. 20*,21*,22*	May 31, June 1*,2 Sept. 2*,3,4,5	May 11*,12*,13 July 30*,31*,Aug. 1
	June 25*,26*,27 Sept. 27*,28*,29*,30*	April 16,17,18 Aug. 30*,31,Sept. 1	June 28*,29*,30*, July 1 Oct. 1*,2,3
May 10*,11*,12* July 30*,31*,Aug.1		May 14,15*,16 Aug. 2,3,4,5	June 14*,15*,16 Sept. 17*,18*,19
April 9,10*,11 Sept. 6*,7*,8*,9*	June 21,22*,23* Sept. 24*,25*,26		May 18*,19*,20* Aug. 6*,7,8
May 7*,8*,9 July 27*,28*,29	May 21*,22*,23 Aug. 9*,10*,11*,12*	June 17,18,19,20 Sept. 20*,21*,22	
June 21*,22*,23 Sept. 24*,25*,26	May 4*,5* July 22*,23*,24*,25	April 5,6,7 Aug. 20,21,22*	April 23*,24*,25 July 6*,7*,8*
April 12*,13*,14* Aug. 27*,28*,29	April 20*,21*,22* July 9*,10*,11	April 23,24,25 July 6*,7,8	April 9*,10*,11* Aug. 30*,31*,Sept. 1*
June 7*,8*,9* Sept. 10*,11*,12	April 23*,24*,25 July 19*,20*,21*	April 19*,20*,21 July 9,10*,11	May 4*,5* July 15*,16*,17,18
June 4*,5*,6 Aug. 23*,24*,25	June 8*,9* Sept. 9*,10*,11*,12	May 4*,5 July 15*,16,17,18	April 20*,21*,22 July 9*,10*,11
April 23*,24*,25 July 5*,6*,7*	May 28*,29*,30 Aug. 31*, Sept. 1*,2*	May 10*,11,12 July 30,31, Aug. 1	May 31, June 1*,2* Aug. 20*,21*,22
April 20*,21*,22* July 2*,3*,4*	April 6*,8 Aug. 27*,28*,29(dh)	May 7,8,9 July 26*,27,28	May 28*,29,30 Aug. 17*,18*,19
April 26*,27 July 8*,9*,10,11	April 9*,10,11 Aug. 17*,18*,19	May 25,26,27* Aug. 13,14,15	April 6*,7*,8 Sept. 3*,4*,5

July 13 - All - Star Game at Baltimore

OFFICIAL 1993

WEST

	AT ATLANTA	AT CINCINNATI	AT HOUSTON
Florida	April 28*,29* July 2*,3*,4,5*	April 26*,27* July 15*,16*,17*,18	April 16*,17*,18 Aug. 17*,18*,19*
Montreal	May 17*,18*,19* Aug. 6*,7*,8	April 5,7*,8 Aug. 20*,21*,22	May 31, June 1*,2 Sept. 3*,4*,5
New York	June 14*,15*,16* Sept. 17*,18*,19*	April 16*,17,18 Aug. 16*,17*,18*	June 4*,5*,6 Sept. 6,7*,8*
Philadelphia	May 14*,15*,16 Aug. 3*,4*,5*	May 31*, June 1*,2* Sept. 3*,4*,5	April 5*,6*,7* Aug. 20*,21*,22
Pittsburgh	April 26*,27* July 15*,16*,17*,18	April 28*,29* July 2*,3*,4,5	April 30*,May 1*,2 July 6*,7*,8*
Chicago	April 12*,13*,14* Aug. 27*,28,29	April 30*,May 1,2 July 19*,20*,21*	April 28*,29* July 22*,23*,24,25
St. Louis	April 30*,May 1,2 July 19*,20*,21*	June 3*,4*,5*,6 Sept. 7*,8*	April 26*,27* July 2*,3*,4,5
Atlanta		May 25*,26*,27* Aug. 13*,14*,15*	May 10*,11*,12* July 29*,30*,31, Aug. 1
Cincinnati	June 10*,11*,12*,13 Sept. 14*,15*,16*		May 6*,7*,8*,9* July 26*,27*,28*
Houston	June 25*,26*,27 Sept. 28*,29*,30*	June 29*,30*,July 1* Oct. 1*,2,3	
Colorado	June 29*,30*, July 1* Oct. 1*,2*,3	May 14*,15*,16 Aug. 2*,3*,4*,5	May 25*,26*,27* Aug. 13*,14*,15
Los Angeles	April 8*,9*,10*,11 Aug. 17*,18*,19*	June 18*,19*,20 Sept. 20*,21*,22*,23	May 14*,15,16 Aug. 3*,4*,5
San Diego	May 31*, June 1*,2*,3 Sept. 3*,4*,5	May 10*,11*,12*,13 July 30*,31, Aug. 1	June 15*,16*,17* Sept. 17*,18*,19
San Francisco	May 28*,29*,30 Aug. 31*, Sept. 1*,2*	June 15*,16*,17 Sept. 17*,18,19	June 18*,19*,20 Sept. 20*,21*,22*,23*

* NIGHT GAME
NIGHT GAMES: Any game starting after 5:00 P.M.
(dh) Doubleheader (tn) Twi-Night Doubleheader

BOLD BLACK FIGURES DENOTE SUNDAYS

NATIONAL LEAGUE SCHEDULE

WEST

AT COLORADO	AT LOS ANGELES	AT SAN DIEGO	AT SAN FRANCISCO
April 23*,24,25 July 6*,7*,8	June 7*,8* Sept. 9*,10*,11*,12	June 4*,5*,6 Sept. 6*,7*,8*	April 12,13,14 Aug. 20*,21,22
April 9,10,11 Aug. 30*,31*, Sept. 1*	April 28*,29* July 15*,16*,17*,18	April 26*,27* July 22*,23*,24*,25	April 30*, May 1,2 July 19,20,21
April 12*,13*,14*,15 Aug. 20*,22	May 4*,5* July 22*,23*,24,25	April 30*, May 1*,2 July 19*,20*,21	April 28*,29 July 15,16*,17,18
May 28*,29,30 Aug. 17*,18*,19	April 30*, May 1*,2 July 19*,20*,21*	April 28*,29 July 15,16*,17*,18	May 4*,5 July 22,23*,24,25
May 31*, June 1*,2* Sept. 3*,4*,5	April 16*,17*,18* Aug. 23*,24*,25*	April 12*,13*,14*,15 Aug. 20*,22	June 3*,4*,5,6 Sept. 6,7*
April 26*,27* July 2*,3*,4,5*	June 25*,26*,27 Sept. 27*,28*,29*	June 28*,29*,30 Oct. 1*,2*,3	June 11*,12,13 Sept. 13*,14*,15
April 28*,29 July 22*,23*,24*,25	April 13,14*,15* Aug. 27*,28*,29	April 16*,17*,18 Aug. 23*,24*,25	June 8,9 Sept. 9*,10*,11,12
May 6*,7*,8,9 July 26*,27*,28*	June 4*,5*,6 Sept. 6*,7*,8*	June 7*,8* Sept. 9*,10*,11*,12	April 15*,16*,17,18 Aug. 23*,24,25
June 21*,22*,23 Sept. 24*,25*,26	May 17*,18*,19* Aug. 6*,7*,8	June 24,25*,26*,27 Sept. 28*,29*	May 20,21*,22,23 Aug. 9,10,11
June 11*,12*,13 Sept. 13*,14*,15*,16	June 21*,22*,23*,24 Sept. 24*,25,26	May 21*,22*,23 Aug. 9*,10*,11*,12	May 17,18*,19 Aug. 6*,7,8
	May 21*,22*,23 Aug. 9*,10*,11*,12	May 17*,18*,19*,20 Aug. 6*(tn),8	June 24,25*,26,27 Sept. 28*,29
June 14*,15*,16* Sept. 17*,18*,19		June 10,11*,12*,13 Sept. 13*,14*,15*	May 7*,8,9 July 26,27*,28
June 18*,19*,20 Sept. 20*,21*,22*	May 24*,25*,26* Aug. 13*,14*,15		June 21,22*,23 Sept. 24*,25,26,27*
May 10*,11*,12*,13 July 30*,31*, Aug. 1	June 28*,29*,30* Sept. 30*, Oct. 1*,2,3	May 14*,15*,16* Aug. 3*,4*,5	

July 13 - All-Star Game at Baltimore